MW00976741

Communication
for the Workplace

Thomas L. Means, Ed. D.
Louisiana Tech University
Ruston, Louisiana

VISIT US ON THE INTERNET
www.swep.com
www.thomsonlearning.com

South-Western
EDUCATIONAL PUBLISHING
Thomson Learning™

Australia • Canada • Denmark • Japan • Mexico • New Zealand • Philippines
Puerto Rico • Singapore • South Africa • Spain • United Kingdom • United States

Business Unit Director: Peter D. McBride
Executive Editor: Eve Lewis
Project Manager: Penny Shank
Consulting Editor: Leslie Kauffman
Editor: Timothy Bailey
Production Manager: Patricia Matthews Boies
Art & Design Coordinator: Bill Spencer
Manufacturing Coordinator: Gordon Woodside
Marketing Manager: Mark Linton
Cover & Internal Design: LouAnn Thesing
Development & Production Services: Litten Editing and Production, Inc.
Composition Services: GGS Information Services

Photo Credits: Page 285, Courtesy of International Business Machines Corporation. Unauthorized use not permitted. Page 286, ELMO USA. All other photos copyright PhotoDisc Inc. 1997–'99.

Copyright © 2001
by SOUTH-WESTERN EDUCATIONAL PUBLISHING
Cincinnati, Ohio

South-Western Educational Publishing is a division of
Thomson Learning.
Thomson Learning is a trademark used herein under license.

ALL RIGHTS RESERVED

No part of this work may be reproduced, transcribed, or used in any form or by any means—graphic, electronic, or mechanical, including photocopying, recording, taping, Web distribution, or information storage and retrieval systems—without the prior written permission of the publisher.

ISBN: 0-538-72322-X

1 2 3 4 5 6 7 8 9 WT 07 06 05 04 03 02 01 00 99

Printed in the United States of America

For permission to use material from this text, contact us by
- Web: www.thomsonrights.com
- Phone: 1-800-730-2214
- Fax: 1-800-730-2215

Brief Contents

Table of Contents

Preface

Employers tell us that communication is one of the most important skills they look for in job applicants. Unfortunately, many students lack the communication skills that will make them competitive in the job market. The goal of Communication for the Workplace *is to help students improve their skills so that they can communicate effectively on the job.*

Today's students will be working in an environment that requires them to collaborate in teams, solve problems, gather information, and use sophisticated technology to communicate with and service their internal and external customers. To meet this need, *Communication for the Workplace* supplements the traditional teaching of writing with new and innovative approaches.

    Communication for the Workplace includes thorough coverage of workplace communication, along with video case studies, critical-thinking case studies, Internet and e-mail applications, a glossary of technical terms, and an appendix on the basics of grammar. We've even developed a web site specifically designed for students and instructors using *Communication for the Workplace.*

Highlights

Communication for the Workplace includes exciting features and an innovative layout to make teaching and learning versatile and accessible. Comprehensive student and instructor resources complete the package.

- Chapters that are divided into sections to make content more accessible
- Chapter opening cases
- Essential chapter on researching and using information
- Special chapter on graphics
- Focused chapter on customer service
- Extensive instruction on writing reports and proposals
- Separate chapter on diversity
- Specific chapter on technical writing
- Internet and e-mail integration into activities
- Critical-thinking questions and case studies at the end of each chapter

- Career case studies and a continuing case at the end of each chapter
- Workplace Communication in Action Video tied to the video cases at the end of most chapters
- Video Casebook that includes additional cases not included in the student textbook
- Technology glossary
- Grammar appendix
- Documentation appendix for APA, MLA, and *The Chicago Manual of Style*
- PowerPoint presentation for each chapter
- Student Note Taking Guide, which enables students to take notes from the PowerPoint presentations
- Online Learning/WebCT
- Two- and four-color acetate transparencies

Features of the Textbook and Its Accompanying Package

Communication for the Workplace contains features that make it a powerful tool for teaching business communication. These features include:

- **Easy-to-read style and colorful illustrations.** The chapters are written in everyday language. Numerous bulleted or enumerated lists highlight important concepts. Chapters are further broken down into sections, which are usually around ten pages long. By having such short sections, the content of the text is divided into small, digestible units. Color photos, artwork, and figures provide visual reinforcement and act as a starting point for class discussion.
- **Integration of ethics and cross-cultural issues.** To provide students with forethought on these topics, concepts on ethics and diversity are incorporated into the text and in marginal notations.
- **Integration of technology.** Concepts about technology and exercises requiring the use of technology are integrated throughout the text. The technical terms used to express these concepts are defined in the Technical Glossary appendix at the end of the text.
- **Introductory case.** Each chapter begins with a case study. To solve the problems described in the case, students must apply the concepts in that chapter. Questions that follow the case challenge students to think critically to develop answers. The questions are answered, as appropriate, at the end of each section of the chapter. A summary of the case appears at the end of the chapter.

- **Career case studies**. Each chapter contains end-of-chapter cases related to "career clusters," requiring students to put themselves into various areas of profession while addressing communication concerns.
- **Continuing case**. Each chapter ends with a continuing case that follows the start-up and progress of a small business. Students are asked to answer questions and complete activities related to the owners' use of communication in running the business.
- **Chapter vignettes**. Each chapter includes at least two boxed features dealing with issues in the areas of diversity, technology, and ethics.
- **Ineffective/effective models**. Poorly written and well-written messages are illustrated side-by-side to provide students with models of good writing. Callouts highlight important features within the document models.
- **Correct and consistent document formats**. All document illustrations in the text and transparencies model correct formatting.
- **Opportunities to write and revise**. Many opportunities to write, edit, revise, and proofread are provided throughout the book, particularly in the end-of-chapter applications and the Study Guide.
- **Marginal notations**. The following icons identify marginal notations that enhance the chapter content and keep students focused:

 Technology

 Diversity

 SCANS

 Chapter Objectives

TEAMWORK

- **Complete but concise coverage.** *Communication for the Workplace* is divided into fifteen chapters. Each chapter is divided into sections, each dealing with an important business communication concept.
- **Checkpoints within sections.** Checkpoints located within sections provide immediate feedback, thereby enhancing learning. Students can check their answers to Checkpoints in Appendix E.
- **SCANS (Secretary's Commission on Achieving Necessary Skills).** These basic skills and competencies are highlighted throughout the chapter text and in marginal notations. Most of the end-of-chapter applications require the usage of these skills.
- **Chapter content and summary keyed to objectives.** Using a special icon, section objectives are highlighted at the point in the chapter where they are discussed. In the chapter summary, each objective is repeated and the pertinent chapter content summarized.
- **Checklists.** The checklists serve as concise reviews of the key elements or steps in various forms of communication.
- **Variety of activities.** Activities at the end of each chapter provide students the opportunity to work in teams, use technology, develop proofreading and editing skills, and exercise their critical-thinking skills.
- **Discussion questions.** Each section ends with discussion questions that require students to recall and apply concepts presented in the section, providing an opportunity for classroom discussion of key concepts.
- **Critical-thinking questions.** At the end of each chapter, critical-thinking questions require students to expand their thinking about the concepts presented in the chapter. These questions are excellent discussion generators.
- **Specialized glossaries.** Two glossaries are included in the appendices of the text—one for key terms and the other for technology terms. These glossary terms appear in bold type in the chapter text.
- **Video case.** To provide another opportunity to apply business communication concepts, a video case is included at the end of most of the chapters. This case offers another learning media for students. Using a related video clip from the Workplace Communication in Action Video, students analyze, problem-solve, and apply communication concepts to respond to the video case questions.

Student Resources

The student supplement learning package provided with *Communication for the Workplace* includes enrichment activities that provide additional opportunities for students to learn and apply the principles of effective communication.

- **Student Note Taking Guide.** This note taking guide is tied to the PowerPoint presentation provided for each chapter. The guide provides students with reduced images of the PowerPoint slides with space for taking notes beside each slide.
- **Study Guide.** The printed Study Guide provides students with additional opportunities to apply concepts from the chapter.
- **Online Learning/WebCT.** This browser-based instructional tool is appropriate for distance education or as an enhancement to classroom instruction, delivering interactive exercises, online reference documents, web links, presentation slides, and more. It is available in HTML format or as a WebCT cartridge.
- **Communication for the Workplace Web Site.** Accessed from South-Western Educational Publishing's web site, www.swep.com, the site contains additional activities, instructor support, and updates for links listed in the chapter Internet activities.
- **WebGuide: Your Online Career Search.** This real-time CD-ROM gives students the power to connect with the best resources on the Internet for the very latest in career information, resume writing and interviewing strategies, and job opportunities.
- **words@work.** This software package connects students to the skills needed to succeed in the workplace. Interactive lessons and exercises reinforce essential grammar, workplace writing, and employability skills. The 40 interactive lessons include 400 extensive grammar and writing exercises as well as a reference section and glossary including links to related Internet resources.

Instructor's Resources

The resources available to instructors using *Communication for the Workplace* include the following items:

- **Instructor's Manual.** The comprehensive instructor's manual contains general teaching suggestions and chapter-specific teaching outlines and solutions.

- **Instructor's Resource CD. PowerPoint presentations** for each chapter are available on the Instructor's Resource CD. The **PowerPoint97 Viewer** is provided free for users who do not have the PowerPoint program. The Viewer will allow users to view but not edit the PowerPoint presentations. **Chapter tests** are provided on the CD in Microsoft Word, WordPerfect, and Microsoft Works. Additional **grammar activities** are also provided on the CD.
- **Electronic Test Bank.** The electronic test bank includes all of the questions found on the Instructor's Resource CD test bank and gives you the ability to edit, add, delete, or randomly mix questions.
- **Video and Video Casebook.** The Workplace Communication in Action video features real companies dealing with realistic business situations. The Workplace Communication in Action Casebook and the video cases in the student text are related to the video and require students to analyze, problem-solve, and apply communication concepts.
- **Two- and Four-Color Acetate Transparencies.** Over 100 transparencies are available to assist with the discussion of chapters. Formatted letters and memos, checklists, and summaries of key concepts support and supplement the chapter material.
- **Annotated Instructor's Edition of the Study Guide.** Solutions overprint the student exercises in the Annotated Instructor's Edition of the Study Guide.

Acknowledgments

Many comments from instructors and students have proved valuable in the development of *Communication for the Workplace*. Special thanks go to the following individuals who provided formal comments.

Vanessa Arnold, The University of Mississippi

Paige P. Baker, Trinity Valley Community College

Sandra Banham, Northwest Mississippi Community College

Janice A. Bittner, Bradford Hall Career Institute

Janice Brown, Athens Area Vocational-Technical College

Billie Miller Cooper, Consumnes River College

Ann Cunningham, Branell Institute

Virginia Dochety, Sawyer College at Pomona

Donna Rose Echeverria, Vatterott College

T. T. Eiland, Citrus College

Andrew Halford, Paducah Community College

Helen T. Hebert, EAI/Remington College

Pam Joraanstad, Glendale Community College

Rita Lambrecht, Northeastern Junior College

Donna Madsen, Kirkwood Community College

Arenda Maxwell, American Institute of Business

Deborah L. Moeckel, Cayuga Community College

Dale A Neeck, Blackhawk Technical College

Jill Nesheim, Aaker's Business College

Douglas Okey, Spoon River College

Sue B. Palmer, Brevard Community College

Betsy Ray, Indiana Business College

Penny Sherrill, Wright Business School

Jean Sorensen, Grayson County College

Lynn R. Southerland, Middle Georgia Technical Institute

Kristene Sutliff, Southwest Missouri State University

Tony Sweet, National Education Center

Colleen Vawdrey, Utah Valley State College

Carmaletta M. Williams, Johnson County Community College

Dr. Andrea Wise, Georgia College

Nancy J. Zitsch, Computer Learning Network

We wish to extend our appreciation to all those who helped us deliver a quality text and support package. For their expertise and significant contributions, we are deeply grateful to the following individuals:

Linda Barr
Instructor and Senior Lecturer, Otterbein College, Westerville, OH

Jo Ann Judy
B.S. in Business Education, The Ohio State University
M.A. in Education, The Ohio State University
Freelance Writer and Training Consultant, Columbus, OH

Corinne R. Livesay
Instructor of Business, Mississippi College, Clinton, MS

Ned J. Racine
B.A. in English, UCLA; Masters in Writing, UCLA
Technical Writing and Software Trainer, Los Angeles, CA
Last school affiliation: Racine International Institute, Altadena, CA

Julie Roehl Coffin
Educational Consultant, Columbus, OH

Lee Wherry Brainerd
B.A. in Education, Northern Illinois University
K-12 certification in English, ESL/EFL, and French
Last school affiliation: National Education Center, Westwood, CA

chapter 1

Communicating in Your Life

1·1 Communication: Its Importance and Roles in Your Life

1·3 Electronic Communication

1·2 Communication: Responsibilities of Participants, Forms, and Barriers

Sending the Wrong Message

Three months ago, Anna Washington graduated from Winston Business College. Upon graduation, she obtained her first full-time job with IBM. Needless to say, she was very excited about the opportunity.

As the receptionist in the foyer of a new building, Anna works in an attractive setting. She has the opportunity to greet most employees, including upper management, and customers as they enter the building. She answers incoming calls and forwards them to appropriate individuals. Anna's computer is equipped with the usual software—word processing, spreadsheets, databases, presentation graphics, and games such as Solitaire, Hearts, FreeCell, and Minesweeper. She has e-mail and Internet access as well.

Anna sometimes uses her word processing software when the secretarial staff has too much work. While this opportunity doesn't happen too often, she enjoys it when it does come.

After three months, Anna's job has lost some of its appeal. She does not greet employees with the same enthusiasm as she did at first. Neither do her fellow employees respond as enthusiastically to her greetings. Her supervisor becomes irritated when she finds errors in the documents Anna has keyed. Answering incoming calls has become routine, almost boring.

Recently, Anna sent an e-mail to a friend about personal business and her supervisor caught her. She did not say anything at that time, but Anna could tell she was upset. Today, Anna was bored and decided to play Solitaire. She was in the middle of her first game when her supervisor brought a document to key. Her supervisor became upset and lectured Anna as several people, including a member of upper management, walked by. Obviously, Anna was very embarrassed.

Questions

1. How important is communication in Anna's job?

2. How did Anna use communication to reflect her attitude toward her job?

3. Did Anna use audience analysis? If so, did she use it effectively?

4. Does Anna's recent job performance reflect an I- or a you-attitude? Explain your answer.

5. What opportunities did electronic communication offer Anna?

6. What messages did Anna's use of electronic communication send to her supervisor?

1

1·1 Communication: Its Importance and Roles in Your Life

Objectives

After completing Section 1.1, you should be able to

1 List the purposes of communication.

2 Diagram the communication process and identify its main parts.

3 List the two media used for sending messages and the two media used for receiving messages.

▼KEY POINT

The effective communicator gets things done and frequently is an effective leader.

The Importance of Communication

The process you use to send and interpret messages so that they are understood is called **communication**. When communicating, you go through the process so quickly and naturally that you do not realize a process is being used. In the business environment, this process is called **business communication**. Being an effective communicator is critical to you in your personal, academic, and professional lives.

Research indicates that adults spend about two-thirds of each day communicating. Responding to friends, maintaining relationships with co-workers and supervisors, interpreting messages, and persuading customers are all ways people interact. Studies also indicate that managers spend more than 50 percent of their time attending meetings, making telephone calls, writing, and listening.

Communication skills include the ability to use language accurately—use proper grammar, choose words precisely, and spell correctly. They also include the ability to speak, teach, counsel, debate, and listen. Whether you realize it or not, your success in life is dependent upon your communication skills.

The Purposes of Communication

We all use communication for five basic purposes: (1) to establish and build goodwill, (2) to persuade, (3) to obtain or share information, (4) to establish personal effectiveness, and (5) to build self-esteem.

To Establish and Build Goodwill

Objective

1

▼KEY POINT

Effective use of goodwill turns coworkers into friends.

Your ability to establish and build relationships affects every aspect of your life. Whether in your social, academic, or professional life, this ability determines the depth of your relationships with your friends, loved ones, family, classmates, and coworkers. Good relationships result in **goodwill**—the favorable reputation that an individual or a business has with its customers. Any communication that helps to develop a better relationship between you and your receiver builds goodwill.

To Persuade

Motivating or persuading others to act in a certain way depends on your ability to convince them that they will benefit from such an action. When others—whether social friends or family, classmates or teachers, supervisors or co-workers—feel that you are sincerely concerned about them personally, your relationship becomes more valued.

To Obtain or Share Information

Information is one of the most valuable resources we have. You must communicate to obtain the information you need and to share the information you have. You need this valuable resource to function successfully with friends, at school, and at work.

To Establish Personal Effectiveness

When you receive a message that is accurate, easy to understand, and error-free, you form a positive image of the sender. If you receive a message full of errors, you suspect that the sender is careless or thoughtless. Thus, whether in a social, academic, or professional setting, a positive image is very important.

To Build Self-Esteem

Positive comments or reactions from others increase your self-esteem. Such positive reinforcement causes you to feel good about yourself and your chances for success. This confidence has a positive impact on your social relationships, your academic associates, and your co-workers.

In summary, you spend a great deal of time communicating. How you communicate critically impacts your social, academic, and professional lives.

SCANS
Employability

Interpersonal: Working on Teams
A key to your success on the job is your ability to work and get along with your co-workers.

Personal Qualities: Self-Management
Your communication skills tell your subordinates, co-workers, and supervisors what kind of person you really are—organized, disorganized, careful, careless, thoughtful, thoughtless, etc.

The Communication Process

Before the communication process begins, you create or develop an idea. To communicate the idea, you will use the communication process. The communication process, illustrated in Figure 1.1, consists of five components: (a) the sender, (b) the message, (c) the receiver, (d) the feedback, and (e) the channel.

Usually, the communication process is interpersonal (between persons). However, it may occur between a person and a machine, such as a computer. It may also occur between two machines. Computers, printers, and fax machines can exchange information.

Objective

The Sender

The sender is a person or thing that originates a message and initiates the communication process. When you are the sender, you have major responsibilities in the communication process. These are described in more detail in Section 1.2.

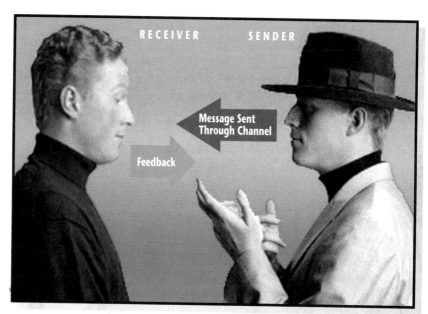

FIGURE 1-1 The main components of communication are sender, message, receiver, feedback, and channel.

Using nonverbal symbols to deliberately mislead receivers can cause others to question your honesty.

DIVERSITY

The meanings associated with nonverbal symbols vary according to culture and nationality. For example, in some cultures it is important to be on time. In others, it is customary to be late.

The Message

A message is composed of a set of symbols. These symbols can be verbal or nonverbal. Verbal symbols are words used when speaking or writing. Letters, memorandums, reports, brochures, catalogs, manuals, and annual reports are composed of verbal symbols. These symbols are also used when speaking face-to-face or on the telephone, participating in a conference or meeting, or delivering a speech.

Nonverbal symbols such as gestures, posture, facial expressions, appearance, time, tone of voice, eye contact, and space always accompany verbal symbols. Whether you realize it or not, you use nonverbal symbols to send and determine attitudes.

All messages contain nonverbal symbols that help the receiver interpret verbal symbols. If verbal and nonverbal symbols conflict, receivers generally believe the nonverbal symbols over the verbal symbols. For example, a sales representative may say that your account is very important but then keeps you waiting. The representative's nonverbal communication may cause you to question the representative's sincerity, and you may decide to take your business elsewhere.

The Receiver

A person or thing to whom a message is sent is the receiver. When you are the receiver, your responsibility is to give meaning to the verbal and nonverbal symbols used by the sender. (Techniques to accomplish this task are discussed in Section 1.2 of this chapter.) The meaning receivers give to messages depends on their respective educational backgrounds, experiences, interests, opinions, and emotional states.

Miscommunication results if the receiver gives the message a different meaning than the sender intended.

The Feedback

Feedback is the response of a receiver to a message. Feedback may be nonverbal (a smile, a frown, a pause, etc.) or it may be verbal (a telephone call or a letter). Any response—even no response—is feedback.

Feedback is a critical component of your communication because it helps you determine whether the receiver has understood the message. If the receiver looks confused (nonverbal feedback), you know that you need to clarify, provide additional information, or modify the message. To be meaningful, feedback must accurately reflect the receiver's reaction to the message.

The Channel

The mode a sender selects to send a message is called the channel. Letters, memorandums, and reports are the most common channels for written messages. One-to-one conversations, telephone conversations, and meetings are common channels of oral messages. E-mail, videoconferences, and voice mail are common channels of electronic messages.

Selecting the appropriate channel becomes more significant as the importance or sensitivity of your message increases. When trying to resolve a sensitive issue with a client, for example, you must carefully weigh the merits of communicating by telephone or by letter. Using the telephone indicates a sense of urgency and allows immediate feedback. On the other hand, a letter enables the sender to explain a position and provide a written record of the message. Often, using both channels is appropriate. You might discuss the situation over the telephone and then follow up with a letter.

TECHNOLOGY
E-mail is being used more and more as a channel of communication. It is easy to send a message and "copy everyone." However, this practice can damage your image as a co-worker.

Checkpoint 1

The Purposes and Process of Communication

Answer the following questions:
1. When communicating, what are the types of symbols that make up a message?
2. When communicating, how important is channel? Why?
3. What is the purpose(s) of each of the following communications?
   a. You greet a customer by saying, "May I help you?"
   b. Your shop supervisor tells you that you are doing a good job.
   c. A company puts its web page on the Internet.

Check your answers in Appendix E.

Communication Media: Their Importance to Your Success

Objective

3

INTERNET

For additional insight into overcoming the fear of public speaking, go to **http://www.toastmasters.org**

SCANS
Employability

Basic Skills: Speaking
When interviewing for a position, employers are usually looking for a confident, teachable person. How you express yourself (speak) in an interview will be used by the interviewer as a reflection of your self-confidence and "teachability."

Basic Skills: Writing
Your written documents become a record by which your supervisors will judge your ability to communicate.

As humans, we have two means by which to send messages and two means by which we receive them. To send messages, we speak and write; these messages are accompanied by nonverbal symbols. To receive messages, we read or listen. These media are critical to you in your professional, academic, and personal lives.

Speaking

The way you send your messages using oral skills over a period of time creates an image. This image is a key to your success. For example, in your professional life, the way you present your messages orally tells your co-workers and supervisors how well you are organized. The accent or pronunciation of words that accompanies your language and your word selection conveys a level of professionalism. You create a professional image by speaking and using words correctly.

In the academic setting, you are in the process of learning to create a professional image. Nevertheless, your assignments are used to evaluate you and where you are in this process. Your pronunciation and word selection when presenting yourself orally reflect your development.

In our personal lives, acceptance is very important. We want to be with those who accept us the way we are. In this setting, the way you speak is important to your acceptance. For example, when in relaxed settings with friends, we know we "fit in." Also, in intimate or important personal situations, your ability to say exactly what you feel is essential for your success.

Writing

Though writing is the least used communication media, it receives a great deal of attention in our schools. Why? In a professional setting, your writing (memorandums, letters, and reports) becomes a written record of your communication skills.

In an educational setting, writing is required extensively. You usually have written reports or projects in many courses. Thus, your grades—a major factor used to judge your success in education—are influenced by your writing skills.

In your personal life, your ability to write an effective letter can deepen a relationship, earn the respect of a friend, and reflect your attitude. Also, sometimes it is easier to tell someone how you feel in a letter rather than face-to-face. In such situations, your writing skills are very important. You want that good friend to know exactly how you feel.

Reading

One of the means to receive a message is through reading. In a professional setting, reading is a part of every job. You will be required to read and understand memorandums, letters, and reports. You will be expected to read effectively. Also, in this age of information, you will need to read continually in order to stay up to date.

In an academic setting, you read constantly. The challenge is to stay focused in order to gather the information needed from the text, articles, and handouts you read. Much of your academic performance is based on your reading skills.

Reading is important in your personal life also. By reading newspapers, magazines, and books, you broaden your knowledge and become a more interesting person. Because you will have more information to share, others may view you more positively and seek your opinion or seek the information you may have.

Listening

The other means to receive a message is through listening. Though the most frequently used means of communication, it is the least taught. Listening is more than just hearing; it also requires understanding. In a professional setting, listening is critical. When receiving an oral message, your response must be correct. If you fail to listen to customers or clients, you may lose their business.

In an educational setting, listening effectively is critical. Effective listening results in doing the right assignment, doing the assignment correctly, understanding the sender's message, and taking notes effectively. Doing these activities well results in learning and, most of the time, good grades.

In a personal setting, listening deepens relationships. The power of listening in our personal relationships is immense. When we listen to someone, we say nonverbally, "You are important." The failure to listen sends a message to a person that he or she is unimportant.

TECHNOLOGY

One of the jobs in greatest demand is computer information systems workers. For those who choose this career area, reading is critical. To fail to read about the development of hardware and software for just a short period can cause a person to become quite dated.

Checkpoint 2

Usage of Communication Media

Indicate the media you would use for the following messages and explain your selection.
1. You want to ask your supervisor for a day off.
2. You need to give the head of the Sales Department your sales figures for last month. They are quite good.
3. You want to tell a subordinate, Les, that he can have a day off as he requested.
4. You must tell Anna (see case study on page 1) that she cannot play computer games while on the job.

Check your answers in Appendix E.

Personal Qualities: Responsibility, Integrity
Your supervisors will constantly use your nonverbal communications to determine your attitude about your job.

> ## CASE 1:
> ## *A n s w e r s*
>
> ### Responses to Questions 1 and 2 in Chapter Opener
>
> 1. **How important is communication in Anna's job?**
>   The main part of Anna's job is communication. Almost everything she does is seen by others and used by them to assess her performance. Anna greets employees and customers, answers incoming calls, and helps the secretarial staff with computer work. These responsibilities all require Anna to have good communication skills.
>
>   Anna's errors in keyed documents send the message that she is either careless or sloppy—a message she does not want to send to her supervisor.
>
> 2. **How did Anna use communication to reflect her attitude toward her job?**
>   Anna's attitude toward her job seems to be declining. This message is sent nonverbally by her actions. For example, she is less enthusiastic when greeting employees. She seems bored to the point of sending personal e-mail and playing games. These nonverbal signals all indicate that Anna is losing excitement for her job.

DISCUSSION QUESTIONS

1. Which of the five purposes of communication is most important? Justify your answer.
2. When you send a message but your receiver gives you no feedback, how do you interpret the receiver's reaction?
3. Which of the communication media do you use the most? the least? Do your responses reflect the amount of time dedicated to the teaching of these skills in schools?

1·2 Communication: Responsibilities of Participants, Forms, and Barriers

As Section 1.1 indicates, communication is critical to your success in all aspects of life. Thus, understanding your responsibilities as a participant in communication, understanding the forms of communication, and being aware of barriers to effective communication will aid you in becoming a better communicator.

Responsibilities of Participants

In the communication process, there are two participants—senders and receivers. For the communication process to be effective, each has important responsibilities.

The Sender's Responsibilities

The sender's responsibilities in the communication process are critical and sometimes dependent upon personal judgment. However, the better you learn to fulfill these responsibilities, the better communicator you will become.

Because the sender initiates the communication process by sending a message, he or she selects the media for the message and the verbal and nonverbal symbols used in the message. To select these well, the sender must (1) analyze and understand the receiver—a process sometimes called *audience analysis*, (2) analyze and understand the environment in which the message will be sent, and (3) encourage and interpret feedback.

Audience Analysis

Because no two audiences are alike, the more you know about your receiver, the better you will be able to analyze your audience. **Audience analysis** is the process used to examine your receiver or audience. Knowing his or her background interests, attitudes, and emotional state will help you select symbols that your receiver will accept.

Objectives

After completing Section 1.2, you should be able to

1. List the three major responsibilities of senders and two major responsibilities of receivers.

2. Define the forms of communication.

3. List the two types of barriers to communication and provide examples.

Objective

1

KEY POINT

In the communication process, the sender's job is the most difficult because he or she is trying to analyze and understand others (the receivers).

DIVERSITY

Is Diversity Really Important?

For whom is diversity important? Is it important only to large, multinational corporations? Is it important to a national company? Is it important to a small company?

The multinational corporation views the world as a global marketplace. As a result, it is concerned about its ability to do business across cultures. To expand its markets and to continue increasing profitability, it must compete successfully in many countries. Thus, multicultural knowledge, understanding, and skills are great assets to multinational corporations.

The smaller, yet nationwide, company must compete and be profitable within its country's borders. The company must find a way to make its products and services attractive to potential customers from different backgrounds and ethnic and technology-oriented groups. A solid diversity-conscious advertising plan and the use of e-commerce are important tools in capturing these growing markets.

Diversity is also important to the small business within a community. The diversity within the population of the United States is dynamic. Its continual change presents many opportunities to small businesses. Think about how the market has changed. Who eats fried chicken—something that used to be a southern dish? How popular is Taco Bell? The economy and the demands of its members are increasingly diverse. To depend upon just one culture or segment of that economy limits the potential profits or existence of even a small company. ■

Questions that you should ask when analyzing the background of your receiver are

1. How much education does the receiver have?
2. Does the receiver have education that relates to the topic of this message? If so, how much?
3. Does the receiver have work experience that relates to the topic of this message? If so, how much?
4. Have I interacted with this receiver before? If so, what is our relationship?

Answers to the preceding questions will assist you in selecting the appropriate words for your message. The words you select for your message reflect your attitude about the receiver and the message.

Questions that will help you identify your receiver's interests are

1. What are the concerns of the receiver?
2. What are the needs of the receiver?
3. Does the receiver have a particular motive?
4. Does the receiver have a desired outcome?

DIVERSITY

The questions about "interests" are critical when analyzing an audience composed of differing cultures or nationalities.

A receiver's level of interest is an important element of audience analysis and is dependent upon the situation. As time passes, the situation and interests may change. For example, an individual who wants to sell a home has basic concerns: price and timing. However, if the seller has a deadline in another city to take up a new job, concerns and even the seller's needs will change as the deadline approaches. Motives and desired outcomes may change from "profit" to "sell as soon as possible."

Questions that will help you identify the receiver's attitudes are

1. What are the beliefs, biases, values, and viewpoints of the receiver?
2. What words will make a positive impression? a negative impression?
3. Are there ideas that can be used to communicate effectively with the receiver? If so, what are they?

Factors that affect a receiver's attitudes are personality, status, power, expectations, nationality, and culture. To illustrate, let's use nationality and culture. Generally speaking, Italians might indicate that something is "difficult to accomplish" rather than telling someone "no." Europeans stand closer to individuals than do Americans. Thus, nonverbal symbols have different meanings based on nationality and culture.

Lastly, you must consider the receiver's emotional state. Questions that will reveal the receiver's emotional state are

1. Will the message make the receiver happy? sad? pleased? upset? Will it affect the receiver at all?
2. Is the receiver in a satisfactory mood to receive the message? If not, do I have time to wait?

This assessment determines the order and timing of your message. In most cultures, when giving pleasant news or routine news to the receiver, the sender presents the main idea first, followed by the supporting information. When giving a message that will make the receiver unhappy or angry, most cultures require that reasons for the bad news be given before the bad news itself.

If the receiver is in a good mood, now is the time to send your message. If he or she is in a bad mood, perhaps you could wait. The question is, "Do you have the time to wait?"

One common pitfall when adjusting for your audience is the I-attitude. When conveying messages, senders need to employ the you-attitude. The you-attitude focuses on the needs, interests, and concerns of the receiver; the I-attitude focuses on the sender. Look at the following examples.

TECHNOLOGY
Using electronic media is very easy, and so using such means to send an *inappropriate* message is becoming more and more common. Use them thoughtfully.

I-Attitude	You-Attitude
I am pleased to inform you that your Tech Credit Card has been approved.	Welcome to the Tech family. Come in and use your Tech Credit Card soon.

(continued)

I-Attitude	You-Attitude
I am sorry. I cannot ship your order until July 1. We are temporarily out of stock of those items.	On July 1, your order will be shipped. The delay is caused by high demand for those items.
We can sell you each box of chocolates for $5, and you can charge your customers $10, leaving $5 for profit.	Make $5 profit on each box of chocolates—your cost is $5 and your selling price is $10.

As these examples illustrate, the you-attitude reflects the needs, interests, and concerns of the receiver. Learn to use the you-attitude in your communications, and you will be perceived as a person sincerely interested in your customers, clients, and friends.

After answering all these questions about your receiver, you are ready to apply the answers and adjust your message based on the background, needs, interests, and concerns of your receiver. Though you may not realize it, you probably have used audience analysis before. Answer this question: "Have you ever put off giving someone a message because he or she is in a bad mood?" If you have, you were using audience analysis to make your decision. You were taking the receiver's emotional state into consideration and deciding to postpone the message. Nevertheless, though most of us have used audience analysis in the past, generally we need to become much more skilled in applying information about our receivers. Background, interests, attitude, and emotional state all make significant contributions to the understanding of your receiver. Effective application of this knowledge will aid you in your effectiveness as a sender.

Message Environment

Another factor a sender must consider when sending a message is its environment.  **Message environment** refers to the physical and social setting in which a message is sent.

When considering physical environment, the sender must ask this question: "Is the environment such that my message will be understood and receive the desired reaction?" If the answer is "yes," then the message should be sent. If it is "no," then it should not be sent. Many things affecting the environment could indicate it is necessary to delay the sending of a message. Below are some examples:

1. When an assembly line is behind schedule, you probably do not want to ask your supervisor for time off.
2. When your supervisor is ill, it is probably not a good time to make suggestions on how to improve production or to ask for a raise.

Another factor of message environment is the social setting. For example, an office party, in most situations, would not be a good place

↓ KEY POINT

Sending a message in the wrong environment illustrates a lack of tact or understanding.

to conduct office business. Sometimes the golf course is a good place to conduct business; other times it is not. The sender must analyze the environment in which he or she is considering sending a message and then react accordingly.

Soliciting Feedback

A challenge for senders is to keep the communication process open by sincerely wanting feedback from receivers. Your attitudes greatly impact the likelihood of your receiving honest feedback. Critical to your ability to receive feedback are your interpersonal communication skills. If receivers feel you are open, sincere, honest, and attentive to their needs, interests, and concerns, you increase your chances for honest feedback.

The Receiver's Responsibilities

The receiver's responsibilities are important and can be more easily controlled than those of the sender. Basically, the receiver's responsibilities are to read and listen effectively.

Reading

Focusing and ensuring understanding are the keys to effective reading. For most of us, it is a matter of discipline. If you want the information badly enough, then you will be willing to pay the price to get it; that price is your time. If you need to, read with a dictionary beside you. When you come upon a word you do not understand, look it up. After

SCANS
Employability

Thinking Skills: Seeing Things in the Mind's Eye
Effective leaders know how to get and use feedback. They view it as an opportunity to see themselves as others see them.

Deceptive feedback can damage a company, a receiver, or a sender.

For suggestions on how to improve your reading skills, go to
http://www.abbylearn.com

Some social situations are conducive to business discussions; others are not. Be sensitive to the mood and purpose of the event, as well as the people who are with you. Act professionally in all social situations with co-workers.

looking up a word a few times, you will soon remember what it means and will not have to look it up again.

Listening

Listening can be a little more self-threatening. When you do not understand a message and you really want to understand it, you must expose your lack of understanding by asking questions. Such an admission can be intimidating. Thus, effective listening can be challenging to us because of our egos. Two techniques can be used to ensure effective listening: (1) clarify for understanding and (2) check for understanding.

To clarify for understanding means that you, as the receiver, know you do not understand some aspect of the message. Hence, you must ask questions. Too frequently, senders assume that "I have said it; therefore, you understand." Such an attitude leaves the burden for effective communication on the receiver. When you are in such a situation, you must ask questions for clarification.

Good listeners also check for understanding. When in listening situations, good listeners paraphrase the message. This action will help to ensure that the sender was clear. If the sender was not clear, the paraphrasing will indicate a problem in communication. Then it is the sender's responsibility to clarify.

KEY POINT

Failure to ask questions when you do not understand indicates that learning is not as important as your ego or fear of looking "dumb."

---

3 Checkpoint

Responsibilities of Participants

Match the responsibility with the participant.

Responsibility	Participant
1. Listening effectively	Sender
2. Assess message environment	Receiver
3. Solicit feedback	
4. Read accurately	
5. Apply audience analysis	

Check your answers in Appendix E.

Objective

Forms of Communication

Forms of communication you encounter are external or internal and formal or informal. These messages may be written, oral, or electronic.

External and Internal Communication

External communication originates within a company and is sent to receivers outside the company. Communication with clients, customers, sales representatives, governmental agencies, advertising agencies, and transportation agencies outside the company is external.

Internal communication originates and is sent to receivers within a company. For example, a memorandum from a supervisor to an employee is an internal communication.

Formal and Informal Communication

Formal communication occurs through established lines of authority and can be written or oral. As Figure 1-2 illustrates, communication may travel down, across, or up lines of authority.

Communication that travels down the hierarchy from a superior (supervisor, manager, or executive) to subordinates is *downward communication*. Instructions from a project manager to project team members travel downward. Policies established by the board of directors and company officers are relayed downward to department managers and then to other employees.

Communication among peers—persons of the same status—is *lateral communication* (sometimes call *horizontal communication*). A memorandum from one department head to another is an example of lateral communication. Lateral communication encourages cooperation between departments and divisions of an organization.

Upward communication refers to communication from subordinates to supervisors. When employees convey to their superiors suggestions

↓KEY POINT

For written business messages, the memo is the most common format.

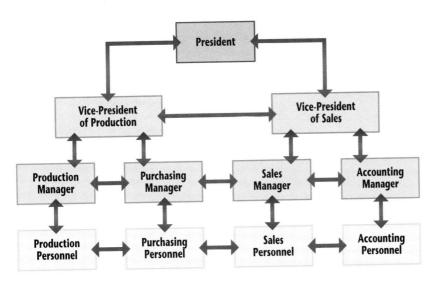

red = downward communication
blue = upward
green = lateral

FIGURE 1-2 Formal communication travels within the lines of a hierarchy. Informal communication does not follow any lines within a hierarchy.

for improving production, their attitudes and feelings about their jobs, or their perception of the organization, they are communicating upward. Likewise, a manager's recommendation to company officers is upward communication.

Informal communication does not follow established lines of authority. It may be written or oral. Sharing interests over lunch or during breaks and socializing after work are examples of informal communication. Often referred to as the *grapevine*, informal communication is usually a rapid communication channel, although not always an accurate one.

Written, Oral, and Electronic Communication

Letters, memorandums, and reports are common forms of written business communication. **Letters** are external documents that may be addressed to business associates, customers, and clients.

Memorandums, often called *memos*, are internal documents used to communicate with one or more co-workers. Because co-workers are the receivers, memos are usually less formal than letters.

Reports are designed to provide meaningful information to a group of people. They may be formal documents, such as research studies or proposals to top management, or informal documents, such as memo reports.

Agendas, minutes of meetings, speeches, brochures, business directories, legal documents, office manuals, and announcements are other forms of written communication used in business. Written communication is used in the workplace for three reasons:

1. It provides a record of the information exchanged. For example, a price quoted in a written bid cannot be disputed.
2. It can be revised until the final message is logical and clear. This factor is especially important when complex information must be explained.
3. It enables the receiver to analyze a message and refer to it as many times as necessary.

Generally, **oral communication** can be sent quickly and provides immediate feedback to the sender. You may use oral communication (one-to-one conversations and telephone conversations) when seeking opinions, explaining procedures, providing counseling, or building relationships.

Written messages may be composed, edited, and transmitted on computers. These written electronic messages are forms of *electronic mail* or *e-mail*. These messages may be internal or external. Oral messages may be sent over the telephone and stored electronically in a computer for playback later on a *voice mail* system. E-mail and voice mail are discussed in greater detail in Section 1.3 and throughout the book.

DIVERSITY

Be aware that acceptable letter format and content varies from culture to culture and nation to nation.

TECHNOLOGY

Though you may use e-mail a great deal, do not become careless in your content. Receivers will use these messages to evaluate your communication skills.

Checkpoint 4

Forms of Communication

Identify each message according to the following categories:

> Downward, upward, or lateral
> Internal or external
> Oral or written

1. A conversation between supervisors of differing departments
2. A letter from the vice president of sales to a client
3. A memo from employee to supervisor informing the supervisor that the employee will be on jury duty next Thursday
4. A report from a vice president to the president of the company
5. An e-mail from an entry-level worker to his supervisor

Check your answers in Appendix E.

Barriers to Communication

Although the primary goal of communication is for the receiver to interpret the message as the sender intended, frequently this goal is not achieved. Communication barriers are obstacles to the communication process. Learning to recognize external and internal communication barriers will help you plan your messages and become a more effective communicator.

Objective 3

External Barriers

Conditions outside the receiver and the sender that detract from the communication process are called external barriers. Examples include environmental factors, such as lighting, heat, humidity, comfort, and noise.

The appearance of a written document also may be an external barrier to communication. A document can create an external barrier if it is smudged; contains errors in content, spelling, or grammar; or is presented in an inappropriate format. You could become so distracted with the appearance of the document that you fail to comprehend its contents.

Another external barrier to communication within an organization is a "closed or authoritarian climate." In such an environment, decisions and policies often are made and implemented by command. Consequently, workers may stop offering suggestions because they may feel that making suggestions is useless.

Conversely, in an open climate in which ideas and information are welcomed, communication flows easily. Workers feel that supervisors and management are receptive to their ideas, which facilitates communication. Most managers in progressive organizations realize the importance of maintaining open communication. They know that being sensitive to employees' attitudes and ideas encourages creativity and growth.

Internal Barriers

People have different personalities, educational backgrounds, experiences, cultures, statuses, and biases. These **internal barriers** affect a sender's willingness and ability to express messages and a receiver's ability to interpret them accurately.

In meetings, extroverts (outward, outspoken, and outgoing individuals) are apt to express ideas and appear to be very knowledgeable. Introverts (inward, quiet, and shy individuals) may not express their opinions until someone asks for them. One-to-one conversation is easier for extroverts than introverts. To avoid becoming a communication barrier, extroverts need to make sure they think before they speak. For introverts to avoid becoming a barrier, they need to make sure they speak.

Another internal barrier to communication can be the motivation or interests of the receiver. If the receiver is interested in the topic or project, he or she will listen and probably participate in any discussion. If he or she is not interested, he or she may not listen or participate.

SCANS
Employability

**Thinking Skills:
Problem Solving**
As your ability to recognize and overcome barriers to your communications improves, your ability to communicate effectively also will improve.

Communications at meetings can be especially difficult to manage. At any one meeting, barriers to communication may be the result of environmental factors, internal factors of individuals, as well as the interaction of participants at the meeting.

Checkpoint 5

Barriers to Communication

Which type of barrier, internal or external, is each of the following?
1. The receiver feels sick.
2. The room is so hot that it distracts the listener.
3. The street noise is so loud the listener cannot hear the radio.
4. The reader cannot concentrate because of a personal problem.
5. The reader thinks the letter contains too many spelling and grammar errors.

Check your answers in Appendix E.

CASE 1:

Answers

Responses to Questions 3 and 4 in Chapter Opener

3. **Did Anna use audience analysis? If so, did she use it effectively?**

   Yes, Anna did use audience analysis. She tried to interpret the attitudes of others she was attempting to serve. For example, she interpreted that others were not reacting to her greetings as enthusiastically as they first did. Did she use audience analysis effectively? Probably—you cannot really tell unless you were there to observe the situation.

4. **Does Anna's recent job performance reflect an I- or a you-attitude? Explain your answer.**

   Anna's recent job performance reflects an I-attitude. Sending a personal e-mail and playing a game on the job reflect concerns for her wants rather than the needs of others.

SCANS
Employability

Interpersonal Skills: Working on Teams, Serving Customers
In general, workers who have the you-attitude have good interpersonal relationships with their customers, peers, and supervisors.

DISCUSSION QUESTIONS

1. Of the three responsibilities of the sender, which is most important?
2. When would you use a letter to send a message? When would you use a memo? When would you use an oral message rather than a written one?
3. What is the communication challenge for an extrovert? an introvert?

1·3 Electronic Communication

Objectives

After completing Section 1.3, you should be able to

1 Identify equipment and software used to create and edit documents.

2 Identify technologies used to send and store documents electronically.

3 Identify technologies used to send oral messages electronically.

Objective

1

↓ KEY POINT

The technology you now use will change dramatically in the near future.

Creating and Editing a Document

Technology has had a tremendous impact on the way messages are created and edited. To create documents, we use computerized workstations with software, scanners, and voice recognition equipment. To edit documents, we use word processing software. Editing includes keying, proofreading, and revising a draft document to achieve its final form.

Creating a Document

In today's business world, documents are frequently created using a computer, an electronic workstation, a scanner, or voice recognition equipment.

Computers

Computers are machines that perform rapid, often complex, electronic processes to facilitate or automate procedures. They range in size and power from large supercomputers to small notebook computers that can fit in your hand (palm tops). Computerized workstations are becoming more and more popular as computers become smaller, more powerful, and less expensive. The most common part of a workstation is the **personal computer** (PC), also called a *microcomputer*. The personal computer has made office technology less expensive and more accessible to workers at all levels.

Electronic Workstations

An **electronic workstation** is a computerized workstation that consists of a keyboard, monitor or display screen, printer, central processing unit, and storage device. The **screen**, also called a monitor, displays the document as it is keyed. The **printer** produces the hard copy (printed copy).

A **central processing unit** (CPU) contains computer chips that control the operating functions of a workstation. These microprocessors work with the software (programmed instructions) to process text, perform mathematical calculations, and sort information. As information is keyed, it is recorded on a storage device. The storage device may be internal (hard disk) or external (floppy disk).

TECHNOLOGY

Your Computer—A Pain in the Neck?

For Sale: Wrist Support—$35; Mouse Support—$25; Foot Rest—$40; Monitor Risers—$30; Ergonomic Keyboard Tray—$130; Arm Support—$100; Polaroid Glare Screen—$150. All these items are for those suffering from the pain of using a computer.

While long hours on a computer can be fun and enable us to do our work quickly and efficiently, those same long hours can cause physical discomfort for some people. Research indicates that physical condition, medical conditions (diabetes, arthritis, and scoliosis, for example), hobbies (weightlifting, handball, playing the guitar), and our ability to relax or not to relax impact the probability of experiencing physical discomfort while using a computer. Common body areas in which computer pain occurs are the neck, shoulders, arms, and hands.

Three suggestions for avoiding this type of pain are:

1. Relax your arms while using your computer. This will reduce muscle strain and conserve energy.
2. Position equipment so that you feel comfortable.

Although setting up a workstation seems simple, place equipment thoughtfully—especially the mouse, keyboard, and screen.

3. Vary your work so that you avoid sitting for hours in the same position. Balance your muscle usage by moving around and changing the physical demands on your muscles.

Additional information about this type of pain and how to avoid it can be found at **http://www.me .berkeley.edu/ergo/ tips/tips.html**. ■

Scanners

A scanner converts printed text into a digital form that can be read by a computer or word processor. As text is scanned, it appears on the screen in the correct format. Updating a printed manual is relatively easy using a scanner. The scanner reads the printed pages and records them in digital form on a disk. The keyboarder calls the manual to the screen and keys only the revisions.

An image scanner can read graphs, charts, or photographs. Once scanned, these images can be integrated into text documents. Hand-held and desktop scanners are available. Scanners are commonly used in checkout stations in retail stores.

Voice Recognition Equipment

Voice recognition technology allows spoken words to be reproduced in printed form on a computer screen. As you speak into a microphone or a headset, the voice sounds are converted into digital impulses that are then compared with sound patterns recorded in the computer's memory. If the two match, the spoken words will be displayed on a computer screen.

▼KEY POINT

Wal-Mart, JC Penney, Dillard's, Kroger, and other major companies use scanners to identify prices at checkout points and to maintain inventories.

TECHNOLOGY

The voice recognition technology available today is somewhat limited. However, progress is being made almost daily.

Most software is copyrighted and cannot be legally copied. However, some software, called shareware, can be legally copied and shared.

DIVERSITY

Some word processing software provides the capability to key in foreign languages.

TECHNOLOGY

- Many word processing software packages now contain document analysis software that checks for spelling and grammar and determines reading difficulty.

- Your city or county tax department probably has a database that contains property records for all residents. This database will be used to determine your taxes.

Editing a Document

Editing includes keying, proofreading, printing, and revising a draft document to achieve a final form. Software is used to edit documents.

Software provides instructions to a computer on how to perform particular functions. Software interacts with the logic of the computer to perform the desired operations. The software entitled Windows makes the computer and its software more *user friendly*. It enables several software packages to run at the same time. Using a mouse or another device, the computer can move easily among programs. For example, a user can use word processing and a database program at the same time.

Word processing software enables the user to enter, format, revise, and print text efficiently. Text can be added, deleted, moved, revised, italicized, converted to bold, put in contrasting typefaces, and much more. Microsoft Word and WordPerfect are popular word processing software programs.

An integrated software package, often called a *suite*, contains word processing, spreadsheet, database management, and graphics programs. These programs can run simultaneously, and documents in one program can be integrated (merged) into another. Integrated software packages include Microsoft Office, Lotus SmartSuite, and Corel Office Suite.

Spreadsheet software creates an electronic worksheet consisting of rows and columns. Rows are read across and columns are read down. The point at which they intersect is called a *cell*. Formulas are entered within cells to add, subtract, multiply, and divide the various columns and rows. By using formulas, you can change one figure in a spreadsheet and all related figures will be updated automatically. Spreadsheet programs include Excel, Lotus 1-2-3, and Quattro Pro.

Database management software provides a way to store and retrieve information using a computer. Client or customer information often is stored in a database. Specific information needed, such as the date of the last order or payment, can be retrieved quickly by searching the database. Among the database software programs available are Microsoft Access, dBase, and Oracle 8i.

Graphics software is used primarily for two purposes: (1) to analyze data, and (2) to create visual aids to support presentations. Analytical graphics software converts numbers, which may originate from a spreadsheet or a database, into meaningful charts and graphs, such as line charts, bar charts, and pie charts. Such visuals enable managers and other professionals to analyze data easily. Presentation graphics software is used for creating visual aids, such as transparencies and slides. Graphics software packages include PowerPoint and Corel Draw. See Chapter 10 for a discussion of the creation and use of visual aids.

With desktop publishing software, a personal computer and a high quality printer can produce documents of typeset quality. Businesses use desktop publishing software to produce newsletters, brochures, reports, advertisements, and other publications that previously were prepared by commercial printers. Text can be formatted in different type sizes and styles. Spacing between lines, called *leading*, can be adjusted to add more or less white space to give the desired effect. Copy can be formatted in newspaper columns, and graphics and scanned images can be combined with text.

TECHNOLOGY
Because of networking and the Internet, many personal computer users have access to large databases and powerful computers.

Checkpoint 6

Production of Documents

Match the equipment or software on the left with the correct function or definition on the right.

1. Graphics   a. Software that enables text to be keyed, stored, and revised easily

2. Desktop Publishing   b. A device that reads and converts paper documents into a form that can be read by a computer

3. Personal Computer   c. Software that designs illustrations or charts

4. Word Processing   d. A CPU that uses word processing and other software applications

5. Scanner   e. Software that can produce documents of typeset quality

6. Spreadsheet   f. Software that provides an electronic worksheet

Check your answers in Appendix E.

Sending a Document Electronically

Traditional means of sending documents, such as hand delivery, interoffice mail, the U.S. Postal Service, and private carriers like Federal Express, are still widely used. Distribution by electronic methods, however, provides faster and more efficient delivery.

Communication sent electronically travels over an office network, a local network, or a wide area network. In an office network, a company has a public directory on its network where someone can post a document and other employees can access it. This process eliminates sending multiple copies to several people and makes for quicker access. It also allows employees to update information on a timely basis, so everyone has access to current information. The computers connected to this network can be in the office or in employees' homes.

A local area network (LAN) connects various workstations within a building or nearby buildings. A wide area network (WAN) connects a nationwide or worldwide network. These networks use telephone lines, microwaves, and satellites as means to convey messages.

To learn more about networks and other electronic communication, see **http://www.zdnet.com**

Electronic Mail

Electronic mail (e-mail) is a system by which written messages are sent, received, and stored by means of a computer. An e-mail message is keyed and edited at a workstation and then transmitted to one or more receiving workstations. The receiver views the message on a monitor and may save, delete, print, or respond to the message. E-mail allows the sender to transmit messages almost instantaneously and avoids the problem of "telephone tag" (repeatedly calling and missing the receiver).

An electronic mail system may be an internal system that runs on a LAN, or it may be a public system. For a subscription fee, an e-mail service enables users to send, receive, and store messages in these services' mailboxes. Electronic mail messages can also be transmitted through the use of the Internet, which is connected to thousands of computers around the world.

Many Internet providers provide e-mail as part of their service package. Users can access card catalogs from many libraries and transcripts of U.S. Supreme Court opinions, as well as send e-mail messages to fellow students and instructors on college campuses. An Internet connection and the Internet address of other users allow you to collaborate with students in your class or other universities. The vast amount of information available through the Internet attracts new users regularly.

File Transfer Protocol

Electronic mail is only one of the many communication options available on-line. File Transfer Protocol (FTP) allows users to transmit large files over the Internet. One user uploads files to a shared FTP site for others to download. FTP sites can be password protected to limit file access.

Fax Machine

Exact copies of documents can be sent electronically using a **fax machine** (facsimile). A facsimile device scans an image and converts it to digital form. The digitized image travels over telephone lines and is converted back to its original form on the receiving end. Facsimiles can be sent using a facsimile machine or a computer modem. Although a facsimile device can transmit any form of printed information, it is particularly useful for sending graphics or images, such as blueprints, engineering drawings, and photographs.

Storing a Document

Messages usually must be saved so they can be retrieved later for reference or distribution. The most common storage method is to file printed documents in file cabinets, on shelves, or in trays or boxes. However, because of the high costs of storing paper, other means of

KEY POINT

Your ability to use e-mail correctly will be a major part of your success in many organizations.

storage and retrieval, such as magnetic disks, microforms, and optical disks, often are used.

Magnetic Disks

Information keyed on a computer usually is saved to a flexible or hard magnetic disk for later reading or printing. A floppy diskette (flexible disk) is a removable storage medium that can store at least 260 pages. A hard disk provides storage for thousands of pages. A hard disk usually is built into a computer and cannot be removed.

Microforms

Microforms are methods used to reduce the size of documents for storage. Documents that must be stored for extended periods of time often are microfilmed. The reduced images of paper documents are stored on microfilm, which may be formatted into microforms, such as roll film, microfiche, or jackets. Checks and accounting records often are microfilmed and stored for specific periods of time.

Optical Disks

Optical disk technology combines a scanner with a computer workstation. A document is scanned into a computer, viewed on a screen, indexed for accurate retrieval, and stored on a disk. To store a document, a laser beam burns the images into a disk. Capacity of an optical disk depends on the disk size—5.25, 8, 12, or 16 inches. Optical disks can store all forms of information— text, data, and images.

TECHNOLOGY
The 3.5-inch disk is the most popular size flexible disk and is a common storage medium.

Sending Electronic Oral Messages

Sending an oral message using electronic means has become very common. Pagers are devices used to notify the receiver that he or she has a message. The message itself can be delivered using a cellular phone or voice mail. Occasionally, a business will need to set up an electronic conference using teleconferencing or videoconferencing.

Objective
3

Pagers

Pagers themselves do not send an oral message; they simply alert the receivers that they have a message. Like a telephone, pagers have numbers that distinguish them from other pagers. When placing a call to a person who has a pager, dial the number of the pager. When the connection is made, you simply enter the number the receiver is to call. Advanced pager systems let callers send a very brief message also. After senders complete their messages, the pager vibrates or beeps to get the receiver's attention. Receivers then read the number they are to call and the brief message.

KEY POINT

Cellular phones provide convenience and security; however, using them at inappropriate times can send the wrong message.

TECHNOLOGY

Electronics retailers now offer pagers, cellular phone service, and sometimes voice mail as a package. Of course, a monthly rate is charged for these services as well.

Cellular Phones

Cellular phones are portable phones that allow receivers and senders to make phone calls while away from the traditional telephone. Cellular phones have become an extremely popular method of oral communication for business and personal use.

Nevertheless, users must take care when using cellular phones. The phones themselves are becoming inexpensive, but the cost of using them can be very expensive. Another disadvantage is the nonverbal message their usage can send. If during a meeting, a person leaves to answer a cellular phone call, he or she sends the message that the phone call is more important than the meeting.

Voice Mail

Voice mail is the oral version of e-mail and takes the place of an answering machine. Voice mail is a computerized system that records a message when the receiver of a telephone call is not available when the call comes in. Like an answering machine, voice mail lets the telephone ring a set number of times before activating. Then, instead of taping the message like an answering machine, a computer records the message. It will also leave a message for the absent receiver to call the computer to get his or her voice mail. Most systems allow receivers access to their "voice mail box" from remote locations.

Some voice mail systems use the number pad on a telephone to route callers to various parts of a business. The message you receive might sound something like this, "If you are calling about your checking account balance, press 1. If you are calling about your savings account balance, press 2. If you need to talk to accounting or bookkeeping, press 3."

Teleconferences and Videoconferences

Occasionally, a business will want to set up a teleconference or videoconference among its employees. Multiple receivers and multiple senders can converse as if having a normal telephone call or face-to-face conversation. The main advantage of one of these conferences is that it saves time of the participant. A main disadvantage is that they are usually very expensive.

A **teleconference** uses the telephone to link two or more locations. The simplest form of teleconference is an **audioconference**, which is a long-distance telephone conference call. If more than two persons are involved, speakerphones may be used.

A **videoconference** is a more sophisticated form of a teleconference. Video conferencing allows participants at different locations to see as well as hear each other. Voices, images, and data are transmitted over telephone lines. Videoconferences may be full-motion video or freeze-frame video. Full-motion is the most sophisticated form of videoconference because every continuous movement is broadcast. With freeze-frame video, images change every few seconds.

Sending and Storing Electronic Messages

Match the equipment and technologies on the left with the correct function or definition on the right.

1. Electronic mail
2. Facsimile
3. Flexible diskette
4. Teleconferencing
5. Hard disk
6. Voice mail
7. Pager

a. A device that transmits an exact copy of text or graphics electronically
b. A storage medium that is built into a computer
c. A method of using the telephone or another media to link two or more persons
d. A telephone system that stores messages electronically
e. A system by which messages can be sent and received electronically
f. A removable storage medium
g. A portable device that alerts receivers that they have a message

Check your answers in Appendix E.

CASE 1:

Answers

Responses to Questions 5 and 6 in Chapter Opener

5. **What opportunities did electronic communications offer Anna?**

   Anna had the opportunity to prove herself as a professional, dependable individual by using the editing features of the software to produce an error-free document and by using the multiple technologies to communicate effectively.

6. **What messages did Anna's use of electronic communication send to her supervisor?**

   Anna's use of electronic communication told her supervisor that she was not very professional and lacked self-discipline. The sending of a personal e-mail was somewhat minor, but it indicated a lack of self-control. The playing of the game was a significant display of the lack of discipline. Some might even consider it unethical because she was being paid to work.

SCANS
Employability

Technology: Applies Technology to Task
Computer skills will be critical to your job success. Most of those skills will be based on your ability to use software packages effectively.

DISCUSSION QUESTIONS

1. What type of electronic equipment can be used to create and edit written documents?
2. What are the major types of software used to create and edit electronic documents?
3. Why are teleconferencing and videoconferencing becoming more common?

CASE 1:

Summary

Anna does not understand how nonverbal communication is used to evaluate her job performance. Her excitement for the first few weeks on the job is expected. Anna's real challenge came after the initial excitement had worn off—a challenge she has failed to meet successfully.

Instead of showing boredom with her job, she needs to find things to do that will enhance her job performance. But what could Anna do to make her supervisor view her as a valued employee? What would you do?

Instead of playing games, Anna could use her computer and surf the Internet for information on being a receptionist and ways to improve her job performance. She could also find good books to read—books that would help her learn about the business world and, specifically, her employer. If her supervisor had seen Anna reading Steven Covey's *The Seven Characteristics of Highly Effective People* instead of playing a computer game, her opinion of Anna might have been different. There are many things Anna could do to use her time more effectively.

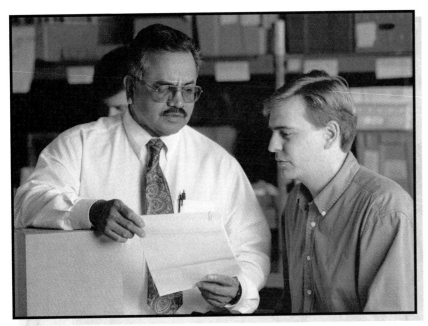

A major key to effective communication is giving feedback. Feedback helps the sender of the message determine whether the receiver has understood the message.

Chapter Summary

Section 1.1 Communication: Its Importance and Roles in Your Life

1 **List the purposes of communication.** The purposes of communication are to establish goodwill, persuade, obtain or share information, establish personal effectiveness, and build self-esteem.

2 **Diagram the communication process and identify its main parts.** For an illustration of the communication process, see Figure 1-1 on page 4. The key parts of the communication process are sender, message, receiver, feedback, and channel. Each plays an important part in the communications you send.

3 **List the two media used for sending messages and the two used for receiving messages.** Two media are employed when sending communications—speaking and writing. Two are used when receiving communications—reading and listening. All four are important to your effectiveness as a communicator.

Section 1.2 Communication: Responsibilities of Participants, Forms, and Barriers

1 **List the three major responsibilities of senders and two major responsibilities of receivers.** To communicate effectively, the sender must use audience analysis, examine the message's environment, and encourage and interpret feedback. The receiver must read and listen effectively.

2 **Define the forms of communication.** You need to be aware of the forms of communication so that you can use them appropriately. The forms of communication are external and internal and formal and informal. External communication originates within an organization and is sent to receivers outside the organization. Internal communication originates within an organization and is sent to receivers within that organization. Formal communication travels through established lines of authority, but informal communication does not follow these lines.

3 **List the two types of barriers to communication and provide examples.** Barriers to communication might cause your communication attempts to fail. Considering them when trying to communicate will help you to send effective messages. The two types of communication barriers are external and internal. External barriers are conditions outside of the receiver or sender that detract from the communication process. A loud noise that prevents a message from being heard is an example of an external barrier. Internal barriers are those that exist inside the sender or receiver. For example, if the receiver is ill, listening skills are negatively affected. Thus, the receiver might not concentrate enough to understand a message.

While learning this information is important, the key is its application. You must send effective messages in your professional environment, your academic setting, and your personal life. To be effective in any of these settings you must realize that they are continually changing and that, as a result, you must adjust accordingly. Because of these changing environments, being an effective communicator requires constant accurate evaluation of the situation.

Section 1.3 Electronic Communication

1 **Identify equipment and software used to create and edit documents.** Equipment used to create a document include computerized work stations, scanners, and voice recognition equipment. The software packages used to create and edit documents include word processing, spreadsheet, database management, graphics, and desktop publishing.

2 **Identify technologies used to send and store documents electronically.** Documents can be sent electronically using an office, a local, or a wide area network. Documents may be stored on floppy diskettes, hard disks, microforms, or optical disks.

3 **Identify technologies used to send oral messages electronically.** While pagers do not send oral messages, they do notify receivers that there is an electronic oral message for them. Cellular phones, voice mail, teleconferencing, and videoconferencing are technologies used for sending oral electronic messages.

Critical Thinking Questions

1. In most job situations, how important is communication? Why?
2. In the communication process, why does the receiver have more control than the sender?
3. If you can use electronic communication effectively and are up-to-date on its new technologies, how can that benefit you while on the job?
4. How should message environment impact the messages you send?
5. What are the key uses of a pager and a cellular phone in communication?

Applications

Part A. Write a short paragraph on each medium of communication. In each paragraph, explain how important that medium is or will be in your career and why.

Part B. Analyze yourself as a communicator. Identify the internal barriers that have been a challenge for you and explain why they are a challenge. Then identify internal barriers that have not been a challenge to you and explain why they are not a challenge.

Editing Activities

1. Edit the following paragraph by correcting all spelling, punctuation, and grammar errors.

   Just as the earths' waters are made up of various oceans, seas, and lakes, so to is the Internet composed of various neetworks, ranging from the large (goverments and multinational corporations) two the middling (educational institutions and medium sized busiensses) too the small (nonprofit organizations and small businesses.) In turn, these networks are connected together via cables and telephone trunk lines that are not unlike the waterways and channels that connect the oceans, seas, and lakes.

words@work

If you are using *words@work*, complete the activities on Editing, Proofreading, and Spelling in the Grammar & Usage section.

2. Edit the following paragraph by correcting all spelling, punctuation, and grammar errors.

    The big difference between navigating the seas and navagating the internet is the sped of the journey. A around-the-world cruise, for example, might take weeks, but a file or a E-mail note can easily go around the globe in just a few seconds. Thanks to the connections between networks, those that travle on the Net, unlike their seafaring counterparts, can travel thousans of miles per second without leaving their chiars. You can go from Calefornia to Australia, pick up a file; copy it to London and Frankfurt, and do it all before your coffe gets cold.

Case Studies

TECHNOLOGY

1. Case 1 contains two situations. Respond to each situation as instructed.

    Situation A: You are a trainer in the human resources division of your company. You have been asked to develop a training session on communication. Your company has e-mail as well as the normal types of communication. You want to teach the session attendees when and when not to use e-mail.

    a. Develop a situation in which the use of e-mail would be appropriate.
    b. Develop a situation in which the use of e-mail would not be appropriate.

    Situation B: As an employee of your company, you have an e-mail to send to a member of your staff; however, the would-be receiver of the e-mail is in a very bad mood. Does this factor impact your decision about sending an e-mail? If so, explain how.

2. As a sales representative of your company, you want to send a message to a very important customer. This particular customer is a good friend of your company's president—they play golf together often. Also, this customer consistently uses you and your company when placing large orders for supplies. In your opinion, the two of you have a very good relationship.

    However, the last time you paid him a visit "just to make sure everything is going well," he seemed very impatient. He seemed to want you to leave "so he could get on with what he had to do."

    Now, two days after your visit, your company has started a sales campaign on many of the products your customer purchases from you. The prices are great but the sale will last only two weeks. Would you contact this customer? If so, how? by letter? by memo? by e-mail? with a personal visit? with a telephone call? Justify your answer.

COMMUNICATION FOR HEALTH SERVICES CAREERS

Since her childhood, Samantha Lopez has wanted to be a nurse. Four years ago, after a lot of schooling and work, her dream came true. She graduated from Iowa Creek College with a degree in nursing. After a short time, Samantha realized that her job would be more secure if she were a registered nurse—an RN. So Samantha went back to school, and two years ago, she completed her RN training.

Just last week, a member of the hospital's administration called Samantha into his office and approached her with a new job opportunity—head nurse for the second floor, D wing. As Samantha thinks about the job opportunity, she wonders if she has the skills necessary for the new position. She enjoys talking and working with patients and is a successful RN—partly because of her interpersonal skills. Samantha wants a second opinion. She has come to you and asked, "What do you think I should do?"

1. In Samantha's present job, how are communication skills important?
2. In the new position offered to her, are communication skills important? Justify your answer.
3. How do the communication skills required for the two positions differ?
4. Should this difference be an important part of Samantha's decision?

COMMUNICATION FOR ENGINEERING AND INDUSTRIAL CAREERS

Alex Palowski has worked for Benton Manufacturing Company for five years as an assembly-line worker. The hours are convenient and consistent. Alex's job is to dip the metal casings of clothes dryers into a vat of white primer paint. Although Alex likes his situation, he is concerned about his future. His pay has not increased to keep up with inflation, and the benefits seem to be getting smaller. Alex has decided that he wants to improve his situation within the company.

Alex has a high school diploma and some on-the-job training. All of his supervisors are not only paid more but also have taken some college classes. Thus, he decides to go back to school, and he enrolls in some night classes at a junior college. His long-term goal is to get a bachelor's degree in management.

1. Besides getting additional education, what else can Alex do to improve his situation and start setting himself up for his future?
2. How important is communication to Alex's goal of improving his situation? Explain your answer.

Video Case

Hearing Without Listening

Andre Chambers had extensive experience as a sound engineer with several television stations in large midwest cities. His dream, however, was to work for the Sci-Fi Network. When he learned they needed a lead sound engineer, he moved quickly.

Andre knew that persistence often made the difference in landing a job, so he contacted the network's Human Resources manager, Ms. Slansky. Ms. Slansky seemed rushed and asked to postpone their conversation, but Andre felt the need to describe his experience and skills right then.

Afterward, it was difficult to reach Ms. Slansky, and when Andre did speak with her, she talked only about the Sci-Fi Network's needs, nothing that Andre felt could help him land his dream job.

Finally, Andre offered to fly to New York for an interview with the Director of Technical Services (DTS) for the network. Andre's sample tape of his work didn't seem to be what the DTS wanted. Whenever Andre spoke of his skills, the DTS talked about the role the lead sound engineer played in the production process, information Andre felt he could learn once he was on the job.

A week later, Andre learned his dream position had been filled. He wondered why no one had told him the information he needed to land the job.

Questions

1. Andre believes there was a problem with the sender during his communication with the Sci-Fi Network. Do you agree? Why or why not?
2. In the video clip, Sandy Dean is a persistent job seeker. So is Andre. Explain why you think one man has his dream job and the other doesn't.
3. Did Andre understand the purposes of communication? List the purposes he neglected.
4. Choose a partner. Take 3–4 minutes each to describe your dream job to your partner. The listening partner may *not* take notes! When everyone has finished, introduce your partner to the class by describing the partner's dream job.

Setting Up Shop

Eva Negron cannot wait to get her new business started!

She graduated from college last month with a bachelor's degree in computer science. She had paid many of her college expenses by working part-time at a campus coffee shop. After graduating, she interviewed for several jobs, but none of them appealed to her. Then she came up with a great idea: she would combine her major with what she had learned by working at the coffee shop.

Eva plans to open a shop filled with computers in Milwaukee, her hometown. She will call the shop NetCafe. For a small hourly fee, her customers will be able to access the Internet in a relaxed atmosphere where they can also sip specialty coffees. In addition, they will be able to munch on fresh bagels and other delicious bakery items.

Eva's target customers are mostly people who want to join the online community, but lack the skills or equipment—or both. Her employees (just Eva at first) will be available to answer customers' questions and help them navigate the Internet, using FTP, Telnet, Gopher, browsers, and other utilities.

The customers will also be able to use the NetCafe's word processing programs, spreadsheet and graphics software, color printers, and scanners. Shortly after opening, the shop will begin offering courses in using the Internet and various software applications.

Eva hopes local businesspeople will also use her shop as a comfortable meeting place. They will be able to use NetCafe's computers to access their own files at off-site databases. Business travelers will also be able to check their e-mail while they sip their favorite coffee.

Eva has talked her uncle, Ramon, into going into a partnership with her. Until recently, Ramon had been the manager of a small restaurant in Milwaukee. It had been torn down as part of an inner-city renovation plan.

Eva and Ramon will be general partners, which means they will both be responsible for operating the business and liable for any of its debts. Eva will manage the computer aspect of the business, while Ramon will be in charge of the coffee shop.

Two of Ramon's friends, investors from his former restaurant, have agreed to be limited or silent partners in this new business. They will not be involved in the day-to-day operations, but they will provide most of the money for rent and the computer setup. Then they will share in the profits.

1. What are the roles of speaking, writing, reading, and listening in this new business?
2. What communication barriers might Eva face as she works with her uncle? What barriers might she face as she helps her customers master the Internet?
3. What challenges should Eva expect in providing services in electronic communication?
4. Tell a partner why you think Eva's shop will or will not succeed. Then ask your partner to summarize your ideas. Next, listen to your partner's opinion and summarize it. What are some things that would make this kind of exercise more difficult?

Communicating in a Diverse Workplace

Succeeding in a Global Business Environment

A highly successful German automotive company recently merged with a U.S. carmaker. Members of the German team met with American staff members in Detroit.

Anita Boaz had been employed at the Detroit site for seven years, moving from administrative assistant to manager. As a result of the merger, Anita's new supervisor would be a newly relocated German manager, Hans Dortmann. She was very comfortable in the relaxed atmosphere of the American office but was a little nervous about meeting the German visitors. She worried that their English wouldn't be good enough for her to understand easily.

Anita's first meeting with Mr. Dortmann was set for a Friday—casual day at the Detroit office. Anita chose some nice slacks to wear, instead of jeans. Traffic was unusually heavy; Anita was a few minutes late for the meeting. The door was closed. She knocked once and went in. The Germans, all dressed in conservative business suits, were sitting at a conference table. Anita reached out her hand to Dortmann and said with a smile, "Good morning, Hans. It's good to meet you! I'm Anita Boaz."

Dortmann rose hesitantly, then responded with a brief greeting and sat down. Anita was baffled by his chilly reaction. Then she decided maybe he wasn't used to working with women at the management level. Anita was disappointed. She came away thinking Dortmann and the other Germans were rude and standoffish. At the same time, the Germans were put off by what they felt was rude behavior on her part.

A few weeks later, the company offered some sessions on cultural orientation. Anita learned the following about German businesspeople:

- They have a high regard for authority and structure.
- They greet each other formally, using titles such as "doctor" or "professor" when appropriate.
- They enjoy working with data and other concrete "evidence."
- They tend to separate business and pleasure, saving humor and social talk until after the business is done.

Over time, Anita and her colleagues in Detroit developed a friendlier relationship with the Germans. But first they had to establish respect for one another.

Questions

1. What assumptions does Anita make about her new supervisor and German businesspeople in general? Why are those assumptions inaccurate?
2. How is Anita's situation typical, given the current trends in business in the United States?
3. What potential communication barriers exist in this situation? Does Anita do the right things to overcome those barriers? Explain.
4. How might Anita and her new supervisor benefit from their differences? What must they do to recognize and learn from each other's strengths?

Cultural Differences at Home and Abroad

Objectives

After completing Section 2.1, you should be able to:

1 Define "cultural diversity," "multicultural," and "multinational."

2 List population trends that indicate the U.S. workplace is becoming more multicultural.

3 Identify three projections for the global workplace of the twenty-first century.

4 List, describe, and give examples of differences among cultures.

Objective

1

▼ KEY POINT

Cultural diversity requires us to value the differences in people, not just tolerate those differences.

Objective

2

Cultural Diversity

We live and work in a society of **cultural diversity.** With cultural diversity, people from different backgrounds have different languages, customs, values, manners, perceptions, social structures, and decision-making practices. As travel and communication around the world become easier, businesspeople are more likely to encounter people from other cultures. The company you work for right here in the United States may be owned by a company based in Europe or Asia. Your coworkers may have been transferred from company headquarters in London or Taipei. Or you may work with people whose parents or grandparents immigrated—along with millions of others—to the United States in recent decades.

Wherever your coworkers are from, they likely have had unique experiences, and they certainly have their own ideas about how things should be done. Accommodating people's experiences and ideas is one of the greatest challenges in the culturally diverse workplace.

The United States is very much a **multicultural** society—a society made up of people from many cultures. More than one million people immigrate to the United States each year. Today, more than 20 million U.S. residents were born in other countries. There are at least 300 different cultures in the United States. Members of those cultures all have different views of proper business etiquette, based on their upbringing and cultural traditions.[1]

According to the U.S. Census Bureau, Hispanics will make up the largest minority group in the United States by the year 2010. Immigrants from China, Korea, and India are adding to an already substantial population of Asian Americans. The same is true for immigrants from Eastern Europe and other areas. The U.S. Department of Labor predicts that African Americans, Hispanics, and Asian Americans will make up more than a quarter of the workforce by 2005. All of this means that the American workplace of the twenty-first century will be more diverse than at any other time in the country's history. Are you ready?

---

[1]M. Kay duPont, "Minding Your Cultural Ps and Qs," *Office Pro*, February 1999, pp. 10–13.

The World as a Global Workplace

International business takes place across the political borders of nations. New technologies make it easier than ever to make products and transport them to people on the other side of the world. Those people on the other side of the world also are manufacturing products that Americans buy. When a businessperson believes that he can sell a product to just about anyone in the world, he is thinking of the world as a global marketplace. That kind of thinking results in a global workplace.

Multinational Companies

A **multinational** company is one that conducts business in two or more nations. Some successful multinational companies are General Electric, Coca-Cola, Microsoft, and Disney. These companies were pioneers in creating the truly multinational corporation. They weren't satisfied just doing business with several countries. They each became an enterprise with a workforce and a corporate culture that reflect the diversity of the markets in which they operate as well as the workforce that keeps those markets supplied.

Diversity in Your Own Global Workplace

Every day, workers in this country interact globally—whether that means ordering products from abroad or visiting an international web site. The chances are great that you will interact in the workplace with people from other nations or with Americans who are from different cultures.

To work effectively with others from different cultures, the first step is to recognize, understand, and accept differences. Then you must deal sensitively with people from other backgrounds. It takes all of us to create a successful multinational environment.

Projections for the Twenty-first Century

What are the projections for the workforce in the twenty-first century?[2]

- Technology, especially the Internet, will enable more businesses to enter the global marketplace.
- There will be an explosive growth of companies doing business across borders.
- Continuing development of a world marketplace will require development of an international workforce.

As companies expand across the globe, challenges to communication grow as well. The Internet helps us find and share information better than ever before. However, crossing cultural boundaries means more than sending e-mail to another country or looking at a web site from across the globe. Whether you are dealing with peers in international locations or foreign-born colleagues in the United States, effective communication requires special planning and understanding.[3]

DIVERSITY
Non-U.S. citizens own roughly 13,000 companies in the United States. These companies employ 5 million Americans.

Objective

TECHNOLOGY
In addition to providing information, the Internet presents opportunities for new ways to do business.

---

[2]"60 HR Predictions for 2008," *Workforce*, January 1998, pp. 50–51.
[3]Paula Jacobs, "Cross-Cultural Connection," *InfoWorld*, May 11, 1998, pp. 110–111.

1 Checkpoint

The World as a Global Workplace

Answer the following questions.
1. Which of the following is an accurate statement about the population of the United States?
    a. More than one million people immigrate to the United States each year.
    b. African Americans, Hispanics, and Asian Americans will make up half the workforce by 2005.
2. Which of the following is an accurate statement about business in the twenty-first century?
    a. All people in all nations will be linked by the Internet.
    b. The continuing expansion of global business will guarantee the multicultural nature of the workforce.

Check your answers in Appendix E.

Cultural Differences

Objective

4

Visit the Multicultural Pavilion on the Web at **http://curry.edschool.virginia.edu/go/multicultural/.** Click on "Awareness Activities" to increase your knowledge of and sensitivity to people from diverse cultures.

People from cultures different from your own are likely to have different values and to make different assumptions than you do. For example, most Americans would be pleased to receive a compliment on an item of clothing they are wearing. However, if you are talking to someone from Asia, that person may divert her eyes, murmur, and hurry away. Many people from Asian cultures believe that accepting praise in front of others is a sign of being vain.

To communicate effectively, you must recognize barriers to communication. Cultural differences can be communication barriers because they prevent or hinder an effective exchange of ideas or information. Once you know that, though, you can begin to overcome the challenges of communicating across cultures. It is important to remember that all people want to feel valued, respected, and understood. The challenge is knowing what words or actions will be perceived as "respectful and helpful."

Language Differences

People all over the world speak more than 3,000 languages. Though English is widely spoken across the globe, it is the native language of only about a dozen nations. Figure 2-1 shows the languages most widely used in the United States and in the world. Note the differences between the two lists. Keep in mind that the percentage of non-native-English speakers in the United States is increasing. Outside of the United States, although English is studied widely, about 5 out of 6 people do not understand it.

Most Widely Used Languages in the United States	Most Widely Used Languages in the World
1. English	1. Mandarin (Chinese)
2. Spanish	2. English
3. French	3. Russian
4. German	4. Spanish
5. Italian	5. Hindi (India)

FIGURE 2-1 Most Widely Used Languages

Body Language

When we communicate with body language—by using gestures or the position of our bodies—we use nonverbal communication. The way we say words and the hand movements, posture, and facial expressions that accompany our words often have greater significance than the words themselves. In addition, the less English that people understand, the more they rely on body language.

Visit The Web of Culture at **http://www.webofculture.com** for more examples of how common gestures vary in meaning across cultures.

TECHNOLOGY

Diversity on the Internet

In an ideal world, the best way to learn about another culture is to get to know a person from that culture who is willing to share information, impressions, and experiences. In the absence of that opportunity, technology provides new ways to learn about people from other cultures. Numerous web sites provide virtual tours of other countries. In addition, some sites focus specifically on diversity both in American society and in the workplace. Following are two extensive sites that provide specific information about the be-

liefs, customs, and behaviors of people from other cultures.

• The first is the Multicultural Pavilion on the Web at **http://curry.edschool.virginia.edu/go/multicultural/**. This site is a rich mix of ideas and information. It includes quotations and proverbs from people and cultures around the world. It even has a multicultural song index. Features of the site also include awareness activities for site visitors to do, data archives, on-

line articles, an on-line discussion board, and links to numerous other multicultural sites.
• Another valuable web site is The Web of Culture at **http://www.webofculture.com**. A click on "Reference" leads visitors to topics such as consulates, cuisine, holidays, languages, religions, time zones, and weather. Or a click on "Education" sheds light on gestures or takes visitors to other multicultural resources, both print and online. ∎

Don't assume that people from all cultures know and use the same types of nonverbal communication that you do. Gestures are *not* universal. An acceptable American gesture, such as the "OK" sign, would likely be perceived as poor manners by someone from France, where that gesture signifies "worthless" or "zero." In other countries, the American OK sign represents an obscene or lewd comment.

If you do business with Islamic people, be aware that they consider the feet unclean. If you touch someone with your foot, apologize. Do not cross your feet at the ankle. This would display the soles of your feet, which is considered rude.

Even how people indicate "yes" and "no" may differ significantly from culture to culture. To signal "yes," a Greek may tilt the head to either side. To signal "no," he may slightly nod the head upward, or just lift his eyebrows.

You may think that greeting business associates would be a simple procedure. How hard can it be to smile, look pleasant, and shake hands? Watch out! People from various cultures have their own ideas about the "proper" way to greet people. Figure 2-2 gives examples of the variety of greeting styles you may encounter.

KEY POINT

In spite of a smile's different meanings, it is still the best sign of general goodwill. Don't forget to use it, especially when being introduced to people.

Argentina	Shake hands briefly and nod to all present. Close friends shake hands or embrace.
Brazil	A long, warm handshake is common, upon both arrival and departure.
Canada	Shake hands firmly. People may just smile and nod in informal business situations, or if they have greeted someone with a handshake earlier in the day.
France	Shake hands lightly and quickly. Be sure to greet each person present.
India	Only the most Westernized of businesspeople shake hands. Instead, expect to use the *namaste* (pronounced nah-mas-tay). Fold palms together below your chin and nod or bow slightly.
Japan	Some Japanese may extend their hand for a light handshake. If not, watch how the person bows and return the bow to the same depth. This indicates that you consider yourself of equal status. As you bow, lower your eyes and keep your palms flat on your thighs.
Saudi Arabia	Most Saudi businessmen shake hands in Western fashion. Only some Saudi men will shake hands with Western women.

FIGURE 2-2 Greeting Customs Around the World
Source: Roger Axtell, *Do's and Taboos Around the World,* Elmsford, NY: Benjamin, 1985.

Facial Expressions

Americans are taught to maintain steady eye contact with others, while people from many other cultures, such as those from Asia, believe less contact is more respectful. Many Americans get confused when others don't give them the eye contact they're expecting. Accept the lack of eye contact as a cultural difference and don't change your usual way of communicating. Non-Americans generally expect Americans to make eye contact. Just don't let your eye contact turn into staring.

Americans usually smile to show pleasure and good nature, but that's not true of all cultures. The importance of a smile and the fine points of timing vary from culture to culture. For example, Middle Easterners might use a smile to soothe someone, thus avoiding conflict. To smile at a French person on the street is considered an inappropriate intrusion. Some cultures use a smile to acknowledge a message that has not been truly understood. Asians may smile when they are happy, sad, apologetic, angry, frustrated, thankful, or even confused.

Personal Space

Personal space is the space immediately surrounding a person, within which other persons should not intrude. The size of a person's personal space varies depending upon personal preference and cultural background. Moving into a person's personal space may cause that person to be uncomfortable.

Most Americans appreciate personal space of 18 inches to three feet. In a business setting, they don't like having others closer than a couple of feet. Generally, Americans don't like crowded elevators or center seats in airplanes, buses, and cars. When possible, they often try to leave an empty seat between themselves and a stranger.

Western Europeans have the same comfort zone as most Americans—18 inches to three feet. Middle Easterners of the same sex, Mediterraneans, and some Hispanic cultures are comfortable with a personal distance of less than 18 inches. Most of the rest of the world prefer more than three feet of personal space. However, the Chinese are used to very limited personal space and are generally comfortable with physical closeness. People from cultures that have relatively less personal space than Americans may be insulted if an American steps back to create more space.

Business Cards

Americans are casual with business cards. Chinese people take business cards very seriously and exchange them early in a meeting. With Asian coworkers, however, don't offer your card until asked or you may appear too aggressive.

Business cards are also very important in Japan. Hold the business card with the thumbs and forefingers of both hands. Present it so that

DIVERSITY

In Japan a business card represents the individual in a much deeper and more meaningful way than it does in the West. The Japanese use a special business card case, which elevates and displays others' business cards when received.[4]

---

[4]Cynthia L. Kemper, "Business Cards Can Be Key in Global Communication," *Communication World*, October/November 1998, p. 24.

the recipient can read the printing on the card, and bow slightly. A Japanese recipient will accept the card in the same way and read it carefully. When you receive a card from a Japanese person, be sure to examine it closely and avoid putting it away quickly. If you're in a meeting, place the card on the table or desk in front of you for further reference.

2 *Checkpoint*

Cultural Differences

Indicate whether each statement is true or false.
1. It is best to ignore barriers caused by cultural differences so as not to draw attention to the differences.
2. The OK sign is perceived the same way in France and the United States.
3. A nod always means "yes."
4. While Americans are taught to maintain steady eye contact, Asians believe less eye contact is more respectful.
5. A smile is universal and means the same in any culture.
6. In general, Hispanic persons are comfortable with a personal space of less than 18 inches.
7. To avoid offending a Chinese or Japanese businessperson, carefully examine a business card that is presented to you before putting it away.

Check your answers in Appendix E.

CASE 2:
Answers

Responses to Questions 1 and 2 in Chapter Opener

1. **What assumptions does Anita make about her new supervisor and German businesspeople in general? Why are those assumptions inaccurate?**
   Anita makes the following assumptions: Hans might not be able to speak or understand English very well because he is from another country; Hans is more used to dealing with male managers than female ones; Hans understands and agrees with the concept of casual office dress; the Germans will be

eager to make friends in Detroit; the Germans have the same ideas as Americans do about proper greetings and personal space. The assumptions are inaccurate because Anita doesn't stop to think that people from Germany might not have the same values and procedures as Americans do.

2. **How is Anita's situation typical, given the current trends in business in the United States?**

More and more companies are able to operate internationally, either by phone, fax, e-mail, and Internet, or by actually sending employees to work in other countries. Also, the American workforce is becoming more multicultural as tens of thousands of people from other countries immigrate to the United States each year. Unfortunately, people—and the companies they work for—don't always recognize the value of training employees to function in multicultural situations. Misunderstandings arise, not because two parties can't agree on business terms, but because they simply don't understand each other.

DISCUSSION QUESTIONS

1. In what ways is the world becoming more culturally diverse? What evidence of this trend do you see in your own life?
2. What are some common American facial expressions or gestures that have other meanings to people from other cultures?
3. What is personal space? How do personal space requirements differ?
4. How should a businessperson present and receive business cards with a colleague from Asia?

2·2 Effective Cross-Cultural Communication

Objectives

After completing Section 2.2, you should be able to:

1 Define "cross-cultural communication."

2 List and explain four guidelines to help people communicate effectively across cultures.

3 Identify strategies for effective global communication.

Objective

1 👉

Objective

2 👉

↓KEY POINT

Effective cross-cultural communication requires special skill and extra patience.

Communicating Across Cultures

Cross-cultural communication occurs when two individuals from different cultures communicate, whether verbally, nonverbally, or in writing. Because they don't belong to the same culture, they don't share the same assumptions, values, beliefs, feelings, or ways of thinking and behaving. These differences make the communication process challenging.

Most Americans have not been trained to communicate with people from other cultures. Because most Americans do not speak a language other than English, the first barrier often is language. When talking to someone whose first language is not English, some special communication skills are required. There is an element of sensitivity needed toward people who use English as a second language. In addition to the language differences, there are barriers created by cultural traditions, values, and basic assumptions about what is proper and improper. Some of these issues are so subtle that people don't even realize that their values affect the judgments they make.

Guidelines for Cross-Cultural Communication

Effective cross-cultural communication begins with having an open attitude about communicating and about the people with whom you are communicating. Learn to find a common ground on which to communicate. This may require you to adapt your usual methods to suit different situations. Here are some guidelines to keep in mind as you approach the challenge of communicating across cultures.

Learn About and Accept Cultural Differences

Now that you are aware of some of the differences among cultures, resolve to learn more about people from nations other than your own. Use Internet sources such as *The Web of Culture* to further explore cultural differences. Read books and magazines about other cultures. See foreign movies and videos. Take every opportunity to talk to people from different countries. Be willing to help internationals with their English speaking and writing skills, if they ask.[5]

---

[5]Mark Rowh, "Our Expanding World: How You Can Get the Global Edge," *Career World*, January 1999, pp. 22–25.

Be Sensitive Toward People from Other Cultures

Avoid generalizations about groups of people. Even positive stereotypes can be misleading or even damaging. For example, the fact that German people like to work with data and figures does not mean that all of them are accounting experts.

Avoid discussion about politics, religion, and any other potentially sensitive issues during business conversations. Be sensitive to ethnic, religious, and moral values of others. Remember that not everyone celebrates the American holidays of Thanksgiving and Independence Day. Similarly, Christmas and Easter are Christian religious holidays that not everyone shares. While people from other cultures may be aware of those holidays, don't assume that everyone gathers with family, exchanges gifts, or celebrates in any other way during those seasons.

Be Prepared for Language Barriers—And Get Past Them

Dealing sensitively with other employees whose first language is not English makes the workplace a more comfortable place. Because people from some cultures consider feedback or criticism damaging to their reputations, don't correct their English unless they have specifically asked you to do so. Instead, to foster understanding, paraphrase or restate what someone has said to ensure you both understand what is going on.

It may not be necessary for you to learn another language, but at least learn to speak certain key phrases to share with international coworkers or visitors. Learning the phrases that appear in Figure 2-3 could be perceived as a sign of respect and of friendliness. At the very least, it is a courteous gesture and may make someone feel more comfortable.

Language	Hello	Good-bye	Thank you
Arabic	marhaba	ma-Assalamah	(no equivalent)
Chinese	ni hao	zai jian	xiexie
French	bonjour	au revoir	merci
German	guten Tag	auf wiedersehen	danke
Hindi	namaskar	namaskar	dhanya-vaad
Italian	ciao	arriverderci	grazie
Japanese	konnichiwa	sayoonara	domo arigato
Korean	an jung	anyong-i-kaeseyo	go mop sum nee dah
Portuguese	oi	atE' logo	obrigado
Russian	privet	dosvidaniya	spasibo
Spanish	hola	adios	gracias

FIGURE 2-3 Key Phrases in Eleven Languages

TECHNOLOGY

Cross-cultural information is more accessible than ever via the Internet. You can visit an educational site about a country or culture, or take a virtual tour of a foreign country.

DIVERSITY

If you do business in another country, it is a nice gesture to learn about the country's history. For example, be aware of whether that country has an independence day and how people commemorate the occasion.

SCANS
Employability

Interpersonal: Works with Cultural Diversity
Learning a second language may make you more employable.

Keep Messages Simple and Short

Whether speaking or writing to people whose first language is not English, keep your language simple and to the point. If you are speaking, pronounce words especially carefully. Use uncomplicated language and be ready to reword your message if the recipient doesn't understand.

In written messages, use short sentences and paragraphs. Avoid slang, jargon, abbreviations, and acronyms. Here is an excerpt from an e-mail message sent from a manager in Maine to a colleague in France. How many opportunities for misunderstanding can you identify?

> The cut date for the first batch is ASAP. The date for the second ship is 11/8/01.

Tamara, in Maine, used two slang expressions in her message. First, she used "cut date" to mean "cut-off date" or "deadline." Then she used "ship" to mean "shipment." She used the abbreviation "ASAP" for "as soon as possible." Finally, she abbreviated the date, leaving it unclear whether she was following the American convention—month/day/year —or the continental style—day/month/year.

KEY POINT

Use formal business English that is clear and concise in all correspondence with people from other countries.

---

3 Checkpoint

Cross-Cultural Communication

Indicate whether each of the following helps or hinders cross-cultural communication.

1. Learn a second language to communicate effectively with people from another culture.
2. Make reference to positive stereotypes about groups of people.
3. When talking to people whose first language is not English, talk as you normally would so as not to insult the other person.
4. Assume that people from other countries are well-informed about American ways and customs.
5. Paraphrase or restate the words of a person whose first language is not English.
6. Learn to speak key phrases, such as "hello," "good-bye," and "thank you."

Check your answers in Appendix E.

Strategies for Global Communication

Objective

3

Now that you know how to *approach* communicating with someone from another culture, here are some specific suggestions to help you succeed. In some cases, the information in this list is just a reminder that you may need to do some research to be able to communicate effectively. Cross-cultural communication does take extra effort.

1. *Be adaptable.* American communication tends to be informal, direct, and verbal. In cultures that are more formal, slow down. Take your lead from your international colleagues. Find out what others value in their business communication and adapt your style to theirs.

2. *Use your best English-speaking habits.* Speak somewhat slowly and clearly when speaking to people whose first language is not English. If you must, use specific technical terms to discuss business. When not discussing business, however, use a relatively simple vocabulary and short sentences.

3. *Do not use acronyms, slang, and jargon.* Don't use them even if the person you're communicating with speaks English fluently. Avoid the American tendency to use military and sports terms in business communication. In addition, avoid idioms—words or phrases whose meanings are something different than the literal meanings of the words. For example, think about what it means to "hit the road" or to "take five."

4. *Be aware of a culture's forms of nonverbal communication.* Recognize that even seemingly harmless gestures such as a smile or a nod may send a message other than what you intend. If you are not familiar with a culture's nonverbal communication habits, err on the side of caution.

5. *Use visual aids.* If you are trying to communicate with someone whose first language is not English, don't be afraid to resort to sketching or drawing a picture. Sometimes it even helps to write a difficult word down. The person's comprehension of written English may be greater than his or her understanding of spoken English.

6. *Recognize that people from cultures other than your own have different assumptions.* If you are invited to someone's home, should you take a gift for your host or hostess? What type of gift? If you gave a bouquet of all white flowers to your hostess in Norway, why would she be offended? If you are introducing people, who should be introduced first, the older gentleman or the woman in the group? Basic understandings about social procedures as well as business matters vary from culture to culture. Do some research, or ask a reliable source for advice.

7. *Be careful about using humor.* There are many issues to consider when using humor. First, many businesspeople prefer to separate business and social matters. Save the humor for the social time. Second, jokes are very difficult to understand for someone who doesn't know the language completely. Third, "the one about the guy walking down the street" may seem funny to you, but it may seem senseless or, worse yet, offensive to your listeners. Joking about something that other people take seriously can put a permanent dent in a business relationship.

8. *Maintain personal contact.* Technology allows us to communicate with people all over the world without actually having personal contact with them. People of some cultures are uncomfortable with the impersonal nature of such communication. Make the effort to communicate face-to-face, by means of a videoconference, or at least by voice periodically.

DIVERSITY
In many countries, people beckon by extending the arm and hand, palm downward, and wiggling the fingers.

DIVERSITY

Managing Diversity in the Workplace

As the makeup of the American workforce changes, people react to the changes but do not necessarily embrace them. Handling diversity in the workplace is a process, and it requires change at all levels of a company. That change must take place in company policy and structure as well as in the behavior and attitudes of all employees.

The American Society for Training and Development (ASTD) has developed two approaches to training workers for managing diversity. One approach, an awareness-based approach, is designed to make employees more knowledgeable and more aware of diversity issues. This is the first step toward helping employees become more sensitive to their diverse coworkers. Awareness-based training focuses on:

- providing information
- revealing assumptions and biases
- evaluating attitudes and values
- correcting myths and stereotypes

Skills-based training is designed to give employees the tools they need to interact effectively in a diverse workplace. This approach reinforces the concepts taught in awareness-based training. Then the employees are asked to take the next step: to change their behaviors. Skills-based training focuses on:

- increasing knowledge of and sensitivity to diversity
- adoption of appropriate attitudes toward diversity
- building or reinforcing interaction skills ■

Source: "Basic Models for Managing Diversity Training" and "Tips for Starting a Diversity Program," *The Network Newsletter* 1, no. 1 (April 1995); The Workplace Diversity Network: A Project of Cornell/LR and The National Conference; available from **http://www.ilr.cornell.edu/depts/wdn/NetNews/1_1/ProblemSolving.html**; Internet; accessed 16 September 1999.

4 Checkpoint

Strategies for Global Communication

Indicate whether each statement is true or false.

1. If a non-American client seems pretty familiar with English, it is okay to relax and speak just as you would to an American colleague.

2. It is best to be formal and conservative in behavior when conducting business with people from other countries.

3. It is best to avoid drawing a picture to help someone whose first language is not English; it would more than likely insult the person.

4. Jokes are best saved for social time, after business is finished, and only once you are well acquainted with your business colleagues.

Check your answers in Appendix E.

CASE 2:

Answers

Response to Question 3 in Chapter Opener

3. **What potential communication barriers exist in this situation? Does Anita do the right things to overcome those barriers? Explain.**

   The most likely communication barrier is language, of course. In addition, cultural differences are likely to hinder communication. Those cultural differences include ideas and attitudes about punctuality, privacy, appropriate office attire, personal space, and proper greetings. Because Anita and Hans have different ideas about these five issues, the issues are communication barriers. The only attempt Anita makes to avoid offending the German visitors is when she chooses to wear nice slacks instead of jeans to the meeting. Beyond that, Anita does nothing to overcome potential communication barriers. In fact, she doesn't even stop to think that any differences (or barriers) might exist beyond the language difference.

DISCUSSION QUESTIONS

1. What is cross-cultural communication? Why does it present special challenges for both senders and receivers?
2. Why does the use of slang, jargon, or abbreviations in written correspondence complicate cross-cultural communication?
3. How might learning about another culture help you communicate with a person from that culture?
4. Name at least five strategies for communicating effectively with someone from a different culture. Explain the purpose of each strategy.

2·3 Other Diversities in the Workplace

After completing Section 2.3, you should be able to:

1 List benefits of diversity in the workplace.

2 Recognize types of diversity in the workplace and understand the challenges diversity creates.

3 Use communication tips for handling diversity.

Objective

KEY POINT

Company executives as well as all levels of employees must be committed to what is called a culture of inclusiveness—an environment in which people's differences are not just accepted, but welcomed.

Benefits of Diversity

A spokesperson at AT&T recently made this statement:

> ... [W]e believe that diversity is key to the success of any corporation. We want to be able to work in an environment where we are all respected and people can work to their maximum potential. That's what keeps us going.[6]

Creating a workplace that all employees perceive as fair and equitable, no matter what their differences are, is very important. More and more companies are addressing the needs of diversity in the workforce.

Once viewed as negative, a diverse group of employees is now seen as an asset. Corporations that want to operate around the globe need to have diverse sources of talent and information to be successful. Roger Wheeler, General Motors Chief Tax Officer, said this about diversity:

> It is well established that, over time, **heterogeneous** [dissimilar] groups outperform **homogeneous** [similar] groups. They are better at problem solving, better at decision making, and better at generating creative ideas. . . .[7]

Diversity in the American workplace is a fact. Even if you are not exposed to international diversity, your coworkers probably come from different ethnic backgrounds, practice different religions, and hold different views on politics, work, and problem solving. To some extent, we take these differences for granted. Everyone is an individual, after all. Recognizing the source or nature of diversity, however, can help make our work relationships smoother and more productive.

---

[6]Kenneth Hein, "Making Diversity Work," *Incentive*, February 1997, p. 18+.
[7]Roger D. Wheeler, "Managing Workforce Diversity," *Tax Executive*, November/December 1997, p. 493+.

Challenges of Diversity

In addition to differences in culture and nationality, you are likely to encounter other types of diversity in the workplace. What are some other diversities?

- race or ethnicity
- gender
- physical abilities
- social class
- age
- socioeconomic status
- religion
- personality

All individuals should have an opportunity to progress in their careers in direct proportion to their ability to contribute to the objectives of the company.

Although diversity is viewed as an advantage in an organization, it can sometimes adversely affect communication among members of an organization. Sometimes we are uncomfortable around people whose habits, beliefs, or customs are different from our own. Our discomfort usually arises because we don't understand the differences, or weren't prepared to encounter them. In some cases, our discomfort or our inability to communicate with a colleague arises because of a **stereotype.** A stereotype is an oversimplified belief about a group of people. For example, the notion that all Scandinavians are blonde is a harmless stereotype. The notion that engineers are men who wear dark-rimmed glasses and have short hair is a stereotype that is often inaccurate. That stereotype isn't fair to a female engineer, for example, who can't be expected to conform to someone else's idea of what an engineer "ought" to look like. Stereotypes lead us to judge people as members of a group rather than as individuals.

While growing up, we often acquire stereotypes about people who are different from us. These learned stereotypes hinder understanding. Although people within a group may have certain characteristics, each person is unique in personality, experience, ability, and current life situation.

DIVERSITY

Americans are stereotyped by various peoples of the world as careless, self-indulgent, competitive, always in a hurry, besieged by crime, and materialistic. Would you want people to draw conclusions about you personally, based on those stereotypes?

Diversity Tips

Communication skills are especially important when you communicate with people of diverse backgrounds. In addition to just writing or speaking effectively, you need to add elements of sensitivity, understanding, and tolerance in your communication. It is important to remember not to patronize or talk down to people who do not speak your language fluently. Instead, think of new ways to communicate that help you and your listener understand and be comfortable with each other. Following are some strategies for communicating with diverse coworkers and colleagues. Consider how each tip could help in a workplace situation, whether in an office in the United States, in Canada, or in Korea.

Objective

Affirmative Action and Workplace Diversity

According to the Civil Rights Act of 1964 and other supporting legislation, certain businesses and institutions that receive federal funds are required to maintain affirmative action programs. Specifically, that means that those businesses and institutions may take race, sex, and national origin into account when hiring employees. The program is designed to promote the interests of women and members of minority populations in a workforce dominated by white males.

Over the years, accusations of "reverse discrimination" have been made. White males have said that they were excluded from job opportunities because their employers had to maintain quotas of female and minority employees at certain levels. In some cases, these claims have stood up in court. Other cases have not.

The ultimate question is, "What's fair?" Should the most qualified candidate get the job, regardless of race, sex, or national origin? Or should companies be required to hire a certain percentage of women or members of minority groups?

As the makeup of the American workforce changes, should the affirmative action rules change? As minority groups make up a larger share of the employee pool, perhaps they don't *need* the protection of affirmative action. Should affirmative action be abandoned, with the assumption that employers will carry out fair hiring practices?

The whole issue goes back to workplace diversity and how Americans deal with it. Do we develop an inclusive society in which all peoples are welcomed and their contributions accepted? Or do we close our society and require people to have to *earn* our acceptance by proving their skills or acquiring wealth or meeting our expectations in some other way? ■

14 Simple, Specific Diversity Tips for Writing and Speaking[8]

1. *Remember that diversity has many levels and complexities, including cultures within cultures.* Did you know there is a significant Hispanic subculture in New Zealand? What might or might not a person of Hispanic heritage from New Zealand have in common with a person of Hispanic descent who lives in Mexico? in Spain?

2. *Don't separate people.* Avoid phrases such as "Jewish people understand that. . . ."

3. *Admit what you don't know.* Many people from outside the United States have a relatively large knowledge base about America from seeing television programs and movies. In general, Americans are less informed about people from other nations because we do not watch their films or television programs.

---

[8]"14 Simple, Specific Diversity Tips for Writing and Speaking," from *Workforce Online*, http://www.workforceonline.com, copyright May 1999. Used with permission of ACC Communications/*Workforce Online*, Costa Mesa, CA. All rights reserved.

4. *Notice what people call themselves.* Use the same term a person uses to identify herself: Persian or Iranian; Hispanic or Chicana.

5. *Don't make assumptions based on a person's appearance, name, or group.* Don't assume that because a person is of a certain ethnicity, he or she necessarily practices a certain religion or supports a certain political party. Even more importantly, don't assume that a person's religious or political tendencies indicate whether that person is "good," "bad," conservative, or radical.

6. *Don't patronize people.* Avoid phrases such as "Surely you understand...."

7. *Don't doubt the authenticity of what you hear.* Each person is the highest authority on what she or he feels.

8. *Be willing to have your biases changed.* It is not a sign of weakness to change your opinion about a person or a group of people.

9. *When writing, replace judgments with facts.* Describe a person as "retired" or as a "senior citizen" (if relevant), rather than as "elderly."

10. *When writing and speaking, consider whether some references and adjectives should be deleted.* For example, in an article about how single mothers cope with work and family, is it necessary to specify that one of the interviewees is Hispanic and one is Vietnamese? No, not unless that information is vital to the accuracy of the article.

11. *Use parallel titles and terms.* Sometimes men are referred to using their first and last names, but women are referred to with just their first names. Avoid such bias.

12. *Think about your use of "we."* A statement such as the following can be alienating to non-Christians: "As we approach Christmas, contact the HR department if you want to help with party planning."

13. *Do not use judgmental words.* Sometimes when we describe people or their actions, we unwittingly judge their actions or demean them.

14. *When writing, have someone review your work who may have a different perspective.* A second opinion is often helpful in detecting unintentional bias in your writing.

Checkpoint 5

Other Diversities in the Workplace

The following sentences are taken from company memos. Identify the words in each sentence that show bias or that may be offensive to diverse recipients.

1. When dealing with elderly customers, be sure to treat them with respect.

2. Our company has many skilled technicians as well as some excellent female technical assistants.

3. We will no longer play Christmas carols through the office intercom out of respect for our Jewish colleagues.

Check your answers in Appendix E.

CASE 2:

A n s w e r s

Response to Question 4 in Chapter Opener

4. **How might Anita and her new supervisor benefit from their differences? What must they do to recognize and learn from each other's strengths?**

   Anita has expertise in dealing with the employees and general operations at the plant in Detroit. Hans Dortmann has expertise, but not when it comes to working with a plant full of *American* workers. No doubt, however, his experience from working in the German plant can contribute to the productivity of the Detroit plant. Anita and Hans need to recognize each other as experts. On a less businesslike level, Anita and Hans should acknowledge that they don't know much about each other's culture. Once that admission is made, they should make themselves open to learning from each other.

DISCUSSION QUESTIONS

1. What are the benefits of diversity in the workplace?
2. Name the kinds of diversity you might encounter in the workplace. What are some challenges that face workers of diverse backgrounds?
3. What are some ways to overcome diversity when communicating in a workplace setting?

2·4 Working Effectively in Teams

Workplace Teams

Workplace teams are a trend in American companies. From manufacturing to service industries, nearly every organization realizes the benefits of using teams to increase productivity and to be competitive in the marketplace.

Every team is different, depending on the personalities and styles of its individual members. You may have participated in teams that "worked" and teams that didn't. What was it that made one team productive and another less productive? Which team was more enjoyable to be a part of?

Look at the profiles of the following two teams. Look for similarities between these teams and your own experiences.

The members of Team 1 hum along in their daily tasks without much fanfare. They pass work back and forth to each other, verify information by telephone, or work in pairs on specific projects—all with little wasted effort.

Team 1 members know what they do well and what other members do well. When they meet, they are relaxed. They accomplish work easily and laugh a lot. The team's results have had a visible impact on company performance. In a crisis, Team 1 rallies to do what it takes to accomplish the immediate goal, but its everyday functioning is not in "crisis mode." People find being on this team satisfying. Other employees wish they could be part of Team 1.

Team 2 members are easy to identify because they are usually in a meeting. They have motivating team slogans on the wall, but frequently leave meetings angry, frustrated, or disgusted. When team members get together in pairs, they spend time blaming one person or the other for the team's failure to get much accomplished. Several members have approached their supervisor about having one of the team members removed.

Why are some teams successful while others are not?

Objectives

After completing Section 2.4, you should be able to:

1 Identify five stages in effective team development.

2 Name and describe five roles needed for effective teams.

3 List qualities shared by successful teams.

4 Define "virtual team."

KEY POINT

Many managers believe that the results produced by an effective, cohesive team can be greater than the results produced by individuals working separately.

Virtual Office "Space" for Virtual Teams

One of the challenges of managing or working on a virtual team is keeping track of schedules, documents, and lines of communication. Do the original or current copies of documents reside with one person who circulates them to other team members? Or does everyone have a copy of all documents all the time, with updates distributed by appropriate personnel? Anyone who has ever worked on a team knows the confusion that arises when different people are looking at different versions of a report or proposal. For virtual teams, is this just a chronic condition that exists because they do not share physical office space? How can virtual team members ever tell whether they have the most current version of a document?

The answer to the problem is to establish virtual office "space" in which to conduct virtual team business. That space is on the Web, of course. A number of commercial sites allow subscribers to establish virtual offices. For a monthly fee, subscribers get a certain amount of storage space for shared files and discussion groups. In addition, team members can establish a shared calendar and hold synchronous chats in private conference rooms. Virtual team members can also use a threaded discussion list or bulletin board to keep each other informed of progress or post queries to the group.

Virtual teams are relatively new on the work front. It only makes sense that the answers to managing these teams involve the technology that makes the teams possible in the first place. ■

Source: "Building a Virtual Office for Virtual Teams," Lawrence Ragan Communications, Inc.; available from **http://www .ragan.com/newsletter**; Internet; accessed September 1999.

Effective Work Teams

Objective

1

SCANS
Employability

**Interpersonal:
Working on Teams**

Employees in the twenty-first century must be able to do more than "work well with others." They must be able to collaborate in spite of cultural and personal differences.

Effective work teams don't just happen. Team members seldom come out of the first meeting knowing that they are finally participating in one of those great teams that gets things done and enjoys visible success. It may take many meetings before anyone has that feeling. Most teams go through several stages before they become effective, productive bodies. Those stages have to do with giving the individuals on the team time to get acquainted and to establish their group roles.

1. *Stage 1.* Team members learn about each other. They exchange ideas and information about themselves and about the team's tasks.
2. *Stage 2.* Team members begin to get down to work. The team establishes goals and tasks. During this stage, individuals may face the conflict of sacrificing individual goals for team goals.
3. *Stage 3.* Team members establish or fully clarify their roles and tasks. The team agrees how to proceed. Individuals take responsibility for specific tasks.

4. *Stage 4.* The team carries out its work. Team members deal with disagreement by compromising. Team members share information and support each other in various ways as they carry out individual and group tasks. Open discussion and exchange of ideas continues.
5. *Stage 5.* The team develops its own identity—as a team rather than as a group of individuals. Team members identify with the team and are committed to its goals.

Team Membership

Successful teams are made up of individuals who have different backgrounds. In an organization, effective work teams have to be based on function, purpose, or individual expertise rather than on personality. All people are different, and organizations can use these differences to advantage in work team situations.

Objective
2

Each person who is part of a team fulfills some sort of role on that team. To be successful, any team has several roles that must be filled. Figure 2-4 describes those roles and how each contributes to a team's overall make-up. These roles are seldom assigned, but most groups include people who naturally assume these positions.

The Leader	This person makes sure everyone understands the objectives and that all team members are committed to the task.
The Challenger	The challenger is not afraid to question ineffective techniques or strategies. He or she is always trying to improve the team.
The Doer	The doer gets the team back on track after distractions and keeps everyone focused on the task at hand.
The Thinker	This person carefully considers other members' ideas and seeks to improve them by making tactful suggestions.
The Supporter	The supporter eases tensions. He or she also makes sure the team members maintain good working relationships.

FIGURE 2-4 Roles for Individuals on Successful Teams

Characteristics of Effective Teams

Do effective work teams simply have the best individual employees on them? Or are the best teams the ones whose members are all friends even before the team is formed? There is no magic formula for building a good team. However, most effective work teams do share some characteristics. Many high-performance teams tend to have the following qualities in common.[9]

Objective
3

[9]"Make Sure Your Work Teams All Have These Qualities . . . and These People," *Manager's Intelligence Report,* May 1998, p. 4.

- Members have a shared team vision and a commitment to clear, challenging objectives.
- Work is done in a supportive atmosphere. There is a strong, positive group identity.
- The team members learn from successes and failures by reviewing their procedures after each project.
- Team members are constantly striving to improve performance.
- The team is stable; team members have worked together for an extended time.
- Team members are able to talk about their differences. This part of effective team functioning is the hardest and usually takes longest to develop.

Virtual Teams

Objective

TECHNOLOGY

Working in virtual teams requires good communication skills because you don't have the advantage of meeting face-to-face with team members.

A **virtual team** is one whose members don't share a physical work space but work together on specific or long-term projects using communications technology. This technology can range from such basic technology as faxes and telephone conference calling to video-conferencing and Internet-based technologies using e-mail and web pages.

Virtual teams are most likely to exist in multinational companies that need to overcome large geographical barriers. However, these teams are growing in popularity throughout the United States as well. Chapter 5 of this text will recommend ways to handle e-mail, an important communication tool for members of virtual teams.

6 *Checkpoint*

Working Effectively in Teams

Indicate whether a statement describes an effective team or an ineffective team.

1. The team learns from its successes and failures.
2. Team members are individuals who do not necessarily agree on the team's vision.
3. Before beginning work on the team, members get to know one another.
4. Team members are people with similar skills and attitudes so that conflict will not arise.
5. The team is made up of people who have different backgrounds.

Check your answers in Appendix E.

DISCUSSION QUESTIONS

1. Discuss the differences between Teams 1 and 2 mentioned in the opening paragraphs of this section. What could have caused Team 1 to be more successful than Team 2?
2. Do you agree with the five stages of effective team development? Why or why not?
3. Have you ever been a team member? Was your team successful? Why or why not?

CASE 2:

Summary

Because Anita was not familiar with German customs, she should have been on her best behavior at the initial meeting. She should have worn business attire for this important meeting, and she should have taken every precaution to make sure she arrived on time. Once she did arrive, Anita might have taken a cue from the closed door. She should have knocked, then waited to be admitted. Finally, she should have waited to be introduced. Her eagerness to be friendly made the Germans uncomfortable. As a hostess, Anita should have let the visiting Germans set the tone for the meeting.

After participating in employee training on the differences between German and American cultures, Anita learned that Germans don't tend to mix their social lives with business. Therefore, she learned to behave more formally at work and to save informality for after-work activities with her new German coworkers. She found that many of these colleagues enjoyed the warmth and friendliness of the Americans as long as business and pleasure were kept separate.

Chapter Summary

Section 2.1 Cultural Differences at Home and Abroad

1 Define "cultural diversity," "multicultural," and "multinational." We live and work in a world of cultural diversity, meaning that people from different nations have different languages, customs, values, manners, perceptions, social structures, and decision-making practices. Multicultural means that our society is made up of many cultures. Multinational companies conduct business in more than one country.

2 **List population trends that indicate the U.S. workplace is becoming more multicultural.** More than one million immigrants arrive in the United States each year. More than 20 million United States residents were born in other countries. There are at least 300 different cultures in the United States. Hispanics will make up the largest U.S. minority group within the next ten years. Immigrants from China, Korea, India, and Eastern Europe are immigrating to the United States in increasing numbers.

3 **Identify three projections for the global workplace of the twenty-first century.**
1. Technology, especially the Internet, will enable more businesses to enter the global workforce.
2. There will be an explosive growth of companies doing business across borders.
3. Continual emergence of a world marketplace will require development of an international workforce.

4 **List, describe, and give examples of differences among cultures.** There are inherent differences in language, customs, values, manners, perceptions, social structures, and decision-making practices. Outward differences experienced in business situations include language, body language, facial expressions, space perception, and use of business cards.

Section 2.2 Effective Cross-Cultural Communication

1 **Define "cross-cultural communication."** Cross-cultural communication is a process by which two individuals who do not belong to the same culture communicate with each other, either orally or in writing.

2 **List and explain four guidelines to help people communicate effectively across cultures.**
1. Learn about and accept cultural differences. Use resources such as books, newspapers, magazines, videos, and the Internet.
2. Be sensitive toward—and tolerant of—people from other cultures. Be aware of possible ethnic, religious, and moral differences.
3. Be prepared for language barriers. Listen carefully; learn to speak "key" phrases.
4. Keep messages simple and short. Pronounce words carefully; use short, simple sentences; avoid slang, jargon, abbreviations, and acronyms.

3 Identify strategies for effective global communication.
1. Be adaptable in your communication style.
2. Use your best English speaking habits.
3. Do not use acronyms, slang, and jargon.
4. Be aware of a culture's forms of nonverbal communication.
5. Use visual aids.
6. Recognize that people from cultures other than your own have different assumptions.
7. Be careful about using humor.
8. Maintain personal contact.

Section 2.3   Other Diversities in the Workplace

1 List benefits of diversity in the workplace. Businesses and organizations need diverse sources of talent and information to be successful. Diverse groups are better at problem solving, decision making, and generating creative ideas.

2 Recognize types of diversity in the workplace and understand the challenges diversity creates. In addition to culture and nationality, diversities include race or ethnicity, gender, physical abilities, social class, age, socioeconomic status, religion, and personality.

3 Use communication tips for handling diversity.
1. Remember that diversity has many levels and complexities.
2. Don't separate people.
3. Admit what you don't know.
4. Notice what people call themselves.
5. Don't make assumptions based on a person's appearance, name, or group.
6. Do not patronize people.
7. Don't doubt the authenticity of what you hear.
8. Be willing to have your biases changed.
9. When writing, replace judgments with facts.
10. When writing and speaking, consider whether some references and adjectives should be deleted.
11. Use parallel titles and terms.
12. Think about your use of "we."
13. Do not use judgmental words.
14. When writing, have someone review your work who may have a different perspective.

Section 2.4   Working Effectively in Teams

1 Identify five stages in effective team development.
1. Members get to know one another.
2. Members set goals and tasks.
3. Members clarify roles and responsibilities.
4. The team carries out its work.
5. Members identify with and support the group.

2 **Name and describe five roles needed for effective teams.**
1. The leader makes sure everyone understands objectives and members are committed to the team's work.
2. The challenger questions ineffective team strategies and works to improve the team.
3. The doer keeps the team on track.
4. The thinker considers others' ideas and tries to improve them.
5. The supporter eases tensions and helps team members maintain good relations.

3 **List qualities shared by successful teams.** Members have a shared team vision. Work is done in a supportive atmosphere. The team learns from successes and failures. Team members are constantly striving to improve performance. The team is stable; team members have worked together for an extended time. Team members are able to talk about their differences.

4 **Define "virtual team."** A virtual team is one whose members don't share a physical work space but who work together on projects using telecommunications technology.

Critical Thinking Questions

1. How do people from diverse cultures differ from each other?
2. How can you communicate more effectively with people from other cultures?
3. What are the projections for diversity in the workplace and how can you be prepared to work in a diverse society?
4. Other than cultural diversity, what are other diversity issues and how should they be addressed?
5. What strengths would you bring to a workplace team? How would you help to improve an ineffective team?

Applications

DIVERSITY

Part A. You have just been informed that the empty cubicle next to yours will soon be occupied by a new employee from your company's international headquarters. Create a fictitious person of another culture as your new coworker. Give this person a name and a nationality. Conduct research to discover what cultural differences you should expect. Assume that the person has a working knowledge of English, but no real, day-to-day experience with the language or with American culture. What will you do to simplify communication between the two of you?

Part B. You work for a medium-sized company with about 500 employees. The company's management feels that employees could benefit from some diversity training to better deal with the different types of employees in the workplace. You have been asked to serve on a committee to provide suggestions for overcoming barriers to communication created by diversity in the workplace. What suggestions will you offer other committee members? Consider also how the diversity training should be delivered. Should employees be required to attend seminars? Or will a memo or newsletter do the job? Include your suggestions for distributing the information along with your specific ideas about overcoming communication barriers.

Part C. You and several other employees have been asked to do a feasibility study to determine whether your company will benefit substantially from conducting business on the Internet. Last year you attended a seminar on teams in the workplace and you know that it will take some time for this new team to get up and running. It is your job to e-mail the other four team members with an initial work plan, along with meeting schedules and agendas. Compose an e-mail that proposes the tasks and goals of your team's first four meetings. Keep in mind the five stages that teams go through before they become truly effective and productive.

Part D. Languages Unlimited is a company in Columbus, Ohio, whose employees translate documents and act as interpreters. The interpreters sometimes work in courtrooms or in hospital emergency rooms. At other times, they serve almost as cultural mentors when a company hosts international visitors. Write a letter of application to Kristine Wilson, the president of Languages Unlimited. Convince her that your sensitivity to multicultural issues in the workplace and your broad knowledge of world cultures makes you the perfect candidate for a position in her company.

DIVERSITY

TECHNOLOGY

TEAMWORK

DIVERSITY

Editing Activity

Edit the following memo, which was issued to employees prior to a visit from a company's international distributor.

> As most of you're aware, June 14th–16th is the date on which our colleagues from Indonesia will visit. They will be in the office, shadowing indiviuals from each department. As our main distributor in Asia, Emarnco is real important to us. We want our visitors to feel good about our products as well as about us, who make them. For that reason, following are some reminders to help you make a good impression on and communicate effectively with our visitors.
>
> 1. Our guests are native Malays and prefer to be called that. Don't call them Asians or Indonesians.

words@work

If you are using *words@work*, complete the activities on Diversity in the Workplace in the Workplace Success section.

2. People from the Indonesian culture are comfrtable with silence. If you ask a questoin, give the person time answer. Indonesians consider it polite to leave a respectful pause before respondign.

3. In general, while our guests are here, plan to spend more time being a host or hostess than working. Showing respect, being polite, and not being hurried or rushed are all important to Indonesians. For that reason, it may seem as if you spend a great deal of time being introduced and making the acquaintance of the the visitors. Don't feel that you need to look especially bussy or productive to impres them. They are here to get aquainted, not to check our production schedules.

Case Studies

DIVERSITY

1. During a crowded cocktail party in Mexico, Elaine noticed her business client waving to her from across the room. Talking with someone else, she saw the wave and thought, "How friendly!" and waved back. A little while later he waved again—more adamantly and vigorously. Again, she waved back more enthusiastically. In the days that followed, her client wouldn't return phone calls and canceled appointments with her.

   Why do you think the client became cool to her?

TEAMWORK

2. Maria and Carlos were given the task of developing a flow chart for a new software program. They were to put together a team quickly, develop the flow chart in a matter of weeks, and find developers to write the program. Maria was in charge of the team, and Carlos was a technical expert. They didn't know each other very well before the project, nor did they know about the other's capabilities or how they worked with others.

   In the first meeting, Maria took charge, getting input from all team members and handing out assignments. Carlos said little throughout the meeting and stalked out angrily after it was over.

   When Maria caught Carlos in the hall and discussed an idea she had, he seemed to understand what she was saying. But a week passed, and nothing happened. Maria felt that Carlos was trying to undermine the team by deliberately doing nothing. Carlos felt that Maria was stupid, or worse, that she didn't care very much about the project.

   The team became divided between those who liked Maria's leadership style and those who respected Carlos's expertise. The project dragged on with little being accomplished.

   Why do you think Maria and Carlos had problems working together? What could they do to improve the situation?

3. In what country would you most like to do business in the future? Choose a nation that interests you. Then visit the David M. Kennedy Center for International Studies at **http://www.byu.edu/culturgrams**. Read or print the CULTURGRAM that corresponds to the country you chose. Based on the information in the CULTURGRAM, prepare an oral presentation to orient your classmates with the business etiquette and social norms of that country. As with any oral presentation, a visual aid will enhance the information you present.

TECHNOLOGY

DIVERSITY

Career Case Studies

COMMUNICATION FOR NATURAL RESOURCES AND AGRICULTURE CAREERS

Jill Terrell started her own landscaping business in Atlanta about 10 years ago. Her company has grown, and she now has eight full-time employees, plus another dozen seasonal employees. When she hires seasonal help, Jill is careful to choose people who are willing to work hard and who have some interest in landscaping and in working with their hands.

For the past several seasons, most of Jill's seasonal employees have been Hispanic. Jill chose them carefully, as always, and has been pleased with her work crews. They follow directions well, learn new skills willingly, and work hard. Jill's problem, though, is getting the seasonal employees to work well with the full-time employees.

The full-time employees are mostly landscape designers. They often go to job sites to supervise the work crews. Though the seasonal workers are respectful, the designers have complained that the workers are uncooperative. Jill guesses that the designers simply feel left out. When the workers talk among themselves, they speak in Spanish. They bring their own lunches and keep to themselves during breaks and lunchtime. In addition, Jill's office manager seems to have difficulty communicating with the seasonal workers about withholdings, taxes, and other payroll issues.

Jill's business has been steady enough that she would like to expand her full-time staff. A couple of her seasonal workers are her first choices for those positions. But she's worried that the good team atmosphere of the company won't be the same, that the Hispanic workers won't really feel part of the group.

1. What can Jill do to help her current full-time staff feel more comfortable with the seasonal workers?
2. If Jill hires some of the seasonal workers as full-time staff, what further steps can she take to ensure that *all* of her employees work well together?

Video Case

Seeing the Person Behind the Gender

Millennium Design, the company that employs Marie and Max in its warehouse, engineers and markets desk accessories for businesses and home offices. In its 25-year history, Millennium Design has never hired a female engineer. To create more diversity among its engineers and designers, the company president asked Oliver Rainer, the director of engineering, to increase the number of female engineer managers on his staff. Oliver interviewed and hired Emily Lu.

Once they started working together, however, Oliver became uncomfortable. Emily found it difficult to make eye contact with him. She seemed uneasy when Oliver complemented her successes in front of her staff. Oliver was also concerned that Emily seemed too friendly with her staff. He wondered whether Emily was a tough enough manager.

Several months after Max and Marie's visit to the Human Resources department, Oliver spotted Max in the cafeteria. Oliver had heard about Max's conflict with Marie. Oliver told Max of his problems with Emily, expecting a sympathetic ear. Oliver believes he and Emily simply have a cultural and gender difference—that all Asians, particularly women, are retiring and nonconfrontational. Oliver asks Max.

"Maybe it's not 'Asians' or 'women,' " Max answers. "Maybe Emily is just different from you."

Questions

1. Do you think that working at Millennium Design—where there has been little diversity—has affected Oliver's interpretation of Emily's behavior? Support your opinion.
2. Can you think of another explanation for Emily's behavior that is not based on her race or gender?
3. Imagine a conversation between Oliver and Emily. Take the role of one person and describe what you would say to the other.
4. In a team of 3–4 people, search the web to find information on company diversity policies. After sharing research and brainstorming, your team will draft a "Workplace Diversity Statement" for Millennium Design.

Continuing Case....

Cultural Communication?

Eva and her Uncle Ramon have chosen October 1 as the grand opening of their new business, the NetCafe. By mid-September, workers had set up the computer stations throughout the shop. Some of the stations stand alone. Others are in clusters so that several customers —maybe coworkers from a nearby business— can talk with each other as they work. All of the stations provide space not only for papers and files, but also for mugs of steaming coffee and plates of tasty pastries that will be available at the shop.

Ramon already has his coffee makers installed. He will contract with several companies to get a variety of coffees. He is still negotiating with a bakery for pastries.

Eva's computers will interface with the Internet through cable modems instead of phone lines. Using cables will be cost-efficient over time and speed up access to the Internet.

Two weeks ago, Luis Colon, a salesman from the cable provider, had come to the shop to talk with Eva about the cable installation. He was from Puerto Rico, like Eva's family. He had even visited the small town where some members of her family still lived.

"Well, Eva," he said, "you don't have to worry about a thing. We'll get this all taken care of for you." He had patted her shoulder and given her a big smile.

Eva had smiled back, but it bothered her that Mr. Colon had called her by her first name. Patting her like a child didn't help, either. She had been worried that people would not take her seriously because of her age and maybe her gender. Now it seemed that she had reason to worry.

The installation of the cable wiring had been scheduled for September 26, but no workers appeared that day. Eva called the company the next morning. The scheduler promised the installers would be there that afternoon.

Eva stayed at the shop until 6:30 p.m., waiting for installers who never came. She was furious as she drove home—and worried that NetCafe would not be ready to open on time.

Early the next morning, Eva called the cable provider again. She asked for Mr. Colon this time. "Your workers have to install the cable this morning!" she told him, trying to keep the anger out of her voice. "The shop opens in three days!"

"Eva, Eva! You worry too much," he said. "Are you sure you're Puerto Rican? Don't you know that tomorrow always comes?"

"Get them here today!" Eva told him through clenched teeth.

1. What assumptions does the salesman seem to make about Eva?
2. Do you think the salesman is more influenced by Eva's age, her gender, her ethnic background, or another factor? Explain your answer.
3. Members of a group can have mistaken assumptions about other members of the same group. Describe an example that is unrelated to Eva and the salesman. Why might this happen?
4. Write a letter from Eva to the salesman. Without insulting him, explain the mistakes in his assumptions.

chapter 3

Nonverbal Communication

3·1 Nonverbal Communication: A Key to Accurate Communication

3·2 Listening: An Important Interpersonal Skill

Nonverbal Communication on the Job

As supervisor of a cleaning crew at Ace Janitorial Services, you must evaluate two relatively new employees.

The first employee, Joe, is from the United States. English is his native tongue, and he understands it well. Sometimes Joe does not get to work on time, but the only time he misses work is when he is sick. His clothes are usually a little soiled, his hair is normally uncombed, and he likes to wear sunglasses and listen to a Walkman while he works. He usually gets his work done, and the quality of his work is acceptable. However, sometimes he's a bit careless when using cleaning chemicals because he has not listened or did not understand instructions. He is very friendly with his coworkers and loves to socialize but does not seem to care too much about his job.

The other employee, Cheng, is from mainland China. Cheng has been in this country for only one year, and his English is not too good. When he's given instructions on the usage of cleaning chemicals and supplies, he listens intently, smiles, and nods his head "yes." But many times he does not understand. As a result, he often needs help in learning how to use the chemicals and supplies correctly. Otherwise, Cheng's work is very good. He nearly always finishes and then goes on to help others finish. His clothes are somewhat worn but always clean and tidy. Like Joe, Cheng is very friendly but is limited in his ability to socialize and develop friendships with coworkers because of his English skills. However, coworkers seem to like him and enjoy his enthusiasm for life in the States.

Questions

1. How would you evaluate these two employees?

2. In your evaluation, how important are the nonverbal symbols of each employee?

3. What kinds of listeners are these employees?

4. In your evaluation, how important are the listening skills of each employee?

3·1 Nonverbal Communication: A Key to Accurate Communication

Objectives

After completing Section 3.1, you should be able to:

1 Describe the roles of nonverbal communication.

2 Indicate the nonverbal symbols sent in written messages.

3 List nonverbal symbols sent in spoken messages.

4 Explain why nonverbal communication is important to you.

Objective

KEY POINT

A firm handshake, a delicately seasoned sauce, the beep of a computer, or the salty smell of the ocean all convey a message without a word being spoken.

The Roles of Nonverbal Communication

Nonverbal communication is composed of the messages we send without or in addition to words. These messages have a strong impact on us as receivers. Often, actions speak so loudly that they drown out spoken words. This happens because we use nonverbal symbols as a means to determine what the sender really feels and the degree of importance the sender attaches to the message and to us.

Spoken or written symbols make up the verbal part of a message and are accompanied by nonverbal symbols. However, a nonverbal message may not have a verbal counterpart. Nonverbal symbols—body language, appearance, touch, space, time, voice—exist in written and oral communication as well as in the environment.

Receivers interpret nonverbal symbols by using their senses: sight, hearing, touch, taste, and smell. If you hear a secretary say, "Great!" and see the secretary smile while a computer merges a list of addresses with a letter, you'll conclude that the mail merge is successful. If you hear a secretary say, "Great!" in a disgusted tone and see him or her frown, you'll probably conclude that the mail merge is unsuccessful. The receiver interprets the message based on sight (seeing the smile or frown) and hearing (the tone of voice).

People's opinions usually are based on the nonverbal symbols they observe and how they interpret them. Studies have found that when judging attitudes, people base 93 percent of their judgment on nonverbal symbols and 7 percent on spoken words. Verbal and nonverbal symbols should be interpreted in relation to each other. Nonverbal symbols may reinforce, contradict, substitute for, or regulate the verbal part of a message.

Reinforcing the Verbal Message

Nonverbal symbols usually reinforce the verbal message. Pointing to a door as you state, "The office is the second door on the left" reinforces the verbal message. Pounding the table while making a statement reinforces a verbal message and emphasizes it as well.

Contradicting the Verbal Message

Sometimes the verbal and nonverbal symbols do not agree. You may say, "That's fine," but if your voice is strained and you look away from the receiver, which symbol will the receiver believe—the verbal or the nonverbal? Research indicates that when verbal and nonverbal symbols conflict, the receiver usually believes the nonverbal message.

Substituting for the Verbal Message

Nonverbal symbols sometimes act as substitutes for verbal messages. Gritting your teeth or throwing your hands in the air indicates frustration; clenching your fists, anger; tapping your foot or a pencil, impatience; and nodding or smiling, agreement.

Regulating the Verbal Message

Nonverbal symbols may be used to regulate or control oral communication between the sender and receiver. These regulators may signal when you want to speak, when you want others to continue speaking, or when you want to withdraw from a conversation. For example, reestablishing eye contact with the receiver indicates that you will conclude your remarks shortly. Nodding in agreement encourages another person to continue; however, checking your watch or closing a portfolio means you are through listening.

SCANS
Employability

Basic Skills: Speaking
Be sensitive to your nonverbal messages that conflict with the verbal message. They play a major part in creating your professional or work image.

DIVERSITY

Overcoming Diversity Challenges

"In general, you're not adding a lot of value by adding a person who is just like everybody else who already works there." "It's an advantage to have more ideas to be able to select from." But while this advantage of diversity is well publicized, turning it into reality is sometimes accompanied by challenges.

Occasionally, diversity causes friction in the workplace. Organizations actively recruit women and minorities, yet the turnover rate for these employees is two to three times the rate for white males. Most of the time, causes for the high rate are not discrimination, open sexual harassment, or hostile environments, but something as simple as the ways of working over a period of time that create barriers to success. For example, companies that make "promotions contingent on traveling or relocation may be inadvertently discriminating against women or working parents whose family responsibilities require stability of location and a regular schedule."

Only when an organization's management is committed to making women and minorities feel "part of the group" will the true advantages of diversity in the workplace occur. ■

Source: Based on an article appearing in *Business First of Buffalo*, June 28, 1999.

- Have you ever sent a non-verbal message that conflicted with the verbal message? How did you do it? Was the real message you were sending to the receiver the nonverbal message? Probably!
- We learn regulators in our childhood. We use them so automatically that we are unaware of them.

DIVERSITY

Because of differing meanings of nonverbal symbols, study a culture before traveling to foreign destinations. By so doing, you may avoid offending members of other cultures.

1 *Checkpoint*

The Roles of Nonverbal Communication

Indicate whether each statement is true or false.
1. All verbal symbols are accompanied by nonverbal symbols.
2. When a hitchhiker raises an arm and fist, and extends a thumb, the hitchhiker is using nonverbal communication that substitutes.
3. When determining a person's attitude, people base more of their opinions on words than on nonverbal symbols.
4. Speakers can use nonverbal symbols to contradict a verbal message.
5. The nonverbal symbol of eye contact often is used to regulate communication.

Check your answers in Appendix E.

Nonverbal Symbols in Differing Cultural and International Settings

Though used the same way in most cultures, nonverbal symbols differ among cultures. In some cultures, for example, arriving late for a social or business engagement is polite; in others, it is considered rude.

Another common difference involves personal space. The intimate or personal space of North Americans is larger than the intimate or personal space of others.

In other cultures, appropriate eye contact varies from ours. American receivers need to have eye contact about 75 percent of the time. With the French, eye contact should be maintained 100 percent of the time. With Chinese, Japanese, or other Asians, it should be maintained only about 10 percent of the time. Too much eye contact with members of Asian cultures is very offensive.

Nonverbal Symbols in Written Messages

Objective

The appearance and correctness of a written document as well as the timeliness of the response send critical nonverbal messages and deserve careful attention. Letterhead stationery, plain sheets, and envelopes should be made of high-quality bond paper and have the same color. The typefaces and design of the letterhead and logo should convey a professional image. Drawings, photographs, charts, and graphs should be appropriate to the content and enhance the message. The print should be crisp and easy to read.

Documents should not include any errors in capitalization, grammar, number expression, punctuation, spelling, or word usage. Accurate content, especially amounts, addresses, and other facts, is essential. Error-free documents send a nonverbal message that the sender is reliable and considers quality important. Documents that contain errors send a negative message about the sender.

Nonverbal Symbols in Spoken Messages

Several nonverbal symbols—body language, touching, use of space and time, and voice and paralanguage—have an impact on oral messages. The following paragraphs discuss each of these symbols.

Body Language

Body language includes facial expressions and gestures. Interpreting body language is surprisingly complex, because a single motion can have many different meanings.

Facial Expressions

People can reveal their feelings through various facial expressions. A frown usually indicates negative feelings; a smile, happy feelings. Nervous smiles convey weakness or insecurity.

Eyes provide a most revealing facial expression and often are called "the windows of the soul." Eyes reveal feelings such as excitement, boredom, and concentration. Eyebrows also send various messages. Raised eyebrows may mean nervousness, surprise, or questioning; pinched together they may imply confusion or indecision.

Direct eye contact conveys interest, friendship, or confidence. A lack of eye contact may mean disinterest or boredom. In business, the amount of eye contact varies depending on a person's status. Because subordinates want to tell their supervisors that they like them, they generally make more eye contact.

Gestures

A gesture is the use of your arms and hands to express an idea or feeling. Crossed arms may indicate concentration or withdrawal; a hand placed against the side of the head can imply forgetfulness; trembling or fidgeting hands sometimes indicate nervousness.

Leaning toward a person who is speaking conveys an open attitude. Nodding confirms listening and sometimes agreement. On the other hand, folding your arms or shaking your head from side to side indicates a closed attitude or disagreement.

We use gestures to determine the real meaning in a message. No matter what words you may use, your eyes and your face reveal what your true feelings are. When we attempt to use gestures to deceive or hide the truth, they will undermine our message.

TECHNOLOGY
Be careful when sending electronic messages. Like any written message, they contain nonverbal messages that help or hinder your career.

Objective

DIVERSITY
The appropriate amount of eye contact is culturally based. (See page 74 in this chapter.)

SCANS
Employability

Personal Qualities: Self-esteem
Eye contact during a job interview is extremely important, because it is a way for the interviewer to measure the applicant's self-confidence.

KEY POINT

Facial expressions and gestures reinforce or contradict verbal messages. Thus, they help receivers identify the sender's true feelings.

DIVERSITY

Facial expressions and gestures are very culturally oriented. For example, an Asian greets one with a bow of the head; the American offers to shake a hand. What happens when people of these two cultures meet?

Sexual harassment is an ethical issue because it infringes on personal freedom and can have a demeaning or demoralizing effect.

Touching

The handshake is the most acceptable form of touching for both men and women in a business environment. It is a gesture used to greet someone and to close a discussion. A person who extends a firm handshake and simultaneously establishes eye contact projects a cordial, confident image. However, a weak, soft handshake suggests listlessness or mental dullness. A cold, wet handshake may indicate nervousness and possibly a feeling of inferiority.

Other forms of touching such as hugging or backslapping are generally not acceptable in business. A person of higher rank, however, may put his or her hand on a subordinate's shoulder as a sign of encouragement or support. A coworker could do the same thing with another coworker. A coworker should not put his or her hand on the shoulder of the supervisor. Such action could be considered too familiar. Businesspersons also must avoid touching that can be interpreted as condescending or as sexual harassment. Sexual harassment can be defined as any unwanted verbal or physical actions associated with sex.

Space

One aspect of space is the physical distance between individuals. In general, people stand relatively close to people they like and leave more space between themselves and people they fear or do not like. When unable to arrange space comfortably, as in a crowded elevator, people adjust by using other nonverbal symbols such as avoiding eye contact, staring at the passing floor numbers, or remaining silent.

People avoid speaking or making eye contact in these situations because their territory, or their own space zone, is being violated. The size of this space depends on the activity and the relation with the other persons involved. For North Americans, the space zones are as follows:

1. *Intimate Zone—0 to 18 inches.* To be comfortable at this close range (as in Figure 3-1), people must have an intimate relationship—close friends sharing confidences, a parent reassuring or scolding a child, a husband and wife having a disagreement. Touch and smell are the senses most used. Verbal communication is usually soft or even murmured.

2. *Personal Zone—18 inches to 4 feet.* To stand this close, participants must be well acquainted. Words are spoken softly.

3. *Social Zone—4 to 12 feet.* The social zone is common for most business meetings or social gatherings. When people converse in their social zone, they have some reason for speaking. If a stranger enters a social zone, people usually break eye contact or turn away. For example, if you notice a stranger as you walk on the sidewalk, you watch the stranger from a distance of about 20 feet. As the stranger approaches, however, you break eye contact. If you speak to a stranger who is within your social zone, you use a formal, businesslike voice.

4. *Public Zone—more than 12 feet.* From a distance of more than 12 feet, people may look at each other, but they do not maintain eye contact. Interaction is avoided. Communication between a speaker and an audience is within the public zone.

When a coworker stands too close or too far from you, he or she probably feels your relationship is on a different level. You may feel the relationship is on a personal level, but he or she feels it is on a social level. Consistently standing too close to a coworker could be interpreted as sexual harassment.

In an office environment, the size, location (corner office, distance from the top manager's office, and so forth), and use of space may be a sign of a person's status. Generally, the more spacious an office, the higher the status. Persons of higher status also may enter a subordinate's space unannounced.

KEY POINT

Meetings usually are held in the office of the person with the higher status because it is more convenient for that person.

FIGURE 3-1   For this situation to be comfortable, what assumption are you making?

**Personal Qualities:
Self-management**
In the American business culture, continually arriving late
sends a nonverbal message
that you are disorganized,
lazy, or disrespectful. Being
consistently on time sends a
nonverbal message that you
are organized and "on the
ball."

Time

How you use time is another aspect of nonverbal communication. If someone asks you to do something as soon as possible, you feel urgency. If someone asks you to do something immediately, you might stop what you are doing and fulfill the request. Arriving on time for appointments and job interviews and responding promptly to requests communicate your sense of responsibility and respect for other people's time as well as your own.

The use of time also shows status. Higher-status persons typically determine the length of a meeting. On the other hand, executives often work longer hours than do lower-status persons.

Voice and Paralanguage

Maybe you have heard the saying, "It's not what you say, but how you say it that counts." **Paralanguage** involves the nonverbal symbols that accompany a verbal message and reveal the difference between what is said and how it is said. Paralanguage includes pitch, stress, rate, volume, inflection, rhythm, and pronunciation. It also includes laughing, crying, sighing, grunting, yawning, belching, and coughing. Even silence, pauses, and hesitations are part of paralanguage. Paralanguage is critical to the correct interpretation of a message.

To understand the effect of paralanguage, repeat the following sentence aloud four times. Each time, stress the underlined word. Note how the meaning of the sentence changes.

I cannot do this.

I cannot do this.

I cannot do this.

I cannot do this.

2 Checkpoint

Nonverbal Symbols

Indicate whether each statement is true or false.
1.   Paralanguage is the study of how something is said.
2.   Touching is a type of nonverbal communication that can be used to reinforce.
3.   The stationery used for a company's documents is a nonverbal symbol.
4.   In the North American culture, the personal zone is 4 to 12 feet.
5.   When measuring attitudes, people give more importance to how words are spoken than to the words themselves.

Check your answers in Appendix E.

Using Nonverbal Symbols to Establish Your Image

Your nonverbal communications are extremely important because, whether you realize it or not, you use them to establish your image. If you ask yourself, "What kind of worker do others think I am?" you are examining your image. Important aspects of your image are based on level of confidence, eye contact, friendliness, enthusiasm, sincerity, body actions, and appearance. As you read this information about image, reflect back on your responses to the questions in the chapter opener—you're a supervisor and have to evaluate two employees.

Objective 4

Culture and Ethics: Alma's Plight

Because values, customs, and ethics differ from culture to culture, ethical issues that arise in international organizations can be quite complex. Thus, when conducting international business or even working for an organization that is owned or controlled by an overseas operation, one needs to be sensitive to cultural differences.

Consider the plight of Alma, an accountant employed by a Japanese electronics producer. Alma worked in the San Francisco office and was responsible for U.S. taxes and incentives allowed by the tax laws. She was ex-

tremely competent and consistently received excellent annual evaluations. She was certain she would be considered for promotion.

Alma thought her break had come at last when she was invited to the headquarters of the corporation in Japan. When she arrived, she was surprised to discover that her itinerary contained errors and that she was scheduled for the next week rather than the present. Finally, after many sightseeing tours and too many nights in a hotel, she was ushered into her counterpart's office. He was very gracious but did not have any-

thing important to say. Alma lost her composure and demanded to know why she was not meeting with his superior. He tried to explain to Alma that she had been assigned to him and that the leaders of the corporation were not "Westernized" enough to feel comfortable with a female executive. No promotion was forthcoming. Needless to say, Alma was very disappointed.

Even though our world is becoming more and more multicultural, many different beliefs, codes of ethics, and ways of doing business are still to be sorted out and changed. ■

Do you realize that there are companies that consult with individuals and companies about their image? Search the Internet using "image" as the key word.

SCANS
Employability

Personal Qualities: Self-management

How confident do you appear to others? How did you build this image? When you're on the job, how important is this image?

KEY POINT

- Do you have coworkers or supervisors who are negative? What are your feelings about them? Do you work well with them?
- Are any of your coworkers also your friends? Why do you consider them to be friends? When you do the same for others, they will consider you to be their friend.
- Do you know people who are enthusiastic? Do you work well with them? Is it important for you to be enthusiastic?

Level of Confidence

"No one knows you like yourself." Because this statement is true, others use your self-confidence level as a basis for determining your competence and abilities. If they perceive you to have an air of self-confidence, they believe that you perceive yourself as competent and confident. If you believe this about yourself, then others will believe it unless you prove otherwise.

Too Much Confidence

Too much confidence can hurt you. If others see you as cocky, inflexible, or as a "know it all," they will see you as self-centered and unrealistic about your own abilities. They will probably respond to you negatively and with serious questions about your "ability to work with others" or your "ability to get the job done." Thus, they will wonder if you really have the ability necessary to be successful, or if you have a personality that allows you to learn and grow.

Too Little Confidence

If you are perceived as having too little self-confidence, you have sent nonverbal messages that say, "I don't believe in myself." If others believe that you do not believe in yourself, they will question why they should believe in you.

Some of the nonverbal messages that say "I lack self-confidence" are being too nervous in a normal situation and overreacting to stage fright. This nervousness is reflected by a quivering voice, shaking hands, perspiration, inability to think clearly, inability to respond to questions, or locking up. If you lack self-confidence, neither you nor your receivers will find the communication exchange pleasant or productive. It will be something that is feared.

Negative thinking and unrealistic expectations are two causes of a lack of confidence. We all need to recognize that everyone makes mistakes—we forget, we overlook things, we mispronounce words, we make keying mistakes, etc. While we are human, we need to feel positive about ourselves. No matter who you are, you can make a contribution. What is it? Find out. Analyze yourself; identify your strengths and build on them.

Friendliness

Another important aspect of an effective image is friendliness. *Friendly* is defined as supporting, helping, or kindly. When you send a nonverbal message that you are supporting, helpful, or kind, you are considered to be friendly. When you are congenial, cordial, pleasant, or kind to others, they are drawn to you. To be perceived this way often means that you must focus on the needs of others rather than on your own needs. We send nonverbal messages that say "friend" when we smile; when we have a relaxed approach; and when we desire honest, open feedback.

Enthusiasm

Enthusiasm is an aspect of image that can set you apart from others. Real enthusiasm is contagious. When you enthusiastically present your ideas, receivers will sense your enthusiasm and feel positive about those ideas and you. When you're truly excited about an idea and eagerly present it, your feelings spread quickly to others. Smiles, raised eyebrows, and eyes that are wide open and sparkle are nonverbal symbols of enthusiasm.

Sincerity

Sincerity is a critical part of your image. For you to be credible, you must be perceived as sincere—which may take time. Open, honest communication sends a nonverbal message that you are sincere. In order to declare you "sincere," receivers need time to observe. If your actions and words contrast with one another, you will be viewed as insincere. If they match, you are considered credible and sincere.

Appearance

According to research, people generally believe that well-groomed people of either gender have more socially desirable personality traits than do individuals who are poorly groomed. Thus, your appearance also is critical to your image and the expectations others will have of you. The first impression others have of you is particularly important. Your dress helps to establish others' first impression of you. It also is an important part of your "total package."

Regarding appearance, what you do with what you have is the key. If you do the best you can, others will respect your appearance. Personal grooming—being clean and neatly dressed and selecting clothing and accessories that are tasteful—must be appropriate.

Proper diet, rest, and consistent exercise are the keys to maintaining an attractive body. In addition, your clothing must be appropriate to your work and for your organization. In most businesses, appropriate clothes are conservative in fabric, color, and style.

Look at Figure 3-2. Which of these workers is ready for work? Which is not? What role did appearance play in your decision?

Body Actions

Body actions are used to determine confidence level. Those critical to confidence level are eye contact and posture.

Eye Contact

Eye contact is one of the most important nonverbal symbols. As already mentioned, if done appropriately, it sends a message of confidence, interest, honesty, and sincerity. If not done properly, it sends a message of the lack of confidence, weakness, boredom, fear, insincerity, or dishonesty. Thus, inappropriate eye contact can be devastating to your image.

ETHICS

Do you know someone who is phony or insincere? How do you feel about that person? Most unethical people are judged so because they are seen as phony or insincere.

SCANS
Employability

Personal Qualities: Social

When you disagree with someone, ask why they think the way that they do. If you really listen to the answer and paraphrase what they say, you will be seen as a sincere person who is really interested in others.

SCANS
Employability

Personal Qualities: Self-management

How important is eye contact? What messages has someone sent you with just eye contact?

Go to
**http://www.thompsonortho
.com/smile.htm**
and learn something that
may surprise you.

FIGURE 3-2 Which of the workers is ready for work? What was the basis of your decision?

TECHNOLOGY

The trend in e-mail is toward voice and video. Remember that when you send any electronic message using video, eye contact is very important.

In one-to-one situations, effective eye contact builds interpersonal trust and confidence in each other. In small-group situations, look each person in the eye, maintaining eye contact long enough to give that person a feeling that you are talking with him or her personally. In large group settings, make sure that you look at individuals in all parts of the room. This action makes members of the group feel that they are being talked to and not ignored.

Although eye contact is one of the most difficult nonverbal skills to achieve, it is critical to your success. Exercise the self-discipline necessary to develop strong eye-contact skills.

Posture

Posture is the way you stand or sit; it conveys your confidence level. Poor posture may be a sign of timidity, laziness, or nervousness. To project a positive self-image, sit and stand naturally but straight and tall.

Nonverbal Symbols in the Environment

The business environment is a form of nonverbal communication. Furnishings and decor; the arrangement of tables, chairs, and so forth; the level of lighting, temperature, and sound; and the use of color contribute to the way people feel in a setting.

Furnishings

Furnishings and decor often are a part of business strategy. For example, in a typical fast-food restaurant, the tables are close together, the lighting is bright, and the seats are molded plastic. The environment is carefully planned to encourage fast turnover of customers. In contrast, a fine restaurant may have a more spacious environment, dim lighting, padded armchairs, fine china, tablecloths, and fresh flowers.

Color

Color establishes a mood within an environment. Soothing colors such as beige, off-white, or light yellow are especially suitable where people perform stressful or tedious work. Excessive use of light blue can have a dulling effect, tending to make workers feel sluggish. Red and orange are stimulating colors, appropriate for areas where people spend a short amount of time (e.g., a cafeteria) or perform creative work.

Music is used by businesses to influence customers. March music or music with a fast beat is used to move people quickly. Slow, mood music is used to encourage people to stay. Is that ethical?

Checkpoint 3

Your Image and Nonverbal Symbols

Indicate whether the following statements are true or false.
1. Eye contact is an important part of your image.
2. Businesses use decorations as a means to project an image.
3. A person who feels that he or she knows everything has a very good level of self-confidence.
4. If you are enthusiastic about your topic, you increase the probability of your audience becoming enthusiastic about it also.
5. If you focus on others rather than yourself, you will be perceived as "friendly."

Check your answers in Appendix E.

CASE 3:

Answers

Responses to Questions 1 and 2 in Chapter Opener

1. **How would you evaluate these two employees?**
    Joe: His main message is that he is somewhat committed to his job. He enjoys people but does not seem to enjoy his job. Cheng: His main message is that he enjoys what he is doing and is trying as hard as he knows how. The main problem is his understanding of English.

2. **In your evaluation, how important are the nonverbal symbols of each employee?**
    The nonverbal symbols are the basis for determining their images. Thus, they are very important.

DISCUSSION QUESTIONS

1. How important is nonverbal communication? Justify your answer.
2. Are nonverbal symbols important in both written and spoken messages? Explain.
3. What nonverbal symbols help you to establish a credible personal image?

3·2 Listening: An Important Interpersonal Skill

Objectives

After completing Section 3.2, you should be able to:

1 Identify the reasons for and the benefits of listening.

2 List the barriers to effective listening.

3 Describe effective listening techniques.

The Importance of Listening

What is the most frequent form of communication—reading, writing, speaking, or listening? If you said listening, you are correct. Research indicates that people spend about 70 to 80 percent of their waking time communicating. Of the time spent communicating, 45 percent is spent listening; 30 percent is spent speaking; 16 percent, reading; and 9 percent, writing. Managers, however, spend approximately 60 percent of their workday listening. Generally, the higher you climb in the corporate hierarchy, the more time you'll spend listening to others.

The Listening Process

Listening is the process of hearing and focusing attention to understand and remember an oral message. Four steps are required in the listening process:

1. *Hearing* is a function of the ears. In an office, you may hear people talking, telephones ringing, a door closing or opening, or other sounds.
2. *Focusing attention* involves concentrating on the speaker and what he or she says. To focus your attention, you must ignore unrelated sounds, background noise, and other distractions.
3. *Understanding* means that you can attach meaning to the speaker's message. For example, a person may hear and focus on someone speaking in an unfamiliar foreign language, but the message is not understood and becomes meaningless.
4. *Remembering* is essential. If you cannot accurately paraphrase something you have just heard, you have not really listened. Figure 3-3 illustrates the listening process.

Types of Listening

The two types of listening—casual and active—have different uses. Casual listening is what you do most frequently. **Casual listening,** sometimes called passive listening, is listening associated with

Objective

1

KEY POINT

- Hearing is the only part of the listening process that is physical. The other three parts depend upon your self-discipline.
- The basis for improving your listening skills lies within you only. No one else can do it for you.

Hearing and Focusing Attention	Understanding	Remembering
You force distractions into the background. You keep the message in the foreground.	You make the connections between important pieces of information.	You bring back to mind the important points of the message.

FIGURE 3-3 The Effective Listening Process

For additional information about listening and how to improve your listening skills, search the Internet using "listening" or "listening skills" as the keywords.

DIVERSITY

Cultural differences make effective listening—understanding and recalling a message —more complex.

conversation and entertainment. Watching a movie or making small talk between classes or at lunch are examples of casual listening. The casual listener expends little energy or effort. Although the listener may comprehend the message, remembering it is not critical. Casual listening is relaxed. When you are engaged in informal conversations, however, you must be careful not to listen so casually that others think you are not paying attention.

Active listening requires understanding and remembering and has purpose. Doctors actively listen to their patients; interviewers actively listen to what an applicant says. To understand the difference between casual and active listening, recall a time that you listened very intently because you had something to gain from what was said—you were motivated to listen by your own self-interest.

When you listen actively, your mind is alert and absorbs what the speaker says. You empathize with the speaker by trying to understand the speaker's perspective, attitudes, and emotions. Empathetic listeners also realize the importance of listening rather than talking.

Active listening, however, involves an element of risk. The listener risks seeing the world as the speaker sees it. When a listener actually senses the feelings of another person and appreciates what the other person's experiences mean to that person, the listener may change his or her beliefs.

Active listening also requires the listener to notice and interpret the nonverbal cues of the message. Speakers express attitudes in various ways: pauses; tone of voice; emphasis given or not given to words; and nervous habits and utterances such as repeatedly saying "okay" and "um," fidgeting with pointers, grasping the lectern too tightly, and so forth. The following situation provides an example of five steps used to employ active listening.

1. Jose sends a message.
2. Yu-lan listens to Jose's words and to the way he uses them. She also watches the nonverbal cues sent by Jose's face, hands, and so forth.
3. Yu-lan analyzes the verbal and nonverbal messages and decides what she thinks Jose is saying.
4. Yu-lan summarizes to Jose what she thinks was his intended message.
5. Jose decides if Yu-lan's summary is correct. If Yu-lan is correct, Jose signals that it was correct. If Yu-lan's summary is incorrect, Jose says, "No, it is. . . ." At this point, Yu-lan repeats steps 2 through 5. This process is repeated until Jose agrees with Yu-lan's summary.

Reasons for Listening

People listen to relax, to obtain information, to express interest, and to discover attitudes. When you listen to good music, usually you are listening to relax. Listening to the sounds of summer or the rhythm of the tides helps clear your mind of worry and relieves stress.

People listen to gather information. Adults gain an estimated 90 percent of information by listening. Gathering information for an assignment, participating in an interview, and obtaining feedback from a customer are examples of listening for information.

You listen to let people know that you are interested in what they have to say and that they are important. Listening and responding to friends or associates over lunch is not only enjoyable but also conveys the message that their thoughts and feelings are important to you. Such informal conversations establish a bond between people that makes communication in informal and formal situations easier.

Finally, people listen to discover attitudes. Attitudes often are expressed in the nonverbal cues of the message. Alert listeners observe these cues and try to identify the speaker's real feelings.

Benefits of Listening

Listening greatly affects the quality of your relationships with others. Through listening, you can better understand your own feelings, attitudes, and beliefs, as well as those of others. Friendships thrive when people take the time to share and understand each other's feelings. Family members build strong bonds by responding to each other's needs. Likewise, good listening helps businesses develop their most important resource—their employees. Employees who believe their opinions count develop greater self-esteem and contribute more to the organization. Customers who think a company understands and meets their needs will return for future business dealings. Those who feel ignored do not return.

TECHNOLOGY
As voice messages become more frequent, your active listening skills will become even more important.

DIVERSITY
Ignoring a person from another culture will probably destroy your relationship with that person more quickly than if you weren't speaking with someone of your own culture.

KEY POINT

Listening and nonverbal communication are interrelated. For example, in judging attitudes, we observe people's nonverbal cues. Observing nonverbal cues thus becomes part of the listening process.

TECHNOLOGY
Listening plays a vital role in our personal and work lives. First came voice mail, then computers with sound. Now e-mail is available with sound. What new technological advancements will require listening skills?

Listening affects the quality of decisions. To make good decisions, you must gather meaningful and accurate information. Gathering accurate information requires alertness and the ability to ask the right questions. Those who can listen to employees and managers at all levels will be able to make the best use of the information available to them.

Good listening skills are essential for success in business. Those who receive and interpret instructions and information correctly win the respect of their supervisors. Successful supervisors listen to both their subordinates and their managers. Similarly, effective salespersons listen in order to gather meaningful feedback from customers and relay it on to appropriate decision makers in the company. Employees who have good listening skills make prime candidates for promotion.

The Nature of Listening

Objective **2**

Some people assume they are good listeners because they have been listening all their lives. Yet, research by Ralph Nichols, the founder of the study of listening, and others indicates that initially people remember and understand only about half of what they hear. After a few weeks, they remember about one-fourth of what they originally heard.

TECHNOLOGY

How Do You Deliver Bad News—Electronically? Face-to-Face?

Researchers of a study entitled *Straight Talk: Delivering Bad News Through Electronic Communication* found that senders are uncomfortable when having to deliver bad news and often "distort or delay news to avoid the unpleasant task." And, receivers seldom like receiving such news.

The authors concluded that electronic communication can increase the "honesty and accuracy" of bad news. They found that less "cushioning of the blow" in electronically transmitted bad news results in more straightforward messages.

Delivering bad news face-to-face is currently a nonverbal way of saying "this news is important," but this may change. The researchers believe that when managers discover better messages being sent electronically, they may prefer most bad news to be delivered through this medium. ■

Source: Adapted from "Delivering Bad News by E-mail Is More Accurate, Less Painful Study Suggests," *Science Daily Magazine*, 25 June 1999.

Effective listening requires remembering; and remembering, in turn, requires effective listening. To become a good listener, beware of barriers that make listening difficult, understand the listening process, and use the appropriate kind of listening.

Barriers to Effective Listening

Missing an important appointment, discounting a valuable suggestion, overlooking the feelings behind the words, and interpreting a situation incorrectly are just a few examples of problems that occur because of poor listening. Researchers have identified various barriers to good listening. As you read about these barriers, evaluate yourself as a listener.

Attitudes about the Speaker

"My, he looks as if he didn't get enough sleep last night." "She speaks so slowly; doesn't she know I've got work to do?" "You wouldn't know he's educated from his language." When listeners have private conversations with themselves, they miss what the speaker is saying.

A speaker's appearance, mannerisms, tone of voice, and body language can distract the listener. Poor grammar or inappropriate word choice also can cause individuals to stop listening and mentally criticize the speaker.

Attitudes about the Topic

"I can't program using C++; programming is too complex." "Oh, insurance! Don't talk to me about that dull subject." Messages that sound technical often intimidate listeners. Uninteresting or boring messages cause people to tune out the speaker. In a similar manner, listeners often lose patience with messages that are too detailed or too long.

Environmental Distractions

Have you ever attended a luncheon at which the speaker began his or her presentation while the desserts or beverages were being served? Have you ever tried to finish a conversation with the telephone ringing in the background? If so, you know how unrelated activities and noise can interfere with your ability to listen. Likewise, excessive heat or coolness and noise are distracting.

Personal Barriers

Deafness or a partial hearing loss is a physical barrier to listening. A headache or another temporary physical discomfort also inhibits listening. Each of us also tends to block out messages for various psychological reasons. Additional personal barriers include the following:

1. *Prejudices or Differing Opinions.* Most people have preconceived ideas about certain topics. If a speaker challenges a strongly held belief, the listener may simply tune out the speaker. Often the listener begins preparing a rebuttal even before the speaker has finished.
2. *Assumptions.* Assumptions made in advance can account for a 75 percent decline in listening. People often disregard messages when they think they already know the information.

↓KEY POINT

Would you like to reduce your study time? When you become a better listener, you remember more; thus, you reduce the amount of your study time.

SCANS
Employability

Personal Qualities: Responsibility
The first step to overcoming your personal barriers to effective listening is to recognize them and admit that you have them.

↓KEY POINT

*   Have you ever tuned out an instructor because of his or her appearance or teaching style? How much did you learn from that person? How much did you miss?
*   How do you feel when no one listens to you? Good listeners improve a speaker's ability to express thoughts clearly. Help the speaker—be a focused listener.

When we ignore someone because of a personal prejudice, are we being ethical?

Why do people ignore each other? If we assume we already know the answer and do not listen, how much information do we miss? We'll never know!

3. *Lack of Attention.* Mind wandering is another deterrent to effective listening. Worrying about a personal problem or daydreaming about more interesting ideas can cause your mind to wander.

To overcome these personal barriers, you must listen with an open mind. When you listen with an open mind, you can learn and grow. If you fail to listen with an open mind, you cannot learn or grow.

Note-taking Techniques

Someone who tries to record everything that is said often hears only about one-third of what is said. Conversely, some listeners record only the main ideas and fail to record enough supporting information to make the main ideas meaningful or clear.

4 Checkpoint

The Importance and Nature of Listening

Indicate whether each statement is true or false.
1. Adults spend more time listening than speaking.
2. Attitudes toward a speaker or toward a topic seldom affect listening skills.
3. Preconceived ideas can create a barrier to effective listening.
4. The last step in listening is understanding.
5. Active listening may result in personal change.

Check your answers in Appendix E.

Objective

To look at listening tips for students, go to **http://coehp.idbsu.edu/ssp/listening.htm**

KEY POINT

Learn while listening by using your spare time to review what has been said.

Effective Listening Techniques

To be productive, people need to become effective listeners. Understanding the listening process and knowing the barriers to effective listening are not enough. Listening is a skill that requires continuous practice. To become a good listener, you must know your own personal weaknesses and practice good listening habits. Follow these suggestions to improve your listening skills.

Share the Responsibility

Although the speaker has most of the responsibility for conveying meaning, effective listeners realize their vital role in the communication process. Listeners must be able to attach meaning to what has been said.

People talk at a rate of about 100 to 150 words a minute and think at a rate of about 300 to 500 words a minute. Thus, the listener has spare time available. Rather than letting their minds wander, effective listeners use this spare time in ways that benefit comprehension. To increase comprehension, use your time effectively by focusing on the main idea, evaluating the message, and providing feedback.

Focus on the Main Idea

Some speakers develop their points in a disorganized manner, mixing the unimportant with the important. Therefore, to be a good listener, you must be willing to wait for the main idea and not be distracted by unimportant details. Separate fact from opinion. When taking notes, record the main ideas and enough supporting information to make the main ideas meaningful. Concentrate on the message, not on the speaker's delivery or appearance.

Evaluate the Message

Compare the speaker's message with the information you already know or believe about the topic. When you have some knowledge of the topic, do not ignore the speaker by assuming you already know what he or she will say. Instead, relate what you already know to what the speaker is saying. Do not judge a speaker until he or she is finished.

Observe the speaker's nonverbal symbols. A natural, relaxed style and good eye contact show that the speaker feels confident about the message. On the other hand, nervous mannerisms may cause you to question the validity of the message.

Provide Feedback

When you understand the message, smile or nod your head to let the speaker know. Feedback tells the speaker that you are listening and that you understand the message. To assure understanding, ask questions for clarification, summarize main ideas, paraphrase the message, or restate the message as you understand it. Statements such as, "If I understand you correctly, you mean that . . ." can provide valuable feedback and aid understanding.

Overcome Poor Listening Habits

Listening is a skill that requires practice. Becoming an effective listener requires changing attitudes toward speakers, attitudes toward topics, and personal habits that result in poor listening. Here are some suggestions for becoming a better listener:

1. Find common interests.
2. Judge content, not delivery.
3. Delay judgment until the speaker is finished.
4. Listen for the main idea of the message.
5. Take notes on only the important points.
6. Concentrate on listening; stay alert.
7. Avoid physical and environmental distractions.
8. Listen with an open mind; do not let prejudices or assumptions cause you to miss the message.
9. Use your spare time to analyze, evaluate, and review the message.
10. Talk less; listen more.

Listening in Specific Situations

In the business world, you will find two common listening situations— listening in a small group and listening in a conference setting.

↓KEY POINT

Without focusing, you greatly increase your probability of not understanding a message.

SCANS
Employability

Information: Acquires and Evaluates

When your supervisor gives you an assignment, make sure you understand it by paraphrasing it back to the supervisor. If you do not understand the assignment, ask for clarification.

Listening in a Small Group

When in a small group, all of your communication skills, including your listening skills, are on display. Thus, when in this type situation, you need to exhibit strong communication skills. The listening skills you need to demonstrate in this setting are

- Practice active listening.
- Listen for ideas and feelings.
- Use effective eye contact (see pages 81–82).
- Employ body language that says you are listening.

Listening in a Conference Setting

As an employee, your training will never stop. As a result, you will attend conferences designed to enhance your competencies. When attending a conference, you will need to listen effectively in order to learn and grow. Listening skills that are especially important when in a conference setting are

- Determine your objective for being at the conference.
- Choose comfortable seating.
- Choose seating where you can see the speaker and any visual aid that may be used.
- Avoid judging the speaker's subject, his or her ability to present, and his or her appearance.
- Take notes effectively.
- Ask questions if permitted and if necessary.
- Learn the content of your notes by keying them.

5 Checkpoint

Effective Listening

Indicate whether each statement is true or false.

1. Listeners have almost no spare time when comprehending a message.
2. Effective listeners ignore a speaker if they already know what the speaker will say.
3. Feedback is important because it tells the speaker that you are listening to his or her message.
4. Effective listeners often must change their attitudes toward speakers.
5. Effective listeners often judge speakers even before they begin.

Check your answers in Appendix E.

A n s w e r s

Responses to Questions 3 and 4 in Chapter Opener

3. **What kinds of listeners are these employees?**

   Joe: This employee is probably average or below. He sometimes does not listen very well because of a lack of interest, which could be read nonverbally as laziness.

   Cheng: This employee currently is unable to understand some messages because of a lack of English skills. However, he is probably not a lazy or unmotivated listener. Eventually, he will become a very good listener.

4. **In your evaluation, how important are the listening skills of each employee?**

   In this situation, the listening skills of both Joe and Cheng hurt their overall evaluations. Because of this weakness, the performance of both is not what it could be. In Joe's case, it is a nonverbal symbol that could be read as apathy or laziness. In Cheng's case, it is a sign of the lack of an ability that will improve with time.

DISCUSSION QUESTIONS

1. Is listening important? Justify your answer.
2. Although the listening process is composed of four simple steps—hearing, focusing attention, understanding, and remembering—why do we remember only a fourth to a half of what we hear?
3. What can we do to become effective listeners?

Summary

In most job situations, nonverbal communications and listening are keys to your success. First, they are keys to your understanding of the messages that are sent to you. In this situation, Joe has an advantage over Cheng because he should have a better understanding of the nonverbal symbols used in the sending of messages in the workplace. Cheng, because he is from China and does not have an "American" background, is at a disadvantage because he is just learning the meaning of the nonverbal symbols used in his workplace environment. Thus, his listening skills are limited because it will be difficult for him to attach meaning to the spoken messages sent to him.

The second reason nonverbal communications are important is that we use them when sending a message. Again, Joe should be familiar with the meanings of symbols when he uses them. Cheng is not. Thus, Joe should be able to send messages more accurately than Cheng.

The third reason nonverbal communications and listening are important is that they are used to identify a worker's attitude. The noverbal symbols and Joe's attitude when listening imply a mixed attitude toward his job. He usually gets the work done but doesn't show a lot of interest in his job. Cheng, on the other hand, seems quite happy with his job but tries to cover up a lack of understanding of messages sent to him by nodding his head "yes."

Thus, it seems quite clear that both nonverbal communication and listening have important roles in the workplace.

Chapter Summary

Section 3.1 Nonverbal Communication: A Key to Accurate Communication

1 **Describe the roles of nonverbal communication.** All messages, whether written or oral, contain nonverbal symbols. We use these symbols to reinforce our messages, to contradict our messages, to substitute for verbal messages, and to regulate our conversation.

2 **Indicate the nonverbal symbols sent in written messages.** Examples of nonverbal symbols in written messages are letterhead stationery; color and type of paper; font selection; company logo; quality of print in the letterhead; and errors in capitalization, grammar, number expression, spelling, punctuation, and word usage. Other nonverbal symbols in written messages include accuracy of content—especially amounts—addresses, dates, and other facts.

3 **List nonverbal symbols sent in spoken messages.** Nonverbal symbols always accompany verbal messages. One of the major types of nonverbal symbols sent in verbal messages is body language. Body language includes facial expressions, gestures, and posture. Other nonverbal symbols that accompany verbal messages are appearance, touching, space, time, and voice and paralanguage.

4 **Explain why nonverbal communication is important to you.** Nonverbal communication is important because it is the means primarily used to establish your image.

Section 3.2 Listening: An Important Interpersonal Skill

1 **Identify the reasons for and the benefits of listening.** We listen to relax, to obtain information, to express interest, and to discover attitudes. Therefore, your listening skills affect the quality of your relationships, the quality of your decisions, and your ability to succeed on the job.

2 **List the barriers to effective listening.** We control most barriers to listening. Our attitudes about the sender or speaker, our attitude about the topic, our prejudices or differing opinions, the assumptions that we make, our lack of attention, and our note-taking techniques all affect our listening skills. The only barrier that is external to us is an environmental distraction.

3 **Describe effective listening techniques.** The listening process involves hearing, focusing attention, understanding the message, and remembering. We can improve understanding by (1) focusing on the main idea, (2) evaluating the message by comparing it with what we already know, and (3) providing feedback. Effective listeners also share the responsibility for communicating and overcome poor listening habits that inhibit good listening.

Critical Thinking Questions

1. How does nonverbal communication interact with listening?
2. Is nonverbal communication more important than listening? Is listening more important than nonverbal communication? Are they equally important? Justify your answer.

Applications

Part A. Identify the nonverbal symbols in each situation listed below. Choose from these nonverbal symbols: (a) furnishings, (b) body language, (c) space, (d) touching, (e) voice and paralanguage, and (f) appearance.

1. a hand laid gently on a shoulder
2. a grunt
3. a new worker slouched in a chair
4. a leather couch
5. the distance between two coworkers during a conversation
6. a pressed shirt

Part B. Indicate the role of the nonverbal symbol in each situation listed below. Choose from these roles of nonverbal symbols: (a) contradict, (b) regulate, (c) reinforce, and (d) substitute.

1. A subordinate asks you a question. Instead of saying, "I have to think about the question," you respond by folding your hands together and placing them behind your head.
2. After a bad day, you arrive home, walk by your spouse without hugging him or her, and exclaim, "What a day!"
3. As you talk with a friend, your friend nods his head, agreeing with what you are saying.
4. While consoling your child, you hug him or her gently and pat him or her on the back.
5. You are speaking with one of your peers. As you are finishing what you want to say, you glance at your peer.

Part C. Visit an office, a retail store, or a restaurant. Write a short report describing the effect of the environmental factors and the image created by the environment.

Part D. Get on the Internet and go to one of your favorite web sites. (If you do not have any favorites, you could use **www.latech.edu** or **www.compaq.com**.) Study the web site. Then write a memo to your instructor indicating (1) the web site you chose and (2) how nonverbal symbols were used at the web site. Also indicate the nonverbal messages that were sent by the web site.

Part E. Engage a friend or an acquaintance in a social listening experience. Then develop the conversation into a serious discussion. Try to maintain the serious discussion for three minutes. Write a one-page report. In the report, answer the following questions:

1. Were you able to maintain the conversation at the appropriate level? If so, how did you do it? If not, what prevented you from doing it?
2. Of the two types of listening, which was the easier to maintain, casual or active? Why?

Part F. Observe someone's listening skills for about 15 minutes. Indicate whether the listener was involved in casual and/or active listening. Rate the listener as good, fair, or poor. Justify your answers by using the keys to effective listening and the characteristics of poor and good listening.

TECHNOLOGY

TEAMWORK

Editing Activities

1. Edit the following paragraph, correcting all spelling, punctuation, and grammar errors.

   If you take a computer course at a college or university, your might be eligible for a account on its computer system. This is a great way, to get to the internet because most reasonably large colleges and universitys have Internet connections. You might have to use one of there computers, or you might be able to dial in from home using you own computer and modem.

2. Edit the following paragraph, correcting all spelling, punctuation, and grammar errors.

   Freenets are, as there name implies, free! If you are lucky enough to have one in you're area, you have hit the jackpot. To find out if there is a Freenet in your locality, check with compute stores, user groups, and the Chamber of commerce. The problmes with Freenets is that there are not many of them, they can be erratic in the service they provide, they often come and go with notice, and logging on is often difficult because of a lack of phone lines.

words@work

If you are using *words@work*, complete the activities on Active Listening in the Workplace Success section.

Case Studies

TEAMWORK

1. This activity involves role-playing involving a restaurant manager, an assistant manager, and two applicants. The restaurant, a fast-food restaurant, needs a new employee. The duties of the new employee are to meet the public and operate a cash register. After studying the resumes of all the applicants, the top two applicants were judged to be equal. The manager decides to call them both in for interviews. For training purposes, the manager decides to have the assistant manager join in on the interviews. The manager will ask five questions; the assistant manager, three.

   After observing this activity, divide into groups of three or four and discuss each candidate by answering the following questions: (1) What are the strengths and weaknesses of each candidate? (2) If you were the manager, which applicant would you hire? (3) What were the major factors in making that decision? (4) What were the major factors in rejecting the other candidate?

   After answering the questions, as a group, write your instructor a memorandum report indicating (1) the applicant you would hire, (2) why you chose that applicant, and (3) why you did not choose the other applicant. Use the simplified memorandum format.

TECHNOLOGY

2. You have an acquaintance that you have known for more than ten years. He feels very close to you and considers you a good friend. Unfortunately, you do not feel the same way about him. One of the reasons is that he is always talking and never listens to you. Even when he does let you talk, his mind seems to wander, or he seems to be getting ready for "his next topic."

   In the past, you have noticed that he "has tuned you out" because he felt he knew what you were going to say or because he already knew about that topic. You wonder what he says about you because he has commented to you that he cannot listen to people "who are dressed strangely" or have strange personalities. Probably the most irritating characteristic of his personality is his inability to agree. If you say yes, he says no; if you say no, he says yes.

   He has just been fired from his second job in three months and the same reason was given each time: "You do not listen!" In a moment of humility, he approaches you as his friend and asks, "Am I really a bad listener? If I am, how can I learn to listen better?" He sincerely wants you to be honest with him.

   What would you tell him? Does nonverbal communication play a role in your response? How? To help him improve his listening skills, what specific suggestions would you give him? For additional tips, go to **http://www-rohan.sdsu.edu/~rbutler/listen.htm**. This site focuses mainly on listening in an academic setting but contains some ideas that can be used to help your friend.

COMMUNICATION FOR BUSINESS AND MARKETING CAREERS

Ollie Ridingbull and his financial group are opening a restaurant just outside Glacier National Park. New roads have made this area accessible. The restaurant is located next to an upscale lodge that accommodates 400 guests. The restaurant is one of two eating places in the area. The other is an ordinary café that serves a basic menu such as hamburgers, hot roast beef sandwiches, and chicken-fried steaks.

The lodge was built by a Native American consortium and has a Native American atmosphere. Its architectural design is rustic: log cabins; paintings of mountains, deer, elk, and cougar; and pinewood furniture with big fluffy cushions.

Mr. Ridingbull wants his restaurant to continue the Native American theme and to offer exceptional food and service to his affluent and sophisticated patrons.

1. As you think about Mr. Ridingbull's new business, how important is listening?
2. How important will nonverbal communication of his staff be? Justify your answers.

COMMUNICATION FOR HUMAN AND SOCIAL SERVICES CAREERS

Julius Stallworth is majoring in law enforcement in college. He plans to attend Career Day, at which 40 law enforcement agencies will have booths. The people sponsoring these booths will talk with and gather resumes of prospective employees.

Julius has prepared a resume to give agencies that express an interest in him. However, he has never attended Career Day before and does not know what to expect.

Now that the day is almost here, he is nervous and has come up with several questions about what he should do. He turns to you, his best friend and asks—

1. What should I wear?
2. What kind of image should I try to project? What are the key elements of this image?
3. What kind of listening should I expect—casual or active? Why?
4. How can I ensure that I understand the messages sent to me by those sponsoring the booths?
5. How can I say nonverbally to those agencies that I understand their messages?
6. Should I take notes?

Video Case

Listening In a Critical Situation

Lisa Navarro has been a paramedic with CareLine for five years. When her partner left CareLine, Lisa was anxious about how she and her new partner would work together. But when Carrie arrived fresh from her training, Lisa was relieved—the women made a strong team from the beginning.

Carrie was a quick learner, and she obviously cared about the people she helped. Gradually, though, Lisa grew concerned with one of Carrie's crucial skills. Carrie was a poor listener. She interrupted patients and had a habit of looking away from them. Lisa could feel patients withdraw.

Lisa began making suggestions to Carrie about the importance of listening in their work, about how listening was more than gathering information. Carrie agreed with Lisa each time but continued her ineffective listening.

Lisa considered her own communication skills and realized she could be a better listener with Carrie. After a week of careful listening, Lisa discovered that Carrie was afraid of making a mistake and possibly losing a patient. In trying to be perfect in every situation, Carrie had come to see her patients as a test of her competency, rather than human beings.

Questions

1. Based on what you saw in the video, why do you think Lisa believes listening and nonverbal communication skills are so important to CareLine ambulance crews?

2. In a team of three or four, discuss what qualities each likes most in a good listener. Consider nonverbal cues and body language. Then have each team member research the same issue at home or with friends. As a team, create a chart of the qualities of the ideal listener, breaking down the qualities by verbal and nonverbal characteristics.

3. Drawing upon the information in the video and your knowledge of Chapter 3, draft a persuasive memo to the CareLine staff, describing the benefits of good listening skills. Print your draft.

Continuing Case....

A Class in Communication

The NetCafe has been open for two weeks now, and business has been good! Uncle Ramon has hired a college student to help him serve coffee and pastries during their busiest time, early mornings. In fact, some people stop by just to pick up something good to eat on their way to work. Ramon has joked to Eva that they should put in a drive-through window.

Eva's computers are increasingly busy. Sometimes two or three friends come in to sip their favorite coffee while they shop on the Internet. Every day, more college students turn up to use the computers. Eva knows she will soon have to set up some rules so they don't dominate her equipment.

Eva is teaching her first class this afternoon, an introduction to the Internet. Only three people signed up, but Eva doesn't mind. She has no experience as a teacher, so she hopes that the small class will help her get used to her role.

The students are Isako Harada, a young Japanese woman who speaks English fairly well; Clara Borden, a grandmotherly type who says to call her Clara; and Kevin Wall, a man of about 30 and hasn't said anything so far.

Eva has seated her students near each other at a cluster of computers. As she explains how to log on, she is glad to see Isako watching intently. She notices, though, that the young woman is watching Eva's hands and has not once looked her in the eye. Isako must be really shy, Eva decides.

Clara is frowning, which Eva guesses is a sign of concentration. Kevin is leaning back in his seat with his arms folded across his chest.

"Do you have any questions?" Eva asks as she looks directly at Kevin. He just shrugs.

Clara raises her hand half-way. "I was wondering," she almost whispers. "How do you get a password? I just . . ."

Eva interrupts and quickly answers her. She hopes Clara didn't notice Kevin rolling his eyes at such a basic question.

Just before the end of class, Eva watches her students try out the techniques she has showed them. Isako is a fast learner, while Clara is trying hard. Eva is surprised to see Kevin make several mistakes. After class, she asks him if he uses a computer at work.

"Well . . .," he mumbles.

Just then, Eva notices Clara heading for the coffee counter. "Bye!" Eva calls. "See you next week."

Eva turns back to Kevin, but he's already on his way out the shop door.

The following week, Eva is discouraged when only Isako shows up for the class.

1. Do you think Eva misread Isako's nonverbal message of not looking her in the eye? Explain your answer.
2. Eva asks, "Do you have any questions?" What nonverbal message does she send along with her question?
3. Do you think Eva's verbal messages or her nonverbal messages had a greater influence on which students returned for the second class?
4. Send Eva an e-mail with some gentle but specific suggestions that will help her improve the attendance in her classes.

The Writing Process

Sending Written Messages That Work

Atlee Corporation is a consulting company with offices in several major cities in the United States. An old firm, it is considered conservative and somewhat elite. The company directors have finally bowed to pressure and agreed to institute a casual dress day for employees. The directors issued the following memo.

TO: All employees of Atlee Corporation
FROM: Atlee Board of Directors
DATE: October 5, 2001
SUBJECT: Implementation of Causal Dress Day

After much consideration, we, the Board of Directors, agree that the implementation of a casual dress day will neither interrupt business nor damage our reputation. For that reason, employees may participate by wearing less formal attire on the last first and third Friday of each month.

    Should any employee violate any of the rules stated herein, disciplinary action may be taken. If this arrangement is to work in an an acceptable manner, certain rules must be followed. First, employees who have contact with outside clients on the designated casual dress days may not participate in casual dress day under any circumstances. Women may not wear clotheing that would be considered revealing. In addition, short ("mini") skirts, shorts, halter tops, tight jeans, and anything resembling swimwear is not allowed. Male employees should wear comfortable slacks and shirts or sweaters, depending on the season.

    If you have questions or comments regarding any information in this memo, direct them to Susan in the San Francisco office (ext. 237) or to Mr. Alazar in the Boston office (ext. 526).

Questions

1. Is this business message receiver-oriented? What is the message's objective?
2. Does this message contain any bias? What evidence do you find?
3. What is the tone of this message? Are the sentences easy to read, or do they contain unnecessary elements?
4. Does this message contain opening, developmental, and closing paragraphs? Are they effective?
5. Does this memo include the five *W*s? If so, what are they? If not, what is missing?
6. What content and mechanical errors does this memo contain?

4·1 Prewriting: Planning and Organizing Messages

Objectives

After completing Section 4.1, you should be able to:

1 Understand the prewriting stage of the writing process.

2 Plan messages by identifying the objective and main idea.

3 Choose supporting information in messages.

4 Adjust messages for the receiver and write receiver-oriented messages.

5 Organize messages.

The Writing Process

Good writers recognize that writing is a process. Writing is not a series of steps so much as a cycle of tasks. At any time, a writer may go back to a previous task to rethink the plan or change what she has already written. This is true whether the writer is turning out business proposals or scripts for television commercials. The stages or tasks in the writing process are prewriting, drafting, revising, editing and proofreading, and publishing or presenting. Figure 4-1 shows the cycle of writing tasks and the way in which they build on each other.

Most jobs become easier when they are broken into stages or steps. This is just as true for writing as it is for building a wall. A bricklayer first sets up guidelines for a wall, then makes sure the bricks are on site, then mixes the mortar. Only then does he begin to lay the bricks, one at a time, to build the wall. If the bricklayer skipped any of these steps, or tried to do them all at once, he wouldn't be a very good bricklayer, would he?

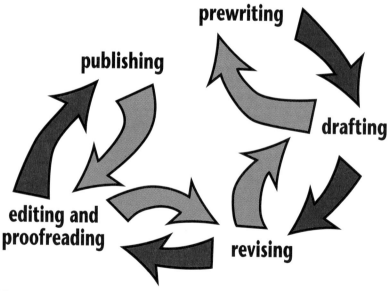

FIGURE 4-1 Cycle of writing tasks

Just like the bricklayer's job, a writer's job is easier when she recognizes that there are certain steps to take. One can't simply begin writing a business letter without preparation. That would be like laying bricks without guides or mortar.

Writers who recognize and use the writing process may still make errors, and they will still spend time revising their writing. Chances are better, however, that their final product will be a well-organized document that expresses ideas clearly and contains all the information it should.

Prewriting

Have you ever sent a message that you wished you had not sent? Maybe you wished you had stated your ideas differently. Do you feel uneasy about your written communications? The problem may be that you don't take time to plan before you write.

The **prewriting** stage is the one during which writers plan their message. Before a writer puts thoughts and ideas down on paper, she should conduct research, gather data, or collect any information she needs to write her message. That allows the writer to begin writing with all of the facts in hand.

For many business messages, no research is necessary. Writers often know everything they need to know for everyday correspondence. That makes the job a little easier. The prewriting stage is also the time to determine the objective and main idea of a message. You will read more about objectives and main ideas later in this chapter.

To make sure their writing is focused and effective, writers of business messages should consider these questions before they begin to write.

- PURPOSE: What is my purpose for writing? (What is my objective?)
- AUDIENCE: Who is my audience, and what response do I want?
- LENGTH: How long should this message be, or how long does it need to be?
- MEDIUM: What form is best for this message—proposal, letter, memo, e-mail message?

Use the acronym *PALM*, for purpose, audience, length, and medium, to help you remember what to think about. It is probably a good idea to jot down the answers to these questions, especially if the message is long or complex. Having notes to refer to can keep a writer on track and on task.

For someone who is writing a brief business message, the prewriting stage is quickly over. The writer collects her thoughts and is ready to write. For longer messages or for particularly important or complicated ones, writers benefit from some further thought and organization.

Objective

TECHNOLOGY
If you are comfortable composing on computer, use your software to help you prewrite. Create a table, or cut and paste ideas from one place to another on the page. Or, you may simply list your ideas, then print them out and take the next step on paper.

KEY POINT

Use a cluster or "spider" diagram to help connect related thoughts or ideas.

Some writers prefer to outline their ideas. Others use a graphic organizer, such as a two-column chart or a cluster or "spider" diagram, to organize their thoughts before they write. Every writer has a different preference, and different types of messages may require different types of organizational tools. What's important is that the writer takes the time to organize *before* she writes. Writing the message will be easier, and the first draft will be cleaner, if the writer takes time for this upfront organizing.

1 Checkpoint

The Writing Process

Answer the following questions.
1. What is the cycle of tasks in the writing process?
2. What happens during the prewriting stage?
3. What does PALM stand for?

Check your answers in Appendix E.

Planning Business Messages

Objective

2

In addition to considering audience, length, and medium for a business message, business writers have a few other issues to consider as they plan a message. Identifying the objective, or purpose, as mentioned in the previous paragraphs, is an integral part of planning. Business writers must also determine the main idea, choose supporting information, and adjust the message for the audience, or receiver.

Identify the Objective

The objective is what you want to achieve through a message. The objective may be to (1) promote goodwill, (2) inform, (3) request, (4) record, or (5) persuade.

Every business message should promote goodwill. *Goodwill* is the expression of good wishes, warm feelings, and concern for the receiver. It contributes to the success of the company you work for and the stability of your job because it strengthens business relationships. Goodwill helps attract and keep customers and encourages good working relationships among company employees.

You can determine the objective of a message by asking yourself what you hope to accomplish with the communication. Figure 4-2 lists the objectives of business messages, with an example of each.

KEY POINT

Failing to plan a business message is like not thinking before you speak. Figure out what you want to happen before you speak or write.

Objectives		Examples
To promote goodwill	**To inform**	A message tells a customer when a shipment of flea collars for cats will be delivered.
	To request	A letter asks for the price of a set of office furniture.
	To record	A memo restates the time and place of a meeting that was agreed upon in a telephone conversation.
	To persuade	A message describes the features and qualities of a new kitchen appliance.

FIGURE 4-2 Objectives of business messages

Checkpoint 2

Identify the Objective of a Message

Identify the objective of the messages that the following sentences contain.

1. Free calendars from Barb's Diner will be available on June 1.
2. We are out of the winter gray stock you ordered for your letterhead. We hope you will accept our popular metallic mist as a substitute.
3. The following are highlights of the interview I conducted with Juan Rios.
4. Please send me your latest catalog.
5. Your report was very helpful, and we will call you when we need this service again.

Check your answers in Appendix E.

KEY POINT

It is important to be able to distinguish between types of business messages, both when you write them and when you receive them.

Determine the Main Idea

After determining the objective of a message, the next step is to identify the main idea. The main idea is the central theme or most important thought. For example, in a message informing your customer about the delivery of pet supplies to a pet store, the main idea is the time the delivery will arrive.

Choose Supporting Information

Supporting information includes essential facts that explain, reinforce, or justify the main idea in terms receivers can understand and from which they can benefit. As you gather information during the prewriting stage, keep your receiver's needs in mind. Ask yourself what the receiver needs to know to be able to respond to your message.

SCANS
Employability

Information: Organizes and Maintains
Being able to organize and maintain information, then interpret and communicate information, are skills every employee must master.

Objective

Objective

4

DIVERSITY

Knowing an audience and its culture helps a writer communicate more clearly.

Adjust the Message for the Receiver

Practice empathy—put yourself in the place of the receiver—when adjusting the content of a message to your receiver. Through empathy, you can see the situation from the receiver's perspective and compose the message accordingly. When you adjust the content of your messages, you will write considerate, receiver-oriented messages.

Considerate messages address the receiver's level of interest, involvement, knowledge, or opinions regarding the subject. Considerate messages use supporting information that receivers will benefit from, understand, and appreciate. Figure 4-3 contains a list of questions to ask yourself as you adjust a message for your receiver.

1. How much knowledge, experience, background, and education does the receiver have about the subject of your message?
2. What does the receiver need to know about the subject?
3. What opinions or attitudes might your receiver have about your subject?
4. How does the receiver feel about you or your department, company, or products?
5. How can your message benefit the receiver?

FIGURE 4-3 Questions for adjusting messages for the receiver

Plagiarism and the Future

So much information is available to researchers today that it is hard to keep track of it all. It is easy to conduct an Internet search, for example, and click on link after link until you can't remember where you've been. All the while, you have been scanning and reading web sites to see if they meet your needs. You are certain to pick up thoughts and ideas as you go. Is it okay to include those ideas in the report you're writing? After all, who's to know whether the

words are your own or "borrowed" from one of dozens of web sites you may have visited?

The answer is, "It's not okay." If you pass off someone else's words or ideas as your own, you are plagiarizing. It doesn't matter whether the words are stolen from an encyclopedia, a news magazine, or a web site. If you use the words without crediting the source, you are plagiarizing. If the source is not copyrighted, the plagiarism is unethical. If the

source is copyrighted, the theft is illegal.

Printed materials and multimedia materials, such as CD-ROMs, generally carry a copyright. Many web sites do, but some don't. Even for those web sites that *are* copyrighted, there is really no way to prohibit the illegal downloading, copying, or use of text. It is up to researchers to follow the law and to conduct research ethically, whether online or off. ∎

The following message is written in two ways to reach two different receivers. The first message is written to a small business owner who is not familiar with the subject of the message. The second message is written to an advertising executive who knows a great deal about the subject. The objective of both messages is to persuade. The main idea is to promote television advertising as the most effective and economical way to increase business.

Message to small business owner: Television advertising can increase your business substantially by reaching more prospective buyers more times and for fewer dollars per thousand viewers than any other advertising medium.

Message to advertising executive: As you know, the cost of television advertising is justified on the basis of reach, frequency, and CPT.

Another way to orient messages to your receivers is to address them directly. Use second-person pronouns (*you* and *your*) instead of first-person pronouns (*I* or *we*). Review Chapter 1 for examples of how to create receiver-oriented messages, or messages that display a you-attitude.

Some direct-mail offers, such as sweepstakes, include strong receiver-oriented messages. Such offers, even though legitimate, can mislead consumers.

Checkpoint 3

Plan the Message for the Receiver

Rewrite each of the following messages as a courteous, receiver-oriented message.

1. Our company requires all employees to show their ID cards to the guard at the entrance of the building.
2. I have your custom-printed business cards ready.
3. We want to ensure that your stay at Dalton's B&B is pleasant; so if it isn't, we'll give you a coupon for a free dinner.

Check your answers in Appendix E.

Organizing Messages

After identifying the content of the message, your next step is to determine the order in which to present the information so that the message achieves its objective. The order depends on how you expect the receiver to react (favorably or unfavorably) to the message. Most business messages are organized using direct, indirect, or direct-indirect order.

Objective

5

- Use direct order to relate both positive and routine messages.
- Use indirect order to relate negative as well as persuasive messages.
- Use direct-indirect order in a document that includes both positive and negative messages.

DIVERSITY

People in some cultures value courtesy and politeness highly. A direct message in such a culture might include an *extensive* expression of goodwill in the first paragraph.

Direct Order

To organize a message using **direct order**, present the main idea first and follow it with supporting information. Favorable, or positive, messages and neutral messages are organized in direct order. By beginning with the positive message, the sender establishes a positive tone immediately. Routine messages also are organized in direct order. It's assumed that the receiver will respond in a positive or neutral manner. Chapters 5 and 6 contain detailed information and examples of messages that use direct order.

Indirect Order

A message organized in **indirect order** presents the supporting information before the main idea. Unfavorable, or negative, messages and persuasive messages are organized using indirect order. Stating supporting information before a negative message helps prepare the receiver for the negative message. This preparation helps the receiver *accept* the negative message. See Chapters 5 and 6 for examples of messages in which indirect order is used.

Direct-Indirect Order

Use **direct-indirect order** when you have both a positive message and a negative message for the receiver. In these situations, present the positive message first, using direct order. Then, to present the negative message, use indirect order. Give the reasons for the negative message, then state the negative message itself. Use of the direct-indirect approach increases the chance that the receiver will understand the message and accept its outcome. See Chapter 6 for an example of a letter written in direct-indirect order.

Figure 4-4 is a summary of the different ways to organize a business message.

Direct Order	Indirect Order	Direct-Indirect Order
1. Main idea	1. Neutral beginning	1. Positive message main idea
2. Supporting information	2. Supporting information	2. Supporting information for negative message
3. Goodwill closing	3. Main idea	3. Negative message main idea
	4. Goodwill closing	4. Goodwill closing

FIGURE 4-4 Organizing business messages

Organizing Messages

Indicate whether each paragraph is organized in direct or indirect order.

1. June and Debra have similar personalities. Both are willing to work long hours and in an industrious manner. Also, they are very organized.

2. A new building is needed. In the old building, the wood is deteriorating and will need to be replaced. The floors are rotten and cannot be refinished. In fact, fixing the existing structure will cost 30 percent more than building a new structure.

3. The president's duties include representing the company to the media, welcoming visiting dignitaries, working with the board of directors to develop policies and procedures, and so forth. The duties seem endless.

4. John always gets to work on time, and he is never late for an appointment. He is very punctual.

Check your answers in Appendix E.

CASE 4:

Answers

Response to Question 1 in Chapter Opener

1. Is this business message receiver-oriented? What is the message's objective?

This business message certainly does *not* have a you-attitude. It seems oriented more to the board of directors than to the receivers. The use of the words *we* and *our* in the first sentence make that fairly clear. The message's objective is to inform. The board of directors is so busy giving itself credit and passing out cautions that the objective is somewhat unclear. Furthermore, the board failed to promote goodwill.

DISCUSSION QUESTIONS

1. How can writers benefit from using the writing process as a cycle of tasks instead of as a series of steps?

2. Why should every business message include an expression of goodwill?

3. What can result if a message is not properly planned or organized?

4. Describe one nonconfidential business message you have received. What is the message's objective? What is its main idea? How is the message organized? Share your evaluation of the message with your classmates.

Drafting: Choosing Words

Objectives

After completing Section 4.2, you should be able to:

1 Use prewriting notes to create a draft.

2 Write courteous messages.

3 Create a positive tone.

4 Choose bias-free language.

5 Choose precise and concise words.

Objective

KEY POINT

Some writers consider the drafting stage a period of discovery. Though their purpose and main idea stay the same, writers may change their argument, their tone, or their method of organization during the drafting stage.

Drafting

Now is the time to put your thoughts on paper. During the **drafting** stage, writers uses prewriting notes or organizational tools as they write their message in sentences and paragraphs. Whether a writer handwrites or keys text on a computer, the most important thing is to get her thoughts onto the paper.

It is best to try to write a draft all in one sitting. Your thoughts will flow more coherently if you don't have to interrupt yourself. Keep your prewriting notes nearby. If you find that you need more information, don't stop to do research. Write yourself a note and move on to the next idea in your message. In Figure 4-5, note how the writer is putting her ideas down without worrying about typographical errors or spelling. She also includes notes to herself to verify facts at a later time.

The whole point of drafting is to develop your ideas. You are not yet concerned about error-free spelling, perfect grammar, or a neat copy. You do, however, want to achieve an appropriate tone, or voice, for the message. And your ideas should land on the paper in some kind of logical order.

To enter the childrens art contest, children may submit original artwork that features their favorite elements of nature. Children may take their subjects from their own back yard or from a favorite park or other naturale setting. Artwork may be in any medium, form, or style, as long as it adheres ot the theme of "What I love About Nature." [Is there a size limit on artwork?]

Entries should express a respect for and appreciation of nature. They will be judged on the basis of that that message as well as on their originality and creativity. Entries must be received by [Get entry deadline date from marketing dept.].

FIGURE 4-5 Sample draft of a business message

Some writers focus on writing an attention-getting opening paragraph as they begin to draft. Others prefer to save their opening paragraph until last, after they know how the message turned out. When it comes to a closing paragraph, make sure that you tie up all loose ends. Do you need to restate or summarize the main points? Perhaps you want to leave your receiver with one final question to consider, or with directions about what action you want the receiver to take next.

Include as many specific details in your draft as you can. Choose your words carefully, but without getting stuck on any one word. If you can't find just the right word, use one that's close and circle or underline it. That will signal you to check a thesaurus or dictionary when you revise your draft. Though you can always change things later, the words you choose help shape the tone and style of your message. As you draft, remember to use words that promote goodwill and that encourage your receiver to accept your message.

Checkpoint 5

Drafting

Each of these writers is drafting a business message. Tell what action each writer should take in the following situations.

1. Shannon isn't sure how to spell the word *corroboration*.
2. Austin needs to get the latest sales figures from Leah in the Sales Department.
3. Stephanie isn't satisfied that her proposal ideas are strong enough.

Check your answers in Appendix E.

Courteous Words

Courteous words are positive, considerate, and bias-free. Courteous business communications address receivers by their proper titles, capture the receivers' attention, and encourage a positive response. Remember, the first step in showing courtesy is saying "please" and "thank you."

Courteous words show receivers that you appreciate them. This is important whether your receiver is a customer, a client, a coworker, or an unknown customer service person.

Objective

Positive Words

As you have already learned, the purpose of every business communication is to promote goodwill. Never deliver an entirely negative message or express anger or other strong emotions in a business communication. Always keep a courteous, positive, and professional tone even when your message is negative. The receiver will have a positive response (or at

Objective

SCANS
Employability

**Interpersonal:
Teaches Others**
Providing feedback to
coworkers is a common
workplace requirement.
Doing so in a positive, constructive manner is vital to
good employee relations.

least a less negative one) if the tone of a message is positive. The following statements show how positive words make negative messages
polite and businesslike.

NEGATIVE WORDS	**POSITIVE WORDS**
You cannot have a refund because you don't have a receipt.	You will receive a refund when you send the receipt.

Proper Titles

Show receivers respect by using their proper titles. Use the titles *Mr.,
Mrs., Ms.,* or *Miss* before last names if the receivers have no professional title. If the receiver has a professional title such as *doctor, reverend,
professor, governor, senator,* or *judge,* use the title abbreviations before the
last name. Appendix C provides more information on titles and their
abbreviations.

Think of words in written materials as having the same impact as facial expressions, vocal tone, and body language in personal exchanges. Choose your
words wisely to avoid miscommunication.

Generally, use a person's title and last name in the following cases:

1. When you have not met the receiver.
2. When you wish to show respect.
3. When the receiver is older than you.
4. When responding to a letter in which the sender used his or her title and/or last name.

Use a person's first name in the following situations:

1. When you have met the receiver more than once and feel he or she would not be offended.
2. When the receiver's age is about the same as or less than yours.
3. When the receiver has previously identified himself or herself to you by first name.

Bias-Free Words

Courteous business communications do not offend the receiver by showing biases or by making the receiver feel singled out in a negative way. Attitudes to beware of include biases against gender, race, age, and disability.

Gender Bias

Men and women can be hired for any job for which they are qualified in today's workplace. Women are pilots, police officers, engineers, doctors, and lawyers. Men are nurses, secretaries, elementary school teachers, and the principal caretakers of young children. The words used for today's workers should be free of gender bias to reflect the reality of the workforce. Use neutral words, such as those suggested in the following list, to identify workers.

GENDER-BIASED WORDS	NEUTRAL WORDS
actress, female vocalist	actor, vocalist
foreman	foreperson, supervisor
waiter/waitress, stewardess	server, flight attendant
salesman, policeman	salesperson, police officer
manmade	manufactured, synthetic
executives and their wives	executives and their spouses

Neutral nouns need neutral pronouns. If you use a singular neutral noun, the pronoun will need to include both masculine and feminine forms to be neutral, as in the phrase "his or her." Avoid using two pronouns by using a plural noun. Plural pronouns, such as *them* or *theirs*, are neutral. These sentences show how to eliminate double pronouns by using neutral nouns:

SINGULAR PRONOUNS	PLURAL PRONOUNS (NEUTRAL)
Each student sat in his or her chair.	The students sat in their chairs.
A doctor uses his or her expertise with every patient.	Doctors use their expertise with every patient.

KEY POINT

If in doubt, use a more formal title than a less formal title or manner of address.

Objective

It is unethical to single people out because of a difference in gender, race, age, or ability.

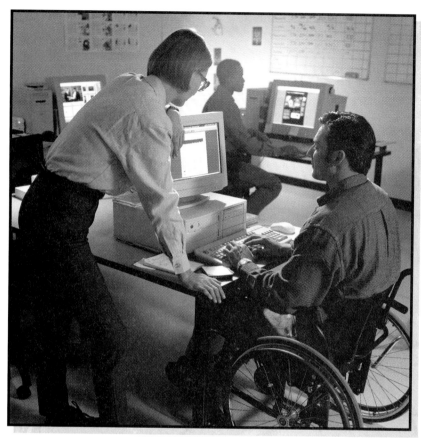

Remember this tip to prevent biases from creeping into your communications: If age, race, gender, or disability is irrelevant, don't mention it.

Race and Age Bias

A simple way to avoid biases of race and age is to avoid mentioning race or age unless it is essential to your meaning. The following sentences show how to avoid race and age biases.

BIASED WORDS	UNBIASED WORDS
We hired an Asian American lawyer.	We hired a lawyer.
Have you met the little old man?	Have you met the man?

Disability Bias

Avoid disability bias by avoiding reference to a disabling condition. If you must mention the condition, use unbiased words as shown in the following examples.

BIASED WORDS	UNBIASED WORDS
afflicted with, suffering from	has
crippling defect, disease	condition

↓KEY POINT

It is possible to recognize differences without calling attention to them.

Courteous Words

Rewrite these sentences to make them courteous and bias-free.
1. Bring me the report.
2. Ms. Jennifer Chang, Minister, will conduct the session.
3. The old Indian attorney was an expert trial lawyer.
4. The lady professor is afflicted by Lyme disease.
5. An employee requesting family leave must file the required paperwork at least one month prior to her requested leave.

Check your answers in Appendix E.

Appropriate Words

Appropriate words for business communications are precise and concise. Using appropriate words ensures that your readers understand your message.

Precise Words

Precise words are exact and specific. They let you say exactly what you mean in vivid and informative language. For example, instead of using the word *concerned*, you might really mean *anxious*. Instead of using the word *store*, you can specify which store and write *Hatcher's Jewelry Store*. Instead of using the phrase *due date*, use a phrase such as *within ten days* to show the precise time. The following sentences are more interesting and informative when rewritten in precise language.

IMPRECISE	PRECISE
Sales have increased substantially this year.	Sales have increased 45 percent this year.
Our new telephone system has great sound quality.	Our new telephone system has clear sound quality.

Concise Words

Good business communications use concise words. Concise means brief, to the point, or short. Concise words, nonetheless, are comprehensive; they carry the writer's full meaning. To write concise messages, eliminate redundancy. Redundancy is needless repetition. Sometimes writers use two or three words whose meanings

Objective

KEY POINT

For writers who plan their messages carefully, precise words come almost naturally.

TECHNOLOGY

Many word processing programs include dictionary and thesaurus tools to help as you work on a document. More extensive programs are available on CD-ROM.

TECHNOLOGY

Drafting in the Computer Age

Computers give writers powerful tools for drafting. How effectively writers use these tools depends on how well they use the software's features. Here are some tips for making your computer work for you when you draft.

- Set your margins as they will appear in your final document. That way, if space or length is an issue, you will always know just where you stand.
- Double-space your drafts. This makes them easier to read and allows room for notes when you revise.

- Establish a date field in the header. By creating a field, the date will automatically update itself every time you open the document. Also, if you print your draft more than once, you can tell which copy is which.
- You may choose to show revisions on screen. Most word processing programs allow you to do this by marking a check box. Once you make this selection, your program will strike through deletions instead of removing them. If you change your mind,

you can restore the text with one or two keystrokes.

- It's a good idea to save cut or scrapped text in another file, especially if the scrapped text is more than a sentence or two. Suppose you write several paragraphs in the middle of a paper and then decide they've gone in a direction you don't want to pursue. Cut and paste those paragraphs to another file. You may change your mind later, or you may find another place for them. ■

overlap when one word is all they need. The following list includes some redundant expressions and concise words to use in their place.

REDUNDANT EXPRESSIONS	CONCISE WORDS
free gift	gift
consensus of opinion	consensus
for the purpose of	to
in all probability	probably
past history	history

Appropriate Words

Rewrite the following sentences, substituting precise or concise words for words that are imprecise.

1. Topek motor scooters get good gas mileage.
2. Please ascertain if Bill can reserve the hotel for our conference.
3. I do not know whether or not I will apply for that job.
4. Customers who place their orders by November 30 receive a free gift.

Check your answers in Appendix E.

CASE 4:

Answers

Response to Question 2 in Chapter Opener

2. **Does this message contain any bias? What evidence do you find?**

This message contains gender bias. Women are referred to as "women," whereas men are "male employees." The board feels the need to restrict the type of casual clothing female employees may wear, implying that they would exercise poor judgment or be less professional about casual day than male employees. Finally, a female employee is referred to by first name only and a male employee by his surname.

DISCUSSION QUESTIONS

1. What are a writer's goals when writing a draft? Why is a draft sometimes called a "rough" draft?
2. What is the value of positive words in effective business communications?
3. Why should you use proper titles and bias-free words in communications?
4. What are redundant expressions, and why should you avoid them in business writing?

4·3 Revising: Creating Concise Sentences and Complete Paragraphs

Objectives

After completing Section 4.3, you should be able to:

1 Revise a draft to improve organization and flow.

2 Write concise sentences by eliminating unnecessary sentence elements.

3 Describe the sentence and paragraph structure of business messages.

4 Include the five *Ws* (*who, what, where, when,* and *why*) in messages.

5 Vary sentence style and paragraph length.

6 Use transitions to connect sentences and paragraphs.

Objective

Revising

You have invested time in planning, organizing, and drafting a business message. You feel pretty good about your document. It is time now to review your draft. Remember, it's just a draft—a first attempt at shaping a message. Remember, too, that in writing, there is almost always room for improvement.

To **revise** is to make changes. Many writers spend at least as much time revising as they do creating their first draft. The revising stage is when a writer makes sure her message says exactly what she wants it to say. How much time a writer spends on revising may depend on the length of the message, its complexity, its importance, or the writer's "investment" in the message. A cover letter may be brief, but it is *so* important to an eager job candidate. On the other hand, an interoffice memo requesting supplies probably requires less effort.

Before you revise a draft, put it aside for at least a few hours, if possible. This helps you look at the material from a fresh perspective, even though you probably know it very well. Taking a break from your draft is especially important for longer letters or documents.

To begin, read your draft all the way through. Try to step back and put yourself in the place of the receiver. Consider the overall effect of your message. Is the message focused? Are there gaps in logic? Do the paragraphs flow? Is all of the information vital to the objective and main idea, or do you stray from the point? Will your receiver be able to follow the message and respond appropriately? Reorganize sentences or paragraphs as needed and read the draft again. Once more, look for logic, flow, and the general "feeling" of the message.

After you form your initial impression and make any large-scale changes, analyze your draft one paragraph at a time. Are your opening and closing paragraphs effective? Does each paragraph pursue a single topic? Read each paragraph aloud to make sure your sentences flow smoothly. Does the paragraph flow logically from the preceding paragraph? Does it prepare the reader for the *next* paragraph? Add or remove information as necessary.

Finally, look a little more closely at your style. Did you vary your sentence length? Are your words precise and interesting? As you revise, you can improve your writing sentence by sentence and paragraph by paragraph. Concise sentences and strong paragraphs are the key to producing a message that is clear and appealing.

Concise Sentences

You have learned that the word *concise* means "brief, to the point," or "short." When you write, express one clear thought in each sentence. Concise sentences are effective in business because they are emphatic and easy to remember. They capture and hold the attention of receivers who are too busy to read long, complicated messages.

Unnecessary Elements

Unnecessary sentence elements, such as redundancies, empty phrases, and wordiness, weaken business communications. The following paragraphs will help you recognize and avoid unnecessary elements.

Redundancies

When writers use the more formal language appropriate for business correspondence, they sometimes get lost in their words. The result can be redundancies that seem to add formality, but add no meaning. In fact, redundancies can confuse the writer's message. How many redundancies can you see in the sentence at left?

Redundant
During the month of June, employees can preview the full and complete Annual Report for the year 2000 before it is distributed to stockholders.

Better
During June, employees can read the complete 2000 Annual Report prior to its distribution.

Empty Phrases and Wordiness

Empty phrases clutter sentences without adding meaning. "I believe," "in my opinion," "there are," and "here is" are examples of empty phrases. The meaning behind these phrases is usually implied, so you don't need to use them when you write. Another way to cut down on sentence clutter is to substitute a word or short phrase for a longer clause. The following sentences show how to avoid empty phrases and wordiness.

Empty Phrase   I believe the best plan is to establish guidelines for situations such as this.

Better   The best plan is to establish guidelines for such situations.

TECHNOLOGY
Even if you compose your draft on computer, it is a good idea to print your draft and make your initial revision notes on hard copy. As readers, we respond differently to on-screen text than we do to printed text.

Objective

KEY POINT
Watch for adjectives and adverbs that repeat the meaning of your verbs. For example, "Write a written evaluation." or "Review the chapter again."

TECHNOLOGY

Most word-processing programs include a word count tool. Sentences of 20 words or less communicate most effectively. Check your average sentence length as you revise a document.

Wordy	When you present complex information, you need to ask yourself if a graphic illustration would make it easier to understand.
Better	Use a graphic illustration to make complex information easier to understand.
Empty and Wordy	To my knowledge, there are three possible solutions.
Better	Three possible solutions exist.

Passive Voice

To cut down on wordiness, use the active voice rather than the passive voice. When you write in the active voice, the subject of the sentence *performs* the action of the verb. In passive voice, the subject *receives* the action. Using the active voice helps you be direct and keeps your sentences from being too wordy. Here is an example:

Passive	The best idea was submitted by Vernon.
Active	Vernon submitted the best idea.

8 Checkpoint

Unnecessary Elements

Identify the empty or wordy phrases in each sentence.
1. Overall, in my opinion, Ralph Rodriguez is by far the best-qualified candidate for the job that is open.
2. The many helpful new office supplies you will need for work are in the supply cabinet at the end of the hall.
3. The house that was built during the Victorian era was renovated for office space.

Check your answers in Appendix E.

Complete Paragraphs

Writers must carefully choose the sentences that make up a paragraph. The sentences must flow logically and smoothly. To be complete, a paragraph must have unity and coherence. Complete paragraphs create messages that are well structured and contain all the information necessary for the receiver to respond. In the following sections, you'll see how to write complete paragraphs and messages.

Sentence Structure in a Paragraph

A **paragraph** is a group of one or more sentences that expresses one idea. Each sentence in a paragraph should contain one thought that relates to and helps complete the main idea of the paragraph. A paragraph can be as short as one sentence, but most contain at least three. Most paragraphs include a beginning sentence, one or more middle sentences, and an ending sentence.

In business writing, the beginning sentence of a paragraph is usually a topic sentence. It gets right to the point by stating the main idea.

The middle sentences develop the topic sentence or main idea of the paragraph. These sentences give the receiver a description, an example, or other information to support the main idea.

The ending sentence brings the paragraph to a close. It is a short summary of the other sentences in the paragraph and sometimes restates the beginning sentence in a different way.

Paragraph Structure in Business Communications

A message can consist of only one paragraph, but most complete business messages have opening, developmental, and closing paragraphs.

Opening Paragraph

In business messages, the opening paragraph tells the receiver the subject of the communication. An opening paragraph should be short—only two to five typed lines. An opening paragraph of a longer message may include a greeting or a reference to an earlier conversation or correspondence. Nonetheless, the subject of the communication follows the brief greeting.

Developmental Paragraphs

A developmental paragraph contains important information or explanations about the main idea of the message. These paragraphs are usually four to eight lines. A developmental paragraph supports the main idea by providing the following types of information.

- Specific facts and details
- Reasons
- Steps or stages
- Examples

Closing Paragraph

The closing paragraph ends a communication with a summation or reference to the main idea stated in the opening paragraph. The closing paragraph prevents a communication from ending abruptly. It gives you an opportunity to thank the reader and perhaps to make a statement about the reader's favorable response to the message. The closing paragraph should be short, like the opening paragraph.

Objective 3

TECHNOLOGY

One-paragraph electronic, or e-mail, memos are a vital business tool. Learn to write complete, one-paragraph messages so that you can compete in the world of instant communication. Send your message in 50 words or less.

↓KEY POINT

Make sure your paragraphs *look* good as well as sound good. Look at a finished memo or letter to see if it looks balanced. Split an especially long paragraph into two, or break out information into a numbered or bulleted list.

Necessary Information—Who, What, Where, When, and Why

Objective

4

Complete business messages often include the five *W*s: *who, what, where, when,* and *why.* A message that contains the five *W*s can be as concise as the following sentence:

> Please attend a meeting in conference room 421 at 3 P.M. Tuesday, August 2, to discuss sales goals.

Many business messages require several paragraphs to cover the five *W*s. As always, adjust the message for your receiver. In some cases, the receiver may not need all five pieces of information.

Variety

Objective

5

Complete messages contain a variety of sentence types. You will hold your readers' attention if you vary the length and structure of your sentences as well as the structure of your paragraphs.

It is best to keep sentences at 20 words or less. At the same time, it adds interest to have some noticeably short sentences—perhaps 10 words or even fewer. Using sentences of different lengths keeps your writing from feeling choppy or monotonous. As you vary sentence length, your sentence structure naturally varies as well. Alternate simple sentences with compound and complex sentences.

Varying paragraph length also keeps your writing from being choppy. We've already said that the opening and closing paragraphs of a message should be relatively short. When writing your middle paragraphs, plan them so that they average about six to eight lines each. Mix in a short, two- or three-line paragraph sometimes to add interest. A short paragraph also is a way to emphasize an important point.

Clear Paragraphs

Objective

6

To be clear, a paragraph must have unity. Unity occurs when sentences in a paragraph express one idea. The expression of that idea must come about by means of a logical order of thought.

A **transition** is a word or phrase that connects sentences in paragraphs, and in turn connects paragraphs in a message. A transition indicates the relationship between one thought and the next. Transitions help your readers move easily from one sentence—and one thought—to the next. Figure 4-6 contains a list of common transition words and phrases, organized by the type of relationship they suggest.

KEY POINT

The purpose of business communication is to give information to the reader as quickly and clearly as possible.

Relationship	Transition Words and Phrases	
Contrast	but however in spite of	on the contrary on the other hand nevertheless
Cause-Result	because of consequently for this reason	hence therefore thus
Explanation	also for example for instance	to illustrate too
Listing	besides first, second, etc.	in addition moreover
Time	since finally	first, second, . . . , last
Similarity	likewise	similarly

FIGURE 4-6 Transition words and phrases

There's handwriting near Time: "Before / after"

Checkpoint 9

Complete and Clear Paragraphs

Read the following paragraph. Then answer the questions.

(1) This, our most fundamental value, is reflected in the growth of our variable compensation and recognition programs. (2) We start by respecting our people and their contributions. (3) Since 1992, we have introduced seven new programs, and annual awards have grown from $2.5 million to more than $10 million.

1. Is the paragraph clear? Use the sentence numbers to indicate a more logical order for the sentences.
2. What transition words are used in the paragraph to create unity?

Check your answers in Appendix E.

Key Point box on right

KEY POINT

We use transitions regularly in our everyday speech. Listen for them in your conversations.

A n s w e r s

Responses to Questions 3, 4, and 5 in Chapter Opener

3. **What is the tone of this message? Are the sentences easy to read, or do they contain unnecessary elements?**
    The tone of the message is neither conversational nor particularly friendly. The board members used many large words and lengthy phrases and sound as if they are "talking down" to the receivers. The writers used passive voice frequently and included empty phrases that clouded the intent of the text. The sentence in paragraph two that begins "First, employees who have contact . . ." is long and unwieldy, with 24 words.

4. **Does this message contain opening, developmental, and closing paragraphs? Are they effective?**
    The message does contain opening, developmental, and closing paragraphs. They are not, however, particularly effective. The opening paragraph should be more direct. The message, after all, is positive. The developmental paragraph is not well organized. The first sentence should be last. The paragraph might better be broken down into a list. The closing paragraph does not restate or summarize the main idea, nor does it express any goodwill.

5. **Does this memo include the five *W*s? If so, what are they? If not, what is missing?**
    The memo covers *who* and *why*, but fails to cover *what, where,* and *when* adequately. When does casual day begin? What constitutes "contact with outside clients"? Does that mean outside the office or in the office? Violation of rules is mentioned, but enforcement of the rules and the nature of disciplinary action are not explained.

DISCUSSION QUESTIONS

1. Why is it important to be concise in business communication?
2. As you revise sentences in a draft, how can you make them more concise?
3. What happens when a writer sends an incomplete business message?
4. What are the five *W*s, and why are they important to writing complete business messages?
5. What strategies can you use to make sure you have included necessary information and used variety in your business writing?

4·4 Editing and Proofreading

Editing

Now that you have organized, drafted, and revised your message, the next step of the writing process is editing and proofreading. With this step, you begin preparing your message for publication.

To **edit** is to alter or refine a written message to improve it. Because you took care of large issues, such as organization and paragraph structure, during the revision stage, editing takes place on a smaller scale. When you edit, you are really fine-tuning your message at the level of sentences, phrases, and words.

Keep your editing tools at hand when you edit. These tools may include a language handbook or style guide, a dictionary, and a thesaurus. You may wish to refer to Appendix C: Grammar and Mechanics in this text for answers to specific grammar and mechanics questions. An editing checklist is another useful tool; it helps to know what you are looking for. Here is a checklist to use whenever you edit your work.

1. *Listen for awkward sentences.* Reading aloud helps you catch awkward sentences. If you stumble over something, chances are the spot needs editing.
2. *Check sentence types and lengths.* Are all your sentences about the same length? If so, create some variety. Are any sentences very long and complicated? Perhaps they need to be split into two sentences.
3. *Look at sentence beginnings.* If you have started many sentences with the same word, change the sentences. Some sentence beginners need to avoid overusing are *I, my, the,* and *there.*
4. *Check compound and complex sentences.* Make sure the ideas in compound sentences are related, and that they are connected with an appropriate conjunction. In complex sentences, check for appropriate subordinating conjunctions and relative pronouns.
5. *Look for slang and informal language.* Business communications should not contain slang, jargon, or the level of informal language we use in everyday speech.
6. *Watch for overused words.* Be original. Replace overused words and phrases with fresh, vivid language.

Objectives

After completing Section 4.4, you should be able to:

1 Edit your own business communications for clarity, completeness, and tone.

2 Proofread for content and mechanical errors.

3 Use different methods of proofreading.

4 Use proofreaders' marks.

Objective

1

7. *Check for clarity, completeness, and tone.* Consider your receiver's viewpoint. Is the message clear? Will the receiver know, without a doubt, what to do or how to respond to your message? Does the message's tone promote goodwill?

Once you edit your message, you are one step closer to having a document that will be well-received by your audience. The next step, proofreading, will ensure that your document is error-free.

---

10 Checkpoint

Editing

Name three improvements that could be made in clarity, tone, or style in this memo.

TO: All Employees
FROM: Human Resources office
DATE: July 17, 20—
The new vacation request forms are available. You need to fill one out for each vacation request you want to make and be sure to do it ahead of time. It gets tough processing so many vacation requests at the last minute right before the holidays.

Check your answers in Appendix E.

Proofreading

Objective

2

KEY POINT

Editing is the final review of the main ideas and content of a message. Proofreading is part of the editing process, but focuses on reviewing and correcting errors in the final draft.

Proofreading is the process of reviewing and correcting the final draft of a written message. It is usually the last step in preparing a piece of business communication for your readers. Allow time for proofreading so you turn out error-free communications. Errors reflect badly on you and may cause confusion for your receivers.

A document may contain many kinds of errors. When you proofread, it is best to look for one kind of error at a time. First, look for general content errors. Common general content errors include missing, repeated, or substituted words; transposed words; incorrect proper names; and incorrect use of words.

Second, look for mechanical errors. Some common mechanical errors are incorrect spacing, missing parts of a business letter, misspelled words, incorrect or missing punctuation, and incorrect capitalization. Mechanical errors are hard to catch. It takes a careful proofreader to detect errors in his or her own writing.

Proofreading Methods

The following list describes six of the most effective proofreading methods.

Objective 3

1. *Scroll the screen.* Move the cursor down the screen of your computer monitor as you proofread each line. Moving the cursor down one line at a time helps you slow down and focus on each line without getting distracted by other things on the page.
2. *Read aloud.* Reading forces you to slow down and examine words more carefully. *Hearing* the words can help you catch awkward sentences as well as omitted or repeated words.
3. *Compare drafts.* Check the final draft copy against the previous, edited copy. This method also helps you make sure that you incorporated all edits when you revised.
4. *Proofread the hard copy.* It never hurts to proofread the printed document, even if you have proofed on screen. In particular, you may detect format errors that weren't apparent on screen.
5. *Proofread backwards.* Proofread each line from right to left, or start at the end of the document and proofread the entire message backwards. Instead of seeing the words that you remember writing, you will have to see each word separately. This method is especially effective when checking for spelling and typographical errors.
6. *Use two proofreaders.* One proofreader reads aloud from the previous, edited copy while the other checks the final copy. The reader indicates punctuation, format changes, and special type treatment, and spells out proper names and any unfamiliar words.

Proofreading and Word Processing Programs

Almost all word processing software programs include a spell checker, and many include a grammar checker as well. These programs or functions are useful, and you should become familiar with them and make a habit of using them. Do not assume, however, that they will replace your own editing or proofreading. Spell checkers will catch obvious spelling or typographical errors, but they will not help you with most proper nouns. Nor will they help you with word substitutions. What if you typed *estate* instead of *state*, or *stripes* instead of *striped*? Only you can detect such errors by proofreading carefully.

The same is true of grammar checkers. Most of these programs detect repeated words, and they may point out an especially long sentence. It is up to you, then, to decide whether to revise that long sentence or keep it. Grammar checkers cannot evaluate your choice of words or the logic of your sentences. Again, it takes time from a careful writer, editor, and proofreader to make sure that a message is properly organized and error-free.

KEY POINT

- The most common errors found when proofreading are (1) word or letter omission or addition, (2) transposed letters or numbers, and (3) misspelled words.
- Most mechanical errors are found in (1) additional occurrences of a misspelled word, (2) long words, (3) capitalized words, (4) numbers, and (5) material that has been revised.
- The more familiar you are with your document, the harder it is to proofread. Your eye tends to see what you *think* is there, not necessarily what actually is there.
- Using two proofreaders is especially helpful if a document contains technical information, equations, or tabular information.

TECHNOLOGY
Writers must have the knowledge and ability to produce clear, correct business messages. Spelling and grammar checkers are useful tools, but they cannot organize information or verify its accuracy.

Proofreaders' Marks

Proofreaders' marks are a type of shorthand for editors. The symbols can be written quickly, and they take up very little space. The symbols are standard, so you can understand other people's proofreaders' marks and they can understand yours. Learn to use the proofreaders' marks that appear on the inside back cover of this text.

---

11 *Checkpoint*

Proofreading

Rewrite each sentence as it appears in this list. Then use proofreaders' marks to indicate any corrections that need to be made.

1. The key to the supply cabinet if in the desk drawer.
2. dr. Helen Wong will introduce the the speaker.
3. New salery levels be will announced
4. The latest model truck has improved breaks.
5. Formal busniess attire is recommended.

Check your answers in Appendix E.

CASE 4:

Answers

Response to Question 6 in Chapter Opener

6. What content and mechanical errors does this memo contain?

In the subject line, *Casual* is spelled "Causal." An extra word (*last*) appears in the second sentence, causing confusion as to when casual day is to occur. The word *an* is repeated in the second sentence of the second paragraph. The word *clothing* is misspelled.

DISCUSSION QUESTIONS

1. What is the purpose of going through the process of editing and proofreading?
2. What should proofreaders look for on the first pass? on the second? Is it really necessary to proofread more than once?
3. What proofreading method do you prefer? Describe the process you use, and explain why you prefer it.

4·5 Publishing

Finalizing Your Message

Up until now, you have been paying attention to getting your message on paper and making sure it is logical and mechanically correct. Now you are ready to publish your work. To **publish** your message is to deliver it to the receiver, or make the message available to the public. To make sure you are ready to publish, you must evaluate your message from a physical or visual viewpoint. Your finished product should not only *sound* good when your receiver reads it. It should also look good.

An Error-Free Message

Now that you are ready to publish, your final document should clearly communicate your objective and main idea. Its tone should be appropriate, and the language level and type of information must be suited to the audience. You have worked hard during the writing process to make sure that your message meets these criteria.

The final document should also be error-free. As you prepare the final copy, double-check the spellings of proper nouns, such as people's names or the names of companies. Make sure you do more than just glance at headings, inside addresses, and document headers or footers. Sometimes writers are so involved in the content of their message that they forget to check for errors in these very obvious places. Think how annoying it is, though, to receive a letter in which your own name or address is misspelled.

A Good-Looking Document

A final document must *look* good. The paper should not be thin, nor should it be wrinkled or stained. The ink on the paper, whether from a pen or a printer, should be dark, not faded. There should be no stray ink marks on the page.

Paper

The quality of paper you use varies with the type of business message you are sending. Résumés and formal business communications should be printed on the highest quality paper. The company you work for

Objective

KEY POINT

Virgin or recycled paper that is high in cotton content is suitable for formal business letters and for letterhead. The speckled or marbled varieties can be attractive, but they may detract from your message.

will likely have letterhead on high-quality paper that is preprinted with the company's logo, name, address, and so on. Internal memos and routine reports are usually printed on a lower quality, less heavy paper. Nonetheless, they must be neat and attractive.

Margins

Take a look at any book or magazine around you. Notice that each page contains a certain amount of white space. A reader's eye needs this white space to help focus on the printed words. Notice, too, that the printed lines of text are not usually more than about 4.5 inches wide—and they're usually much shorter than that. Magazines, in particular, set text in two narrow columns to make the text easier to read.

You need to set up your business communications with these same ideas in mind. You want your document to be easy for your receiver to read. In addition, you want it to be attractive. Leaving some white space in your document makes it more attractive than if you cram a page full. Most of your white space will be at the top, bottom, and sides of your pages. Most style guides recommend one-inch margins all the way around. In addition, you should leave an extra line space above any headings or subheadings within your document. In a long or particularly dense document, you may also wish to leave a blank line space between each paragraph. For specific types of documents, see Chapters 5, 6, 9, and 10, which contain information about memos, letters, routine reports, and formal reports and proposals, respectively.

Formatting

If you work for a large company, it may have company guidelines about how to set up business letters. The company may also specify what font to use. If the decision is up to you, choose a nondecorative font with variable letter spacing, such as Times, Times New Roman, or Helvetica. For the font size, use 12 point.

In business letters, use the same font throughout the letter. For longer documents, such as reports or proposals, using different fonts in certain ways can make your document more attractive and more legible.

Graphic artists and journalists know that in headlines or headings, a sans serif font, such as Helvetica, gets more attention and is easier to read than a serif font. For that reason, many publications, including newspapers, use a sans serif font for headlines. The text of a document, then, should be in a serif font, such as the Times font shown in this sample paragraph.

Helvetica for Headings

In addition to being set in a sans serif font, headings are often set in boldface as well. This ensures they get the attention they deserve.

TECHNOLOGY

Software programs usually have default margins established. More than likely, these defaults are a standard one inch on all four sides of the page. This is appropriate for most business correspondence.

Objective

The Final Document

All of this may seem like a lot of trouble for a simple interoffice memo. However, appearance and correctness is just as important for that document as it is for an annual report or a job application letter.

To summarize, your finished document should display the characteristics shown in Figure 4-7, whether it is a résumé, a letter of request, a sales brochure, or an internal memo.

A final document is...

- ■ error-free. It contains no errors, and there is no sign of any corrections having been made.

- ■ clear and concise. It contains the right kind of information for the audience, and the audience knows just what to do with that information.

- ■ neat. It is printed on good paper with dark ink.

- ■ attractive. It has even margins, appropriate font types and sizes, and helpful titles or headings.

FIGURE 4-7   Characteristics of a document ready to be published

Checkpoint 12

Publishing

Answer these questions.
1. What characteristics should the content of a final document display?
2. What should the physical appearance of a final document be?
3. What can writers do with headings to make their documents more attractive and more legible?

Check your answers in Appendix E.

Enhancing Your Message

Even the most clearly written message can benefit from a well-placed illustration, figure, or table. In addition to adding visual appeal, graphics can add information, make a concept easier to grasp, or summarize complex information. Refer to Chapter 8, Developing and Using Graphic and Visual Aids, for information about creating specific types of figures, tables, and charts.

Objective

KEY POINT

It is best to place figures at the top or bottom of a page. This makes your pages look more uniform. It also helps you plan and save space for the figures.

When you use graphics in a report, for example, each item, whether it is an illustration, map, chart, or graph, should have a number and a title or caption. All graphics should be numbered consecutively within a document. Your captions or titles should be parallel. That is, always use a sentence fragment or always use a complete sentence to identify or label graphics.

In the text of the report, you should refer to a figure by number just before that figure appears. Place the figure as close as possible to its first text reference. Do not, however, break a paragraph to do so. In some cases, a figure will have to fall on the page following the text reference. For that reason, avoid introducing the figure with a phrase such as this: "Figure 8, below, clearly shows that the statistics support our reasons for investing." In fact, the figure may not be "below," but on the next page.

If you borrow ideas, copy a figure, or acquire data from another source, give credit to the source. Include a source line immediately beneath the figure. Cite the author or editor, publication date, publisher, and page number, if appropriate.

When you think about using graphics, keep your audience in mind, just as you did when you were drafting your document. Make sure the graphics are helpful, not just decorative. And make sure they enhance your message, and that they do not detract from your carefully prepared written message.

13 Checkpoint

Enhancing Your Message

Answer these questions.

1. How can written messages benefit from graphics?
2. What is the correct placement and labeling of a graphic within a written message?
3. What should you do if you borrow ideas or data from another source?
4. What should you do before you add graphics to your written message?

Check your answers in Appendix E.

DIVERSITY

Appealing to All Types of Receivers

Everyone processes information differently. Some people are really good at taking in visual information. Others need to hear something to comprehend it well. Still others are hands-on learners who need to touch something or actually do something, such as perform a set of computer commands, before they understand a concept.

When you write and publish a message for multiple receivers, keep in mind the fact that different kinds of visuals help different kinds of people. Keep a file of business communications that contain graphics. Highlight the graphics that seem particularly helpful. Be prepared to alter or vary them to suit your own purpose.

Be creative as you develop graphics. Instead of a standard two- or three-column chart, perhaps a set of items connected by arrows, to show a progression or connection, would be more effective. If you have a bulleted list with fairly lengthy items, perhaps you could box each item. If the items describe a process or a series of steps, you could set the boxed items in stair-step fashion to show movement.

Avoid creating "busy" graphics. Your software may allow you to add all sorts of symbols, shading, special fonts, and so on, but don't add too much. If you find one of your graphics is getting too busy, perhaps you need to simplify it, or maybe you need to use more than one graphic to convey your ideas. Graphics must be legible and functional. If they are too fancy or too busy, your receivers won't get anything out of them.

Don't assume that every receiver will view a graphic in the same way. Vary the type and style of your graphics to appeal to all kinds of receivers and the way they absorb information. ■

DISCUSSION QUESTIONS

1. What is the purpose of the publishing step of the writing process?
2. If a business message is clear and concise, why does it really matter what it looks like?
3. What impressions might receivers make if a business message is sloppy or inaccurate?
4. What business communications have you received that made an impression—either positive or negative—because of their appearance?

Summary

The Board of Directors of Atlee Corporation sends a strong *sender*-oriented message. It almost seems as if the memo has a negative message. The positive message is clouded in the board's own misgivings about the need for a casual day and about the possible abuses—or so the Board thinks—of casual day. In addition, the writers of the memo do not include anything to promote goodwill among the employees.

It is appropriate for a company to establish guidelines for a policy such as a casual day. The guidelines should be laid out in an easy-to-read list in a positive, or at least a neutral, manner. If violation of the guidelines must result in disciplinary action, the possible disciplinary actions should also be stated, in detail.

Naming a contact person for questions or follow-up is helpful. However, the closing paragraph would benefit from a restatement of the main idea, as well as from an expression of goodwill. If the Board members had used the writing process or if they had at least edited thoughtfully, they would likely have produced a more effective memo.

Chapter Summary

Section 4.1   Prewriting: Planning and Organizing Messages

1 **Understand the prewriting stage of the writing process.** During prewriting, writers collect information and consider the purpose, audience, length, and medium for their business messages.

2 **Plan messages by identifying the objective and main idea.** Every business message should promote goodwill. Additional objectives of messages are to inform, to request, to record, or to persuade. The main idea of a message is its central theme or most important thought.

3 **Choose supporting information in messages.** Supporting information includes essential facts that explain, reinforce, or justify the main idea. Writers need to choose supporting information that is suited to the receiver and to the situation.

4 **Adjust messages for the receiver and write receiver-oriented messages.** All ideas and information in a message should be presented in a receiver-oriented manner that emphasizes the benefits to the receiver. Keeping the receiver's interests in mind helps writers create considerate messages.

5 **Organize messages.** Organize messages in direct, indirect, or direct-indirect order. The organization needs to match or be suitable for the objective of the message. A positive message is best delivered in direct order—main idea first, then supporting information. A negative message should be in indirect order—supporting information first, then the negative main idea—to help the receiver accept the message.

Section 4.2 Drafting: Choosing Words

1 **Use prewriting notes to create a draft.** Writers should concentrate on getting ideas down on paper in a roughly logical order during the drafting stage of the writing process.

2 **Write courteous messages.** Effective business communications use courteous and correct words. Courteous words are polite and positive; they address receivers by their proper titles and show no biases.

3 **Create a positive tone.** Use positive words to write a message that is courteous and professional. A letter with a positive tone, even if the message is negative, is easier for a receiver to accept.

4 **Choose bias-free language.** Expressing biases in the workplace is not acceptable. When we write, our language must not indicate biases regarding gender, race, age, or disability. Choose neutral words and phrases rather than biased words.

5 **Choose precise and concise words.** Appropriate words for business communications are precise—they describe vividly just what the receiver needs to know. And appropriate words are concise—they convey the message without redundancies or wordiness.

Section 4.3 Revising: Creating Concise Sentences and Complete Paragraphs

1 **Revise a draft to improve organization and flow.** Read paragraphs for topic sentences, logic, and smooth transitions between thoughts. Consider the overall impression of your message's tone.

2 **Write concise sentences by eliminating unnecessary sentence elements.** Express one clear thought in each sentence. Use concrete words to build concrete sentences—sentences whose meaning is clear and easily understandable by receivers. Consider whether your receiver requires dates, times, locations, addresses, quantities, and so on.

3 **Describe the sentence and paragraph structure of business messages.** Paragraphs may vary in length, but in general, they should have a beginning sentence, middle sentences that develop the main idea, and an ending sentence. Business messages that are more than brief memoranda should include an opening paragraph, developmental paragraphs, and a closing paragraph.

4 **Include the five Ws (Who, What, Where, When, and Why) in paragraphs and messages.** The five *W*s—meaning *who, what, where, when,* and *why*—comprise the necessary information to include in most business messages.

5 **Vary sentence style and paragraph length.** To keep readers interested in your message, vary sentence length. The average sentence length should be about 14 or 15 words. Including some shorter and longer sentences keeps your writing from becoming choppy. Vary paragraph length as well. Opening and closing paragraphs are generally shorter than developmental paragraphs.

6 **Use transitions to connect sentences and paragraphs.** Transition words and phrases connect sentences by showing relationships between ideas. They help readers move easily from one thought to the next.

Section 4.4   Editing and Proofreading

1 **Edit your own business communications for clarity, completeness, and tone.** To edit is to alter or refine a written message to improve it. As you edit, focus on main ideas and content as well as the finer points of structure and wording. Ensure that your message is clear, complete, and courteous.

2 **Proofread for content and mechanical errors.** The most effective way to proofread is to look for one kind of error at a time. Take one pass looking for content errors such as missing or repeated words, transposed words, and incorrect proper names. Then proofread for mechanical errors such as incorrect spacing and missing information as well as spelling, grammar, and capitalization.

3 **Use different methods of proofreading.** The six methods of proofreading are (1) Scroll the screen, (2) Read aloud, (3) Compare drafts, (4) Proofread the hard copy, (5) Proofread backwards, and (6) Use two proofreaders.

4 **Use proofreaders' marks.** The use of standard proofreaders' marks is an efficient way to mark corrections or changes on your own or someone else's work.

Section 4.5   Publishing

1 **Generate error-free, attractive business communications.** To ensure an error-free document, double-check spellings of proper nouns, and verify the accuracy of headers and footers.

2 **Format a document appropriately.** Use high-quality paper and allow one-inch margins at the top, bottom, and sides of the page. Use sans serif fonts for headings and serif fonts for text.

3 **Incorporate graphics to enhance a business message.** Use graphics to enhance a business message, not just to decorate it. Place figures as close as possible to a text reference. Number figures consecutively and provide captions or titles in a consistent style.

Critical Thinking Questions

1. Describe the writing process. How can you use it to complement your strengths and weaknesses as a writer?
2. What different objectives might business messages have? Give a brief explanation. Give examples of messages that have each type of objective.
3. Many business communicators feel that adjusting the message for the receiver is the most important part of business writing. Why do you think this is so?
4. What effect does a polite and positive message have on a receiver? What are some strategies for sending positive messages, even if the main idea of a letter is negative?
5. Why does reading aloud or backward help you proofread better?

Applications

Part A. The organization you work for just held a fund-raising raffle. A name was drawn at the end of the day. The winners—a married couple—were not present, and it is your job to write a letter to the couple. Use direct order in your message. Before you write, jot down your objective, the main idea, and any supporting information (such as what the winners must do to claim the prize). Make up details as necessary to complete a two- or three-paragraph message.

Part B. The winners of your organization's raffle prize have lost their raffle ticket. The organization's policy is to award prizes only when the prize claim ticket is turned in. Plan and write a letter to the winners to explain the policy. Choose an appropriate method of organization. Create a courteous, positive tone in your message.

Part C. Your boss has just shared with you a great idea she has for how to make your department more efficient. As she leaves your office, she says, "Get together with Goodall and Martinson. Lay out this plan and see what they think. Then get back to me. Thanks."

TECHNOLOGY

1. Compose an e-mail message to Goodall and Martinson. Set a time for a meeting, and let them know, briefly, what it is about. Be sure to include the five *W*s in your message.
2. Following the meeting, compose an e-mail to your boss. Let your boss know how your coworkers reacted to the idea. Build strong, logical paragraphs. Use direct or indirect order, depending on whether your message is positive or negative.

Editing Activities

words@work

If you are using *words@work*, complete the activities on Writing in the Workplace in the Writing at Work section.

TEAMWORK

Part A. Rewrite the following paragraph so that it has sentence variety and effective transitions.

Electronically prepared letters are becoming commonplace in today's society. Electronically prepared communications are an expected part of today's society. A major challenge for communicators will be to make these electronically prepared communications successful. They can make them effective by using the same skills as those needed for preparing communications in the traditional manner.

Part B. Proofread the following message to correct general content and mechanical errors. Work in teams of two. One person should proofread the message using proofreaders' marks to indicate changes. The second person should interpret the proofreaders' marks, make the changes on the computer, print a copy, and mark other changes, if necessary. Teammates should exchange the revision until they agree the document is correct.

Welcome to Atten Motrgage compnay. for you're infromatoin and knowlege we have inclosed herewith a brochure to answer any questions I think you might have about you new mortgage laon? You loan number is located the uper left left hand cornor of the the payment coupon. payment coupons will be maled to You under seperate cover and must acompany all payments.

Case Studies

TECHNOLOGY

1. For years Steve has dabbled in carpentry—just simple projects, but he finds the activity relaxing and rewarding. Recently, he agreed to build a playhouse for a neighbor's children. The children were delighted, and everyone in the neighborhood thinks it's the greatest playhouse they've ever seen. Several people have encouraged Steve to market his design or offer his services to other people. Steve thinks it'd be great to get paid for designing playhouses.

Steve searches the Web. A number of companies offer playhouses in several different designs, but no one seems to offer truly custom-designed playhouses. He decides to establish his own web site to market his services as a playhouse designer.

Because Steve's playhouse design service seems to be a new concept, he is not sure just what to include at his site. He decides to keep it simple.

Playhouses by Steve

I can design any playhouse you want. I have done carpentry as a hobby for years. Recently I built a playhouse for a neighbor. Everyone in the neighborhood says it's great. Send e-mail if you want me to design a playhouse.

Has Steve left anything out? Improve Steve's message, keeping in mind Steve's audience, his objective, and his main idea.

2. Dresden Press started out years ago as a typesetting firm. The company has successfully made the transition to the computerized and electronic age. A core staff of ten employees keeps busy maintaining customer accounts, overseeing projects, and supervising desktop publishers. To keep up with her clients' demand, Cher Markham, the president, hires full-time employees on a temporary basis to work as desktop operators. Though these employees need special skills, Cher finds that it is too expensive to keep them on staff during the slower periods of business.

Each employee signs a contract specifying the rate for working on a specific project and the project duration. The contract also states that the employee will be given notice two weeks prior to his or her termination. As project end dates approach, there is often much anxiety among the desktop operators. When Cher decides it's time, a letter goes out to the desktop operators whose projects are ending and whose services will no longer be needed. Write a termination letter to one of Cher's desktop operators. Decide on your objective and main idea before you begin writing. Remember to promote goodwill, because you may need to hire that person again.

Career Case Studies

COMMUNICATION FOR HUMAN AND SOCIAL SERVICES CAREERS

Tina Dancy works as a preschool teacher at a privately owned child-care center. The center provides care for infants through five-year-olds from 7:00 a.m. until 6:30 p.m. As lead teacher in the four-year-old room, Tina works a shift from 8:00 a.m. until 4:30 p.m. That allows her to guide her students through the main activities of the day. Two other teachers work in the room—one from 7:00 until after lunch, the other from 10:30 until closing.

One of Tina's four-year-olds, Austin Mallory, has been displaying some aggressive behavior for the last several weeks. On some days, he has completely disrupted class by overturning paint trays and refusing to sit quietly during story time. Of greatest concern to Tina is that Austin has begun to hit his classmates with his hands and whatever is handy. Tina's room is full of child-safe toys, but if the toys are used as "weapons," one of the children could be seriously injured.

Austin's parents have been told that their son is having difficulty paying attention and that he is rough with his classmates. They seem concerned, and they listen to what the teachers have to say. Tina conveys her concern for the childrens' safety to the center's owner who agrees that the parents should be fully informed of his behavior. The owner leaves it up to Tina to write the letter.

Write the letter to Mr. and Mrs. Mallory, informing them of Austin's behavior, your concerns, and what actions the teachers take when Austin exhibits inappropriate behavior at the center. It is important that the letter doesn't come across as a complaint. Suggest any actions the Mallorys might take to redirect Austin's undesirable behavior. Keep in mind that the Mallorys are paying customers.

COMMUNICATION FOR HEALTH SERVICES CAREERS

Malcolm Tanner is a nurse at Riverside Hospital, one of several large hospitals in a big city. He has worked there for seven years now and has a pretty good attitude toward his job. Of course, it's not that he and his coworkers don't have complaints. Like other hospital workers all over the country, they work long, hard shifts, and they don't get rich doing it, that's for sure.

Lately, the morale among the fourth-floor staff has been declining. There are rumors that a huge healthcare corporation is going to buy the hospital. The workers are all worried and fear there will be staff reductions. Or they are afraid that new management will come in and make unreasonable changes to the way the nursing staff operates.

Malcolm thinks it's silly to get upset and waste time worrying about things that may not even be true. He decides to e-mail his supervisor, Norma Trepicchio, who has just returned from vacation. Normally Norma is very supportive of her staff, so Malcolm feels comfortable approaching her. Malcolm wants to let her know that everyone is worried about these rumors and that morale is low.

Write Malcolm's e-mail. Make sure the memo is constructive and not just negative. Your purpose is to inform. You may also wish to persuade Norma to take some action to improve staff morale.

Communicating with Customers

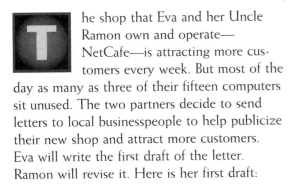he shop that Eva and her Uncle Ramon own and operate—NetCafe—is attracting more customers every week. But most of the day as many as three of their fifteen computers sit unused. The two partners decide to send letters to local businesspeople to help publicize their new shop and attract more customers. Eva will write the first draft of the letter. Ramon will revise it. Here is her first draft:

Dear Customers,

You may not have heard of us, but we have opened a new shop in this community. We are a one-of-a-kind business that you have never seen before in this area. We offer a complete range of computer services that you will not find anywhere else.

For example, for a small but fair fee, you can access the Internet through our top-of-the-line computers. They are equipped with a variety of browsers and the latest utilities. In addition, you can use our graphics and spreadsheet software. Our shop also has color scanners, color copiers, and other equipment.

While surfing the 'net, you can also treat yourself to a steaming cup if your favorite coffee and a fresh bagel or a light and flaky pastry.

We plan to serve three groups of customers:

1. New users, who can learn to use computers by attending out classes or talking with our knowledgeable staff. This group includes the elderly, most of whom do not know a bit from a byte.

2. Knowledgeable users, who want the latest technology and software.

3. People who feel isolated and want a chance to use computers in a social environment.

We'd be glad to show you our setup. We can't afford to offer you free computer time due to the fact that we are a new business. However, we'll give you a free cup of coffee as a gift just for stopping by. Just bring thin letter with you and see what we have to offer. You'll be glad you did!

Sincerely,

The Owners of NetCafe

1. Is Eva's letter receiver-oriented? Explain your answer and provide examples.
2. Point out some examples of unnecessary negativity in the letter.
3. Who would most likely be interested in learning about the three groups of customers that the shop hopes to attract?
4. Which of the five *W*s are missing here?
5. What are three errors in the letter that would not be caught by a spell-checker?
6. Revise this letter to be more receiver-oriented and positive. Your prewriting stage should include thinking of reasons why the intended readers would visit NetCafe. Then use these reasons to help introduce the shop to potential customers.

chapter 5

Writing Memos and E-mail

5·1	Uses of Internal Documents	**5·3**	Abuses of Internal Documents
5·2	Formatting and Writing Effective Internal Documents	**5·4**	Writing Meeting Communications

Communicating Too Fast

Nancy DiMelio has earned a glowing reputation as manager of the Computer-Aided Design (CAD) department at Lloyd Engineering. Her four busy computer operators use expensive state-of-the-art computer hardware and software. Others within the company are curious about the hardware and software the CAD department uses, but because of her department's workload, Nancy must limit the time her staff can spend demonstrating or explaining CAD.

Recently, as Nancy read the more than forty e-mail messages she receives each day, she discovered an e-mail from Lance Chow, her most senior worker. Lance reported that Connie Reyes, a member of the Mainframe Support department, had asked to "borrow" a copy of the new CAD software. Borrowing violated Lloyd Engineering's strict rules about software licenses.

Nancy composed an e-mail message to her supervisor. In part, she wrote, "Connie Reyes is a CAD artist wannabee. Instead of breaking company rules and asking to borrow $970-worth of software, Connie should pay more attention to her own work." Nancy also mentioned that Lance did exactly what he was supposed to do by forwarding the problem to her. Nancy sent the e-mail message to her supervisor and a "bcc" to Lance.

Nancy began receiving angry e-mail messages from the Mainframe Support department. They were angry that she would criticize one of their workers. Nancy's reputation with the Mainframe Support department had just suffered major damage. Later, Lance sheepishly appeared in Nancy's office and told her he had accidentally forwarded her e-mail to Connie. Lance apologized and Nancy reassured him, "The mistake, Lance, was mine."

Questions

1. E-mail offers almost instant communication with others. Do you think that immediacy contributed to the situation Nancy created?

2. What is a "bcc," and when do you use it?

3. Nancy admits, "The mistake, Lance, was mine." What can Nancy do in the future to prevent this situation from recurring?

4. Do you believe e-mail should be used for all communications?

Uses of Internal Documents

After completing Section 5.1, you should be able to:

1 Explain how memos are used in internal communication.

2 Explain how electronic memos, e-mail messages, are used in internal communication.

3 Describe when to use memos and e-mail messages.

Objective

1

Internal Documents

The two most common internal documents—those written for use within an organization—are memos and e-mail messages. The memo, sometimes called a memorandum, is a business document that has traditionally been the most common communication inside a company's walls. However, with the advent of Internet technology, electronically sent e-mail messages are quickly replacing the memo as the communication of choice. In either case, effectively written messages are a necessity for clear communication within any business setting.

Business Memos

Memorandums (memos) are informal messages sent to persons within an organization. A memo is a quick, easy way to communicate with a colleague or a supervisor in your own department, in another department, or in another company office. Memos can be sent via **hard copy** (printed on paper) or electronically (via computer and modem or network connection).

Memos usually are more concise and less formal than the letters you would write to someone outside your organization. In addition, memos do not include the receiver's complete address or other elements that are needed when communicating with someone outside the company. Consequently, the memo is a streamlined, efficient way to send a message to an internal audience.

More and more companies are using **electronic mail (e-mail)**, a computerized communication system for sending and receiving memos and other messages. To use e-mail, the sender keys the memo onto a special screen, such as the one shown in Figure 5-1. With the touch of a few keys, the message is sent instantly to the receiver's **electronic mailbox**, a computer file that holds messages sent to a particular person. The receiver can view the memo on the screen (printing it out if necessary) and respond using e-mail.

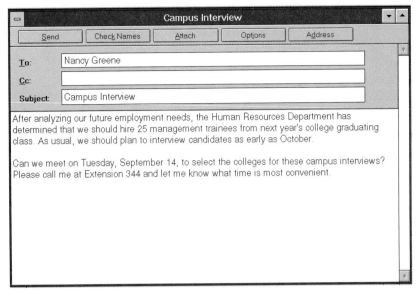

FIGURE 5-1 In many companies, employees can send memos to colleagues by usng an e-mail system.

TECHNOLOGY

As software and hardware makers strive for greater compatibility among the various e-mail applications and multiple computer servers, e-mail should become even more reliable in the future.

On the Internet, an international address contains a two-digit country code. For example, *fr* for France and *uk* for United Kingdom.

E-mail Messages

Objective

As more workers **telecommute** (work from computer stations in their homes) or have their own personal computers at work, e-mail is beginning to take over formal memo writing in many companies. E-mail messages are composed, transmitted, and usually read on a computer screen.

There are several advantages to sending e-mail memos:

- Messages can be sent to several people simultaneously.
- E-mail can be sent readily to anyone listed in your **address book**, the feature that lets you store frequently used e-mail addresses.
- Messages are sent in **real time**—information is exchanged instantaneously.
- Multiple messages can be sent with just a few keystrokes.
- E-mail can be sent globally.
- Messages can be sent day or night, whether the receiver is available or not. The message is held in an electronic mailbox, the computer storage file that holds the e-mail until the receiver opens the system and reads the mail.
- E-mail can be sent or received on both networked and stand-alone computers equipped with modems (transmitters of electronic signals via telephone lines).
- Documents from other software programs (such as a spreadsheet) can be attached to the e-mail message.

KEY POINT

- E-mail messages can be archived (saved), printed out for a permanent record, or forwarded to another receiver.
- A memo can be written directly into the e-mail body, or it can be attached from another software application where it was first created.

TECHNOLOGY

A memo may be prepared using a memo template from a word processing software program, such as Microsoft Word, Corel WordPerfect, and Lotus.

SCANS
Employability

Thinking Skills: Problem Solving

A sender can broadcast one e-mail message to all computers in a company, whether they are in the same building, in the same state, in the same country, or worldwide.

For people who telecommute (work from computer stations in their homes), e-mail provides a means of frequent correspondence with clients and coworkers.

- Whether long or short, documents can be transmitted in seconds.
- E-mail memos may convey a sense of urgency and importance that hard-copy memos or letters don't.
- Internal e-mail systems are relatively inexpensive.

Memos—When to Use Them

Objective

3

Memos, whether hard copy or electronic, are an efficient medium of internal business communication for several reasons:

- Memos can be sent to more than one receiver.
- Memos take less time to format and key than letters.

- Memos are less expensive, time-consuming, and complex than conference calls or meetings.

Memos are messages that supervisors and peers will use to judge your on-the-job performance; therefore, use them with care. Also, choose carefully the people to whom you send these internal documents. The content and tone of your memos *must* not be offensive to anyone. Knowing how and when to use memos is critical to success in your career.

Memos are used (1) to provide a record; (2) to advise, direct, or state policy; (3) to inform; and (4) to promote goodwill.

Provide a Record

Memos often are used to record certain events that have occurred or specific things people have said. For example, suppose that you took part in a meeting to revamp your company's maternity/paternity leave policy. You might send a memo to your supervisor containing the ideas discussed and any recommendations made. After this memo was filed, it could be retrieved and used as a record if needed.

DIVERSITY

The business world of every culture uses a message format for internal written communications. Most of these formats are similar to the memo format. Did North Americans borrow the idea for the memo from another culture, or did other cultures take it from the North American culture?

TECHNOLOGY

A Web Forum to Call Your Own

You've just come home from the movies, and you want to warn all your friends to avoid seeing "The Night the Purple Octopus Devoured Peoria."

Using the miracle of e-mail, you send off your movie review to dozens of friends all around the world, with just one keystroke: Send. You are surprised to receive many argumentative responses to your "Purple Octopus" review! It seems every-

one wants to be a film critic, and they all want to discuss movies among themselves. However, you don't have the spare time it would take to organize and forward your friends' e-mail messages. Is there a way for your e-mail list members to interact with each other?

There is. It's called Delphi Forums and it's free! You can be the forum master of an online film-review forum at an easy-to-use site that can be ac-

cessed by any member from anywhere. Members can chat among themselves. And members don't even have to log on to the forum to check for new messages; Delphi notifies you by e-mail when you have forum mail.

For more information about how to create your own forum, go to **www.delphi.com** and learn about its powerful communication tools. ■

Advise, Direct, or State Policy

Memos also are used to advise, direct, or state policy. Employees often write memos to advise supervisors or peers on particular topics or procedures. For example, suppose the supervisor of your department has requested your advice on the changes in the new maternity/paternity leave policy. After your investigation, you send your supervisor a memo with the recommended changes.

Supervisors commonly use memos to direct. For example, as a supervisor, you might write a message to direct the human resources department to draw up legal and administrative guidelines for the new leave policy.

Memos also are used to state policy and explain procedures. As a supervisor, you might write a memo that explains to your employees the new leave policy and the procedures necessary to implement it.

Inform

Memos frequently are used to inform. For example, assume that Nita, one of your office managers, will be taking maternity leave for two months. The message you write informs department members of the situation and states who will replace Nita during her absence.

Promote Goodwill

Another use of memos is to promote goodwill. Send a goodwill message to congratulate someone who has accomplished something outstanding or to thank someone. You might write a goodwill memo to thank all of the committee members who contributed to the research and design of the new leave policy.

SCANS
Employability

Basic Skills: Writing
Use a memo as the main written medium for providing information to coworkers.

One way to conserve natural resources and reduce waste is by sending e-mail memos.

SCANS
Employability

Personal Qualities: Social
Use goodwill memos and e-mails to promote good interpersonal relationships with coworkers. For example, send an occasional message to acknowledge birthdays and other special occasions.

---

1 Checkpoint

Uses of Memos

Identify the purpose of the memo in each situation.
1. A memo to provide employees with a new set of directions for obtaining reimbursement for medical expenses.
2. A memo to employees in the Information Systems Department telling them the new departmental supervisor is Beth Kirk.
3. A memo to a coworker thanking her for her support on a project.
4. A memo to your supervisor stating your belief that the workload should be more evenly distributed. You have expressed your feelings on this topic before and your supervisor ignored it.

Check your answers in Appendix E.

CASE 5:

Answers

Response to Question 1 in Chapter Opener

1. **E-mail offers almost instant communication with others. Do you think that immediacy contributed to the situation Nancy created?**
   The immediacy of e-mail remains one of its greatest benefits and one of its hazards. For example, if Nancy had written a memo or a letter to her supervisor, she would probably have taken more time to contemplate its message and tone. But once she clicked on her e-mail software's Send button, the message was gone and impossible to retrieve.

   In addition, an e-mail message can be easily (and in this case accidentally) forwarded to people who were never intended to see it. Nancy should have double-checked her e-mail to ensure that her message and tone would have been suitable for an unexpected reader.

DISCUSSION QUESTIONS

1. Why are memos used for internal communication?
2. Discuss the specific advantages of an e-mail message over a hard-copy memo.

5·2 Formatting and Writing Effective Internal Documents

Objectives

After completing Section 5.2, you should be able to:

1 Identify the parts of a memo.

2 Understand traditional and simplified memo formats.

3 Explain ways to organize memos and e-mail messages.

4 List and explain the guidelines for writing effective memos and e-mail messages.

Objective

TECHNOLOGY
If you use a template to create a memo, you can customize the template to save and use for future similar documents.

Parts of a Memo

Most memos contain a heading, a body, and one or more notations. These memo components present important information in an organized way, and they show receivers exactly where to look for the details they need.

Memo Heading

The four standard components in a memo heading are TO, FROM, DATE, and SUBJECT. Each component guides the writing process by prompting the writer to include the needed information. To draw attention to the heading, you may want to use double spacing and capitalization in the heading components. The information following each component appears in uppercase and lowercase.

The TO Line

The TO line contains the name of the person or people who will receive the memo. Depending on the style preferred by your company, you can write only the receiver's full name, add an appropriate courtesy title, add the receiver's title, or add the receiver's department name:

TO: Evan Wherry

TO: Mr. Evan Wherry

TO: Evan Wherry, Customer Service Manager

TO: Evan Wherry, Human Resources Department

When sending a memo to everyone who holds a particular job, you can omit individual names and address the memo to those who hold that particular job title:

TO: Service Managers

When sending a memo to everyone in a particular department or location, you can omit individual names and address the memo to everyone in that department or in that location:

TO: All Customer Service Personnel

When sending a memo to many people, avoid listing all the addresses by referring to a distribution list positioned at the end of the memo:

TO: Committee Members—Distribution Below

The FROM Line

The sender's name appears on the FROM line. Generally, you should not use a courtesy title with your own name, unless that is your company's style. However, you may need to include one or more pieces of information such as a job title, a department, a location, or a telephone extension:

FROM: Drew Sage, Security Manager, Extension 988

The sender should sign his or her initials beside the printed name on the FROM line or at the end of the memo.

The DATE Line

Put the date that you write the memo on the DATE line, showing the full name of the month, the day, and the year.

DATE: March 6, 20—

The SUBJECT Line

The SUBJECT line shows the topic of the memo. Word the subject as a phrase instead of a complete sentence. Make the subject brief and to the point, so that your receiver can quickly identify the purpose of the memo:

SUBJECT: Dental Insurance Program

Memo Body

Communicate your message in the body of the memo. Memos need no salutation; simply double-space after the heading and start the body of the memo. The body is usually single-spaced; however, the body of a very short memo may be double-spaced.

Memo Notations

Place the keyboard operator's reference initials below the body of the memo, and add any notations below the initials. For example, if a document is attached to the memo with a staple or a paper clip, note this by adding the word *Attachment* below the keyboard operator's reference initials.

The distribution list, if any, appears below any notations. The names on this list are usually alphabetized. However, some companies prefer to organize distribution lists according to rank or department. Thus the name of the highest-ranking person could appear first, followed by other names in descending order of rank in the company.

SCANS
Employability

Personal Qualities: Self-management
Signing your initials beside your printed name helps personalize the memos you write. It also shows that you have reviewed the memo and verified its accuracy before sending it.

Memo Forms

Memos may be prepared on a preprinted form that already contains the heading. Also, some businesses use memo forms that meet their specific needs. One example is a message-reply memo, which consists of multiform paper (either with carbon or carbonless). The sender fills in the heading and the message and keeps a file copy. The receiver then replies on the form and removes a file copy before returning the memo to the original sender.

Formatting Memos

Memorandum formats can follow one of two styles: traditional or simplified. In the *traditional* style, the heading appears at the top of the page. In the *simplified* style, the heading components are omitted. The simplified style is produced more easily on a computer or a word processor because of its uncomplicated format.

Traditional Memo Format

You can use the traditional memo format with letterhead stationery or plain paper. Figure 5-2 shows an example of a traditional memo on letterhead. When a company uses e-mail, its e-mail software often includes a preformatted memo screen for the writer's convenience.

The following guidelines will help you prepare a memo using the traditional format:

1. Use a 1½-inch top margin on a plain sheet or two lines below the letterhead.
2. Use 1-inch side margins.
3. Key *TO:*, *FROM:*; *DATE:*; and *SUBJECT:* in capital letters vertically down the left margin.
4. Key all heading information 10 spaces from the left margin.
5. Double-space between the *TO, FROM, DATE,* and *SUBJECT* lines, between the heading and the body of the memo, and between paragraphs in the body.
6. Start all paragraphs at the left margin; do not indent text.
7. Key the operator's reference initials two lines below the body of the memo; key additional notations below these initials.
8. Try to limit a memo to one page.

Simplified Memo Format

Because of the widespread use of personal computers, the simplified memo format is increasingly popular. This format, shown in Figure 5-3, can be produced easily on automated equipment using either letterhead stationery or plain paper.

The following guidelines will help you prepare a memo using the simplified format:

1. Use block format (all lines, including paragraphs, begin at the left margin) with 1-inch side margins.

Objective

TECHNOLOGY

Laser printers can be loaded with letterhead stationery when you want to print a more professional looking memo.

SCANS
Employability

Basic Skills: Writing

The same organization may use more than one form or format for its memos, or it may specify the form or format that will be used universally throughout the company.

MOUNTAIN LIGHT & POWER
1500 West Central Boulevard
Brigham City, UT 84302-1500
801-555-9800 Fax: 801-555-9843

TO: Board Members—Distribution Below

FROM: Sergio Reyes, General Manager *SR*

DATE: September 4, 20—

SUBJECT: Storm Emergency Brochure

Our Public Relations office has prepared a new brochure outlining storm emergency guidelines for household and industrial customers in our service area. Although such emergencies are rare, we want to help our customers and employees prepare for any problems that may arise during the winter storm season.

The attached informative 20-page brochure is free. If you need additional copies, please call Kimberly Albano at Extension 56.

js

Attachment

Distribution: Sandra Chasen
             Peter Donnelly
             Leon Garcia
             Michelle Stanton
             Virginia West

FIGURE 5-2 A memo in traditional format on letterhead stationery

---

MOUNTAIN LIGHT & POWER
1500 West Central Boulevard
Brigham City, UT 84302-1500
801-555-9800 Fax: 801-555-9843

September 4, 20—

All Mountain Light & Power Employees

EMERGENCY BROCHURE

Our Public Relations office has prepared a new brochure outlining storm emergency guidelines for household and industrial customers in our service area. Although such emergencies are rare, we want to help our customers and employees prepare for any problems that may arise during the winter storm season.

The attached informative 20-page brochure is free. If you need additional copies, please call Kimberly Albano at Extension 56.

Sergio Reyes

Sergio Reyes, General Manager

js

Attachment

FIGURE 5-3 A memo in simplified format on letterhead stationery

2. Omit *TO, FROM, DATE,* and *SUBJECT*.
3. Place the date two lines below the letterhead or 1½ inches from the top (line 10) of a plain sheet.
4. Show the receiver's name four lines below the date.
5. Place the subject line in all uppercase letters or in uppercase and lowercase letters two lines below the receiver's name.
6. Begin the body of the memo two lines below the subject line.
7. Place the name of the sender four lines below the body.
8. Place the keyboard operator's reference initials a double space below the printed signature line.

---

2 *Checkpoint*

Traditional and Simplified Memo Formats

Indicate whether each statement is true or false.
1. Use 1½-inch side margins with both the traditional and the simplified memo format.
2. Omit *TO, FROM, DATE,* and *SUBJECT* in the simplified memo format.
3. Because of its uncomplicated format, the traditional memo style is produced more easily on a computer or word processor.
4. Place the keyboard operator's reference initials a double space below the body in the traditional memo format.
5. The date appears on line 10 in the simplified memo format when using plain paper.

Check your answers in Appendix E.

Guidelines for Planning and Organizing Memos and E-mail Messages

Objective

As is true of any message, you must first plan your message before you can organize an effective memo or e-mail message. Planning a memo or an e-mail message requires four steps:

1. Identify the objective. What do you hope to accomplish in sending this message?
2. Identify the main idea. What do you want the receiver to do or to understand?
3. Determine the supporting information. What does the receiver need to know about the main idea to respond to or understand your message?

4. Adjust the content to the receiver. What do you want the receiver to gain from this message?

After planning, you need to determine how to organize your message to achieve its purpose. As with letters, a memo or e-mail message can be organized in either the *direct order* or the *indirect order*.

Direct Order

Use the direct order in a memo that contains good news for the receiver or that makes a routine request. The direct order presents the main idea first, followed by supporting information. In the memo below, the main idea in the first sentence makes a routine request.

TO: Lee Racine, Supplies Clerk

FROM: Bobby Davis

DATE: May 16, 20—

SUBJECT: Supplies Needed by Publishing Services

Please prepare an order of supplies for the Publishing Services Department. The following supplies are needed:

1. Five packages of company letterhead stationery
2. Twelve cartridges for Zippy Laser Printers (Model 500)
3. Seven packages of plain bond stationery
4. Eighteen boxes of envelopes with the company's return address

I know you are busy and have no assistants to deliver this order; therefore, Casey MacDonald, a department member, will come to the supply room tomorrow at 9 a.m. to pick up the order. Thank you for your help.

lwb

Indirect Order

Supporting information appears before the main idea in the indirect order. Use the indirect order in memos that contain bad news for the receiver or that try to persuade the receiver. In bad news situations, prepare the receiver by giving the reasons for the bad news before presenting it—the main idea. In persuasive situations, receivers are more apt to do what you want if they understand the reasons before being asked.

Thinking Skills: Creative Thinking
Because memos are used to judge your skills, they become a basis for promotions, raises, important assignments, and so forth. Write effective memos that are assets, not liabilities.

↓KEY POINT

Brainstorming means setting aside some time for creative thinking and discussion. During this time, no idea is too extreme. Analyze ideas created during brainstorming after the brainstorming session.

DIVERSITY
Other cultures use the direct-indirect order in memos, but the North American culture does not. To other cultures, tact is more important than presenting only one main idea.

Keep It to Yourself: How to Guard Your Computer Privacy

Your employer, bank, creditors, and the IRS occasionally have a legitimate need for your personal data: your name, phone number, address, income, social security number, and mother's maiden name. Almost no one else does. Therefore, it is up to you to safeguard your privacy when you are writing an e-mail or surfing the Internet. Here are some pointers on how to protect the personal in your personal life:

- Never share personal data until you know who you're dealing with and what that person plans to do with the information. Any time you respond to an offer of samples or services and provide personal data, you are giving away some privacy.

- Don't expect your boss, your ISP (Internet Service Provider), or your software to guard your privacy. Locate online references to yourself and delete your records from any sites, lists, or companies with which you are uncomfortable.

- Select and guard your passwords well—they are the keys that unlock your identity.

- Don't write personal e-mail communications at work unless you are comfortable with the possibility of your boss or another company employee reading them.

- Frequent sites that state their policy toward customer or user privacy. ■

As shown below, messages written in the indirect order have three parts and are presented in this sequence: (1) a neutral beginning, (2) supporting information, and (3) main idea (bad news). The neutral beginning should not state or imply the main idea. However, it should introduce the topic of the memo.

DIVERSITY

Because bad news is difficult to relate, North Americans prefer to present reasons for the bad news as quickly as possible. Members of other cultures sometimes consider this attitude abrupt or unsympathetic.

REDUCTION IN PERSONNEL

I certainly appreciate all the input you gave us on the staff-reduction decision we had to make. As you know, headquarters asked us to reduce staff by 10 percent. If we could leave your department status quo, we would. However, two members of your staff must be retired or dismissed. I will meet with you on Monday, June 9, to identify specific individuals.

Neutral Beginning	I certainly appreciate all the input you gave us on the staff-reduction decision we had to make.
Supporting Information	As you know, headquarters asked us to reduce staff by 10 percent.
Main Idea	If we could leave your department status quo, we would. However, two members of your staff must be retired or dismissed. I will meet with you on Monday, June 9, to identify specific individuals.

Guidelines for Writing Memos and E-mail Messages

After planning and organizing a memo, writing and editing become your focus. The following guidelines will help ensure that you write clear, concise memos that receivers understand.

- *Restrict a memo to one main idea.* The writer of an e-mail message may get a response, because it is so easy to respond to e-mail. The writer of a hard-copy memo, however, sometimes does not know if the receiver understood the memo. To simplify and help ensure understanding, try to put only one main idea into a memo.
- *Compose a short, clear subject line.* The subject line of a memo should reflect the main idea. The sentence that contains the main idea and the subject line of the memo should be similar, and they should use the same key words.
- *Make the body stand alone.* A memo should be written clearly enough for the receiver to understand it even if the receiver does not read the subject line. Unity, simple language, effective organization, and coherence make the body of a memo stand alone.
- *Use tables and visual aids.* When you need to communicate with statistics or other quantitative data, arrange the data in a table or a visual aid. Explain the table or visual aid, as in Figure 5-4. Refer to Chapter 8 for detailed information on types of visual aids.
- *Use headings in long memos.* Divide a memo that is longer than one page into sections. Insert headings before each section to guide the receiver. If a memo is complex, construct an outline before beginning to write it.
- *Number items in a list.* Use enumerations or bullets to separate steps in a process, a list of items, and so forth.
- *Proofread your message.* After all this work, be sure to proofread or have a colleague proofread your message. Errors and typos *always* interfere with clear communication.

Objective 4

ETHICS

Our court system often uses memos as written records. Think of all the cases against people in the federal government in which memos were used as evidence—Watergate, Iran-gate, Whitewater, and so forth.

KEY POINT

"Write to express, not impress!" (Author unknown) Effective writing is clear and concise, not long and complex.

TECHNOLOGY

Most word processing software programs allow users to insert bullets (dots, squares, diamonds) before items in a list. Bullets also help separate items.

Electronic mail is only one of the many communication options available on-line. Other options made possible by the Internet include ftp sites for sending large files or graphic images. These may be quicker and less costly than overnight mail services.

CB
Central Bank Corporation
412 West Central
Fullerton, CA 92632-1412
714/555-4500 • Fax: 714/555-6328

TO: Tom Harrison

FROM: Angela Chin

DATE: January 28, 20—

SUBJECT: Profit of the Rustin Branch

The profit of the Rustin Branch for 20— was $22,850. The gross income for the branch was $151,000, and the total of goods returned was $13,500. Although the profit margin is not as high as in other branches, sales in this branch are growing quite fast. Profit for this branch next year should be excellent.

The following pie chart illustrates the profit of the branch in dollars and in percentages.

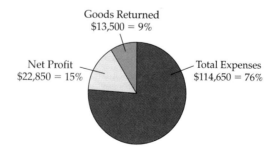

Goods Returned
$13,500 = 9%

Net Profit
$22,850 = 15%

Total Expenses
$114,650 = 76%

FIGURE 5-4 A memo containing a visual aid

Use the checklist below to help you write effective memos and e-mails.

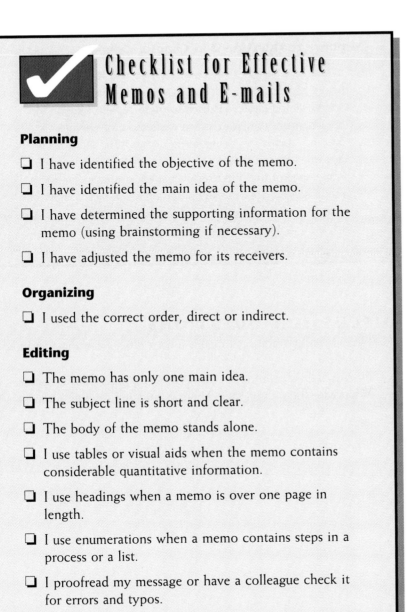

Checklist for Effective Memos and E-mails

Planning

❏ I have identified the objective of the memo.

❏ I have identified the main idea of the memo.

❏ I have determined the supporting information for the memo (using brainstorming if necessary).

❏ I have adjusted the memo for its receivers.

Organizing

❏ I used the correct order, direct or indirect.

Editing

❏ The memo has only one main idea.

❏ The subject line is short and clear.

❏ The body of the memo stands alone.

❏ I use tables or visual aids when the memo contains considerable quantitative information.

❏ I use headings when a memo is over one page in length.

❏ I use enumerations when a memo contains steps in a process or a list.

❏ I proofread my message or have a colleague check it for errors and typos.

CASE 5:

Answers

Response to Question 2 in Chapter Opener

2. **What is a "bcc," and when do you use it?**
   Before photocopiers and word processors arrived on the office scene, carbon paper was used to make copies of important documents as they were being created on a typewriter. In fact, *bcc* stands for "blind carbon copy." The word *blind* describes a copy that is sent to an individual without the knowledge of the other recipients. For example, someone might send a bcc as a way of letting a supervisor know of a situation.

DISCUSSION QUESTIONS

1. How does the traditional memo format differ from the simplified memo format?
2. Discuss the guidelines for writing and editing effective memos.
3. What care should you take when writing and sending e-mails?

5·3 Abuses of Internal Documents

Objectives

After completing
Section 5.3, you
should be able to:

1 Identify and describe
the abuses of memos
and e-mail messages.

2 Understand possible
remedies for abuses.

3 Identify some common
abuses particular to
e-mail messages.

When Not to Use Memos and E-mail Messages

Even though memos and e mails are the most frequently used form of written business communication, people sometimes abuse them. Abuse occurs when these messages are (1) written too frequently, (2) written to gain attention, (3) written by a committee, and (4) rewritten for each level of management.

Written Too Frequently

The convenience of memos and e-mail sometimes results in writing too many of them, with copies to too many others. With e-mail especially, writers may get careless with word choice, content, and proofreading. Sometimes they become aggressive or even abusive with their language. These senders fail to realize that e-mail memos are frequently sent on by the receiver to others. To remedy these abuses, give e-mail memos the same careful attention that you give to traditional memos.

Today's employees may easily feel overwhelmed by the number of messages they receive from telephones, voice mail, and e-mail. Whenever memos, whether e-mail or hard copy, are overused, an entire organization may suffer from communication overload. Communication overload is a mental condition that occurs when a person receives so many messages that he or she fails to take the time necessary to read or comprehend them.

Supervisors often make the mistake of sending a memo a second time because employees have ignored the first. Then, if the second memo works, the supervisor may assume that he or she needs to send two memos to get a message across—an attitude that obviously results in communication overload.

The solution to communication overload is fewer communications, not more. Another possible solution is to post *one* memo, if appropriate, on a community bulletin board.

Objective

Objective

SCANS
Employability

Personal Qualities: Responsibility
Avoid communication overload by discussing and planning social and sports activities with colleagues during lunch or over the telephone; do not send an e-mail message or a memo.

Sometimes workers use memos to raise their status above others—especially when seeking promotions. They hope to achieve this status by writing memos that use a condescending tone or that discuss the actions or attitudes of fellow workers.

Written to Gain Attention

Too often, an ambitious person will view memos as a way to call attention to what he or she is doing for the company or as a way to receive recognition from a supervisor. As a result of such usage, supervisors can become disgruntled with the sender—the employee. In the attempt to gain recognition, the worker can be viewed as a problem rather than an asset. A memo to gain attention often includes numerous *I's*, *me's*, and *my's*. Read and compare the ineffective and effective examples below.

AN INEFFECTIVE MESSAGE

SUBJECT: A Change in Line Production

I am pleased to say that I have some suggestions that would drastically increase production. I have been with the company about three weeks now and have made several important observations. I think these suggestions could increase production by at least 50 percent. Let me know when we can get together to discuss my ideas.

AN EFFECTIVE MESSAGE

SUBJECT: A Change in Line Production

Thank you for posting the announcement for incentive awards in our department. I would like to enter the competition with some suggestions that could increase line production by perhaps as much as 50 percent. Please let me know when we can get together to discuss these ideas. Thank you.

Written by Committee

"Too many cooks spoil the broth," the expression goes. And memos written by committee are often spoiled or poorly written. Committee members may be competitive or may disagree on memo style and content because of egos, not reason. The memo may be cluttered and unfocused, making it difficult for the receiver to understand its purpose and content.

The body of the ineffective memo shown on page 165 was written by committee. The opening paragraph does not state the objective of the memo. Even the subject line provides no indication of the topic. What does this memo really say? Is the committee deadlocked? Is this a final report, or is it a report of temporary conditions?

While the ideas in the memo are quite clear, its purpose and the committee's plan for the future are unclear. The solution to this problem is to let one person represent the committee and write its memos. Does the effective version accomplish this?

AN INEFFECTIVE MESSAGE

The committee has met several times to discuss various pros and cons of the possibility of flexible scheduling. The results of this four-person committee are most interesting.

Tommy has strong feelings and believes that flexible scheduling would result in a loss of productivity. Norma tends to agree with Tommy but wonders if employees would be self-directing.

Nicola also has strong feelings, but she has the opposite opinion of Tommy. She says she may have research to back up her view that flexible scheduling improves productivity. Alex tends to agree with her.

lwb

AN EFFECTIVE MESSAGE

Our four-person committee has met several times to discuss the possibility of flexible scheduling. There have been some good arguments on both sides of the issue, but, unfortunately, we are deadlocked in our voting.

Would you agree to appointing a fifth member to break the tie and help us resolve this important matter? Please call me at Ext. 2556 when you have thought about this. Thank you.

lwb

Rewritten for Each Level of Management

Sometimes messages need to be sent to each employee level of a company—from entry-level workers to the president. In these situations, the sender of the memo may be tempted to rewrite the same memo for each level. Such reasoning is faulty. Be sure to write such a memo that is clearly directed to and appropriate for its audience.

SCANS
Employability

Basic Skills: Writing
When writers try to be formal, they often shift from the active voice to the passive voice. Remember to use the active voice as much as possible; it is concise and clear.

DIVERSITY

Creative Support for Creative Entrepreneurs

"The human being is very creative," says Muhammed Yunus, the founder of Grameen Bank—which lends money to poor people who want to start businesses. "We all meet challenges, and we all solve problems. We're all basically entrepreneurs." Grameen Bank has helped rural entrepreneurs from all over the globe form small support groups and get loans for their projects. *Grameen* means "village" in Yunus's native tongue, Bengali.

Having once studied and taught economics in the United States, Yunus returned to his homeland of Bangladesh in 1971. He realized that the economic theories he was teaching at a rural university did not make much sense when he would step out of his classroom and into the village. Soon he began giving small, interest-free, no-collateral loans to villagers who needed "seed money" to start a business.

Eventually, Yunus took out personal loans to pass on to villagers, from banks that claimed that poor people were not creditworthy. Yunus's own research and experience proved them wrong:

"Nobody is better at managing money than the poor." Yunus learned that, with a little help, these villagers could demonstrate the courage, creativity, and ambition to maintain their own businesses and cooperatives.

Some 20 years later, Grameen Bank has helped over 10 million women and men across the United States and in 50 other countries. These resourceful entrepreneurs convene a new kind of "board meeting," designed to make decisions that support and encourage the grass roots businesses they represent. ■

Common E-mail Abuses

Objective

With the proliferation of e-mail, you may note that some abuses are more particular to e-mail than to memos. Here are some common e-mail abuses:

- Spamming, or sending mass, unsolicited messages, which are called *spam*
- Rambling on and on or changing subjects
- Writing in one continuous paragraph
- Writing a message that might offend other receivers if the message were forwarded to them

- **Shouting**, or using all capital letters when writing an e-mail message
- Making grammatical, punctuation, or spelling errors because of the usual immediacy of e-mail writing
- Using emoticons frequently or inappropriately. (An **emoticon** is an icon, built by combining various letters and symbols, used to reflect emotion in personal or informal e-mail.)
- **Flaming**, or sending angry or insulting messages, often anonymously

TECHNOLOGY

- Some writers use emoticons (keyboard characters arranged to look like a face) to express emotions:
  :-D = I'm happy
  :-(= I'm unhappy
  :-+ = I'm tired
  :-O = I'm surprised

- Some e-mail systems have a feature that can trace the senders of flaming messages.

A virtual team uses technology to link its members together. The team need not share physical space to interact.

Checkpoint 3

E-Mail Abuses

Complete the following sentences.
1. Avoid using all capital letters, or _____.
2. Be careful in an e-mail not to ramble or constantly change _____.
3. Many e-mail users hate receiving e-mail "junk mail," or _____.
4. Writing a continuous e-mail message in one long _____ may lose your reader.

Check your answers in Appendix E.

CASE 5:

A n s w e r s

Response to Question 3 in Chapter Opener

3. **Nancy admits, "The mistake, Lance, was mine." What can Nancy do in the future to prevent this situation from recurring?**

Quite simply, Nancy can pause and consider before she clicks her e-mail's Send button. She can reexamine the message and tone of her e-mail before she sends it. For example, the use of the word *wannabee* was a poor choice. Nancy's reexamination of her message should also involve subtler issues. In any written document, without the receiver's hearing a person's voice or reading body language and expression, many subtleties of communications disappear. When Nancy reviews her e-mail, she should look at the tone and feeling of her message, as well as the words she chooses.

DISCUSSION QUESTIONS

1. Discuss when it is *not* appropriate to write a memo.
2. Identify and describe some common abuses of memos.
3. Discuss your experiences with spamming, shouting, or other e-mail abuses.

5·4 Writing Meeting Communications

Meetings

Meetings are an important method of exchanging information in any business setting. There are board meetings, conferences, training sessions, and staff meetings. A meeting may consist of a supervisor and one employee, a group of colleagues, or employees and their vendors or clients. In today's global economy, many companies are adopting a team approach, where employees from different departments, and even from different locations, work together to solve problems, exchange ideas, and share responsibilities.

As a business communicator, you may participate in various kinds of meetings and belong to several committees within your organization. For instance, you may belong to a *standing committee*, which is a permanent group that meets regularly, such as a project planning committee. You may also report to an *ad hoc committee*, a temporary group meeting for a specific purpose, such as a holiday party committee. A *task force* is a group charged with completing a specific task.

As mentioned in Chapter 1, many companies now use teleconferencing or videoconferencing for business meetings, to save on travel time and expense. These meetings are conducted among attendees at different locations, via computer, telephone, and video.

In all of these meetings, whether you are the group leader or an attendee, two internal documents you will use are agendas and minutes.

Meeting Notices

Notification of a meeting is usually given by either memo or e-mail. The notice should include the date, time, and location of the meeting or teleconference. It can be accompanied by a copy of the meeting's agenda.

After completing Section 5.4, you should be able to:

1 Describe several kinds of meetings.

2 Develop and write meeting agendas.

3 Draft minutes to report meeting results.

Objective

DIVERSITY
Thanks to the Internet and other technologies, we are truly a "global village" in our business communications. The most effective communicators may want to learn the foreign languages, business customs, and body language of colleagues and clients from other countries.

Agendas

An **agenda** is the order of business to be discussed during a particular meeting. The person who organizes the meeting usually prepares and distributes the agenda in advance, so that participants can prepare for the meeting. The agenda can be sent to the meeting attendees as hard copy or as an e-mail attachment.

Agendas help keep people focused on the scheduled topics. Both the leader and the participants can use the agenda as a written guide.

SCANS
Employability

Thinking Skills: Decision Making
The agendas for regular weekly or monthly meetings may vary little, so participants often can anticipate what topics will be discussed. In contrast, agendas for one-time meetings are less predictable; these agendas should be distributed in advance to allow participants time to prepare.

TECHNOLOGY
Microsoft Word is one word processing program that offers agenda templates, as well as a Wizard with a form for taking minutes.

Planning and Organizing Agendas

To plan an agenda, determine the meeting objective and prepare a list of topics to be discussed. Determine if committee reports need to be reviewed during the meeting. Think, too, about any new topics that participants may introduce. You may want to ask colleagues how long their topics will probably take. Finally, allow time for routine announcements.

Because an agenda is used as a discussion guide as well as a planning document, you will want to include every topic that should be discussed during the meeting. Also include information about the meeting date, time, and place. Be sure, however, not to include too much detail on the agenda.

The first item should be the call to order. After the roll call and approval of minutes from the previous meeting, add any entries for chairperson or subcommittee reports. Unfinished business—topics not resolved in prior meetings—is next, followed by new business. Most agendas end with announcements and adjournment.

Formatting Agendas

Agendas for formal meetings typically follow a structured format. Figure 5-5 shows a sample format for an agenda. Although formats vary, the name of the meeting generally is worded as a phrase. For example, a meeting about finding new employees could be titled "Recruitment Meeting." Center the day of the week, date, time, and location information under the meeting title. Number the items in the agenda below the heading.

Not every agenda contains each entry shown in Figure 5-5. On the other hand, many agendas are even more detailed. For example, the agenda for a major, ongoing project may show the name of the person who will report on each topic next to each entry.

Agenda
Sales Planning Meeting
Friday, January 6, 20—
10:30 a.m.
Soares Conference Room

1. Call to Order

2. Roll Call

3. Approval of Minutes from December Meeting

4. Chairperson's Report

5. Subcommittee Reports

    A. Sales Forecasting

    B. Supplier Evaluation

6. Unfinished Business

7. New Business

    A. Total Quality Management Program

    B. Product Distribution Analysis

    C. Other New Business

8. Announcements

9. Adjournment

FIGURE 5-5 Format for an agenda

A search on the World Wide Web will reveal many sites that discuss the fine points of writing agendas, proposals, and minutes.

4 *Checkpoint*

Agendas

Indicate whether each statement is true or false.
1. An agenda is the order of business for a meeting.
2. The first item on any agenda is the roll call.
3. In planning an agenda, do not consider new business at this time.
4. An agenda should include the meeting's date, time, and place.

Check your answers in Appendix E.

Objective

Minutes

Minutes are the official record of the proceedings of a meeting. They summarize topics discussed, decisions made, and actions to be taken. Minutes are sent to every meeting participant as well as to people who were invited but could not attend. On occasion, minutes also are sent to nonparticipants such as senior managers or peers whose work is affected by decisions made during the meeting.

KEY POINT

Minutes are intended only to summarize what occurred in a meeting, not to provide a word-for-word account of who said what and when.

SCANS
Employability

Personal Qualities: Self-management
Meeting participants also can take turns performing the role of recording secretary.

Planning and Organizing the Minutes

Planning begins even before the meeting. Decide who will take notes during the meeting—either a company assistant or a volunteer from the group.

Usually the minutes begin with the time, location, and the names of people present and absent, including the leader. The body of the minutes is organized according to the order in which topics were discussed. Generally, items are discussed in the order shown on the agenda. The minutes also should reflect any topics that were discussed out of order.

Formatting the Minutes

By following a few formatting guidelines, you can make minutes easy to read. Figure 5-6 shows the format for minutes of a meeting. Use 1-inch side margins, a $1\frac{1}{2}$-inch top margin, and single spacing. Center the name of the meeting and/or organization in *all caps* at the top. Below that, center a subheading (optional), such as "Minutes of the Executive Board." Center the date two lines below the heading. Use uppercase and lowercase letters for a subheading.

Start the body four lines below the subheading, single-spacing the text and double-spacing between paragraphs. Use headings to identify the various parts of the meeting. Key the headings in all caps, or use uppercase and lowercase letters and underscore them as shown in Figure 5-6. Four lines below the last line, add a signature line and key the name of the person who recorded the minutes.

MINUTES OF INFORMATION SYSTEMS COMMITTEE

August 14, 20—

Call to Order

The meeting was called to order by Chairperson Michele Isenberg at 10:00 a.m. in Room 24.

Members present were Bob Benson, Kay Hall, Henri Laborde, Ted Mead, Matt Neary, Rebecca Reynolds, and Lisa Ybarra. Ex-officio members present were Amelia Durang, Maling Huang, and Morris Lappe.

Minutes of the June 14, 20—, meeting were approved.

Report on Data Center Facilities Upgrade

Dr. Hall distributed the Request for Proposal draft, which will be sent to mid-range server vendors.

Mr. Neary reported on the bidding process to select a vendor to upgrade the data center's electronic security systems.

Program of Work/Goals

Ms. Isenberg distributed the corporate auditors' Data Center Process Integration report. Section 4 of the report has questions to be answered and forwarded to the auditors. Each committee member took a subsection of Section 4 to respond to.

Unfinished Business

Next Meeting

The next meeting will be held on October 15, 20—.

The meeting was adjourned at 11:35 p.m.

Lisa Ybarra
Lisa Ybarra, Recording Secretary

FIGURE 5-6 Format for minutes of a meeting

TECHNOLOGY

A High-Flying Office at the Airport

If Laptop Lane has its wish, business travelers will have less unproductive downtime—even at the airport. A new technology at some of the larger commercial airports helps commuters turn airport downtime into valuable office time.

Thanks to Laptop Lane, you can write, print, and send off your e-mails and memos from an airport lounge.

Laptop Lane is currently renting private cubicles outfitted with PCs, phones, printers, faxes, and high-speed Internet access to travelers. The service is available in the major airports of Chicago, Atlanta, Cincinnati, Seattle, and Denver. Laptop Lane plans to expand to other airports at a rapid pace to meet the demand for such high-tech computing services.

In 1999, the cost for Laptop Lane services was about $2 for the first five minutes and 38 cents for each additional minute. These fees cover all charges for long-distance calls made within the United States, printing, faxing, and online connections. For more information, visit **www. laptoplane.com**. ∎

CASE 5:

Answers

Response to Question 4 in Chapter Opener

4. **Do you believe e-mail should be used for all communications?**

Students can take either side here. Those suggesting that e-mail should be used for all communications (perhaps because of its speed and the advantage of sending global e-mail) should, however, suggest that care be taken before sending an e-mail. A communication distributed electronically requires the same consideration and review as a memo or letter.

Those arguing the other side may mention that e-mail can be mistakenly sent to readers besides the intended recipient. Also, the speed with which e-mail travels might tempt the communicator to send his or her message without careful review. Lastly, some issues are more easily and effectively resolved face-to-face.

DISCUSSION QUESTIONS

1. What is the purpose of an agenda?
2. Discuss why you think minutes of a business meeting are important to keep.

CASE 5:
Summary

Nancy needs to mend fences with the Mainframe Support department and Connie Reyes. She should apologize and explain her frustration with the CAD department's work-load. Nancy should ask her supervisor to write an e-mail to all managers reminding them that the CAD department follows Lloyd Engineering's strict rules about software licenses. Finally, Nancy needs to follow the etiquette of e-mail writing and never again write a message she wouldn't want repeated.

Chapter Summary

Section 5.1 Uses of Internal Documents

1 **Explain how memos are used in internal communication.** Memos are used for internal communication within an organization to communicate with a colleague or a supervisor.

2 **Explain how electronic memos, e-mail messages, are used in internal communication.** Electronic memos, or e-mail messages, are also used for internal communication within an organization. There are several advantages to e-mail: they can be sent globally to several people at once; they can be sent at any time and held in an electronic mailbox; and they can be transmitted in seconds, with or without attachments.

3 **Describe when to use memos and e-mail messages.** Both memos and e-mails have four purposes: (1) to provide a record; (2) to advise, direct, and state policy; (3) to inform; and (4) to promote goodwill.

Section 5.2 Formatting and Writing Effective Internal Documents

1 **Identify the parts of a memo.** Most memos contain a heading, a body, and one or more notations.

2 **Understand traditional and simplified memo formats.** Memos can be formatted in the traditional or simplified style. The traditional memo format can be used with letterhead stationery or plain paper. The simplified format, which is easily produced on computers or word processors, also can be used with letterhead stationery or plain paper.

3 **Explain ways to organize memos and e-mail messages.** When planning memos and e-mails, use the four-step process for planning all messages: (1) identify the objective, (2) identify the main idea, (3) determine the supporting information, and (4) adjust the content to the receivers. Memos can be written in the direct or indirect order. Write memos in the direct order when they contain good news for the receiver or make routine requests. Write memos in the indirect order when they contain bad news for the receiver or are trying to persuade the receiver.

4 **List and explain the guidelines for writing effective memos and e-mail messages.** Guidelines for writing memos and e-mails include (1) restrict message to one main idea; (2) compose a short, clear subject line; (3) make the body stand alone; (4) use tables and visual aids; (5) use headings in long messages; (6) number items in a list; and (7) proofread your work.

Section 5.3 Abuses of Internal Documents

1 **Identify and describe the abuses of memos and e-mail messages.** Memos and e-mails are misused sometimes. Common misuses occur when memos are (1) written too frequently, (2) written to gain attention, (3) written by committee, and (4) improperly rewritten for each level of management.

2 **Understand possible remedies for abuses.** As much care should be taken with composing and sending memos and e-mails as with any written communication. The writer needs to think about when a memo or e-mail message is appropriate and to whom.

3 **Identify some common abuses particular to e-mail messages.** E-mails have their own particular kind of abuses, including spamming, shouting, and flaming. E-mails can be sent too quickly, possibly without as much consideration as hard-copy messages; they can also be accidentally forwarded to the wrong receiver.

Section 5.4 Writing Meeting Communications

1 **Describe several kinds of meetings.** Businesses hold a variety of meetings, such as staff meetings, board meetings, conferences, training sessions, standing committee and ad hoc committee meetings, and task forces.

2 **Develop and write meeting agendas.** An agenda is the order of business for a meeting and may be used as a guide for and record of that meeting.

3 **Draft minutes to report meeting results.** Minutes are the official record of the proceedings of a meeting. They can be formatted using headings to identify various parts of the meeting.

Critical Thinking Questions

1. When might it be better to communicate with a traditional memo, rather than an e-mail message?
2. When might it be better to communicate with an e-mail, rather than a traditional hard-copy memo?
3. How might the language used in a memo to a colleague differ from that used in a letter to a client?
4. What might be said in a business meeting that should not be included in the minutes?

Applications

Part A. List the main idea and use for each e-mail:

1. Congratulations on your promotion. We would like to hold a small celebration in your honor in the marketing conference room on Tuesday at noon.
2. My recommendation was to open a new branch in Lancaster, but I have no problem with your decision to open one in Juniper instead. Juniper also has excellent potential. If I can help in any way, let me know.
3. The annual vacation-leave policy requires employees to apply for leave at least two weeks before the suggested vacation time and to receive preapproval of all annual vacations. Please use Form 908941-B for this approval. If emergencies occur and you cannot provide the two-week notice, use Form 908942 to receive emergency approval.

TEAMWORK

Part B. Divide into groups of three or four members. Assume that you are departmental supervisors and that you have received the following memo from your supervisor. Rewrite the memo for your subordinates. Each group will revise the memo for a specific purpose, which your instructor will provide. Each group will not know the purpose assigned to other groups.

TO: Janice Davenport, Supervisor

FROM: Stephanie Fergason, Vice President of Human Resources

DATE: July 24, 20—

SUBJECT: New Preferred Providers of Health Care Services

Please write a memo to your subordinates telling them that Green Clinic and Washington General Hospital have recently become Preferred Providers of Health Care Services (PPHCS).

This means that when employees enrolled in our health care plan use Green Clinic and Washington General Hospital, they will receive health care services at a lower cost. Also, it means that all covered employees need to do is show their membership card to the PPHCS organization and all insurance claims will be filed for them. In summary, if our employees use the PPHCSs, they will receive low-cost health care services without worrying about insurance claims.

Part C. Proofread the following memo and make any necessary corrections. Then prepare an agenda from the topics in the memo.

To: Joanna Burke

From: Benjamin Soto

Subject: New-product promotion meeting

Date: January 12, 20—

With the national introduction of our Cool-Touch Toaster four months away, we need to complete our promotion plans. Please schedule a new-product promotion meeting for Thursday, January 19, at 2:00 PM in Conference Room B. I would appreciate it if you would take notes during the meeting, which I will chair.

We should review the minites from last month's meeting and invite the chairpersons from the Advertising and In-store Promotion Subcommittees to report the results to date. I will report on the production schedule and show a sample of the new packaging.

Because we did not reach a decision about the warranty period, when we discussed it last month, we need to discuss this at the upcoming meeting. In addition, we should decide what to do about Sales Incentives, which was also discussed at last month's meeting. I may have announcements to make regarding new product ideas and we should allow time for any new topics.

Editing Activities

I. Find the spelling errors in the following e-mail message body; then list the words, correctly spelled, on a separate sheet of paper.

   The meddical records department will be closed on Monday, October 10. You can get a copy of any pashient's record on that day by using the central computer sistem or by calling the shift superviser on extention 29. The depaartment will reopen at 6 a.m. on Tuesday, October 11.

II. Team with a class member to evaluate the following memo written by a subordinate to his supervisor. Evaluate the memo by answering the following questions: Is this an effective memo? Why or why not? Does this memo illustrate an effective use of memos? Why or why not? Write a memo to your instructor that contains your evaluation.

words@work

If you are using *words@work*, complete the activities on Memos and E-mail in the Writing at Work section.

TEAMWORK

TO: Carlos Tibbets, Sales Supervisor

FROM: Russell LeBeau, Sales Representative

DATE: September 12, 20—

SUBJECT: Attendance at the San Francisco Trade Show

Thank you for permitting me to attend next week's trade show in San Francisco. I'm sure it will be the most exceptional trade show ever. All of our main competitors will be exhibiting their most advanced technologies. I am very excited!

The knowledge that I gain there will really help me. I sure am happy that the company is paying my expenses—five nights in a $150-a-night room would be too expensive for me.

Case Studies

1. Assume that you, Guido Novello, head the layaway department in a large retail store, Healy's Emporium. Write a memo to all members of your department. Explain that management has decided that employees cannot take annual vacations during November and December because of the holiday season. Use the indirect order and positive language to write this memo in the simplified memo format.

2. A salesperson of a small insurance company obtained names, addresses, and telephone numbers of employees in your department. The salesperson calls the employees, implies that he is calling with your approval, and states that his insurance rates are the cheapest—even cheaper than the rates provided in the company's benefit package. Neither of these inferences are true; he does not have your approval, and the insurance rates provided in the company's benefit package are cheaper. Write an e-mail message to your subordinates informing them of the situation and these facts. Invent any details you may need.

TECHNOLOGY

Career Case Studies

COMMUNICATION FOR NATURAL RESOURCES AND AGRICULTURE CAREERS

Reclaiming Arrow Lake has been the focus of Laura Marino's work ever since she was named chief biologist of the Arrow Mountains district. Where once the lake had been a thriving resort area, few campers or people who fish used the facilities at the time she started her job.

One of her priorities was restocking the lake with fish once found naturally there. After a three-year program of removing excess vegetation from the lake and clearing debris which slowed the flow of water into the lake, the lake was restocked. Once the fish took hold, people fishing and campers returned to the lake. The reclamation was such a success that Laura was often consulted by other biologists statewide.

Last week, however, her staff noticed dead fish floating at the perimeter of the lake. Each day the problem has worsened and without more information, Laura does not know what action to take. To start her research, Laura is writing an urgent memo to the ten Arrow Lake wildlife rangers, to see what they might know about it.

1. What should be the main idea in Laura's memo?
2. What questions might she ask the wildlife rangers?
3. What graphics would you recommend Laura add to her memo?

COMMUNICATION FOR ENGINEERING AND INDUSTRIAL CAREERS

TECHNOLOGY

Steven Hiza is an electrical engineer for the construction manager of his city's new subway system. Steven ensures that the subway's sophisticated electronic monitoring system—the transit system's first line of defense in protecting passengers and equipment in case of an emergency—tracks even minute changes in the stations and tunnels.

During his weekly inspection of progress on the monitoring system, Steven notices that the system's fiber optics still have not been completely laid. Although the installation of the rest of the system is ahead of schedule, Steven knows the system will not be completed on time unless the cable is installed more quickly.

Steven must inform his supervisor immediately through e-mail. He knows that his supervisor hates bad news, so Steven must present his information in a positive light, perhaps mentioning some good news, too. Write Steven's bad-news e-mail, inventing details as you need them.

Video Case

Writing an International Memo

Oscar Torres has his dream job at ElectroGuard, a company that manufacturers highly sophisticated security systems. As Director of International Training, Oscar prepares account executives (AEs) to work and succeed in the Caribbean, Mexico, and South America.

When the Vice President of Sales invited Oscar out for lunch, Oscar expected a relaxing meal. Instead, he received a shock. Effective in 10 days, ElectroGuard begins marketing its systems in Europe. Oscar tried to explain the amount of training this would require, but the Vice President of Sales had no choice. This edict came straight from the company president. AEs will begin arriving in Europe in 10 days.

Oscar returns to his office, his head swimming with ideas. How can he quickly communicate what the AEs will need to know? Oscar opens his word processing application and begins writing a memo.

Questions

1. Oscar chose a memo as the medium for his communication. Why do you agree with his choice, or why would you have chosen to write a letter or an e-mail?

2. Imagine that you are Oscar. Draft a memo to the account executives who will soon be traveling to Europe. Based on your viewing of the video, list the five general areas the AEs should research before they visit a new country and why each area is important. Print your draft.

3. Using the Internet, look for sources that can help you augment the five general areas your AEs could research. Example search phrases are "cross-culture in business" or "foreign business customs." A sample URL is **www.webofculture. com**. Add any new areas of research to Oscar's memo. Print your draft.

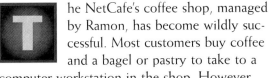

Communicating over Coffee

The NetCafe's coffee shop, managed by Ramon, has become wildly successful. Most customers buy coffee and a bagel or pastry to take to a computer workstation in the shop. However, many people are coming to the shop just to enjoy one of Ramon's many varieties of coffee. Ramon has set up small tables and chairs specifically for the comfort of these customers.

Although business is doing well, Ramon is having problems with one of his coffee suppliers. This company, Kenya Koffee, is located on the east coast of Africa, where a special coffee bean grows. Ramon places his orders with Kenya Koffee through e-mail. Using e-mail is a new experience for him, so he was surprised when his niece and business partner, Eva, told him he was participating in e-commerce.

"E-commerce," she explained, "is any business conducted over the Internet."

Ramon is just glad that e-mail makes it much easier and faster for him to place orders. However, three weeks ago Ramon e-mailed a coffee order to Kenya Koffee, but the order hasn't shown up yet. He sent them a reminder about it last week. Still, no coffee order has appeared. Ramon has not heard one word from Kenya Koffee, either.

This afternoon, two of the shop's best customers came in just for a cup of the strong Kenyan coffee—and left without it, annoyed. Ramon gritted his teeth and hurried to one of the shop's computers. He quickly typed out this e-mail:

Date: July 1, 20—
Subject:
To: Kenya Koffee
From: Ramon Negron, Co-owner, NetCafe

I AM DESPARATE FOR THAT COFFEE ORDER I PLACED WITH YOU NEARLY THREE WEEKS AGO! WHAT IS TAKING SO LONG? Please send it to me as soon as you cane. My customers keep asking for the Kenyan blend. I'm afraid they will stop coming in unless I can get for them very soon! It's one of the most popular brands I sell. Also, are you ever going to send me information about that new blend of local cofee that you expected to get in? I would like to have a sample to see how my customers like it. Is the meantime, I MUST get the Kenyan blend I ordered by the end of the week. If not, I will look for another supplier!! :-(:-(:-(

1. What, if anything, is missing from the heading of Ramon's e-mail?
2. Which order does Ramon use for his e-mail: direct or indirect? Explain whether you think he made a good choice.
3. What would you suggest to Ramon concerning the formatting of his e-mail?
4. How would you describe the tone of Ramon's message? What would you change? Why?
5. Did Ramon take the time to use the spell-check on his e-mail? Did he read it himself for errors? How can you tell?
6. Rewrite Ramon's message, applying what you have learned about e-mail. Make whatever changes you think are necessary. Then, explain why your version is better than Ramon's.

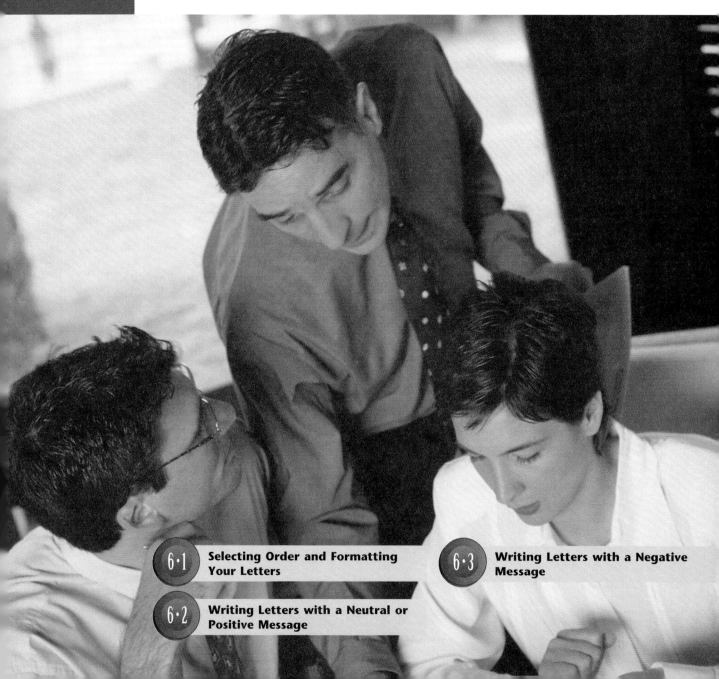

Writing Letters to Your Clients and Customers

chapter 6

6·1 Selecting Order and Formatting Your Letters

6·2 Writing Letters with a Neutral or Positive Message

6·3 Writing Letters with a Negative Message

Maria's Reactions to Letters

Recently Maria Gonzalez changed jobs. After completing her business technology degree, she left her position as a checkout clerk at a local supermarket. Now she works in the secretarial pool at a financial services office in Yuma, Arizona.

As expected, Maria's company uses letters for external messages. Most of the recipients of these letters are in the United States; however, some recipients are in Mexico. Maria keys letters written in English only. Because she keys documents for many workers at the office, Maria has noticed many inconsistencies. Maria has also noticed that many letters contain specific formatting instructions, which often vary.

Because of her Mexican heritage, Maria feels comfortable with most of the long letters sent to Mexico. Nevertheless, at times, she feels that a letter she has keyed for a recipient in Mexico is somewhat short and not very well written.

The letters dictated by some of the executives in Maria's office are always short and sometimes seem a little blunt and tactless. Other people's letters are always long and wordy, sometimes running to two and three pages. She has also noticed that some people dictate letters with varying lengths.

Maria has noticed one other thing—that most authors of the letters she keys are white Americans. Most of the time Maria feels these letters are too short and a little blunt. She wonders if this concern is the result of her having a different heritage.

Questions

1. Are Maria's concerns about the varying formats justified? Is there one correct format?

2. If there is more than one correct format, how do you determine which one to use?

3. Are the same steps used in planning all types of letters?

4. How are letters with a neutral or positive message alike? How do they differ?

5. Why does Maria consider some of the letters with a negative message a little short and somewhat blunt or tactless?

6. Should a writer consider culture or nationality when writing his or her letters? If so, why?

Selecting Order and Formatting Your Letters

After completing Section 6.1, you should be able to:

1 Identify the use of letters.

2 Select the correct order for letters.

3 Describe the standard and optional parts of a business letter.

4 Use the block, modified block, and simplified block letter formats.

5 Prepare a business envelope.

Objective

1

Objective

2

Use of Letters

Business letters are used to communicate written messages to persons outside an organization. Letters are also used to communicate formal written messages to employees within an organization. Business letters are considered to be more formal than memos.

Business letters are printed on letterhead stationery, which includes the company name, address, telephone number, e-mail address, and logo. A letterhead may also show the company facsimile (fax) number, the company slogan, or the names of company officials and departments. The letterhead and the letter's appearance are important because a receiver starts to form an opinion of the sender and the company by looking at the letter.

Identifying the Order of Your Letters

A letter can be written in direct order or indirect order, depending on whether the message is neutral, positive, or negative. (Refer to Chapter 4 for a review of direct and indirect order.) When identifying the type of letter you are going to write, think about how the receiver will respond. The diagram below will help you decide the type of letter you should write and the order of your letter.

How the Receiver Will Respond	The Type of Letter You Write	Letter Order
Main idea makes a routine request	Neutral message	Direct
Main idea is an order of merchandise or a positive response to a request	Positive message	Direct
Main idea is perceived as an acknowledgment or an act of friendship	Positive message	Direct
Main idea contains a negative message for the receiver	Negative message	Indirect

Letter Parts

The standard parts of a business letter are the dateline, letter address, salutation, body, complimentary close, signature block, and reference initials. A business letter also may include these optional parts: attention line, subject line, company name in signature block, enclosure notation, copy notation, postscript, and second-page heading. Figure 6-1 illustrates many of these letter parts.

Dateline

The dateline shows the date of the letter. Position the dateline about two inches from the top of the page, or at least two lines below the letterhead. The exact placement depends on the letter length. The horizontal placement of the dateline depends on the letter format used.

Letter Address

The letter address is the part of the letter that contains the complete name, title, and address of the receiver. Position the letter address four lines below the dateline. Place each part of the letter address on a separate line, beginning at the left margin.

Include the receiver's personal or professional title (*Mr., Ms., Dr., Mrs.*) in the letter address. The job title can appear either on the same line with the name or on the line below, whichever gives better balance. Allow one space between the two-letter postal abbreviation and the ZIP code. Use the ZIP+4 code if you know the last four digits.

> **KEY POINT**
>
> If you are writing to a woman and you do not know the personal title she prefers, use Ms.

Ms. Maureen Saunders, Treasurer
Central Tennessee Bank
396 Stewart Avenue
Franklin, TN 37064-7109

Use ALL CAPS for the letter address if the letter is sent in a window envelope or if computerized equipment is used to merge the letter with a list of mailing addresses. This format uses no punctuation.

MS MAUREEN SAUNDERS TREASURER
CENTRAL TENNESSEE BANK
396 STEWART AVENUE
FRANKLIN TN 37064-7109

Attention Line

The attention line is an optional part of the letter address that directs the correspondence to a particular individual when the letter is addressed to an organization. Begin the attention line at the left margin on the second line of the letter address. For example:

Central Tennessee Bank
Attention Ms. Maureen Saunders
396 Stewart Avenue
Franklin, TN 37064-7109

- Think of the salutation in a letter as a way of saying "hello" to the receiver.
- Use a first name in the salutation only when you are certain that the receiver believes you have a personal relationship.

Salutation

The salutation acts as the greeting to the receiver. The salutation should agree with the first line of the letter address. If the first line of the address does not contain a person's name, use the neutral salutation *Ladies and Gentlemen*. If the letter is addressed to a job title, use the title in the salutation; for example, *Dear Service Manager*. The formality of the salutation depends on the relationship between the sender and the receiver of the letter. As a guide, use the name that you would use if you were addressing the person face to face.

Key the salutation at the left margin and two lines below the letter address. A colon follows the salutation if mixed punctuation is used; no punctuation follows the salutation if open punctuation is used. The example below shows two letter addresses and salutations.

Brennan's Supermarket
1018 Eighth Street
Monroe, WI 53566-0011

Ladies and Gentlemen:

Produce Manager
Brennan's Supermarket
1018 Eighth Street
Monroe, WI 53566-0011

Dear Produce Manager

Subject Line

The optional subject line contains the topic of the letter. Key the subject line in all capital letters two lines below the salutation at the left margin. Omit the word SUBJECT. For example:

Mr. Mario Petrocelli
570 Orchard Boulevard
Northbrook, IL 60062-4110

Dear Mr. Petrocelli:

OVERSEAS TRAVEL REGULATIONS

Body

The body contains the message of the letter. Single-space the body of the letter and double-space between paragraphs. Place the letter attractively on the page using side margins of 1, 1½, or 2 inches, depending on the length of the letter.

Complimentary Close

The complimentary close is the formal closing. It is keyed two lines below the body of the letter, and only the first letter in the first word is capitalized. Use a comma after the complimentary close when using mixed punctuation; omit the comma when using open punctuation.

Frequently used complimentary closes include the following:

Sincerely   Sincerely yours   Cordially

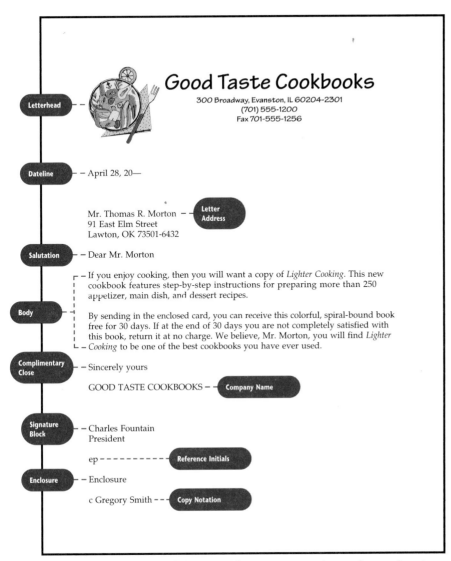

FIGURE 6-1 Letter in block format with open punctuation and named parts

Company Name

A company name may appear after the complimentary close if company letterhead is not used. If used, the company name is keyed in all capital letters a double space below the complimentary close. The first letter of the company name should align with the first letter of the complimentary close.

Signature Block

The signature block contains the writer's signed name, keyed name, and title. Key the writer's name four lines below the complimentary close. Omit the title *Mr.* before a man's name, unless the name can be confused with a female name. *Miss, Mrs.,* or *Ms.* may be used before a woman's name, depending on the writer's preference. Place the writer's official title on the line below his or her name.

Reference Initials

The operator's **reference initials** indicate who keyed the letter. Key the initials in lowercase and position them at the left margin two lines below the printed signature line. If the initials of the person writing or dictating the letter also are included, key them in capital letters and separate them from the operator's initials with a colon (GK:er).

KEY POINT

Use the enclosure notation in the plural (Enclosures) when you enclose more than one item.

Enclosure Notation

An **enclosure notation** indicates that an additional item is included with a letter. Key the word *Enclosure* (or its abbreviation, *Enc.*) two lines below the reference initials when including an item.

Copy Notation

A **copy notation** indicates that a copy of the letter is being sent to someone other than the addressee. Two lines below the reference initials or enclosure notation, key the notation as a *c* for *copy* or *pc* for *photocopy* followed by the name of the person receiving the copy.

c Alex Andros	c Toni Bailey
pc Sally Williams	Carlos Santiago

For *blind copy*, use *bc*. A blind copy (bc) notation should appear on the copy (but not on the original) when you do not want the addressee to know that you sent a copy to someone else. For example:

bc Carolyn A. Northcott

SCANS
Employability

Thinking Skills: Decision Making
Postscripts rarely are used in normal business letters, but they often are used in sales letters.

Postscript

For emphasis, you may add a **postscript**, a sentence or paragraph at the end of the letter that reinforces the message in the body. New information should not be included in a postscript. Position the postscript two lines below the last notation. The letters *P.S.* may be omitted.

Second-Page Heading

Use a second-page heading when the letter continues onto a second page. Use plain paper of the same quality as the letterhead. Key the addressee's name, the page number, and the date one inch below the top edge of the page, and single-space all three elements at the left margin. The heading also can be keyed on one line—name at left margin, page number at center, and date at right margin. Continue keying the body two lines below the heading. For example:

KEY POINT

Use a similar heading on later pages if your letter is longer than two pages. Put the appropriate page number in the heading of each page.

Miss Matilde Delgado
Page 2
June 2, 20—

or

Miss Matilde Delgado	page 2	June 2, 20—

Letter Parts

Identify each letter part.
1. FEBRUARY ORDER
2. Enclosure
3. Dear Mr. Yamagushi
4. c Josephine Ray
5. Sincerely
Check your answers in Appendix E.

Business Letter Formats

Like memos, business letters may be prepared in different formats. The three basic letter formats are block, modified block, and simplified block. When writing a letter, try to select the format that will be the most pleasing to your receiver.

Block Format

In block format, all lines begin at the left margin. Refer to Figure 6-1, page 189, for an example of block format. (The figure also identifies the letter parts.) Usually, paragraphs are not indented in this format.

Modified Block Format

In modified block format, all lines begin at the left margin except for the dateline, the complimentary close, and the signature block, which begin at the center of the page. This format is fairly efficient because only one tab setting at center is required. Paragraphs may begin at the left margin, or they may be indented five spaces. The indentation is optional because paragraphs are separated by a double space. Figure 6-2 on page 192 shows an example of a modified block letter.

Simplified Block Format

The simplified block format omits the salutation and the complimentary close. Designed for efficient processing, the simplified block format often is used when preparing letters by merging addresses from a database with a form letter. As in the block format, all lines begin at the left margin. The spacing between letter parts is the same as that in block or modified block format.

Refer to Figure 6-3 as you read these guidelines for preparing letters in simplified block format:

1. Place the dateline on line 13 (2 inches from the top of the page) so that the letter address is positioned for use with a window envelope.

Objective 4

TECHNOLOGY
Even when using electronic equipment to prepare the letter, the block format is fast and simple to use because you do not need to set tabs.

MAIN STREET CLOTHIERS
15 Main Street, Arlington, VA 22210-3428
(703) 555-3200, Fax (703) 555-3392

June 29, 20—

Mr. Robert DeSousa
89 Gateway Street
Arlington, VA 22210-1452

Dear Mr. DeSousa:

We are delighted to enclose your new Main Street Clothiers credit card. You may use this card in both the Arlington and Crystal City locations.

Because of your fine credit record, you will be able to charge as much as $3,500 in clothing and accessories. Simply present your credit card to any salesperson at the time of purchase.

Our annual summer clearance sale starts on July 1, and we hope you will stop in early for the best selection. Thank you for doing business with Main Street Clothiers.

Sincerely,

Mary Ann Loudon

Mary Ann Loudon
Credit Manager

MAL:jp

Enclosure

FIGURE 6-2 Letter in modified block format with mixed punctuation

MAIN STREET CLOTHIERS
15 Main Street, Arlington, VA 22210-3428
(703) 555-3200, Fax (703) 555-3392

June 29, 20—

MR ROBERT DESOUSA
89 GATEWAY STREET
ARLINGTON VA 22210-1452

NEW CREDIT CARD

We are delighted to enclose your new Main Street Clothiers credit card. You may use this card in both the Arlington and Crystal City locations.

Because of your fine credit record, you will be able to charge as much as $3,500 in clothing and accessories. Simply present your credit card to any salesperson at the time of purchase.

Our annual summer clearance sale starts on July 1, and we hope you will stop in early for the best selection. Thank you, Mr. DeSousa, for doing business with Main Street Clothiers.

Mary Ann Loudon

Mary Ann Loudon
Credit Manager

MAL:jp

Enclosure

FIGURE 6-3 Letter in simplified block format with address for window envelope

2. Do not include a salutation and a complimentary close.
3. Place a subject line keyed in ALL CAPS or in uppercase and low-ercase letters two lines below the letter address.
4. Position the writer's name and title four lines below the body in either ALL CAPS or in uppercase and lowercase, depending on the writer's preference.
5. When writing a letter using this format, it is a good idea to per-sonalize it by incorporating the receiver's name within the body of the letter.

A format for a friendly or personal letter is found and explained at
www.englishplus.com/ grammar/00000142.htm

Business Envelopes

When preparing a business envelope, key the receiver's personal or professional title and the job title as they appear in the letter address. If the letter address contains an attention line, type this information on the line below the receiver's company name on the envelope.

Key the address on the envelope using all the information in the letter address. The address should be keyed in all capital letters, and all punctuation should be omitted in order to comply with the official

Objective
5

Ethical Conduct—It Starts at the Top

Ethics is a major component of many individual corporate cultures. An organization's ethical decisions determine its ethical behavior. In other words, it's not what you say; it's what you do. The NCAA and the ITT Corporation are good examples.

The NCAA is the organization that governs college sports. Its large rulebook contains guidelines for ethical behavior, yet the reputation of college sports continues to have

problems. Some college leaders pay athletes to come to their schools and help the schools attain national rankings. University officials are sometimes aware of this cheating but ignore it because they want the publicity that accompanies a national ranking.

For the ITT Corporation, the opposite has happened. In the past, this corporation was believed by some to operate unethically. Then Rand V. Araskog became its chair and

introduced a 16-page "code of conduct" that defined what employees should and should not do. He also told top management to conduct business correctly and to "bend over backwards" to develop a good public image. His efforts were successful and ITT's image changed greatly.

Ethics starts at the top. A dedicated leader can make a difference, even in a multinational corporation. ■

U.S. Postal Service format. Include the ZIP code or the ZIP+4 code on every envelope.

With a **standard business envelope** ($9\frac{1}{2}''$ by $4\frac{1}{8}''$), the receiver's name and address should begin on line 13 or 14. Key all information single-spaced in block style, four inches from the left edge of the envelope, as shown in Figure 6-4.

Self-adhesive labels often are used when mailing a letter to many recipients. For example, labels may be used for a mailing to customers telling them of an upcoming sale. These labels should be placed approximately in the same spot on the envelope as the recipient's address would be keyed. Many word processing software packages contain programs that will print the addresses of customers or clients on labels. If you are sending a special letter to a customer, these same word processing software packages also have templates that will print the letter address on an envelope.

KEY POINT

The standard-sized business envelope is commonly known as a Number 10 envelope.

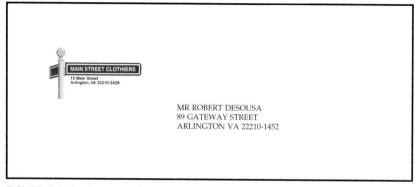

MAIN STREET CLOTHIERS
15 Main Street
Arlington, VA 22210-3428

MR ROBERT DESOUSA
89 GATEWAY STREET
ARLINGTON VA 22210-1452

FIGURE 6-4   Business envelope

2 Checkpoint

Letter Formats and Business Envelopes

Indicate if each statement is true or false.
1. In the block format, all lines begin at the left margin.
2. Paragraphs in the modified block format are always indented.
3. Paragraphs in the simplified block format are always indented.
4. The salutation and complimentary close are omitted in the simplified block format.
5. Each line in the envelope address is separated by one double space.

Check your answers in Appendix E.

CASE 6:

Answers

Responses to Questions 1 and 2 in Chapter Opener

1. **Are Maria's concerns about the varying formats justified? Is there one correct format?**

   Maria's concerns are justified to some extent. While several formats are acceptable for letters to recipients in the United States, writers must make sure they use a correct format—block, modified block, or simplified block.

2. **If there is more than one correct format, how do you determine which one to use?**

   The key to this answer is to know your receiver. Select the format that your receiver will like the best. If you do not know which one he or she will like the best, you will have to select one. The block format is used most of the time because it is personable yet simple.

DISCUSSION QUESTIONS

1. What are the standard parts of a business letter?
2. Describe how the block, modified block, and simplified block letter formats differ.
3. How is the information in the letter address used when preparing the business envelope?

Writing Letters with a Neutral or Positive Message

Objectives

After completing Section 6.2, you should be able to:

1 Plan letters with neutral or positive messages.

2 Organize letters with neutral or positive messages.

3 Write letters with neutral or positive messages.

Objective

Objective

Planning Letters with Neutral or Positive Messages

Communication is receiver-oriented; therefore, senders should view messages from the receiver's perspective. This perspective helps the sender obtain the desired response from the receiver. The four steps in planning letters that contain neutral or positive messages are to identify the objective, identify the main idea, determine the supporting information, and adjust the content to the receiver. These steps are applied in the following example:

Identify the Objective	To make an offer of employment.
Identify the Main Idea	To offer the applicant a position as a training director in the Services Department.
Determine the Supporting Information	Impressed with the applicant's knowledge of the company and good work attitude; annual salary of $28,000; paid semimonthly; starting date is July 1; conditions of employment; and decision needed within one week.
Adjust the Content to the Receiver	Applicant is knowledgeable about the job requirements and the company. Applicant will be eager to hear from us.

Organizing Letters with Neutral or Positive Messages

After using the four steps for identifying the content that goes into these letters, now it is time to present this information in the correct order. Letters with neutral or positive messages are organized in direct order—the main idea is presented immediately, followed by the supporting information, and concluded by the closing.

Main Idea

In effective letters with a neutral, positive, or routine message, the main idea appears clearly and concisely in the first or second sentence. Emphasize the main idea by keeping introductory paragraphs short— one or two sentences (usually no longer than four lines).

DIVERSITY
In the North American business culture, writing in a clear and concise manner is very important. This concept is especially true when composing main ideas.

Checkpoint 3

The Main Idea

Indicate whether each sentence would be a good or poor opening for a response to a request for customer credit information (a letter with a neutral main idea). If poor, explain why.

1. We appreciate your confidence in our credit information.
2. Thank you for requesting credit information on John Rogers.
3. The credit information on John Rogers is enclosed.
4. We receive many requests for credit information each day.
5. You can rate John Rogers as an excellent credit risk.

Check your answers in Appendix E.

Supporting Information

After conveying the main idea in the first paragraph, the next step in planning is to provide information that will clarify the main idea and help the receiver. Supporting information should furnish necessary explanations, state conditions of the main idea, or answer questions.

This section may have one or more paragraphs. For clarity, make sure each paragraph has a central idea, repeats key words, and enumerates important points. For psychological appeal, make these middle paragraphs no longer than eight lines.

Goodwill Closing

The closing of a letter provides an excellent opportunity to build goodwill. The closing should be friendly and courteous and leave a favorable impression with the receiver. In addition, it should identify any required action. Using the receiver's name adds a personal touch. Figure 6-1 on page 189 shows a letter that uses that technique.

Correspondence from a company that sells products or services may include a soft sale in the closing. A *soft sale* is an attempt to sell a product or service, but it is not strong or pushy. The following is an example of a goodwill closing that contains a soft sale:

> Thank you, Mr. Ruiz, for your order. By the way, you may want to visit our store during our Anniversary Sale between the 15th and 29th of May. All personal computers and word processors will be reduced 25 percent.

KEY POINT

Receivers usually scan letters before reading them carefully. Keep paragraphs relatively short so that receivers develop a positive attitude toward your letters.

4 Checkpoint

Goodwill Closings

Indicate whether each sentence would be a good or poor closing for a letter that supplies requested credit information. If poor, explain why.

1. The next time I need credit information from your agency, you'll certainly hear from me.
2. If you need additional information, please ask.
3. Please ask if you need more information on John Rogers.
4. We appreciate your request.
5. John Rogers will be an excellent credit customer.

Check your answers in Appendix E.

Writing Letters with Neutral or Positive Messages

Objective

3

There are several types of letters with neutral and positive messages. Six of these are discussed here: (1) routine requests, (2) claims, (3) orders, (4) positive responses, (5) friendship letters, and (6) acknowledgment letters.

Letters with Neutral Messages

A **routine letter** contains a neutral message—the main idea is neither positive nor negative. In routine messages, the sender is sure the receiver will respond as the sender wants. Thus, the receiver does not need to be persuaded to do something. Examples of routine letters are routine requests and claims.

Routine Requests

A **routine request** is a request for an action that will be done willingly. This type of request is presented in the direct order. "Will you . . ." is the main idea of a routine request. To aid the receiver in the response, the writer must provide sufficient detail for the receiver to understand the request and respond easily. Providing details means anticipating the receiver's questions and responding to them. For example, if you asked someone to speak, you would need to provide the receiver with answers to the following questions:

1. What is the topic?
2. What is the background, knowledge, and expected size of the audience?
3. What is the date, time, and location of the presentation?
4. Will the speaker be paid? If so, how much?
5. If travel is involved, who will arrange and pay for accommodations?

SCANS
Employability

**Interpersonal:
Serving Customers**
Receiver-oriented supporting information in a request helps the receiver judge the sender in a favorable light.

In a routine request, reveal the main idea quickly, provide necessary supporting information concisely, and close in a polite, helpful manner. The following plan is used for these requests:

Main Idea	States the request politely and directly and provides reason for the request, if appropriate.
Supporting Information	Specifies information required to obtain a complete response, such as times, dates, benefits to the receiver, and terms of payment.
Goodwill Closing	Ends pleasantly and indicates the action the receiver should take.

Figure 6-5 on page 200 contains an example of a poorly written routine request. Figure 6 6 on page 201 contains a well-written routine request.

Claims

A **claim letter** is a special request for a refund, an exchange, or a discount on merchandise or services. Customers and clients use the direct order in claim letters to communicate to the receiver that they expect an adjustment—a positive settlement to a claim.

Main Idea	Asks for an adjustment.
Supporting Information	Explains the problem or the reason for the request and identifies the damage (if damage occurred).
Goodwill Closing	Ends with a positive statement and indicates how to correct the situation.

A claim letter should have a positive but firm tone. The following example is the body of a well-written claim letter:

Please replace the 2x4s in the exterior walls with 2x6s.

Yesterday, my wife and I stopped by the construction site of our new home and noticed that 2x4s were being used in the exterior walls. As indicated on the blueprints, 2x6s are to be used in the exterior walls.

As I was walking around, I realized that you are well ahead of schedule. That is very exciting because we are eagerly awaiting the opportunity to move into our new home. Thank you for the good work you are doing.

If you have any questions, call me at my office number (555-3983).

SCANS
Employability

Basic Skills: Writing
In positive responses to claim letters, tone is extremely important. It tells the receiver how willingly the sender made the requested adjustment.

MARIO LOPEZ

**6306 Claramont Avenue
Cincinnati, OH 45208-1841**

September 5, 20—

Ms. Alicia DeVon
3402 East 25th Street
Taylorsville, SC 29646-0926

Dear Ms. DeVon

Last night's *Taylorsville Gazette* included an article on your speech to a local investor's club. The article discussed the investment strategies you have employed in your highly successful career. It also contained some of your thoughts on mutual funds and state bonds; however, I would like some additional details—more than what was printed in the paper.

Do you have any copies of your speech or handouts that were given to members of the club? I'm sure they would be very interesting.

Yours truly

Mario Lopez

Mario Lopez

FIGURE 6-5 Poorly written routine request letter in block format with open punctuation

MARIO LOPEZ

**6306 Claramont Avenue
Cincinnati, OH 45208-1841**

September 5, 20—

Ms. Alicia DeVon
3402 East 25th Street
Taylorsville, SC 29646-0926

Dear Ms. DeVon:

Please send me a copy of the handouts you provided at your recent presentation to the Taylorsville Investment Club. I would really appreciate a copy of your investment strategies and your insights on mutual funds and state bonds.

Unfortunately, I had to miss the meeting but read the article in last night's *Taylorsville Gazette.* While the article was very complimentary, it did not contain much detail. Because many members have told me that I had missed some very valuable information, I am making this request.

For your convenience, a self-addressed, stamped envelope is enclosed. Thank you very much for taking the time to talk to the club. I look forward to receiving the information.

Sincerely yours,

Mario Lopez

Mario Lopez

FIGURE 6-6 Well-written routine request letter in block format with mixed punctutation

Letters with Positive Messages

A receiver will react favorably to a letter that contains a positive message. Examples of documents that contain positive messages are orders, positive responses to requests, and goodwill letters. For these letters use the direct order:

Main Idea	Says "yes" to the receiver.
Supporting Information	Provides any details the receiver needs to carry out specific instructions.
Goodwill Closing	Ends with a helpful, positive closing. If the sender sells goods or services, the closing should contain a soft sale.

Orders

Companies usually place orders by using a form called a *purchase order*. Occasionally, a small company or an individual will use a letter to place an order. "Please send me . . ." is the main idea of an order letter. Provide complete supporting information to ensure an order will be filled correctly and to avoid wasting time and money. Formatting the middle paragraph as a table provides clarity and completeness. An order letter is organized in the direct order:

Main Idea	Asks the receiver to fill the order.
Supporting Information	Supplies specific details needed by the receiver. For each item ordered, indicate the stock number or catalog number, a description including the size and color where applicable, quantity ordered, unit cost, total cost, method of shipment and shipping address, and method of payment.
Goodwill Closing	Ends with a statement indicating the action the receiver should take.

Figure 6-7 on page 204 illustrates a poorly written order letter. Figure 6-8 on page 205 illustrates a well-written order letter.

Positive Responses to a Request

A positive response letter tells the receiver the sender is saying "yes" to a request. The direct order is used for positive responses:

Main Idea	Gives a positive response to the request.
Supporting Information	Provides necessary information so that the receiver knows what the sender is offering and expects. Also makes necessary requests.
Goodwill Closing	Ends with a courteous, positive statement and possibly a reminder of any action the sender wants the receiver to take. If the sender is a profit-seeking organization, the closing should include a soft sale.

KEY POINT

- Failing to place ordered items in an easy-to-read table can cause the shipping clerk to miss part of your order.
- Forms for purchase orders and procedures for completing them usually are included in the operations manual of an organization.

If you wanted help in writing a letter to a Chinese businessperson, the web site **www./saacnet.com/executive summary.html** could help you.

KEY POINT

A soft sale is an easy way to remind a customer of a company's products or services.

Figure 6-9 on page 206 is an example of a poorly written positive response to a request for someone to speak at a conference. Figure 6-10 on page 207 is an example of a well-written positive response. Note that the supporting information confirms such details as the date, time, and place and makes a request of the receiver.

A positive response to a credit request is a letter that contains a positive message. The following example contains the body of a positive response for a charge account. It is poorly written.

Thank you for your application for a charge account at Al's Building Supplies. When we receive such applications, we always examine them very carefully.

All our accounts have credit terms of 2/10, net/30. After examining your credit background, we were surprised to find such a good credit history. As a result, we are giving you a $15,000 limit on your account.

We hope to see you soon.

The following example presents a well-written positive response to a credit request. The supporting information includes a description of restrictions on the account and the payment terms. The closing includes an effectively written soft sale.

Your Al's Building Supplies charge account is ready for you. Thank you for your interest in our products.

For new accounts, the terms are 2/10, net/30. Because your credit rating and references are excellent, the limit for your account is $15,000.

Enclosed are catalogs of our products. If you have any questions about them, call 1-800-555-0300. Our trained salespeople will be happy to help you.

Goodwill Letters

A goodwill letter can be an acknowledgment or a friendly message designed to build relationships. Effectively written goodwill letters help increase the receiver's positive feelings toward the sender. Goodwill letters may express congratulations, sympathy, welcome, or appreciation. They may also extend invitations or acknowledge an order or receipt of something. The expression is the main idea of a goodwill message.

When a person sends too many goodwill letters, the receivers may question the motivation behind them.

Tamara Hindelworth

4509 EAST KEYNOTE DRIVE
TEXARKANA, KY 42601-9051

July 9, 20—

Whitlock Catalog Sales
708 North 14th East
Odgen, UT 84625-0096

MERCHANDISE ORDER

I was looking at your recent sales catalog and became very excited when I saw that you had Winthrop Drill sets for $49. I could use three sets of these drills as I am going to use them for Christmas gifts for my sons.

Also, I saw that you carry Osborne bone china dishes. I love your Morning Glory pattern and want 2 sets of eight place settings at $75 each. These dishes will be used for my daughter and granddaughter for Christmas.

I have enclosed a check for the total amount that includes the $25 for shipping. Thank you.

Tamara Hindleworth

Tamara Hindleworth

FIGURE 6-7 Poorly written order letter in simplified block format

Effective

Tamara Hindelworth

4509 EAST KEYNOTE DRIVE
TEXARKANA, KY 42601-9051

July 9, 20—

WHITLOCK CATALOG SALES
708 NORTH 14TH EAST
OGDEN UT 84625-0096

MERCHANDISE ORDER

I was leafing through your most recent sales catalog and saw some amazing buys. Please send me the following merchandise:

Item No.	Item Description	No. Ordered	Cost per Unit	Cost
456-t	Winthrop Drill Set	3	$49.00	$147.00
9071	Osborne Bone China Service for Eight	2	75.00	150.00
	Shipping Costs			25.00
	Total Costs			**$322.00**

Please send these items to

Tamara Hindleworth
4509 East Keynote Drive
Texarkana, KY 42601-9051

I have enclosed a check for the total amount. I look forward to receiving these items soon. Thank you.

Tamara Hindleworth

Tamara Hindleworth

FIGURE 6-8 Well-written order letter in simplified block format with letter address for a window envelope

**Microcomputer
Services Company, Inc.**

13450 Grant Boulevard
Greenville, SC 50298-1345
864-555-1134
Fax 864-555-1178

September 10, 20—

Ms. Elizabeth Shiflett
4103 East Waketon Avenue
Greenville, SC 50293-4303

Dear Elizabeth

We appreciate your coming to interview with us for our position of training
director in the Office Services Department. There were many really well-
qualified individuals that applied for this position. We were surprised by
competition for this position.

During your visit, we were impressed with your knowledge of our company and
of the management techniques that we use. Your positive attitude is very apparent.

Thus, we would like to offer the position to you. If you accept our offer, your
starting date would be July 1. If this date is inconvenient, please let us know—
we have flexibility. Your annual salary will be $27,000, and you will be paid
$1,125 semimonthly.

Please let us know your decision in writing by Wednesday, October 1.

We anxiously await your reply and hope that you will accept our offer. If you
have any questions, call me at (864) 555-1134.

Sincerely

Harry James

Harry James
Vice President of
Administrative Services

rk

FIGURE 6-9 Poorly written positive response letter in block format with open punctuation

Effective

Microcomputer
Services Company, Inc.

13450 Grant Boulevard
Greenville, SC 50298-1345
864-555-1134
Fax 864-555-1178

September 10, 20—

Ms. Elizabeth Shiflett
4103 East Waketon Avenue
Greenville, SC 50293-4303

Dear Elizabeth

Congratulations! You have been selected for the position of training director in
the Office Services Department.

During your visit, we were impressed with your knowledge of our company and
of the management techniques that we use. Your positive attitude is very apparent.

Your starting date is July 1. If this date is inconvenient, please let us know—
there is some flexibility. Your annual salary will be $27,000, and you will be
paid $1,125 semimonthly.

Please let us know your decision in writing by Wednesday, October 1.

Elizabeth, we eagerly await your reply and hope that you will accept our offer.
If you have any questions, please call me at (864) 555-1134.

Sincerely

Harry James

Harry James
Vice President of
Administrative Services

rk

FIGURE 6-10 Well-written positive response letter in block format with open punctuation

Friendship Letters

A **friendship letter** says nonverbally to your receiver, "I want a positive interpersonal relationship with you." This type of letter may or may not need supporting information. For example, when expressing sympathy, details are inappropriate. Yet, details in an invitation are critical because the receiver needs to know who is invited, when and where the occasion will be held, and how to dress.

The following congratulatory message needs no supporting information:

Main Idea	Congratulations on your recent promotion to Supervisor of Office Services.
Goodwill Closing	You truly deserve this promotion, and those who will work for you will be fortunate to have you as their supervisor.

The following invitation includes necessary supporting information:

Main Idea	You are invited to a small surprise party celebrating Mark Mortonsen's recent promotion.
Supporting Information	It will be held on the third floor in the cafeteria at 4:15 p.m. on Wednesday, August 25.
Goodwill Closing	Come and help us congratulate Mark. RSVP by Monday, August 23, ext. 5068.

Acknowledgment Letters

An **acknowledgment letter** tells a sender that a message has been received. The main purpose of an acknowledgment is to maintain or build goodwill. An acknowledgment also may be used to inform the receiver that a request cannot be filled right away. These messages often are used to acknowledge orders and credit applications. The supporting information usually reveals the reasons for the delay, and the goodwill closing contains a soft sale, as shown below.

Main Idea	Thank you for your order. We are pleased to have you as one of our customers.
Supporting Information	The demand for the earthenware plant holders has far exceeded our supply. Your order will be sent May 15, the day we expect our shipment.
Goodwill Closing	In the meantime, look over the enclosed flyer announcing our "Spring Fling Sale." Place your order now to enjoy 50 percent savings on several items.

The checklist below will help you compose effective letters that contain a neutral or positive message. Questions in the planning stage will help you determine the content of the message and adjust it to your receiver. The writing stage will help you to organize and present the message in a complete, considerate manner. The editing stage will help you make your writing correct and concise.

Checklist for Neutral or Positive Messages

Planning Stage

❏ Have I identified the objective of the message?

❏ Have I identified the main idea of the message?

❏ Have I identified the supporting information needed by the receiver?

❏ Have I adjusted the main idea and supporting information to the needs and background of my receiver?

Writing Stage

❏ Have I presented the main idea in the first or second sentence of the first paragraph?

❏ Have I presented all supporting information the receiver will need in order to do what I want?

❏ Have I presented the supporting information after the main idea?

❏ Is the ending friendly, courteous, and personable?

Editing Stage

❏ Is the language clear and concise, and is the message in the appropriate tone?

❏ Are format, grammar, punctuation, and spelling correct?

❏ Are the first and last paragraphs no longer than four lines each?

❏ Are other paragraphs no longer than eight lines?

5 Checkpoint

Letters with Neutral or Positive Messages

Indicate whether each statement is true or false.

1. Use the indirect order for letters with a positive message.
2. In routine requests, the receiver views the main idea of the letter neutrally.
3. All goodwill letters require supporting information.
4. In an order letter, some of the supporting information should be placed in tables.
5. A claim letter should be written in the indirect order when the sender asks for a refund.

Check your answers in Appendix E.

TECHNOLOGY

Technological Advances Create Dilemmas for Companies

In today's world, technological advances are continual. Computer chips become smaller but store more and more information. Computer usage in automobile production is becoming increasingly common. Companies seek these inventions because of potential profitability.

But what all can companies do with the advances they create? In a way, they are free to do with them as they choose, but there may be consequences. For example, during the Cold War, Toshiba Corporation developed a technology for milling-machine tools that brought millions of dollars worth of sales from many countries—including Russia.

Russia, then, was able to build quieter submarines. The sale of this technology violated regulatory rules of trade with the Communist Bloc countries, resulting in a conflict between Toshiba and the United States Senate. The Senate threatened to ban Toshiba's products from the United States for two to five years. To avoid this punishment, Toshiba promised to sell its technology only to approved countries. ■

CASE 6:

Answers

Responses to Questions 3 and 4 in Chapter Opener

3. Are the same steps used in planning all types of letters?
Yes, the steps for planning letters are the same; however, the content will vary.

4. How are letters with a neutral or positive message alike? How do they differ?
These letters use the same steps for planning, use the direct order, and generally have the same content—a main idea, supporting information, and an ending. They may use any of the formats (block, modified block, and simplified block). They differ in that some goodwill letters need no supporting information.

- -

DISCUSSION QUESTIONS

1. Where is the main idea placed in letters containing neutral or positive messages? Why?
2. What supporting information should be included in (a) an order? (b) a routine request? (c) a positive response to a request? (d) a goodwill letter?
3. Why is a goodwill closing important?

Writing Letters with a Negative Message

Objectives

Objective

1 ☞

Planning Letters with Negative Messages

A **letter containing a negative message** conveys news that will disappoint the receiver. Letters that deny requests, decline to supply information, refuse credit, or reject a proposal are examples of this type of letter. Careful planning and organizing are required to convey the disappointing news and yet maintain goodwill. Achieving this goal is challenging, especially when the receiver of the letter has a different cultural heritage. People from other cultures may view the average U.S. businessperson's use of concise writing as somewhat short and abrupt.

The tone of a letter that contains a negative message should reflect a sincere concern for the receiver's interests. Your aim is to present the unfavorable news positively and in a manner the receiver will view as fair and, if possible, in the receiver's best interests.

The steps in planning these messages are to identify the objective, identify the main idea, determine the supporting information, and adjust the content to the receiver:

KEY POINT

Laws guide society through tough times. Well-written letters that contain negative messages are like laws—they get businesses through tough times, yet maintain goodwill.

Identify the Objective	Convey the unfavorable news yet maintain goodwill.
Identify the Main Idea	State the refusal in a positive way that reflects the receiver's best interests.
Determine the Supporting Information	Determine what, if any, additional background information the receiver may need; determine logical reasons for the refusal; and determine possible benefits to the receiver.
Adjust the Content to the Receiver	Determine the receiver's values and concerns. Adjust the supporting information accordingly.

Organizing Letters with Negative Messages

Letters that convey a negative message are organized in the indirect order. Indirect order presents the reasons or details that explain the unfavorable news before stating the negative news itself. The reasons are presented first to prepare the receiver for the unfavorable news. The direct order is used in letters that contain negative messages only when the sender knows the receiver prefers the direct order.

When organizing a letter in indirect order to convey unfavorable news, follow these steps:

1. Begin with a neutral opening.
2. Explain the reasons for the negative news.
3. State or imply the negative news.
4. Close on a positive note; if possible, offer an alternative.

Neutral Opening

The objectives of the opening are to establish rapport and to focus the receiver's attention on the topic of the letter. To establish rapport, the opening paragraph should contain a **neutral opening**—implying neither a positive nor a negative response to the receiver. A neutral opening does not mislead the receiver into thinking the response is positive, nor does it discourage the receiver by revealing the negative news.

In the openings of letters containing a negative message, maintain a positive tone by avoiding the use of negative words or phrases such as *unable, regret to tell you, a problem exists,* or *unfortunately.* Instead, use positive, neutral words and phrases such as *appreciate, agree with you,* and *thank you.*

Avoid opening a letter containing a negative message by referring to the date of the receiver's previous communication. For example, "Thank you for your letter of August 10" is an overused opening. This opening does not introduce the topic of the message. The following opening introduces the topic:

Your application for a charge account received our immediate attention.

Assume that the sender is writing to refuse a request to serve on a committee. Examples of bad and good neutral openings for this situation follow:

Bad Openings	Good Openings
Serving on such an important committee would be a real pleasure.	Thank you for asking me to serve on the Improvements Committee.

DIVERSITY
In Latin American cultures, writers do not use direct order for letters that contain negative messages. To state the negative news before explaining the reasons behind the news is considered extremely offensive.

KEY POINT
If you state your negative response or imply it in the opening, the receiver may become so upset that he or she stops reading.

Bad Openings	Good Openings
The Improvements Committee is an important committee on which to serve.	I agree with you. The Improvements Committee is very important.
I wish I could serve on the Improvements Committee.	I appreciate the opportunity to serve on the Improvements Committee.

6 *Checkpoint*

Neutral Openings

For the following situation, rate each neutral opening as good or poor. If poor, explain why.

Situation: You are a manager for a company that gives seminars on effective business communication. Dr. James Jiang, a professor at Northeast College, has requested techniques for writing letters containing negative messages. Because your business depends upon teaching such information, you cannot share the techniques.

1. I have been asked to respond to your letter of August 15.
2. Writing effective letters containing negative messages is a demanding task.
3. GoodCom Seminars, Inc., always gives consumers what they want.
4. Writing effective letters containing negative messages is an interesting challenge.
5. I wish I could send you the techniques you requested.

Check your answers in Appendix E.

Reasons for the Negative Message

The supporting information in a letter containing a negative message provides the reasons for the negative news. This section may have one or two paragraphs, depending on the complexity of the letter. Present the receiver with a logical explanation of the reasons why you cannot grant the request. Keep the letter unified by concentrating on one or two main reasons.

If possible, emphasize how the reasons will ultimately benefit the receiver. Also, do not use company policy as a basis for denying a request. Although citing company policy may be appropriate in some cases, always explain how this policy benefits the receiver. If the message does not explain company policy, the goodwill between a company and its customers may be damaged.

In the following examples, the reasons on the left are company-oriented rather than you-oriented. The reasons on the right are you- or receiver-oriented.

Poorly Written Reasons	Well-Written Reasons
We would like to repair your cellular phone, but company policy forbids it.	Providing free repair of cellular phones out of warranty would add greatly to the retail prices of our phones. For example, . .
If we replaced your sprinkler or refunded your money, we would be doing the work of the shipping company. Write to them and ask them to refund your money. They have insurance to cover their costs.	We chose the company that ships our merchandise carefully. This shipper guarantees its service yet keeps your costs low. The shipping invoice on your sprinkler indicates that it was in working condition when it was shipped. Consequently, you will need to contact the shipping company to request a replacement or refund.

> **KEY POINT**
>
> The most important elements in a letter with a negative message are the reasons for the negative response. If these reasons are explained well, the receiver will accept the negative news; if they are explained poorly, the letter may damage goodwill.

Checkpoint 7

Reasons for the Negative Message

For the following situation, rate each reason for the negative message as good or poor. Explain your rating.

Situation: You are a manager for a company that gives seminars on effective communication. Dr. James Jiang, a professor at Northeast College, has requested techniques for writing letters containing negative messages. Because your business depends upon teaching such information, you cannot share the techniques.

1. We receive many requests for the techniques used in our seminars. When we have supplied them in the past, our seminar attendance has decreased.

2. GoodCom Seminars, Inc., is dedicated to helping customers improve their communication skills. Customers attend our seminars to increase their efficiency and to gain a competitive edge.

3. Giving you our techniques would decrease our potential profits.

4. The policy of GoodCom Seminars, Inc., prohibits sharing techniques.

5. We appreciate your interest in our presentation materials. They were developed over many years and are the primary reason executives attend our seminars.

Check your answers in Appendix E.

SECTION 6.3 • WRITING LETTERS WITH A NEGATIVE MESSAGE   **215**

**Personal Qualities:
Social**
Learn to think in positive terms.
You and your coworkers will
be much happier.

The Negative Message

After learning the reasons for the negative message, the receiver should be mentally prepared to receive the actual refusal. If the reasons are logical, the refusal will evolve almost naturally. Soften the negative message by implying it rather than stating it directly. Convey the message quickly using positive language if possible.

To imply the bad news and to avoid using negative-toned words, (1) use an "if" clause, (2) use the passive voice, or (3) focus on what you can do rather than what you cannot do.

Avoid using the personal pronouns—*I, me, my, mine, we, our, ours, us, you, your,* and *yours*—when using negative language. These personal pronouns combined with negative language can insult the receiver.

In the following examples, those on the left are poorly written. Those on the right are well written.

↓**KEY POINT**

- Most of the time, it is possible to use positive language and avoid negative language altogether.
- In well-written letters that contain a negative message that must include negative language, the reasons for the negative response are more important. When using negative language, make sure the reasons for the negative response are receiver-oriented.

Poorly Written "No's"	Well-Written "No's"
I cannot send you your order today.	If I could, I would send your order today.
	Your order will be sent as soon as our new shipment is received.
	Your order will be sent as soon as we receive the shipment from our supplier.
Because your camera is no longer under warranty, I cannot grant your request for a replacement. I have to deny your request because your camera is not under warranty.	If your camera were still under warranty, it would be replaced. Only cameras under warranty are replaced free of charge.

8 *Checkpoint*

The Negative Message

Write each of the following sentences using only positive language.
1. I cannot send your order until September 5.
2. Don't hand in your assignment until it is finished.
3. Because he was less qualified, he did not get the job.
4. We can't send you the paper you requested because we are sold out.
5. The concert must be cancelled because the lead singer is sick.

Check your answers in Appendix E.

The Closing

The closing of a letter containing a negative message should be courteous and helpful. The purpose of the closing is to maintain or rebuild goodwill. After refusing the receiver's request (the negative news), change the emphasis and close on a positive note.

To maintain a positive tone, (1) do not mention or remind the receiver of the negative news again, and (2) do not apologize because you cannot accommodate the receiver. If a mistake has not been made, an apology is not appropriate. If you did make a mistake, you owe the receiver an apology. However, place the apology in the middle paragraphs—not in the closing.

The closing should have a sincere tone. Avoid overused closings such as, "If you have any questions, please don't hesitate to call." Use a similar statement but with a positive tone: "If you have any questions, please call." Avoid using conditional words such as *hope, think,* and *maybe.*

Offer the receiver another option. Most problem situations have more than one solution. Presenting another option shifts the emphasis from the negative news to a positive solution.

The following examples illustrate both poorly written and well-written closings:

Goodwill is the one and only asset that competition cannot undersell or destroy. Only you can let goodwill slip away.

Poorly Written Closings	Well-Written Closings
Even though we cannot fill your order, we have enclosed our newest catalogue.	Because part No. 1403 is no longer being manufactured, part No. 1402 is being used as a substitute. The substitute part is only $15 and functions just as well as part No. 1403. If you would like to order part No. 1402, call me at 1-800-555-9021. Your order will be shipped the day you place your order.
I'm sorry that we cannot fill your order, but we have enclosed our newest catalogue.	
Even though we cannot fill your order, if there is anything I can do, please let me know.	

If the receiver is a customer, you may close the message with a soft sale by mentioning a related product, a discount, or some other relevant item that would interest the receiver. In this situation, your job is to get the customer in the store or using your services again.

Poorly Written Closings	Well-Written Closings
Some of our materials are greatly reduced. Come in and see them soon.	Our latest sales brochure is enclosed. Note that some of our materials are reduced by by as much as 50 percent. Come in and see them soon.
We appreciate your business. Come in and see us soon.	

9 Checkpoint

The Closing

Based on the following situation, rate each closing as good or poor. Explain all ratings.

Situation: Once again, you are a manager for a company that gives seminars on effective communication. Dr. James Jiang, a professor at Northeast College, has requested techniques for writing letters containing negative messages. Because your business depends upon teaching such information, you cannot share the techniques.

1. My sincere hope is that this response meets with your satisfaction.

2. As you may know, our seminars are very effective. Attend one and you not only will learn the techniques but also will gain insights into the techniques themselves. A list of the times and places of the seminars, an enrollment card, and a coupon for a 25 percent discount on enrollment are enclosed.

3. Dr. Jiang, several other companies might share their techniques. Have you tried SITCOM Co. or LITCOM, Inc.? Their addresses are enclosed.

4. I am truly sorry that I cannot grant your request.

5. Our library is extensive, and we often allow researchers to use it. If you are interested, please call to arrange a time convenient for you.

Check your answers in Appendix E.

Writing Letters with Negative Messages

Objective

3

Letters with negative messages that need special attention are messages that (1) decline a request and (2) refuse credit.

Declining a Request

The reasons for declining a request are the most important aspect of **request denial letters**. The success of the message depends on whether the receiver judges these reasons as valid. Figure 6-11 on page 220 illustrates a poorly written letter that declines a request and Figure 6-12 on page 221 illustrates a well-written letter that declines a request.

Refusing Credit

Credit may be refused for several reasons. The credit application may contain incomplete information or insufficient credit references. The references may not be verifiable, or they may be bad. The employment record may not be strong enough or verifiable. The applicant may have excessive debt obligations, delinquent credit obligations, or insufficient income.

SCANS
Employability

Basic Skills: Writing
Initially, writing effective letters that contain a negative message will take more time than writing other letters. As you write more and more of them, however, the process will become easier and less time-consuming.

If credit must be refused, the receiver has a right to know why. The sender's responsibility is to explain the reasons tactfully. The goal is to refuse credit but maintain the person as a cash customer. Here is an example of the body of a well-written letter that denies credit.

> Thank you for your order for Stonecut Flooring. You certainly have selected a quality product that is extremely durable.
>
> Your credit application has been reviewed. As you probably know, financial experts suggest that individuals maintain an income-to-debt ratio of about 3 to 1. Because your obligations extend beyond one-third of your income, we suggest that a cash purchase be made.
>
> Please let us know if you wish to place a cash order now. In addition to flooring, we have many other quality products for your home at low, discounted prices.
>
> As a cash customer, you will receive the same quality merchandise, courtesy, and low prices.

The checklist on page 222 will help you to compose effective letters that contain a negative message.

Credit laws require credit lenders to inform receivers of their rights when they have been refused credit. If these rights are explained in legalistic language and are not clear, help the receiver by writing the refusal letter in clear, easy-to-understand language; then, enclose the required statements on a card.

Writing Letters with Both Positive and Negative Messages

Once in a while, you may have to write a letter that contains both a positive and a negative message. The steps for planning this type of letter are the same as for other messages (see page 212 for the steps). However, in these situations, you will have two main ideas instead of just one—the positive message is the first idea and the negative message is the second. When organizing these letters, use the negative message plan but use the positive message for the neutral beginning. In the following example, the positive message is that part of an order is being filled; the negative message is that part of it isn't being filled.

Good News Beginning	Thank you for your order of four Greg Fisher CDs and three Viewmaster CDs. The four Greg Fisher CDs are being shipped to you today.
Reasons for the Bad News	The demand for the Viewmaster CDs has far exceeded expectations. As a result, the supply of these CDs is presently depleted.
The Bad News	However, a new shipment will arrive on Thursday of this week. Your Viewmaster CDs will be mailed to you the day they arrive.
Soft Sale	A catalog of our new arrivals is enclosed. Some are as much as 50 percent below retail prices. Find those that you would like and send us your order soon.

Lee's Electronic Store

906 North Main Street
Boswell, AR 72790-0001
870-555-2342
Fax: 870-555-5710

April 26, 20—

Mr. Alex White
3692 South Whitestone Drive
Allentown, TN 37662-1240

Dear Mr. White:

    I received your request for a refund of $159.58 for the video cassette player you bought at our recent "Clearout Sale." I'm sorry, your request cannot be granted.

    When we have a sale such as the "Clearout Sale," signs are posted all over the store which clearly state that all sales are final. Thus, even though all video cassette players have a one-year warranty, this guarantee does not apply during major sales. ALL SALES ARE FINAL!

    Mr. White, I am sorry for this misunderstanding. But do come in and see us again. We are having another big "Clearout Sale" next week.

Sincerely,

John Lee

John Lee
Manager

FIGURE 6-11 Poorly written letter declining a request in block format with mixed punctuation and indented paragraphs

Effective

Lee's Electronic Store

906 North Main Street
Boswell, AR 72790-0001
870-555-2342
Fax: 870-555-5710

April 26, 20—

Mr. Alex White
3692 South Whitestone Drive
Allentown, TN 37662-1240

Dear Mr. White:

Your request for a refund or replacement of a video cassette player was brought to my attention. You bought an excellent player when you purchased the X-100.

When a sale such as the "Clearout Sale" is held, prices are cut drastically in an effort to clear out selected models of merchandise. During these sales, signs are posted at many places throughout the store stating that all sales are final. To provide refunds or replacement on sales merchandise would drive up consumer prices 50 percent. For example, a $150 item would cost $225.

Mr. White, if the video cassette player had been purchased at a regular retail price, a refund or replacement would have been possible. However, if you will bring the video cassette player in, we will repair it free of charge.

Enclosed is a certificate for 25 percent off your next purchase at Lee's. Presently, we are having a 33 percent off sale on computers and software. Come in, use your certificate, and take advantage of this opportunity.

Sincerely,

John Lee

John Lee
Manager

FIGURE 6-12 Well-written letter declining a request in block format with mixed punctuation and indented paragraphs

Checklist for Writing Negative Messages

Planning Stage

❏ Have I identified the objective of the message?

❏ Have I identified the main idea of the message?

❏ Have I identified the supporting information needed by the receiver?

❏ Have I adjusted the main idea and supporting information to the receiver?

Writing Stage

❏ Is the opening neutral and does it introduce the topic of the message?

❏ Does the supporting information focus on one or two receiver-oriented reasons for the negative message?

❏ When giving the negative message, have I used positive language?

❏ When giving the negative message, have I used an *if* clause or the passive voice (if possible)?

❏ When giving the negative message, have I told the receiver what could be done rather than what couldn't?

❏ Is the closing helpful and courteous? (Including a soft sale is appropriate in a letter to a customer.)

❏ Does the closing offer an alternative if possible, contain no apology, and avoid reminders of the negative message?

Editing Stage

❏ Is the language clear and concise? Is the tone positive?

❏ Are the format, grammar, punctuation, and spelling correct?

DIVERSITY

Overcoming Groupthink through Diversity

The United States Bureau of Labor Statistics has made some interesting predictions. By the year 2000, 85 percent of those entering the workforce will be women, minorities, and immigrants. Only 15 percent will be white males. By the year 2005, 27 percent of the workforce will be made up of groups now considered to be minorities. Women will make up approximately 48 percent of the workforce, and more than 22 million workers will be over age 50.

This change comes with advantages. For example, a problem often faced by groups is "groupthink," or members who think alike because of similar backgrounds. Some people believe the *Challenger* space shuttle disaster was caused, in part, by groupthink—that the thinking patterns of those involved were so much alike, potential problems could not be anticipated.

An advantage of diversity, such as that predicted by the Bureau of Labor Statistics, is that team members who come from different backgrounds do not think alike. Thus, ideas are analyzed from differing perspectives. ■

CASE 6:

Answers

Responses to Questions 5 and 6 in Chapter Opener

5. **Why does Maria consider some of the letters with a negative message a little short and somewhat blunt or tactless?**
   Because Maria is of Mexican heritage, she expects this type of letter to be longer than the average American businessperson would expect it to be. Thus, she views some of the letters as somewhat tactless and blunt.

6. **Should a writer consider culture or nationality when writing his or her letters? If so, why?**
   Yes. The expectations of the receivers often depend upon the culture or nationality.

DISCUSSION QUESTIONS

1. What are the steps in planning a letter containing a negative message?
2. Why is the indirect order used in most letters that contain a negative message?
3. Explain the purpose of the opening, supporting information, and closing of a letter that contains a negative message.

CASE 6:
Summary

If Maria had a better understanding of letter writing and the formats used when writing letters, she would probably be more comfortable with her job. She would understand that letters will vary in length because of purpose and will vary in appearance because of format.

In a world that is becoming more and more globalized, the impact of nationality or heritage on communications becomes increasingly important. For example, Maria feels that some of the letters that white Americans are writing are abrupt or short. In the Mexican culture, letters are generally longer—especially letters that contain a negative message. Remembering to adjust your message for your receiver is extremely important when communicating with a person of a different heritage.

Chapter Summary

Section 6.1 Selecting Order and Formatting Your Letters

1 Identify the use of letters. A letter is a format that is common in the business world. This format is used for external communication. Thus, messages sent to individuals outside of an organization are using the letter format.

2 Select the correct order for letters. When determining the type of letter you are writing, try to perceive the letter as the receiver will view it. When the receiver views the letter as containing a neutral or positive message, use the direct order. When the receiver views the letter as containing a negative message, use the indirect order.

3 **Describe the standard and optional parts of a business letter.** The standard parts of a letter include a dateline, letter address, salutation, body, complimentary close, writer's name and title, reference initials, and copy notation. The optional parts of a letter are attention line, subject line, company title, enclosure notation, postscript, and second-page heading.

4 **Use the block, modified block, and simplified block letter formats.** The three acceptable letter formats are called block, modified block, and simplified block. In the block format, every line of the letter begins at the left margin. In the modified block, the dateline, the complimentary close, the company title if included, and the writer's name and title start at the middle of the page. All other parts begin at the left margin. In the simplified block format, all parts begin at the left margin, but the salutation and complimentary close are omitted.

5 **Prepare a business envelope.** The business envelope is $9\frac{1}{2}$ by $4\frac{1}{8}$ inches. Place the address on line 13 or 14. Begin four inches from the left side of the envelope. All information should be keyed in capital letters, omitting any punctuation marks.

Section 6.2 Writing Letters with a Neutral or Positive Message

1 **Plan letters with neutral or positive messages.** The steps for planning letters that contain a neutral or positive message are (1) identify the letter's objective, (2) identify its main idea, (3) determine its supporting information, and (4) adjust the content for the receiver.

2 **Organize letters with neutral or positive messages.** When organizing letters with neutral or positive messages, use direct order. In the direct order, the main idea of the message comes before its supporting information.

3 **Write letters that contain neutral or positive messages.** When writing letters that contain neutral or positive messages, ask yourself these questions:
1. Have I presented the main idea in the first or second sentence of the first paragraph?
2. Have I presented all supporting information the receiver will need in order to do what I want?
3. Have I presented the supporting information after the main idea?
4. Is the ending friendly, courteous, and personable?

Section 6.3 Writing Letters with Negative Messages

1 **Plan letters containing negative messages.** The planning of a letter that contains a negative message follows the same four steps as a letter that contains a neutral or positive message. The steps are (1) identify its objective, (2) identify its main idea, (3) determine its supporting information, and (4) adjust the content for its receiver.

2 **Organize letters containing negative messages.** The organization of a letter that contains a negative message differs from a letter that contains a neutral or positive message. Letters that contain a negative message are written in indirect order which means that the supporting information is given before the main idea. Letters with a neutral or positive message are written in the direct order.

3 **Write letters containing negative messages.** When writing letters with a negative message, ask yourself these questions:
  1. Is the opening neutral and does it introduce the topic of the letter?
  2. Does the supporting information focus on one or two receiver-oriented reasons for the negative news?
  3. When giving the negative news, have I used positive language?
  4. When giving the negative news, have I used an *if* clause or the passive voice?
  5. When giving the negative news, have I told the receiver what could be done rather than what couldn't?
  6. Is the closing helpful and courteous? (Including a soft sale is appropriate in a letter to a customer.)
  7. Does the closing offer an alternative, contain no apology, and/or avoid reminders of the negative message?

Critical Thinking Questions

  1. Why is the formatting of a letter important?
  2. Why is the opening of a letter containing a positive message different from an opening of a letter containing a negative message?
  3. Are the objectives of most letters similar? Justify your answer. Are the main ideas of most letters similar? Justify your answer.

Applications

Part A. Indicate the type of letter each sentence might open: order, acknowledgment, positive response, request, and claim.

1. Please replace this faulty lock.
2. I would like to open a charge account with your company.
3. Your account has been adjusted as you requested.
4. Here are the prints you ordered.
5. Your order for 12 two-drawer Ez-Clos file cabinets has been received.
6. Please credit my account for the cost of one 16-oz. container of Restoration Carpet Cleaner.

Part B. As the owner of Clean Business, Inc., you have received a letter from Dr. J. J. Mortichi, President of the Mortichi Clinic. He is worried about the health hazards of cleaning solutions used at the clinic. Write to him to explain that the cleaning solutions your employees use are proven safe and effective. Use the modified block format, and make up any information you need, including the letter address.

Part C. In your role as a worker in the registrar's office of Westlake Community College, you received a letter from a transfer student who wants to know the registration dates for the coming term. Use the block format to provide this information in a letter to the student. Make up any information you need to write this letter.

Part D. Compose a letter congratulating a friend on a recent promotion, anniversary, birthday, or other event. Supply all necessary information.

Part E. Assume that you are a loan officer for Stonehead First National Bank. You have received a request for a $25,000 home improvement loan from Mr. and Mrs. James Kennedy of 973 East Ashbrooke Drive, Tennison, VA 22812-3735. Write Mr. and Mrs. Kennedy, acknowledge receipt of their application, and explain that processing will take about ten days.

Part F. Write Mr. and Mrs. Kennedy, using the address shown in Application Part E, and tell them their loan has been approved. Advise them that they must sign the loan agreement within 14 days. Because they are such a good credit risk, tell them of other loans available to them, such as car loans, small investment loans, and boat loans.

Part G. Rosa Bennett has written you, the manager of Katina's Fashions, to request a charge account. Write Ms. Bennett and ask her to complete and return the enclosed credit application. Explain that application processing takes about two weeks. Ms. Bennett lives at 4391 North Plum Tree Avenue, Apartment #6, Rio de Piedras, CA 92383-0413.

Part H. Write Ms. Bennett at the address shown in Application Part G, and tell her the credit application with Katina's Fashions, 391 East Kamala Lane, San Jacinto, CA 92383-0413, has been approved. Her account will have a $500 limit. The interest rate on the unpaid balance at the end of each billing period—30 days—is 18 percent a year.

Part I. Mays Printing Service prepared and printed a resume for Ms. Pam Donaldson. The resume was printed exactly as she specified. She proofread the resume but overlooked a mistake in the spelling of a previous employer's name. The resume was printed with the mistake, and she has asked for a refund. As manager of Mays Printing Service, write Ms. Donaldson, 1607 North Benard Avenue, River City, TN 37415-0551, and refuse her request.

Part J. Look at the letter contained in Figure 6-8—a letter to Whitlock Catalog Sales from Tamara Hindleworth. Write Ms. Hindleworth a letter of acknowledgment.

Part K. Using the letter in Figure 6-8, write Ms. Hindleworth a letter telling her that the drill sets will be shipped immediately. Also tell her that because of great demand, Whitlock is temporarily out of the dish sets, but you expect a shipment of them in two weeks. You will send her dish sets then.

Part L. You are Ms. Hindleworth, who placed the order described in Figure 6-8. When you received the dish sets, one of the plates in one of the sets was broken. Write the company you ordered the dish sets from and ask for a replacement.

Part M. As credit manager for Best Foods, Inc., write Ms. Chantel Washington, 445 Ocean View Lane, New Beach, CT 06513-1413, and refuse her request for credit. At present, she has many charge accounts that are charged to their limits. She might not be able to make the payments if you allowed her additional credit.

Part N. Ms. Kathy O'Neal, 2903 North Woodhaven, Mount Whitney, WA 98273-9998, bought a dress from your department at Elaine's Dress Shoppe. All dresses are altered to fit the customer. After Ms. O'Neal had the dress altered, she decided it was the wrong color. She has returned the dress and has asked for a refund. As manager of Elaine's, write to her and refuse the request.

Part O. Ashad Mostika of 2148 Western Golf Avenue, Chicago, IL 60505-6131, a recent immigrant to this country, has sent you a credit application. Write Mr. Mostika and refuse his request because of his lack of credit references.

Edit and rewrite the following letter. First, format it in block format with open punctuation. Then format it in modified block format with mixed punctuation and paragraphs beginning at the left margin.

words@work

If you are using *words@work*, complete the activities on Business Letters in the Writing at Work section.

April 14, 20—/Mr. Marvin Fontana/98 Barfield Road/Atlanta, GA 30328-5187/Dear Mr. Fontana

Welcome to First Bank. We have enclosed a brochure that will answer any question's about your new checking account.

In addition to that brochure, enclosed you will find your "Everywhere" automated teller machine card with this letter. Let us point out that you can use your "Everywhere" card at any First Valley Bank branches. In addition, you can use them at any other teller machines anywhere that displays the "everywhere" logo.

Thank you once more for chosing First Bank. We are pleased to be able to serve your banking need.

Sincerely/Nancy Tallman/Customer Service

Representative/cp/Enclosure

1. (a) Send an e-mail to the Admissions Office of a university asking them to send you admissions materials, registration dates, and brochures about the university. Put the e-mail in letter format. Print a copy of your e-mail to hand in to your instructor.
    (b) Write your instructor a memo in the simplified format, answering these questions:
    1. What type of letter are you writing?
    2. What order should you use?
    3. What is its main idea?
    4. What is the supporting information?
    (c) After you have received the materials from the university, evaluate them. Then write your instructor a letter telling him or her if you would or would not attend that university. Justify your answer based on the materials you received. Put your response in a letter in the simplified block format. Use the subject line "EVALUATION OF A UNIVERSITY."

TECHNOLOGY

2. Below is a letter written to a customer who has requested that two midnight blue, no-wrinkle sheets be replaced. (a) In a traditional format memo, indicate the problems in the letter. (b) After completing part (a), rewrite the letter so that it is well written. Put it in modified block format with open punctuation and indented paragraphs.

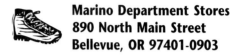

Marino Department Stores
890 North Main Street
Bellevue, OR 97401-0903

January 12, 20—

Mrs. J. T. Thomas
444 North Summit Street
Bowling Green, OH 43402-0001

Dear Mrs. Thomas

We have the two midnight blue, no-wrinkle sheets that you returned to us with the request that we exchange them for new ones.

We can imagine how disappointed you must have been with them, but we can explain the difficulty. You have been sending the sheets to a laundry that evidently washes them using a standard wash cycle and a strong bleach.

The washing instructions clearly visible on the labels say "WASH IN GENTLE CYCLES ONLY AND USE NO STRONG BLEACHES." Did you call this to your laundry's attention? Some laundries use gentle cycles and avoid strong bleaches only when specifically instructed to do so.

Using a standard cycle and strong bleaches sometimes keeps other cotton fabrics white and clean. But on these sheets, the standard cycle causes wrinkling and the strong bleaches cause fading.

In view of your past record with us, however, we are sending you two new midnight blue, no-wrinkle sheets free of charge. Just follow the instructions on the label, and the sheets will give you excellent service.

Cordially

William Hollinsford

William Hollinsford
Complaint Department Manager

COMMUNICATION FOR ENGINEERING AND INDUSTRIAL CAREERS

Luisa Medina is a sales representative for Tel City Machinery, a company that produces machinery for the manufacturing of industrial tools. Yesterday, she and other sales representatives were told of a flaw in the design of one of the machines. Now each representative must write a letter to those companies that have purchased the machine and tell them of the problem. The presidents of these companies will be unhappy because it will take two or three days to repair each machine. During this time, each company's production will be hindered.

Luisa realizes that the presidents she must write to are very different individuals. David Alfonso is an accommodating person. He has a strong personality but is open to suggestions and concerned with how his message affects others. Marshall Johnson is the opposite of Mr. Alfonso. Mr. Johnson is formal, direct, and tactless. His main attitude in leading is, "Let's get it done now. Don't waste time—time is money."

1. What kind of letter is Luisa writing to these presidents?
2. Will the letters she writes Mr. Alfonso and Mr. Johnson be the same? Justify your answer.

COMMUNICATION FOR NATURAL RESOURCES AND AGRICULTURE CAREERS

You have worked for the National Park Service for 25 years and have moved up the hierarchy to become the Head Ranger for a national park. One of your responsibilities is to propose to your regional director a budget for each year's operation of the park. To formulate this budget, you always seek mini budgets from the rangers responsible for each sector of the park. When you put their mini budgets together, you get a feel for the financial needs for the entire park.

Six months ago, you received the mini budgets, compiled them, and submitted your proposed budget to your regional director. In that proposal, you asked for an 8 percent increase in your annual budget. Although this is more than a cost of living increase, it seems necessary because of the increasing number of tourists who visit the park.

You have just received your budget for the coming year. You did not get the 8 percent requested—you got 5 percent. The monies for some of the increases were provided, but those requested for other park operations were not. Now you must inform the other rangers.

1. What type of message are you going to give the rangers?
2. How will you organize this message?

Video Case

Up Close and Personal

Many businesses like Superior Livestock Auction rely heavily today on information technologies to market their products and services. So when Erika Tasmajian began running her grandfather's produce business, Fresh Everyday, she was eager to apply what she had learned in her college classes.

Fresh Everyday had a number of long-time customers, but it had been slowly losing business to national chains. Erika's strategies were designed to expand the Fresh Everyday client list. She created a web page listing specials and bulk prices for restaurants, automated the telephone system to answer calls more quickly, and added a fax machine and the capability of video conferencing. Fresh Everyday did attract new customers, but Erika noticed fewer orders from long-time customers.

Over dinner Erika discussed the problem with her grandfather. She learned that he had always kept in touch with his customers through a stream of letters. Courtesy letters accompanied each invoice. Informational letters advised of special sales. Thank-you letters sent after major holidays thanked customers for their business.

Questions

1. Based on the video and your experience, what human qualities are critical to the success of a business like Superior Livestock Auction or Fresh Everyday? Do you think information technologies can take the place of these qualities?
2. Do you think there is a connection between fewer orders from long-term customers and fewer letters being sent to customers? Why or why not?
3. In the video, Superior Livestock Auction embraced several new technologies to further its business. Do you think these technologies eliminated Superior's use of letters to communicate with its customers? Why or why not?
4. Draft a letter thanking Fresh Everyday's restaurant customers for their purchases during the Thanksgiving holiday. Select an appropriate format. Print your draft.

Continuing Case....

Communicating with Partners

Dominic Lula and Opal Morales are the two silent partners in Eva and Ramon's NetCafe. Dominic and Opal invested $35,000 each in the new shop.

Opal lives in Milwaukee and visits the shop at least once a week. After taking one of Eva's introductory computer classes, Opal is enthusiastically "surfing the 'net."

Dominic lives south of Milwaukee in Kenosha. He does not own a computer and has no intention of buying one. He has not been in the shop since its grand opening. The only reason he invested in NetCafe, as he had told Eva many times, is that he and Ramon are old friends. Dominic, like Opal, had also invested in Ramon's former restaurant.

"Give me a restaurant any day," says Dominic. "Computers? Who needs 'em?"

The NetCafe has just finished its first quarter in business. It did well in some areas, and not so well in others. Eva and Ramon decide to write a brief quarterly report in the form of a letter. They will send the same report to Dominic and to Opal.

January 4, 20—

Dominic Lula
287 DeSales Street
Kenosha, Wisconsin 67843

Dear Dominic,

We wish all our news was good. The NetCafe has finished its first quarter in business.

We regret to tell you that the income from hourly computer use and the computer classes has not been as high as we had hoped. We had projected an income of $23,000 a month, but we took in an average of only $18,126 our first three months. At the same time, we paid monthly cable fees of $1,100, rental fees of $12,000 for the computers and other equipment, $1,229 for supplies, $1,500 for staff (Eva), and another $1,950 to rent the shop and pay the electric bill and related expenses.

Ramon and I are sure that our customers' recommendations and our new ads in the local paper will bring more people into the NetCafe to use the computers. Every week the hours of use seem to increase. I will start teaching an additional course next quarter, too.

The coffee shop, however, is doing very well. Ramon now offers twelve varieties of coffee and dozens of different pastries and bagels. He has hired one full-time and one part-time employee to help him prepare and serve. After subtracting the costs of supplies, equipment, and staff, the coffee part of our business had a profit of $1,878.

We apologize for this poor start. We have several ideas to increase our profits. We hope our news next quarter will be entirely good!

Sincerely,

Eva and Ramon

1. Does Eva use a consistent format in her letter? Explain your answer.
2. What kind of message does Eva present in her letter, especially from Dominic's point of view?
3. Discuss how Eva presents this message and offer general suggestions for improvement.
4. Using your suggestions in Question 3, rewrite this letter to make this bad news more acceptable for Opal and especially for Dominic.

chapter 7

Researching and Using Information

7·1 Planning and Defining the Search

7·3 Organizing, Evaluating, and Using Information

7·2 Locating Sources of Information

Asking the Right Questions

Gloria is an executive assistant for Jameson Recovery Associates. Her company helps businesses develop contingency plans to prevent natural or manufactured disasters from terminating their business operations.

Jameson provides consulting, training, and software services. The company helps develop plans for the information and records that would need to be recreated in order for a business to continue functioning in the event of disasters.

Gloria has been in her current position for three years. Although she loves her job, she has been hoping for an opportunity to show her supervisor that she is ready to assume some more challenging responsibilities.

One of the sales executives, Jim Galloway, is preparing to make an important presentation to a large software company. When he asks Gloria to assist with the initial research, she jumps at the chance.

Jim speaks with Gloria on Monday morning, asking her to locate information on the company and prepare a report for his review by a week from that Friday. He tells her that the company is headquartered in Chicago, is publicly held, and has been in business since 1979.

Gloria is so excited by the project that she neglects to ask Jim some key questions to aid in her research. She wonders what her first step should be, where she should begin her search for information about the company, what specific information would be helpful, and how much information would be needed to prepare a thorough report.

After speaking with Jim again, Gloria learns that he wants information on the company's growth (past, present, and planned), financial stability, and corporate officers. He wants to know of planned expansions, mergers, sales, takeovers, or any rumors of such activity. He will use this information to present a detailed plan to the company on safeguarding its business operations in the event of a disaster.

Questions

1. What questions should Gloria have asked Jim Galloway during their initial conversation regarding this research project?
2. How should Gloria decide what information she needs, what is most important, and how she should proceed?
3. Based on the information she needs, where should Gloria begin her search?
4. What other types of resources might provide the information Gloria needs?
5. How should Gloria determine the data to include in her report to Jim Galloway? Should she include recommendations in her report?
6. For this type of report, is it necessary for Gloria to cite her sources? If so, how should she present the information?

Objectives

After completing Section 7.1, you should be able to:

1 List the basic steps in any research project.

2 Define keywords and explain their use in an information search.

3 Explain the purpose and importance of a timeline in planning a research project.

Objective

↓KEY POINT

Breaking the research project into five basic steps makes it more manageable.

SCANS
Employability

Systems: Understands Systems
Developing a solid plan of action before beginning alleviates false starts and can save your employer time and money.

Steps in a Search

We live in the Information Age. As we enter the twenty-first century, we have access to more information than at any other time in history. We have instant access to current events by way of a wide range of media, including television, radio, newspapers, and the Internet.

With so much information available, searching for and locating the precise bit of information we need can seem like an overwhelming task. That's why it is critical for you to develop the necessary skills to access information sources, to understand how to determine the accuracy of those sources, and to be able to conduct a logical and efficient search for information.

Researching and finding information requires us to systematically sort through what is available in order to locate, organize, evaluate, and use the data that answer our questions, explain our theories, or reinforce our positions. The five basic steps in a research project are (1) planning the search, (2) locating sources of information, (3) organizing the information, (4) evaluating the sources, and (5) using the information.

Planning the Search

Planning is perhaps the most important step in your research. You should resist the temptation to jump into the search without giving careful thought to where and how you will conduct your search for information. By making sure you understand your assignment, carefully developing your search strategies, and scheduling your time wisely, you will be able to accomplish your goal.

A poorly planned search can result in frustration as well as wasted time and energy. Would you begin a long trip without mapping your route? If you did, you would most likely lose your way, head in the wrong direction, or wander in circles. The same thing can happen if you leave on a "research trip" without a plan. So take the time to map your strategies before you begin!

Understanding the Assignment

First, make sure you completely understand your research assignment as well as the focus of the research. For example, if you are searching for information on farming, are you interested in information on organically grown produce? Or are you trying to locate facts about crop rotation? If your research involves computer technology, are you looking for sources on maintaining data security or on developing computer software? Your focus will affect your search. If the topic of your search is too broad, you will become frustrated by having to wade through a long list of sources that may have little to do with your search. Ask yourself the following questions:

1. What question am I trying to answer?
2. What information will I need in order to answer this question?
3. What is the best method to use in locating this information?
4. Where might I find the best sources of information?
5. What is the most logical "first step," and how should I proceed?

If you are unable to answer these basic questions about your search, you may not have a clear understanding of your assignment, your purpose, or your focus. Before proceeding, you may need to return to the person who assigned the research project and ask for clarification.

Checkpoint 1

Steps in a Search for Information

Indicate whether each statement is true or false.

1. The most important step in the research process is organizing the information into a useable format.

2. With so much information available, locating the facts and data you need is a simple task.

3. The focus of your research should become clear to you as you proceed with your search.

4. Before beginning a research project, you should determine the best method for finding the information you need.

5. If you are unable to answer basic questions about your search, you should seek clarification before proceeding.

Check your answers in Appendix E.

Using Keywords to Define the Focus of the Search

Make notes of questions, ideas, or thoughts you might have relating to your research project, and list any keywords that may relate to your search. **Keywords** are search terms or phrases that in some way relate to your research topic. They help you focus on the central point of

Objective

KEY POINT

- Think of keywords as points on a map that will help you navigate to your intended destination.
- Because the brain has a relatively short attention span, it works best in brief, intense bursts of activity.

SCANS
Employability

Thinking Skills: Creative Thinking

These creative-thinking techniques can be used in many areas of business to generate ideas and solve problems quickly.

your research—the area of primary interest. For example, if you were searching for information on traffic safety, you might think to list keywords like *traffic, safety, accident,* and *automobile.* The more clearly defined your list of terms, the easier and quicker you will arrive at the answer you need. Always remember, the better the directions, the smoother the trip!

Once you have established your list of keywords, try to develop a list of related words that can be used either to broaden or narrow the scope of your search. You might find it helpful to use a webbing or clustering technique when developing your list of keywords and related terms. These creative-thinking techniques allow your mind to generate many ideas in a quick burst of creativity. They also can help you more clearly define your focus by generating ideas to include in your report that you may not yet have considered. Figure 7-1 is an example of a web that develops keywords for a research project on traffic safety.

To use a **webbing** or **clustering technique**, begin by drawing a circle in the center of a sheet of paper and writing the topic of your research in the center of the circle. Now begin drawing lines from that central idea to form related terms. Write as much as you can for as long as you can without stopping to evaluate the clusters. You may find that you have uncovered key words or connections that you might not have otherwise thought to use.

For example, your web might reveal additional words or phrases related to your research topic such as *seat belt, air bag, child safety seat, speed limit, highway, MADD* (Mothers Against Drunk Drivers), *vehicle inspection, unsafe driving, road rage, motorcycle, helmet, bicycle,* and *pedestrian.* From this new list of words, you may decide to focus your report on traffic safety from the perspective of determining which safety measures are most effective in preventing accidents and saving lives.

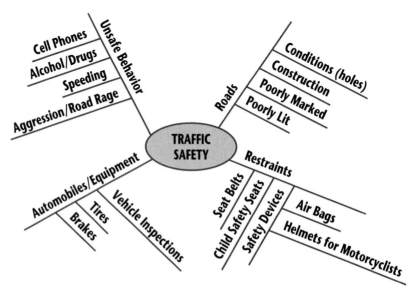

FIGURE 7-1 A creative-thinking technique for a research project on traffic safety

Spam—It Isn't Just for Lunch Anymore

As anyone who has an e-mail account knows, spam no longer refers exclusively to processed meat in a can. Instead spam is the expression used to describe the junk e-mail that clogs the arteries of our computerized mailboxes.

Each time we access our accounts, we must wade through message after message hawking everything from weight-loss gimmicks to sure-fire investment offers. These spammers, as they are known, have found what would appear to be the perfect way to advertise their products to us *at our expense*. But now several states are fighting back, and more appear to be following.

According to an Associated Press article published in the February 25, 1999, edition of the *Seattle Times*, many states are passing anti-spam laws. While the states of Washington and Nevada may impose civil penalties, both Virginia and California now consider spamming a crime that could result in jail time.

For more information on spam and anti-spam legislation, enter the keywords *spam* and *law* in your search engine or subject index. To review the full text of the *Seattle Times* article, enter **www.seattletimes .com** and search the archives under the keyword *spam*. ■

After you have completed this exercise, review the relationships between words and phrases. You may want to rank the terms, selecting the keywords to begin your search and using other related words or phrases to narrow or broaden the search as necessary.

Developing Deadlines and Timelines

Once you have established a clear deadline for the completion of your project, you should develop a timeline to help you complete the research and report on time. A **timeline** is a tool used for planning and scheduling the completion times for each phase of a project. It lists the specific dates by which each task and phase must be completed.

To set up a timeline, it is easiest to begin at the end and work backward. That is, begin with the date on which your report must be completed. Working backward from that date, indicate the dates on which all research information must be gathered, organized, evaluated, and used.

For example, if your report must be completed on May 1, calculate backward from May 1 to determine the date on which you must begin writing the report, and note that date on your timeline. Next, calculate backward from the date you will begin writing to decide when all research must be completed, organized, and evaluated. Again, note those dates on your timeline. From those points, you can determine when you need to begin the research. Figure 7-2 shows an example of a timeline for a research project.

Objective

SCANS
Employability

Personal Qualities: Self-management
Most business projects are time sensitive. Effective employees know how to manage their time well to meet project deadlines.

PROJECT NAME: _____

Tasks to Be Completed	Date for Completion
Planning the Search:	
Determine focus of research	April 20
Develop list of keywords and phrases	
Decide research strategies/methodologies	
Locating Sources of Information:	
Library research—public, university	April 21
Web searches	April 22
Complete research—all data and information gathered	April 23
Organizing the Information:	
Prioritize sources of information	April 24
Organize facts in logical order	
Evaluating the Sources:	
Evaluate sources for validity and reliability	April 24
Check sources for bias, dated material	
Using the Information:	
Write first draft of report	April 27
Make revisions to first draft of report	April 28
Write final draft of report	April 29
Proofread final draft of report	April 30
Submit written report	May 1

FIGURE 7-2 Timeline for a sample research project

2 Checkpoint

Planning the Search

Complete each of the following sentences.

1. A(n) _____ is a tool for scheduling each phase of a research project.

2. Critical-thinking techniques such as _____ allow your mind to generate ideas in a quick burst of creativity.

3. _____ are search terms that relate to your research topic.

4. When designing a timeline, you should begin with the proposed completion date and work _____ to establish deadlines for each phase of the research project.

5. Once you have determined a list of keywords, you may generate related words to either _____ or _____ the search.

Check your answers in Appendix E.

Answers

Responses to Questions 1 and 2 in Chapter Opener

1. **What questions should Gloria have asked Jim Galloway during their initial conversation regarding this research project?**

   Jim told Gloria the date on which he needed the report and provided her with some brief information about the company. However, there were many important questions that Gloria, in her excitement, forgot to ask. By not communicating clearly with Jim about this project, Gloria runs the risk of preparing a report that will not include the needed information.

   Gloria should have asked about the focus of the project—the specific information Jim wants her to locate. She also should have discussed with him the purpose of the information, how it will be used, and the depth of information that he needs in the report.

2. **How should Gloria decide what information she needs, what is most important, and how she should proceed?**

   These are questions that Gloria initially was unable to answer because she had not discussed the project adequately with Jim. After returning to him with a list of clearly defined questions, Gloria now knows that he wants information on the company's growth, financial stability, and corporate officers. He also wants to know if there are any planned expansions, mergers, sales, or takeovers, or any rumors of such activity. Armed with this information, Gloria should be able to proceed to the appropriate resources and begin gathering information for her report.

DISCUSSION QUESTIONS

1. Before beginning a research project on foreign business customs, what information will you need? What questions must you answer before starting the project?

2. List all of the keywords you can think of on the topic of computer security. Do you think your list would have been more expansive if you had used a creative-thinking technique like webbing or clustering? Why?

3. What tools or techniques have you used in the past to manage your time on a project? How have they worked? How do they compare to a timeline?

7·2 Locating Sources of Information

Objectives

After completing Section 7.2, you should be able to:

1 Identify primary and secondary sources of information.

2 Discuss the resources available for conducting research at public libraries.

3 Explain how subject indexes and search engines are used in an information search on the Web.

4 List the advantages and disadvantages of advanced search features.

Objective

KEY POINT

Using information from a variety of sources provides depth and balance to your research.

Sources of Information

Because there is so much information available from many different sources, determining the best source for your particular research project can be a challenge. Libraries, including public and university libraries and special collections, offer many valuable resources, from books and journals to electronic databases. Likewise, the Internet provides a wealth of information from many different sources around the world. Depending on your research question, your best source of information may be an individual or an organization. As you begin conducting your research and gathering information, you probably will find that your report will be enhanced by including information from a variety of sources.

There are two basic types of information: secondary information and primary information.

Secondary Information

Secondary information includes sources of information that are already in published form. Secondary sources of information include

- books
- periodicals
- encyclopedias
- dictionaries
- handbooks
- almanacs
- directories
- government publications
- electronic databases
- web sites

Primary Information

Primary information involves the firsthand gathering of data. These unpublished sources of information can lead you to experts in the area you are researching who can provide you with valuable insights, opinions, and access to cutting-edge information that may not yet be in published form. Primary sources of information include

- interviews
- surveys
- observations

Interviews

Depending on your objective and the focus of your research, interviews can be an excellent source of information. By interviewing experts in the field you are researching, you can gain valuable information that may not be readily available from other sources. Conducting interviews with employers or employees within a particular business sector can reveal important trends and also may offer a unique perspective on the industry as a whole.

Interviews with sources outside an organization, such as customers, can lend yet another angle to your research project. For this reason, many companies regularly seek their customers' opinions on their products, prices, and services to help them better serve their markets.

Surveys

This method of gathering information can be conducted in person, in writing, or by telephone. Surveys usually involve the design of a carefully worded questionnaire to be completed by the survey subjects. Although the knowledge gained from a well-produced survey can be invaluable, designing, distributing, collecting, and compiling the questionnaires generally takes a considerable commitment of time and money. Therefore, before selecting this method of research, it is

SCANS
Employability

Basic Skills: Listening
Good listening skills are required for conducting successful interviews. Pay close attention not only to what your interview subject says but also to gestures, facial expressions, and body language.

DIVERSITY
Survey questions must be carefully worded to avoid bias relating to gender, age, race, or national origin.

Always ask permission beforehand to tape-record an interview. Be sure you have batteries and a fresh tape. Take notes in case of equipment failure.

important to know if you have adequate time and financial resources available to successfully complete this type of project.

Observations

Observations involve careful monitoring of the activities of another person or persons. *Job shadowing*, which is one familiar form of observation, can provide valuable information about the job duties of the people being shadowed. By spending time observing these people as they go about their daily tasks at work, you can gain insight into the position, the organization, and the industry as a whole. In addition, by observing people on the job, you may discover problems in the organizational structure, work flow, or operating procedures that can offer information on improving morale or productivity.

Knowing Where to Look

When beginning a research project, it is usually better to begin your search by checking *secondary sources* of information. These published sources contain a wealth of data that will provide valuable background information for your project. Depending on the scope of your project, secondary sources may, in fact, provide all the information you need. After consulting secondary sources, you may find that you need to conduct primary research. The published sources then offer a solid basis for gathering additional information by interviewing individuals, conducting surveys, or observing people in the workplace or elsewhere.

As you locate sources for your research project, you should organize the information in a systematic way. When you are ready to write, you will have all the information you need at your fingertips. One way is to write each source on an index card or separate piece of paper. On the card, note key points as well as the title, author, page references, publisher, date, and any other relevant information. For interviews, note the date of the interview, the name and title of your interview subject, and any facts or quotes that you will use in your report.

The Library

Objective

The public library offers a multitude of resources for research. These include periodicals, handbooks, almanacs, directories, government publications, companies' annual reports, and electronic databases.

If you are searching for information on a business, you might begin in a directory, such as *Standard and Poor's Register of Corporations, Dun and Bradstreet's Million Dollar Directory, Directory of Corporate Affiliations*, or *Thomas Register of Manufacturers*. You also could begin in an electronic database such as *Hoover's Online* or *Reference USA*, which profiles millions of U.S. and Canadian companies. Your library most likely has subscriptions to a number of electronic resources available on CD-ROM or through on-line services, which are updated frequently.

KEY POINT

By carefully recording your observations, you can later construct a job description or the work-flow patterns of an organization.

The public library offers a wealth of research resources, including reference books, electronic databases, and, often, access to Internet resources.

For publicly held companies, the library may be able to provide a copy of the latest annual report to stockholders. It also may provide access to *Compact Disclosure*, a database that offers detailed financial data from Securities and Exchange Commission (SEC) filings. For privately held companies, this information probably will not be available. Because privately owned companies are not required by the SEC to disclose financial information, the only data available may be information the companies elect to make public. However, using the library's indexes to newspapers and business periodicals, including electronic databases such as *InfoTrac* and *UMI ProQuest Direct*, you can search for articles that may reveal information about the business dealings of these companies.

If the company has a web site, it too can be a good source of information and may allow you access to current press releases about the company. However, it is important to remember that information

Publicly held companies are those whose stock is traded on stock exchanges like the New York Stock Exchange or American Stock Exchange, or over-the-counter. Access the various stock exchange web sites at **www.nyse.com**, **www.amex.com**, or **www.otcbb.com** for a look at the stock values of some of these companies.

available at a company's web site is self-reported; it will most likely present the organization favorably. To get a more balanced view of any company, always look for additional sources of information. Books, journals, reports, and documents on specialized topics that may not readily be available at the public library most likely can be found through a university library or business collection. Figure 7-3 lists some tips for locating information on a company.

The Encyclopedia of Associations also is an excellent reference for locating sources for interviews. It contains an extensive listing of professional associations along with contact information. These associations offer a wealth of information about their respective industries and can refer you to the leaders within their profession. Your public library also may have access to an on-line database such as *Associations Unlimited* that you can use to locate sources.

One other major asset that all libraries have is librarians—those amazing people who can answer any question, find any reference, track down the most obscure volume, and locate resources on any topic. Librarians are trained to help you find information, so take advantage of their talents and consult them!

3 Checkpoint

Sources of Information

Indicate whether each statement is true or false.
1. Job shadowing is a type of primary information research.
2. A survey is the quickest and easiest method of gathering information.
3. You should begin your research project by checking primary sources of information first and then searching secondary sources.
4. A good source of information about a publicly held company is the company's latest annual report.
5. Primary information involves the firsthand gathering of data.

Check your answers in Appendix E.

Finding It on the Web

Objective

3

The World Wide Web can be a dream come true or a nightmare, depending on how well you are able to navigate the wealth of information available. Assuming you have planned your search well and have determined that a good place to look for information is on the Web, how should you begin?

You may begin your search by accessing a **URL**, or uniform resource locator, for a specific web site. The URL is the web address,

TIPS FOR LOCATING COMPANY INFORMATION

Is the company publicly traded?
If yes, a wealth of information is available in the company's annual reports to stockholders and at *Compact Disclosure*, a database that provides financial data from Securities and Exchange Commission filings.

Is the company a subsidiary of another organization?
If yes, information about the company may be available under the name of the larger organization. Check under both company names.

Where is the company headquartered?
If you have not yet discovered the location of the company's headquarters, check one of the many business directories such as *Standard and Poor's Register of Corporations, Dun and Bradstreet's Million Dollar Directory, Directory of Corporate Affiliations,* or *Thomas Register of Manufacturers* for a company profile. You also may be able to access this information through an electronic database such as *Hoover's Online* or *Reference USA*.

These business resources also will provide information on estimated sales, earnings, number of employees, year founded, business description, divisions, and subsidiaries.

Does the company have a web site?
If yes, the company may provide the information you need at that site. Most company web sites contain a page called "About the Company" or "Company History" that provides background information about the organization, divisions, headquarters and remote locations, and officers of the company. Other pages at the site may provide information about products and services offered by the company and may include access to company-generated press releases.

Has anything been reported recently in the business press regarding the company?
Newsworthy events such as expansions, mergers, takeovers, or rumors of such activity generally are covered in the national business press—particularly for publicly held companies. However, a more in-depth picture of a company's business activities (and the effects they may have on the local community) may be found in the city or regional newspaper where the company is located. To locate newspaper and magazine articles about the company, check one or more of the databases your public library may be able to access such as *InfoTrac* or *UMI ProQuest Direct*. You also should determine the name of the local newspaper and check its archives for articles about the company.

FIGURE 7-3 Tips for locating company information

usually written in the form of <u>www.webaddress.com</u>. To enter a URL, access your Internet service provider and type the web address you want. When written within other documents, URLs typically appear as underlined and colored text. By clicking on the URL with your mouse, you can be connected directly to that web address by way of your usual Internet service provider.

If you do not have a specific URL or web address to access, you will most likely begin your search for information in a **search engine**, such as AltaVista (**www.altavista.com**), HotBot (**www.hotbot.com**), or InfoSeek (**www.infoseek.com**); or a **subject index**, like Yahoo! (**www.yahoo.com**) or Excite (**www.excite.com**). Although many people refer to subject indexes as search engines, the distinction between the two relates to how each resource compiles information.

Search engines compile information by sending out *spiders* or *crawlers*—software that combs the Web to locate and index web sites. Subject indexes like Yahoo! rely on humans to compile catalogs manually by reviewing information and determining which sites to include. Subject indexes also have categorized sites to make it easier for you to find information on a particular subject.

If you look at the opening screen in Yahoo! (see Figure 7-4), you will see categories ranging from Arts & Humanities to Recreation & Sports, each with several subcategories listed. By clicking on *Newspapers*, for example, you can access a second screen that offers several options for accessing a list of newspapers by region, by type (from college and university papers to tabloids), or alphabetically. With just three quick clicks of the mouse, you can be at the web site for almost any major newspaper in the country.

By entering one or more of your keywords, you can use each of these search tools to produce a *hit list* of potential information regarding your research subject. (A **hit** refers to each item in the list of Internet sources that meets your search criteria.) You will no doubt find that using just one search engine or subject index does not provide you with all the information you are seeking. Therefore, you will need to check more than one source when conducting your search for information.

Although much of the information accessible via the Web is available free of charge, some specialized sites charge a fee for information. You will need to determine the amount of money you are able to commit to this research project if you feel this information is vital to your report. You also might check with your public library to see if it subscribes to that particular research service.

Once you locate web sites on your specific research topic, you may find **links**, or quick connections, to other related sites that will be helpful in your search. These links usually appear as underlined text, often in color, and may be particularly useful for following a thread of information to gather additional data. These links may provide helpful information that you may not have considered previously.

A review of the opening screen for each search engine or subject index reveals both similarities and differences. Visit at least one search engine and one subject index, and compare them.

Visit two search engines or subject indexes, and enter the same keyword in each. Carefully note the number of hits that are generated and compare the hit lists. You will find that some hits are the same, but many are different.

TECHNOLOGY

While we think of libraries as sources of books, journals, and newspapers, the library also is an excellent resource for locating the latest on-line information on a topic.

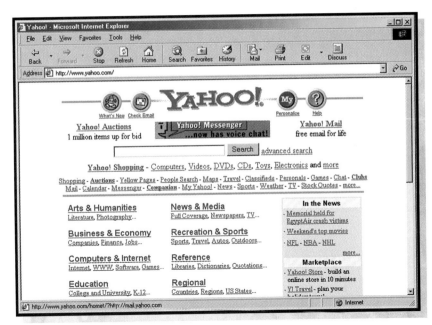

FIGURE 7-4 Home page for YAHOO! subject index
Reproduced with permission of Yahoo! Inc. ©1999 by Yahoo! Inc. YAHOO! and the
YAHOO! logo are trademarks of Yahoo! Inc.

Web Rings

Web rings are a group of web sites, usually on the same or a related
topic, that have been linked together to form a closed ring of sites.
Once you are inside a web ring on a specific topic, it is easy to move
from one site to another within the ring to access a wide range of
information on your search topic. If you are able to locate a good
web ring on your specific research topic, it can provide you with a
wealth of information and reduce the hours you spend searching for
information.

You can search for web rings on your search topic using any of the
search engines or subject indexes. Enter your keyword and the word
webring in the search box. An alternate route to access a wide range of
web rings is to visit the *WebRing* site www.webring.com. There you
will find an extensive list of web rings on a variety of topics.

Here are some other sites that provide valuable links to information:

- **The Internet Public Library Reference Section (www.ipl.org/ref/).**
  This site provides access to almanacs, biographical information, cal-
  culators and conversion tools, census data and demographics, federal statistics, and various dictionaries, encyclopedias, and periodical
  directories. It also includes access to information on thousands of
  businesses, including Fortune 500 companies.
- **The Library of Congress (www.loc.gov).** This site provides access
  to an extensive on-line catalog as well as valuable research tools
  and other services for researchers. It also offers links to the on-line
  catalogs of numerous other libraries, including public libraries, university libraries, and business collections worldwide.

▼ KEY POINT

Web rings and their value to
your research can vary. Look
for Web rings that include
sites sponsored by reputable
organizations.

Visit WebRing at **www.
webring.com** and review
the directory of Web rings
available at that site.

- **Research-it** (www.iTools.com/research-it). This site provides a wealth of research tools including access to a dictionary, thesaurus, biographical dictionary, currency exchange information, stock quotes, maps, telephone listings, and links to *Bartlett's Quotations*.

TECHNOLOGY

Heading for the Mall Without Leaving Home

The personal computer has changed forever the way many of us do business. Now instead of fighting the traffic, weather, and crowds at the malls, many of us are settling back in our desk chairs and letting our fingers stroll through thousands of Internet "shops." This trend shows no sign of stopping. For years, "home shopping convenience" meant wading through the pages of catalogs that arrived in our mailboxes in ever-increasing numbers—particularly as the holidays approached. In the mid-1980s, home shopping took on new meaning as television viewers were introduced to 24-hour-a-day, 7-day-a-week shopping convenience on The Home Shopping Network and QVC, both of which offer everything from jewelry and kitchen appliances to clothing and exercise equipment.

With lower prices—and dazzling variety—available through Internet shopping sites, more and more people now shop at home with the touch of a keyboard or click of a mouse. At any hour of the day or night, shoppers can surf through the halls of virtual malls or specialized shopping sites offering everything from gourmet foods to vacation getaways. Looking for a book, video, or music CD? You can find it fast on a number of sites, including **Amazon.com**, **Barnesandnoble.com**, or **Borders.com**. Click, click, click, and your order is complete and on its way to your doorstep.

Can't find the time to visit the neighborhood grocery store? No problem. Order your groceries online and have them delivered to you in a matter of hours. Looking for a hard-to-find item—coins, antiques, collectibles? Locate it on one of many trading sites, such as **eBay.com**, where buyers and sellers "meet" to deal.

E-commerce, as this phenomenon is known, has become so commonplace that many businesses fear they cannot compete unless they have an on-line presence. In a few short years, the Internet has become the new "Main Street," only instead of companies selling their goods within a single community, they now are doing business around the globe. ■

Advanced Search Features

When an on-line search produces a hit list that is either too large to manage or too small to be useful, you may need to more clearly focus your search in order to locate the sources of information that will be most useful for your research. This can be accomplished through the use of advanced search techniques, which allow you to enter more than one keyword or phrase.

Boolean Operators. Boolean operators may be used to connect two or more keywords or phrases to either broaden or narrow the scope of your search. The most common Boolean operators are AND, OR, and NOT (or AND NOT).

Using the term OR broadens your search, producing a larger hit list of sources, because only one of the search terms you enter needs to be present. For example, if you enter the terms *chocolate* OR *candy*, the software will return a list of hits that includes web sites containing either the word *chocolate* or the word *candy*, but not necessarily both words within the same hit.

If you are searching for information on computer monitors and you enter the words *monitor* OR *screen*, you could generate a hit list of sites relating to touch-screen products, screen savers, drug screening, and screening and monitoring of diseases. For this reason, it is important to select keywords carefully or your search may result in a long list of useless sources that have little to do with your research topic.

The Boolean operator AND is used to narrow the search by requiring that all search terms be present in each source on the hit list. For example, if you entered *branch* AND *tree*, the list would include only hits containing both the word *branch* and the word *tree*. Hits containing only one of the terms would not be listed, thus eliminating references to branch locations of banks or other businesses. This strategy produces a shorter list that may be more on target. Be careful, however, not to eliminate some useful sources that may not include both terms in the text.

When you want to eliminate a specific term from the hit list, it may be appropriate to use the Boolean operator NOT or AND NOT. For instance, if you entered the search terms *tree* AND NOT *bonsai*, the resulting hit list would include all sources containing the word *tree* but not those referring to bonsai trees.

Truncation and Wild Cards. Truncation is a method of broadening the search by using a base or root word followed by a wild card that allows the software to search for several similar key words that begin with the same root. The **wild card** is a symbol, most commonly an asterisk (*), that commands the software to return a list of resources containing all words that begin with that root or base word. For example, entering the search term *pollut** would result in a hit list containing all the terms beginning with the base word *pollut*, including *pollutant*, *pollute*, *polluter*, and *pollution*. This is a handy tool to use when there are a number of similar words that may be relevant to your search.

Objective

4

▼KEY POINT

Using more than one keyword in a single search allows you to pinpoint the information you need without having to sort through long lists of references. To benefit your search, choose the keywords you will connect with great care.

▼KEY POINT

Because some search engines or subject indexes handle advanced searches differently, you should review instructions at each search engine or subject index web site before proceeding with an advanced search.

4 Checkpoint

Finding It on the Web

Match each term on the left with the correct item on the right.

1. _____ URL   AND, OR, NOT
2. _____ wild card   Alta Vista
3. _____ Boolean operators   base or root word
4. _____ search engine   web address
5. _____ truncation   *

Check your answers in Appendix E.

CASE 7:

Answers

Responses to Questions 3 and 4 in Chapter Opener

3. **Based on the information she needs, where should Gloria begin her search?**

   Because it is a publicly held company, Gloria could find a great deal of the information Jim Galloway wants about the company from its most recent annual report. This should be available at her local public library.

4. **What other types of resources might provide the information Gloria needs?**

   Gloria might check the stock exchange web site for a history of the company's stock. She also should check the indexes to business journals and major newspapers for articles that report planned changes in the business, such as mergers, expansions, or sales.

DISCUSSION QUESTIONS

1. Many research tools are available in print form at the library as well as on the Web. Why might you use one resource over another?
2. If you were investigating the career of air traffic controller, what method of gathering information would you use first? Why?
3. To search for information on jobs in the computer industry, what keywords might you use? How would you limit the search to computer jobs in Atlanta only?

Organizing, Evaluating, and Using Information

Organizing and Prioritizing Information

Once the research is completed and you have located all the information you need, the task of organizing the sources begins. This can seem like an overwhelming job, especially if you have gathered information from many different sources. However, if you have maintained detailed cards or pages for each source, you should be able to decide easily on the structure of your report.

Begin by looking for connections among your various sources. Have you located the same or similar information from a number of different places? Clip those cards or pages together. Place your cards or pages in order from beginning to end in a logical manner that will guide your reader through the report. Every report you write should have a beginning or introduction, a middle or statement of facts, and an end. Prioritize your information so you are "telling the story" in a way that will not confuse your readers.

You may present your findings for someone else to review. However, you also may be asked to arrive at a conclusion and make recommendations based on your research. If so, present sound reasoning for your recommendations by making sure your conclusions are tied to facts presented in your report.

Evaluating Sources of Information

When gathering information from secondary sources, you should constantly evaluate the information you find. Ask yourself these questions:

1. Is it true and accurate?
2. Is it reliable? Is it provided by a reputable source?
3. Is it current or dated?
4. Is it biased?

Always check the validity and reliability of your sources. Simply put, **validity** means that the information presented is an accurate representation of facts. **Reliability** indicates that the information is free of error

Objectives

After completing Section 7.3, you should be able to:

1 Discuss a method of organizing and prioritizing research information in a report.

2 Explain the importance of validity and reliability in evaluating research information.

3 Identify key copyright issues involved in using published information.

Objective

SCANS
Employability

Information: Interprets and Communicates
Companies make decisions to commit time and resources based on reports presenting data, drawing conclusions, and recommending actions. Make sure your research is accurate, and your report is clearly and concisely written.

Objective

Web-publishing software is now so inexpensive and easy to use that almost anyone can launch a web site. You should carefully scrutinize each source of information before using it.

TECHNOLOGY

Looking at the last three letters of the web address may provide a clue to the source of the information and how reliable that source may be. The suffix *gov* refers to government-sponsored sites; *edu* is reserved for educational institutions, and *org* applies to nonprofit organizations. The suffix *com* is found at commercial sites.

Objective

When using a direct quote from a source within your report, always set it apart in some way, such as enclosing it within quotation marks, and include the source credit, including page number if appropriate, after the quotation.

Visit the web site for the U.S. Copyright Office at **www.loc.gov/copyright** for more information on copyright laws.

and that if repeated, the research would result in the same findings. If most of the information you find offers the same or similar information, that is a good indication that it is reliable. If there is one source that offers dramatically different data, you should question its reliability.

For example, anyone can launch a web site and publish information in a professional-looking format. However, the information may be completely inaccurate. Just because it is "published" doesn't mean it should be used without question. Responsible researchers constantly ask questions to determine if information is valid and reliable before using it.

Check to see if the information is provided by a reputable source. Is the research information provided by a university or a government agency? Can you tell who publishes the web site? Is that person's name, title, affiliation, and contact information clearly listed?

If the information you have found is outdated, it may be of little use to your research project. Pay attention to dates of publication as well as the dates on which the information was placed on the web site.

Finally, ask yourself if the information from the article, book, or web page you are using is well balanced and lacks bias. You may discover bias relating to age, gender, race, or national origin. You also may notice bias simply in the way information is slanted in the presentation. Anyone can publish information espousing his or her own viewpoint. Avoid using information that presents an obvious bias.

Using Information

When using information you have retrieved from a secondary source, it is necessary to cite your source and give credit to the authors in your report. (See Appendix D for various styles of citations.) Using the words of an author without that author's consent and without crediting the source of the information is called **plagiarism**. It leads the reader to believe that the words are your own. This is unprofessional and unethical behavior.

Using the work of an author without authorization and without crediting the source of the information also is a violation of **copyright** laws. The authors of original works, both published and unpublished, are guaranteed copyright protection under the law of the United States as provided by the U.S. Copyright Office.

Crediting the author of information gathered from a web site can be a tricky situation. The author or the source of the information may not be clearly spelled out at the site. Nevertheless, it is irresponsible to use the information without citing your source. If the author is unclear, at least note that the information was retrieved from a web site and list the URL of the site. Likewise, if information is provided to you by way of an interview or e-mail, those notations should be made when crediting the information.

Using Information

Indicate whether each statement is true or false.

1. Copyright protected documents must contain the copyright notation ©.

2. Reliability of sources indicates that the information is free of error.

3. It isn't necessary to credit the author of information obtained from the Web.

4. You should avoid using information that presents an obvious bias relating to age, gender, or race.

5. When using information that you have retrieved from a secondary source, you must properly credit the author in your report.

Check your answers in Appendix E.

CASE 7:

A n s w e r s

Responses to Questions 5 and 6 in Chapter Opener

5. **How should Gloria determine the data to include in her report to Jim Galloway? Should she include recommendations in her report?**

   After collecting all of the information requested, Gloria should review her sources and evaluate them for validity and reliability. If any of the information does not clearly indicate a source or deviates greatly from other information she has collected, she may want to eliminate that particular information or mention her findings and misgivings in the report. (This could be the situation if she discovers any unsubstantiated rumors about the company.)

   Although Jim has not specifically asked Gloria for recommendations, if she is able to draw any conclusions from the data collected and can make a sound recommendation based on the facts presented in her report, her initiative could be rewarded.

> **6. For this type of report, is it necessary for Gloria to cite her sources? If so, how should she present the information?**
>
> Yes. Regardless of the length or type of report, any information presented should be attributed to the source from which it was taken. Depending on the amount of data she will present in her report, Gloria may be able to include references to the source within the body of the report, or she may wish to attach a detailed bibliography.

DISCUSSION QUESTIONS

1. Would you consider information found at a web site with the suffix *edu* more reliable than information from a site ending in *com*? Why?
2. What is meant by bias? Why is it important for information to be free of bias?
3. Why is it always important to credit the source of your information?

CASE 7:
Summary

In her excitement at being asked to work on Jim Galloway's presentation, Gloria initially forgot that the most important step in any research project is proper planning. Because she didn't ask Jim to clarify the specific information he needed, she initially was confused and didn't know where to begin. Only after determining his needs and the intended use for the information was Gloria able to begin the research process with a clear plan for locating the requested data.

When conducting research, it is important to follow each step in the research process: (1) plan the search, (2) locate sources of information, (3) organize the information, (4) evaluate the sources, and (5) use or present the information in an appropriate format.

By taking the time to discuss the project again with Jim and determine the specific information he wanted, Gloria should be able to produce a thorough and accurate report that may help convince her supervisor to give her more responsibilities.

Chapter Summary

Effective research skills are an important part of business communications. The ability to execute a successful search for requested data quickly and accurately is essential in today's Information Age.

Section 7.1 Planning and Defining the Search

1 **List the basic steps in any research project.** The basic steps in any research project are (1) planning the search, (2) locating the sources of information, (3) organizing the information, (4) evaluating the sources, and (5) using the information.

2 **Define keywords and explain their use in an information search.** Keywords are search terms or phrases that relate to the search topic. They are used to focus the search. Several keywords or phrases may be used together to either broaden or narrow the scope of the search.

3 **Explain the purpose and importance of a timeline in planning a research project.** A timeline is a planning and time management tool designed to keep the research project on track by scheduling the completion time for each phase of the project.

Section 7.2 Locating Sources of Information

1 **Identify primary and secondary sources of information.** Primary sources of information involve original data gathered by the researcher, including interviews, surveys, and observations. Secondary sources of information are those already in published form. These include books, periodicals, encyclopedias, dictionaries, handbooks, almanacs, directories, government publications, electronic databases, and web sites.

2 **Discuss the resources available for conducting research at public libraries.** The public library offers a wide variety of resources including books, periodicals, directories, almanacs, and government publications. It also provides access to electronic databases and the Internet.

3 **Explain how subject indexes and search engines are used in an information search on the Web.** Subject indexes and search engines are research tools used to locate information on the Web. By entering keywords or phrases into the subject index or search engine, you can locate a list of web sites that relate to your search topic.

4 **List the advantages and disadvantages of advanced search features.** Advanced search features allow you to either broaden or narrow the focus of your information search. Broadening the search enables you to locate more sources, while narrowing the search allows you to tightly focus on your specific search topic. However, by broadening the focus, you may produce a hit list that is too large to manage and contains information unrelated to the focus of your search. By narrowing the focus, you may eliminate several sources that could have provided valuable information.

Section 7.3 Organizing, Evaluating, and Using Information

1 **Discuss a method of organizing and prioritizing research information in a report.** By maintaining a record of each information source and your findings on a separate index card or page, you should be able to review your information quickly and organize it based on the order it will be presented in your report. Plan your report so there is a logical flow of information from beginning (introduction) to middle (statement of facts) to conclusion and recommendations.

2 **Explain the importance of validity and reliability in evaluating research information.** Validity and reliability are absolutely essential in good research. They ensure that the information is accurate and free of errors. Without validity and reliability, your research findings would be worthless.

3 **Identify the key copyright issues involved in using published information.** Authors of original work are guaranteed copyright protection under the law. Using an author's work without permission and without properly crediting the source of the information is a violation of those laws.

Critical Thinking Questions

1. What is the importance of each phase of the research process?
2. When might personal interviews be your first choice for a research method?
3. When searching for information on privately held companies, what disadvantages are you faced with?
4. How would you more tightly focus your information search if an initial web search produced a list of 5,000 hits?
5. What is the danger of including older, or dated, information in a report?

Part A. Using a webbing technique, develop keywords and phrases for each of the following topics:

1. employee benefits
2. customer service skills
3. office dress code

Part B. Select one of the topics from Part A on which to conduct an information search. Decide on the focus of your research and list the keywords you will use to begin your search and the keywords you will use to broaden or narrow your search. Conduct secondary research on your topic, using either library resources or the Web to locate information from at least three sources. Turn in your notes and bibliographical information on index cards.

Part C. Write an e-mail request for an interview. After completing your secondary research, locate the name of an individual you think would be a good interview subject for a report on your selected topic. Write an e-mail request to that person, outlining the focus of your study and requesting an appointment for a brief in-person or telephone interview.

Part D. Using the information you have located, prepare a short report on your selected topic.

Part E. Using the bibliographical information you have gathered in Part B, prepare a bibliography to accompany your report, properly citing each source, including any personal interviews, observations, and web sites where you may have retrieved information.

TECHNOLOGY

Editing Activity

Read the following e-mail requesting information. What necessary information has been omitted from this request? Rewrite the e-mail, adding relevant facts to make the request clear and complete.

> Jim,
>
> Please prepare a report as soon as possible on the situation in our Midwest office. I will be meeting with the president soon and will need the most current data to review before that meeting.
>
> Thanks,
>
> Hector

words@work

If you are using *words@work*, complete the activities on Finding Information in the Workplace Success section.

Case Studies

DIVERSITY

1. Greg Richardson works for Worldwide Interpreting, a foreign language interpreting and translating service located in Houston, Texas. His company provides document translation services in a number of foreign languages and interpreting services to government offices, hospitals and medical offices, schools, and businesses in the Houston area.

    The company has grown at a steady rate since opening five years ago. The owners are planning to expand the business to at least two new cities within the next year and a half. Ms. Harada, one of the owners, has asked Greg to conduct some preliminary research and develop a list of ten potential sites for the new offices.

    She indicates that the list should include cities with a large number of foreign-born residents to assure that there will be adequate need for Worldwide's services. The cities also should be large enough to offer a wide variety of business opportunities, including government offices, educational institutions, and medical facilities. Finally, after Greg has prepared the list of cities, Ms. Harada would like to know how many other translating or interpreting services are currently doing business in those cities.

    Based on this information, where should Greg begin, and how should he proceed?

2. Dolores Lopez works for a large meat manufacturing company outside Denver, Colorado. The company produces beef and pork products, both fresh and frozen, for sale to food brokers and retail outlets throughout the United States.

    The officers are interested in expanding internationally. They are aware that the demand for U.S. meat products in foreign markets has grown considerably over the past several years. However, having sold their products only in the domestic market, they are unsure of the regulations involved in selling beef and pork products abroad.

    The company is specifically interested in selling its products in Russia, Korea, and Saudi Arabia. They have asked Dolores to gather information and prepare a report for them regarding the advisability of expanding the business in this direction. Specifically, Dolores needs to determine (1) the inspection and certification requirements, (2) the packaging and labeling requirements for each package of meat and each carton being shipped overseas, and (3) any restrictions on the sale by either the United States or the country of import.

    Armed with this information, where and how should Dolores begin her search?

COMMUNICATION FOR HEALTH SERVICES CAREERS

Frank Myers works in the human resources department of Mercy Medical Center, a large metropolitan hospital. In the last two years, Mercy Medical Center has experienced a 50 percent turnover in its nursing staff. This has resulted in numerous problems for the hospital.

Due to this constant turnover, there have been shortages of nurses to adequately care for patients; a lack of continuity of care; a constant need for recruiting, hiring, and training new nurses; and low morale among the staff.

Although the human resources department conducts exit interviews with each employee who leaves Mercy Medical Center, Frank believes that many of these employees have not provided full and complete information about their reasons for leaving. He has decided to address this issue by conducting a survey within the nursing staff of the hospital to try to determine the causes of the problem.

1. Is a survey the best way to gather the information Frank needs? Why?
2. What steps can Frank take to assure the success of the survey?

COMMUNICATION FOR MEDIA AND VISUAL ARTS

Denise Franklin is an advertising assistant at the New Horizon Advertising Agency. Her firm has been hired by a national insurance company that sells supplemental health insurance policies to design an advertising campaign aimed at senior citizens. As part of its overall campaign, the New Horizon team plans to run print ads in several daily newspapers in areas that are highly populated by senior citizens.

The project manager has assigned Denise the job of developing a list of potential newspapers in which to place the client's ads. Because she needs to stay within the client's budget for this project, Denise must carefully select the publications in which New Horizon will place the ads in order to reach the largest possible number of people in her target group.

1. With that in mind, what is Denise's first step?
2. How can Denise locate the newspapers to most effectively reach her target audience?

Video Case

Researching to Stay Ahead

Isabel Medina is the general manager for Hot Chill, a five-store chain selling sports apparel. Because the stores are located near mountain resorts, their primary income has come from clothing worn during winter sports. The stores' owners have just informed Isabel that they want her to begin selling sports equipment as well, including Black Diamond's mountain climbing gear. They gave her a deadline of four months.

Although Isabel welcomes the challenge of selling a new line of product, she intentionally positioned Hot Chill's focus away from the highly competitive sports equipment market and its sometimes thin profit margin. She must structure a timeline for these tasks: research what equipment to sell, purchase the new equipment, stock the stores, advertise, poll customers for their reactions to the new products, develop a plan for Hot Chill to exploit its competitors' weaknesses, and research those strengths and weaknesses.

Questions

1. Based on the video you have just seen, name ways in which Black Diamond does research. For each item you list, describe whether Black Diamond is gathering secondary or primary information.
2. What types of primary and secondary research do you recommend to Isabel to help her develop an effective sales and marketing strategy?
3. With two or three other classmates, create a questionnaire that Isabel could use to interview local climbers about their equipment buying habits. Think about the types of information that Isabel will need to determine what equipment will be most popular in Hot Chill.
4. Using the Internet, search for sites that sell mountain climbing equipment. You might try www.rei.com, www.bluewater-climbing.com, or www.shopems.com. Alone or with a partner, help Isabel with her competitive analysis. Create a table comparing features and prices for harnesses and ropes.

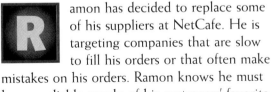

Wading Through Web Sites

Ramon has decided to replace some of his suppliers at NetCafe. He is targeting companies that are slow to fill his orders or that often make mistakes on his orders. Ramon knows he must have a reliable supply of his customers' favorite coffees or they will go elsewhere.

As a result of working with Eva, Ramon has learned some basic computer skills. He decides to use NetCafe's computers to search on-line for new suppliers. He will search during the late morning, when his coffee counter is fairly quiet. Eva wants the shop to have its own web site to advertise its products and services. As part of his search, Ramon intends to gather information about the kinds of information their web site might offer.

Ramon begins his search by typing in the keyword *coffee*, using the search engine InfoSeek. The search quickly results in a list of ten major categories of information, including coffee grinders and coffee magazines. It also offers 634,409 specific web sites! As Ramon scrolls down the first ten web sites, he sees sites as varied as the Harvard Women's Health Watch and the Gevalia Coffee Company. Many of the listings, he notices, are chat rooms for people who like to drink coffee.

An hour later, the NetCafe is filling up with customers, many of whom have come in for a mug of coffee. Ramon is still wandering from web site to web site. He has not located one supplier with whom he is sure he wants to do business. He gives up and concentrates on serving his thirsty customers.

1. Working with a partner, conduct an online search for coffee suppliers and information about the varieties of coffee that they supply. On a sheet of paper, document your search to show the search engine(s) and the Boolean techniques or advanced search features you used. List the web sites you accessed and the links you used between sites. Make your documentation complete so others could follow your path.

2. Select five of the best coffee suppliers you have located and print a copy of their web sites. For each source, answer these questions:

   a. Does the supplier seem to cater to people buying coffee for their own use or does it offer good prices for wholesale buyers at coffeehouses?

   b. How valid and reliable does the web site seem to be? Is it mostly a subjective advertisement? Does it offer many products that are only loosely related to coffee? Or does it offer mostly factual information about the coffee it supplies?

   c. How many and what kinds of links does the web site provide?

   d. How well does the web site use graphics? Describe its strengths or weaknesses.

   e. What kinds of ordering options does the web site provide?

   f. What aspects of this web site could the NetCafe use in its own web site?

chapter 8

Developing and Using Graphic and Visual Aids

8·1 Purposes and Placement of Graphic Aids

8·2 Developing Graphic Aids

8·3 Using Visual Aids for Oral Presentations

Improving the Progress Report

Alex Mason, acting as spokesperson for his work team, has just finished giving a ten-minute progress report to the company's top managers at their regular monthly meeting. As he leaves the meeting, Alex recalls the day, more than three months earlier, when he volunteered to give the very first progress report on his work team's project. Alex's intention had been to take his turn first and then not have to give the progress report for any of the remaining months of the project.

Before he knew what hit him, however, Alex had an unwritten job responsibility added to his job description: official team spokesperson. After that first meeting no one ever raised the issue of who would present the report at the monthly meeting. In fact, whenever the discussion shifted to what should be included in the progress report, everyone matter-of-factly referred to Alex's presenting the information.

Alex believes he is doing a good job at including the key project update information the managers need to know. He is not quite so sure, however, that he is doing a good enough job of presenting the information. The handout he prepares for his presentation each month is full of impor-

tant numbers and statistics. The oral presentation he gives pretty much follows his handout.

Having worked with the numbers throughout the month, Alex is very familiar with them by the time he presents them in the meeting. He's troubled, though, by the EGO (eyes-glazed-over) look he has observed in many audience members during the part of his report where he rattles off the numbers.

Alex decides that between now and next month's meeting, he will need to find a more effective way to present the numbers and statistics portion of his progress report—in both the handout and the oral presentation.

Questions

1. Why do audience members often tune out a speaker when a great deal of numerical or statistical data is included in an oral presentation?

2. What graphic aids might Alex consider using in presenting the numbers portion of his next monthly report?

3. How might Alex apply the ancient Chinese proverb, "One showing is worth a hundred sayings"?

8·1 Purposes and Placement of Graphic Aids

Objectives

After completing Section 8.1, you should be able to:

1 Discuss why graphic aids are used in the communication process.

2 Describe how to place and identify graphic aids in written documents.

3 Explain how graphic aids can mislead an audience.

Objective

↓ KEY POINT

Research indicates that what you show your audience carries about *three times* more impact than what you tell them.

Why Use Graphic Aids?

A **graphic aid** provides a visual representation of the words in your message. Graphic aids provide an efficient means of presenting dense amounts of information in a way that can help the audience understand your message. Because most people remember what they *see* much longer and better than what they *hear*, graphic aids are important for you to know how to use as you work to improve your communication skills.

Communicators increasingly use the various types of graphic aids discussed in this chapter for three reasons:

1. Audiences expect that messages should be delivered in clear, easy-to-understand, visually stimulating formats. No matter how interesting the content, few people revisit an Internet web site that contains only text, stay tuned to a television program made up entirely of "talking heads," or spend money on magazines that have no photographs.

2. Technology has made the creation and delivery of graphic aids easier and more accessible than ever before. Software programs, such as Microsoft Excel, have built-in charting programs that allow you to quickly and easily convert numerical data into colorful, easy-to-understand graphs. You can insert graphs into reports and letters or use them in computer presentations. Placing graphic aids on your web site for anyone who has Internet access or attaching them to an e-mail message are common practice.

   Every graphic aid discussed in this chapter can be created using a personal computer, provided you have the appropriate software programs and the necessary hardware such as a color printer or scanner. The technology margin notes throughout this section, together with the text discussion, will alert you to ways the computer can assist you in developing and delivering your graphic and visual aids.

3. Communicators recognize that the odds of keeping their audience's attention while at the same time getting their point across are much higher when they use graphic and visual aids.

Using Graphic Aids in Written Documents

When you use graphic aids in written documents, you should follow several guidelines in placing and identifying them. Doing so will ensure that the reader benefits as much as possible.

Placing Graphic Aids

You must first decide whether the graphic aid should be placed within the body of your document or in an appendix. The main factor to consider is where the reader would prefer and most benefit from its placement. If the graphic aid relates to a major point being presented, then most likely it should be placed in the body of the document. If the purpose of the graphic aid is to provide details that few would need to reference, then place it in the appendix.

When you refer to the graphic aid within the written text, remember to place your statement referring to the graphic aid *before* the actual graphic aid appears. Also make the reference to the graphic aid flow smoothly into your discussion, as illustrated in the two examples that follow:

> The demand for Product X increased an average of 2.5 percent for each of the past six quarters as illustrated in Chart 7.

> The demand for Product X over the past six quarters increased an average of 2.5 percent. (See Chart 1 in the Appendix for a detailed comparison by sales region.)

When the placement of the graphic aid is to be in the body of the document, place the graphic aid on the same page as its reference. When that is not possible, then place the graphic aid on the page immediately following its first mention. Finally, avoid dividing a graphic aid between two pages.

Identifying Graphic Aids

Graphic aids contain the following four parts:

1. *A unique number for referencing purposes.* Choose a numbering system and be consistent with this format throughout the document. For example, you may choose to call all graphic aids *Figures* and number them consecutively throughout. Another option is use the two designations *Table* for all graphic aids that are in table format and *Figure* for all graphic aids that are not tables. If the document contains only one section, then number the figures consecutively (*Figure 1, Figure 2, Table 1, Table 2,* etc.). When there is more than one section or chapter, use a system such as *Figure 1.1, Figure 1.2* for the first section and *Figure 2.1, Figure 2.2* for the second section, etc. The only exception to this numbering requirement occurs when

Check out these visually oriented web sites: **www .exploratorium.edu/exhibits** (some features available from this site require plug-ins, such as Shockwave, RealAudio, and QuickTime); **www.nordstrom .com** (shopping on-line).

SCANS
Employability

Creative Thinking
Employers are looking for employees who can communicate information effectively. Going through the thought and preparation required to create visual aids can contribute to a better-organized presentation than a presentation using no visual aids.

DIVERSITY
Because a "picture is worth a thousand words," you can save your audience much time by providing visuals. Those in your audience whose first language is not English will especially appreciate your efforts to present ideas visually as well as in writing or orally.

Avoiding Copyright Crimes

Many presenters, who have not secured appropriate permissions or licenses from the copyright owners, include in their presentations such items as photographs scanned from magazines; graphics, audio files, and video clips downloaded from the Web; or CD music from their personal collections. Claiming ignorance of copyright laws does not reduce the consequences for breaking the laws.

Basic facts about copyright law include:

- Copyright law is broken whenever an individual photocopies, distributes, customizes, publicly performs, or displays someone else's original work without permission.

- Copyright protection lasts for the lifetime of the author or creator, plus 70 years. After those 70 years, it passes into what's called the "public domain," free to be used by anyone without permission.

- Copyright is violated whether or not you charged money in your reuse or duplication of copyright works.

- Placing information about the source of the original work, without having secured permission from the copyright owner, will not protect you from being prosecuted.

Excluding the fine for actual damages, copyright violation penalties can range from $20,000 to $100,000 per hit, depending on the type of violation. In addition, commercial copyright violations involving more than 10 copies and a value of more than $2,500 is now a felony in the United States. ■

For more information on copyright issues, visit Brad Templeton's the "10 Big Myths about Copyright Explained" at **www .templetons.com/brad/ copymyths.html**.

KEY POINT

Descriptive, yet concise, graphic aids titles assist your reader in understanding your ideas.

the document contains only one graphic aid, in which case no number need be assigned.

2. *A title for each graphic aid that describes its contents.* The title may be all uppercase, or uppercase and lowercase, and should contain enough detail for the reader to be able to understand the graphic aid without having to read the explanation in the text.

3. *The graphic aid.* For example, the table, pie chart, flowchart, or picture is normally placed below its number and title.

4. *A source line.* This part is not included if the content of the material in the graphic aid originated with the author of the document. However, you must include a source line whenever you obtain the material from another source. The word *source* is usually placed beneath the graphic aid and is in uppercase letters followed by a colon and the source. For example:

SOURCE: XYZ Company, *1999 Annual Report,* p. 9.

Using Graphic Aids to Mislead

Figure 8-1 illustrates how a graphic aid can be created in a misleading way. Note in these two graphs that the vertical axis (the line that goes from bottom to top) represents the number of people who attended the conference, and the horizontal axis (the line that goes from left to right) shows the five years for which attendance figures are provided. When looking at the left graph, casual viewers comparing the height of the bars that represents how many people attended the conference might get the impression that nearly four times as many people attended in 1999 than in 1995. Because the vertical axis starts at "400," the graph misrepresents the actual increase in attendance. The graph on the right provides a more accurate picture of the increase by beginning the vertical axis at "0."

Because some readers will only skim your document, giving more attention to the graphic aids than to the written text, graphic aids often have more impact than their accompanying text. In addition, your readers usually will remember visual images longer than written text. For these reasons, you must analyze your graphic aids to ensure you have designed them to present an accurate picture of what the data represents. Your ethical responsibility is to report data as clearly and accurately as possible.

Objective 3

TECHNOLOGY
Software graphing programs provide a means for changing the starting value of the vertical axis from zero to another value. For example, a line graph illustrating the Dow Jones Industrial Average on a given day (see **www.thomsoninvest.net/index.sht**) is an exception to the rule that the axis must start at zero.

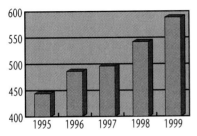

This graph misrepresents the data.

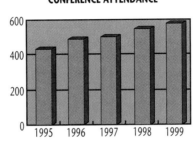

This graph accurately presents the data.

FIGURE 8-1 Bar graphs can be misleading.

ETHICS

If you must omit part of a scale because of excessive data, you can make sure your reader recognizes that fact by drawing a slash or a wavy line on the axis, as illustrated in the broken bar graph in Figure 8-9.

Purposes and Placement of Graphic Aids

Answer the following questions:
1. Graphic aids
   a. provide a visual representation of words
   b. present dense information more clearly
   c. can be created using a personal computer
   d. all of the above

2. True or False. The main factor to consider when placing a graphic aid is where it will fit.

3. Four parts of a graphic aid are (a) a unique number for referencing purposes, (b) a __?__, (c) the graphic aid, and (d) a __?__ line.

Check your answers in Appendix E.

CASE 8:
Answers

Response to Question 1 in Chapter Opener

1. **Why do audience members often tune out a speaker when a great deal of numerical or statistical data is included in an oral presentation?**

   Audience members have difficulty visualizing meaning for the numbers or statistics they hear. When meaning escapes the audience, they lose interest in what is being said. One way for speakers to keep audience attention is to provide the visual meaning as they present the data.

   For example, if a speaker were to present the data in a table format that organizes the numbers or statistics into meaningful relationships, the audience would be able to visualize the significance of the data.

DISCUSSION QUESTIONS

1. Why do graphic aids often have more impact than their accompanying text?
2. Is an audience's demanding increased usage of visual images a positive or negative characteristic of the communication environment in which we live and work? Justify your answer.

8·2 Developing Graphic Aids

Choosing the Best Graphic Aids

If you have ever used a software application, such as Microsoft Excel's charting feature, to create graphic aids, you know how easy these programs are to use and how professional looking the end product can be. Users can create a wide variety of graphic aids after spending just a couple hours in learning how to use a charting program.

Even though such powerful charting tools are only a mouse click away, you still need to know the basic graphic aids principles presented in this chapter because the computer can do only what you tell it to do. When using these charting programs, for example, you must choose the type of graphic aid you want generated from the information you key into the program.

To choose the best graphic aid, you must know what you want your receiver to understand from the graphic. In other words, you

Objectives

After completing Section 8.2, you should be able to:

1 Choose the graphic or visual aid that will best accomplish your communication objective.

2 Create tables to present cumbersome information in an organized, easy-to-follow format.

3 Create the three types of charts often used in business reports.

4 Create line and bar graphs in their various formats.

5 Identify miscellaneous graphic and visual aids used in reports.

Objective

Presentation and graphic software give you the ability to create professional graphics for your reports and presentations.

must identify the objective you hope to achieve and choose a graphic aid suited to that purpose. Figure 8-2 outlines the types of graphic aids covered in this chapter, with objectives for each.

Tables

Objective

A **table** is an arrangement of information into rows and columns for reference purposes. Your table should have clear and concise descriptors for the identifying title as well as for the labels at the top of each column, as illustrated in Figure 8-2.

TECHNOLOGY

With most software applications, the easiest way to correctly align numbers in a table is to select the cells in which the numbers appear, and then choose the right alignment option.

Graphic Aid	Objective
Table	To show exact figures or to present cumbersome information in an organized, easy-to-follow format
Organization chart	To show lines of authority and relationships among departments and employees within an organization
Flowchart	To illustrate a procedure or process
Pie chart	To show how the parts of a whole are distributed
Line graph	To illustrate changes in quantities or values over time
Bar graph	To compare one or more quantities
Map	To show geographic relationships
Picture	To provide a realistic view of a specific item or place
Drawing	To emphasize details of an idea or procedure

FIGURE 8-2 Objective determines appropriate graphic aids. (Example of table in portrait orientation)

SCANS
Employability

Technology: Applies Technology to Task
In addition to expecting employees to communicate their ideas orally and in writing, employers also expect employees to communicate using graphic, pictorial, and multimedia methods.

The information contained in Figure 8-2 could have been presented in a lengthy paragraph made up of nine sentences. However, the information is communicated more effectively and is easier for the reader to reference when presented in a table instead of in paragraph format. The same is true for the information contained in Figure 8-3.

Tables can be presented in either **portrait orientation** (the short edge of the paper is at the top of the table, as in Figure 8-2) or **landscape orientation** (the long edge of the paper is at the top of the table, as in Figure 8-3). You choose the orientation that best accommodates the number of columns in your table. Lastly, whenever your table contains numbers, be sure the digits are aligned correctly:

Incorrect Alignment	Correct Alignment
10,397.20	10,397.20
542.00	542.00
3,492.79	3,492.79

Marketing Department
Vacation Planner
Number of Days Taken for 2002

Employee	Jan-02	Feb-02	Mar-02	Apr-02	May-02	Jun-02	Jul-02	Aug-02	Sep-02	Oct-02	Nov-02	Dec-02	2002 YTD
Chan, Danelle	3				3							4	10
Carducci, Bevin	2							14					16
Daanske, Kirsten				5									5
Frinsky, Tracy									3			4	7
Gonzales, Maria		10					10						20
Grant, John												10	10
Herrera, Joey				5		3							8
Jackson, Irvin										5		5	10
Kirk, James T.	4					12							16
Kitching, William									4		3		7
McMillan, Cynthia		2					5						7
Picard, Jean-Luc										8		7	15
Santana, Ariel									15				15
Slavoric, Olga						8							8
Smith, Hannibal			2		2			2					6
Wong, Susie			4				4						8

FIGURE 8-3 Table in Landscape Orientation

Charts

Objective

3

Find and analyze an organization chart, such as the one at **www.xerox.com/downloads/ charts040999.ppt**

TECHNOLOGY

A well-known software application for drawing flowcharts is Visio®. Go to the web site at **www.visio.com/products/ standard/** to learn more about using the computer to draw flowcharts.

Three types of charts are commonly used in business reports. They are organization charts, flowcharts, and pie charts.

Organization Charts

An **organization chart** is used to illustrate the relationships and official lines of authority and communication among employees and departments of an organization. The chart can represent the entire organization or only one department or division within the organization. Figure 8-4 illustrates XYZ Company's organization chart. The boxes in the organization chart may list position titles or employee names and position titles. The higher the level of the box in the chart, the higher the level of authority that position has within the organization.

The solid lines between boxes at different levels represent lines of authority and formal communication. Positions at higher levels can give work orders to those positions at lower levels if they are connected by direct lines. Horizontal lines represent communication channels between positions that are at the same authority level.

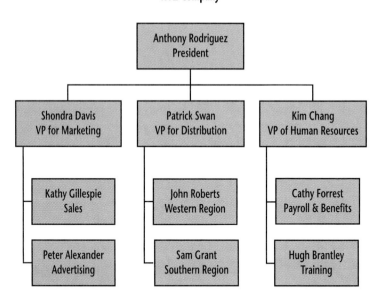

FIGURE 8-4 Organization Chart

Flowcharts

A **flowchart** is a step-by-step diagram of a procedure or process. The flowchart simplifies complicated procedures by summarizing each step of the procedure and allowing the user to see the order in which the steps must be followed. For example, if a new procedure were to be presented to employees in eight paragraphs of explanatory text, preparing a flowchart that presents each step of the procedure would help to ensure that steps are not omitted by those who only skim the eight paragraphs. Figure 8-5 is a flowchart diagramming the procedure for changing a flat tire.

Procedure for Changing a Flat Tire

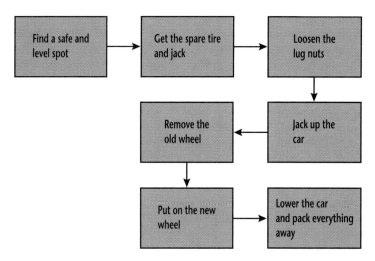

FIGURE 8-5 Flowchart

Pie Charts

A **pie chart** shows how the parts of a whole are distributed and how the parts relate to one another. Figure 8-6 shows a sample pie chart. Generally, the parts (which should be limited to no more than seven) are represented by percentages. A pie chart can easily present such statistics as a breakdown of family income into various expense categories.

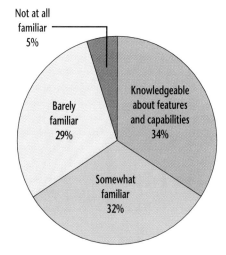

FIGURE 8-6 Pie Chart

KEY POINT

If you want to emphasize or call attention to a particular section of the pie chart, you can "explode" the pie section by slightly moving it out from the rest of the chart.

When you construct a pie chart, place the largest pie section so that its left edge lines up with the twelve o'clock position on the pie circle. Then place decreasing pie sections clockwise from there.

Graphs

Objective 4

A **graph** provides a means for comparing data. The most common types of graphs are line and bar graphs, both of which come in several varieties. Strive for simplicity of design in creating your graphs. You want the reader to be able to interpret the information easily.

Line Graphs

A **line graph** is useful for showing changes in a quantity or value over time. This type of graph often is used to show fluctuations or trends in sales, costs, or production over a period of months or years. In graphs depicting trends, the horizontal axis is used to show the time or quantity measured; the vertical axis is used to show amounts.

A **single-line graph** shows the movement of only one quantity or value over time. Shading or coloring may be used to add emphasis to the single-line graph, as shown in Figure 8-7.

A **multiple-line graph** shows the movement of two or more quantities or values over time. In this type of graph you can differentiate the lines by choosing different line styles (dashed, solid, dotted), different colors (red, green, and yellow), or different styles and colors (dashed red line, solid green line, and yellow dotted line). Use a **legend** to identify what each line represents, or label the lines within the graph area, as illustrated in Figure 8-8.

DIVERSITY

The U.S. Census Bureau provides data on trends in minority population at **www.census .gov/pubinfo/www/hotlinks. html**. Find specific trend data of interest to you and use it to create a line graph that shows your findings.

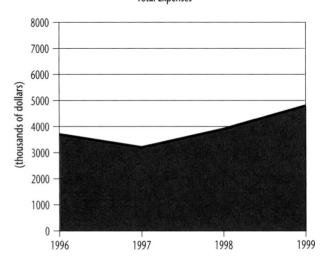

Andrews Supply House, Inc.
Total Expenses

FIGURE 8-7 Single-line Graph

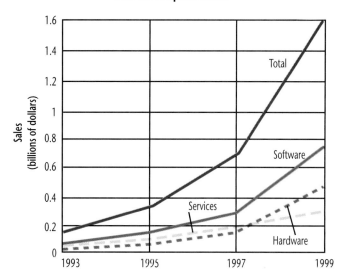

**Growth of
Portable Computer Market**

FIGURE 8-8 Multiple-line Graph

Bar Graphs

A **bar graph** is used when you want your audience to be able to compare the data represented in the graph. The most common types of bar graphs are the simple bar, broken bar, multiple bar, and stacked bar. The bars can be constructed either vertically or horizontally in all of these graph types. To avoid mispresenting information in the graph, as discussed in Section 8.1, the quantities or amounts axis should begin with zero.

A **simple bar graph** compares only one set of data. The **simple vertical bar graph**, in which the height of the bar indicates quantity, is shown in Figure 8-9. The second graph in Figure 8-9 presents the same data in a **simple horizontal bar graph**, in which the length of the bar indicates quantity. (Even though all the remaining bar graphs can also be constructed horizontally, this first example is the only one showing the two formats.) A **broken bar graph**, as shown in Figure 8-9, is used to indicate omission of part of each bar if some quantities are so large that they would go off the chart.

A **multiple-bar graph** is useful for comparing more than one set of data at various points in time. You may want to add color to the bars to distinguish among the sets of data being presented and then use a legend to identify what the color represents. Comparing more than four sets of data in one graph makes the graph too cluttered and difficult to read. Figure 8-9 shows a multiple-bar graph.

A **stacked bar graph** divides each bar into the parts that contributed to each total bar. For example, Figure 8-9 not only shows

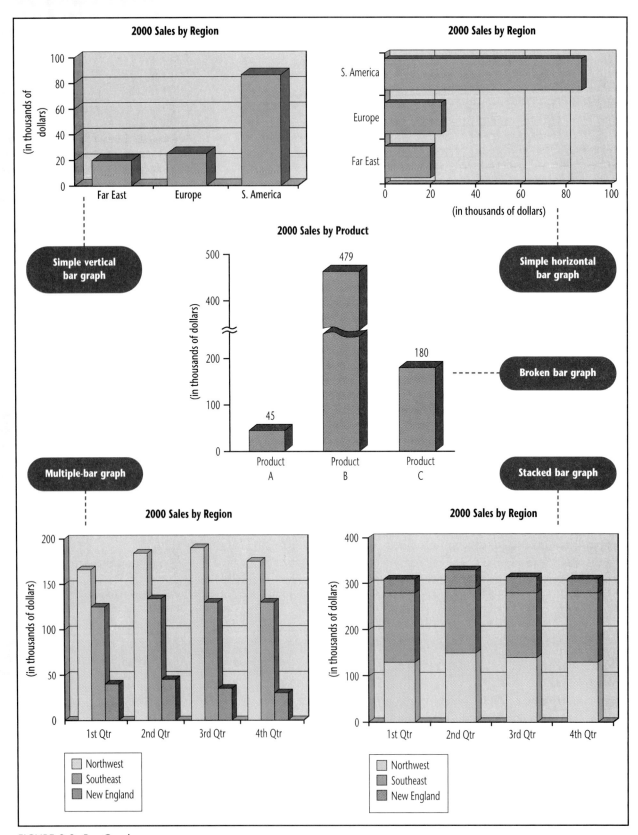

2000 Sales by Region

2000 Sales by Region

Simple vertical bar graph

Simple horizontal bar graph

2000 Sales by Product

Broken bar graph

Multiple-bar graph

Stacked bar graph

2000 Sales by Region

2000 Sales by Region

FIGURE 8-9 Bar Graphs

the total sales in each quarter of 2000, but the graph also provides a breakdown within each bar indicating the contribution each region made to the total sales. In interpreting the graph, you can easily see that the Northwest region consistently had greater sales than the other two regions. Notice that with this type of chart, as in the multiple-bar graph, you'll need to distinguish among the sets of data being presented by using color and a legend.

Miscellaneous Graphic and Visual Aids

Although used much less frequently than tables, charts, and graphs, the three miscellaneous graphic and visual aids presented in this section can enhance your communication when used in appropriate situations. These miscellaneous graphic and visual aids are maps, photographs, and drawings.

Maps

A **map** shows geographic relationships and is especially useful when your audience may not be familiar with the geographic areas in your report. The map shown in Figure 8-10 communicates much information visually in an easy-to-grasp and more interesting format than a lengthy written explanation would be able to do.

Photographs

A **photograph** is used to provide a realistic view of a specific item or place and to make the document more appealing to read. Four sources of easy access to photographs are the digital camera, professional photograph collections available on CD-ROM, the scanner, and the World Wide Web.

Go to the U.S. Bureau of Labor Statistics (**www.bls .gov/regnhome.htm**) or the U.S. Census Bureau (**www .census.gov/datamap/www/**) to see how effectively maps are used to organize and communicate the information from these organizations.

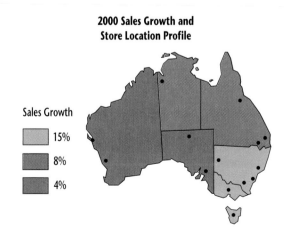

FIGURE 8-10 Map

Find out how to use the
photographs and other
media that you find on the
World Wide Web appropri-
ately and legally. A detailed
article is available at **www.eff
.org/pub/CAF/law/ip-primer**;
many copyright and fair use
resources are available at
**http://fairuse.standford.edu
/multimed/**.

- A **digital camera** stores images digitally (the format a computer can use) rather than recording them on film. Once you take your picture, you can download the photograph to your computer system, manipulate it with a graphics program, insert the photograph into a document, and print the document.

- CD-ROM collections, such as the *IMSI MasterClips* 303,000 (**www.imsisoft.com**), include clip art, scaleable drawings, and high-resolution photographs. Depending on the source of your photographs and how you are using them, you may have to pay a fee for their use.

- A **scanner** captures images from photographic prints, posters, magazine pages, and similar sources for computer editing and display. Scanners usually come with software, such as Adobe's Photoshop product, that lets you resize and otherwise modify a captured image before inserting it into your document.

- The World Wide Web opens your computer to another excellent resource. Many web sites provide photographs that you may download for free (such as **www.xoom.com**); others such as the Time collection (**www.thepicturecollection.com**) charge a fee for the photographs you use.

See Figure 8-11 for a photograph used to give a realistic view of the people and technology used in a videoconference.

FIGURE 8-11 Videoconferencing saves companies money by reducing travel costs. It virtually eliminates the scheduling problems encountered when trying to bring people from outside a company together in one place for a meeting.

DIVERSITY

Culturally Correct Presentations

When making presentations in cross-cultural environments, speakers must be aware of differences in cultural expectations and practices. Guidelines to follow include:

- Simplify and clarify your content by using simple sentences and restating key points.
- Speak more slowly and deliberately than usual, using more pauses and being careful to enunciate clearly.
- Remember that body language is not universal. For example, in Greece a head nod indicates "no" rather than "yes." A "thumbs up" is a rude gesture in Australia.
- Adjust eye-contact habits. Direct eye contact, for example, can be considered an invasion of privacy in cultures found in Japan or the Philippines.
- Adapt presentation style to meet audience members' expectations regarding an appropriate level of formality. Formality level in some cultures, for example, would lead audience members to feel uncomfortable if the speaker were to dress too casually, mingle with the audience during break, or use animated gestures and tell jokes during the presentation.
- Win points with your audience by being patient, polite, and showing respect for cultural differences. ■

For more information on international presentations, use the search feature at **www.presentations .com** and type in the search words "international audiences."

When you are making presentations to a culturally diverse group of people, make sure you simplify your presentation, speak slowly, and use your body language and eye contact accordingly.

Drawings

A **drawing** is useful for communicating a complicated idea or a procedure. Manufacturers of bicycles, for example, provide consumers detailed drawings to assist them in putting their bicycles together. Providing a photograph of the assembled bicycle would not provide enough detail to get the bicycle put together properly. A simpler example provided in Figure 8-12 illustrates how to load a CD into a CD-ROM drive. The drawing provides more detail about the procedure than a photograph showing the CD already loaded into the CD holder could provide.

**Loading CD into
CD-ROM Drive**

FIGURE 8-12   Drawing

2 Checkpoint

Developing Graphic Aids

For each objective, identify an appropriate graphic type.
1.   Illustrate the steps in a new procedure.
2.   Organize cumbersome detail into an easy-to-follow format.
3.   Show geographic relationships.
4.   Emphasize details in assembling a product.
5.   Provide a realistic view of a specific place.
6.   Show lines of authority and relationships among departments.
7.   Show how the parts of a whole are distributed.
8.   Illustrate changes in quantities or values over time.
9.   Compare one or more quantities with another.

Check your answers in Appendix E.

CASE 8:

Answers

Response to Question 2 in Chapter Opener

2. What graphic aids might Alex consider using in presenting the numbers portion of his next monthly report?

Of the graphic aids described in Section 8.2 that applied to the presentation of numbers, Alex could consider using any of the following, depending on what he is trying to accomplish in presenting the numbers:

- Table—Alex could arrange the numbers in rows and columns, so that the audience can see how the numbers and statistics relate to one another.
- Pie chart—Alex could use this graphic aid if illustrating the proportion or distribution of the values is necessary.
- Line graph—Alex should use this type of graphic if he needs to show changes in quantity or value over time. This is probably necessary in comparing the numbers from last month's report with this month's.
- Bar graph—The managers probably need to compare numbers over the life of the project as well, so more than likely Alex also could use this graphic aid.

DISCUSSION QUESTIONS

1. Identify the three types of charts commonly used in business reports and give a brief description of each.
2. Of the graphic aids described in this section, which type or types do you come across most frequently in the books and periodicals you read most often? Which type is easiest for you to understand? Which is most difficult to understand?
3. Have you ever tried a charting software program? If yes, identify them and describe your experience.

Using Visual Aids for Oral Presentations

After completing Section 8.3, you should be able to:

1 Choose an appropriate visual aid that will enhance your oral presentation and help the audience to better understand your message.

2 Prepare visual aids to ensure they are well received by your audience.

3 Use visual aids in a professional manner during your oral presentation.

Objective

↓ KEY POINT

People remember 10 percent of what they read, 20 percent of what they hear, 30 percent of what they see, and 50 percent of what they see and hear.

Choosing the Best Visual Aids

Humans can process visual images 60,000 times faster than text. Studies conducted by 3M to determine the effectiveness of visual communication have shown that the effective use of visual aids can make speakers appear more professional, better prepared, more persuasive, more credible, and more interesting than those who do not use visuals.[1] Visual aids support and clarify the speaker's ideas and help audience members to visualize the message.

The four-step visual aids process is (a) deciding whether your oral presentation requires visual aids, (b) choosing the best visual aids, (c) preparing your visual aids, and (d) presenting your visual aids.

If you can answer "yes" to any of the following questions, then visual aids should be used in the presentation:

- Will visual aids help clarify your message?
- Will visual aids add interest to your presentation?
- Will visual aids help the audience remember what you say?

The rest of this section covers what you need to know in order to complete the remaining three steps of the visual aids process.

Many types of visual aids can be used to allow audience members to view the text, charts, graphics, or other images that accompany your spoken words during your oral presentation. Among the more common options are: (1) posters and flip charts; (2) transparencies, slides, and computer presentations; (3) objects; (4) chalkboards, whiteboards, and electronic whiteboards; and (5) handouts.

Posters and Flip Charts

Posters and flip charts are similar in size, and both generally are displayed on an easel. For posters, prepare your visuals ahead of time. For flip charts, you can either prepare your visuals ahead of time and flip through the pad as you speak, or you can draw your visuals as you speak.

---

[1]*Brilliant Meetings: The Art of Effective Visual Presentations* (Austin, TX: 3M Austin Center, 1993), 12.

Transparencies, Slides, and Computer Presentations

Generally, the content of all three of these visual aids is very similar and is created using a software program such as Microsoft PowerPoint. The difference lies in how your audience sees the visual aid.

- With **transparencies**, presentation visuals are transferred to clear acetate film and those images are projected on screen using an overhead projector.
- With **slides**, images are transferred to 35mm slides, placed in a slide carousel, and projected on screen using a slide projector.
- With a **computer presentation**, the computer is connected to projection equipment that allows your audience to see the slides you have prepared in your presentation software program. As your slides appear on your computer monitor, your audience sees the projected image enlarged on screen. Figure 8-13 illustrates one option for projecting your computer presentation using a laptop computer, a projector, and a projection screen.

Many computer presentation software programs allow you to create a **multimedia presentation**, which lets you add to your text and graphics such features as sound, **animation** (movement of text or images on a slide), and **video clips** (brief video features that usually include sound). Adding these special features results in a much more visually stimulating presentation than can be achieved with transparencies and slides.

↓KEY POINT

If you choose a visual aid, such as a flip chart, that requires you to write down ideas as you speak, make sure you write legibly and spell correctly. If you have trouble with either skill, choose a different visual-aid option.

Check out the web site at **www.genigraphics.com** to learn more about a company where you can send your PowerPoint file and have them reproduce the electronic slides onto transparency acetate film, 35mm slides, and posters.

TECHNOLOGY

Your computer must have sound and video capabilities before you can use it to create and project multimedia presentations. The speakers on your computer are usually too weak to project enough volume to your audience, so you will need to wire your computer to the auditorium's amplifier system.

FIGURE 8-13 Presentation graphics created on computer can be projected onto a large screen for viewing in a meeting.

Objects

Audience members can view three-dimensional objects presented from the front of the room or even passed among audience participants, provided the object is large enough and the crowd is small enough. With smaller objects and larger audiences, however, the object should be projected on screen using a visual presenter, such as the one illustrated in Figure 8-14.

Chalkboards, Whiteboards, and Electronic Whiteboards

The familiar grade-school visual-aid medium that in the old days was referred to as a "blackboard" now has an electronic version. Using chalk on a green or black erasable surface has progressed to using colorful markers on an erasable whiteboard. Using special markers on an erasable **electronic whiteboard** captures the images and allows the user to print out a hard copy of what is written on the board.

Handouts

You may want to give handouts to your audience members so that they have visual documentation of your presentation. When you give the audience your handout depends on how you'd like them to use it:

- At the beginning of your presentation, audience members can use the handout to follow your points and to add additional notes.
- During your presentation, the handout can emphasize or add detail to a particular point you are making.
- At the conclusion of your presentation, the handout can supply reference materials that your audience can use later.

Go to **www.mmm.com/ meetingnetwork/ presentations/pmag_improve _handouts.html** and read the article on improving audience handouts.

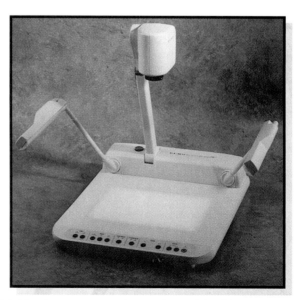

FIGURE 8-14 Visual presenter used to project a 3-D object

Choosing the Appropriate Visual Aid

When deciding which of these visual aids will be best in your situation, answer these questions:

■ *Which options do you have available in the location where you will be making your presentation?* Some of the options, such as a computer presentation or an electronic whiteboard, require that you have access to the necessary electronic equipment. On the other hand, if you're using posters on an easel, no special equipment is required.

■ *Which option will be best in helping your audience to understand and remember your message?* You might prefer using the familiar chalkboard or whiteboard option; however, if some other option would help your audience to more easily understand and remember your message, then use another more appropriate visual aid.

■ *How many people will be in your audience and how large is the room?* If you're speaking to a small group, a poster or flip chart would be appropriate. For larger audiences, those options would be inappropriate.

■ *How much detail do you have to give your audience?* Because the print has to be so small, transparencies, slides, and computer presentations do not work well when you have many numbers and lots of detailed information to present.

■ *How much time do you have to prepare your visual aids?* Writing down key points on a whiteboard as you speak requires no preparation time. Preparing transparencies or slides would require a great deal of preparation time.

■ *Should I use more than one type of visual aid?* All of these visual aids options can be used either alone or in various combinations. For example, you could give a handout that contains copies of the slides you will use in your computer presentation. Or you could add variety to a lengthy presentation by using a flip chart for the first half and overhead transparencies for the second half.

Preparing Your Visual Aids

Here are some preparation guidelines that apply to any visual aids option you may choose:

1. *Keep your visual aids simple and brief.* The more detail and unnecessary information you include, the less your audience will want to look at your visual. Your job in preparing visual aids is to make what you are presenting easy to understand and as concise as possible. For example, instead of writing out a complete sentence for one of your points, use only key words to convey the meaning. Your oral explanation that accompanies the point will provide the necessary details. Likewise, if you have something complicated to communicate, instead of placing it all on one slide, consider how you might break down the complex idea into smaller segments. Then present the information in, say, three parts instead of one.

KEY POINT

The only visual aid that works well with lots of detail is a handout; however, you have to be careful when you give the handout to your audience. If the handout is given at the wrong time, it can distract your audience. Participants will be reading the detail instead of listening to your presentation.

Objective

TECHNOLOGY

Go to **www.officeupdate .microsoft.com/ downloaddetails/pp97qs.htm** for a slide show demonstration of Microsoft PowerPoint that includes PowerPoint basics; a guided tour of important features; and lists of tips, tools, and tricks.

When trying to explain a complex idea, displaying a complicated visual aid with small print is worse than displaying no visual at all.

Be careful to give appropriate credit to the sources of information you use to create your visual aids. Doing so not only avoids charges of plagiarism but also adds credibility to your presentation because of how thoroughly your sources are documented.

Objective

KEY POINT

You must give your audience enough time to absorb the information on each visual aid. If you advance too quickly, your audience will get frustrated by how little time you give them to understand the ideas presented. They will eventually give up trying to understand.

2. *Make sure everything is large enough.* The best way to test whether the size is adequate is to set up your visual aids in the front of the room in which you will be making your presentation and then go sit in the back seat in that room. If you can comfortably see everything (text, pictures, labels on your graphics, objects, etc.), then you have done well. If you have to squint to see anything, redo your visual aids so that everyone in your audience will be able to see them.

3. *Use color for emphasis.* Your audience members will expect colorful visual aids. Take advantage of the widespread availability of technology and tools—such as color scanners, color printers, and color markers—that allow you to add color to your visuals. Use good taste in coordinating your color schemes. Do not overdo the color so that it becomes a distraction instead of an enhancement.

4. *Always include a title; use a source line if necessary.* Your visual aids should always be titled. You would not, for example, have a line graph with no title, nor a list of bulleted points with no title. Use a source line only if you used a reference source for the content.

5. *Prepare an acceptable number of visual aids.* The two extremes you should avoid are (1) preparing so many visual aids that your audience gets buried in them, and (2) preparing so few visual aids that your audience gets bored. For example, if you have prepared a computer presentation for a 20-minute presentation that requires your flashing up a new slide every 12 seconds for the entire 20 minutes, your audience will get burned out in the first 5 minutes because they've already had to absorb the content of 25 slides. As a general rule, you should present a new visual about every 2 minutes.

Presenting Your Visual Aids

Finally, as you present your visual aids, keep in mind some basic guidelines for using your visual aids in a professional manner.

1. *Display your visual aids at the right time.* Visual aids can easily become a distraction if you display them before you are ready to discuss their contents. For example, if you place a poster on an easel at the beginning of your presentation but will not be using the poster until after the introduction, some people in your audience will be distracted by the poster during your introduction. A better approach would be to have a blank poster board covering the poster until you are ready for it.

2. *Display the points on your visual aids at the right time.* A visual aid also can become a distraction if you display all the points before you're ready to talk about them. For example, if your transparency has three bulleted points that make up the outline of your presentation and you display the entire transparency as you begin talking about point one, some people in your audience will be distracted by looking ahead to see what's next. Instead, reveal only the point

you are talking about, and cover the two remaining points with a sheet of paper. Move the piece of paper down the sheet as you talk about each remaining point. In computer presentations, you can use a feature called *build* that allows you to easily program a slide so that your bulleted points come in one at a time.

3. *Practice using your visual aids before the audience arrives.* You need to have a "dress rehearsal" for your presentation, particularly if you are using visual aids. Go to the presentation room and practice how you will use your visual aids. Make sure you know how to turn everything on and off, to focus the image, and to position equipment so everyone in the room can see your visual aids. If you are going to use some of the more technology-dependent options, such as an electronic whiteboard or a computer presentation, make sure you test everything well in advance of your presentation.

4. *Face the audience when using your visual aids.* Audience members prefer to see the front of you. When you speak, they can hear you better if you are facing them rather than the screen behind you. When using a pointer, hold the pointer in the hand closest to the visual aid to avoid turning your back to the audience. Read from your transparency while facing the overhead projector (and thus your audience) rather than turning around to read from the screen. Likewise, read from your computer monitor rather than turning toward the projected image as you speak.

↓KEY POINT

The best way to determine whether you're using visual aids correctly is to have someone videotape you giving your presentation. In viewing yourself on videotape, you will be able to analyze your use of the visual aids and what you could do to improve.

SCANS
Employability

Basic Skills: Speaking
Exhibiting excellent presentation skills can enhance your visibility on the job and contribute to your chances of being promoted to positions requiring the ability to communicate to large groups of people.

When using visual aids in a meeting, be sure to focus your attention on the audience, not on the visual aid.

Checkpoint

Using Visual Aids for Oral Presentations

Answer the following questions:

1. Which of the following is *not* a characteristic of a multimedia presentation?
   a. animation
   b. sound
   c. projection of three-dimensional objects
   d. video clips with sound

2. True or False. As a general rule, you should present a new visual about every two minutes.

3. The four guidelines for presenting your visual aid are (a) display your visual aids at the right time; (b) display the _____ on your visual aid at the right time; (c) _____ using your visual aids before the audience arrives; and (d) _____ the audience when using your visual aids.

Check your answers in Appendix E.

CASE 8:

Answers

Response to Question 3 in Chapter Opener

3. **How might Alex apply the ancient Chinese proverb, "One showing is worth a hundred sayings"?**

   At a minimum, Alex should use visual aids to present the numbers portion of next month's progress report. Depending on what equipment is available, and on what he already knows how to use or can learn to use before next month, any of the options mentioned are appropriate for this type of presentation.

   Among the simplest visual aids are the poster, flip chart, chalkboard, whiteboard, or electronic whiteboard. The options requiring more expertise are transparencies, slides, and computer presentations. Alex already uses handouts; however, it appears that he is just listing numbers on the handouts. He should use one of the graphic aids discussed in Section 8.3 to illustrate the data in a more meaningful way.

TECHNOLOGY

Keeping Up with Changes in Presentation Technology

According to a survey conducted by the 3M Meeting Network (**www.3m.com/meetingnetwork**), multimedia projectors (also known as LCD projectors or video projectors) are second only to overhead projectors as presenters' most-often-used tool for delivering presentations.* Multimedia projectors connected to a laptop computer can, for example, project onto a screen an electronic slideshow using PowerPoint, Astound, or Freelance Graphics.

Whether you're one to whom this presentation technology is brand new or you're one who already has a good idea of what you want to buy, you'll find a wealth of information at **www.presenting solutions.com**.

From this site you can:

- Learn the meanings behind all the technical jargon, such as "lumens," by choosing the glossary link.
- Visit the Speaker's Lounge to get tips on presentations and advice and information about LCD projectors, film recorders, digital imaging, and photography.
- Sign up to receive special reports by e-mail. Among the reports you can receive are Presenting Solutions Annual Portable Projector Report, Quarterly Reports, and Hot Product Announcements—a good way to keep up with the latest products on the market and improvements in presentation technology.
- Visit the Virtual Demo Room, designed to work with 56K or faster modems, where you can see what various projectors actually do, for example, under different light levels. Presenting Solutions uses streaming audio and video where users can see how a particular product performs or side-by-side comparisons of products. ■

*Jon Hanke, "Survey Offers Glimpse of the Average Presenter," *Presentations* (June 1999), p. 13.

DISCUSSION QUESTIONS

1. As an audience participant, which visual aids do you prefer the speaker to use? Why?
2. What are the two extremes you should stay away from in preparing visual aids?

Summary

Because using visual aids would help Alex clarify his message, add interest to it, and help the audience remember what he says, he should use visual aids during next month's progress report. When choosing which visual aids would best suit his purpose, he should consider which options are available. He should consider which option would work best based on the size of his audience and the size of the room. He also should consider the level of detail he needs to show, how much time he can give to preparing his visual aids, and whether using more than one type of visual aid would be appropriate.

In preparing the visual aids, he should remember to keep them simple and brief, as well as large enough. His visual aids should use color and include appropriate titles. He should plan on preparing approximately one visual aid for every two minutes of his presentation. He should decide whether the data would be appropriate to present in a table format, a pie chart, line graph, or bar graph.

Alex should practice using the visual aids prior to the meeting. He should face the audience at all times, display the visual aids at the right time, and reveal only the points or information he is talking about. His practice session should include making sure the equipment he is using (whether it's an overhead projector with transparencies, a flip chart on an easel, or a computer presentation) is working properly. He should make sure that he is situated in the best position so that all of his visual aids can be seen easily by those in the back of the room.

By following these steps, Alex will be able to communicate the information at each monthly meeting in an effective and professional manner.

Chapter Summary

Section 8.1 Purposes and Placement of Graphic Aids

1 **Discuss why graphic aids are used in the communication process.** Graphic aids are used in the communication process because (a) they can help your audience visualize your message; (b) most people remember what they *see* much longer and better than what they *hear*; (c) audiences expect messages to be delivered in clear, easy-to-understand, visually stimulating formats; (d) technology has made the creation and delivery of graphic aids easier and more accessible than ever before; and, (e) communicators can keep their audience's attention and get their point across better with graphic and visual aids than without them.

2 **Describe how to place and identify graphic aids in written documents.** Place graphic aids either as close as possible to their mention in the text, or in an appendix. Identify them with a consistent numbering system when more than one graphic aid appears in the document. Each graphic aid should have a title identifying its contents and a source line if the graphic aid is based on another source.

3 **Explain how graphic aids can mislead an audience.** Starting the vertical axis at some other number than zero on a bar graph is an example of one way to mislead your audience. Because the audience often compares the size of the bars in the graph to interpret the relationship of the numbers, the proportions are misrepresented when the axis does not begin at zero. (Figure 8-1 is an example of how graphic aids can visually distort data by having the vertical axis begin at some point other than zero.)

Section 8.2 Developing Graphic Aids

1 **Choose the graphic or visual aid that will best accomplish your communication objective.**

- A table is used if the objective is to show exact figures or to present cumbersome information in an organized, easy-to-follow format.
- An organization chart is used to show lines of authority and relationships among departments and employees within an organization.
- A flowchart is used to illustrate a procedure or process.
- A pie chart is used to show how the parts of a whole are distributed.
- A line graph is used to illustrate changes in quantities or values over time.

- A bar graph is used to compare one or more quantities with another.
- A map is used to show geographic relationships.
- A picture is used to provide a realistic view of a specific item or place.
- A drawing is used to emphasize details in an idea or procedure.

2 **Create tables to present cumbersome information in an organized, easy-to-follow format.** Arrange information into rows and columns, and use clear and concise descriptors for the identifying title as well as for the labels at the top of each column. Use landscape orientation when you have too many columns to fit across the page in portrait orientation. Lastly, whenever the table contains numbers, be sure the digits are aligned correctly.

3 **Create the three types of charts often used in business reports.**

- Organization charts use boxes with names and job titles or departments that are connected with lines. This type of chart illustrates the relationships and official lines of authority and communication among employees and departments of an organization.
- Flowcharts present a step-by-step diagram of a procedure or process. The flowchart simplifies complicated procedures and allows the user to see the order in which the steps must be followed.
- A pie chart shows how the parts of a whole are distributed, and how the parts relate to one another. Generally, the parts are limited to no more than seven and are represented by percentages. The largest part of the pie should start in the twelve o'clock position with decreasing amounts placed clockwise from there.

4 **Create line and bar graphs in their various formats.** Line graphs show changes in quantities or values over time and can be either a single- or multiple-line graph. Bar graphs are used to compare data. The simple vertical and simple horizontal bar graphs compare only one set of data. The broken bar graph, multiple-bar graph, and stacked bar graph are other variations used.

5 **Identify miscellaneous graphic and visual aids used in reports.**

- A map shows geographic relationships and is especially useful when your audience may not be familiar with the geographic areas in your report.
- A photograph provides a realistic view of a specific item or place and makes the document more appealing to read.
- A drawing is useful for communicating complicated ideas or procedures.

Section 8.3 Using Visual Aids for Oral Presentations

1 **Choose an appropriate visual aid that will enhance your oral presentation and help the audience to better understand your message.** Visual aids options include posters and flip charts; transparencies, slides, and computer presentations; objects; chalkboards, whiteboards, and electronic whiteboards; and handouts.

2 **Prepare your visual aids to ensure they are well received by your audience.** Preparation guidelines include: (a) Keep your visual aids simple and brief. (b) Make sure everything is large enough. (c) Use color for emphasis. (d) Always include a title; use a source line if necessary. (e) Prepare an acceptable number of visual aids.

3 **Use visual aids in a professional manner during your oral presentation.** Usage guidelines include: (a) Display your visual aids at the right time. (b) Display the points on your visual aids at the right time. (c) Practice using your visual aids before the audience arrives. (d) Face the audience when using your visual aids.

Critical Thinking Questions

1. Look through one of your textbooks (other than this one) and find a graphic aid to critique. Were you able to quickly grasp the meaning of the data presented? What techniques were used to make the graphic aid visually appealing (colors, artwork, etc.)? Did the graphic aid accurately represent the data, or was some form of visual distortion evident?

2. Do you think bypassing the textual explanation of graphic aids and looking only at the graphic aid is common practice? Conduct an informal poll of several friends to find out whether your opinion was supported or contradicted. Explain how your findings might affect your use of graphic aids in your own written documents.

3. What keeps people from learning how to use software applications that have greatly simplified the process of creating organization charts, tables, pie charts, line graphs, and other graphic aids?

4. As an audience participant, which of the preparation guidelines have you seen presenters violate most frequently? Why do you think the guideline is violated so frequently?

5. As an audience participant, which of the guidelines for presenting visual aids in a professional manner have you seen presenters overlook most frequently? Why do you think the guideline is overlooked?

Applications

TECHNOLOGY

Part A. Use a software program of your choice that gives you access to charting tools and create the following charts. One option is Microsoft PowerPoint, which provides mini-applications to complete the organization and pie charts.

- A simple two-level organization chart for "Southcentral Bank" that includes only job titles. On level one, make a box for the "President and Chairman of the Board." On level two, include five boxes: "VP Loans," "VP Investments," "VP Trust," "VP Marketing," and "VP Operations."
- A pie chart for "Budget Allocations" that shows the following allocations stated in percentages: Rent, $950; Utilities, $150; Savings, $200; Food, $250; Clothing, $125; Entertainment, $75; Car Payment, $225; Miscellaneous, $90.

TECHNOLOGY

Part B. Send to your instructor an e-mail message to which you attach the charts you created in Part A.

Part C. Look through a recent business magazine, such as *Fortune, BusinessWeek,* or *Forbes,* or any magazine or newspaper, such as *Time, Newsweek, USA Today,* or your local newspaper. Find three different examples of any of the charts or graphs discussed in this chapter. For each chart or graph, identify its type (for example, pie chart, stacked bar graph, multiple-line graph); and write a paragraph to accompany each chart. Your paragraph should either (a) critique the effectiveness of the chart; or (b) briefly summarize and introduce the chart as you would if the chart were in one of your own documents.

Editing Activity

words@work

If you are using *words@work,* complete the activities on Visuals in the Writing at Work section.

Assume you are going to give a presentation entitled "How to Get Organized." Your presentation will include six guidelines, and you have decided to use a flip chart for your visual aid. Before the presentation, you will write at the top of six flip-chart pages one guideline per page prior to the presentation. As you give your presentation, you will jot down ideas related to each of the six guidelines.

Following are the six points of your presentation. Edit each point so that only the key words remain. These key words are the only words, then, that you would write on your flip-chart pages.

1. Select areas to organize that will give you the most benefit for the time you will spend in getting and keeping them organized.
2. Get rid of the clutter in the areas that you are going to organize.

3. Don't think about the entire organizing task; instead, focus on getting one small portion done at a time.
4. Establish a system that is simple to maintain and simple to explain to others who may have to use it.
5. Practice maintenance habits that will help you stay organized.
6. Determine the most comfortable and productive level of organization appropriate for you.

Case Studies

TECHNOLOGY

1. Jan Anderson feels a sense of satisfaction as she reflects on the completion of her first year working in the life insurance and securities industry. Scrolling through the client list on her laptop computer, she recalls the many individuals and couples she has worked with during her first year on the job. She remembers selling life insurance policies to many of her clients and updating policies for others who had major changes in their family situations. For many others, Jan recalls setting them up in investment and savings programs for their retirement or for their children's college education.

   One thing about this job that has surprised Jan somewhat is how much time she has spent educating her clients, many of whom were unaware of basic financial principles about saving and investing as well as uninformed about insurance basics. During her sales calls, Jan uses educational materials published by the companies whose products she sells. She takes the most informative materials and places them in clear protective sheets in a notebook. She finds it convenient to flip through the pages, explaining what is needed for each client, and skipping pages when necessary.

   Jan has recently begun thinking about how she might update and liven up her presentations by using her laptop computer for the information portion of her sales presentations. Never having used her computer for that purpose, Jan needs some advice on where to begin.

   a. If you were advising Jan, what basic ideas would you ask her to consider as she begins preparing a computer presentation to use during her sales calls?
   b. What guidelines should you make sure Jan is aware of regarding the use of her laptop as a presentation tool?

TECHNOLOGY

2. Grant's boss, Maria, called him into her office on a Thursday afternoon. "Grant," Maria began, "you've been with us for nearly six months now and have gone to several of our monthly development sessions. Do you think you'd like to give next month's presentation? Brad and I were talking yesterday and thought with your skills and knowledge that you'd be a good candidate to give the next presentation. It would give you some visibility and help everybody get to know you a little better. What do you think?"

"Yes, I could probably find time to get a 45-minute presentation together for next month," responded Grant. "What topic did you have in mind?"

"It's actually two topics rolled into one," Maria explained. "The main topic is creating presentations, but we'd also like you to include an explanation of how you researched the Internet to find sources for your training session. This subtopic will help those who want some pointers on how to be more efficient at finding what they need from the Internet. Maybe you could prepare a handout with appropriate Web addresses for employees to study the topic further on their own. If you point them in the right direction, many will do further study—especially those who are finding that their jobs are requiring them to give more and more presentations."

Grant said, "I like that idea, Maria. But before I give you a definite yes, I'd like to get on the Net and see what's available on the topic of creating presentations. If I find enough good information, I'll be glad to take on this extra assignment. Let me check into it and get back with you tomorrow afternoon with what I've found."

"That sounds fine, Grant," said Maria, "I should be back in my office after 3 tomorrow afternoon. Stop in anytime after that and let me know where we stand on this."

a. Assume the role of Grant, and use a search engine to find sites such as the ones listed here. You might try **http://37.com/** where you type your search phrase once and get results from up to 37 different search engines.

   http://www.mmm.com/meetingnetwork/presentations/ creating.html

   http://www.tcp.ca/1997/9704/9704pres/create/create.html

   http://www.tacoma.washington.edu/compserv/handouts/ office97/create/index.html

b. Print out three or four of the most helpful articles you find on the topic of creating presentations. As Grant, prepare what you'll say to Maria when you go back to let her know whether you'll take on the assignment she's suggested.

Career Case Studies

COMMUNICATION FOR HEALTH SERVICES CAREERS

Andrea Mitchell is the director of the health-and-fitness education department at the health-care facility in her hometown. One of her main responsibilities is to schedule 15 to 20 classes and support group meetings every quarter. Scheduling involves first deciding what classes to offer based on need and demand. Once the classes have been selected and a rough timetable sketched out, she must find qualified individuals to teach the courses when they're offered. After matching instructors with courses and adjusting times when necessary, she finalizes the schedule and develops the promotional pieces that go out to the community.

A recent promotional piece included course descriptions, meeting times, and other necessary information for the classes and meetings for October through December. She categorized the classes under appropriate headings related to heart-health education; classes specifically for women; family courses, such as childbirth and sibling adjustment; cancer support group meetings; and fitness and nutrition classes.

The classrooms have several visual aids options available; however, Andrea knows that although many of the instructors are very knowledgeable about their topics, they know little about using visual aids in teaching. She wants to schedule a one-hour training session in which she covers basic guidelines for the supplies and equipment: flip charts, overhead projectors with transparencies, and electronic whiteboards.

Prepare an outline for Andrea to use during her training session for the instructors.

COMMUNICATION FOR BUSINESS AND MARKETING CAREERS

Peter Chapman, employed in the hospitality and tourism industry for nine years, recently took a position as vice president for marketing at a new resort in Branson, Missouri. Peter has been hired to lead the marketing effort as the resort begins building phase three of the condominium units and doubling the size of the existing health-club facility. Other on-site amenities at the resort include an indoor pool, racquetball and tennis courts, an 18-hole golf course, a restaurant, and a beautiful lake that is perfect for swimming, boating, and fishing.

Peter's main task is to design a promotional package that will attract guests to the facility and encourage them to buy into the timeshare concept. Timeshare ownership is when an individual or family pays a one-time fee of $12,000 to $20,000 for a one-week-per-year ownership of one condominium (including access to all the on-site amenities) at the resort. Title includes lifetime ownership for the purchaser, and the ownership can be sold to another individual or willed to a relative after the original owner dies.

1. Advise Peter as to what graphic or visual aids his sales staff could use to communicate the benefits of timeshare ownership over traditional vacation formats, such as staying in hotels or camping out.

2. Help him familiarize potential purchasers with all the resort has to offer.

Video Case

Creating a Guide for Effective Presentations

Susanna Marguiles, Memorial Hospital's Patient Relations Director, has a role she does not want. Susanna enjoys planning, designing, and supervising all patient outreach programs. Among her duties, Susanna makes presentations to patients in the hospital as well as presentations to health-related groups in the community. To fulfill her responsibilities, Susanna has taught herself a range of graphics programs, including presentation software. Now she is acknowledged as the in-house expert at creating effective presentations. That is the problem. Susanna understands when the busy Chief of Medicine asks her for help with a presentation, but unfortunately, everyone else also comes to her for help.

Susanna decides to create a brief guide for designing effective presentations. She reasons that if she can teach others to create excellent presentations, she will have more time to finish her own assignments.

Questions

1. Based on what you've learned from Chapter 8 and what you've observed from Susanna's presentation, create an outline of the topics that should be included in Susanna's guide for effective presentations.
2. As part of her guide, Susanna wants to present five tips for using visual aids effectively. What five tips would you recommend?
3. Many colleagues asking for Susanna's help do not distinguish between a written report and a presentation. Based on your knowledge of Chapter 8, explain the difference between the two forms of communication.
4. As part of her guide, Susanna has decided to include an example of an effective presentation created with presentation software. Working with two or three other teammates, first create an outline of five graphics (or visual aids) to accompany Susanna's presentation about the safety of blood transfusions. Then, using computer software, create the presentation.

Continuing Case....

Counting on Coffee

The NetCafe has been open for a year now. Next week, Eva and Ramon will hold their first annual meeting with their two limited or silent partners, Dominic Lula and Opal Morales. The meeting will begin with dinner, followed by reports from Eva and Ramon.

The two active partners have provided the silent partners with three quarterly reports during the year. Eva and Ramon are not worried about how Opal will respond to the final figures on their first year in business. Opal is very proud of the computer skills she has gained through the NetCafe. She clearly understands the potential of this new business.

Dominic, however, still thinks they should ship the rented computers and other equipment back to the company that owns them. Then they could concentrate on the important business of the NetCafe: the coffee counter.

Eva and Ramon are spending a lot of time preparing their presentations. They know that visuals will add interest and clarity. They just need to decide which visuals to use and how to organize them.

First Quarter

Computer use fees	$14,700
Scanners/copiers	3,990
Computer classes	1,350
Coffee	22,920
Pastry/bagels	14,250

Second Quarter

Computer use fees	$15,360
Scanners/copiers	4,350
Computer classes	1,800
Coffee	23,220
Pastry/bagels	14,580

Third Quarter

Computer use fees	$16,230
Scanners/copiers	4,830
Computer classes	2,700
Coffee	23,550
Pastry/bagels	15,420

Fourth Quarter

Computer use fees	$19,110
Scanners/copiers	5,370
Computer classes	3,750
Coffee	23,700
Pastry/bagels	15,810

1. Here are the sources of NetCafe's income for its first year. Develop a visual aid to show this information:

Hourly computer use fees	31%
Scanner and copier fees	7%
Computer classes	5%
Coffee sales	40%
Pastry sales	9%
Bagel sales	8%

2. Now develop a visual that compares these rounded income figures for each quarter:

3. Write a summary of the visual you prepared for Exercise 2. Compare the quarterly increases in each category in a way that will help convince Dominic that the NetCafe should continue offering computer services.

4. Suggest two other visuals that Eva and Ramon might include in their presentations to help explain the NetCafe's first year in business.

Writing Routine Reports

Reports and Peter's New Job

Peter Chang is an employee of the U.S. Department of Agriculture in the northern section of the San Joaquin Valley in California—one of the most productive agricultural areas in the world. Recently, Peter was promoted to the position of agricultural loan clerk. In his new position, he has many reports to read— reports from farmers who are applying for loans; status reports from farmers who have received loans; and reports from his employer, the federal government, on new loan programs.

After reading so many reports, Peter wonders, "Why are reports so different?" Some are long, some are short. Some are simple, some are complex. Some are easy to read, some are difficult to read. Some are coherent, some are not. Some make recommendations, some do not. Why are reports so different?

Peter also has reports to write. For example, each month, he must send his office manager a memo report informing her of the content of loan reports submitted by recipients and the content of reports from loan applicants. Several times a month, Peter also has to send short, in-formal manuscript reports to the office manager.

Think about Peter's situation and respond to these questions:

Questions

1. How important are reports to Peter's situation?

2. Is there a process that would help reports to be more consistent?

3. Why does the language in the reports sent to Peter by his employer seem "cold" or formal?

4. Why do some reports look like memos? Why do some look like letters? Why do others look different from memos and letters?

9·1 Planning Informal Reports

Objectives

After completing Section 9.1, you should be able to:

1 Explain how to classify reports according to their style, purpose, and format.

2 Identify the steps in planning an informal report.

3 Explain the differences among data, conclusion, and recommendation.

Objective

1

KEY POINT

Some reports you write will be for managers only one level above you; others will be for managers two or three levels above you. Know your audience and adjust accordingly.

Types of Reports

A *report* is a document that provides the facts about a specific situation or problem for consideration by a specific group of people. Reports are business tools that enable managers to make decisions or solve problems. Reports can be classified according to their style, purpose, and format.

Style

The two styles of reports are formal and informal. **Formal reports** generally are long, analytical, and impersonal. A formal report often contains preliminary parts such as a title page, an executive summary, and a table of contents, as well as supplementary parts such as a bibliography and an appendix.

An example of a formal report is a company's annual report to stockholders or a report to a government regulatory agency. Another example is an *external proposal*, a report that analyzes a problem and recommends a solution to people outside the writer's company.

Informal reports are shorter than formal reports and are written in a less formal style. Unlike formal reports, informal reports generally have no preliminary or supplementary parts because they usually are concerned with everyday matters that require little background. In addition, an informal report is organized differently from a formal report.

A sales report is an example of an informal report. In a sales report, the writer summarizes sales for a specific period, such as the number of cars sold by an automobile dealership during the previous month. Another type of informal report, an *internal proposal* (also known as a *justification report*), is used to analyze an internal problem and recommend a solution. For example, a shift supervisor might write an internal proposal to convince a factory manager to buy new equipment.

Purpose

Reports can be either informational or analytical. **Informational reports** present information (facts), so they include very little analysis. For example, a bank manager may ask the head cashier to prepare an informational report about the average number and value of money orders sold each day. The components of an informational report are the topics (subjects) or the areas investigated.

Another type of analytical report is a recommendation report, which analyzes a problem and recommends a solution.

CHAPTER 9 • WRITING ROUTINE REPORTS

Analytical reports analyze a problem, present facts, draw conclusions, and make recommendations. In contrast to an informational report, which just presents the facts, an analytical report also suggests what might be done to solve the problem. The components of an analytical report are the problem's probable causes and solutions.

Format

Informal reports can be written in several different formats, or arrangements, including *memo, letter,* and *manuscript* formats. Formal reports are longer and more complex than informal reports, so they are written in manuscript format.

Steps in Planning Informal Reports

Before writing a report, you must do some preliminary work. Even if you are simply reporting facts, you must gather those facts and then arrange them in an easy-to-follow, logical sequence. When planning a report, you should (1) identify the problem; (2) decide on areas to investigate; (3) determine the scope; (4) plan the research; (5) develop a preliminary outline; (6) collect the data; and (7) analyze the data, draw conclusions, and make recommendations.

Identify the Problem

The first step is to identify the problem to be studied and the objective of the report. As in planning letters and memos, determine why you are writing the report and what you hope to accomplish.

Prepare a written statement of the problem you will analyze in your report. Depending on the preferences of your company and your supervisor, this statement may be expressed as an infinitive phrase, as a question, or as a statement.

Infinitive Phrase	The purpose of this report is to determine if the accounting department needs new computers.
Question	This report will answer the question, "Does the accounting department need new computers?"
Statement	This report will determine if the accounting department needs new computers.

Decide on Areas to Investigate

Your next step is to decide exactly what to investigate. Only after you understand the problem and the scope of the investigation can you plan your research and identify specific areas to investigate.

Determine the Scope

Scope refers to the boundaries of the report—what will be included and excluded. For example, a report about the use of computers in all departments will require more research and have a wider scope than a report that examines computer use in just two departments.

SCANS
Employability

Personal Qualities: Responsibility
Most reports you write will be informal, but using correct grammar, punctuation, and format is still very important.

▼KEY POINT

When you write a brief, informal report for a manager in your organization, use one of the memo formats shown in Chapter 5 unless the organization uses its own format.

Objective

▼KEY POINT

You should be able to express any problem statement in a single sentence. If you cannot, try to simplify the problem until you can.

▼KEY POINT

To do too much or too little (not identify the scope) in a report will be frustrating to you and the receiver of the report.

SCANS
Employability

Thinking Skills: Problem Solving

Managers, when assigning a report, usually specify the scope. If they do not, ask about the scope.

DIVERSITY

Geographical order is useful for reports that deal with different countries. A report on sales in Japan, the United States, and China can be organized according to the sales in each country.

TECHNOLOGY

Speadsheet software packages frequently provide both the data and the data analysis for an analytical report.

Plan the Research

Once you know the scope of your report, develop a plan for getting the facts you need. List the questions that need answers and execute the steps you need to find those answers. Also consider how much time and money you have. Then develop a schedule for collecting the data, analyzing the results, and writing and finishing the report on time.

Develop a Preliminary Outline

Now you are ready to prepare a preliminary outline to organize the facts you uncover in your research. This preliminary outline will likely differ from the final outline you use to write your report. The preliminary outline is simply a way of organizing the topic you decided to investigate.

Outlines for Informational Reports

The outline for an informational report can be arranged in one of five ways:

1. *Chronological Order.* Organize the facts in relation to time; that is, what happened first, next, and so on.
2. *Order of Importance.* Arrange the facts in order of importance, from the most to the least important or vice versa.
3. *Logical Sequence.* Group the facts according to the logical order of steps—first, second, third, and so on.
4. *Category.* Separate the facts into categories; for example, stocks, bonds, and certificates of deposit.
5. *Geographical Order.* Organize the facts by location.

Outlines for Analytical Reports

When outlining analytical reports, you can organize the facts in one of two ways. One method is to use a **hypothesis**, a possible cause or explanation of the problem. The second method is to use **alternatives**.

Hypotheses. In this method, phrase each possible cause as a hypothesis in your outline. The following outline shows two *hypotheses* (the plural of hypothesis) for a drop in auto sales. Under each hypothesis are the questions that must be answered to prove or disprove the hypothesis.

I. Our prices are too high. (Hypothesis)
    A. What are our prices?
    B. What are our competitors' prices?
    C. How important is price to our customers?
II. The quality of our product is low. (Hypothesis)
    A. What is our repair record?
    B. How does our repair record compare with that of competitors?
    C. What are the results of product evaluation?

Alternatives. To evaluate alternative solutions to a problem, arrange your preliminary outline according to the relative merits of each alternative. For example, to determine where in your school building to install new computers, one alternative is to research the number of courses in each subject that use computers. Another alternative is to research the number of students enrolled in each course that uses computers. This example shows how to outline these alternatives:

I. Number of Classes Taught Using Computers
   A. Paralegal Courses
   B. Business Courses
   C. Health Courses
II. Number of Students Enrolled
   A. Paralegal Courses
   B. Business Courses
   C. Health Courses

Figure 9-1 shows two frequently used outline systems—the alphanumeric system and the decimal system. Use the system best suited to the problem or preferred by your company.

DIVERSITY
In the American business culture, we are so "solutions oriented" that we sometimes fail to identify the best alternative.

Alphanumeric	Decimal
I. xxxxxx	1.0 xxxxxx
A. xxxxxx	1.1 xxxxxx
B. xxxxxx	1.2 xxxxxx
1. xxxxxx	1.2.1 xxxxxx
2. xxxxxx	1.2.2 xxxxxx
a. xxxxxx	1.2.2.1 xxxxxx
b. xxxxxx	1.2.2.2 xxxxxx
(1) xxxxxx	1.2.2.2.1 xxxxxx
(2) xxxxxx	1.2.2.2.2 xxxxxx
II. xxxxxx	2.0 xxxxxx
A. xxxxxx	2.1 xxxxxx
B. xxxxxx	2.2 xxxxxx
C. xxxxxx	2.3 xxxxxx
1. xxxxxx	2.3.1 xxxxxx
2. xxxxxx	2.3.2 xxxxxx

FIGURE 9-1 Outline Systems

Outline Formats
The preliminary outline follows either the topical format or the discussion format. In a **topical outline**, *headings*—the words that start each section—describe in a few words the topics you have investigated. A **discussion outline** provides more information about the topics and the *subtopics*, the topics that are included under each heading. The discussion outline takes longer to write but is often more helpful to the report writer. These formats are shown on the following page.

Topical Outline	Discussion Outline

I. Characteristics of Voice Mail
  A. Speed
  B. Cost
  C. Equipment
	I. Voice mail offers the latest technology for sending messages.
	  A. It offers speed.
	  B. It costs no more than a telephone call.
	  C. Special equipment is needed.

SCANS
Employability

Systems: Understands Systems
To determine which outline format to use, you can check your company's style manual or look at outlines in reports written by other employees.

1 *Checkpoint*

Planning Reports

Indicate whether each statement is true or false.
1. The first step in writing a report is to identify the problem and the report's objective.
2. Identifying the scope enables the report writer to determine how much money to spend on gathering facts.
3. When outlining an informational report, always arrange the facts in geographical order.
4. A hypothesis is a possible cause or explanation for a problem.
5. When planning an analytical report, your preliminary outline will probably be identical to the one you will use to write your report.

Check your answers in Appendix E.

Collect the Data

The next step in planning a report is to perform the *research* by collecting appropriate data. Two sources of data are available—primary and secondary. **Primary research** involves gathering fresh, new data, whereas **secondary research** involves locating data that already has been gathered and reported.

Primary Research

If the facts you need are not available in books, magazines, or other sources, you may need to conduct primary research. To conduct this type of research, you might talk with experts, customers, or suppliers; observe what happens in a particular situation; or experiment to see what works.

Secondary Research

Research completed by others also can be useful. Consult books, periodicals, other reports, and electronic sources to gather information. Computer database services, available at many libraries, often offer a more thorough search of the literature than may be available in printed form in the library.

Conducting primary research is very complex and requires expertise in research methodology. For example, go to **http://www.soc.staffs.ac.uk/**

DIVERSITY

Hey, Everybody Knows All xxxxxx Are . . . .

Do you have general perceptions about any types of individuals? What about other groups? What kinds of jokes do you tell?

When you have set opinions about any group or type of individual, you are stereotyping. Stereotyping is having the same ex-pectations of everyone within a type or group of individuals.

But when we have the same expectations of everyone within a group, our assumptions are false. No two people are alike. Every person is unique. When we stereotype individuals, we lose the chance to enjoy another person or to gain another client or customer. Further, we risk being offensive, whether in writing or in speaking. Expanding our awareness and appreciation of different people, cultures, and beliefs helps us grow both personally and professionally. ■

Look for information on business and specific organizations in the *Business Periodicals Index*, the *Reader's Guide to Periodical Literature*, *The Wall Street Journal Index*, as well as other books, directories, catalogs, and indexes. The U.S. government publishes reports on a variety of subjects. In addition, some of the most useful sources of information are found inside a company, including internal reports, memos, and reports to stockholders. CD-ROMs, databases, and the Internet are resources that may provide useful data for a report. When using the Internet as a resource, a **search engine** is a great tool for finding information on your research topic. A search engine is software that allows you to search the Internet for information using key words.

▼KEY POINT

Some companies maintain a library where you can look at important documents and reference materials from every department.

Bibliography Cards

As you conduct your research, you will need a method of identifying your sources. You can identify your sources by preparing a *bibliography card* for every source. These cards provide the details for the bibliography that the formal report will include.

For each source that you use, prepare a bibliography card similar to the one shown in Figure 9-2. For books, list the author's full name (last name first), the book title (underlined), the publisher's location and name, and the publication date. For example:

King, Julie Adair. <u>WordPerfect Suite 8 for Dummies</u>. Chicago, IL: IDG Books Worldwide, Inc., 1997.

BIBLIOGRAPHY CARD

King, Julie Adair. <u>WordPerfect Suite 8 for Dummies</u>. Chicago, IL.: IDG Books Worldwide, Inc., 1997.

NOTE CARD

King   What Suite 8 does

<u>WordPerfect Suite 8 for Dummies</u>

This package includes programs to handle just about every computing job you can imagine. If you are upgrading from Version 7, you are going to be surprised at the changes. p.10.

FIGURE 9-2 Examples of Bibliography Card and Note Card

When you use information from a magazine article, list the author's full name (last name first), the article title (in quotation marks), the magazine title (underlined), the publication date, and the page numbers:

Brown, D. "Outsourcing Professional Services." <u>Internal Auditor</u>. Dec. 1998: 61–64.

When you use an electronic source, list the author's name, the title of the article, the title of the full work, and the date of the publication. Indicate if the source is on-line or CD-ROM, and specify the path to the information. For example:

Sanderson, Brenda. "Working with the Electronic Bulletin Boards." <u>Today's Electronic Media</u> [On-line] Available http://www.tem .com/sandi.htm. Cited 1999 Aug. 10.

Note Cards

Prepare a separate *note card* for each point you plan to mention in your report. In most cases, you will summarize the information you locate in a secondary source, as illustrated in Figure 9-2. When you want to use material directly from the source, **paraphrase**—change the words—and give credit to the author. Avoid **plagiarism**, which is presenting another person's work as your own, by clearly identifying your sources. Copyright laws protect the writer's interests. Even if the information does not fall under the copyright laws, ethical behavior requires you to give credit to its source.

Analyze Data, Draw Conclusions, and Make Recommendations

Unless you have been asked to provide only an informational report, the last step in preparing to write a report is to analyze the results, draw conclusions, and make recommendations.

Is a little plagiarism ethical?

Objective

Analyze Data

Once you have your research results—the **data**—look for logical links between facts and figures. If you are working with numerical data, compare and contrast figures. Then organize the material in a way that helps the reader. For example, if you researched the high turnover rate of production supervisors in your manufacturing company, you might put the data into three categories: salaries of different supervisory jobs in the company, salaries offered by competing manufacturers, and the number and kinds of promotions supervisors have received at each job level.

Draw Conclusions

After you have analyzed the data, you may arrive at a **conclusion**, an opinion based on interpretation of data. Here's a possible conclusion for the study of high turnover among production supervisors:

> Production supervisors in our company have limited advancement opportunities.

Make Recommendations

Include recommendations in a report if you have been asked to do so. A **recommendation** offers suggestions of what should be done. Recommendations should be related to conclusions, as in the following:

> I recommend that supervisory positions within our company be reorganized to provide opportunities for career advancement.

SCANS
Employability

Systems: Understands Systems
When writing a report, include recommendations only when specifically requested. To provide them when not requested can be offensive to the receiver.

Checkpoint 2

Collecting and Analyzing Data

Indicate whether each statement is true or false.

1. Primary research involves gathering fresh data.
2. Secondary research involves locating data that already has been gathered and reported.
3. A conclusion is based on data.
4. Data lead to conclusions; conclusions lead to recommendations.
5. You need not note the source of information that you paraphrased.

Check your answers in Appendix E.

CASE 9:

Answers

Responses to Questions 1 and 2 in Chapter Opener

1. **How important are reports to Peter's situation?**
   Reports are very important in Peter's job. He receives reports from farmers and ranchers when they provide the necessary information to obtain a loan from the Department. Reports are the way Peter checks to see that loan recipients are using their loans monies appropriately. Reports from his supervisors also inform him about new governmental loan programs.

2. **Is there a process that would help reports to be more consistent?**
   Yes. If individuals would consistently use the seven steps for planning reports, reports would be more consistent. The seven steps are (1) identify the problem and write a problem statement for the report; (2) decide on areas to investigate; (3) determine the scope; (4) plan the research; (5) develop a preliminary outline; (6) collect the data; and (7) analyze the data, draw conclusions, and make recommendations.

DISCUSSION QUESTIONS

1. Why are reports classified according to style, purpose, and format?
2. Do findings, conclusions, and recommendations differ? If so, how?

Organizing Informal Reports

Most business reports are informal reports and have one of two purposes. They present information that has been requested, or they analyze a problem and report the findings. The organization and the format of these reports vary depending on the nature of the message and the people who will receive them.

Like business letters and memos, informal reports are organized around a main idea and supporting information. If the report is an informational report, the main idea is the information that has been requested. If the report is an analytical report, the main idea is a summary of the conclusions and recommendations. The supporting information of either report explains or details the main idea.

Informal reports may be organized in either the direct order or the indirect order. The organization you choose depends on how receptive you expect your reader to be.

Direct Order

If the report is routine (weekly sales report) or if you expect the reader to respond favorably, use the direct order and present the main idea first. Busy managers prefer reading this type of report since the main ideas appear at the beginning and save time. Most business reports are written in this order.

Informational reports such as progress reports commonly use direct order. In these reports, the results (or main ideas) appear at the beginning. Analytical reports that are expected to have a favorable response also are organized in direct order. The main ideas (conclusions and recommendations) appear first, followed by the supporting information.

Indirect Order

Use indirect order when you expect an unfavorable response or when the receiver may need persuasion to accept the main idea. You can buffer the main idea by presenting the data and the reasons first.

Use indirect order in an internal proposal when management is likely to be hesitant about approving the project or the budget. You might also use indirect order for a *troubleshooting report,* an analytical

Objectives

After completing Section 9.2, you should be able to:

1 Explain when to use direct or indirect order to organize an informal report.

2 Know when to use the personal and impersonal writing styles in informal reports.

3 List the parts of an informal report.

4 Describe when to use the letter, memo, and manuscript formats for informal reports.

Objective

SCANS
Employability

Information: Interprets and Communicates
When you're preparing an informal report, use a receiver orientation, emphasizing what the receiver needs to know.

report in which you investigate a problem and propose a solution. Imagine, for example, that your recommendation is to close a company operation, and that you do not expect management to be receptive to the idea. In this case, you would use the indirect order, placing your recommendation—to close the operation—at the end of the report.

Outlining and Writing Informal Reports

Once you decide how to organize your report, you are ready to outline it. Outlining helps you identify and position the topics and subtopics you will include. After placing the main idea and the supporting information in a logical sequence, you can begin writing the report.

Report Outlines

As you start to outline an informal report, use the preliminary outline you developed to guide your research. More than likely, the outline will need some revision because of what you learned from collecting and analyzing the data. Once you have revised the outline, you can use it as a guide for writing the final report.

Outlines for informal reports organized in direct or indirect order are shown in Figures 9-3, 9-4, and 9-5. Most informal reports can be written using one of these outline methods.

Figure 9-3 is an outline for an informational report organized in direct order. Notice that the introduction and the main idea come first, followed by the research findings.

SCANS
Employability

Basic Skills: Writing
Because most managers prefer to read the main idea first, most reports are written that way—in direct order.

KEY POINT

Use a positive tone in your reports, even when you are sending negative messages.

SCANS
Employability

Thinking Skills: Problem Solving
Outlines are a great aid in structuring your reports. They help with clarity and coherence.

I. Introduction

II. Main Idea: AllWrite, Preferred Word Processing Software

III. Findings: Word Processing Needs for Our Office
    A. Lengthy document production
    B. Frequent revisions
    C. Special features needed (mailmerge, macros, sorting)
    D. High-speed, letter-quality print (laser printer)

IV. Findings: Comparison of Four Word Processing Packages
    A. Word processing software package A
    B. Word processing software package B
    C. Word processing software package C
    D. Word processing software package D

V. Closing

FIGURE 9-3 Outline of Informational Report in Direct Order

Figure 9-4 is an outline for an analytical report organized in direct order. The main idea consists of conclusions and recommendations followed by findings and supporting details.

Figure 9-5 is an outline for an analytical report organized in indirect order. The findings and supporting details precede the conclusion and recommendation, which together make up the main idea.

Writing Style

Informal reports usually are written in a relatively **personal style**, using any pronoun you choose. If your report is about a serious problem or if it is going to a senior manager, you may want to use a degree of formality. In this case, you would write your report in an **impersonal style**, without using **first-person pronouns** or **second-person pronouns**. (Look under **third-person pronouns** in the glossary for a listing of pronouns you can use when writing in this style.)

↓KEY POINT

Remember that a discussion outline provides more detail than a topical outline and can help you actually write the report.

Objective

I. Introduction

II. Main Idea
    A. Conclusion: Production supervisors in our company have limited advancement opportunities.
    B. Recommendation: Supervisory positions should be revamped to provide opportunities for career advancement.

III. Findings and Supporting Details
    A. Production supervisors' salaries compare favorably with those of competing organizations.
    B. Fringe benefits are satisfactory.
    C. Opportunities for advancement are limited.

IV. Closing

FIGURE 9-4 Outline of Analytical Report in Direct Order

I. Introduction

II. Findings and Supporting Details
    A. The company's third- and fourth-quarter sales are down.
    B. Projections for the coming year show slower sales.
    C. The company has too much inventory in stock.

III. Main Idea
    A. Conclusion: We are overproducing cars in our Lakeview plant.
    B. Recommendation: Close the Lakeview plant and lay off plant workers.

IV. Closing

FIGURE 9-5 Outline of Analytical Report in Indirect Order

DIVERSITY

Use only third-person pronouns when preparing a report for someone in another country. Using first- or second-person pronouns can imply a familiarity that in many cultures is considered inappropriate for business relationships.

The impersonal style keeps a report from sounding like one person's opinion because it does not refer to *I*, *me*, or *you*. By avoiding personal references, a report written in an impersonal style emphasizes the facts rather than the writer. This style makes the report sound more objective than a report written in a personal style.

Decide whether to write in the present or past tense. Use the past tense when writing about events in the past and the present tense for events that are still occurring. Avoid switching back and forth between tenses in a single section. Switching can confuse your readers, who may have difficulty following the timing or sequence of events.

3 *Checkpoint*

Organizing and Writing Informal Reports

Indicate whether each statement is true or false.

1. Use direct order when you expect your reader to be receptive to your report.
2. Use a personal writing style to emphasize the facts rather than the report writer.
3. Write informal reports in either the present or the past tense and avoid switching between tenses.
4. An informational report in direct order starts with the main idea, followed by supporting information.
5. An analytical report in direct order starts with the introduction, followed by findings, and then the main idea.

Check your answers in Appendix E.

The organization and format of business reports can vary depending on the nature of the message and the people who will receive them.

Formatting Informal Reports

Informal reports may be formatted like letters, memos, or manuscripts. The format depends on the receiver and the length of the report.

Parts of an Informal Report

Regardless of the format used, informal reports have three main parts:

1. Opening (the introduction)
2. Body (findings and supporting details)
3. Closing

The length of the opening will vary according to the purpose of the report. For a brief memo report, the opening might be only a subject line. For other informal short reports, the opening may include the following information: the subject of the report, the purpose of the report (the reason why the report is important), and a preview of the main ideas of the report. If you use direct order, include the summary of findings or conclusions and recommendations in the opening.

The body of a report includes the findings and supporting details that resulted from the research. Your revised outline will provide the organizational plan for this section. This section is usually the longest and must be well organized so the report is easy to understand.

A report's conclusions or recommendations should flow logically from the data presented in the body of the report.

KEY POINT

The closing is your last
chance to make a positive,
lasting impression on the
reader, so choose your final
words with care.

Objective

4

KEY POINT

Including information about
expected future action is a
good way to clarify the
writer's or reader's responsibility for follow-up.

SCANS
Employability

**Information Interprets
and Communicates**
Many internal proposals are
written to justify large purchases or investments in
equipment or inventory.
These reports are longer
than typical informal reports
and are better suited to the
manuscript format.

The closing of a report is important because it is the final opportunity to leave an impression on the reader. If you are writing a report
in direct order, you should reemphasize the main ideas in this last
section. If you are using indirect order, you should first present the
summary of findings (informational reports) and then the conclusions
and recommendations (analytical reports). Make sure that any conclusions or recommendations flow from a logical presentation of the data
in the report body. If the report includes several conclusions or recommendations, use a list format for simplicity.

Letter Reports

External reports, those written for people outside the organization, often are written in letter format. (See Chapter 6 for details on formatting letters.) These reports are called **letter reports**. In general, an informal report written in letter format should be five pages or less. If
you need more than five pages, use the manuscript format. Manuscript
format allows you to separate the various parts of the report so readers
can follow the organization of your material.

The opening may mention who asked for the report and the
date the report was assigned. The report body is the report itself.
This middle section includes findings and supporting details and
may include an analysis of the situation being studied and recommendations to resolve problems. The ending is similar to the closing
in any letter. If possible, the ending should mention some expected
action on the part of the reader or writer. See Figure 9-6 for an example of a letter report.

Memo Reports

A **memo report** is a short internal report, which is sent to others
within the organization, and is written in memo format. These reports
are informal primarily because of their format, not necessarily because
of their content.

Use the memo format for routine internal reports that are five
pages or less. (See Chapter 5 for detailed information on formatting
memos.) If your report needs to be longer, use the manuscript format.
An example of a memo report is shown in Figure 9-7.

Manuscript Reports

Manuscript reports are short reports written in manuscript format and
are usually longer than memo or letter reports but not as long as formal reports. Internal proposals, for example, frequently are formatted
as manuscript reports.

The opening may include the following information: the subject of
the report, the purpose of the report (the reason why the subject is
important), and a preview of the main ideas of the report. If you are
writing in direct order, include the summary of findings or conclusions
and recommendations in the opening. See Figure 9-8 for an example
of a manuscript report.

Pacific Food Services

1518 West Southland Boulevard
Evansville, IN 47711-7818
(812) 555-6106

TO: All Dieticians
FROM: Isabel Gomez, Chief Dietician
DATE: August 12, 20—
SUBJECT: High School Visits

Every high school in Sales District 3 has signed up for our free annual menu consultation. With the information we provide about menu items, serving size, and ingredients, the schools are better able to plan their monthly food purchases. In turn, we learn more about the students' and teachers' special dietary needs.

Because of the need to complete these visits before school begins, I have arranged the following schedule for high school visits.

Dietician	Schools	Dates
Allman, Trudy	Central High School	August 19
	Packer Regional High School	August 20
Maroni, Carlos	Campbell High School	August 19
	Morrow High School	August 20
Sogo, Rinji	Avondale High School	August 19
	Jonesboro High School	August 20
Davis, Robert	Forest Park High School	August 19
	Riverdale High School	August 20

FIGURE 9-7 Memo Report

RCG Raleigh Consulting Group
216 North Main Street
Raleigh, NC 27612-7643
(919) 555-7922

December 14, 20—

Mr. Donald A. Stevens
Human Resources Manager
Southern Textiles
6 Elm Street
Kinston, NC 28501-1463

Dear Mr. Stevens

Opening — Here is the report you requested on recommended training programs for new shift supervisors. After talking with your plant manager and with one dozen newly promoted supervisors, I recommend that you consider a two-day management and communication course.

Management Training

Body — Because new shift supervisors have no management background, an intensive one-day training program would provide management ideas that they can apply immediately. This program would cover basic management functions and information on managing for quality improvement.

Communication Training

New shift supervisors must be able to communicate with workers, peers, top management, and union representatives. A one-day training program would give these supervisors the speaking and writing skills they need to be effective. This program would cover oral and written communication, listening, and feedback.

Closing — Our manufacturing clients have found that two consecutive days of training immediately after a promotion can provide the tools that new supervisors need to be productive right away. Please call me at (919) 555-2580 so that we can discuss how to tailor this course to your mill's specific needs. Thank you for giving us the opportunity to work with you.

Sincerely

Dr. Joan Carter

Dr. Joan Carter, President

wa

FIGURE 9-6 Letter Report

SPECIFICATIONS FOR NEW CREDIT RECORD STORAGE FACILITY

Opening

To accommodate seasonal variations in credit volume and to allow for future growth in credit sales, the Credit Department proposes that a new credit record storage facility be constructed in the regional office. This facility would store credit and collection records for up to 1,000 regional customers. The specifications for the proposed storage facility are outlined in this report.

Body

Physical Specifications

The proposed storage facility should meet the following specifications:

Space. An area of 700–900 square feet is needed.

Furniture and Equipment. Provide two rectangular workstations with seating for two at each workstation. Workstations should each be equipped with one microfiche reader, one microfiche storage file, one personal computer, and one laser printer. The two computers should be linked with the central credit processing system. Each workstation requires two work chairs. In addition, one 3′ × 6′ table for file preparation is needed.

To hold credit applications that must be retained for two years, provide 10 linear feet of reinforced steel shelving. The shelving should be 8′ high with 16″ between shelves. The lowest shelf must be positioned at least 4′ above floor level.

To hold customer correspondence about credit disputes or collections, provide six 4-drawer letter-size file cabinets. To hold returned mail from credit and collection accounts, provide two rolling storage bins.

One multi-line telephone should be installed at each workstation. These telephones should be linked with the regional office's voice-mail system.

Provide one facsimile device for transmission of credit documents. The facsimile must be equipped with a ten-page document feeder and a letter-size tray to hold incoming faxes.

Security. This file storage facility must be secure both day and night. Provide one card-activated locking system with a manual override in case of power failure.

2

Wiring. Appropriate wiring should be provided for the following equipment:

Personal computers and printers
Microfiche readers
Facsimile equipment

Environmental Factors

The proposed file storage area should meet the following specifications for other environmental factors.

Climate. The heating, ventilation, and air conditioning system must accommodate a temperature range between 68–78 degrees Fahrenheit (20–26 degrees Centigrade), and a humidity level of 40–60 percent.

Flooring. Linoleum or vinyl tile should be provided in the area. All furniture and equipment must be set on two-inch risers to prevent water damage in case of flooding.

Lighting. Indirect, nonglare lighting supplemented by task lighting is needed at the workstation. For all other areas in this facility, provide standard ceiling lighting.

Construction Schedule

Every year, the Credit Department experiences heavier demand for record storage as a result of increased credit and collection activity during the fall and winter months. To accommodate this seasonal demand, the facility should be ready by September 15.

File Transfer Schedule

The Credit Department will require two business days to transfer current customer records from the downtown office to the new storage facility in the regional office. Customer correspondence records and microfiche files will be moved on the first day; customer applications will be moved on the second day.

Closing

Summary

A storage facility constructed according to the specifications described in this report would allow the Credit Department to adequately service 800–1,000 customers. With the availability of this storage facility, the Credit Department could comfortably accommodate both seasonal storage demands and expected growth ir future credit sales.

FIGURE 9-8 Manuscript Report

Formatting Informal Reports

Indicate whether each statement is true or false.

1. Memo reports should be five pages or less in length.
2. Manuscript reports usually are longer than memo or letter reports but not as long as formal reports.
3. Informal reports have three main parts: the opening, the body, and the findings.
4. The ending of a letter report is similar to the closing in any letter.
5. In a report written in direct order, the ending should reemphasize the main ideas.
6. Put the conclusions and recommendations in the opening of a manuscript report written in indirect order.

Check your answers in Appendix E.

CASE 9:

Answers

Responses to Questions 3 and 4 in Chapter Opener

3. **Why does the language in the reports sent to Peter seem "cold" or formal?**
   The language is "cold" because it is the impersonal style. This is the style most commonly used in governmental reports.

4. **Why do some reports look like memos? Why do some look like letters? Why do others look different from memos and letters?**
   Reports look like letters and memos because they can be formatted using the rules for formatting letters and memos. The reports that look "different" probably employ the manuscript format.

DISCUSSION QUESTIONS

1. Why are reports written in both direct and indirect order?
2. Why do you have three choices when selecting a format (memo, letter, or manuscript) for an informal report?

TECHNOLOGY

Send It Today!

Have you ever fallen behind schedule and had a long report due within a very short period? Were you able to get it to the receiver on time?

Sam Williams works for an engineering firm in London, England. Sam needed to have a major report to his San Francisco office on a Thursday, but he could not get the necessary data to run his analyses until Tuesday. After running the analyses, he still had to write the report. Did he get it to San Francisco on time?

After receiving and analyzing the data on Tuesday, Sam wrote the report and keyed it on Wednesday. Then, Thursday morning, he had two choices: He could fax the report or send it over the Internet. Either way, Sam's report would go halfway around the world in just a few seconds. With today's technology, communication is almost instantaneous. ■

CASE 9:

Summary

Peter's questions about the reports he receives from his customers and the government reveal that he does not understand the writing of informal reports. The information in this chapter would really help him improve his work performance. For example, if he understood the use of language style and formatting options, he would better understand how a customer (a farmer in this situation) is approaching him. This understanding could also help Peter when he writes reports to his supervisor and others. He would know how to use language style and formatting to help him set the right tone in his reports.

Chapter Summary

Section 9.1 Planning Reports

1 **Explain how to classify reports according to their style, purpose, and format.** The two styles of reports are formal and informal. The purposes of reports are to provide information (informational) and to analyze (analytical). Their possible formats are memo report, letter report, and manuscript.

2 **Identify the steps in planning an informal report.** The seven steps for planning a report are (1) identify the problem; (2) decide on areas to investigate; (3) determine the scope; (4) plan the research; (5) develop a preliminary outline; (6) collect the data; and (7) analyze the data, draw conclusions, and make recommendations.

3 **Explain the differences among data, conclusion, and recommendation.** Data are composed of facts, data lead to conclusions, and conclusions lead to recommendations.

Section 9.2 Writing Informal Reports

1 **Explain when to use direct or indirect order to organize an informal report.** If you expect the reader to respond favorably to what you are writing, use direct order. If you expect the reader to respond unfavorably to what you are writing or to have to be persuaded, use indirect order.

2 **Know when to use the personal and impersonal writing style in informal reports.** If your report is about a serious problem or is going to a senior manager, you probably want to use an impersonal style. Otherwise use a personal style.

3 **List the parts of an informal report.** The parts of an informal report are the opening, the body, and the closing.

4 **Describe when to use the letter, memo, and manuscript formats for informal reports.** Use the letter report format when the receiver of the report is outside the organization and the report is five pages or less in length. Use a memo report format when the receiver is within the organization and the report is five pages or less. Use the manuscript format for reports longer than letter or memo reports but shorter than formal reports.

Critical Thinking Questions

1. Why are the steps for planning all types of informal reports the same?
2. Why are first-person and second-person pronouns usually part of an informal report yet generally not used in reports that use formal language?
3. Is planning just as important when writing a short, simple report as it is when writing a long, complex report? Justify your answer.

Applications

Part A. For Part A, do the following:

1. Select a topic for a short informal analytical report.
2. Start planning the report by identifying the problem and writing a statement of the problem.
3. Define the scope.
4. Prepare a preliminary topical outline for organizing your research.
5. Answer the questions, "Should you arrange the material according to hypotheses or alternatives? Why?"

Part B. Conduct secondary research for the problem identified in Part A using no fewer than five sources. Provide the data you made up or found.

Part C. Using the research you have conducted for the problem identified in Part B, analyze the data, draw conclusions, and make recommendations.

Part D. Develop a preliminary discussion outline for a report on the reasons for lower holiday sales at downtown stores. Organize the report around these hypotheses:

1. The weather kept people from shopping downtown. Possibly the snow on December 20 and again on December 22 discouraged shoppers. Another possibility is that the frigid temperatures during the first two weeks of December hurt sales.
2. The downtown stores closed too early. Other retailers may have stayed open later, drawing customers from our stores. Also, our downtown locations were not open as late as our mall stores.
3. Our staffing was inadequate. We should find out if our downtown stores hired extra help for the holiday season. We should also investigate if we had enough staff during the busiest times of the day and during the busiest days of the week.
4. We needed more merchandise. For example, we should check our stock of best-selling books to see if we sold out before the end of

December. Did we order extra quantities of gift books in time for the holidays?

Part E. Plan a brief informational report to your instructor on one of the following topics:

Business curriculums (curricula) at your campus

Enrollment trends at your campus

Parking facilities on your campus

Library facilities on your campus

1. Prepare a preliminary outline to guide your research. Then conduct primary research (by interviewing people on campus) or secondary research (by checking reports and other materials).
2. Decide whether to use direct order or indirect order to organize this report; explain your choice.
3. Modify the preliminary outline if necessary so it can be used to write the report.
4. Determine the main idea that you want to convey in this report.
5. Write your problem statement for this report.
6. Determine what format should be used for the report. Support your recommendation.

Editing Activities

1. Edit the following notes on secondary research sources and format them as they would appear in a report bibliography.

   Re-inventing the corperation written by John Naisbitt and Patricia Aburdene, published by Warner Books in New York, 1985.

   The Leadership Factor was published by the Free Press, in New York in 1988. The auther of this book is John P. Kotter.

   A book published by Touchstone (located in New York) in 1990: When giants learn To Dance by author Rosabeth Moss Kanter.

2. Edit, proofread, and rewrite the following short report.

   Hear is the report you requested on recomendd electronic mesage systems ofr your organization. After surveying the number and types of messages your company snds I recomend that you consider adding e-mail and fax machines. Becuase you're organization sends many memos among 8 branch offices e-mail would speed up communiction. Additionally, it would be inespenxive and convinient.

   You're offices often send ilustrations and graphics to each other. Faxsimile machines would speed up the prosess, provide high quality imaging, and lower costs.

words@work

If you are using *words@work*, complete the activities on Reports in the Writing at Work section.

Case Studies

1. As manager of the automotive repair shop for the local Auto-X dealer, you have a thriving business. Yesterday, the owner of the dealership asked you to prepare a report summarizing the past year's activities in the automotive repair shop. You have had some very good achievements this past year, but you have also had some problems.

   The good things that have happened are

   - All 12 workers in the shop have had at least two training courses this year, preparing them for the new models coming out next September.
   - On a questionnaire given to all customers, the average rating by customers of the services rendered by workers in the shop was 5.5, with 7 being the highest score possible. This rating is in the "very good" range.
   - Just over 95 percent of the repairs to vehicles were complete within the timeframe stated to customers.
   - Income from the automotive repair shop increased 25 percent.

   The problems are

   - The customers' overall rating of the mechanical aspects of cars manufactured by Auto-X Motor Company fell 25 percent—from 5.0 to 3.75 (with 7 being the highest score possible).
   - The average rating by customers of Auto-X Motor parts was only 3.4, with 7 being the highest score possible. This rating fell in the "poor" range.
   - While income for the automotive repair shop increased, profit from the shop fell 20 percent (costs increased 40 percent).
   - Labor turnover within the shop continues to be a problem. This year the turnover rate was 60 percent. The average number of years a worker has worked in this shop is 1.4 years. When workers were asked about their reasons for leaving, most gave "wages" as the main reason. Some indicated that they could make as much as $3 an hour more in other shops. Also, some (40 percent) indicated that the "working atmosphere" of other shops was much better.

   (a) If you were writing this report, which of the following approaches would you use: direct order, analytical, formal, letter report, manuscript, or impersonal writing style. Justify your answer.
   (b) Write the report for the owner.

2. Go the web site **http://newsweek.com/**. Scroll to the bottom of the screen and click on "Index." From the Print Edition-US link, select an article and read it. Make a bibliography card and as many note cards as needed for an informal memo report you will write. From the Print Edition-International link, select an article and read it. Use a different article than the one used in the Print Edition-US. Make another bibliography card and as many note cards as necessary for the article from the International Edition.

    Write a four-part memo report to your teacher about these articles.

    In Part A of your memo, respond to the following questions about the article in Print Edition-US:

    ■ What was the purpose of each article?
    ■ What was the main idea of each article?
    ■ How did the authors support the main idea of each article?
    ■ After you read each article, what did you learn?

    In Part B of the memo, respond to the same four questions about the article in Print Edition-International.

    In Part C of the memo, tell what you learned from the articles.
    In Part D of the memo, tell what you learned from this exercise.

TECHNOLOGY

Career Case Studies

COMMUNICATION FOR HEALTH SERVICES CAREERS

You and your spouse live in a suburban area near a city of 450,000 residents. You have lived there 15 years and plan to stay at least until you both retire. You enjoy the family-type living style of your neighborhood.

Your spouse is a general dentist. The clients are primarily children, but parents also come in for annual checkups and normal minor dental work. Your spouse's income is between $100,000 and $125,000 per year.

You work for an organization that promotes health within the city. You have just read an extensive report that indicates that 50 percent of the cavities in the baby teeth of children could be eliminated if cities would use fluoride in their water-supply systems. The report is quite thorough, well done, and credible. Usually, when you read such a report, you write your boss a memo suggesting actions the city could take to improve the health of its residents.

1. What drawbacks to you would there be for writing this memo?
2. In light of these drawbacks, should you write the memo?

COMMUNICATION FOR ENGINEERING AND INDUSTRIAL CAREERS

Eric Tath oversees the city's utility operations. Every month, he must send a written status report to the city manager. In the report, he must indicate the income of the operations; its expenses including fuel, salaries, and maintenance; the number or watt hours consumed by customers; the average cost of a watt hour, etc. These statistics are usually compared with the data of the same month in the previous year. In almost every month, sales and income increase over those of the previous year.

Eric has always used the memo-report style, but lately, he has been thinking another form might be more effective.

1. Do you think using a form would be a good idea?
2. If you were Eric, would you want to use a form if the statistics were negative?

Continuing Case....

Analyzing Potential Customers

Eva has hired Le Liang, a recent college graduate in computer sciences, to help her at the NetCafe. His main job is helping customers use the shop's computer software applications. In his first two weeks on the job, Le has proved to be patient and knowledgeable.

Le has also observed several of Eva's classes. Now he has some ideas that he'd like to explore. While he was going to college in Los Angeles, Le explains to Eva, he lived in an older section of that city. He got to know a large group of older people who lived there. Le thinks that the NetCafe can attract more people in this generation to use the shop's computer services.

Eva is always interested in ways to increase the number of computer users at the shop. She asks Le to write an informal report, explaining what he would do to attract older people to NetCafe.

Help Le plan and write his report by completing the seven steps below. You might work with a partner on this project. Remember that you do not have to cover all the topics mentioned. After doing some preliminary research, you will choose some promising ideas and focus on those.

1. Identify the problem. Write a statement that concisely explains the problem Le plans to address.
2. Decide on areas to investigate. For example, you might focus on possible reasons for older, possibly retired people to come to the NetCafe. In this case, you would consider and research ways that older people use—or could use—the Internet in particular and computers in general. For example, they might use the Internet to research their genealogy, or they might use e-mail to keep in touch with friends and family.

   Or you might use this report to explore why many older people avoid computers and ways that the NetCafe might overcome these obstacles. For example, are older people reluctant to use computers because of a lack of technical knowledge? Or do they not see how the Internet and computers could be helpful in their lives? Is the availability and cost of using computers a factor?
3. Determine the scope of your report. Decide what topics you will and will not include in your report for Eva.
4. Plan your research. How will you gather the information for your report? For example, will you use the Internet, other reference sources, or interviews with older family members, neighbors, or the staff at a senior center?
5. Develop a preliminary outline. List the main topics you plan to discuss in the order you think you will discuss them.
6. Collect your data. Gather information from the sources you have chosen, which may be primary, secondary, or both.
7. Analyze your data, draw conclusions, and make recommendations. Tell Eva which services are likely to attract more older people to the shop, based on your research. You might also suggest some services that probably would not work, judging from what you have learned.

Writing Formal Reports

Writing Reports—A Major Function of a Business

rock Smith has a profitable business—Smith's Property Management. Business is strong, but it requires Brock and his staff to work long hours and perform hard mental work. The company oversees the financial and progress aspects of the construction of major projects. It also manages day-to-day operations of large and small apartment complexes.

Many of Brock's clients are retired businesspeople who have large investments in their rental properties. These individuals usually are very concerned about their properties and how they are being managed. To provide clients with feedback on their investments, Brock and his staff write reports. One of the company's largest expenses is the cost of the time needed to write these reports.

This past week Brock and his staff put in more than 20 hours writing a formal report to a client who is building a large apartment complex. Brock is managing the project. The report includes information on how the building is coming along, how real costs are running in comparison to estimated costs, the anticipated completion date, etc.

The previous week was the first week of the month. That week is always difficult because monthly reports on the previous month's activities are sent to all clients.

Thus, overtime last week amounted to about 40 hours for the staff.

At last the weekend is here, but Brock finds himself at the office on Saturday morning completing a special report for a client who is considering selling a piece of property. He wanted Brock to provide information on the profitability of the property for the last five years.

While Brock is taking a short break to get mentally revived, he starts thinking about his business and how the demand for reports is beginning to eat into his profits. He wonders if there is anything he can do. He decides he will ask his staff members if they have any ideas on Monday.

Questions

1. How often should Brock and his staff write formal reports?

2. Should all parts of a formal report be included in the reports that Brock and his staff write?

3. What type of special report is Brock currently using in his business?

4. How could computers assist Brock in the preparation of reports?

5. Are there special reports that could help Brock do a better job of managing his business?

10·1 Writing Formal Reports

Objectives

After completing Section 10.1, you should be able to:

1 Decide when to use a formal report.

2 Prepare the possible preliminary and supplementary parts of a formal report.

Objective

SCANS
Employability

Systems: Understands Systems
When companies have preferred requirements for formatting reports, follow the requirements carefully.

Planning, Organizing, and Writing Formal Reports

Formal reports are more complex and longer than informal reports. Because of this complexity, you may need to allow more time to plan, organize, and write a formal report than you would need to prepare an informal report.

The steps for planning and organizing formal reports are identical to those used for informal reports. The steps for planning are:

1. Identify the problem
2. Decide on areas to investigate
3. Determine the scope of the report
4. Plan the research or data gathering
5. Develop a preliminary outline
6. Collect the data
7. Analyze the data, draw conclusions, and make recommendations

Details on these steps were presented in Section 1 of Chapter 9.

When planning a formal report, choose either the direct order or the indirect order and refine your outline. Details on these steps were presented in Section 2 of Chapter 9. When you have finished with these procedures, you are ready to write your report.

Formal reports are sometimes used when writing to top management of an organization. They also are needed when your receiver expects to receive one. However, because of the amount of time required to write a formal report, it should be used only when absolutely necessary.

As with an informal report, the organization and the writing style you choose for a formal report can vary, depending on the nature of the message and the people who will receive it. Both informational and analytical formal reports are longer and more complex than informal reports. As a result, formal reports are formatted differently from shorter, informal reports. Style manuals have been written for the formatting of formal reports. Some of them are *Publication Manual of the*

American Psychological Association (APA),[1] the *Handbook for Writers of Research Papers (MLA),*[2] and *The Chicago Manual of Style.*[3] The formal report in this text uses the MLA guidelines. For some specifics on using *APA* and *Chicago,* see Appendix C.

Direct and Indirect Order

When organizing a report, you can use either direct or indirect order. Formal informational reports usually follow the direct order because they contain information that readers expect; readers, therefore, should react favorably. Formal analytical reports that probably will receive a favorable response also are organized in the direct order. On the other hand, use the indirect order in a formal report when you expect an unfavorable response or when you may need to persuade the reader to accept the main idea.

Writing Style

Many important business decisions are made on the basis of the information presented in formal reports. With so much at stake, these reports need to sound impartial and professional. Thus, formal reports usually are written in an **impersonal style**, without personal pronouns such as *you* and *I.* An impersonal writing style focuses attention on the facts rather than on the writer. It also makes the report sound more objective than a report written in the personal style.

KEY POINT

Other personal pronouns to avoid when using a formal writing style are *we, us, our, me, my, mine, your,* and *yours.*

Parts of a Formal Report

A formal report has three major parts: preliminary parts, body or text, and supplementary parts. Figure 10-1 shows the parts of a formal report.

Objective

KEY POINT

Not every formal report contains all the preliminary and supplementary parts. You should include only those parts that pertain to the report you are preparing.

Preliminary Parts	Body or Text	Supplementary Parts
Letter of transmittal	Introduction	Bibliography
Title page	Findings and analysis	Appendix
Table of contents	Summary, conclusions, and recommendations	
Executive summary		

FIGURE 10-1 Parts of a Formal Report

[1]*Publication Manual of the American Psychological Association,* 4th edition, Washington, DC: American Psychological Association, 1994.

[2]Joseph Gibaldi, *Handbook for Writers of Research Papers,* 4th edition, New York: Modern Languages Association for America, 1995.

[3]*The Chicago Manual of Style,* 14th edition, Chicago: University of Chicago Press, 1994.

Preliminary Parts

The **preliminary parts** are the parts of a formal report that appear first, providing the reader with information about the report body. Preliminary parts include a letter or memo of transmittal, a title page, a table of contents, and an executive summary.

A **letter of transmittal** or **memo of transmittal** transmits the report to the reader. This document conveys what you would say if you were giving the report directly to the reader; therefore, it is usually less formal than the report itself. A letter of transmittal would accompany a report to readers outside the organization; a memo of transmittal would accompany a report for internal use. Use direct order for the letter or memo of transmittal, beginning with a statement such as, "Here is the report you asked me to prepare about . . ." Include a brief statement of the report objective, followed by a short summary of the report. End by thanking the person who requested the report and offering assistance if needed. Figure 10-2 shows a sample memo of transmittal.

A **title page** is the report page that shows the report title; the name, title, and organization of the person for whom the report was written; the writer's name, title, and organization; and the date the report is submitted. Figure 10-3 shows a sample title page. You may use the title page as the report cover if the report is short or if the report is for internal use. Otherwise, use a cover made of heavier paper or plastic. Label the cover with the report title and, if desired, with the writer's name and the date.

A **table of contents** is a list of the report's content. You can prepare the table of contents after the report is written by listing the main headings shown in the report body and the page number where each heading occurs. Figure 10-4 shows a sample table of contents.

The **executive summary**, sometimes called a *synopsis* or an *abstract*, is a brief overview of the report. The purpose of the executive summary is to convey the key points of the report to the reader. The executive summary is especially important when a report is long and technical because it allows busy readers to grasp the main points quickly without reading the entire report. The executive summary should use the indirect approach for reports written in indirect order and the direct approach for reports written in direct order. Figure 10-5, on page 338, is an example of an executive summary.

The Report Body

The **report body**, which contains the actual report, consists of three parts: the introduction; the findings and analysis; and the summary, conclusions, and recommendations.

The **introduction** states the purpose of the report. Figure 10-6 (shown on pages 339–340) illustrates an introduction to the body of the report.

KEY POINT

A letter of transmittal should follow the format for letters shown in Chapter 6. If, however, the report is only for internal readers, the letter of transmittal may be in the memo format shown in Chapter 5.

KEY POINT

In some companies, you may be asked to submit all formal reports inside a preprinted report cover bearing the company name and logo.

Meade Legal Services

1100 Court Street
Cincinnati, OH 45201-1100

TO: Richard Bryce, Senior Vice President
FROM: Katie Goodman, Manager of Office Services
DATE: May 15, 20—
SUBJECT: The Effect of Information Processing

On March 23, 20—, you asked me to prepare a report on the impact of information processing in selected legal offices in the United States. You also asked that my report determine the impact of information processing on business education curricula offered by NABTE institutions.

The completed report, which is attached, shows that information processing has had a significant effect on legal offices and on business education curricula. The report also includes recommendations for ways in which NABTE institutions can match their curricula to the needs of legal offices in their local areas.

Thank you for the chance to study this important issue. If you have any questions about the report, please call me at extension 454.

tr

Attachment

FIGURE 10-2 Transmittal Memorandum

THE IMPACT OF INFORMATION PROCESSING IN SELECTED
LEGAL OFFICES AND NABTE INSTITUTIONS

Prepared for

Richard Bryce
Senior Vice President
Meade Legal Services

Prepared by

Katie Goodman
Manager of Office Services
Meade Legal Services

May 15, 20—

FIGURE 10-3 Title Page of a Formal Report

TABLE OF CONTENTS

Preliminary Part

Body

Supplementary Parts

ii

FIGURE 10-4 Table of Contents

EXECUTIVE SUMMARY

The purpose of the study was to determine the impact that information processing has made in selected legal offices in the United States. Further, the study sought to ascertain the impact that information processing has made on business education curricula offered by selected NABTE institutions.

Methods and Procedures

The participants for the study were information-processing specialists employed in legal offices throughout the United States and NABTE representatives from selected collegiate institutions. The legal participants were randomly selected from the Martindale-Hubbell Law Directory, 1998. The NABTE representatives were randomly selected from NABTE institutions located in or near the capital city in each state.

Each legal office participant completed a questionnaire, and each NABTE representative completed a business education questionnaire. The t-test, McNemar test, and Stuart-Maxwell test were used to analyze the data.

Results and Conclusions

The results of the study revealed that attorneys hired high school graduates or two-year secretarial graduates who knew how to answer the telephone, operate a workstation, file documents electronically, use various computer software packages, and key straight copy at speeds of 60 to 80 words a minute. The data also revealed that, in general, the firms had not established evaluation standards for information-processing specialists and had not increased the number of these specialists since purchasing electronic workstations. The firms also had not increased the salaries of information-processing specialists. Further, the findings revealed that the cost of processing information in legal offices had decreased since the implementation of electronic workstations.

The responses received from the NABTE representatives revealed that business educators trained office technology and comprehensive business education majors to operate information-processing equipment, use software packages, and key documents at production rates. No changes were noted for teaching basic business or basic English skills.

iii

FIGURE 10-5 Executive Summary

INTRODUCTION

Advanced technology has caused many changes in the twentieth century. Equipment has changed from manual to electric and, in the eighties, from electric to electronic. Information processing and communication methods have progressed to an extremely high level of sophistication (Simcoe, 1999). Some legal offices have become fully automated while others strive for a similar setting. According to Moody (1998), office automation is an extension of the technologies refined and developed to electronically process data and words.

Statement of the Problem

The problem of this study was to determine the impact information processing has made in selected legal offices in the United States. Further, the study sought to ascertain the impact that information processing has made on business education curricula offered by selected National Association of Business Teacher Educators (NABTE) institutions.

Specifically, the study seeks to determine the training and entry-level skills needed for employment, the functions and operations performed, and the equipment and software used by information processing specialists in legal offices before and after the implementation of the electronic workstation.

Scope

The report will study the impact that information processing has had on the legal office but will not include the impact of other automation technologies on the legal office. Participants identified in the study were from large cities; therefore, this study will not address the impact of information processing on legal firms in small cities.

The study also will determine any changes in tasks performed before and after information processing was implemented.

(Continued on the next page)

FIGURE 10-6 Introduction to the Body of the Report

Limitations of the Study

The limitations of the study are as follows:

Legal Firms. The legal office participants invited to participate in this study were randomly selected from the Martindale-Hubbell Law Directory, 1998. Also the legal firms had to be located in the capital cities in the United States or the largest city in the state where an NABTE institution was located.

NABTE Representatives. The business educators invited to participate in the study were selected from the NABTE Directory. One NABTE institution located in the capital city or a city near the capital per state was identified for the study.

Definitions

These definitions were listed to assist the reader.

1. After information processing means after the implementation of information-processing operations (concepts, equipment, procedures).

2. Before information processing means before the implementation of information-processing operations.

FIGURE 10-6 *(Concluded)*

The introduction discusses several topics, including any or all of the following:

Authorization	Statement of who authorized the report and the time and manner of authorization
Statement of the Problem	Reasons for writing the report and the goals to be accomplished
Scope	Information the report does and does not cover
Limitations	Factors affecting the scope of the report, such as a limited amount of time or a limited budget
Definitions	List of unfamiliar terms and their definitions

The **findings and analysis** section of the report body (illustrated in Figure 10-7) presents the findings and the supporting details and examines these results. The **summary, conclusions, and recommendations** section (illustrated in Figure 10-8) summarizes the findings, draws conclusions, and makes recommendations.

Supplementary Parts

A formal report may also contain **supplementary parts** that follow the report body, such as a bibliography or an appendix. The **bibliography** is a list of sources used in preparing the report, shown in alphabetic order by authors' names.

Figure 10-9 on page 344 shows a sample bibliography. (MLA guidelines call this section "Works Cited".) A bibliography shows readers where the information in the report comes from and where to look for additional information.

An **appendix** contains material related to the report but too long to be included in the body. Examples include questionnaires or a glossary of terms. Figure 10-10 (page 344) shows a sample appendix.

KEY POINT

When your report relies on primary research such as a survey, your appendix should include a copy of the questionnaire. Including the questionnaire helps readers understand how the data were gathered.

Checkpoint **1**

Planning, Organizing, and Writing Formal Reports

Indicate if each statement is true or false.

1. Formal reports usually are written in a personal style, using first-person pronouns such as *I, me,* and *you.*   *False*

2. A formal report has three main parts: preliminary parts, body, and supplementary parts.   *True*

3. An executive summary explains how information was collected for the report.   *False*

4. An appendix and a letter of transmittal are two supplementary parts of a formal report.   *False*

5. A bibliography lists the sources of the information in a formal report.   *True*

Check your answers in Appendix E.

FINDINGS AND ANALYSIS

The responses received from legal office participants relating to the cost of processing information since the implementation of information processing are shown in Table 1. The data presented are classified by National Business Education Association regions. Fifty percent of the legal office respondents indicated a decrease in the cost of processing information, while 28 percent reported no change had occurred in this area.

A summary of the data supplied by legal respondents reported an increase in the number of information-processing specialists employed in 21 percent of the legal offices since implementing information processing, while 23 percent revealed a decrease. Fifty-six percent of the office respondents reported no change in the number of specialists employed.

Table 1

PERCENTAGE OF LEGAL RESPONDENTS REPORTING
THE COST OF PROCESSING INFORMATION
SINCE ELECTRONIC OPERATIONS WERE
IMPLEMENTED IN LEGAL OFFICES

Legal Offices by Regions	Increase in Cost	Decrease in Cost	No Change	Total Percent
Eastern	29%	42%	29%	100%
Mountain Plains	19%	39%	42%	100%
North-Central	25%	63%	12%	100%
Southern	21%	49%	30%	100%
Western	19%	55%	26%	100%
Mean	22%	50%	28%	100%

FIGURE 10-7 Findings and Analysis Section of the Report

SUMMARY, CONCLUSIONS, AND RECOMMENDATIONS

This study was designed to determine the impact information processing has made in selected legal offices in the United States. Further, the study sought to ascertain the impact that information processing has made on business education curricula offered by selected NABTE institutions.

The conclusions of this study provide the basis for the following recommendations:

1. The NABTE institution representatives participating in this research study and their business education department chairpersons need to study the skills, functions, and operations performed by information-processing specialists in legal offices. The study should determine if the needed skills, functions, and operations are being taught in business education programs.

2. The NABTE institution representatives participating in this study and their business education department chairpersons need to analyze the current business education curricula to determine a procedure to eliminate voids in the legal secretarial curricula.

FIGURE 10-8 Summary, Conclusions, and Recommendations Section of the Report

6

APPENDIX

Functions and Operations Performed by Information-Processing
Specialists in Legal Offices

Please place check marks in the appropriate columns to indicate functions and
operations secretaries/word-processing specialists in your legal office perform
BEFORE INFORMATION-PROCESSING (IP) and AFTER IP.

R = Rarely
O = Occasionally
F = Frequently

	BEFORE IP				AFTER IP	
	R	O	F		R	O	F
1. Answering the telephone							
2. Transcribing handwritten copy							
3. Transcribing rough draft							
4. Transcribing from machine dictation							
5. Transcribing from telephone							
6. Receiving oral directions							
7. Composing correspondence							
8. Transcribing material received from an attorney							
9. Transcribing material received from a paralegal							
10. Proofreading others' work							
11. Operating a computer							
12. Using word-processing software							
13. Using software other than word processing							
14. Filing manually							
15. Filing electronically							
16. Performing other functions on a computer							
17. Operating a photocopier							
18. Operating a microfiche reader/printer							
19. Operating an optical disk system							
20. Other _____							

FIGURE 10-10 An Appendix of a Report

5

WORKS CITED

Anderson, R. I. "Information Processing." *National Business Education Yearbook.*
Reston, Virginia: National Business Education Association, 1996: 55–56.

Brostrom, Gail C. and Erica Parker. "The Importance of Communication Skills
in the Business World." *National Business Education Yearbook.* Reston, Virginia:
National Business Education Association, 1996: 1–12.

Callens, Emily. "The Use of Workstations in Legal Offices." *New York Times
Magazine,* 6 July, 2000: 40+. *New York Times Ondisc.* CD-ROM. UMI-Proquest,
Feb. 2000.

Gauge, Thomas, and Tyler L. Callens. "Statistical Methods in Cancer Research."
The Analysis of Case-Control Studies. Lyon: International Agency for Research
on Cancer, 1990.

Gillstrap, Ryan T. *A Comparative Study of Major Task Requirements of Information-
Processing Specialists and the Traditional Secretary.* Dissertation. University of
Georgia, 1990.

Parker, Brett T. and Joseph Clair Otto. "Are Schools Meeting Needs of the
Business Community?" *Business Education Forum* (Feb. 1997): 23–24.

U.S. Department of Commerce. Statistical Abstract of the United States,
1991–1992. Washington, D.C.: Government Printing Office, 1992.

FIGURE 10-9 The Bibliography of a Report (Entitled By MLA "Works Cited")

Formatting Formal Reports

Formal reports generally follow specific formatting guidelines. A company may develop its own **style manual**, a set of guidelines for formatting documents, to help report writers plan the appropriate margins, spacing, headings, and other details.

Margins

Most formal reports use 1-inch side and bottom margins. Reports that are stapled at the left side use a 1½-inch left margin. The preliminary and supplementary pages and the first page of the body usually have a 2-inch top margin. All other pages use a 1-inch top margin. MLA uses 1-inch sides, top, and bottom margins. If the right margin is uneven, it should be no narrower than one inch.

Spacing

Formal reports may be double-spaced or single-spaced, depending on your organization's preference—a preference that should be stated in its style manual. If a report is double-spaced, indent paragraphs. If the report is single-spaced, double-space between paragraphs. However, in this situation, paragraph indentions are not required.

Headings

Use headings to help organize and present data. Headings help the reader follow your line of thought as you move from point to point in the report. A *first-level heading* is a heading that opens a major section; for example, a first-level heading is a heading identified with a Roman numeral in your outline. A *second-level heading* is a heading that introduces a subtopic below a first-level heading.

↓**KEY POINT**

Remember to use the appropriate memo or letter margins for the memo or letter of transmittal.

DIVERSITY

When sending a report containing a letter of transmittal to a foreign country, be sure to follow the appropriate spacing for a letter in that country.

Ethics and the Accountant's Audit Report

Accountants often find themselves in difficult ethical situations. As auditors, if they indicate that a company is in a poor financial position, the company may not use them again to audit its records. As a result, income will be lost. If they indicate that a company is in good financial condition and it is not, they can be sued.

To help accountants make correct ethical decisions, The National Association of Accountants (NAA) has adopted a code of ethics for its members. This code covers four areas—competence, confidentiality, integrity, and objectivity.

Accountants often encounter situations involving ethical decisions. In these situations they are obligated not to mislead investors and stockholders. When independent auditors indicate in an audit report that a company is financially sound, they are legally responsible for that statement. Therefore, auditors must be sure of the accuracy of their data to ensure that their audit report reflects the actual financial condition of a company. ■

The same-level headings within a section, such as second-level headings at the A and B level in an outline, should be parallel in form. Parallel headings show readers that the ideas are grouped for a reason. If one heading begins with a noun, for example, then all headings at that level should begin with a noun. If one begins with a verb, then all others should begin with a verb. Each level should have a minimum of two headings. See the following examples.

Parallel Headings	Unparallel Headings

I. Steps in Planning (first-level heading)
  A. Defining the Objective (second-level heading)
  B. Determining the Project Leader (second-level heading)
    1. Vendor (third-level heading)
    2. Outside Consultant (third-level heading)
II. The Feasibility Study (first-level heading)
	I. Planning the Study
	  A. Defining the Objective
	
	  B. Determine Project Leader
	
	    1. Vendor
	    2. Hiring an Outside Consultant
	II. The Feasibility Study

Figure 10-11 shows one way to format report headings.

FIRST-LEVEL HEADING

Key the words of a first-level heading in capital letters and center the heading. Making it **bold** is optional. Allow three spaces (two blank lines) before starting the first paragraph under a first-level heading.

Second-Level Heading

Place a second-level heading at the left margin of the report, capitalize all important words, and underline the heading or print it in bold. Making it **bold** is optional. Side headings are always preceded and followed by a double space (one blank line).

Third-Level Heading. A third-level heading is part of the paragraph. Making it **bold** is optional. Double space before it, underline it, capitalize the first letter of important words, and follow it with a period. Begin the text two spaces after the period.

Fourth-level headings may be needed in your report. If so, capitalize only the first word, underline it, and run the heading into the text of the paragraph.

FIGURE 10-11 Format for Report Headings

Visual Aids

Most formal reports (and many informal reports) include visual aids, graphics such as charts, graphs, tables, and illustrations that help the reader understand and interpret the written information. With computers, the production of graphics is much easier and less expensive. Visual aids and their usage in reports are described in Chapter 8.

↓KEY POINT

Use visual aids to emphasize important points of your report.

Computer-generated visual aids, such as charts, graphs, tables, and illustrations, enhance the effectiveness of reports by making information easier to interpret and understand.

Checkpoint 2

Formatting Formal Reports

Fill in the blanks with the appropriate word or words.

1. A company's _____ usually provides guidelines for the formatting of its documents, including formal reports.

2. The right-side margin for most formal reports is _____.

3. A(n) _____ heading introduces a subtopic of a third-level heading.

4. With parallel headings, if the first heading within a division begins with a noun, other headings must begin with a(n) _____.

5. If a formal report is double-spaced, the paragraphs must be

    _____.

Check your answers in Appendix E.

CASE 10:

Answers

Responses to Questions 1 and 2 in Chapter Opener

1. **How often should Brock and his staff write formal reports?**

   Brock and his staff should not be writing formal reports too often. Maybe once a year an annual report should be written to each client. Other types of special reports—periodic reports, status reports, project reports—that are shorter would probably be sufficient for other parts of the year if used properly.

2. **Should all parts of a formal report be included in the reports that Brock and his staff write?**

   Brock's formal reports should not contain all of the possible parts. The parts included should be based on "need." For example, most of Brock's reports would not need a bibliography. However, most of those same reports would probably need an appendix.

DISCUSSION QUESTIONS

1. Why is it important to have the purpose of a report in its introduction?

2. Why are headings an important part of a long, formal report?

10·2 Writing Specialized Reports

Types of Specialized Reports

Many companies have specialized reports particular to their needs, but a few of them need emphasis. Two basic types of specialized reports are managerial reports and technical reports. **Managerial reports** provide those members of an organization with information to assist them in decision making. **Technical reports** may be written for management or other receivers. However, their basic purpose is to provide analyses of possible solutions to problems, to explain technologies, or to report to shareholders.

Managerial Reports

Some of the major managerial reports (reports written for management) are the staff report, the status report, the audit report, the periodic report, and a plan of action.

Staff Report

The staff report is one of the most frequent reports written for managers. The **staff report** is prepared by a member of a manager's staff. Usually a staff report is in memo-report format; however, it can be adapted to any report format—memo, letter, manuscript, or formal report. Because this type of report is used repeatedly within an organization (as a monthly sales report, for example), word processing templates are commonly set up and used. This type of report generally is written using direct order. Its plan for presentation is as follows:

Introductory Material	The introductory section of a staff report is usually very short. Many companies construct staff reports using word processing templates. For example, if a memo report format is commonly used for staff reports, the **TO**, **FROM**, **DATE**, and **SUBJECT** may appear on the screen when the template for the report is called up.
Summary	Many executives will read only the summary section of a staff report in order to save time. As a result, this section should contain the objective (paraphrased), major findings and conclusions, and recommendations.

Objectives

After completing Section 10.2, you should be able to:

1 Name the two types of special reports and their purposes.

2 Identify basic reports written for management.

3 Designate the three principal technical reports.

Objective

Objective

KEY POINT

The staff report provides managers with information that is essential to their effectiveness.

SCANS
Employability

Information: Acquires and Uses Information
While staff reports may become routine to the writer and receiver, they are critical to the writer's career. They are a tool to measure the writer's job performance.

TECHNOLOGY
A key to your productivity when writing reports will be creating effective templates for your routine or periodic reports.

KEY POINT
This plan of presentation helps the writer of staff reports with logic. Note how the plan leads from findings, to conclusions, to recommendations.

TECHNOLOGY
For the person who wants a career in technology, a status report will be a common writing event.

Objective   Immediately following the summary is the report's objective. This should be a clearly written statement indicating what the report is attempting to do. (For a review on report objectives or problem statements, see page 305 in Chapter 9.)

Findings   After presenting the objective of the report, present the findings. In this section, present only data that is pertinent to the objective of the report. Avoid the temptation to insert data that is not really relevant to the report's objective.

Analysis   Sometimes this section of a staff report is combined with the Findings section. In some cases it may be logical to analyze the findings and their relationship to the problem as you present them. In other situations, it might be better to analyze the impact of findings after they have been presented.

Conclusions   From the facts, the report writer draws conclusions that are the major contributors in making a recommendation.

Recommendation   When appropriate (when asked for or when understood), the recommendation part of the report is its most important part. It becomes an expectation of the receiver. As previously stated, the recommendation is based on conclusions.

Major users of the staff report are all branches of the Armed Forces of the United States. These organizations commonly use the staff report as a way to provide information for their decision makers.

Status Report

As the name implies, a **status report** (sometimes called a progress report) is used to inform readers of the status of a project. Its purpose is to inform managers about the progress on a particular project. This knowledge assists managers in making appropriate decisions about the project. It should tell management the work that has been completed, the work that is being done currently, and the work that should be completed before the next report is due. In this report, significant problems or progress should be presented.

This type of report should be written as often as is necessary to keep management informed. The frequency of the report depends upon the complexity of the project and management's needs. Direct or indirect order can be used in a status report, depending upon the type of message you must give the receiver. However, most status reports are routine and use direct order. A status report can be required at regular intervals—such as daily, weekly, monthly, bimonthly, etc.— or they may not have a set interval. For an example of a status report, see Figure 10-12.

TO: Trudy Brockton, CEO
FROM: John Ford, CIO
DATE: April 14, 20—
SUBJECT: Status Report on Scanners for Checkout Stations

On April 8, you asked me to investigate the possibility of installing optical scanners at all checkout stations for all six of our stores. I have completed the preliminary investigation and am gathering additional data. I am in the process of gathering specific detailed information from companies that could provide and install the scanners. I anticipate having all the needed information from these companies by April 30. By May 6, I expect to have a completed report with a recommendation on your desk.

Should you have any questions or concerns, please call me at extension 3491.

FIGURE 10-12 Status Report

Audit Report

An **audit** is a formal, periodic examination of a company's accounts and financial records. The purpose of the audit is to verify correctness. The purpose of an **audit report** is to report those findings. This type of report is probably the most standardized of all reports. Typically, audit reports are written in direct order. They can vary in length. Many times, however, they are short, standardized statements of an accountant's findings that indicate the correctness of the accounts examined. As a result, the wordings of these statements are very similar. Figure 10-13 on page 352 contains an example of an audit report that covers three years. Although the company's name and the years have been changed, this is an audit report that was part of an annual report.

Periodic Report

The purpose of a **periodic report** is to provide management with information at regularly scheduled intervals. The intervals may be daily, weekly, monthly, bimonthly, etc., but they are consistent. These reports usually follow a set format. Because they are used regularly, they commonly use templates or are on keyed forms. See Figure 10-14 on page 353 for an example of a periodic report.

Accounting firms that conduct audits can avoid ethical dilemmas by following strict standards set by the industry's governing board.

To the Shareholders and Board of Directors of XXX Company

We have audited the accompanying consolidated balance sheet of XXX Company and subsidiary companies as of December 31, 2000, 1999, and 1998 and the related consolidated statements of income, shareholders' equity and cash flows for each of the years then ended. These consolidated financial statements are the responsibility of the Company's management. Our responsibility is to express an opinion on these consolidated financial statements based on our audits.

We conducted our audits in accordance with generally accepted auditing standards. Those standards require that we plan and perform the audit to obtain reasonable assurance about whether the consolidated financial statements are free of material misstatement. An audit includes examining, on a test basis, evidence supporting the amounts and disclosures in the financial statements. An audit also includes assessing the accounting principles used and significant estimates made by management, as well as evaluating the overall consolidated financial statement presentation. We believe that our audits provide a reasonable basis for our opinion.

In our opinion, the consolidated financial statements referred to above present fairly, in all material respects, the financial position of XXX Company and subsidiary companies at December 31, 2000, 1999, and 1998, and the results of their operations and their cash flows for each of the years coded, in conformity with generally accepted accounting principles.

FIGURE 10-13 Audit Report Covering a Three-Year Period

The order used in periodic reports is dependent upon the message you must give. Direct order is used for routine or good-news messages. Indirect order should be used for bad-news or persuasive messages.

Plan of Action

A report that is a **plan of action** reveals the strategies to be used when solving a problem. Such plans could indicate that further investigation is needed or they could reveal how a recommendation is to be implemented. This type of report usually is written in direct order and is basically an informative report. Plan of action reports usually are formatted as memo or letter reports, depending upon who the receiver is. Plans of action generally are short; thus, the formal report format is seldom used.

Daily's Department Store
WEEKLY SALES REPORT

Store: <u>Tacoma, Washington</u>

Sales Period: <u>Annual Sales, 2001 & 2002</u>

Department	Sales, 2001	Sales, 2002	Increase or Decrease	Percent of Increase or Decrease
Children's Clothing	$12,650	$15,906	+$3,256	+$25.7%
Men's Clothing	$19,819	$19,051	−$768	−3.8%
Women's Clothing	$25,412	$30,297	+$4,885	+19.2%
Furniture	$54,981	$93,009	+$38,028	+69.1%
Sporting Goods	$19,762	$21,098	+$1,336	+6.8%
Hardware	$8,794	$8,120	−$674	−7.7%
Totals	**$141,418**	**$187,481**	**+$46,063**	**+32.6%**

FIGURE 10-14 Periodic Report

KEY POINT

In the sales industry, the periodic report is probably the most common type of written report.

Checkpoint 3

Managerial Reports

Match the type of report with its characteristics.

Type of Report	Characteristics
____ 1. Staff report	(a) sometimes called a progress report
____ 2. Status report	(b) report on the periodic examination of a company's accounts and financial records
____ 3. Audit report	(c) tells of a strategy to be used when solving a problem
____ 4. Periodic report	(d) provides management with information at regular intervals
____ 5. Plan of action	(e) prepared for managers by their subordinates

Check your answers in Appendix E.

SCANS
Employability

Information: Acquires and Uses Information
When writing an analyses of alternatives report, you have the opportunity to demonstrate your problem-solving ability—a valued managerial skill.

DIVERSITY

Although systems white papers contain technical subject matter, they generally are written to a receiver that does not have a technical background. Thus, one of your challenges when writing white papers is to write in such a style that the receiver will understand the report.

Objective
3

Technical Reports

The three technical reports described in this chapter are analyses of alternatives, systems white papers, and annual reports.

Analyses of Alternatives

A report that examines possible solutions to a problem is called an **analyses of alternatives**. Because this report may simply discuss alternatives or may make a recommendation after an analysis, it may be written in direct, indirect, or direct-indirect order. These analytical reports can use any format, even a formal report format if it exceeds five pages in length. (As with most messages, the order used in these reports depends upon the type of message.)

Systems White Papers

The purpose of a **systems white paper** is to provide specific, detailed information on a technology. As a result, these papers are generally written in direct order and use a personal, informal tone. Usually, they are descriptive informal reports that can use either the memo, letter, or manuscript formats. However, in some situations, the formal report format can be used. Thus, they can have any of the preliminary or supplementary parts of a formal report.

Sometimes, however, the writer will use a formal tone in order to be perceived as unbiased. This appearance is especially important in this type of report. In such situations, the writer can use a formal report format to provide additional formality to the report. When using a formal report format, use either the company manual or style manuals for formatting guidelines.

TECHNOLOGY

Groupware and CWS

One element of groupware (software designed for groups) is collaborative writing software (CWS). As businesses and organizations increase their use of teams and groups, the need to write a team or group report has grown. CWS enables several members of a team to work on the same document rather than a copy of the document.

CWS can be interactive or independent. If interactive, the software allows two or more members to work on the document at the same time. One member acts as a host. Then when a member wants to contribute something, he or she signals the host, who determines the order in which participants will have access to the document. In between writing sessions, only the host will have access to the document.

If using independent CWS, the document resides on a computer that may be accessed by any team member at any time. This type of availability enables team members to work on the document when convenient. The disadvantage of this system is that team members must check in periodically to see the changes others have made. ∎

Technical reports provide analyses of possible solutions to problems, explain technologies, and inform shareholders.

Annual Report

Every year many companies must write **annual reports** to their shareholders. Typically, these reports are long and formal. They are considered technical because they contain a good deal of financial information. Because they are quite long, they are formatted as a formal report and usually have many of its preliminary and supplementary parts.

This report usually has footnotes and an audit report. The report itself is normally split into two sections—the nonfinancial section and the financial section. The nonfinancial section ordinarily contains a letter to the stockholders from the Chief Executive Officer (CEO), descriptions of the company's managerial philosophy, product descriptions, its successes (and sometimes its failures), prospects and challenges for the future, and a list of directors and officers. Attractive pictures of products and facilities are a standard feature of these reports.

Writers of annual reports may be tempted to use their "showy appearance" to conceal a negative message.

The four basic financial statements typically contained in an annual report are

- an income statement
- a stockholders' equity statement
- a cash flow statement
- a balance sheet

Common characteristics of the financial section are

- a graph or table that summarizes the company's financial data over the past five years
- a discussion and analysis of the results of the company's operations and its financial condition
- recent stock price information
- summaries of unaudited quarterly financial data

The order used in an annual report is determined by its main idea. Like analyses of alternatives, all three orders can be used in annual reports.

4 Checkpoint

Technical Reports

Indicate whether each statement is true or false.
1. An analyses of alternatives may examine one or more possible solutions to a problem.
2. Systems white papers are written in direct order and generally use a formal tone.
3. Both analyses of alternatives and systems white papers use only the memo report format.
4. In an annual report, both financial and nonfinancial information is reported.
5. Annual reports are written in direct order only.

Check your answers in Appendix E.

CASE 10:

Answers

Answers to Questions 3, 4, and 5 in Chapter Opener

3. **What type of special report is Brock currently using in his business?**

   Currently, Brock is using a progress report. The report to the client that is building a large apartment complex is a progress report.

4. **How could computers assist Brock in the preparation of reports?**

   Computers may be used to key and format the reports. If the members of Brock's staff would use templates on regularly occurring reports, a great deal of time would be saved.

5. **Are there special reports that could help Brock do a better job of managing his business?**

   Yes, there are. If Brock would restrict his clients to an annual report at the end of each year and then provide periodic or progress reports during the year, the time spent writing reports could be better planned and would be more manageable and less time consuming.

DISCUSSION QUESTIONS

1. How are managerial and technical reports alike? How do they differ?
2. Are reports written for management important to the writer? Why or why not?
3. In technical reports, why is it that analyses of alternatives and annual reports can use any of the three orders, yet systems white papers use only the direct order?

CASE 10:

Summary

It is important for Brock and his staff to learn how to use reports effectively. As the company develops, reports will be needed more frequently. Thus, to conserve time and money, Brock should learn how to use the various types of reports. He also should learn how to use templates for the preparation of reports.

Chapter Summary

Section 10.1   Writing Formal Reports

1 **Decide when to use formal reports.** Formal reports are used when writing to top-level management or to important audiences outside the organization.

2 **Prepare the possible preliminary and supplementary parts of a formal report.** The preliminary parts of a formal report are letter or memo of transmittal, title page, table of contents, and executive summary. A bibliography and an appendix are the supplementary parts of formal reports.

Section 10.2   Writing Specialized Reports

1 **Name the two types of special reports and their purposes.** The two types of special reports are managerial and technical reports. Managerial reports are written to decision makers to assist them in their decisions. Technical reports are written to provide technical data for their receivers.

2 **Identify the basic reports written for management.** The basic reports written for management are staff reports, status reports (sometimes called progress reports), audit reports, periodic reports, and plans of action.

3 **Designate the three principal technical reports.** The main technical reports are analyses of alternatives, systems white papers, and annual reports.

Critical Thinking Questions

1. If long, formal reports are seldom written, why should you know how and when to write them?
2. Why is a letter or memo of transmittal important? Could it be written using personal pronouns?
3. Of the eight types of special reports presented in the chapter (staff report, status report, audit report, periodic report, plan of action, analyses of alternatives, systems white paper, or annual report), which is the most important? Justify your answer.
4. How do the purposes of a periodic report and a status report differ? How are they similar?

Applications

Part A. Plan and organize a formal report for your instructor on one of the topics you selected in Part E of Chapter 9. Then answer the following questions:

1. How will this formal report differ from the informal report you prepared?
2. Will this report have a section on findings and analyses? Will you include recommendations in your report? Why or why not?
3. Where in this formal report will you show your secondary research sources?
4. Write an outline of your formal report.

Part B. Write a status report for your supervisor, Kyle Larson, using the following information:

1. Topic of the report—Internet usage of employees
2. Date assigned—September 1, 20—
3. Completed so far—(a) first draft of the questionnaire is completed, (b) the questionnaire has been pretested
4. To be completed—(a) questionnaire is to be adjusted according to the results of the pretest, (b) questionnaires are to be sent to all employees, (c) results of the questionnaire are to be tabulated, (d) conclusions on results are to be derived, and (e) conclusions are to be drawn and recommendations made.

Part C. The relationship between local residents and students at a college usually needs improvement.

1. Divide into teams of five or six; then develop two questionnaires—one for local residents and one for students—that explore their feelings on the relationship between the groups.
2. Pretest the questionnaires on a small sample of residents and students. Then administer the adjusted questionnaires to the appropriate respondents—local residents and students.

TEAMWORK

3. While gathering the data, write a status report on your project to the president of your student body and a leader of your local community. In the report, explain what you are doing and ask if they want to see the results of your findings. If they do, ask if they would like conclusions and recommendations in the final report.

4. Write a formal report for either the president of your student body or the leader of the local residents. Include in the report findings and analyses, summary, conclusions, and recommendations.

Part D. The Twilight Restaurant is a "tablecloth" restaurant specializing in seafood and steaks. It is located in New Orleans in the French Quarter and has a seating capacity of about 300.

Each table is covered with a white tablecloth; then a dark green cloth is placed diagonally over the white one. Since the restaurant opened more than three years ago, it has been renting tablecloths and linen from a linen laundry service. Other items provided by the service are white napkins, server tunics, chef's tunics, and dish towels.

The owners are always looking for ways to cut costs and improve profits. They have asked you to determine whether they should continue to use the laundry service or buy their own linens and have them laundered.

In an average week, the restaurant uses about 500 white tablecloths, 500 green tablecloths, 2,750 white linen napkins, 80 server tunics, 40 chef tunics, and 1,000 dish towels. Current costs are $0.50 per tablecloth (white and green), $0.10 per white napkin, $2.50 for a server's or chef's tunic, and $0.10 per dish towel.

You have contacted two restaurant supply houses. They have indicated that purchasing the needed linen supplies would cost around $5,000. They would need to be replaced about every four months. If the restaurant did purchase its own linens, a laundry service would pick up dirty linens twice a week (Monday and Thursday afternoons). The day dirty linens are picked up would be the day that a shipment of clean linens are returned. The cost of this service would be $375 a week.

Write a report to the owners suggesting a plan of action. Use an illustration in your report if it would be beneficial.

Editing Activities

words@work

If you are using *words@work*, complete the activities on Reports in the Writing at Work section.

1. Edit and correct all errors in the following paragraph.

    Before starting a project, check the list of existing templates and sea if one of them are close to what you want. You can save alot of time by making a few changes to an existing document instead of starting form sratch. As you creat projects of your own those saved documents will also become templates who can be easily changed and used for future occasions.

2. Proofread and edit the following message.

A memory function is particulary useful where using pictures that are selected from a floppy disk or CD. When using this fucntion, it embeds a copy of the picture files used in your project within the project file theirselves; so, the orginal picture file is not required the next time your open the file. Thus when selected the package will not require you to insert the floppy disk or CD containing the picture used each time you open your project.

Case Studies

1. **Situation:** Nicki Simpson is a public accountant for several wealthy individuals who have major real estate holdings. One couple owns a mall in Edinboro, Tennessee. In this mall, a major retailer has just moved because it built its own store in a nearby area. As a result, it has ended its lease for the store in the mall. However, there are three other major retailers that have indicated interest in the vacant store. The proposed lease offers from the interested retailers were due yesterday. Below is a review of their lease proposals:

Proposed Lease Content	Carlton Stores	Pensays	Sandies Shops
Monthly rent	$75,000	$95,000	No lease
Length of lease	30 years	20 years	proposal
Cost of needed changes to be made before moving in—costs to be paid by company providing the lease.	$225,000	$475,000	received

Send the owners a status report on the lease situation.

2. You work for a highly successful dress designer, Cleothis Fashions. You are in the "crunch time" of the fall season designs. It is two weeks before the fall show, and your boss, Jamie Cleothis, is at the usual pre-show stage of panic!

Jamie called you yesterday and asked for a report on how all the designs are progressing. Today, you are to write a status report on the ten dresses for which you are responsible. Using the data in the table on the following page, write Jamie a status report in the traditional memo format. Use the appropriate order.

Dress #	Material In	Bodice Finished	Skirt Finished	Dress Finished	Accessories In
1	X	X			X
2	X	X	X		X
3	X	X	X	X	X
4	X	X	X	X	X
5	X				
6	X	X	X		X
7	X	X	X		X
8	X	X	X	X	X
9	X	X	X	X	
10	X				

Indicate in your memo that you are in good shape for the show. Your only major concern is the accessories that are to accompany dresses 5, 9, and 10. You have not received these items yet; you indicate that you will call the providers of these items to make sure they will arrive by Wednesday of next week—one week before the show. Sewing and putting the dresses together will be done in plenty of time for the show.

Career Case Studies

TEAMWORK

DIVERSITY

COMMUNICATION FOR NATURAL RESOURCES AND AGRICULTURE CAREERS

Yesterday your boss, Alex Chin, received a letter from a state agency in Brazil. The writer, Edwardo Heminez, had heard of his success in the treatment of cotton. Chin's product decreases the impact of insects on cotton plants while increasing the number of bolls on each plant. Your boss's research indicates that about 10 percent more cotton is produced on an acre because of the treatment with his product—Co-ton A.

Because the weather in this region of Brazil is similar to the cotton regions of the United States, Mr. Heminez is very interested in trying the product.

While you understand his excitement about Co-ton A, you realize that there are many concerns that must be overcome before it can be shipped to Brazil. First of all, the cost of Co-ton A is about $500 an acre. The cost to produce an acre of cotton in Brazil is about $900 and about $1,500 in the United States. The cotton produced on an acre in the United States is valued at $4,500. The amount of cotton produced in Brazil per acre is valued at $3,500.

There also are other costs. The cost of shipping Co-ton A to Brazil would be about $500 an acre. Then there would be the question of getting the product through customs. Would Brazilian authorities allow the product into Brazil? Mr. Heminez thinks they would. Also, if you ship your product to Brazil, would someone copy it and sell it there? Such action may not only cost you the Brazilian market but possibly other markets across the world.

Write your boss a report that analyzes the alternatives he has. You will need to brainstorm to determine these alternatives. (You may brainstorm for alternatives in groups.) Make recommendations in the report.

COMMUNICATION FOR BUSINESS AND MARKETING CAREERS

TEAMWORK

Divide into groups of three or four. Use the information in Case Study 1 on page 362. Assume you are to write a plan of action report with recommendations on the proposed leases. Assume also that Sandies Shops has submitted a proposed lease after the deadline. The lease proposes that the rent be $125,000 a month for 25 years. The costs of needed repairs before moving in would be $500,000.

1. Indicate the preliminary parts and supplementary parts of a formal report that you would include in your plan of action. Justify your answer.
2. After brainstorming areas you would investigate in order to make your recommendation, develop an outline of the plan of action you would write. In this outline, include the opening with an objective and other parts, the body, and the ending of your report.

Video Case

Selecting Report Format and Tone

Heather and Shaun Healy are devoted members of Pedals for Progress, a nonprofit group that gathers unused bicycles, repairs them, crates them, and sends them to developing nations.

To highlight the purpose of Pedals for Progress, as well as raise money for the group, Heather and Shaun hit on the idea of the Pedals for Progress 20K Ride. Heather believed that a local company would agree to be the corporate sponsor of the event in exchange for good publicity.

Knowing Krell Industries' commitment to the community, Heather decided that Krell would be the perfect corporate sponsor to donate funds and staff time. She suggested that she and Shaun write a report for Nora Clayton, Krell's president. Shaun agreed and gathered information on the costs for conducting the 20K ride. Heather drafted an outline.

Now that brother and sister are ready to collaborate on the report, they cannot agree on the form it should take. Heather sees the report as informational. She believes a short, informal report using direct order and personal style will be better received by the busy Ms. Clayton. Shaun sees the report as analytical. Because of the importance of their request, he wants to write a formal report using indirect order and impersonal style and including considerable material about Pedals for Progress.

Questions

1. Given what you know of Heather and Shaun's purpose and what you just learned from the video about Krell Industries, suggest a compromise form for their report.
2. Why is the tone of the report important? What tone would you recommend to Heather and Shaun?
3. Visit the Pedals for Progress home page to learn more about this organization. Then draft an outline for Shaun and Heather's report. Consider what information will be critical to Ms. Clayton's decision-making process.

Continuing Case....

Reporting on Results

 As a follow-up to their first annual meeting, Eva and Ramon are putting together a report on their first year in business. The NetCafe is a small company, so they did not think they needed a formal annual report. However, Dominic Lula, one of the silent partners, has called the shop several times since that meeting. He asks questions that Eva and Ramon answered in their presentations that night. It's clear that he would feel more comfortable if he had a report he could read and reread. The NetCafe continues to need Dominic's financial backing, so Eva and Ramon want him to feel confident about the business.

At the same time, the other silent partner, Opal Morales, is impatient with long explanations. "Just tell me what I need to know, not all that extra stuff," she said several times during their first annual meeting.

1. Review the list of preliminary and supplementary parts of a formal report below. Decide which parts Eva and Ramon should include in their annual report and explain why. Keep their two main readers in mind. However, be aware that others will eventually be reading this report, perhaps including new investors in the NetCafe—or in a branch of NetCafe.
   a. letter of transmittal
   b. title page
   c. table of contents
   d. executive summary
   e. income statement
   f. stockholder's equity statement
   g. cash flow statement
   h. balance sheet
   i. audit report
   j. bibliography
   k. appendix

2. Should this annual report contain personal pronouns? Why or why not?

3. Should the annual report describe the shortcomings of the business, as well as its successes? Why or why not?

4. Should the NetCafe's annual report include a summary, conclusions, and recommendations? If so, what would be an example of each kind of information, related to the NetCafe?

5. Which parts of this annual report is Opal most likely to read? Explain your answer.

6. Which parts will Dominic be likely to read? Why?

chapter 11

Technical Communication

11·1 Writing to Instruct

11·3 Writing to Persuade

11·2 Writing to Describe

Streamlining Returns

Benjamin Contreras works in the shipping department of a large publisher. When customers return damaged books, the damage often is not obvious to the clerks who unpack them. They sometimes place these books back on the warehouse shelves. The damaged books are then shipped out again to the next customer who orders them. That customer finds the damage, returns them again, and usually complains about the inconvenience.

Benjamin thinks the company could avoid shipping out damaged books by creating labels that identify the books as damaged. The company could send the new labels to customers who want to return damaged books. When the damaged books arrive back at the warehouse with the new labels, the clerks would know to give the customer credit for the return and then destroy the books.

Benjamin's supervisor, Karen Horner, likes this idea and has the new labels made. She asks Benjamin to write a letter to customers, explaining how to use the labels. Karen decides that he also should write a complete set of instructions for returning books. This would prevent customers from shipping by the wrong method, sending the books to the wrong address, and so on. She also asks Benjamin to write a description of the return process for staff in other departments because they often ask questions about it.

Benjamin has read many sets of instructions and assumes that a description of a process would be very similar. He thinks he probably could just give other staff members a copy of the instructions he writes for the customers. Benjamin is concerned about the customers' reaction to the instructions. He often talks with them on the phone and knows they are very busy and tend to be impatient. They may not read the instructions; some may be annoyed at even receiving them.

Questions

1. What questions should Benjamin ask himself before he begins writing the customer instructions for returning books?

2. How can Benjamin make these instructions look easy to follow?

3. Should Benjamin give his new instructions to the other staff instead of writing a process description for them? Why or why not?

4. Will Benjamin's process description have more or less detail than his instructions? Why?

5. How can Benjamin persuade customers to read and follow the new instructions for returning books?

6. What benefits of the new return process might appeal to customers?

11·1 Writing to Instruct

1 List the components of effective instructions.

2 Describe how to write effective steps for instructions.

3 Explain how a manual is similar to and different from instructions.

4 Describe how to make information in a manual easy to locate.

↓KEY POINT

Writing instructions and manuals requires a careful analysis of your intended readers.

The Purpose of Instructions and Manuals

Do you always read the instructions before tackling a task? Or do you find most instructions to be confusing, incomplete, or tedious? Instead of reading the instructions, many people use a trial-and-error approach in trying to install a modem, program a VCR, use jumper cables to start a car, or complete some other task. Or they may glance through the instructions, looking for information that might help them complete the task quickly. As a result, they may complete steps in the wrong order or skip some entirely. Only after their other approaches fail will they resort to reading the instructions.

Instructions tell readers how to do something. **Manuals** are sets of instructions combined with explanations, descriptions, definitions, and other related information. Both instructions and manuals should provide all the guidance readers need in order to carry out the tasks. Your challenge is to write instructions and manuals that are so inviting and easy to use that people decide to read and follow them.

Components of Effective Instructions

Objective

When people read instructions, few read them from beginning to end, even though most instructions caution readers to do this. To encourage people to read a whole set of instructions, the steps must be clear, well organized, and geared to the intended receivers. They must include the information that receivers need—not too much and not too little. The instructions must be written using terms the receivers understand. In addition, instructions must look inviting to read.

Effective instructions include the following components: (1) a clear and limiting title, (2) an introduction and a list of needed tools or materials, (3) numbered steps in sequential order, and (4) a conclusion. Figure 11-1 shows a set of instructions with the components labeled.

Clear and limiting title

- - - - - **How to Install the DEBUG Anti-virus Detector on Your Computer**

The DEBUG Anti-virus Detector was designed for use on personal computers. You can install the detector whether or not your computer already has a virus. - - - - - - ┐
This software will identify any files with a known virus and repair those files, keeping your computer virus-free.

Materials needed: DEBUG CD -
                    DEBUG Disks 1 and 2

Introduction and list of materials

CAUTION: Make backup copies of your AUTOEXEC.BAT files before installing this virus detector.

- - - - - First, install the DEBUG Anti-virus Detector:
1. Choose and carry out one of the following:
    a. To install from a CD, insert the DEBUG CD into the CD-ROM drive.
       The detector setup program will start automatically.
    b. To install from a floppy disk,
       1. Insert the DEBUG Disk 1 into Drive A.
       2. Click Start on the Windows taskbar.
       3. Click Run.
       4. Key A:SETUP in the text box.
       5. Click OK.
2. Follow the instructions on the screen.

Numbered steps in sequential order

If the program detects an active virus during installation, follow these steps to remove it:
1. Turn off your computer.
2. Insert DEBUG Disk 2 into Drive A.
3. Turn on your computer.
    The screen will show this message: Emergency Virus Removal.
4. Press Enter to load the program.
    The program will scan for any active viruses and remove them.

Conclusion

After your detector is installed, it will automatically scan your files on a regular basis and detect and remove any viruses it finds.

CAUTION: Be sure to update your detector periodically. New viruses are constantly being created and spread.

FIGURE 11-1 Components of effective instructions

Clear and Limiting Title

The title for a set of instructions should do more than name the topic. It also should explain what the reader will do with the topic. In addition, the title should be limiting: specific enough for readers to know what it does and does not cover. Compare these titles.

Unclear and too broad:	The ABC Modem
Clear and limiting:	How to Install the ABC Modem
	How to Use and Troubleshoot the ABC Modem

Introduction and List of Needed Tools or Materials

Readers need a brief orientation—two or three sentences—before they begin following a set of instructions. The introduction should explain what the instructions should accomplish (if that is not obvious), who should follow the instructions, and perhaps when and why to follow them. For example, let's say the instructions tell how to reorder parts. The introduction should explain who is responsible for reordering the parts and when the parts should be reordered.

Next, list any needed tools, equipment, or materials so readers can gather them before beginning the steps. Then include any of the following sections that are relevant:

1. *Special Skills or Knowledge Required.* For example, if you expect readers to be familiar with certain software or company procedures, point that out. Otherwise, readers may attempt to follow the instructions without the necessary background knowledge. Refer readers to an appropriate source for any additional information they may need.
2. *Time frame.* Tell readers how long the entire task or individual steps should take, if that information would be helpful.
3. *Cautions.* Warn readers about possible injury or other hazards. If necessary, repeat the warnings in the steps.
4. *Definitions.* Define any terms that might not be familiar to readers, such as *initialize* or *airway*. Try to avoid using unfamiliar terms. They may discourage people from reading the instructions.

Numbered Steps in Sequential Order

To begin, think carefully about what your intended readers need to know in order to accomplish this task. What do they already know about this procedure? Have they completed similar tasks? How is this one different?

Your goal in writing these steps is to provide everything readers need, without overwhelming them with details or unneeded information. One way to streamline your instructions is to avoid including obvious steps, such as "Seat yourself in front of the computer."

KEY POINT

Writers tend to skimp on introductions because they are impatient to get started. However, readers need to know when and why they should follow the instructions.

As you write instructions, you assume some responsibility for the safety of your readers. Make sure you alert them to hazards.

For information from the federal Occupational Safety and Health Administration on safety warnings, log on to **http://www.osha.gov/**

KEY POINT

Considering what readers need and want to know is the first step in all effective writing.

Conclusion

In the last section of your instructions, you will describe the expected results. This will help readers determine whether they have successfully completed the procedure. If your instructions are lengthy, you might summarize the major steps.

Guidelines for Writing Effective Steps

These guidelines will help you write clear, inviting, easy-to-follow steps.

- *Number each step and start it with a verb.* The verb should name an action the reader will complete.

Instead of:	1. Alt and F1 are pressed simultaneously.
Write:	1. Press Alt and F1 simultaneously.

- *Put the steps in sequential order.*

Instead of:	1. Insert the disk into Drive A after turning on the computer.
Write:	1. Turn on the computer.
	2. Insert the disk into Drive A.

- *Describe each step separately so readers will not overlook a step.*

Instead of:	1. Click Start, point to Programs, and click Uninstall.
Write:	1. Click Start.
	2. Point to Programs.
	3. Click Uninstall.

- *Indent any explanations under the appropriate step.* Do not number explanations because the reader may think they are steps. If you wish, put explanations in italics or enclose them with parentheses.

Instead of:	1. After you press F3, the screen will show the first menu.
Write:	1. Press F3.

  The screen will show the first menu.

- *If a step should be carried out only under certain conditions, describe the conditions first.* This is an exception to the start-with-a-verb rule given earlier. If you do not immediately alert readers to a special condition, they might complete the step before they realize it should be performed only at certain times.

Instead of:	1. Enter the order number in Field 6 if the order will be filled by our warehouse.
Write:	1. If the order will be filled by our warehouse, enter the order number in Field 6.

- *If you have many steps or several procedures, group them under subheadings,* such as those used in Figure 11-1.

- *Single-space the information within a step; double-space between steps.*

KEY POINT

The conclusion may simply be a sentence or two that follows the steps and has no separate heading of its own.

Objective

SCANS
Employability

Interpersonal:
Teaches Others
Make sure you understand a process completely before trying to explain it to others. Ideally, you will have performed this process yourself.

Write instructions in ways that help prevent mistakes.

■ *Include diagrams or other graphics whenever they will clarify the instructions.* Place the illustrations as close to the relevant step as possible. Add arrows, numbers, or letters to link the steps to the areas on the illustrations that you are discussing.

■ *Highlight warnings and cautions so readers do not overlook them.* Print a warning in a different color or use all capital letters.

■ *Create a clear, inviting format by using numbers, letters, indentation, boldface, and lots of white space.*

■ *As part of the revision process, ask someone to try following your instructions.* Ask for feedback on ways to improve your final draft.

SCANS
Employability

**Information:
Interprets and
Communicates**
Having someone try out your instructions helps you determine whether you have done an effective job of organizing information and communicating it to others.

1 Checkpoint

Writing Effective Steps

Rewrite these instructions so they are clear and easy to follow.
1. Send the pink copy of the invoice to the shipping department after checking to make sure that the warehouse has enough stock to fill the order.
2. Part 103A should be reordered when only five boxes remain in stock.
3. After you enter the customer's name, the screen will display that customer's purchase history.

Check your answers in Appendix E.

Writing Effective Manuals

Manuals provide guidance in completing several related processes, such as entering a customer order, setting up shipping, and verifying that the order was packed and shipped. A manual might explain how a machine works and how to use, maintain, and repair it. Manuals may be written for experienced or inexperienced readers—or for both.

Like a set of instructions, a manual must have a clear title and be well organized, clearly written, and appropriate for the intended readers. As you plan a manual, carefully consider your readers' needs and skill levels, just as you would in writing instructions.

Most manuals are divided into sections or chapters, one for each main procedure or process. A manual may have a **glossary**, a list of unfamiliar terms, abbreviations, or acronyms. The glossary might be placed at the end of the introduction or the end of the manual. Be sure to include the glossary in the table of contents.

A manual might also include an *appendix*, a collection of supplemental material at the end of the manual. An appendix might consist of examples of forms, floor plans or district maps, lists of company

SCANS
Employability

**Interpersonal:
Working on Teams**
Manuals often are written by teams, with each member writing a different section.

branches or suppliers, or brochures explaining company products. Each category of items in an appendix should be listed separately in the table of contents. For example:

Making Information Accessible in Manuals

Most readers use manuals as a reference when they complete a procedure for the first time or when they encounter problems with a procedure they know how to perform. For these reasons, information in a manual must be easy to locate.

Detailed Table of Contents

The table of contents should include all the headings and subheadings in the manual, along with their page numbers, to make it easy for readers to locate specific topics. The table of contents should also list by title any figures, tables, or diagrams in the manual. If the manual contains many figures or diagrams, they can be placed in a separate list.

Introduction

The introduction to a manual is more elaborate than one for a simple set of instructions, but it should include the same kinds of information. It should explain how the manual is organized, how it can be used and by whom, and what processes or procedures it covers. Each section of a manual might also have its own short introduction.

Objective

4

KEY POINT

A detailed index at the end of a manual, listing the topics and subtopics it covers, also can help readers locate specific information.

DIVERSITY

Interfacing Interculturally

Choosing clear, specific terms for instructions and other business writing is vital when our readers speak—or maybe just read—English as a second language.

We may use synonyms instead of repeating the term over and over. However, synonyms tend to pose problems for international readers. We must use terms consistently. A report, for instance, should always be called a *report*, not a *finding* in paragraph two and a *paper* in paragraph four.

Most readers in the United States will realize that *push*, *click on*, *choose*, and *press* mean basically the same thing in instructions for loading software. However, international readers may assume that the different words have different meanings. To avoid this problem, use one term consistently and define it in a glossary.

Another key in writing for international read-ers is to use specific words. A vague term such as *run* has many different meanings. When readers look it up in a dictionary, they may be stumped as to which definition applies. Instead of *run*, use more specific terms, such as *operate*, *thread*, or *direct*.

Spell out acronyms (words formed from abbreviations) the first time you use them. Also, avoid Latin abbreviations, such as *etc.* and *e.g.* ■

Tabs or Dividers

A tab on the first page of each section can make the sections easy to locate. Colored pages that serve as dividers also help readers find the section they want.

Graphics and Diagrams

Often a picture *is* worth a thousand words. Use graphics wherever they would be helpful. For example, a drawing could show how machine parts should be attached. A flowchart could trace the path of an order through a system. An organizational chart might show how the company staff is organized. Tables might provide codes, contact numbers, temperatures and pressures, or other information that readers will need.

Modifications for Different Experience Levels

A manual might include special instructions for readers with less experience. Basic, step-by-step instructions for certain procedures might be placed in the appendix. A note in the instructions would say "For more information on completing this process, see Appendix C."

KEY POINT

Tables or other information that readers might need at some point, such as a list of branch addresses, can be placed in an appendix. At the appropriate place in the manual, tell readers where to locate this information.

2 Checkpoint

Making Information Accessible in Manuals

Indicate whether each statement is true or false:

1. A table of contents is helpful, but not essential, for a manual.
2. Experienced and new employees can use the same manual.
3. A manual is simply one very long set of instructions.

Check your answers in Appendix E.

Use the checklist below to help you write effective instructions and manuals.

Checklist for Writing Instructions and Manuals

❑ Have I thoughtfully considered what my readers need to know in order to perform this process or these processes?

❑ Have I provided a clear, informative title?

❑ Does the introduction explain who should follow these instructions, when, and why? Does it list needed materials, tools, or knowledge?

❑ Are the steps organized sequentially, numbered, and clearly written? Do they start with a verb? Are explanations indented below steps and not numbered?

❑ Have I included other appropriate components, such as warnings, definitions, graphics, or subheadings?

For a Manual

❑ Have I made it easy for readers to locate specific information and included a detailed table of contents?

❑ Have I adapted the manual for readers with different experience levels?

CASE 11:
Answers

Responses to Questions 1 and 2 in Chapter Opener

1. **What questions should Benjamin ask himself before he begins writing the customer instructions for returning books?**
   Benjamin should ask himself: What do the customers already know about returning books? What do they need to know? What terms will they understand? What kinds of mistakes do customers often make?

2. **How can Benjamin make these instructions look easy to follow?**
   He can write them in numbered steps, indent explanations under each step, use graphics and lots of white space, and include only necessary details.

DISCUSSION QUESTIONS

1. What are the main components of a set of instructions?
2. Why might writers tend to omit the introduction in a set of instructions or a manual?
3. What is the most difficult part about writing instructions?
4. Let's say someone follows your instructions, makes a mistake, and says, "But I thought you meant...." What might be the problem?

Objectives

After completing Section 11.2, you should be able to:

1 Explain how a process description differs from a set of instructions.

2 Describe the components of object and mechanism descriptions.

3 Explain how to write a description of an object or a mechanism.

4 List the components of a process description.

Objective

1

KEY POINT

A process description answers the question "How is an order placed?" A set of instructions answers the question "How do I place an order?"

Types of Description Writing

A **description** is a verbal and visual picture of something. You might be asked to write a description of an object or a mechanism, usually as part of a report or a manual. An **object** is something natural or synthetic that can be seen or touched, ranging from an apple, to a coffee cup, to a pencil. A **mechanism** is a synthetic object that consists of several moving parts working together to perform one or more tasks. A mechanism can be as simple as a pencil sharpener or as complex as a computer.

You might also be asked to write a process description. A **process description** explains how something works. A **process** is a series of events that take place over time and result in a change or a product. A process may be controlled by humans or be a natural event, such as the eruption of a volcano or the formation of acid rain. While a set of instructions explains how to perform a task, a process description explains how something happens. People read process descriptions to find out how something works, not to learn how to perform the process themselves.

A process description might be combined with an object or mechanism description. Most object, mechanism, and process descriptions are accompanied by illustrations or diagrams. Together, the verbal picture and the visual picture help readers visualize an object, a mechanism, or a process and understand how it looks and/or works. All three types of descriptions are used in product brochures, in proposals for new or redesigned products, and as part of instructions for operating or repairing objects or mechanisms.

A description can range from an informal, one-paragraph explanation to a formal report with an introduction, body, and conclusion. As always, you must consider the needs and technical backgrounds of your readers as you plan any description writing. You need to find out what the readers already know about this object, mechanism, or process. You must also determine how they will use this description. For example, will they use it to become more familiar with the parts of a computer, or to compare one type of computer with another? The answers to these questions will help you determine how much detail is enough and which terms to define.

Components of a Formal Object or Mechanism Description

Objective

Formal descriptions usually include these components: (1) a clear and limiting title, (2) an introduction and overview, (3) a part-by-part description, and (4) a conclusion.

Clear and Limiting Title

Like instructions, descriptions should begin with a clear, informative title that tells what the description does and does not cover. Notice how specific the title is for Figure 11-2. This title limits the description to one kind of floppy disk, although other kinds of disks are mentioned in the description for comparison.

Introduction and Overview

To orient readers, begin with the definition and purpose of the object or mechanism, as shown in Figure 11-2. Like the introduction to a set of instructions, this introduction should include basic information. This often includes what the object or mechanism looks like, a general idea of how it works, and its principal parts. Do not state the obvious, such as telling readers that a copier makes copies. Include a labeled illustration here or in the part-by-part description.

KEY POINT

You might include a cutaway or cross-sectional diagram to show internal parts.

Part-by-Part Description

For an object, describe each part separately, as shown in Figure 11-2. Explain each part's appearance and function, describing any **subparts** (parts of parts) as necessary. List the parts in a logical sequence. For example, you might start with the most important or most obvious part. Or you could begin at the top and progress to the bottom, or move from the outside to the inside. Label the parts on one large illustration, or include an illustration of each part.

For a mechanism, you might describe how it looks when it is not functioning, what each part looks like and how they work together, and/or how its parts fit together.

Conclusion

Longer descriptions require a brief conclusion to summarize the main parts and how they work together. A conclusion for a mechanism description might describe one operating cycle.

KEY POINT

Similar to a conclusion for a set of instructions, the conclusion of a short description may be a brief paragraph without a separate heading.

Part-by-part description

Metal Slider
This slider, 1 7/8 inch x 1 1/4 inch, has an opening that is 1/2 inch x 1 inch. A hidden spring pulls the slider into position to protect the Mylar disk.

Label
Adhesive labels can be attached to the disks so users can record the contents.

Conclusion

Conclusion
Microfloppy disks, small and sturdy, store retrievable data magnetically and can be used over and over.

Clear and limiting title

The Double-Sided, High-Density Microfloppy Disk

A microfloppy disk is a thin 3.5-inch disk of Mylar, coated with rustlike material called ferric oxide and encased in a square, rigid, plastic shell. The disk is used to store computer data. As the computer transfers data to the disk, it magnetizes the rustlike material on the disk's surface, creating a pattern that represents the data being stored.

A rectangular cutout near one edge of the plastic shell exposes part of the disk to the read-write head of the computer. The cutout is protected by a metal slider. Before the computer can transfer data to the disk, it must move the slider and expose the part of the disk under the cutout.

Introduction and overview

Other floppy disks include the 8-inch large floppy and the 5.25-inch minifloppy. A microfloppy disk, recording data in high density (HD) on both sides (double-sided), can store 1440K (1.44MB) of information.

The microfloppy disk has four main components:

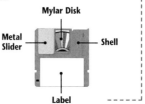

- a protective plastic shell
- a Mylar disk
- a metal slider
- a label

Components of the Microfloppy Disk

Protective Plastic Shell
This rigid shell, slightly more than 3.5 inches square, comes in black and a range of other colors. The opening covered by the metal slider is 3/8 inch x 1 inch. A 1-inch round opening in the back of the shell exposes a metal disk that allows the Mylar disk inside to spin as the computer's read-write head transfers information to it. On the side of the shell opposite the metal slider is a small tab that can be moved to prevent the read-write head from writing over data already on the disk.

Mylar Disk
This thin, flimsy disk is coated with ferric oxide, rustlike iron particles. Each iron particle has a north and a south pole, like a tiny magnet. The computer's read-write head uses a pattern of magnetic pulses to change the orientation of the iron particles to the north or south, forming a pattern that represents the data being stored.

Part-by-part description

FIGURE 11-2 Components of a formal object description

Guidelines for Writing Object and Mechanism Descriptions

These guidelines will help you clearly describe an object or a mechanism.

- *Describe the object or part by its shape, dimensions, size, color, texture, position, and/or material.* To describe an object's shape, you might use words such as *cylindrical, corkscrew, star-shaped, L-shaped, threadlike,* or *concave.* In describing its size, you would include the height, width, thickness, length, depth, area, and weight. Measure accurately. Your readers might use this data to determine if certain parts will fit together.

- *For most of your descriptions, be objective.* A description for a promotional brochure might require subjective terms such as *efficient, practical, attractive, good, poor, awkward, difficult,* or *impressive.* However, in most technical writing, writers avoid subjective terms that reflect opinions, not facts.

- *Be specific and precise, avoiding vague or general terms.* At the same time, use language your readers will understand.

  Instead of: beside the strut

  Write: adjacent to the right side of the strut

  Instead of: cardiac infarction

  Write: failure of the heart muscle

- *Compare the unfamiliar to the familiar.* For example, you might compare recording information on a computer disk with recording music on an audiotape.

Objective

KEY POINT

In writing a description, include what a camera would record. You are writing a verbal picture of the object.

DIVERSITY

Include the metric equivalents of measurements if your readers use this system.

Checkpoint 3

Writing an Object or Mechanism Description

Select the more descriptive word or phrase in each sentence.
1. The pad has a (rough/pebbly) surface.
2. The bolt is (to the left of/beside) the first hinge.
3. The joint between the two pipes is (poor/loose).

Check your answers in Appendix E.

Writing a Process Description

A process description tells how something works and includes the same components as an object or mechanism description. Remember that a process description does not explain how to perform a process; that is the function of instructions. A process description might be a separate document or part of a larger document, such as a repair manual or a sales brochure.

Your first step is determining your readers' needs and levels of experience and knowledge. Find out how your description will be used so you know what details to include and how to present them.

A process description that is meant to provide a general understanding, such as the one in Figure 11-3, will not include technical details. Figure 11-3 is written for beginning computer users so it avoids technical terms and detailed descriptions.

TECHNOLOGY

A Picture or a Thousand Words?

A picture—a drawing, graphic, or illustration of some kind—is truly worth a thousand words, especially when you are writing an object, mechanism, or process description. You can add graphics to your description writing in a number of ways.

For example, many word processing programs include files of pictures, often called "clip art," that you can insert into a document. You can adjust the size of the entire graphic or parts of it, along with its position on the page. Then you can add labels or short explanations in callout boxes. You can also drag arrows from the callout box to the part of the object or mechanism you are describing. Specialized clip art programs are also available with images that you can modify to fit your purposes.

Many word processing programs include drawing tools that you can use to create your own graphics. For example, you might start with a basic shape, such as a three-dimensional cube, and adjust it or add to it to represent a certain mechanism or part of a mechanism. A "paint" program allows you to draw images freehand and then paste them into your document.

If your artistic skills are limited, a device called a scanner can electronically convert a photograph, chart, or other graphic from a reference source into a file in your computer. You can store this graphic and use it as needed. Make sure that the graphic you scan is not copyrighted, that is, protected by law from copying. You must have the permission of the author or artist to use a copyrighted image, and you must cite the source of the image in your document.

So write a thousand words for your object, mechanism, or process description—or use your computer to add a picture! ■

Clear and limiting title

How Data Is Transferred between a Computer and a Floppy Disk

A computer records information on a floppy disk in much the same way that a tape recorder records sound on tape. The computer has a read-write head with a needle that can write new information on the floppy disk and later read information from the disk.

Introduction

The Process

When you slip a floppy disk into its slot in the CPU, or central processing unit, the disk rests on a turntable, or spindle, inside the CPU. When you decide to save your work and key SAVE, the computer's read-write head lowers its needle to touch the disk. An electrical charge passes through the needle, magnetizing the iron particles on the surface of the disk. Each particle has a north pole and a south pole, like a tiny magnet. The magnetic charge positions the particles into a specific, invisible pattern on the disk. This pattern represents the data you are saving.

Step-by-step description

The read-write head remains stationary as the spindle spins the disk. On a new disk, the head starts "writing" at a position close to the outer rim of the disk. This is called track 0. When that track is filled with data, the head lifts and moves to the next track, track 1, which is slightly closer to the center of the disk. The head continues in this way until the disk is filled with data. On a used disk, the head will search for available tracks and record on them.

Most computers now have two read-write heads. One writes on track 0 of the disk's top surface; then the other writes on track 0 of the bottom surface. They continue alternating until both sides of the disk are filled. A double-sided drive requires a double-sided disk, marked DS.

When you open a file that you have saved on a floppy disk, the read-write head moves to the correct track and waits for the disk to spin into the correct position. Then it lowers its needle and "reads" the magnetic pattern on that track, transferring it back into the letters and numbers that appear on your computer screen.

A floppy disk provides a place to store a copy of the files on the computer's hard drive so the files will not be lost if the hard drive "crashes." However, floppy disks must be kept away from stereos, televisions, and telephones because their speakers contain magnets that can scramble the magnetic pattern on the disk.

Conclusion

FIGURE 11-3 Components of a process description

Objective

4

TECHNOLOGY

Much writing in computer science involves process descriptions, such as how data is transferred and translated from one form or system to another.

KEY POINT

If you are describing a natural process, such as the formation of acid rain, modify your introduction accordingly.

SCANS
Employability

**Thinking Skills:
Knowing How to Learn**
Learning a new job often involves reading many process descriptions. Employees must often know how a procedure is completed, even though they will not perform it themselves.

Components of a Process Description

Most process descriptions include these components: (1) a clear and limiting title, (2) an introduction, (3) a step-by-step description, and (4) a conclusion.

Clear and Limiting Title

Contrast the specific title in Figure 11-3 with a more general title, such as "Transferring Data" or "How a Floppy Disk Works." The title should also suggest the technical level of the process description.

Introduction

An introduction should define the process and provide the "big picture" so readers understand the general idea. The introduction also might explain why or how the process is used, who or what performs it, and where or when it takes place, unless that information is obvious. If the process can be divided into steps, they might be listed in the introduction. The brief introduction in Figure 11-3 serves as an overview of the process. A longer, more technical process description would require a longer, more detailed introduction.

Step-by-Step Description

Describe the process sequentially, much as you would describe the steps in a set of instructions. If the process occurs in a continuous cycle, begin with a major step. In a process description, the steps usually are not numbered as they are in a set of instructions. However, if the process is lengthy, each step might have its own subheading. Make sure you explain the relationships between the steps: how one step leads to or causes another.

Include any graphics or illustrations that would be helpful. For example, you might illustrate an internal combustion engine at each stage in its operation, with the changes clearly labeled.

Use present tense to describe a process that is ongoing or repeated.

Instead of: Light *entered* the eye through the iris.

Write: Light *enters* the eye through the iris.

Use past tense to describe a process that was completed in the past.

Instead of: The pH level of the samples *is* determined.

Write: The pH level of the samples *was* determined.

Conclusion

As with object and mechanism descriptions, a longer process description may require a paragraph summarizing the process and perhaps discussing its uses or advantages. The conclusion in a short process description might simply be the final paragraph.

Writing a Process Description

Indicate whether each statement is true or false.

1. People read a process description to learn how to perform a task.
2. A process description can be written in present tense or past tense.
3. In describing a process, begin each step with a verb.
4. A process description should be as technical as your knowledge allows.

Check your answers in Appendix E.

Use the following checklist to help you write effective object, mechanism, and process descriptions.

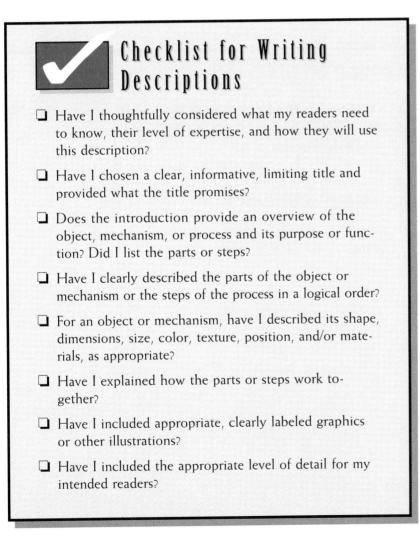

Checklist for Writing Descriptions

❑ Have I thoughtfully considered what my readers need to know, their level of expertise, and how they will use this description?

❑ Have I chosen a clear, informative, limiting title and provided what the title promises?

❑ Does the introduction provide an overview of the object, mechanism, or process and its purpose or function? Did I list the parts or steps?

❑ Have I clearly described the parts of the object or mechanism or the steps of the process in a logical order?

❑ For an object or mechanism, have I described its shape, dimensions, size, color, texture, position, and/or materials, as appropriate?

❑ Have I explained how the parts or steps work together?

❑ Have I included appropriate, clearly labeled graphics or other illustrations?

❑ Have I included the appropriate level of detail for my intended readers?

CASE 11:

Answers

Responses to Questions 3 and 4 in Chapter Opener

3. **Should Benjamin give his new instructions to the other staff instead of writing a process description for them? Why or why not?**

    No. He should write a separate process description because the other staff are not going to follow the instructions to return books. They just need to understand the process.

4. **Will Benjamin's process description have more or less detail than his instructions? Why?**

    The process description will have less detail because it provides a general idea of the procedure, not step-by-step instructions.

- -

DISCUSSION QUESTIONS

1. What are the components of an object, a mechanism, and a process description?
2. How is Figure 11-2, an object description, similar to and different from Figure 11-3, a process description?
3. What kinds of object and mechanism descriptions do you read every day?
4. Explain which of these words would be appropriate in description writing: *nearby, parallel to, rectangular, several.*

11·3 Writing to Persuade

The Purpose of Persuasive Writing

In a work setting, people often try to persuade others to do things. A team leader tries to persuade team members to work overtime on a special project. One employee tries to persuade other employees to use a new form. A salesperson tries to persuade customers to place orders. The collection department tries to persuade customers to pay their bills. Much of this persuasion occurs in memos, letters, and proposals—that is, in writing.

Objectives

After completing Section 11.3, you should be able to:

1 Plan a persuasive letter.

2 Organize a persuasive letter.

3 Organize a sales letter and a collection letter.

4 Plan and organize a proposal.

Persuasive writing often is used in work settings when presenting new procedures or other changes that require acceptance by employees. In such situations, remember to explain why the changes are taking place and how they will benefit employees.

To persuade people to do something, you must be able to identify a reason for them to do it. People will act to meet their own needs, so you must show your readers they have a need to do what you want them to do. This must be *their* need, though, not *yours*. For example, if you ask other employees to fill out a new form because it will make your job easier, they are unlikely to be persuaded. Few new forms will be filled out. However, if you show them how using the new form will make their own jobs easier, they will be much more willing to do as you ask. Needs vary among people, but they are often linked to achievement, recognition, comfort, convenience, physical well-being, or money.

Planning a Persuasive Letter

Objective

To plan a persuasive letter or memo, complete these steps:

Identify the Objective	To get the reader to do something
Identify the Main Idea	To show that the requested action will meet the reader's own needs
Determine the Supporting Information	Choose information that will convince the reader to do as you request.
Adjust the Content to the Reader	Consider the reader's values and concerns and adjust the supporting information accordingly. For example, is a supervisor more interested in simplifying procedures, providing quality customer service, or maintaining department morale? Is a coworker more concerned about avoiding errors or earning a commission?

↓KEY POINT

You will not actually start a persuasive letter by stating your objective. If you make your request right away, before explaining the situation, the reader is likely to say no.

Objective

Organizing a Persuasive Letter

Like letters with a negative message, persuasive letters are organized in an indirect order. This means that you must describe the need convincingly before making your request. In this way, you prepare the reader for the main message before presenting it. After readers understand the need, they will be much more likely to agree to the solution—doing as you request.

To organize a persuasive message (letter or memo), follow these steps:

1. Gain the reader's attention.
2. Show the reader that he or she has a need.

DIVERSITY

People in many other cultures, such as Hispanic and Asian writers, naturally use the indirect order for persuasive letters. They tend to be more receiver-oriented than North American writers.

3. Explain your solution to that need—in other words, your request.
4. Present the supporting information.
5. End by asking for a specific action.

Figure 11-4 shows what can happen if these steps are ignored. Figure 11-5 shows how much more persuasive a message can be if the writer follows these steps.

Gain the Reader's Attention

Introduce the topic of your letter or memo in an interesting and relevant way. Remember that the goal is to capture your reader's interest, not make the request. Here are some possible approaches:

- Describe a problem related to your request that the reader has experienced or mentioned recently. For example, perhaps your supervisor has noted that your department is behind in processing orders.

- Remind the reader of a goal related to your request. You might point out, for instance, that your department has set a goal of each representative calling 80 potential customers a day.

- Present a "what if" situation related to your request. For example: "What if there was a no-cost way to cut the number of customer complaints in half?"

- Tell your coworkers that you know of an opportunity that they will not want to miss.

Although you want the reader's attention, do not use overly enthusiastic advertising-type tactics to begin a business request. Instead, be positive, sincere, honest, and receiver-oriented.

Checkpoint 5

Beginning a Persuasive Message

Rate each opening below as good or poor.
1. I am looking for someone to address the Association of Small Businesses next month. I know you are busy, but would you be our speaker?
2. Thank you for your letter of May 19. I sincerely appreciate it.
3. I believe the overtime policy should be changed.
4. I share your concern about the recent drop in sales.

Check your answers in Appendix E.

Show the Reader That He or She Has a Need

Explain the need—from the reader's point of view. For example, if you are writing a memo to your supervisor, you might point out an increase in customer complaints, a backlog in the service department, the errors that result from the current method of entering orders, or the high cost of repairing the copier during the past three months. Because the supervisor is responsible for the efficient operation of your department, he or she has an interest in solving these problems.

KEY POINT

As you describe the need, include as many numbers as possible. For example, how much have complaints or errors increased? How big is the backlog? How much have copier repairs cost during the past three months?

Ineffective

TO: Sylvia Smith, Human Resources Director
FROM: Kevin Timpkin, Customer Service Supervisor
DATE: November 13, 20—
SUBJECT: Additional staff

In spite of the company's hiring freeze, my department needs additional staff immediately. Not only are we ten days behind with our correspondence, but we're getting further and further behind every day. Although I have tried everything I know to alleviate the situation, I am convinced there is no hope of solving this problem with our present staff. In view of these circumstances, please consider hiring more staff for this department.

FIGURE 11-4 A poorly written persuasive memo

TO: Sylvia Smith, Human Resources Director
FROM: Kevin Timpkin, Customer Service Supervisor
DATE: November 13, 20—
SUBJECT: Suggestions for bringing correspondence up to date

At our last staff meeting, you mentioned that Customer Service is getting behind in answering inquiries and complaints. I share your concern because we are now ten days behind. Our department goal, as you know, is to answer customer correspondence within four days, and we were meeting that goal until recently.

Gain the reader's attention

During the past three months, customer inquiries have increased 115 percent, mostly because of the company's new Doors 2000 software. Unfortunately, complaints have also increased 75 percent, mostly from customers who have purchased this new software. In the same period, our department lost a worker, leaving us with only four full-time employees and me. Although I have been working 60-hour weeks and have encouraged my staff to work as much overtime as possible, we are getting further behind.

Show the reader that he or she has a need

If we hired another full-time staff member, I estimate that at the end of the following month, we would be only six days behind. By the end of the next month, we would be able meet our department goal of answering correspondence within four days. If we also hired a temporary worker for at least one month, we could catch up sooner than that.

Explain your solution to that need

I realize the company has a freeze on hiring, but I believe we could hire both a full-time staff member and a temporary worker for the same salary that our former staff member earned. The money spent on a temporary worker would be well worth the goodwill we would create by answering our customers' inquiries and complaints within four days. As you know, when we answer complaints and inquiries promptly, we encourage our customers to order from us again instead of turning to our competitors.

Present the supporting information

Can we meet on November 18 to discuss this request? The sooner we hire more staff, the sooner we can increase the quality of service we are providing to our customers.

End by asking for a specific action

FIGURE 11-5 A well-written persuasive memo

Explain Your Solution (Your Request)

Now that your reader understands the need, explain how he or she can meet that need—by doing as you request. For example, you might suggest a small product change to reduce customer complaints. Or you could recommend a simpler procedure to allow staff to catch up with a backlog.

Do your homework before writing this part of your persuasive message. The more details you include, the easier it is for readers to visualize your solution, and the more likely they are to agree to it.

For example, you would describe the product change in as much detail as makes sense for your readers. You would outline the new procedure step-by-step. If you are requesting a purchase, such as a new copier, suggest specific models and provide approximate rental or purchase costs. You might even attach brochures for the two copier models that best meet your department's needs. Make it easy for the reader to grant your request.

Present the Supporting Information

To encourage readers to agree to your request, you must do two things: address any obvious obstacles, and emphasize your **primary appeal**—the benefit that will appeal most to this reader.

1. *Address obstacles.* The most common obstacles or objections involve a resistance to change and a lack of time, energy, and/or money. Let's say you are asking other staff to fill out new forms. You must overcome their resistance to change and their concern about the time required to complete the forms. You might point out that the new forms will greatly reduce the current errors that end up consuming so much of their time and result in many customer complaints. Or you might be asking your supervisor for a new copier. Point out how this purchase will eliminate the high repair costs for the old copier and save time now wasted by going to a copy shop to make copies.

2. *Emphasize the primary appeal.* It's very important to identify the benefits that match the values and concerns of your readers. Think of benefits to the readers personally, not just to the company. Suppose your request is to make a small product change. The benefits might include increased sales and commissions and fewer customer complaints to handle. What if you are asking for a new copier? The benefits, in addition to saving money on repairs, might include having equipment that works reliably and improving staff morale.

From all the possible benefits, determine the primary appeal (the main selling point in a sales letter). This is the appeal that is most likely to attract readers' attention and motivate them to act. Let's say you are trying to convince a coworker to serve on a committee. The primary appeal for one person might be the opportunity to influence office policies in general. The primary appeal for another coworker might

> KEY POINT

- Be careful not to point out obstacles that may not have occurred to your readers. Address only the most obvious ones.
- State the primary appeal —and other benefits— from the reader's point of view, not your own. Help your reader recognize that your request meets his or her own needs.

be the opportunity to work toward a certain goal, such as instituting flexible working hours.

Do not assume that readers will automatically recognize the benefits of doing as you request. Point these benefits out and help your readers visualize them in their own lives. Depending on the values and needs of your readers, you might provide research findings that support your request. Or you could mention other departments or other companies that have made this change and benefited from it.

KEY POINT

When your persuasive letter has multiple readers, determining the primary appeal is much more complex. You may have to mention several primary appeals to get all readers on board.

Checkpoint 6

Describing Benefits

Rate each benefit as good or poor.

1. If you allow me to work on a flexible schedule, I will be able to be home when my children get out of school.

2. Please get the statistics to me by April 14 so I can meet my deadline.

3. Telling customers that we have changed medical suppliers will reduce the number of calls we get from people who think we sent the wrong pills.

4. Buying a new copier for the department will really take a lot of stress out of my job.

Check your answers in Appendix E.

End by Asking for a Specific Action

Writers sometimes end their persuasive letters and memos with vaguely hopeful sentences such as these:

"I hope you will give my request serious consideration."

"Please let me know if you have any questions about my request."

These writers are not asking for a specific response. They are likely to get no response at all. The closing of a persuasive message should clearly indicate the action the reader should take to approve or grant the request. The action suggested should be easy to do, such as initialing the memo and returning it to you.

If your request is major or expensive, you might end by asking for an appointment to talk about it. Or you might ask for your request to be discussed at the department's weekly meeting. Or you could tell the reader you will call in two days to discuss your request.

If possible, encourage the reader to act promptly by including a deadline of some kind. Explain how approving your request quickly

KEY POINT

If a request has no deadline, many readers will put it aside until it's convenient for them to respond. That convenient time may never come.

will save time and/or money. For example, you might mention that the copier you recommend is on sale. Purchasing it by the end of the month will reduce the cost by 10 percent. Or point out that as soon as the new forms are created and distributed, the number of errors will begin to drop.

Writing Different Kinds of Persuasive Messages

Persuasive requests are common in the business environment. They might be sent from supervisor to employee, from employee to supervisor, from employee to employee, and from employee to customer or supplier. Sales letters and collection letters are two special kinds of persuasive messages.

KEY POINT

A sales letter is one business communication in which you *should* use modifiers—adverbs and adjectives.

Sales Letters

A **sales letter** tries to persuade a potential customer to purchase a product or service. Like other persuasive messages, it involves gaining the reader's attention, establishing a need, showing how a product or service will meet that need, presenting supporting information, and providing for an easy way for the reader to respond. A sales letter might appeal to readers' senses by describing how something looks, sounds, feels, smells, or tastes. This appeal can range from the warm, cinnamon smell of apple pie to the silky feel of a new blouse.

Figure 11-6 shows how the steps of writing a persuasive message apply to a sales letter.

Collection Letters

The purpose of a **collection letter** is to persuade a customer to pay a past-due bill. Collection letters have four stages: (1) the reminder stage, (2) the strong reminder stage, (3) the discussion stage, and (4) the urgency stage.

The *reminder* letter assumes the customer has simply forgotten to make a payment. It is written in the direct order, as shown here:

Dear Customer,

We greatly appreciate your prompt payments for all of the year 2000. A copy of your January 2001 statement is enclosed. Did you overlook this payment, which was due by February 10?

An addressed, postage-paid envelope is enclosed for your convenience in sending this payment. Thank you for your attention to this matter!

Comfy Feet, Inc.

October 1, 20—

Gain attention and establish a need

Dear Friend,

On your feet for eight hours or more but not foot-weary? Isn't this how you'd like to feel at the end of your workday?

Through extensive research and testing, we have developed a new kind of shoe with you in mind. These comfortable, attractive shoes have shock-absorbing features that cushion and protect your feet all day. More than 80 percent of the doctors and nurses who tried our shoes wanted to keep them! Many wanted to order a pair for a friend or family member, too.

Explain your solution to that need

As an introductory offer, these Quality Label leather shoes are available for only $29.95 a pair. As you can see from the enclosed photographs, they come in styles and colors to please every need and taste.

Present the supporting information

To place your order, just call toll free at 1-800-555-0153. Or fill in the enclosed, addressed, postage-paid form. You will be slipping into your new shoes within a week and enjoying new freedom from tired feet!

End by asking for specific action

Melissa Konrad

Melissa Konrad
Sales Manager

Enclosure

FIGURE 11-6 A well-written sales letter

KEY POINT

In large companies, collection letters for the first two stages are often form letters. The collection department staff write personal letters for the last two stages.

A *strong reminder* is sent when the customer has, for whatever reason, not responded to the first reminder. This collection letter is direct and firm:

Dear Customer,

A copy of your January statement is enclosed. As you can see, your February 10 payment is overdue. By sending us a check for $350, you will bring your account up to date and preserve your credit rating.

A postage-paid return envelope is enclosed. Please send your payment today and clear your account.

The purpose of the *discussion stage* collection letter is to obtain full payment, partial payment as a temporary measure, or an explanation of why the customer has not made the appropriate payment. This letter is organized in an indirect way as a last try at persuading the customer to respond:

Dear Customer,

Your home loan with First Western Bank has been beneficial to both of us. In the past, your payments have been prompt and consistent. In fact, you have been one of our best customers.

Two months have passed, however, since your last payment. Although we have sent you two reminders, we have not received a reply. Is there some reason why you cannot make a payment?

You can preserve your credit rating in one of these ways:

1. Make your past-due payments totaling $700 within ten days.
2. Send one payment of $350 immediately and send the other payment by March 30.
3. Call within one week to let us know why you have missed your last two payments, and to explain your plans for correcting the situation.

We look forward to hearing from you.

KEY POINT

Notice how this discussion-stage letter explains the situation before making the request again. It also mentions a primary appeal: the customer's (last) opportunity to preserve his or her credit rating.

The purpose of the *urgency stage* collection letter is to obtain payment and advise the customer of the consequences if payment is not made immediately. The organization is direct, and the tone is firm.

Dear Customer,

It appears that we have been unable to persuade you to make past-due payments or to tell us why you are unable to make the payments.

The enclosed statement shows the amount now due, $1,050. Unless we receive full payment by April 30, your account will be turned over to the Edwards Credit Agency, a collection company.

To prevent this negative situation, send us your full payment immediately.

Checkpoint 7

Writing Collection Letters

Identify the correct stage for each of these sentences from collection letters.

1. Your account will be sent to Cross Collections.
2. Have you sent us your June payment?
3. Please bring your account up to date.
4. We have valued you as a customer in the past.

Check your answers in Appendix E.

Writing Proposals

Proposals are another type of persuasive writing. A **proposal** is a formal report that describes a problem and recommends a solution. The writer establishes a need and tries to convince the reader to meet that need by taking a specific action. Proposals may be internal, such as from an employee to a supervisor, or external, such as from a consulting firm to a company.

Objective

4

KEY POINT

When you write a proposal, you *propose* or suggest a practical way to meet the reader's need.

Sometimes a company asks for proposals to meet an identified need. These proposals are **solicited**. The company sends out **requests for proposals (RFP)** that outline what it needs. For example, a company might ask suppliers to provide proposals explaining the price, delivery time, quality, and other information for certain materials or services. The company uses these proposals to decide where to make its purchases.

Other proposals are **unsolicited**. The receiver has not requested this type of proposal. The writer of an unsolicited proposal must work harder to establish a need for the proposed action. One example of an unsolicited proposal is a researcher requesting money from a foundation to investigate a specific problem.

Persuade or Prey?

A writer often tries to convince a reader that a certain action will fulfill one of the reader's important needs. The writer can have the reader's best interests in mind—or the writer can be manipulative, preying on the reader's fears. For example, the underlying message in a "persuasive" memo from a supervisor might be "Do this if you want to stay in my good graces—and keep your job."

However, threats rarely work as a method of persuasion. First, they do not result in permanent change. If employees are bullied into following a new procedure, they will do it only when the supervisor is watching. If, though, the memo explains why the new procedure is necessary or helpful or how it truly meets a need, employees are likely to follow it even when no one is watching.

Most people react poorly to threats and manipulation, whether written or oral, and they may put their efforts into undermining a project rather than completing it. They may work more slowly, complaining all the while to coworkers. Or they might overreact. For example, if the supervisor's "persuasive" memo demands a reduction in wasted paper, employees may stop making and distributing copies that are necessary for good communication among team members.

Some persuasive messages, particularly in direct-mail advertising, prey on readers by exaggerating the problem or the benefits of the proposed action or product. "Buy this home insurance," an ad warns, "or you will lose everything you have worked for all your life in the next big storm." Other persuasive messages prey on readers' insecurities. "Buy these pills," another ad urges, "and lose those unsightly pounds."

An ethical persuasive message respects readers. It shows them how an action or product will benefit them but does not try to persuade them with threats, exaggerations, or false promises. ■

Planning a Proposal

Like other persuasive writing, an effective proposal depends on carefully identifying the most compelling benefits for the intended receiver. What is most likely to motivate this receiver to accept this proposal? If the proposal is solicited, the receiver already recognizes the need. However, you must present your solution to that need in a way that emphasizes the benefits you can provide. These benefits might include a lower cost than your competitors, a higher-quality product, or your staff's in-depth knowledge of the receiver's needs and procedures.

If the proposal is unsolicited, you must clearly establish the need and explain the proposed action, again stressing the benefits to the receiver.

Organizing a Proposal

The content and organization of your proposal will vary, depending on what you are proposing. Most, but not all, proposals contain the following elements, which you can also see in Figure 11-7.

1. **Introduction.** Briefly summarize what you are proposing, what it will accomplish, and what types of information are included in your proposal. Immediately begin to stress the benefits to the receiver.
2. **Background.** In this optional section, you might describe the events that led to the current situation, such as changes in the company structure or a product line.
3. **Need.** Describe the problem that your proposal will solve or the need it will meet, from the receiver's point of view.
4. **Scope of Project.** Outline your plan or solution to meet the need.
5. **Action Plan.** List the steps that must be taken to carry out your proposal.
6. **Schedule.** Discuss the amount of time needed to complete the project and the deadline for each step in the action plan.
7. **Cost.** Explain the proposal's total cost and link the cost to the benefits the reader will receive.
8. **Qualifications.** Describe your own qualifications (if you will carry out the proposal personally) or those of your company.
9. **Call for Action.** Just as in a persuasive letter, end with a specific request for the receiver to do something, such as scheduling a meeting to discuss your proposal.
10. **Supporting Information.** Include any necessary supporting information, such as the names of references, in an appendix.

DIVERSITY

When you submit a proposal to a company in another country, include details about your company's history, its financial strength, and the technical strength of its personnel.

Formatting a Proposal

An RFP usually lists the information that must be included in a solicited proposal. Follow the RFP closely so your proposal will not be eliminated because of the way you presented the information. If your proposal is unsolicited, use subheadings to make the document inviting to read and easy to skim, as in Figure 11-7.

Teletalk   1000 Broadmoor Way Omaha, NE 68113-1844 Telephone: (402) 555-1000 Fax: (402) 555-1068

July 12, 20—

Ms. Gloria Quintero
Director of Consumer Affairs
The Foodworks Market
10 Dunstable Highway
Omaha, NE 68111-6409

Dear Ms. Quintero:

As you requested, here is our proposal for conducting a telephone survey to ---------
determine consumer interest in the posting of nutritional information in your
store's produce department. The objective of the project is to provide the research
you need to decide whether to post this information. This proposal describes
the need for and the scope of the project and outlines the action plan we would
carry out to obtain the customer feedback that will help in your decision.

Background
Consumers are more concerned than ever about their health. Many want to use
more fresh fruits and vegetables in the meals they prepare at home. However,
because produce is not packaged in containers, consumers cannot check the
labels for nutritional value. Thus, they have no source of nutritional information
at the point of sale.

Need
Your supermarket has positioned itself as the market leader in customer service.
To maintain this position, you want to investigate whether posting detailed nutri-
tional information in the produce department would be valuable to consumers.

Scope of Project
To learn what adult consumers think about the posting of nutritional information, we propose to plan and conduct a comprehensive survey. It would include
- identifying potential interviewees
- preparing a script for the telephone survey

Introduction

FIGURE 11-7 Solicited proposal in letter form

Ms. Gloria Quintero
July 12, 20—
Page 2

- compiling and analyzing survey results
- preparing a final report for Foodworks' management

To get a balanced sampling, we recommend surveying at least 300 adults. We will need the names and telephone numbers of up to 900 adults so that we can be assured of completing 300 interviews.

Action Plan
After you approve the project, Teletalk will require about three working days to prepare, test, and revise a script for the telephone survey. After testing the survey on 25 telephone contacts and making any necessary changes, we will proceed to complete 300 telephone interviews during five weekday evenings. One week after completing the survey, we will provide a statistical analysis of the results and a written summary of our findings and recommendations.

Schedule
We can begin this project within a week of receiving your approval. You will receive our analysis and summary about three weeks after we begin.

Cost
Our price for planning, completing, and analyzing this survey is $5,000. Additional costs for telephone charges, postage, and other expenses will be billed at the end of the project.

Teletalk has been privileged to conduct more than one dozen surveys for Foodworks over the past three years. As always, we welcome the opportunity to help you in your goal of identifying and meeting the needs of your consumers. Thank you for asking Teletalk to submit this bid.

Qualifications

Sincerely,

Brad Altman

Brad Altman
Vice President

FIGURE 11-7 Concluded

SCANS
Employability

Interpersonal:
Exercises Leadership
Being able to write effective persuasive messages is one way to influence others and provide leadership.

8 *Checkpoint*

Writing Persuasively

Indicate whether each statement is true or false.

1. A primary appeal is the same as a request for specific action.
2. If you ask for a response to your request, most receivers will consider you pushy or aggressive.
3. An RFP indicates that a proposal is solicited.
4. If a proposal is solicited, the receiver already recognizes the need.

Check your answers in Appendix E.

Use the following checklist to help you write convincing persuasive letters, memos, and proposals.

Checklist for Persuasive Writing

❑ Have I thoughtfully considered my receivers' needs and determined the primary appeal of this message?

❑ Does the opening gain the receiver's attention and introduce the topic?

❑ Have I clearly established a need from the receiver's point of view?

❑ Is my solution to that need clear, logical, and practical?

❑ Have I identified the supporting information and adjusted it to the receiver? Did I focus on the identified primary appeal?

❑ Do I end by asking for specific action?

❑ For a proposal, have I included all the appropriate components?

CASE 11:

A n s w e r s

Responses to Questions 5 and 6 in Chapter Opener

5. **How can Benjamin persuade customers to read and follow the new instructions for returning books?**
    He can show them how the instructions will benefit them.

6. **What benefits of the new return process might appeal to customers?**
    Some benefits include better record keeping to avoid misunderstandings and billing problems; using the new labels will prevent customers from receiving damaged books.

DISCUSSION QUESTIONS

1. Philosopher and mathematician Blaise Pascal once said, "People are generally better persuaded by the reasons which they have themselves discovered than by those which have come into the mind of others." How does this apply to persuasive writing?
2. Why is most persuasive writing organized in an indirect order?
3. Do you think a solicited or an unsolicited proposal would be more difficult to write? Why?

CASE 11:

S u m m a r y

By carefully considering the customers' needs, Benjamin writes clear instructions in a step-by-step format that invites the customers to read and follow them. He decides to begin his instructions to the customers with a persuasive message. Benjamin explains how following the procedure will ensure that they receive the proper credit for returning books and avoid being billed for books that were not properly labeled when they arrived back at the publisher.

After learning more about process descriptions, Benjamin decides to write one for the other staff at his company. He realizes that the staff needs to understand the general procedure for returning books. Since they will not be returning the books themselves, a process description is more appropriate than instructions.

Chapter Summary

Section 11.1   Writing to Instruct

1 **List the components of effective instructions.** Effective instructions include a clear and limiting title, an introduction and a list of needed tools or materials, numbered steps in sequential order, and a conclusion.

2 **Describe how to write effective steps for instructions.** Each step in instructions is numbered, starts with a verb, and is listed sequentially. Any explanations are indented under the step, and any special conditions for carrying out the step are placed immediately before the step. Steps can be grouped under subheadings. Graphics are added whenever they would be helpful; cautions and warnings are highlighted.

3 **Explain how a manual is similar to and different from instructions.** Manuals and instructions both explain how to perform tasks, but manuals are longer and more complex, usually covering several related processes. Manuals often include several sets of instructions.

4 **Describe how to make information in a manual easy to locate.** An effective manual includes a detailed table of contents, an introduction, and tabs or dividers. It also includes graphics and may have modifications for different experience levels.

Section 11.2   Writing to Describe

1 **Explain how a process description differs from a set of instructions.** A set of instructions explains how to perform a task, while a process description explains how something works.

2 **Describe the components of object and mechanism descriptions.** Object and mechanism descriptions are verbal and visual pictures. They include a clear and limiting title, an introduction and overview, a part-by-part description, and a conclusion.

3 **Explain how to write a description of an object or a mechanism.** In describing an object or part of a mechanism, you might include its shape, dimensions, size, color, texture, position, or material. Descriptions should be objective, specific, and precise, and measurements should be accurate. You can help readers visualize an unfamiliar object or mechanism by comparing it to something familiar.

4 **List the components of a process description.** A process description includes a title, an introduction, a step-by-step description, and a conclusion.

Section 11.3 Writing to Persuade

1 **Plan a persuasive letter.** To plan a persuasive letter, identify the objective and the main idea, determine the supporting information, and adjust the content to the receiver. It's very important to consider the request from the receiver's point of view. You must select supporting information that will show how granting your request will meet the receiver's own needs.

2 **Organize a persuasive letter.** Persuasive messages are organized indirectly. You must gain the reader's attention, show the reader that he or she has a need, explain your solution to that need (make your request), present the supporting information, and ask for a specific response.

3 **Organize a sales letter and a collection letter.** A sales letter is organized indirectly and focuses on the benefits of the product or service to the customer. Collection letters are written in four stages, from the reminder stage to the urgency stage.

4 **Plan and organize a proposal.** A proposal can be solicited or unsolicited. It describes a need from the receiver's point of view and explains how the writer can meet that need. A proposal may include an introduction, background, need, scope of project, action plan, schedule, cost, qualifications, call for action, and supporting information.

Critical Thinking Questions

1. An employee has written a set of instructions as a series of paragraphs. She defends her approach, saying, "All you need to know is there. Why should I bother putting it in numbered steps?" Does she have a good point? Why or why not?

2. In writing instructions and manuals, is shorter always better? Is longer always better? Explain your answer.

3. Over the next ten years, do you think you will write more sets of instructions or more process descriptions? Why is it important to know how to write both?

4. Descriptions that are part of product brochures often include subjective terms, such as *efficient* and *simple*. Should this type of writing still be considered "technical communication"? Why or why not?

5. What are some situations in which a persuasive message should be organized in the direct order? Explain your reasoning.

6. Is it fair for readers to decide whether to grant your request before they even finish reading your memo or letter? Why or why not?

Applications

TEAMWORK

Part A. Draw a map of the route from the college to your home, and then write a set of directions someone could follow from the college to your home. Put your map out of sight, and exchange directions with a partner. Use your partner's directions to draw a map from the college to his or her home. Then compare maps with your partner. Are the maps you both drew based on the other person's directions similar to the first one you each drew? If not, what changes in the written directions would have enabled you both to draw more accurate maps?

Part B. Locate a set of instructions and rewrite them as a process description.

TEAMWORK

Part C. Select a special process that you understand well but that is unfamiliar to many people, such as how a computer functions, how a television works, how diamonds are rated, or how air pollution affects the ozone layer. Write a description of the process you selected. Then exchange descriptions with a partner. After reading your partner's process, rewrite it in your own words. Then work together to decide whether you each explained your process well enough for the other person to understand and rewrite it correctly.

TEAMWORK

Part D. Write a description of an object or mechanism, using a nonsense word such as *klane* in place of the name of the object or mechanism. Be sure to include all the components of a description, as appropriate. Then trade descriptions with a partner. See if your partner can identify the object or mechanism you described. Then work together to find ways to clarify, organize, and in other ways improve both of your descriptions.

TECHNOLOGY

Part E. You work for a large company. Write an e-mail to your coworkers, persuading them to join a new sports team that is forming at the company. (You can choose the sport.) Be sure to mention benefits that will appeal to the wide range of people who work for your company.

TEAMWORK

Part F. You want your college to add a certain course or to change the scheduling of one or more courses. Work on a team with two or three other students to write a short, unsolicited proposal to the college administration, including all the relevant components. As you plan, think carefully about how your proposed change would benefit the college.

Part G. You are the credit manager for Arrow, a men's clothing store. Write a series of four collection letters to Kevin Green, a regular customer. Your first reminder will point out that a $75 payment on his account was due March 5. Three weeks later, you still have not received a payment, and now the April payment is also due. You send a second stage reminder. Six weeks later, with no response from Mr. Green, you send another collection letter—the discussion stage message. Finally, after three months have passed, you send him an urgency stage letter.

Part H. Obtain brochures and pamphlets from a travel agency or a car dealership. Study them and write a one-page sales letter to potential customers of the agency or dealership, urging them to take a certain tour or buy a certain car.

Part I. Bring in an example of poor writing, such as an unclear set of instructions, a vague process or object description, or an unconvincing persuasive memo or sales letter. Exchange poor examples with a partner and rewrite your partner's example. Then share your rewrite with your partner, pointing out the weak areas of the original and how you corrected them.

TEAMWORK

Editing Activities

1. Edit the following instructions on locating computer files to be printed. Format the instructions as they should appear.

   1. The printer should be turned on.
   2. The Search dialog box will open after you choose File ▶ Find File.
   3. You must make sure that the File Name box contains *.doc.
   4. After you click the down arrow by the Location box, select the disk drive where your files are located.
   5. The computer will search for the files as soon as you click the OK button.

2. Edit this portion of a persuasive memo from a human resources director to all company employees.

   What if you became vary sick at work? Your health—evan you life—might depend on immediate help being nearby. For this reason, the company is offerring training in CPR, or cardiopulmonary resuscitation, to all employees who work hear. The coarse will be held on two Tueday evening from 6:30 to 9:30 am. Their is no charge. Many people have expressed and interest in the class, so sign up in the Human Resources office before the course get filled. If you take the time to learn CPR you may save someones life at work or at home!

words@work

If you are using *words@work*, complete the activities on Instructions in the Writing at Work section.

words@work

If you are using *words@work*, complete the activities on Persuasive Writing in the Writing at Work section.

Case Studies

1. Cassandra had been skilled at using computers since she was a child, so she was delighted to be hired by the Information Services department of a large insurance company. After a few weeks on the job, however, she was surprised to find out how little some company employees knew about computer processes and software interfaces. She mentioned this to Mark, her supervisor, who agreed with her. In fact, Mark had just installed a new software package that traced insurance claims, but he knew that few employees were using it.

    Mark suggested that Cassandra write a set of instructions designed just for the company employees. She worked on them for several days. Twice she thought she was finished, but she kept finding exceptions that she thought employees should know about. She added them to the instructions and included a detailed glossary to help explain the terms she used.

    At last, Cassandra showed her six-page set of instructions to Mark. He read them over slowly and suggested that they have several employees try them out. Cassandra was a little disappointed that Mark thought her instructions needed to be tried out. She was also perplexed when he gave her instructions to three employees who knew little about computer software. "They probably won't even appreciate my good work," she thought.

    What do you think happened when these employees tried out Cassandra's instructions? Why do you think Mark suggested this trial? Give Cassandra some advice about writing effective instructions.

2. Karl is in charge of staff development for his company, which employs 1,200 people and manufactures chemicals. Karl majored in chemistry in college, so he is familiar with the work of the company chemists and technicians. He painstakingly reviews the most recent professional journals and seeks out experts who can help the company staff stay current on issues in the chemical field. In his memos to staff describing the half-day seminars he has arranged, Karl stresses the qualifications of the speakers and the fact that their topics were carefully chosen to benefit company employees.

    However, not many employees register for these presentations —and even fewer attend. Karl has been embarrassed more than once by the low attendance. His manager is also concerned about the cost of bringing in experts to speak to empty seats. Karl suspects that his memos need to be more persuasive, but he isn't sure how to change them.

    Analyze the situation and suggest some causes of Karl's problem. How could he improve his memos? What other ways might he improve staff attendance at the seminars?

COMMUNICATION FOR HUMAN AND SOCIAL SERVICES CAREERS

Katha Barkley coordinates a federal job-training program in her county. The program begins with an 8:00 a.m. work-skills class, followed by on-the-job training at local companies. Participants are permitted to miss the morning class no more than twice a month and be absent from their work assignments no more than once a month.

Nearly one-third of the participants fail to meet the attendance requirements and must be dropped from the program. Katha always calls absentees to encourage them to attend the class and show up at their work assignments. If their attendance does not improve, she sends them a letter stressing the importance of meeting the federal requirements and pointing out that they cannot continue in the program unless their attendance improves. Recently, Katha added a paragraph to her letter, explaining that the program might be discontinued unless more people complete it successfully. Katha feels frustrated because few participants who receive the letter improve their attendance. In fact, many of them never show up again.

1. What do you think is the biggest problem with Katha's letter?
2. How might Katha revise her letter to help improve attendance?

COMMUNICATION FOR MEDIA AND VISUAL ARTS CAREERS

Phil Martinez is the Programs Director for his town's system of 16 libraries. The system has added a new online service for teachers that enables them to order collections of grade-appropriate books focused on certain lesson topics. This new service also provides activity suggestions and a chat room so teachers can share their own ideas and tips. To use this service, teachers must obtain a Personal Identification Number (PIN) to gain access to the online service, which is available only to school districts served by the library system.

Phil wants to encourage teachers to use the new service, and he also wants others in the community to appreciate the many different ways that the libraries serve the town. Phil plans to write an article for the local newspaper, explaining the new service. In the article, he will also describe the steps for obtaining a PIN and for accessing the service.

1. What advice would you give to Phil?
2. What kind of information should he put in the newspaper article?
3. What points should he stress?
4. When he writes the instructions for accessing the service, how can he allow for the different levels of computer knowledge among teachers?

Video Case

Paying the Price for Poorly Written Communication

After 16 years with the Boeing Company as a technical writer, Pamela Hughes has decided to open her own technical writing company. Her first clients are two investment bankers, Donald Troccino and Lydia Ramos. They are considering whether to purchase New Tech Fasteners, a once successful aerospace company now almost bankrupt.

Besides hiring experts in accounting, law, manufacturing, and public relations to help decide whether New Tech Fasteners was a good investment, Lydia and Donald want a technical communicator's opinion. Pamela soon understood why.

Pamela found unclear assembly instructions being shipped with New Tech products. The procedures the firm used internally, including its quality control procedures, featured few illustrations and poor organization. The manuals used by its customer service representatives seemed targeted only for experts. Pamela's conclusion was brief: "New Tech threw away its market through miscommunication. Anyone hoping to rebuild New Tech's market share will have to address its technical communication shortcomings."

Questions
1. Why do you think a company can lose its market through poor communication?
2. Pamela also recommends that New Tech give a new, rewritten customer service manual to every customer service representative. List what you think should be the characteristics of this manual.
3. With a partner, draft a letter to New Tech customers announcing the purchase of New Tech by Ramos and Troccino. Persuade your readers that New Tech is committed to customer service. Invent any details you require. Print out your draft.
4. Find an Internet site hosted by a manufacturing company. Choose and write four sentences or phrases that the manufacturer uses on the web page to *persuade* the viewer to buy its product.

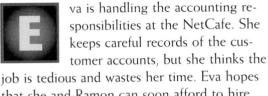

Continuing Case....

Collecting on Computers and Coffee

Eva is handling the accounting responsibilities at the NetCafe. She keeps careful records of the customer accounts, but she thinks the job is tedious and wastes her time. Eva hopes that she and Ramon can soon afford to hire someone else to send out bills and keep track of customer payments.

At the NetCafe, customers can use their shop accounts to charge their hourly computer use, coffee and baked goods, and other services. On the first day of the following month, Eva sends each customer an invoice with all the charges listed. The payment is due by the twentieth of that month, as stated on the invoice. Eva waits at least an extra week for the payment, in case it is delayed in the mail. If she has not received a payment by the end of the month, she sends that customer a reminder.

This month, Eva decides to see if any customers are habitually late in their payments. She thinks maybe she'll send those people stronger reminders.

As she checks the records for the previous months, Eva is pleased to see that nearly every customer who was sent a reminder made a payment within ten days.

However, Eva also notices a disturbing pattern: few of the customers who had to be reminded to pay their bills charged any services in the following months. In most cases, their names do not appear again in her records. Eva hopes that means they started paying in cash rather than not returning to the NetCafe.

As Eva studies the customer names, she has a sinking feeling. She hasn't seen most of them in a long time. They didn't come back, she concludes. How depressing!

Eva decides to take a hard look at her reminder letter to gauge if that might be part of the problem. Here is the form letter that she has typically sent out:

Dear [customer]:

Please be informed that your payment of [amount] for [month, year] is overdue. NetCafe is a small business, as you know, so we cannot afford to have too many overdue accounts.

Please pay your bill so that we can continue to offer you services. We look forward to seeing you in the shop again very soon.

Sincerely,

Eva Negron

1. What should be the goal of a first-stage collection letter?
2. What is the underlying message of Eva's letter? What is her implied threat?
3. Rewrite Eva's letter, incorporating what you have learned about reminder-stage collection letters.
4. Write a strong-reminder-stage collection letter that Eva could use if her new reminder-stage letter does not convince customers to pay their bills.

Presentations and Meetings

The Presentations and Meetings of Salu's Job

Salu Alufopho has worked for Computer Systems Proficiency, Incorporated, just under four years. Last month he received his third promotion. Now he is working at the first level of management and has found his new responsibilities quite challenging. The oral communication skills needed in this new position are much more demanding than before.

Salu meets continually with project managers—those under him—to get their reports. After receiving the status of the projects he is responsible for, Salu then meets with his supervisors and briefs them on each project. Occasionally he is part of a team that presents a proposal to a prospective client. When part of the team, he sometimes gives introductions. However, most of his presentations to clients are briefings on projects.

Although he had a speech class at his business college, Salu does not feel prepared for all the presentations he has to give. He has noticed that Katelynn, one of his supervisors, is really impressive during her presentations. She maintains interest by using quotations, anecdotes, questions, humor, and even statistics. Also, Katelynn always wraps up her presentations clearly.

Salu also has questions about briefings. He feels he knows nothing about this type of oral presentation and had never even seen one before his promotion to management. He also wonders what he could do to plan and organize formal presentations.

With regard to meetings, Salu has never had any training for them. He has attended many of them but has received no training on how to organize or make them effective. As Salu analyzes the meetings he has attended, he knows that some were more successful than others. He wonders what makes a meeting successful? What makes them unsuccessful? What can a leader do to help ensure the success of a meeting?

Questions

1. What should a briefing contain? Are briefings long or short?
2. How can Salu plan and organize the formal oral presentations he must give?
3. What can Salu do to organize the meetings he is responsible for leading?
4. What can Salu do to lead a meeting effectively?

12·1 Oral Presentations

Objectives

After completing Section 12.1, you should be able to:

1 Describe two types of short oral presentations.

2 Discuss planning, organizing, and outlining a formal presentation.

3 Describe three important factors in delivering speeches.

Objective

KEY POINT

- When speakers stay focused, presentations often stay short.
- When giving an overview, be sure not to give away the recommendations or main idea. That is the speaker's spotlight.

Short Oral Presentations

Oral communication is a common business activity. The types of oral presentations you give will depend on your career path. If you supervise others, you may conduct training programs. If you work in a human resources department, you may conduct new employee orientation programs. If you become a high-level executive, you may make presentations to the board of directors, stockholders, media, and civic and professional organizations.

Most oral presentations are simple, straightforward, and short—15 minutes or less. Typical short speeches are introductions and briefings. Begin with an opening that creates interest and prepares the audience for what will follow. Then provide details in the body and summarize the main points in the closing.

Introducing Speakers

When planning an **introduction** of a speaker, determine if you should follow a specific format. Many organizations provide guidelines for introductions to keep them short and uniform. If no formal guidelines exist, consider adapting these suggestions to the situation.

Obtain Information about Speakers

You will be given a resume or biographical sketch. If possible, find out what the speaker would like you to mention. Your purpose is to prepare the audience to accept the speaker and the speech. Too much information causes restlessness in the audience.

Introduce Speakers and their Presentations

Mention information about the speaker, state the title of the presentation, and give an overview of the speech. Provide information that the audience can relate to and that will create interest in the presentation.

Briefings

A **briefing** is a short presentation usually given at a meeting or a conference to bring people up to date on business activities, projects, programs, or procedures. Because briefings are short, highlight key points and provide a few details to support each point. To highlight and focus on key points, you could use a visual aid that lists them.

Formal Oral Presentations

Preparing formal oral presentations is challenging. A long speech may last from 20 minutes to more than an hour. As part of your preparation, determine the objective of your speech, analyze the audience, determine the time available for the speech, gather information, and determine the appropriate mode of delivery.

Planning the Presentation

Planning an oral presentation is like planning a written report. Oral presentations have an introduction, a body, and a closing. You may also use visual aids such as tables, charts, graphs, and photos.

Determine the Objective

What do you want to communicate to an audience? Answering this question will help you determine the objective or purpose of your presentation. (Generally your objective will be to persuade or inform.) Write the objective in sentence form. For example:

Marketing managers should learn about new products and sales goals.

A customer should place an order with us because we have a quality product and fast delivery.

Analyze the Audience

Analyze the expected audience in terms of size, knowledge level, and demographics. How do you want your audience to react to your presentation? How much does your audience already know about the topic? Is the audience's attendance voluntary or involuntary?

The size of the audience determines the approach you take for delivery. If the audience is small (20 or fewer people), you may be able to have more audience interaction. If the audience is large (several hundred), you need a good sound system and some way to make visual aids visible to the entire audience.

If the audience has little or no knowledge of the subject, you need to provide background information. If the audience is familiar with the topic, you may begin talking about the subject directly with little introduction.

Knowing the demographics of the members of your audience can help when preparing your speech. What is the range of ages? How many are men and how many are women? What is their educational level? What are their occupations? Where do these people live or work? What socioeconomic and ethnic groups are represented? What will be their attitudes toward the topic of your presentation? For additional information about audience analysis, see Chapter 1.

Objective

Using an Internet search engine, key in "delivery of presentations." See what you will find.

TECHNOLOGY

PowerPoint presentations, while great visual aids, should not become the focus of your presentations. Content is the focus.

DIVERSITY

Diversity Brings a Need for Negotiation

As organizations diversify, the probability of conflict within the organization and among its employees increases. Thus, the need for conflict management or negotiation increases.

To assist in the resolution of conflict, examine three questions:

1. Is there a real conflict?
2. What is the conflict?
3. What is the cause of the conflict?

Sometimes what appears to be a serious conflict is just a misunderstanding. But if the conflict is real, you need to identify it and what is causing it. Once you have the answers to these questions, you are ready to apply the concepts of negotiation:

1. Avoid the three pitfalls of conflict: positional arguing, bargaining, and being disagreeable.
2. Use the five-step approach for conflict resolution:
   a. Attempt to manage it, but do not suppress it. Examine it carefully.
   b. Keep participants focused on concepts rather than on personalities.
   c. Seek facts by asking probing questions. Support an open-communication atmosphere.
   d. Increase quality listening in the group. Listen for specific differences and link them to the group's thoughts.
   e. Make sure all statements are clear. Coordinate meanings if necessary and check for understanding. ∎

↓KEY POINT

To make sure you stay within the appropriate timeframe, practice your presentation several times, noting its length.

Determine Time Available

Speakers often are allotted a specific amount of time to speak. If you have a few main points and 30 minutes in which to make a presentation, spend 3 to 5 minutes on opening remarks and the introduction. Take 15 to 20 minutes to develop the main points. Use 5 to 10 minutes for conclusions, summary, and questions.

Gather Information

Information for an oral presentation is gathered in much the same way as data for a formal written report. Refer to Chapter 7 for information on gathering data for reports.

Determine Mode of Delivery

Several modes of delivery are available to speakers—impromptu, textual, and memorization.

When you are asked to speak without any notice, you make an **impromptu speech** (sometimes called an **extemporaneous speech**). Take a few moments to gather your thoughts before speaking and avoid rambling by including an introduction, a body, and a closing.

When making a **textual presentation**, you read from a written copy of your speech, from an outline, or from note cards. Reading a speech is not recommended unless the material is highly technical. Even then, maintaining eye contact is essential. Speaking from an outline or notes is effective because you can maintain eye contact while referring to notes to make sure you cover major points.

Memorizing an entire speech is not recommended because you may forget lines or become flustered. Also, a memorized speech often sounds stilted and formal. Memorizing a quotation or opening or closing remarks, however, can be effective.

Organizing the Presentation

All presentations, formal and informal, should have three main parts: introduction, body, and closing.

Introduction

The introduction to a presentation should contain an attention-getter, your topic, your purpose, and then your main points. To open your presentations effectively, you may want to use some proven attention-getters; then, tell the audience your objective and give a preview of what you will cover in the presentation.

Attention-getters hold the audience's attention during a long presentation. Use reliable attention-getters in the opening and throughout your speech. Common attention-getting techniques include:

1. *Quotations.* Use a quotation to illustrate a point. If possible, memorize the quotation and cite the source.
2. *Anecdotes.* Tell a story related to the audience or the topic. People enjoy hearing stories and often understand a point better when they hear a related anecdote.
3. *Humor.* A little humor can relax a serious business atmosphere and make an audience more receptive. Many speakers warm up an audience with jokes and then proceed to a serious topic. However, if you are not an experienced speaker, use humor with discretion and care.
4. *Statistics.* Cite an interesting or unusual statistic when appropriate. People like details, but not too many!
5. *Questions.* Ask a question. A good question can help your audience focus on your topic or make it eager to hear the answer.

Body

The middle part, or body, of a presentation should present the main points. Use the same organizational plans as those used in writing letters and memos—direct or indirect. Limit the main points to three or fewer, and arrange them in a logical sequence. As you progress in the speech, summarize previous points and preview information to come. When you shift topics, provide a transition from one idea to the next.

KEY POINT

- Your audience feels you are "talking" to them when you look at them. To fail to have eye contact may cause their minds to stray.
- The more you say, the less people remember. Plan carefully to make your presentations as concise as possible.

SCANS
Employability

Basic Skills: Speaking
If you're an inexperienced speaker, avoid trying to get an audience's response in an attention-getter. What would you do if the audience didn't laugh at your joke or didn't respond to your question?

Speakers can use long, poorly organized speeches to confuse or cloud positions on issues or policies. Such actions may be self-serving, but are they ethical?

KEY POINT

The more complex or lengthy the presentation, the more important an outline becomes.

DIVERSITY

Remember, the use of direct and indirect order varies according to culture.

Add variety to presentations to hold the audience's attention. You can vary the pace of a presentation by using visual aids, asking questions, and using examples to illustrate key points.

Closing

Close a presentation by reviewing or summarizing the main points. Your objective is to make sure the audience understands the topic and possibly takes some action as a result of your presentation.

Outlining the Presentation

An outline can be a valuable tool when planning a speech. If you use the outline as notes for the presentation, you may find that complete sentences, rather than one- or two-word topic headings, are more helpful.

Develop the outline according to the organizational plan used for the speech—direct or indirect. Use direct order (main idea first) when you expect the audience to be receptive. Use indirect order (main idea later) when you expect the audience to be skeptical or unreceptive.

Suppose that you are the campaign manager for a political candidate and must make a speech on your candidate's chances of winning the election. If the polls indicate that your candidate probably will win, you would develop an outline using direct order. Figure 12-1 shows a presentation outline using direct order.

Suppose, however, that the election is too close to predict. You would use indirect order, placing the main idea later in the speech. Figure 12-1 shows a presentation outline using indirect order.

1 Checkpoint

Short and Formal Oral Presentations

Fill in the blanks with one or more words.

1. Organizations sometimes provide guidelines to keep introductions _____ and _____.

2. Planning an oral report is like planning a(an) _____.

3. If you are giving a long, formal presentation and you start to lose the members of your audience, get them back by using a(an) _____.

4. A(an) _____ outline is better for a formal presentation than a word outline.

5. The closing of a long, formal presentation should include a(an) _____ of the main points of the speech.

Check your answers in Appendix E.

Direct Order

I. Introduction
 A. Attention-getter—my candidate will win!
 B. Objective—to explain why you are going to win
 C. Preview—order the presentation by districts:
    District 1 and District 2
II. Body
 A. District 1
   1. Neutral district
   2. About 15,000 voters
   3. Opponent will receive 53 percent—8,000 votes
   4. My candidate will receive 47 percent—7,000 votes
   5. Opponent will carry District 1
 B. District 2
   1. Your home district
   2. About 15,000 voters
   3. Opponent will receive 27 percent—4,000 votes
   4. My candidate will receive 73 percent—11,000 votes
   5. My candidate will carry District 2 by a wide margin
III. Closing (Summary)
 A. Main idea—My candidate will win!
 B. Objective—to predict the outcome of the election
 C. Preview—paraphrased preview of the election
 D. Summary of data and conclusions

Indirect Order

I. Introduction
 A. Attention-getter
 B. Objective—to explain the anticipated results of tomorrow's election
 C. Preview—order the presentation by districts:
    District 1 and District 2
II. Body
 A. District 1
   1. Neutral district
   2. About 15,000 voters
   3. Opponent will receive 53 percent—8,000 votes
   4. My candidate will receive 47 percent—7,000 votes
   5. Opponent will carry District 1
 B. District 2
   1. Your home district
   2. About 15,000 voters
   3. Opponent claims 40 percent—6,000 votes
   4. My candidate's remaining share is 60 percent—9,000 votes
III. Closing (Summary)
 A. Objective—paraphrase objective
 B. Preview—paraphrase preview of the election
 C. Summary—summarize data and conclusions
 D. Main idea—election is too close to call. Let's really push to get voters out in District 2.

FIGURE 12-1 Presentation outlines—The differences between direct order and indirect order

Delivery of Oral Presentations

Delivery of a presentation is as important as content. Voice qualities, nonverbal symbols, and visual aids can enhance or inhibit delivery. Feedback can let you know if your audience understands and accepts your message. The checklist below provides suggestions for delivering effective speeches.

KEY POINT

The better your delivery, the greater the chance that you'll achieve the objective of your presentation.

SCANS

Employability

Personal Qualities: Self-esteem

Speakers who speak softly give a nonverbal message that they are insecure or shy— neither message benefits a professional career.

Voice Qualities

Your vocal qualities need to portray a confident, competent presenter —an important part of an image (image was discussed in Chapter 3). Speak loudly enough for everyone to hear while still sounding natural. To achieve appropriate volume, look at the person farthest away and project your voice as though you were speaking to that person.

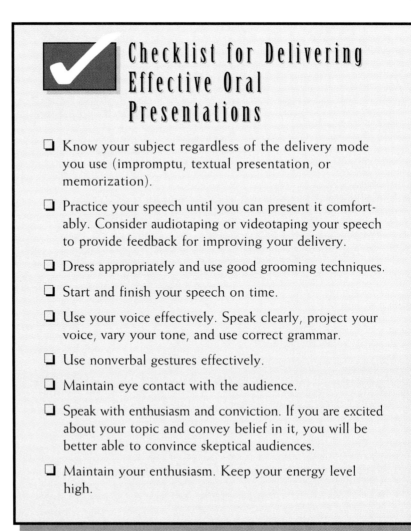

✔ Checklist for Delivering Effective Oral Presentations

❏ Know your subject regardless of the delivery mode you use (impromptu, textual presentation, or memorization).

❏ Practice your speech until you can present it comfortably. Consider audiotaping or videotaping your speech to provide feedback for improving your delivery.

❏ Dress appropriately and use good grooming techniques.

❏ Start and finish your speech on time.

❏ Use your voice effectively. Speak clearly, project your voice, vary your tone, and use correct grammar.

❏ Use nonverbal gestures effectively.

❏ Maintain eye contact with the audience.

❏ Speak with enthusiasm and conviction. If you are excited about your topic and convey belief in it, you will be better able to convince skeptical audiences.

❏ Maintain your enthusiasm. Keep your energy level high.

Speak at a moderate pace. If you talk too rapidly, the audience may not have time to consider all your points and may become confused. Also, you may give the impression that you are nervous.

Nonverbal Symbols

Nonverbal symbols add to or detract from an oral presentation. They indicate how the speaker feels about the situation—relaxed, nervous, or confident. Important nonverbal symbols during oral presentations include eye contact, facial expression, gestures, and posture.

Eye Contact

Maintaining eye contact with members of the audience keeps them involved in your speech. Focus on members of the audience to let them know you want to communicate with them and to read the feedback they give you.

Facial Expression

Use appropriate facial expressions to communicate with your audience. A smile, a frown, a look of concern, or a look of surprise can convey a message.

Gestures

Use gestures to emphasize important points in your speech. Gestures also indicate if you are nervous or calm. Actions such as playing with a visual aid pointer, repeatedly saying "ah" or "um," tapping fingers, looking at visual aids instead of the audience, clutching the sides of a lectern, putting your hands in your pockets, and folding your arms indicate nervousness.

Though you may be nervous about giving a speech because of your fear of public speaking, the key is to hide that nervousness. You can overcome this fear by doing what you are afraid of—speaking in public. Two ways you can channel this nervous energy are:

1. Think positively about your presentation and your performance as a presenter.
2. Focus on the needs, interests, and concerns of the audience—the you-viewpoint.

Posture

Send the right message with your posture. Good posture indicates self-confidence, an interest in your topic, and respect for the audience; poor posture indicates the opposite.

Visual Aids

Visual aids should be used to emphasize, explain, or illustrate points of your presentation. Transparencies, flip charts, chalkboards or whiteboards, slides, and computer presentations are examples of visual aids. Visual aids for presentations were discussed in Chapter 8.

KEY POINT

- Your audience's confidence in you is based on your nonverbal symbols.
- Presenters who appear very nervous send a nonverbal message that their fear of the situation exceeds the importance of their message.

KEY POINT

Failing to practice your presentation with your visual aids is practicing to fail.

Use visual aids appropriately to emphasize a point or explain complex data.

Look at Microsoft web sites that tell you about presentation graphics or other software.

KEY POINT

Only feedback will tell you if your presentation really was effective.

Feedback

Oral presentations allow immediate feedback to the speaker in the form of questions from the audience. When planning a speech, allow time at the end for questions and answers. If the group is very small, you might encourage comments or questions during the presentation. If the group is large, ask the audience in your introduction to hold questions until after the presentation.

2 *Checkpoint*

Delivery of Oral Presentations

Fill in the blanks with one or more words.

1. Content of a speech and its _____ are equally important.

2. _____ should be used to emphasize or illustrate main points of a presentation.

3. _____ reveal how the speaker feels about the speaking situation.

4. _____ during a presentation implies self-confidence.

5. When speaking to a(n) _____ , try to allow questions during the presentation rather than at its end.

Check your answers in Appendix E.

CASE 12:

A n s w e r s

Responses to Questions 1 and 2 in Chapter Opener

1. What should a briefing contain? Are briefings long or short?

A briefing is a presentation usually given at a meeting or a conference to bring people up to date on business activities, projects, programs, or procedures. When giving a briefing, you should highlight key points and provide a few details to support each point of the briefing. Because they are to highlight, they should be short and usually informal.

2. How can Salu plan and organize the formal oral presentations he must give?

To organize a formal presentation, Salu must (a) determine its objective or purpose, (b) analyze his audience, (c) determine the time available, (d) gather information, and (e) determine the appropriate mode of delivery.

DISCUSSION QUESTIONS

1. How are briefings and introductions alike? How do they differ?
2. Why are planning and organizing a formal oral presentation important?

12·2 Effective Meetings

Objectives

After completing Section 12.2, you should be able to:

1 Identify guidelines for effective participation in meetings.

2 Organize a productive meeting.

3 Discuss guidelines for leading a meeting effectively.

Objective

DIVERSITY

The importance of timeliness is based largely on culture. In some cultures, timeliness is important. In others, it is not. However, in the North American business culture, arriving on time for a meeting is extremely important.

Guidelines for Effective Participation in Meetings

When you attend a meeting, you send a message about who you are, your abilities, and your competence level. Meetings are a type of theater where managers observe and evaluate the performance and progress of subordinates. Even in the most ordinary meeting (a weekly staff meeting, for example), what you say and how you say it demonstrate your readiness for more responsibility—or less.

This chapter provides insights into the art of effective communication during meetings. Whether you are a leader or a participant, a meeting—because it takes up the time of those in attendance—is expensive for a company but an opportunity for you. Effective meetings need competent participants, organization, and effective leadership.

Because managers constantly evaluate meeting participants, you need to be a productive participant. To be productive, follow the guidelines presented in this section.

Arrive on Time

If you will arrive late for a meeting, notify the leader. When you enter the meeting, take your seat without interrupting. Timeliness sends a nonverbal message that you are dependable and that you believe the content of the meeting is important. Tardiness sends the opposite nonverbal message.

Participate Actively

Active participation means that you take the responsibility of partial ownership of the meeting. This type of participation requires involvement—a process that begins before you enter the room. For example, when you receive the agenda, prepare a list of questions to ask. If a meeting has been called to make a decision, prepare to support your point of view. Disagreement is okay. Few managers want "yes" people; instead, they want participants who have carefully formed opinions relevant to the topic. Come to a meeting prepared—ready to listen as well as speak—and remain focused on the objective of the meeting.

When you attend a meeting, go prepared to participate.

Improve Decision Making

When participants are reluctant to make a decision, an effective participant acts as an informal leader and tries to move them forward. Start by asking a probing question such as, "Does anyone need more information about the software?"

Sometimes people who make requests also prevent decisions. When the information is available, a participant should say something like, "Now that we have all the information we need about the software, we can proceed to costs."

The opposite problem occurs when the group makes a decision before you feel it is ready. In this case, use delaying tactics to postpone action. You could say, "I've listened carefully to all the information, but I still have some questions. Evelyn, tell me again why you think the software will help us maintain inventory." Even if the group does not agree with you, your hesitation probably will create more discussion.

SCANS
Employability

**Thinking Skills:
Problem Solving**
To ask the right questions at the right time is a sign of an alert, competent employee.

To be flexible in your decision
making reflects a mind open
to learning.

Make a Positive Impact

Meeting participants have a responsibility for making a positive, help-ful influence on the meeting. The following suggestions will help you improve your value as a group participant.

1. *Take a position but be willing to change it.* Groups work best when par-ticipants are open to new information and points of view.
2. *Speak briefly and directly.* Speak in a clear, organized manner so others will want to listen.
3. *Discuss ideas.* To discuss is to exchange ideas; to argue is to become emotional and unreasonable. Arguments often start when partici-pants put their ideas ahead of group objectives and refuse to listen to differing points of view. The moment you engage in an argu-ment is also the moment the group stops functioning. When you argue, you lose credibility.
4. *Avoid personal attacks.* Mutual respect is a key to group functioning. A group cannot move toward its goal if members verbally attack each other.
5. *Engage in fair play.* Give everyone the opportunity to speak; do not dominate the discussion. Keep your remarks concise.
6. *Use body language to your advantage.* Make eye contact when you begin speaking, speak slowly and calmly even when you are excited, and make sure your posture communicates authority and confidence.
7. *Take notes.* To insure you remember key points take notes that will help you remember what is said, complete assignments, and be prepared for the next meeting (if there is one).

Figure 12-2 summarizes the responsibilities and failures of group members at meetings.

RESPONSIBILITIES	FAILURES
Arrive on time.	Arrive late continually.
Focus on the topic.	Engage in personal attacks.
Participate actively.	Fail to make the goals of the meeting personal goals.
Lead the group to competent conclusions.	Fail to help the group reach adequate conclusions.
State positions clearly.	Choose not to share views with the group and remain uninvolved.
Follow an organized agenda.	Ramble from topic to topic. Speak for too long.
Discuss ideas willingly.	Argue with people who disagree.
Engage in fair play.	Dominate the discussion and act unfairly.

FIGURE 12-2 Responsibilities and failures of meeting participants

TECHNOLOGY

Be Careful What You Say in an E-mail or Voice Mail!

In an e-mail message to his superior, a manager described a colleague as a "backstabbing xxxxxxx." The receiver of the message made a hard copy of it and laid it on his desk. Some other employees walked by the desk and saw it. Upper management was informed, and, as a result, all the sender's e-mails were read. To no one's surprise, the man was fired. He sued, but a U. S. District Court ruled that management has a right to read an employee's e-mail and listen to an employee's voice mail. Both e-mail and voice mail can be copied and sent to others without the sender's approval.

Always be careful what you say in your e-mail and voice mail messages. Assume that everything you write or send via e-mail or voice mail might be passed on to everyone. When you have something to say that is confidential, say it in a face-to-face situation—not in a way that ultimately belongs to your company. ■

Source: Adapted from an article by Raju Narisetti, *The Wall Street Journal*, 19 March 1996.

Organize Productive Meetings

If you are responsible for holding a meeting, ask yourself if the meeting is really necessary. Before scheduling a meeting, determine whether the work can be accomplished without a meeting (if an information memo could suffice), or if the same result can be achieved by calling a few people on the telephone. If you can accomplish a task without a meeting, do not call one. If a meeting is needed, define its tasks, determine the type of meeting to hold, choose participants carefully, and use the mechanics of an effective meeting.

Define the Tasks

Assuming that meetings require little or no planning could be your first and biggest mistake. You must define the task or tasks of each meeting.

1. An effective leader recognizes what the group can and cannot do. For example, entry-level managers do not develop company policy. Corporate directors develop company policy but do not gather information; that job usually is done at a lower organizational level.

2. Trying to do too much ensures failure. Restrict the content of a meeting to its designated purpose. Although under certain conditions, a meeting can have two or more purposes, call separate meetings when goals become too broad. The general rule is "one objective—one meeting."

Objective

2

SCANS
Employability

Systems: Understands Systems
As a new supervisor, should you cancel the weekly department meeting if you think it is unnecessary?

Determine the Type of Meeting

With the task of the meeting identified, you can easily determine the type of meeting you need to hold. Meetings can be held (1) to inform, (2) to develop new ideas, (3) to make decisions, (4) to delegate work, (5) to collaborate, and (6) to persuade. Determining the type of meeting you need makes organizing it much easier.

To Inform

At meetings to inform, participants present oral reports that contain needed information. Use a meeting to inform when clarifying written information participants have received previously. This type of meeting also can be used to present new information. Figure 12-3 shows important aspects of a meeting to inform.

To Develop New Ideas

Brainstorming meetings are sessions in which participants suggest new ideas in an open, democratic atmosphere. Use brainstorming meetings to develop new procedures, programs, and so forth.

To Make Decisions

Decision-making meetings bring people and companies together to debate an issue, reconcile conflicting views, and make a decision. Hold a decision-making meeting before developing a new system. Collect information in advance to prepare for the decision-making stage. Critical features of decision-making meetings are listed in Figure 12-4.

Using an Internet search engine, key in "departmental meetings." You will see how individuals are posting the minutes of their meetings to the web for public reading. Is this a technique for picking up membership?

KEY POINT

At brainstorming meetings, a leader should be sure to stress that the goal is inventing, not deciding.

I. Agenda
   A. List speakers, subjects, and the length of time to speak.
   B. Distribute the agenda to scheduled participants before the meeting.
II. Meeting Procedure
   A. Indicate assent through silence.
   B. Ensure everyone is present.
   C. Discuss the information; stick to the topic.
   D. Summarize new information, accomplishments, and follow-up actions.

FIGURE 12-3 Important aspects of a meeting to inform

I. Agenda
   A. List problems.
   B. Receive input and summarize it in a written document.
   C. Distribute the written document before the meeting.
II. Meeting Procedure
   A. Discuss each problem.
   B. Allow junior members to vote first.
   C. Summarize the decision.
III. Action Minutes
   A. Summarize accomplishments and follow-up actions.
   B. Set a follow-up date.
   C. Include a preliminary agenda for the next meeting.

FIGURE 12-4 Important aspects of a meeting to decide

To Delegate Work

Meetings to delegate are held to assign tasks to people or groups, who are then responsible for completing those tasks. Although you can assign responsibilities over the telephone or by memo, you may need to hold a delegating meeting to clarify specific details. Meetings to delegate often are followed by informational and decision-making meetings.

KEY POINT

Effective meeting leaders and participants make sure that assignments are clear and accepted.

To Collaborate

Collaborative meetings are sessions in which participants work together, i.e., to organize complex memos, letters, or reports. Collaborative efforts succeed only if people work together as a team. These efforts waste time if members of a group are not open to improvement.

To Persuade Others

Persuasive meetings involve oral presentations to achieve a group consensus and support for a course of action. For example, a persuasive meeting may present the merits of specific computer hardware or build enthusiasm for purchasing the hardware.

Choose Participants Carefully

Group communication in a meeting works best when everyone has a reason for attending and can contribute to the discussion. When more than one person has the same expertise or point of view, choose only one to join the group to simplify communication. For best results, limit a group to seven people. A larger group often complicates communication.

Corporate culture may affect who can and who cannot be invited to a meeting. In formal, highly structured companies, meetings usually are attended by people on the same organizational level. In less structured companies, participants are more likely to span the entire organization, with less emphasis on seniority and position.

KEY POINT

The success of a group is closely related to the ability of its members to work together.

Use the Mechanics of an Effective Meeting

The mechanics of a meeting set the tone for the meeting and involve scheduling the meeting, selecting an appropriate site, and arranging the furniture.

Schedule Meetings Carefully

Although meetings can be scheduled at any time during the day, certain times are preferable. Early in the morning and right after lunch are popular meeting times. Many businesspeople hold working breakfasts, lunches, and dinners to accomplish two things at once. Meals often are served or brought into the workplace for meetings.

When scheduling a meeting, consider the travel needs of the participants. An 8:00 a.m. meeting that forces people to get up at 5:30 a.m. may be counterproductive. Even if participants arrive on time, they may be too tired to accomplish anything else during the day. Nevertheless, early morning scheduling is not unusual.

KEY POINT

When a scheduling conflict exists, leaders may have to make a choice by determining if personal preference or the preference of meeting participants is more important.

What Should Ben Do?

Ben is an oil industry executive who has worked for his company for 35 years and is only three years away from retirement. Recently, his sales and the productivity of his region in Asia have fallen slightly. He is worried that he might lose his job before retirement.

Four months ago, a presentation Ben made to the government division over oil production resulted in his company being invited to bid on maintaining all the oil pumps of the government—a $10 million, five-year contract. The bid was submitted three months ago.

One month ago, a good friend of Ben's who works for the government told Ben that his bid was a little high. Ben reworked it and lowered it slightly. The friend just called and told Ben that he would probably get the contract, and the friend requested a gift of $75,000. Ben consulted his superiors in the United States. They told him it is against U.S. law to offer such a bribe but also "that he should do what he can do to secure the contract." Ben needs his retirement package. What should he do? ■

In a meeting that involves various presentations, talk with each presenter in advance to find out how much time he or she will need. The final agenda should reflect input from everyone participating in the meeting.

If you need to hold a series of meetings, schedule a time for the next meeting at the end of the current one. To schedule an initial meeting, write a memo or send an e-mail message instead of using the telephone. Scheduling by telephone may take two or three days as you call and recall participants with conflicting schedules.

Select an Appropriate Meeting Site

The decision to meet in your office, in a conference room, in someone else's office, or at an outside location depends on the amount of space needed and the environment that is best for the group. You may need a table to hold papers or an overhead projector available only in a conference room.

Political considerations also have an impact on meetings with clients. Holding a meeting at a client's office delivers the implicit message that you are committed to that client's needs. Think about the image you want to create, and then choose the location for the meeting.

Arrange Furniture Appropriately

Furniture arrangement can enhance a meeting and help you avoid communication barriers. Here are some considerations:

1. The natural place to sit during a meeting in your office is behind your desk. However, the desk communicates that you are in charge of the discussion. To remove the message of power, move to a separate seating area or to a conference room where people can sit across from one another as peers.

2. Even when seating is informal, certain people have traditional places at the table. The leader usually sits at the head of the table; a key ally or the department manager may sit directly across. Wait for the key players to sit before choosing your place.

3. Choose your seat with your purpose in mind. Choose a controlling position if you want to influence the meeting. If you have little to say, choose a spot that allows you to remain unnoticed.

4. Consider also where potential troublemakers will sit. When you expect dissention, orchestrate a seating arrangement that separates troublemakers from one another.

SCANS
Employability

Interpersonal: Exercises Leadership
Seats in the front, in the center of a room, or at the head of a table imply power. Seats that allow participants to remain unnoticed are in the middle of a group or in the middle of a side of a table.

Checkpoint 3

Effective Participation and Organization

Indicate whether each statement is true or false.

1. Because meetings are inexpensive, they often are used by organizations to make decisions.

2. Active participants seldom accept ownership of a meeting.

3. Effective leaders know productive meetings must be long.

4. Effective meetings generally have only one objective.

5. When making seating arrangements for a meeting, separate potential troublemakers.

Check your answers in Appendix E.

TECHNOLOGY
When participating in a videoconference, a nonverbal message about your effectiveness as a meeting leader or participant is sent—frequently to those several levels in the hierarchy above you.

Lead Meetings Effectively

When you are the leader of a meeting, you should realize that the communication that takes place within a meeting is defined by your performance as leader. The more effective you are as a leader, the more effective the meeting will be. As a leader in very formal meetings, you may need to use **Robert's Rules of Order** (a set of rules designed to ease the operation of a formal meeting) for procedures. However, in most business meetings such formality is not necessary.

Objective

Begin Effectively

Convening the meeting is your first act of control in front of a group; do it with direction and purpose. Open the meeting by restating the specific tasks you want to accomplish. Although this information is part of the agenda, repetition will focus the group's attention. Make your statement positive and forward looking even if you anticipate problems. Never start by apologizing for previous mistakes or blaming others for problems. Convene the meeting on time to show your determination to get the job done.

KEY POINT

An agenda can be used to direct participants back to the objective of a meeting if they stray.

Use an Agenda

Use an **agenda** to determine and control the direction of the meeting. Problems arise when meeting participants stray from the topic—when attention drifts to peripheral issues or personal stories. Remain polite and friendly, but keep the group on track. When participants ramble, summarize what you think they have said and ask a question to point them in a specific direction. An effective group leader looks for signs of confusion—puzzled looks, questions that ask for clarification, and drifting attention spans. When members are confused, summarize what the group has accomplished, what is now being discussed, and/or where the discussion is heading.

Stay Focused on the Task or Objective

Members of management are surprised about the number of people who do not know what type of meeting they are attending. For example, when a supervisor convenes a meeting to convey a decision, a staff member may persist in debating the decision. The time for discussion is past! Situations like this occur because the staff member does not realize the type of meeting he or she is attending. The purpose of this meeting is to inform and delegate—not to make a decision.

An agenda tells participants to prepare for a specific type of discussion and to focus on that discussion during the meeting. The agenda is a promise you, as a leader, make to the participants that the meeting will deal with specific issues.

SCANS
Employability

**Interpersonal:
Working on Teams**
Participants need to recognize the kind of meeting they are attending. An inaccurate assessment can make a participant seem uncooperative.

KEY POINT

Difficult people may destroy an otherwise effective group. Deal with difficult people carefully, or a meeting can be a waste of time.

Balance the Discussion

Handling difficult people is the greatest challenge any meeting leader faces. Because you generally cannot hand-pick meeting participants, sooner or later you will encounter people whose personalities or hidden agendas make group success questionable.

Some people want to dominate conversations while others rarely say a word. An effective group leader tries to balance these contributions—to encourage extroverts to say less and introverts to say more. Without intervention, a meeting can become a platform for one person's point of view, thereby making a true consensus difficult to achieve. Encourage people who say little to participate by asking direct, specific questions such as, "Gary, you are our computer expert. Will adding this program overload the existing computer system? Will we have to upgrade?"

When people talk about an area they know well, their shyness often disappears. Although you cannot force people to participate, you can ensure a positive climate and abundant opportunities.

Handling an overzealous contributor is more difficult. You could say something like, "Chris, as you can see by the agenda, we have a lot to cover. I can give you only five more minutes." If Chris continues to talk, redirect the discussion to another person. Interrupt Chris and say, for example, "Your survey points to the need to communicate with consumers. Kelli, can you fill us in on the advertising plan?"

Make Meetings Successful

The leader sets the tone for the meeting through fairness, work ethic, and control. The following factors are critical to the success of your meetings.

Recognize Contributions

Recognize everyone's contributions. Participants who feel their discussion is valued will continue to contribute. Even if a proposal has problems, focus on the positive aspects and lead the group forward.

Maintain High Standards

Do not accept slipshod work or opinions that masquerade as facts. When participants do not have information the group needs, postpone the meeting if possible.

Maintain Order

Follow the agenda as the discussion moves through the various meeting stages. At the conclusion of each item, summarize points of agreement and disagreement and include any actions that will be taken. These internal summaries improve communication. Allow only one person to speak at a time, and discourage private conversations.

End Effectively

At the end of a meeting, summarize what happened and move the group ahead to future action. Your summary should review the discussion so that everyone understands how the group progressed from thought to action. Summarize items that need further consideration, review assignments and deadlines for future work, and set the time and place for the next meeting.

4 Checkpoint

Lead Meetings Effectively

Fill in the blanks with one or more words.

1. When opening a meeting, state its _____ even if it is written on the agenda.

2. The greatest challenge a leader faces is _____.

3. Participants who feel discussion is valued will continue to _____ in a meeting.

4. When participants are unprepared, effective leaders will _____ the meeting.

5. _____ are effective tools when ending a meeting effectively.

Check your answers in Appendix E.

CASE 12:

Answers

Responses to Questions 3 and 4 in Chapter Opener

3. **What can Salu do to organize the meetings he is responsible for leading?**

   The steps for organizing meetings are: (1) define the tasks, (2) determine the type of meeting, and (3) choose participants carefully. Other considerations when organizing a meeting are: (a) schedule a meeting carefully, (b) select an appropriate meeting site, and (c) arrange the furniture appropriately.

4. **What can Salu do to lead a meeting effectively?**

   When leading a meeting, Salu should (a) begin effectively; (b) use an agenda; (c) keep the meeting focused on its objective; (d) balance the discussion; (e) make meetings successful by recognizing contributions, maintaining high standards, and maintaining order; and (f) end the meeting effectively.

DISCUSSION QUESTIONS

1. Are agendas important in long and short meetings? Justify your answer.

2. Are the mechanics of a meeting really important? Justify your answer.

CASE 12:

S u m m a r y

Even though most people do not enjoy giving presentations, it may be an important part of your future. For most, the fear of presenting subsides as they give more and more presentations. In Salu's case and in most situations, as he progresses upward in his company, the number and length of his presentations will increase. It is very important for him to continue to develop his presentation skills.

Salu's meeting skills are equally important. Most people in a meeting or group situation focus only on the objective or task of the group. Salu and all of us also need to consider the behavior of those at the meeting. Being flexible, engaging in discussion, playing fairly, and not being part of personal attacks send positive nonverbal messages.

As Salu continues to advance within his company, his presentation skills and his effectiveness at meetings will be even more important to his career than they are now.

Chapter Summary

Section 12.1 Oral Presentations

1 **Describe two types of short oral presentations.** The two types of short oral presentations are introductions and briefings. An introduction is simply the introduction of a speaker. A briefing is a short presentation given at meetings to update attendees on business activities, projects, programs, or procedures.

2 **Discuss planning, organizing, and outlining a formal presentation.** The five steps in planning a formal presentation are: (a) determine its objective; (b) analyze your audience; (c) determine the time available; (d) gather the information; and (e) determine the mode of delivery. The organization of a formal presentation has three parts: the introduction, the body, and the closing. The introduction should include an attention-getter, the purpose or objective of your presentation, and a preview. The body of the presentation should include your main ideas. The closing should contain a summary, conclusions, and recommendations. When outlining a formal presentation, you will probably find that a discussion outline (several sentences) rather than a topic outline (just main words) will be more helpful.

3 **Describe three important factors in delivering speeches.** Three important factors when delivering speeches are vocal qualities, nonverbal symbols (eye contact, facial expressions, gestures, and posture), and visual aids.

Section 12.2   Effective Meetings

1 **Identify guidelines for effective participation in meetings.** The guidelines for effective participation at meetings are: (a) arrive on time; (b) participate actively; (c) improve decision making; and (d) make a positive impact by taking a position but being flexible, speaking briefly and directly, discussing ideas, avoiding personal attacks, and engaging in fair play.

2 **Organize a productive meeting.** To organize a productive meeting, you should define its task, determine the type of meeting, and choose participants carefully.

3 **Discuss guidelines for leading a meeting effectively.** To lead a meeting effectively, a leader should use an agenda; keep the group focused on its objective; balance the discussion; make the meeting effective by recognizing contributions, maintaining high standards, and maintaining order; and end the meeting effectively.

Critical Thinking Questions

1. Will meetings be important to you in your probable career? If so, how?
2. Will oral presentations be important to you in your probable career? If so, how?

Applications

Part A. Based on a report you have written for this or another class, prepare two outlines of an oral presentation you would give on this report. Prepare one outline in direct order. Prepare the other in indirect order. Which outline is better for this report? Justify your answer.

Part B. Select the better outline from Part A. Prepare and deliver the oral presentation in class.

Part C. Listen to a speech and prepare a written evaluation of the speaker's effectiveness in delivering the speech. To help you, use the evaluation sheet provided in Chapter 12 of your Study Guide.

Part D. Assume that you work for the recruitment office of your school or college. Outline a presentation for student recruitment. Visit the appropriate office to obtain pamphlets, brochures, and so forth, to locate information for the presentation. Develop an outline and visual aids for the presentation.

Part E. Plan, develop, and deliver the oral presentation described in Part D.

Part F. Divide the class into groups and give each group a resume for a fictitious person who will speak to the class. Students are to develop an introduction for the speaker. Groups should be prepared to present their introductions orally.

TEAMWORK

Part G. Bring a product to class. Divide the class into groups that will develop an introduction to a speech designed to persuade people to buy the product. The introduction should contain an attention-getter, an objective, and a preview.

TEAMWORK

Part H. You have just been appointed to chair a committee on a new local softball tournament. You want to make sure each meeting of the committee is well planned and organized. Prepare a checklist to use to ensure that your meetings are organized and that you fulfill your responsibilities as a leader. Organize the checklist into at least two parts—mechanics of organizing meetings and guidelines for effective leaders of meetings.

Part I. Write a memo announcing a meeting for the committee described in Part H. Determine the objective and prepare an agenda for the meeting. Be ready to discuss your memo and agenda with the class.

Part J. Attend a meeting. Observe three or four participants at the meeting. Write a memo evaluating each of the participants. Did they arrive on time? Did they participate actively? Did they improve the decision making? Did they make a positive impact on the meeting?

Editing Activities

words@work

If you are using *words@work*, complete the activities on Speaking at Work in the Workplace Success section.

1. Proofread, edit, and revise the following message.

   Yesterday, I choose to enroll in my employers health insurance program. The two major affects of this decision is that 1) teh cost of this insurance is consistant with what I can afford, and 2) the coverage of this policy will fullfill my families needs. By joinning this program, I am better able to fullfill the needs of my family.

2. Proofread, edit, and revise the following message.

   Did you see the brochure and pamplet on the south Seas. They were extraordinary. There were pictures of waterfalls, beaches, and hotels that were uneque. Sarah is planing to go their on her vacation. I wish I was going with her. However this year, because of a lack of funds, my family and I will be going to the mountians. We will be camping out in tents, and enjoying nature at it's best.

Case Studies

TECHNOLOGY

1. Toastmasters' International is an organization that is heavily involved in public speaking. Their web site address is **www.toastmasters.org**. Look this site up and write a memo to your instructor about it.

   In your memo (1) explain how Toastmasters' International works, (2) tell how to join Toastmasters', (3) explain where the nearest club is, and (4) discuss tips they give on speaking skills.

2. Terry Wood started working for MasterClips, Inc., immediately after graduating from Gonzales Technical College. As a new employee at MasterClips, he soon became a member of a computer programming team. At his first team meeting, he was surprised at the inability of team members to get things done. They started out by discussing the project and their various responsibilities, but arguments arose. After about 15 minutes of arguing, the team leader closed the meeting by saying, "Well, that's enough for today." At the second team meeting, the same thing happened. This pattern continued until yesterday when Terry found out that his team leader had been fired. Now Terry has been asked to take charge of the team temporarily. The supervisor explained that other team members are too emotionally upset with each other and that the team leader needs to be seen as neutral. The supervisor asked Terry to write her a memo before the first team meeting explaining what he would do to improve team meetings. Terry did not dare turn the supervisor down, but he is very concerned about what he should do to help his team. He wants to be sure his meetings are effective. What would you say in the memo if you were Terry?

COMMUNICATION FOR ENGINEERING AND INDUSTRIAL CAREERS

Mostafad Durrat, vice president of personnel at Columbia Products, Inc., is an officer in a two-year-old company that produces parts for automakers. Because the company is relatively new, it has only three levels on its organizational chart. Little opportunity exists for advancement, so loyalty and dedication to the company among production-line workers is weak. The top level is made up of area vice presidents. Under these managers are middle managers—the supervisors of the production divisions. The lowest area on the organizational chart represents the production-line workers who make the parts.

Mostafad and other top managers, concerned about the lack of motivation among the workers, have created a reward system for cost-cutting ideas. A worker who presents an idea that is implemented and cuts costs will receive 25 percent of the first year's savings. The workers in his or her group will split another 25 percent of the savings among themselves.

You have been selected to present the plan to middle management and production-line employees at a companywide meeting. The theme of your presentation is "working smarter, not harder."

1. What areas does your presentation need to cover?
2. Will audience analysis impact your presentation? If so, how?
3. Will you use visual aids? If so, how?

COMMUNICATION FOR MEDIA AND VISUAL ARTS CAREERS

You are the manager of the Allison City Art Center. The purpose of this center is to display the work of many up-and-coming young artists who live in the state.

When started 25 years ago, the center was well funded, and many artists wanted to have shows there. But the past four years have seen a drop in financing. The building needs a lot of work to overcome a depressing atmosphere and to attract a new generation of artists.

You have worked hard with representatives of your state government to gain new and additional funding. Soon, several legislators will visit to determine whether they will support your request.

1. To prepare for the visit, what will you do?
2. Will you make the center look as good as possible, leave it as it normally is, or make it look a little worse than usual? Justify your answer.

Video Case

Adding Graphics to Good Presentations

Sam Turney impressed his small audiences as a frequent volunteer speaker for Memorial Hospital. Sam had a sense his presentations were effective. Still, he was delightfully surprised when Susanna Marguiles, Memorial Hospital's Patient Relations Director, offered to hire him as a full-time member of her staff.

With a communicator of Sam's quality on her team, Susanna wants Sam to expand his work to include groups of all sizes and presentations on a variety of health themes. Susanna also wants Sam to begin using state-of-the-art presentation software and equipment. Sam is anxious because he simply feels more comfortable with small groups and because he knows nothing about presentation software and equipment.

Susanna helps Sam with his first electronic presentation. However, Susanna will be attending a conference in another city when Sam gives his second electronic presentation—a presentation before an audience of hundreds—designed to persuade parents to take child CPR classes.

Sam is terrified as he prepares his presentation. He feels a little better after Susanna calls to give him advice. "You're using the same strong communications skills," she told him, "even if the audience is larger and the equipment is more sophisticated."

Questions

1. Was Sam's speech in the video clip informative or persuasive? What was the specific purpose of the speech?
2. After viewing the video, why do you think Susanna finds Sam an effective communicator?
3. Choose two or three team members. Using Internet resources, research a health topic for a five-minute presentation. Include graphics to illustrate your points. Don't forget the option of using e-mail to reach local authorities during your research. Deliver the speech to the class, dividing responsibilities. Be prepared to describe the type of speech you are giving and your sources.

Continuing Case....

Branching Out

The NetCafe has been open for nearly two years now. Eva has hired one full-time and one part-time technician to help teach classes and answer customer questions. Randy, the full-time technician, has also completed several projects, including PowerPoint presentations, for local businesses. The business owners insist they don't have the staff, time, and/or knowledge to do the projects themselves. (Eva is trying to enroll them in some of NetCafe's classes!)

A young woman named Mika has been working for Ramon at the coffee counter for nearly a year. She takes over on his days off. Ramon has hired other staff, too, allowing the NetCafe to start selling specialty sandwiches. At noon most days, a crowd of people waits impatiently for an empty table—or an empty computer station. The NetCafe concept is working!

Things are looking up in other areas, too. For the past year, Eva has been dating a young man named Nick, who works for a company based in Chicago. Nick was in Milwaukee on company business when he first stopped at the NetCafe. He used its computers to access his e-mail.

Since then, Nick has come into the NetCafe every time he gets in town—and not just to see the computers. Eva has visited Chicago, too, and met Nick's friends and family. Last week, Eva and Nick announced their engagement.

Now Eva wants to open a branch of NetCafe in Chicago. She and Nick have already found a good site for it.

"I can set up the computers," Eva tells Ramon. "And maybe I can borrow Mika to set up the coffee shop. Randy can take over for me here."

Ramon is sorry to see Eva go but excited at the possibility of a new branch. "Maybe I'll come to Chicago and let Mika take over here," he tells Eva with a grin.

They decide to present this idea to their two silent partners, Dominic Lula and Opal Morales, at their second annual meeting. The silent partners are now receiving substantial checks every quarter as their share of NetCafe's profit.

Eva and Ramon believe that Opal will enthusiastically support a Chicago branch. Dominic might admit that the first NetCafe has become successful. Still, he will probably be hesitant about putting up more money for another one. Eva will make the presentation, but Ramon will help her organize it.

1. Should this presentation be in the direct or the indirect order? Why?
2. What possible attention-getters might Eva use in her introduction?
3. Brainstorm a list of possible topics that could be included in this presentation. Keep in mind that Eva must answer any questions the silent partners might have about opening a new NetCafe. Consider what you would want to know if you were a silent partner. For example, you might wonder about NetCafe's competition in Chicago, the location that Eva has chosen, and the schedule for opening the new shop.
4. Choose the topics that should be included in Eva's presentation and put them in order to form the body of the presentation.

chapter 13

Communicating
with Customers

13·1 Customer Service

13·2 One-on-One and Telephone Communication

Customer Service at a Minimum

In his job as sales support associate, Cal helps four busy salespeople at a company that sells flooring, wallpaper, and countertop materials for kitchens and bathrooms. The company, Floors & More, has four locations, each in a different city.

All the salespeople have cubicles, though they spend most of their time making sales presentations in people's homes. Cal's job is to process the salespeople's orders. When a problem—such as a back order—comes up, he puts the paperwork back on the appropriate person's desk. Cal has not learned how to solve the problems, nor has anyone suggested that he do so. He sometimes runs out of things to do. When that happens, he waits in a cubicle until something comes up.

In the showroom, the receptionist, Angelica, also has a cubicle. Angelica answers all incoming calls. The phone rings 10 to 20 times per hour. Most calls are for the salespeople. Angelica takes messages (usually just a name and number) for the absent salespeople. If showroom customers have a question, they often must wait until Angelica is between phone calls. Sometimes, if a caller isn't someone she knows, she puts the call on hold and answers a question with the phone resting on her shoulder.

Occasionally, customers in the showroom approach Cal with a question. Sometimes he just says, "I'm not a salesperson; I can't help you." At other times, Cal tells them they'll have to wait for Angelica or make an appointment with one of the salespeople. The salespeople, however, do not have telephones with them when they are out of the showroom, and Angelica does not schedule appointments for them.

Questions

1. How important is customer service to the owners of Floors & More? How can you tell?

2. What messages does Angelica's behavior send to customers? What could she or the company do to change those messages?

3. What role does technology play in how Floors & More employees communicate with both internal and external customers? How could the company use technology differently or more effectively?

4. How does Cal perform when he has opportunities for one-on-one communication with external customers? with internal customers?

5. What is Angelica's strategy for telephone communication? How effective is her strategy? Explain your answer.

13·1 Customer Service

Objectives

After completing Section 13.1, you should be able to:

1 Explain the importance of customer service,

2 Identify external and internal customers.

3 Explain the qualities of courteous, professional customer contact.

4 Describe the appropriate way to receive customers.

5 Discuss the importance of using ethical behavior when dealing with customers.

6 Explain how to use communication technology in communicating effectively with customers.

Why Is Quality Customer Service So Important?

"Customer service is more important than ever." Pick up any business magazine or company newsletter, and you may read those words. But why? **Customer service**—the performance of activities to ensure customer satisfaction—has been around for a long time. Why is it so important now? Simply put, customer service is more important now because there are more customers and more companies providing customer service.

Having more customers is a good thing for a company, but only if it can keep those customers and attract new ones. Most business experts agree that the way to keep customers is to deliver a quality product by means of excellent customer service. To succeed, a company needs to distinguish itself in some way; providing *quality* customer service is one sure way of doing so.

The number of companies providing services has increased dramatically during the last decade. This number will continue to increase, according to the Bureau of Labor Statistics. As more companies compete to gain your attention—to mow your lawn, repair your computer, or provide your health care—they must find new ways to serve you. The services provided by Abe's Lawn Service and Al's Lawn Service may be the same, so *how* Abe and Al serve you will determine whether one or the other keeps your business or loses it.

Objective
1

Objective
2

External and Internal Customers

When you think of customers, you probably think about people who, for example, want to buy a car, have a car washed, or have it repaired. Each of these is an example of an **external customer**, someone from outside the company who requests information or purchases a product or service.

As an employee, you also have internal customers. An **internal customer** is a supervisor, coworker, or maintenance worker who works for the same company you do. You and your internal customers provide services to each other, sometimes directly, sometimes indirectly.

Think of it this way. You are a one-person customer service provider. You have services to "sell" to anyone who walks up to your desk, into your office, or toward you on the sales floor. If the person approaching you is from the accounting office and she asks you to give her a rundown on a project budget, she is asking for a service and is your customer. Your job is to satisfy her. Make her feel comfortable; make her feel as if you know what you are doing and that you are providing accurate information. She will walk away feeling good, and she will feel confident that she can come to you for reliable information whenever she needs to.

What if you don't satisfy her? After all, she is just one of many people in the accounting department. It's not as if she is your boss. Suppose you throw together some budget figures several days later. The accountant comes back to you with questions, which you can't answer because you weren't really paying attention to what you wrote down. The accountant then wonders if you really understand the budget process, much less the importance of it. She mentions her concerns to your boss. Your boss is embarrassed that one of her employees hasn't measured up. You look bad because you didn't satisfy your customer.

KEY POINT

- Customer service—even more than price and quality of product—is the key to a company's ability to keep its customers.
- A customer is anyone you deal with in the course of doing your job.

Most jobs require people to provide service to both internal and external customers.

SCANS
Employability

Interpersonal:
Serving Customers
Satisfying customers' or clients' expectations is a basic skill that all employees need to master, no matter what their job or industry.

Objective

3

You need to provide quality service to internal customers as well as to external customers. Try to satisfy everyone you deal with by treating people courteously, by providing accurate information, and by using tact and discretion in each and every transaction.

Customer Service and Contact

Every time you communicate with a customer, whether internal or external, you make an impression on that customer. At every point of contact you must provide the same courteous, professional service. This is important whether the contact takes the form of a scheduled meeting, a conversation on the sales floor, an e-mail message, or a brief business letter. Maintaining customer contact in a way that satisfies the customer is just as important as selling a product to that customer or completing a service call.

Customer Contact

Customer contact refers to maintaining customer satisfaction by communicating in a timely manner by whatever means is convenient for the customer. Returning telephone calls, messages, and e-mail promptly is a critical means of ensuring the delivery of quality customer service. Determining what is "timely," however, is up to you. The industry in which you work, the type of products or services you provide, and the type of customer all have an impact on how quickly a good customer service provider responds to communications from customers.

One of the most important factors in customer service is building a relationship of trust with customers. If the customer trusts you, he or she will continue to be your customer. There are three ways to foster trust with a customer. First, make yourself accessible to the customer—make it easy for the customer to get in touch with you. Second, give the customer knowledgeable responses. Third, maintain continuous contact with the customer.

Be Accessible

To be a good customer service provider, you need to be accessible to your customers. **Accessibility** is the ease with which customers can contact you. To make sure that you are accessible to your customers, give them at least two different ways to communicate with you. Provide an office telephone number, a cellular telephone number, a facsimile number, and/or an e-mail address for customers to use. Also, assure your customers that you will respond to any means of communication just as quickly as another. In addition, make sure your customers know what your hours are. They will be disappointed if they call in the morning, only to find out that you don't come in to work until 2:00 in the afternoon.

TECHNOLOGY
Today's telecommunications technologies make it easier than ever to keep in touch with customers, whether they are at work or at home, and whether you are in the office or on the road.

Give Knowledgeable Responses

Knowing your product or service thoroughly makes it easy to give knowledgeable responses to customer inquiries. Sometimes though, the nature of a customer's question or the complexity of the product or service, makes it impossible to respond immediately. Don't guess when giving customers information. Verify prices, stock, availability, size, or whatever pertains to the customer's needs. Think how you would feel, after all, if a customer service provider said something like this: "I'm not sure, but I think it costs $220, and it will be in stock some time next month."

Providing knowledgeable responses also may involve explaining the reasons behind your answers. You may need to simplify technical or complex issues so the customer can understand. At the same time, don't "talk down" to the customer. You can make your message understandable without insulting the customer's intelligence.

Finally, don't bluff, and don't be afraid to say, "I don't know." However, don't let the contact end there. Let that customer know you will find the answer and get in touch with him or her at some specific time in the near future. Then do what you have said you will do.

DIVERSITY

Your customers may have certain expectations because of their cultural background. Be aware of the needs that might arise because of the diversity of your customers.

Maintain Continuous Contact

Contact with a customer may begin with a simple inquiry. If you, the customer service provider, can answer the question immediately, the contact with that customer may end right there. If not, you are responsible for following up and providing the customer with the requested information.

During the initial contact, you should be clear about when the customer can expect something to happen, whether it be a telephone call, an e-mail message, or the receipt of information in the mail. If the follow-up work takes longer than expected, contact the customer just to let her know that her inquiry is still moving forward. Or, if you end up doing something other than what you had indicated to the customer, call and tell her. In general, make the customer feel as if you are taking care of her and that answering her inquiry promptly and accurately matters to you. Figure 13-1 shows how a poor customer service provider communicates with a client. A quality customer service provider, however, has much more contact with the customer.

Policies and Procedures

Every company has policies and procedures that govern how employees serve their customers. As an employee, it is your responsibility to be aware of those policies and to act accordingly. In some cases, a company's policies may limit what you can do

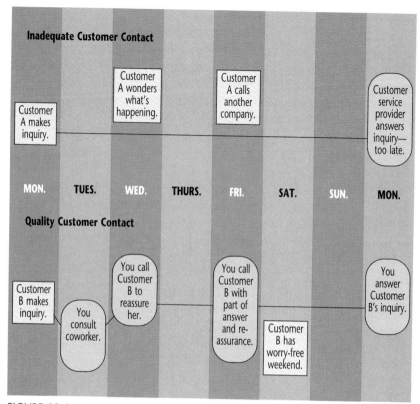

FIGURE 13-1 Two views of customer service

for a customer. For example, a salesperson may not have the authority to offer a free replacement for a defective product, or an account representative may need a supervisor's signature before he can carry out a large cash transaction for a customer. Some policies, as in the latter example, exist to protect the customer or the company from fraud.

In a truly customer-oriented environment, employees have the authority to do "whatever it takes" to attract and keep customers. Quality customer service, then, boils down to the energy and creativity of individual employees. How *you* communicate, how *you* treat each person you deal with—within the confines of your employer's policies—is what matters.

Organizations devoted to serving customers are said to have a strong service culture. A **service culture** is a combination of customer-focused policies and attitudes that penetrate a company, from the executive offices all the way to the furnace room. To help maintain customer-focused service policies, employees receive extra training in customer service. They also are allowed to use their own initiative in solving customer problems and are rewarded for doing so.

KEY POINT

Companies that make customer service a priority have a strong, positive service culture.

Customer Service and Contact

Choose the more appropriate response to each customer inquiry

1. Customer: When can I expect the technician to arrive?

   Response A: You are on the schedule for tomorrow afternoon. I can call you tomorrow morning with a more specific time.

   Response B: The best I can do is to tell you he'll be there sometime between 12:00 and 5:00. You'll have to call in the morning if you want to know exactly when.

2. Customer: When can I reach you tomorrow to give you the measurements?

   Response A: You can just call and leave a message.

   Response B: Here's my card. You can reach me in the morning at my desk, or in the afternoon on my cellular phone number.

3. Customer: What was the profit margin on that project? I need the information for my monthly report.

   Response A: I don't know offhand, but I can find out for you. I'll buzz you in a few minutes.

   Response B: I'm pretty sure it was about 48 percent.

Check your answers in Appendix E.

Customer Interaction

Objective **4**

A customer walks into a store. Two salespeople lean on a counter at the back of the store. They are chatting and do not look up when the customer enters. The customer looks around for several minutes, then leaves. The customer didn't try to speak to the salespeople, so he must not have needed any help.

This scenario is an example of customer interaction. In this case the customer service providers failed to interact. Perhaps they didn't realize that customer interaction begins the moment the customer enters the store. If service providers don't take the initiative, customers will form their opinions and more than likely move on.

Making First Impressions

First impressions *do* count. Job interviewers—and interviewees—know it. So do salespeople. Customers know it, too. They want to be favorably impressed from the moment of contact with a customer service provider. They want to be in pleasant surroundings; they want to feel welcome, whether they are on the telephone or in your office. The first few seconds of your conversation or meeting may well set the tone for the entire relationship with this customer. In fact, they may determine whether you have a relationship with this customer at all. What impression will you make?

Certain actions and behaviors on the part of customer service providers can ensure that those first few seconds of a customer's experience are favorable. Here is what you can do.

Give Customers Prompt Attention

Customers come to get advice or receive help, or to make a purchase. They deserve to be helped as quickly as possible. If they do not receive attention, they may take their business elsewhere. Worse yet, they may tell other people to go elsewhere as well.

What if the sales floor is extremely busy, or the waiting room extremely full? Sometimes taking care of customers as promptly as possible still means they must wait. In such cases, there should be some kind of communication with the customer. People who are kept waiting, without knowing how long they must wait or why they must wait, are sure to become impatient. On the other hand, if a receptionist says, "Mr. Weber is running late today because his son missed the bus and had to be driven to school," most people will understand. Again, the customer deserves prompt attention, even if that attention is just an acknowledgment of her presence.

KEY POINT

Customers need to know they will be taken care of, so acknowledge their presence promptly, even if it's just to say, "Someone will help you shortly."

Truth on the Web

An unhappy customer will tell ten other people about it. A satisfied customer, on the other hand, *might* tell one other person. It's a strong reminder that damage from one dissatisfied customer can significantly outweigh the benefits of many satisfied customers. The equation becomes even more daunting as the Internet increases the pathways of communication.

Unhappy consumers can now take their stories straight to the World Wide Web and broadcast them for thousands of readers. Several newsgroups, as well as a number of web sites, serve as repositories of consumer stories. Some of those stories tell of customer service beyond the call of duty, but most tell of rip-offs, unfair practices, and poor customer service in general.

The existence of these sites raises an issue. Anyone can submit a "story," and no one is checking the truthfulness of the submissions. So what's to stop Company A from planting false stories about competitors to ruin their business? Or what if someone at Company B wants to generate some "good press" by planting a false account of good customer service on one of these sites? How do site visitors know that what they are reading is true?

As long as the Web remains a relatively unmonitored communication tool, its content will be subject to the whims of human nature. As is often the case, the consumer is at the mercy of the seller. Even in a consumer's forum, such as the newsgroups and web sites mentioned here, the consumer must exercise caution and good judgment. ■

Greet Customers Cheerfully

A pleasant, cheerful greeting goes a long way. Assuming a customer has received attention in a timely manner, the greeting is the next step toward setting the tone for the remainder of this customer's contact. A customer service provider who greets customers glumly, or with a "What's your problem?" attitude will probably find himself dealing with customers who are glum and have a lot of problems. Regardless of the situation, greet customers in a friendly, respectful manner.

Providing Service

"Providing service" means different things to different people. No matter what the type of service, though, *quality* customer service involves courtesy, careful listening, and individualized treatment. The key is to combine these elements in every customer interaction.

Be Courteous

You have the ability to set the tone of your customer contact. Think of your customers as guests, and treat them accordingly. Courtesy doesn't have to be elaborate. For example, instead of saying, "I need those papers," you can say, "May I have those papers, please?"

As a professional, it is your responsibility to provide friendly service, even if you are tired or if you have done this a million times before. True professionals put forth their best effort every day, with every customer, every time.

If you are dealing with a dissatisfied customer, you must remain calm. The situation will only escalate if you match the customer's agitation. Remember that you don't have to "win" in a conversation with an irate customer, but you do have to remain professional.

Many customer service providers must deal with diverse customers on a daily basis. Both internal and external customers may be from different cultures or possibly different countries. People with different backgrounds have different customer service expectations. The best policy is for service providers to educate themselves about the cultures their customers represent. When that's not feasible, the next best policy is to include extra courtesy and a level of formality when interacting with people from other cultures.

Listen Carefully

Don't assume that you know what a customer wants or needs. As one customer service consultant advises, "Customers want the feeling that you've never heard this before, or that their situation is so important to you that you're willing to give them your complete undivided attention."[1] More than likely, you will have heard what a customer has to say, maybe thousands of times. But each customer deserves—and will appreciate—your attention.

DIVERSITY

Remember, those of another culture appreciate a greeting based on their culture. Look on page 42 in Chapter 2 for "Greeting Customs from Around the World."

DIVERSITY

Politeness and formality in business transactions are valued highly by people from many cultures. Make an effort to learn the codes of proper conduct if you interact with customers from different cultures.

---

[1]Customer Service Group. 1998. Alexander Communications Group, Inc. "How to Pick up a Dropped Ball: A Four-Step Service Recovery Formula." (*The Customer Communicator*, January 1998), 30 March 1999, http://www.alexcommgrp.com/csg/html/tccarticle.html.

Active listening is important. Nod your head, look concerned, or indicate with other types of body language that you are indeed listening. Avoid tapping your fingers or fidgeting with a pen. Those actions send the message that you are not listening or not interested. Eliminate or do your best to block out barriers to communication. Don't be afraid to say, "Let's step over here where it's more quiet." Your customer will only be grateful that you have made it easier to communicate.

Sometimes it is necessary to key information into a computer as your customer provides it. If that is the case, don't get so absorbed in your computer screen that you forget to make eye contact with the customer. If you must turn to your computer screen for any length of time, excuse yourself and explain briefly what you must do and how long it will take. Your explanation will reassure the customer and will also keep him from interrupting you while you concentrate.

KEY POINT

Maintaining eye contact is an important part of active listening.

Determine the Customer's Purpose

Make sure you understand each customer's specific needs. As an active listener, you should summarize what the customer tells you to make sure you have understood properly. Does the customer want information, or does she need action? Is she expecting to have her problem solved right this minute, or does she want to make an appointment for some other time? If you are unable to act on the customer's request right away, explain why.

Listening is a critical customer service skill. Before you can help someone, you must understand what he or she needs.

Apologize When Necessary

Mistakes happen, and when they do, a good customer service provider acknowledges the mistake by apologizing. It doesn't really matter who is to blame. You need not accept personal blame, nor should you blame someone else. Blaming is unprofessional, and it doesn't help the customer at all. Apologizing is simply a matter of courtesy; it is a way to get past the mistake and begin to rectify the situation. An apology should always be followed up with a statement that assures the customer that you will fix the mistake, correct the error, or "make it right," whatever that may involve. An apology can be as simple as, "I'm sorry that happened, sir. Let me order you a new one."

Use Tact and Discretion

Carry out transactions with customers quietly and discreetly. This action is important whether you are a bank teller, a washing-machine salesperson, or an advertising consultant. The customer's business is no one else's business. Using tact and discretion helps your customers learn to trust you. If they trust you, they are more likely to keep coming back.

Checkpoint 2

Customer Interaction

Indicate whether each statement or situation reflects poor customer service or quality customer service.

1. "Well, I'm sorry you had to wait, but there were other customers here before you."
2. "Good morning, ma'am. I will be with you shortly. Please have a seat."
3. A service provider asks a customer to move away from a busy desk and to explain his situation again.
4. A service provider clears her computer screen and sets up a new file while a customer explains her reasons for returning a product.

Check your answers in Appendix E.

Customer Service and Ethics

We all have a sense of right and wrong. We agree that it is wrong to steal and to cause physical harm to other people. In fact, we agree so much that there are laws against—and punishments for—such actions. Each of us is responsible for obeying these laws. The laws, however, don't cover everything. We also are responsible for behaving according to a set of ethics. **Ethics** are the principles of right and wrong that guide each of us. Be aware that some actions may be legal, but at the same time absolutely wrong, or unethical.

Objective

KEY POINT

Whether an apology is in order or not, acknowledge the customer's feelings. Customers need to feel that you understand and sympathize with their problem.

KEY POINT

Ethics—a person's principles of right and wrong—must guide people in business transactions just as they do in personal relationships.

For some professionals, such as tax advisors or financial consultants, giving advice is what they do. Ethical professionals in these fields make sure their advice is well-grounded in fact and experience, and that they serve their customers' interests.

Ensuring Ethical Communication

Ethics in business begins with communication. Have you ever felt that a repair person was lying to you just to get you to spend more money on his or her services? Did you ever think that a salesperson wasn't giving you a straight story on a product or its availability? If either of these people lied, misrepresented the facts, or otherwise distorted the truth, he or she was acting unethically. Is this kind of behavior illegal? Usually not. Is the person communicating professionally and responsibly, or, in other words, in an ethical manner? Absolutely not.

Most professionals in repair and sales positions are excellent customer service providers. A relative few who follow unethical practices have tainted the reputation of all. Negative stereotypes about dishonest appliance repair technicians and underhanded automobile salespeople, for example, have developed. As with all stereotypes, the image is not accurate and is based on the characteristics of just a few people in the category, not all of the people.

One way to gauge your own professional, ethical behavior is to ask yourself this question: Am I treating my customers as I would want to be treated? If the answer is no, then you need to change the way you communicate with your customers. Being fair and honest is a good place to start. Make sure that you fully disclose all the information your customers need to make informed decisions. You can advise a customer, but make sure that your advice fits the customer's needs, not your own.

Another way to make sure your communication is ethical is to give your customers facts rather than opinions. You must even be careful about interpreting facts for customers. That isn't to say, though, that you can't explain something to a customer. What you must avoid is presenting facts in a way that misleads or deceives the customer.

Maintaining Confidentiality

Ethical business communication includes maintaining confidentiality. Private or secret information is considered confidential information. It should not be shared with anyone who is not authorized to know the information.

Confidential information may come to you from internal sources. You or your coworkers may be developing new product ideas or formulas. Those ideas or formulas are confidential and should not be shared with anyone outside the company, particularly anyone connected with a competing company. In some cases, a company may want developing ideas to remain confidential even from other departments or divisions within the company.

External customers are a vast source of confidential information, particularly in some fields. Customers' medical and health records, financial records, and certain aspects of legal and court proceedings are all considered confidential. If you handle confidential information in the course of your work, it is unethical to share it with anyone without authorization.

Be discreet when dealing with customers. All of your customers' business transactions and personal information should be treated as confidential.

ETHICS

Sharing confidential information, even with just a friend at work, is unethical. Your customers' business is private.

Following a Code of Ethics

We said earlier that everyone has a sense of right and wrong. We use that sense—our ethics—to guide our actions. Companies and organizations also use ethics to guide their actions. To communicate to both customers and employees their sense of right and wrong, some companies write their philosophy down. This written version, called a *code of ethics*, describes an organization's intentions with respect to how it treats customers and employees. Employees are expected to respect and adopt their company's code of ethics while conducting business for the company.

INTERNET

Many professional organizations include their code of ethics on their web sites. Learning about a profession's ethics could help you decide whether that field is right for you.

Checkpoint 3

Customer Service and Ethics

Indicate whether each statement is true or false.

1. A service provider who lies is behaving unethically.

2. A service provider who makes a mistake is behaving unethically.

3. A service provider who lies is breaking the law.

4. It's okay to talk to a coworker at lunch about a customer's financial situation if you don't name the customer.

5. Organizations as well as individuals are expected to operate according to a set of ethics.

Check your answers in Appendix E.

Technology and Effective Communication with Customers

Objective

6

The business world once relied on telephone calls, formal business correspondence, and face-to-face meetings. Today, however, business-people can use many different technologies to communicate with each other and with customers. The proper use of communications technology can be highly effective as well as highly profitable. The improper use of it can leave customers feeling left out, inadequate, or simply ignored.

Telecommunications

Communicating by voice is a direct, and usually convenient, way to contact customers. Telecommunications allow personal contact even over long distances. A service provider can make a telephone call to set up a meeting, to discuss a business proposal at length, or to answer a customer inquiry. Other telecommunications technologies have extended the use of the telephone. These other technologies add convenience, though they allow for less personal contact than a direct telephone conversation.

Voice Mail

When was the last time you made a telephone call and got a busy signal? It rarely happens any more. Individuals and companies use telephone-answering devices to process incoming calls. Your customers may have simple answering machines at home, which record messages on tape. Places of business may have voice mail, a computerized telephone-answering system that directs calls to specific recipients and also allows callers to leave messages. A blinking light on the telephone may alert recipients that they have voice mail. Recipients can retrieve messages from the voice-mail system at any time and from any location.

Most voice-mail systems allow individuals to record their own outgoing message. Keep this message updated daily to provide current information for your callers. It is obvious to your callers that you are unavailable, so record an outgoing message that is somewhat more helpful. Here's an example:

> Hello, this is Isabel Torres. I am out of the office on Wednesday, January 19th, but will be checking my voice mail periodically. Thank you for leaving a message.

There is an art to leaving a message on an answering machine or on voice mail. You may have received hard-to-understand messages on your own answering device. Either the caller talked too softly, too quickly, or too long so that he got cut off in the middle of his

---

> **KEY POINT**
>
> Technology should enhance customer communication, not complicate it.

> **KEY POINT**
>
> Even a recorded message makes an impression on customers. Use your best telephone voice when you record your outgoing message.

telephone number. Figure 13-2 describes what to say and how to say it when leaving voice-mail messages for your customers.

Voice mail is best used to maintain contact or to give brief answers to questions. Lengthy voice-mail messages are sometimes hard to understand and may be inconvenient. A recipient might have to listen to a long message several times to make sure she retrieves all of the information the message contains. In spite of this limitation, leaving a voice-mail message is easier and more efficient than dictating a message to a receptionist. And it certainly is better than getting a busy signal.

Whether recording an outgoing message or leaving an incoming message, communicators should analyze their audience and apply the principles of business communication. Messages should be brief, clear, and complete. They should focus on the receiver, not the sender.

What To Say	What It Sounds Like
Greet the recipient.	Hello, Mr. Andler.
Identify yourself and your company.	This is Cher Marconi from LX Systems.
State your telephone number (even if you are not necessarily asking the customer to return your call).	You can reach me at 555-0192.
Briefly state your purpose for calling. (If your message is long, complicated, or confidential, ask the recipient to return your call at his or her convenience.)	I'm calling to confirm our meeting tomorrow morning at your office at 9 A.M. I have the specifications for your new network all ready.
Leave the door open for communication.	If you have any questions before then, feel free to call.
Close the message in a friendly manner.	Have a nice day.

FIGURE 13-2 A model for an effective voice-mail message

Cellular Phones and Pagers

The common use of cellular phones and pagers means that people are within reach, whether they are at the office, visiting a customer, or somewhere in between. As a customer service provider, these technologies make you more accessible to your customers. If you carry one of these devices while meeting with customers, however, certain rules of etiquette apply.

TECHNOLOGY

Many customer service providers carry cellular telephones with them when they visit customers. If you must accept a telephone call while with another customer, excuse yourself and step away. It is rude to talk on the phone right in front of the original customer.

If you carry a cellular phone, ask yourself whether you *must* receive calls while meeting with customers. Consider how your current customer will feel if you use her time to take care of another customer. Receiving a call during your meeting with a customer sends the non-verbal message that the unknown caller is more important than your customer. If it won't hurt to be out of touch for an hour or so, leave the phone in your car, or turn the ringer off. If you must take calls while you are talking with a customer, excuse yourself and attend to the device. Unless a telephone call pertains to the business you are presently conducting, keep the call short.

Use the same rule for pagers. If it won't hurt to be out of touch, do your current customer the courtesy of turning your pager's beeper off. If you feel it vibrate, you can just reach down and turn it off. Don't try to keep talking while you are looking at your pager to see who called. Again, unless you are expecting a call that pertains to the business you are conducting, don't return the call until your meeting is over.

Be aware of the messages you send when you use cellular phones. It's probably okay to make a call from your vehicle to let a customer know you are running late. But don't try to conduct business of any length while you are driving. You need to attend to your driving. And the customer may feel (and rightly so) that he does not have your complete attention.

Finally, be aware that cellular phone conversations are not necessarily private. Think of cellular phones as mobile radio telephones. Because the transmission travels via radio waves, other people may be able to pick up your conversations on various electronic devices.

Facsimile Machines

Technically, a facsimile, or fax, machine is a method of telecommunication. The difference, of course, is that it transmits printed documents, in digital form, rather than voice messages. Fax machines are particularly useful for communicating detailed information, particularly if it is organized in a chart, table, graphic organizer, or any other illustrated form. The advantage of using a fax machine is that the transmission is immediate, unlike other means of sending printed materials. You can fax a letter to a customer and have an answer within minutes. Or you can fax some figures to a colleague in another city and then discuss them over the phone a few minutes later.

TECHNOLOGY

Even complex print documents can be transmitted quickly and clearly with a fax machine.

Be careful about sending confidential documents by fax. Fax machines are usually shared by a number of people within an office. Anyone who walks past the fax machine has access to the contents of a document that has just been received. If a document contains confidential information, it is best to send it by courier or mail.

Electronic Communication

Communication by electronic means is less personal. At the same time, it is convenient, fast, and increasingly accessible to business people all over the world.

E-mail

More and more of your customers, both internal and external, are likely to have access to e-mail. Whether your customers are at home or at work, they may have e-mail service through the Internet. Your internal customers—your colleagues—may use a companywide network (an intranet), the Internet, or both, to communicate electronically.

There is a tendency to be somewhat informal in e-mail, perhaps because many people use e-mail for personal messages. If your e-mail is work-related and the recipient is a customer, your message should be businesslike in tone and style, just as if you were printing a letter on your company letterhead.

E-mail is particularly useful for "broadcasting," or sending the same message or information to a number of people. However, sending e-mail is similar to leaving a voice-mail message in that it is not interactive like having a conversation is. For that reason, certain guidelines apply. They are listed in the checklist below.

KEY POINT

E-mail is quick and convenient, but should still be businesslike and professional.

Checklist for Sending Effective E-mail

❑ Identify yourself and your company fully. Don't leave it for the customer to figure out from your e-mail address.

❑ State clearly the purpose of your message. Don't write a message so brief that it leaves the recipient guessing what it's about.

❑ State clearly who will take the next action, what that action should be, and when it should occur. In other words, make it clear what the customer can expect.

❑ If you must transmit a lengthy document, ask the recipient if he or she prefers to have it sent as an attachment to an e-mail message. If so, the recipient can then handle the larger document in a more convenient way, rather than having to scroll through screen after screen of e-mail. (Always ask first whether the recipient's e-mail software can process attachments.)

❑ Type in standard format, using upper- and lowercase letters. Avoid sarcasm or other forms of speech that might be misunderstood in print.

❑ Proofread your message. As always, business correspondence should be error-free.

The Internet and the World Wide Web

Technology now allows customer service providers to supply service without *personally* contacting customers. If your company has a web site, that site is a form of customer service—it provides information to your customers. Even though there is no direct contact at first, you must treat visitors to your web site just as you would visitors to your office. Here is how to maintain a customer-friendly web site.

1. Make the site visually appealing. At the same time, make sure that graphic elements don't interfere with the legibility of the text.
2. Post a list of frequently asked questions, or FAQs.
3. Provide access to as much information as possible. Everyone who visits your site should be able to find something useful. Include links to other useful sites.
4. Organize information logically and effectively. Think about what visitors will want to know and how they will navigate the site.
5. Provide current, or "live," information on your web site. Your customers don't want to know what models were available last year or last month. They want to know what's available today, what color it is, and exactly how much it will cost.
6. Respond to e-mail from site visitors. Treat these as if they were telephone messages. Don't put them off because they are less personal and therefore easier to ignore in the midst of a busy day.
7. Treat web site visitors as individual customers, just as you would if they were standing in front of you.

The use of the Internet as a customer service tool will increase as the technology evolves and becomes even more readily available to the population at large. Customer service provided by this means must be conducted as thoughtfully as other forms of customer service.

Technology and Customer Satisfaction

Some people are put off by technology. You will achieve customer satisfaction only if you use technology tools well. The use of technology does not justify being impersonal, uncommunicative, or discourteous. You should use technology to improve and expand your ability to provide quality customer service, not just to do it faster or more efficiently.

Remember that your customers are individuals. Judge each customer's level of comfort with relevant technologies. Don't assume that everyone has a computer at home or is able to locate information on the Internet with ease.

As companies compete for customers, technology will play a vital role in their ability to provide quality customer service. The winners will be those companies that take the extra step.

Many colleges have web sites that are customer service tools. The sites are aimed at attracting new students and keeping alumni informed about campus events.

SCANS
Employability

Technology: Applies Technology to Task
The ability to use technology appropriately is a skill many employers require of their employees.

Checkpoint 4

Technology and Effective Communication with Customers

Decide whether voice mail, a cellular phone, a fax machine, or e-mail is the best way for these service providers to communicate with their customers.

1. A company representative is driving to a meeting with Customer A. He encounters some road construction and is likely to be at least 20 minutes late.

2. A project manager in a large architectural firm frequently has project updates to communicate to all the members of her eight-person team. Their offices are down the hall. The updates include schedule changes as well as technical specifications and other fairly complex information.

3. A media advertising consultant has some revised ad sketches to show to a client. The client is eager and working under a deadline.

Check your answers in Appendix E.

CASE 13:

Answers

Responses to Questions 1–3 in Chapter Opener

1. **How important is customer service to the owners of Floors & More? How can you tell?**

   The company provides a certain level of customer service in a number of different ways. The description indicates, however, that it is not a particularly customer-focused company. There is a showroom, but no employee dedicated to making customers feel welcome or answering their questions. There is a receptionist whose job is to answer the telephone. She does so, but puts forth a minimum amount of effort communicating with her internal customers or reassuring her external customers that their messages will get through. No one has thought to make Cal a more valuable customer service provider, whether to internal or external customers.

2. **What messages does Angelica's behavior send to customers? What could she or the company do to change those messages?**

   Angelica's message to showroom customers is that she is too busy with the telephone to be bothered with questions. The ringing phone is a barrier to communication, and that's not Angelica's fault. By keeping the telephone on her shoulder while she talks to showroom customers, however, she sends the message that she has no desire to answer anything but the briefest of questions. Angelica could be a better service provider to her internal clients by taking more complete messages for the salespeople. The company could restructure its staff so that one person answers the telephone and another person provides customer service to showroom customers.

3. **What role does technology play in how Floors & More employees communicate with both internal and external customers? How could the company use technology differently or more effectively?**

Obviously the telephone is the company's main link with its customers. A more sophisticated telephone system, with voice mail, would ease Angelica's burden in addition to giving customers more direct contact with the salespeople. The salespeople could carry cellular telephones so they could be in more frequent contact with the office. The office computers could be linked with a network so that the salespeople, Angelica, Cal, and others could communicate via e-mail. That would make it easier for Cal to be more active in solving problems when they arise. The company also could maintain a web site, so that customers can see photos of available products, get tips on decorating and remodeling, and send queries to the company for more information.

DISCUSSION QUESTIONS

1. What is the purpose of customer service? What emphasis do you place on customer service in your own life?
2. Why is receiving the customer so important? What two or three aspects of initial customer contact do you think are most important? Explain your choices.
3. How is technology changing the ways that customer service providers communicate with customers? Characterize the changes.

13·2 One-on-One and Telephone Communication

Communication and Your Voice

Professional singers train for years to make the most of their voices. The rest of us might benefit from some training as well. Though we use our voices in different ways, we still use them. Don't we owe it to our listeners to give them something pleasant to listen to? Don't we owe it to ourselves to ensure that people listen to us and understand us when we speak?

Quality

The quality of the human voice varies in a number of ways. Though you may think otherwise, you have control over how your voice sounds. You can change how your voice sounds. In fact, you do it every day. Have you ever listened to yourself? Record your speaking voice and listen. You might be surprised at what you hear.

The **pitch** of your voice is its highness or lowness. Most of us prefer to listen to voices that are neither too high nor too low. Television and radio broadcasters are taught to speak with a somewhat low pitch. A voice that has a high pitch or a pitch that is too low can be difficult or unpleasant to listen to.

In your everyday speech patterns, you change the pitch of your voice. For example, you raise the pitch of your voice at the end of a question. If you are talking confidentially to someone, you probably talk in a low, steady pitch. If you are excited or enthusiastic about something, your pitch may rise. A speaker with no pitch variation is uninteresting and hard to pay attention to.

Another quality of your voice that you can control is its volume. Use an appropriate volume level for each situation. If you are addressing a dozen coworkers sitting around a conference table, speak loudly enough for everyone to hear. Your listeners will think you lack confidence or expertise if you speak too quietly. If you are talking to a customer, only you and the customer need to hear what you have to say. Keep your volume at a conversational level.

The tone of your voice may be the part that customers remember the most. **Tone** is the way your message sounds. When you say, "Can I help you?" is your tone courteous or impatient? Do you sound bored

Objectives

After completing Section 13.2, you should be able to:

1 Recognize vocal qualities that are most helpful to productive communication.

2 Describe the factors that lead to successful one-on-one communication.

3 Identify techniques for communicating effectively on the telephone.

Objective

1

KEY POINT

You can choose how your voice sounds and, therefore, how it affects your listeners.

or truly concerned when you say "I understand" to a customer? Even if you *feel* bored or impatient, you can alter the tone of your voice to send a more positive message. Your success as a customer service provider may depend on it.

Clarity

The way you enunciate when you speak sends a message to your listeners as well. **Enunciation** is the way in which you sound out each part of a word. Clear, correct enunciation makes you sound intelligent, confident, and knowledgeable. Sloppy enunciation makes you sound like a sloppy person. The speed at which you speak affects your ability to enunciate. It is important not to talk too fast, especially on the telephone or when leaving voice messages.

Informal, nonbusiness conversations allow us to be a little less precise in our speech. At work, however, you should always use your best, most correct speech. Avoid shortening words. For example, do not say *hafta* for *have to*, *gonna* for *going to*, and *workin'* for *working*.

Pronunciation is the way you make a word sound. For example, a person might say *asteriks* very clearly, but that is a mispronunciation; the word is *aster<u>isk</u>*. Incorrect pronunciation is distracting to your listeners. It is especially important to pronounce people's names correctly. Don't be afraid to ask someone to repeat her name if you don't catch it the first time, or if you simply aren't sure how to pronounce it.

Most of us probably take our voices and speech patterns for granted. Keep in mind that your speech plays a large role in the impression you make on people. Pay attention to how you speak. Listen to others. What qualities do their voices have? Are they agreeable or unpleasant? Analyzing others' vocal qualities, as well as your own, will help you speak with a voice that is easy and pleasant to listen to.

One-on-One Communication

Whether you are talking to a friend, a family member, your boss, or a customer, one-on-one communication is the most complex form of communication. It also is the most rewarding. Sending appropriate messages through words and body language is critical to making ourselves understood. In turn, accurately interpreting a speaker's verbal and nonverbal cues is a skill we all must master.

Listening carefully, using appropriate body language, and interpreting other people's body language are just as important to good communication as speaking clearly and using appropriate words. The nonverbal messages you send by means of your appearance, posture, and facial expressions are strong messages. A receiver is likely to remember a nonverbal message even after he or she forgets a specific verbal message. A service provider who sits slumped in a chair may *say* all of the right things, but the customer is likely to walk away thinking about how bored—or rude—the service provider was, not about the helpful service he provided.

DIVERSITY

Don't avoid using someone's name because it is unusual or "foreign." Have the person teach you how to say it, but without making a big deal about it. Remember, your name may be just as "foreign" to him.

SCANS
Employability

Basic Skills: Listening and Speaking

Listening and speaking are basic skills that are vital to the success of every employee, regardless of his or her job.

TECHNOLOGY

One-on-One Communication Via Video Screen: Does It Still Count?

During the 1990s, automatic banking became an accepted and expected convenience. Automatic teller machines made it easy for customers to access their accounts from any number of locations at any time during the day or night. This approach to customer service brought about a real change in the nature of banking. The key to customer service became convenience rather than personal attention.

In spite of that convenience, many customers still prefer service from a person, particularly when making deposits. For that reason, some banks are testing "video banking" technology. At a video banking site, a drive-through banking lane is equipped with a video screen. On that screen is a live teller who is actually located in a nearby branch office. The teller attends to a customer, who is instructed to place his or her transaction in a drawer and push it closed. The on-screen teller's image is replaced by news, movie reviews, or product information while the teller takes care of the transaction. The teller's image reappears on the screen when he or she is ready to complete the transaction.

To some, the addition of a live teller, even by video, defeats the convenience and quick service provided by a drive-through banking lane. Others are comforted by the presence of a person taking care of their money. Whether video banking catches on or not is up to consumers. ∎

Parts of a Conversation

Whether a conversation is brief or lengthy, it follows a pattern. Think of a conversation as a process that has a beginning, a middle, and an end. More precisely, it has these five parts, or stages: greeting, introduction, exchange, summary, and closing.

1. *Greeting.* Whether it is a nod of the head, a brief "hi," or a more formal "Good morning, Mr. Harada," a greeting begins every conversation. The tone of a greeting should match the nature of the conversation. For example, a jovial greeting followed by the delivery of bad news would be inappropriate.

2. *Introduction.* Think of the introduction as a transition from the greeting to the topic of the conversation. An introduction may be direct or indirect. Many workplace conversations involve direct introductions: "Are you ready to meet with me about that report now?" Or, an employee who would like some help from a coworker might say, "How's your workload this week?" This question would then lead to the real purpose of the conversation, which takes place in the next stage.

KEY POINT

A conversation may begin with a verbal or a nonverbal greeting.

3. *Exchange.* The exchange usually is the most extensive stage of a conversation. During the exchange, the parties conduct business. Both speakers must use their oral communication skills as well as their listening skills effectively to make the conversation meaningful.

4. *Summary.* During the summary, the sender and receiver may briefly restate what they have discussed, they may state an agreement they have come to, or they may just give a sign that the conversation is almost over. "That sounds good. Let's do that," is a summary that both indicates agreement and signals that the conversation is ending.

5. *Closing.* The closing should be pleasant. Whether it is formal or informal depends on the relationship between the speakers. A handshake, a wave, or a pat on the shoulder may accompany a closing. A closing may also involve verification of what is to happen next, as in, "I'll put that file on your desk. See you tomorrow."

Guidelines for Success

Despite the use of electronic methods of communication, communicating with customers in person is still the most important form of customer contact. To create the impression you need for success, follow these guidelines for one-on-one communication.

1. *Relax.* Though you need to be aware of the message you are sending, being *too* aware of yourself can make you tense. Instead, focus on *sharing* information, on being communicative. Relaxing aids the exchange of information, which is what communication is all about. In addition, if you are relaxed, the person you are talking to is more likely to relax.

2. *Think before you speak.* Whether you are delivering good news or bad, consider how the information will affect your listener and deliver the message accordingly. Also, speak in a way that your listener will understand, whether that means choosing your words carefully or moderating the speed or volume of your speech.

3. *Listen carefully—and actively.* Listening carefully sends the message that you care what the other person has to say. It also fosters a trusting relationship with a customer. Watch the customer's facial expressions and other body language to get the complete message. A customer may say, "That's fine," but her body language may reveal that she is uncomfortable with the solution you have suggested. By recognizing her discomfort, you can take the next step and put her at ease.

4. *Use names.* Learn your customers' names, remember them, and use them. When you meet new customers, use their surnames, particularly if they are older than you. This sign of respect can go a long way toward building a relationship with a customer.

5. *Use eye contact.* Maintaining eye contact is one sign that you are paying attention to—and interested in—what a speaker is saying. It also helps you and the speaker focus on the conversation rather than on nearby distractions. Failing to make eye contact sends the

↓KEY POINT

Address all customers in the same manner. Don't differentiate based on your initial impression of a person's appearance or attitude.

DIVERSITY

The use of surnames and appropriate titles is especially important to people from other cultures. A businessperson from Germany or Japan, for example, would be offended if a business acquaintance used his or her first name.

message that you are nervous, uncomfortable, or perhaps untrustworthy. None of those messages will win customers.

6. *Maintain a conversational, pleasant tone of voice.* Be pleasant and courteous in your speech, even in a hectic environment or even if a customer becomes unpleasant or hostile. Don't speak in a way that indicates you are bored, upset, or impatient.

7. *Be honest and sincere.* Customers value honesty and sincerity. They don't want to feel that you might be hiding something from them. If they trust you—if they believe that you are being honest—they are more likely to listen to your ideas.

Checkpoint 5

One-on-One Communication

Indicate whether pitch, tone, enunciation, or pronunciation is creating a barrier to communication in each situation.

1. "I gotta check with my supervisor about that, sir," said the clerk helpfully.
2. "Please hold, ma'am, while I verify your account number," squeaked the telemarketer.
3. "Your 'realitor' can advise you about home inspections," offered the loan officer in his husky voice.
4. "Who's next? Please step up," ordered the clerk at the returns desk, glancing at the clock.

Check your answers in Appendix E.

Telephone Communication

Telephone communication requires the same listening skills, the same attention to verbal cues, and the same preparation as does one-on-one communication. In fact, you have to be even more careful about listening and attending to verbal cues because you lose the visual element. You can't tell what expression is on your customer's face, so you are completely dependent on what you hear. The person on the other end of the call is completely dependent on what he or she hears from you. Here is how to send the message that will keep your customers coming back for more.

1. *Plan calls.* Before you dial, make sure you have all the information you need. Jot down a list of points to cover during the call. You don't want to have to interrupt the call to get something from the other side of your office. If you are shuffling papers while you talk, the caller may perceive that you are disorganized or simply not paying attention.

Objective

3

↓KEY POINT

When answering calls, try to pick up by the second ring. This sends the message that you want to talk to the caller and that you value the caller's time.

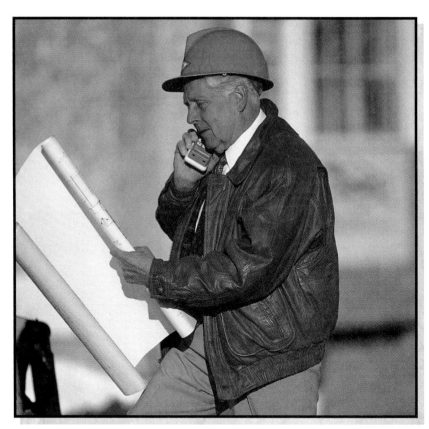

When handling business matters over the phone, it is especially important to listen carefully and to listen for verbal cues that will help you understand how the customer is reacting to your message.

DIVERSITY

Speaking more slowly is sometimes helpful when talking to people whose first language is not English.

2. *Identify yourself and your organization.* Greet the recipient by name and identify yourself immediately. Then briefly state the purpose of your call.

3. *Use a pleasant, low tone of voice.* Your voice conveys your personality, even over the telephone. Talking in moderate tones makes your listeners *want* to listen to you.

4. *Speak clearly and courteously.* Because your recipient must rely only on what he hears, it is more important than ever to talk clearly and perhaps a little more slowly on the telephone than you would in person. Your enunciation of words is especially critical on the telephone. Make sure you speak directly into the mouthpiece.

   As in any customer contact, be polite, and don't forget to say *please* and *thank you.* Also, ask the recipient if she has time for the call right now. If you've caught the recipient at an inopportune time, arrange to speak with her later. Be sure to specify whether you will call again or whether the customer should call you.

5. *Take messages accurately.* Take a message if you need to find information, consult a colleague, or refer the caller to someone else. Your message should contain the following pieces of information: name; organization, if appropriate; telephone number and extension;

date; time of call; an appropriate message; and your initials, as the message taker. Repeat information, especially the telephone number, back to the caller. Don't be afraid to ask the caller to repeat something if you're not sure you heard correctly or if you simply didn't understand what was said.

6. *Transfer calls efficiently.* First of all, make sure you know how to transfer calls correctly. When doing so, tell the caller to whom you are transferring the call and why. Offer the caller your colleague's number or extension, so that the caller can call that person directly next time.

7. *Close conversations cordially.* Again, *thank you* is always appropriate to say to a customer. If there will be further contact with the customer, make sure the customer knows when and how it will occur. Then close with something pleasant, such as, "Good-bye, Mr. Simms. Have a nice day." Always let the caller hang up first.

The main ideas behind communicating with customers—and providing quality customer service—all sound like clichés.

"Treat your customers like guests."

"Treat customers as you would want to be treated."

"Put yourself in the customer's place."

Clichés or not, they are all good reminders. Business communication is by nature cordial, respectful, and professional. Communication with customers should be all that and more.

Checkpoint 6

Telephone Communication

Rate the following methods of telephone communication as good or poor. Consider the employees' attitudes as well as what they say.

1. Kyle prides himself on his speedy customer service. He answers customers' questions as briefly as possible, assuming that the customers just want to be done with their business quickly. He closes his telephone calls by saying, "Okay. Bye."

2. Marly covers the phones whenever the company receptionist is away from her desk. She dislikes this part of her job and feels that she is much too busy to be bothered with it. If her colleagues are not available to take their calls, she takes the caller's name and number.

3. Sarin works at a bank. She answers customer inquiries about account balances, account statements, and various transactions. She hopes to become a bank loan officer in time. She always asks her customers, "Is there anything else I can do for you today?"

Check your answers in Appendix E.

Responses to Questions 4 and 5 in Chapter Opener

4. **How does Cal perform when he has opportunities for one-on-one communication with external customers? with internal customers?**

   Cal doesn't feel—or hasn't been taught to feel—that it is his job to talk to showroom customers. What he doesn't understand is that it is everyone's job to talk to showroom customers. Those customers are the reason that Cal has a job, so he should take care of them. Cal's communication with internal customers isn't what it could be, either. He is "doing his job" by processing the salespeople's paperwork, but he is not really taking care of them or the customers they serve. Because Cal has time on his hands, it would make sense for him to do some problem solving. If Cal could keep the paperwork flowing, the salespeople would have one less thing to do, and the customers would receive their orders more quickly. Also, the salespeople would gain more confidence in and more respect for *their* internal customer, Cal.

5. **What is Angelica's strategy for telephone communication? How effective is her strategy? Explain.**

   Angelica's strategy seems to be to "get it over with." Taking names and numbers for messages is an absolutely minimal method. She doesn't do the customers or the salespeople any favors by not taking more complete messages. She shows less respect to customers she doesn't know by putting them on hold to answer questions for showroom customers. At the same time, the showroom customers find themselves talking to someone with a telephone on her shoulder.

DISCUSSION QUESTIONS

1. What qualities do our voices have, and how do those qualities affect how we communicate?
2. What are two things you can do *before* you speak to a customer in person? Why are those things important?
3. Why is it especially important to speak clearly and somewhat more slowly on the telephone?

Floors & More does not have a very strong service culture. Almost everything about the showroom and the way the employees interact could be more customer friendly. The customers who come to browse the showroom are left to their own devices. In fact, there should be someone in the showroom whose sole responsibility is to take care of customers from the moment they walk in the door.

Angelica has her hands full with the telephone. If the company had a voice-mail system, callers could leave voice mail for specific salespeople. That would cut down on the volume of calls Angelica has to handle. Freed from the constantly ringing phone, Angelica could assist customers by scheduling appointments with the salespeople.

Cal needs to change his attitude. He should make himself useful in whatever capacity he can, including being more helpful to customers. Employees who are versatile, reliable, and who anticipate the needs of those around them are likely to be secure in their jobs.

Chapter Summary

Section 13.1 Customer Service

1 **Explain the importance of customer service.** Customer service is the element that gives companies a competitive edge in a highly competitive economy. Providing quality customer service is a way for a company to distinguish itself and its products or services.

2 **Identify external and internal customers.** External customers are people from outside a company who purchase the company's products or services. Internal customers are an employee's coworkers and colleagues. Both external and internal customers should be treated the same—with respect, courtesy, and honesty.

3 **Explain the qualities of courteous, professional customer contact.** Every point of contact with a customer is important. All forms of contact should be courteous and professional, whether the contact is in person, over the telephone, or in written correspondence. By being accessible, by providing knowledgeable responses, and by maintaining continuous contact, a customer service provider fosters a trusting relationship with a customer.

4 **Describe the appropriate way to receive customers.** To create a good impression, greet customers promptly and cheerfully and provide courteous service. Listen carefully to determine the customer's specific purpose. Apologize for errors or mistakes. Take steps to correct the error and satisfy the customer. Use tact and discretion in all dealings with external and internal customers.

5 **Discuss the importance of using ethical behavior when dealing with customers.** Telling the truth, revealing all information, being fair, and maintaining confidentiality are all part of behaving ethically. Unethical behavior breeds distrust among customers. Unethical behavior may not be illegal, but it is absolutely wrong.

6 **Explain how to use communication technology in communicating effectively with customers.** The common use of telecommunication technologies makes it easier than ever to stay in touch with customers. It is important to use the technologies effectively, however, or you may send the wrong message to a customer. Voice-mail messages should be clear and brief, starting with your name and number. Use cellular phones for checking in, but do not conduct business while driving. Transmit print documents quickly with a facsimile machine, but don't transmit anything confidential. E-mail is fast and convenient. It is best used for relatively short messages. Web sites should provide as much information as possible, so that visitors can find something useful or of interest.

Section 13.2 One-on-One and Telephone Communication

1 **Recognize vocal qualities that are most helpful to productive communication.** A voice pitch that is neither too high nor too low is most pleasant. Speaking at a volume that is appropriate to the situation helps ensure that your listeners stay with you. The tone of voice you use may send negative messages, even if the words themselves are pleasant. You can produce whatever tone of voice you want, regardless of how you feel. Enunciating clearly, not speaking too quickly, and pronouncing words correctly allow your listeners to concentrate on what you are saying, not how you are saying it.

2 **Describe the factors that lead to successful one-on-one communication.** Relax and concentrate on exchanging information. Plan what you have to say and deliver your message in a way the listener will understand. Use active listening and read nonverbal cues to interpret the listener's response. Use people's names; it is a sign of respect. Maintain appropriate eye contact both while listening and speaking. Use a pleasant tone of voice, and speak honestly and sincerely.

3 **Identify techniques for communicating effectively on the telephone.** Plan your calls and make sure you have necessary materials at hand. In your greeting, state your name and the name of your company or organization. Use a pleasant tone of voice, speaking clearly and a little more slowly than you would in person. Be courteous. If you must take a message, take a *complete* message, and read critical parts back to the caller to ensure accuracy. Know how to transfer calls, and do so as efficiently as possible. Always close telephone conversations cordially.

Critical Thinking Questions

1. Why do businesspeople feel that customer service is becoming more and more important?
2. What does the phrase "continuous contact" mean when it comes to customer service? What effect does continuous contact have on a customer?
3. When providing customer service, what communication skills should you use? Explain why.
4. What kind of behavior by a customer service provider would be considered unethical? Explain the situation and why it is unethical.
5. How can—and should—customer service providers use technology to enhance customer satisfaction?

Applications

Part A. Keep a log of the experiences you have with customer service providers for one week. You may have contact with letter carriers, receptionists, bus drivers, telemarketers, coworkers, or any number of other types of service providers. On a three-column chart, identify the customer service provider in the first column. In the second, indicate whether your impression of each service provider was positive or negative. Then, in the third column, note what the person did to create that impression. At the end of the week, take stock of the specific actions and behaviors that shaped your opinions.

Part B. Do some "shopping" in a mail-order catalog, and find a product that you want to know more about. Perhaps you need to know its dimensions, or exactly what material it is made out of. Use the catalog's toll-free number and make an inquiry about the product. Thank the customer service provider for his or her time. Then write a paragraph that describes your call. Rate the customer service provider as excellent, good, or poor, based on the person's response to your inquiry. Give specific reasons for your rating.

TEAMWORK

Part C. Work with a partner to plan and role-play the following situations. The student who assumes the part of the customer service provider should demonstrate excellent customer service by using an appropriate tone of voice, maintaining eye contact, and so on.

1. A customer is opening a new account at a bank and is transferring a large sum of money from another bank to the new account. The customer, a senior citizen, is sitting across a desk from a bank officer, who is entering information on a computer.

2. A sales representative is visiting a couple who claims that the floor they just had installed is defective. The sales representative can tell right away that the floor is indeed defective. She informs the customers that there must have been a manufacturer's error. The couple is gratified to hear the news; however, they are still upset by the problem. The customer service provider proceeds to reassure them and to tell them what will happen next.

Part D. Decide whether each of the following situations is ethical or unethical. Explain your reasons.

1. A washing-machine service technician evaluates a customer's machine and finds that some of the electrical wiring near the motor is damaged from a flood in the customer's basement. He doesn't have the parts on hand, and replacing the wiring is tedious work. He reports to the customer that the whole motor assembly needs to be replaced.

2. The salespeople at an appliance store earn a salary plus commission. Commissions vary depending on the make and model of each appliance. In general, the more basic models of appliances bring a lower commission than the more elaborate or well-equipped models. For that reason, the salespeople convinced the sales manager *not* to display the most basic models. Technically, the appliances are still available to customers.

TECHNOLOGY   DIVERSITY

Part E. A customer visits a web site maintained by a company that builds cedar play structures for children. He sends an inquiry to the company via e-mail, asking whether the company can design a structure to accommodate his son, who is confined to a wheelchair. Compose an informative e-mail response from the company to the customer, Mr. Tobias, indicating that the company can custom-design such a structure. Inform Mr. Tobias how the plan would proceed, once they come to an agreement, and what he should do next. Make up details, as needed.

Following is the body of an e-mail message from an organization's conference department to a customer, a potential conference attendee. Edit, proofread, and rewrite this memo to correct all errors.

> The instructions on the confrence registration from asked attendees to express their first, second, and third choices for housing. you listed only one choice on the form, and that hotel is full. Please reply via e-mail today so that I may know your further preferences. If I do n't hear from you, I will have to assign you to what ever housing is left.

words@work

If you are using *words@work*, complete the activities on Interacting with Customers in the Workplace Success section.

1. At a home improvement store, a sign in the paint department claims that "WE CAN MIX OR MATCH ANY COLOR." The paint desk personnel have a computer they can use to match items that customers bring in, such as curtains, or even an object in a photograph. The only criterion is that the object whose color is being matched be at least one square inch. One customer wants to match a narrow stripe in a piece of wallpaper. She says, "I'd like to match this color," pointing to the quarter-inch-wide stripe. The young employee responds, "Can't help you." In fact, what the employee meant was that the wallpaper stripe was too small of a sample to be able to use the computer to match the color. The customer, a bit surprised and put out by the employee's lack of helpfulness, says, "Okay, I'll go somewhere else," and leaves the store.

    Work with several classmates to develop the following role plays in connection with this scenario.

    a. Role-play the scene just as described.
    b. Now suppose that the employee's supervisor witnessed the exchange. Role-play a conversation in which the supervisor gives some constructive criticism to the employee.
    c. Role-play the initial exchange between the employee and the customer as it *should* have occurred.

2. The Internet can be a powerful customer service tool. Obviously, commercial sites have customer service—and sales—in mind when they create their sites. Many other web sites are service-oriented, even if the sponsor of the site is not overtly selling a product. Visit three of the web sites listed here. Use the list of criteria on page 458 to evaluate each site you visit. In addition, comment on any other factors that affect your impression of the site. Then rate

TEAMWORK

TECHNOLOGY

each site's level of customer service on a scale of 1 to 10, with 10 as an excellent rating. Justify each rating by summarizing your evaluation in one or two paragraphs.

- The Internal Revenue Service **www.irs.ustreas.gov**
- Major league baseball information **cnnsi.com**
- The U.S. Senate **www.senate.gov**
- Public Broadcasting Service **www.pbs.org**
- Detroit Institute of Arts **www.dia.org**

Career Case Studies

COMMUNICATION FOR HEALTH SERVICES

In some industries, such as construction or retail, competition for customers has always been fierce. In the health-care industry, however, competing for customers—patients—hasn't really been an issue until recently. Doctors now advertise to make themselves look accessible to new patients. They no longer rely on acquiring new patients by word of mouth from existing patients. In short, customer service is becoming more of an issue for health-care professionals as they realize that patients want and need to be taken care of in certain ways.

As a pediatrician, Aahmir Gulzar feels fortunate to be involved in a steady industry. Parents will always take their kids to the doctor, he thinks to himself. He and his three associates recognize the need to build their patient base, however. Other pediatricians are advertising in local newspapers. Everyone is busy at Aahmir's practice, Northwest Pediatrics, but still, the doctors feel they should be expanding their business. They agree to invest in a new office so that they are able to expand the practice. A site is chosen in a new commercial subdivision. The next step is to design the office. As part of their new focus on customer service, the doctors want to develop an environment that is customer friendly, for both children and their parents.

1. Design the waiting room or rooms and reception area for Northwest Pediatrics' new facility. Keep your external customers in mind. Consider decorating themes as well as the physical layout of the areas.
2. Write a proposal and accompany it with sketches or overhead drawings. In the proposal, include the reasoning behind your suggestions. Remember that the doctors will want to use the features of their new facility to attract new patients.

COMMUNICATION FOR HUMAN AND PERSONAL SERVICES

The Your Image salon is a well-established, full-service salon that caters to a steady client base. The owner, Jan Claymor, feels lucky that she has had very little staff turnover in the last two years. Her stylists, four women and two men, all seem content with their jobs and with the atmosphere at the salon.

Jan's newest stylist, Steve Edgerton, joined the salon about four months ago when Jan expanded her staff. Steve came well recommended. In addition, quite a number of his former clients followed him to Your Image. Jan is glad to have gotten both a good employee and some more steady clients. Steve seems to enjoy working with all types of customers, from the kids right on up to the older men and women. As a result, clients have been giving Jan good feedback about her newest stylist.

In the back room, however, where the stylists relax and take their breaks, Steve seems to do nothing but complain. Whether it's the weather, the clients, or the stale coffee, he seldom has anything good to say about anything. Some of the other stylists have begun to refer to Steve as "Bad News Steve." They try to take their breaks while Steve is busy so they don't have to listen to his complaining in the break room.

Everyone has noticed that Steve's attitude changes as soon as he is in the presence of a client. The employees all wish that the pleasant Steve would stay, and the "Bad News Steve" would not bother to come into the salon.

1. As Steve's coworker, there are things you would like to say, but you're not comfortable speaking to him directly. You wish you could just leave a flyer in the break room from a "How to Be a Good Coworker" seminar. What would the flyer say? As you develop the flyer, remember that you are trying to change someone's behavior, not his personality.
2. As his boss, what should Jan do or say to make Steve aware that he needs to pay attention to his internal customers as well as to his external customers?

Video Case

The Value of Customer Service

As part of his work toward a Bachelor's Degree in Communications, Kevin Morrissey's university requires that he do a summer internship. Although he had hoped for summer work with a public relations firm or with a company involved in cutting-edge Internet design, his academic advisor strongly suggested an internship with Hot Rods by Boyd.

Kevin soon discovered why his advisor had suggested Hot Rods by Boyd, where customer service really means communication. Much of Boyd's customer service communication is done face-to-face or by telephone.

Unfortunately, because of a fire at a vendor's manufacturing plant, the frames for several Boyd-designed hot rods are late, delaying the completion of several customers' orders. Kevin is asked to call these customers and tell them about the delay.

Kevin is now on the front line of customer service.

Questions

1. What does customer service mean to the employees at Hot Rods by Boyd?
2. Suppose that you are Kevin. You want to write a telephone "DO's and DON'T's" list for yourself. You'll keep it beside the telephone. Based on your knowledge of the chapter, what tips would you write as Kevin?
3. One customer of Hot Rods by Boyd, Arnie Falvo, is out of town. Again as Kevin, write a bad news letter, explaining the delay in Falvo's hot rod being built. Invent any needed details.

Contacting Customers

Dominic Lula and Opal Morales are the silent partners in the NetCafe in Milwaukee. They both want more information from Eva and Ramon before they provide funding for a new NetCafe in Chicago.

Dominic wants to make sure the original NetCafe is as good as it can be. He has asked Eva and Ramon to find out if there are any ways that NetCafe can be improved. (Dominic still hopes that customers will say the computers are taking up too much room. He can't believe that anyone comes to the shop just to tap away on those confusing machines!)

Opal, on the other hand, is ready to set up a new shop in Chicago. However, she is concerned about the possible competition for a shop like the NetCafe. She knows that Eva has already chosen a location for the new shop. Eva's fiancé, Nick, who lives in Chicago, helped her make the selection. The shop will be on the first floor of an old brick building in a renovated area on the city's west side. Opal wants assurance from Eva and Ramon that the people who live and work near this location would become customers of the new NetCafe.

Eva and Ramon decide to use two different questionnaires to gather the information for Dominic and for Opal.

1. Explain whether you think Dominic is justified in making his request.
2. Is Opal being reasonable about her request? Why or why not?
3. Regarding the questionnaire for customers of the current NetCafe (Dominic's request):
   a. Customers are not likely to complete the questionnaire unless they have a reason to do so. Describe a benefit that they would receive by filling in the questionnaire.
   b. Decide how to present the questionnaire to customers. For example, should it be printed on paper so anyone who comes into the shop can complete it? Or should it be mailed out with the monthly invoices? Or should it be sent as e-mail or in another format? Defend your choice.
   c. List the key points you would include on this questionnaire. In other words, what are the standards of quality customer service?
   d. Create a rough draft of this questionnaire by writing the questions and grouping them under appropriate headings. Design a way that customers can rate how well they think the current NetCafe meets each customer service standard.
4. Regarding the questionnaire for potential customers of the proposed NetCafe (Opal's request):
   a. Describe a benefit that potential customers would receive by filling in the questionnaire.
   b. Suggest at least two ways to contact potential customers and persuade them to complete the questionnaire.
   c. Describe the questionnaire. For example, how long should it be? How would you determine the potential customers' needs? How would you determine the level of their interest in the services of the NetCafe?

chapter 14

Employment Communication

14·1   Analyzing Yourself and the Market   14·2   Writing Your Resume

Brad's Job Search

Brad Adams is excited. Next week he will graduate from Hillsdale Community College near Kansas City, Missouri. He will be getting his associate degree in geography. While Brad is excited about graduating, he also is somewhat concerned. The economy in the area around Kansas City is good, but he does not have a job yet.

One of his problems is that he does not know how to go about getting a job.

He wanted to start his job search five weeks ago but did not know how to begin. His friend suggested he go to the library and get a textbook with a resume to use as a pattern. Brad did what his friend suggested. He went to the library, found a book, and wrote a resume listing his qualifications for any job. Two weeks later, he mailed out the resumes along with copies of job advertisements from a local paper. No luck! No interviews and no job.

Questions

1. How well does Brad understand the job-getting process?

2. How good was the advice of Brad's friend?

3. Did Brad start his job-getting process soon enough?

4. Based on his method of writing a resume, do you think Brad's resume is well written?

5. Why do you think Brad has not gotten any interviews?

14·1 Analyzing Yourself and the Market

Objectives

After completing Section 14.1, you should be able to:

1 Analyze your personal and career goals.

2 Identify your qualifications.

3 Analyze the job market.

4 Research potential employers.

Objective

1 👉

SCANS
Employability

Personal Qualities: Self-management
A wise man once said, "He who has no goals ends up somewhere." Who will determine where you end up? Will you set goals for yourself, or will you leave it to chance?

Your Job Search

One of the most exciting and important challenges in your life will be the job search. Whether you are just starting your career or are reentering the job market, finding a job requires preparation and planning. Begin your job search at least three months before you want to start working.

Personal Goals

This chapter explains how to conduct your job search. The first step in any job search is to analyze your personal and career goals. Thinking about your personal goals will clarify what is important to you. Answer these questions by writing personal goal statements:

1. What do I most enjoy doing? (Sample goal statement: I like cars, and I want to continue learning more about them.)
2. What are my interests? (Sample goal statement: I want to be involved in a business.)
3. How important is material success and fame? (Sample goal statement: I want to be financially secure.)
4. Where do I want to live? In the city, suburbs, or country? (Sample goal statement: I want to live in the country.)
5. Do I want to work in an office or outside? (Sample goal statement: I don't want to be in the office all the time.)
6. Do I want to work mainly with people? with machines? with ideas? (Sample goal statement: I want to work with people.)
7. Do I want to travel? Do I want to travel domestically? internationally? both? (Sample goal statement: I want to see all the major U.S. cities.)

Add any questions that will help you identify your personal goals. Put these goals in order of importance.

Career Goals

Just as you did with your personal goals, you should take time to think through what you want out of your chosen career. Write goal statements to answer the following questions:

1. What kind of work do I enjoy? What do I want to be doing five years from now? (Sample goal statement: I enjoy fixing cars, and I want to manage a car repair shop in five years.)
2. Where do I want to work? (Sample goal statement: I want to work in a suburban community near a U.S. city.)
3. How much do I want to earn next year? five years from now? (Sample goal statement: I want to earn $25,000 next year and $40,000 five years from now.)
4. How far do I want to advance? What position do I want to hold five years from now? ten years from now? (Sample goal statement: I want to hold my CPA in five years and head an accounting department within ten years.)
5. What is my ideal balance between personal and work obligations? (Sample goal statement: I want a career that allows a lot of free time for family and friends.)
6. Do I prefer steady, predictable work hours or a varied, flexible work schedule? (Sample goal statement: I want a work schedule that changes from week to week.)

Add any questions that help you clarify what you want from a career. List the most important goals before the less important goals. Compare this list to your list of personal goals to better understand what you want from life and work.

SCANS
Employability

Personal Qualities: Self-management
- Setting goals is not a one-time activity. You should review your goals from time to time, look at the progress you have made toward those goals, think about whether the goals are still important to you, and make any needed changes.
- Goals are achieved by careful planning. Once you have identified your career goals, you should think about the steps you need to take to achieve your goals.

Analyze Your Qualifications

All of us have unique qualifications, skills, abilities, and accomplishments that make us fit for certain jobs. Analyzing your **qualifications** gives you the information you need to prepare a resume and to sell yourself during a job interview.

Begin by creating a file to hold information about your skills, abilities, and accomplishments. This file becomes the basis of your **portfolio** (a folder, computer file, notebook, or small briefcase containing samples of your work, transcripts, letters of recommendation, and other related items). Here are some items to include in your portfolio:

Objective 2

- Academic transcripts
- Letters of recommendation and commendation (school, work, or organizations)
- Previous resumes
- Copies of job application forms
- Awards
- Test scores
- Certificates or diplomas of coursework completed

Next, list at least ten skills, abilities, and accomplishments that have given you satisfaction and that make you marketable. Include accomplishments that reflect your creativity, initiative, and ability to work well with others. You might list a scholarship you have received,

↓KEY POINT

As you analyze your qualifications, remember that few people are top performers in everything they do. Tell the truth about what you can and cannot do so that you and your potential employers can agree on a proper job match.

athletic activities you enjoy or excel in, your grade point average, and other information.

Organizing information about yourself in one place will help you remember important facts as you write your resume. This information also will yield clues about the right career field for you. Your file should include details about qualifications such as education, work experience, achievements and activities, special skills, and personal traits.

Work Experience

When identifying your qualifications, list all your work experience, including temporary or part-time jobs. Include the name, address, and telephone number of each employer; the name of your supervisors; salary history (if requested); dates of employment; and, most important, the major tasks, responsibilities, and skills that you developed or refined for each job. Military experience should be included in this listing.

If you have had no previous work experience, list your unpaid volunteer activities such as teaching Bible school or raising funds for charity. These activities show prospective employers that you can complete work tasks and that you are committed, ambitious, and responsible.

If you have had little work experience, your first resume may list only jobs that are unrelated to your career goals. For example, you might list a job as a cashier even though you are applying to be a receptionist. As you gain more work experience, your resume will show only those jobs that relate to your intended career.

For each job or volunteer activity, list any work-related skills you learned or applied. For example, if you learned or became more skilled in accounting while working at a paid or unpaid job, list this information. These skills are transferable and can be used in other work-related situations.

Education

Employers want to know how you have educated yourself for your career. List the names of schools you attended (after high school), the city and state, certificates and degrees earned, and the dates attended or expected graduation date. You also may include specific courses or skills that relate to your intended career and any special courses or programs you have completed. Include high school information if you have no post secondary education.

Achievements and Activities

In addition to your work and educational qualifications, list your other achievements and activities. For example, if you were treasurer of a club or organization or captain of the tennis team or won a local contest for your artwork, you should list it.

↓KEY POINT

Research indicates that individuals with a four-year college degree are likely to earn $500,000 more during their lifetime than a person with only a high school diploma.

Special Skills and Personal Traits

Next, list at least ten skills, abilities, and accomplishments that have given you satisfaction and that make you marketable. Then consider how your skills, abilities, and accomplishments can be used on the job. Employers are especially interested in your computer and communication skills.

To complete your self-inventory, think about your personal traits. Answer the following questions:

1. Do I have leadership ability?
2. Do I meet deadlines?
3. Do I work well under pressure?
4. Do I enjoy learning new skills? Do I enjoy teaching others?
5. What are my personal strengths and weaknesses?

With a thorough understanding of your skills and traits, you can make a better match with a suitable career field.

If you need them, many career counselors can help you with any part of this self-analysis by arranging for you to take aptitude and personality tests. Self-analysis can help you determine what you want, what you have to offer, and what career is right for you.

SCANS
Employability

Personal Qualities: Self-management
Once you match your goals and qualifications with a particular career field, you may find that you need additional education or work experience to get the job you really want. Consider working at a lower-level position or a part-time job to obtain the experience you need.

Checkpoint 1

Analyzing Your Goals and Qualifications

Indicate whether each statement is true or false.
1. The first step in any job search is to find the jobs available.
2. An understanding of personal traits is one part of a self-analysis that can help you select a suitable career field.
3. Volunteer activities can be listed in the work experience section of your resume.
4. Employers are not interested in your educational courses.

Check your answers in Appendix E.

Analyze the Job Market

Before sending your resume to prospective employers or scheduling any interviews, you need to analyze the job market. Analyzing the job market involves determining actual job openings and gathering information about organizations for which you want to work.

Objective
3

Both types of research are important to your success in getting the job best suited for you. Interviewers are more likely to hire someone who knows something about their company than someone who has not taken time to do basic research. Research can also help you decide if a company is right for you.

Identifying Job Openings

To locate actual job openings, go to school placement offices, check with personal contacts, look in newspapers and professional magazines, search the Internet, and use employment agencies or temp agencies if needed. Jobs are also sometimes obtained through internships.

School Placement Offices

Many schools provide job placement services. Placement offices assist both employers and student applicants by providing opportunities for both to meet. School placement offices also may have access to computerized job banks that enable you to search for openings or send resumes to many employers.

One advantage to a school placement office is that employers and applicants can be screened by knowledgeable personnel, providing a better opportunity for a good match between employer and employee. School placement offices also may have access to computerized job banks that allow students to search for openings or send resumes to many employers at one time.

KEY POINT

Job fairs are a good opportunity to meet with several employers in your chosen field in one day. As you talk with company representatives, you can find out about these employers and, at the same time, learn how your qualifications match their needs.

Job advertisements in newspapers can be a good source of available jobs in your community or across the country, and they can provide information about the companies listed.

Personal Contacts

An informal but often effective way to locate employment opportunities is to talk with people you know. This is called **networking**. Some of the best jobs are never advertised but instead are filled through networking. To organize your network of individuals, use "Wizard." This part of Microsoft Office helps you set up a database of individuals who make up your network.

Newspapers and Professional Publications

Check the job advertisements in your local newspaper as well as in any local, regional, or national business newspapers. Similarly, look through the advertisements in any professional or industry publications that serve your career field. Respond to these advertisements as quickly as possible and be sure to follow the instructions in each advertisement.

Internet

Another source of job openings is the Internet. Specific web sites were established for companies to list job openings. Most of these sites organize the openings based on location or job title. Through these sites, thousands of jobs from all over the country are at your fingertips. Some of these sites are

http://www.hotbot.com
http://www.jobtrak.com
http://www.careermosaic.com

http://www.careerpath.com
http://www.joboptions.com
http://www.monster.com

KEY POINT

Networking can be one of your most powerful tools for locating and landing a good job.

KEY POINT

Industry publications usually contain help-wanted advertisements placed by specialized employment agencies. You also can locate specialized agencies by asking contacts in your career field.

More jobs are listed on the Internet than on any other source.

DIVERSITY

Who Owes Whom an Apology?

Two months ago, new neighbors, the Durrats, moved in next door to Leo and Deborah. They seemed to be a nice family, and friendly. Since this was their first time out of their homeland, Saudi Arabia, Leo and Deborah wanted to welcome them to the neighborhood. They invited the Durrats to the Christmas party they were having for a few of their other neighbors. The Durrats politely thanked Leo and Deborah but indicated they had another commitment that Saturday night. When the time of the party arrived, though, Leo noted that the Durrats seemed to be at home.

Leo didn't think much about it until a few weeks later when he and Deborah invited the Durrats over for dinner. They arrived 20 minutes late, and no one ate Deborah's roast pork. When the Durrats left, Leo and Deborah talked about their dismay with the new family. If you were Leo and Deborah, would you be upset?

What if Leo and Deborah understood that the Durrats are devout Muslims, that Saturday is their day of worship, that they do not eat pork, and that in their country it is polite to be late for a dinner engagement? Is an apology in order? If so, who owes whom? ■

Employment Agencies

Both public and private employment agencies are available to match job seekers with job opportunities for permanent jobs with the employer. State employment agencies frequently have listings of jobs. To contact state employment agencies, refer to the government section of your telephone directory under your state's name.

Private employment agencies charge a fee either to the employer or to the applicant. Before signing an agreement, find out who pays the fee and how the fee is calculated. Do not sign an agreement you may not wish to keep.

Temp Agencies or Temp Services

In this era of cost cutting, many organizations use temp agencies to provide workers needed only temporarily—perhaps for only a short-term project. These agencies employ the workers for the project required by the organization. The agency is the employer, and it pays the worker and provides worker benefits. Sometimes, when the organization likes the temp worker, it hires him or her full-time and pays the temp agency a fee for finding it a good employee.

Internships

More and more companies are offering internships to students. An internship allows a student to work for a company or organization for a set period of time. Usually the student is paid for this work. Internships have become a common source for jobs because, if the company likes the student's work, he or she may be offered a position.

Libraries

Visit school and public libraries to scan the many publications available to job seekers. For example, you can research individual organizations in *The Best 100 Companies to Work for in America* by Robert Levering, Milton Moskowitz, and Michael Katz, Doubleday, 1993. These libraries may also have computer programs about building careers. Talk to the librarian for other sources.

Research Specific Organizations

Objective

Doing research on specific organizations is important to your success in getting the job best suited for you. Interviewers are more likely to hire someone who knows something about their company than someone who has not taken time to do basic research. Also, this research can help you decide if a company is right for you.

Conduct Your Research

To research an organization, visit a local or school library. Check publications such as company annual reports and *The Wall Street*

KEY POINT

Temp agencies are becoming major employers and are a means to move into a good job

KEY POINT

More and more internships are becoming available as organizations realize the benefits of better student education opportunities and improved recruitment of top students.

TECHNOLOGY

Libraries sometimes have databases containing a great deal of information about specific companies and organizations.

Journal. You also can find articles on individual companies in CD-ROM indexes such as *Business Periodicals on Disc* and *Business Newsbank.*

In addition to conducting secondary research, try to talk with people who are familiar with the company, such as employees, suppliers, and customers. Figure 14-1 lists data that every job hunter should know about a prospective employer.

Organize Your Research

Over time, you will gather or collect many notes, advertisements, articles, letters, and other items to which you can refer during your job search. Carefully organize your research in a file for each company, so that the information is available when you need it.

One way to organize your research is to use a separate file for each company. Each file should contain notes and any research materials about that company. As your job search progresses, you can add copies of job advertisements placed by the company in local papers.

KEY POINT

The skills in secondary research that you use when researching a report can be applied to researching individual organizations as well.

SCANS
Employability

Systems: Understands Systems
You should save copies of any letters you write to potential employers as well as any letters you receive. This process will help you keep track of questions that have been asked and other details that may have been addressed in the correspondence.

KNOW THE PROSPECTIVE EMPLOYER

Company Identification
- Name, city, and state of the home office
- Local address and telephone number
- Name of person responsible (if possible) for the department with which you will interview
- Name and title of the person with whom you will interview

Company Classification
- Business, government, or charitable organization
- Unique company features

Company Activities
- Production, sales, service-oriented, or a combination
- Any brand names associated with the company
- Company's competition

Company Size
- Number of employees, which indicates the size of the organization
- Annual sales or production output

Location of Facilities
- Location of the company's branch or regional offices, plants, or outlets

FIGURE 14-1 Information on prospective employers

A library is an excellent source of information for learning about a company that may be your future employer.

2 Checkpoint

Analyzing the Job Market

Fill in the blank with the appropriate word or words.
1. You should research the company identification, company activities, and company size before _____.
2. Keep all company research together in a(an) _____.
3. When seeking employment opportunities by talking with people you know, you are _____.
4. Thousands of job openings from all over the country are available to you through the _____.

Check your answers in Appendix E.

CASE 14:

Answers

Response to Questions 1, 2, and 3 in Chapter Opener

1. **How well does Brad understand the job-getting process?**

   Brad does not seem to understand it well at all. He started late and he did not analyze himself or the job market. He did not use his college's placement center or any other agency to help him.

2. **How good was the advice of Brad's friend?**

   The advice was not good. Writing a resume is not the first step in the job-getting process. Self-analysis and market analysis are the first two steps. Writing the resume is the third step. Also, using a resume in a book as a pattern for a resume is not good. Resumes should be tailored to the needs of the position for which you are applying and to the individual applying for the position.

3. **Did Brad start his job-getting process soon enough?**

   No. If Brad wanted a job when he finished school, he started much too late. You should start at least three months before you want a job.

DISCUSSION QUESTIONS

1. Why does the job-getting process begin with a self-analysis?
2. Should the areas of self-analysis vary? Justify your answer.
3. Is market analysis really an important part of a job search? Justify your answer.

SECTION 14.1 • ANALYZING YOURSELF AND THE MARKET   **489**

14·2 Writing Your Resume

Objectives

After completing Section 14.2, you should be able to:

1 Describe how to organize and prepare a resume.

2 Understand the opportunities provided by electronic resumes.

Objective

KEY POINT

- A resume is not expected to lead to an immediate job offer; the purpose of a resume is to open the door to a job interview.
- Resumes should look conservative, polished, and professional. The exception is in creative professions such as advertising where unusual, innovative resumes may be welcomed.

Organizing Your Resume

Now that you know your personal and career goals and are aware of the job opportunties, you are ready to apply for employment. This section focuses on how to organize, format, and write an effective resume.

A **resume** (sometimes called a *data sheet* or a *vita*) is a concise summary of an applicant's qualifications for employment. It should highlight skills and abilities that you want employers to notice. The resume is a tool you use to sell yourself to employers.

Employers receive many resumes and must scan each of them quickly. Based on the resume's appearance, the reader forms a first impression. For that reason, a resume should be easy to read, attractive, crisp, and clean. Use the following guidelines when writing your resume:

1. Use at least one-inch margins on all sides.
2. Print on high-quality, 20-lb. bond paper. Use colors that are appropriate to business, such as white, off-white, and gray. Use matching envelopes.
3. Use headings, boldface print, different font sizes, underscores, listings with bullets or asterisks, or capitalization to emphasize your qualifications.
4. Limit your resume to one page (unless you have extensive job-related experience).
5. Format your resume attractively on the page, using white space effectively.
6. Use parallel structure in headings and listings.
7. Never use the pronoun *I* as the first word of a sentence on a resume. For example, say, "Filed corrrespondence" rather than "I filed all correspondence."
8. Correct all spelling, grammar, and punctuation errors.

Use a personal computer to prepare your resume so that adjustments to content and format can be made easily.

Resume content may be either general or specific. Use a general resume if you are applying for a variety of jobs; use a specific resume if you have one particular job or type of job in mind.

Many resumes contain the following sections, which are discussed in more detail later in the section: (1) heading; (2) job objective; (3) special qualifications; (4) work experience; (5) education; (6) activities, interests, and achievements; (7) personal information; and (8) references. Think about the content you put in these sections. Be sure to omit any information that might cause a negative reaction. For example, if you have an interrupted work history, omit dates when listing work history.

When you organize your resume, think about its role as a selling tool. Choose an organizational plan that highlights information that will impress employers. Your resume can be organized in one of two ways: in reverse chronological order or in functional order.

Reverse Chronological Order

A resume organized in reverse chronological order presents the most recent work experience first and works backward to earlier jobs. Most resumes are organized this way. If much of your work experience is relevant to the job for which you are applying, use a resume organized in reverse chronlogical order. Resumes in reverse chronological order are shown in Figures 14-2 and 14-3.

Functional Order

In a resume organized in functional order, you present your accomplishments or skills in order of their importance, showing the most important or impressive first. For example, if a job requires strong communication skills, you might organize your accomplishments under headings such as "Writing Experience" and "Public Speaking Experience." Your educational background and job history would appear in later sections of the resume.

Many people, especially those who are just entering the job market or looking for work after a long period out of the job market, organize their resumes in functional order.

If you do not have much relevant work experience but have attended college or taken courses beyond the high-school level, education is your most important qualification. In this case, you should present your educational qualifications before your work experience. In all sections of a functional order resume, you may want to list items in descending order of importance. This technique will emphasize your strengths and deemphasize less important aspects of your background. A resume in functional order is shown in Figure 14-4.

TECHNOLOGY
- Many word processing programs offer a variety of typefaces that can give your resume a professional look. Use an ink-jet or laser printer to make your resume readable.
- Remember to use the spell checker to catch spelling errors before you print your resume. Careful proofreading is also essential because spell checkers are limited.

SCANS
Employability

Personal Qualities: Self-management
Keep a copy of every resume you submit. As you prepare for an interview, you can scan the resume sent to that particular employer as a reminder of what the resume emphasized and deemphasized.

Heading - - - ELENA DIAZ
145 Crabapple Road * Richmond, IN 47374-2187
(Day) 317/555-0148 * (Night) 317/555-0182 * ediaz@wjc.edu

Job Objective - - - CAREER GOAL:

To become a legal secretary at a large law firm with opportunity for advancement.

Special Qualifications - - - QUALIFICATIONS:

Operate microcomputer. Key 70 wpm.
Take shorthand at 100 wpm. Operate transcriber.

Work Experience - - - EXPERIENCE:

Legal Secretary. Charles S. Ballard, Attorney-at-Law, Richmond, Indiana, August 1998 to present.

Format and edit legal documents using computer and word-processing software, file documents with the courts, post to client accounts, make bank deposits, answer telephone, greet clients, make appointments, transcribe from machine dictation, distribute incoming mail, and file correspondence.

Salesperson, Carson's Department Store, Richmond, Indiana, May 1995 to August 1998.

Operated computer terminal, handled transactions with customers, set up displays, and stocked merchandise.

Education - - - EDUCATION:

Waynesboro Junior College, Waynesboro, Indiana.
A.A.S. degree with major in Office Technology.
Will graduate June 2001. Worked full time while attending college. Received Rotary scholarship.

Took elective courses in business law, business application software, and business management.

Activities, Interests, and Achievements - - - ACTIVITIES:

Special Olympics volunteer, 2000. Responsible for scheduling practice meets and coaching sessions.

References - - - References available upon request.

FIGURE 14-2 Resume in reverse chronological order (scannable format)

LOUELLA K. HINES

1247 Madison Road • Columbus, Ohio 43216 • (614) 555-5799 • LHines@mail.com

OBJECTIVE   Computerized Accounting Systems Auditor I

KEY SKILLS
- Education in accounting practices and computer systems
- Programming competence in COBOL and RPG
- Practical experience in EDP accounting applications
- Good knowledge of MS Word, Excel, Access, DOS, and Windows
- Proven interpersonal skills in an auditing environment
- Experienced in AS/400, PC, IBM MVS, and Novell LAN operations

EDUCATION

Bachelor of Business Administration, 2000 • Clermont State University, Columbus, OH
    Major: Computer Information Systems • Minor: Internal Auditing

Relevant Courses of Study:
- Analysis, Design, and Auditing of Accounting Information Systems
- Internal Auditing • Information Systems Auditing • Accounting Applications
- Database Management • Advanced Corporate Finance • Cost Accounting

Senior Internship:
Under the supervision of the Managing Field Auditor of American Interstate Bank, performed internal audits on the safety deposit box operations of five local branches. Reviewed the audit findings with the branch managers. Compiled final report and presented it to the Chief Operating Officer.

EXPERIENCE

Alexander & Swartz, Columbus, OH   9/99 to Present
Part-time Assistant Staff Auditor. Assist in audits of cash, accounts receivable, and accounts payable for mid-sized firms that use AS/400s. Interface with clients, audit RPG programs, and write audit reports as member of the Business Services Assurance and Advisory team.

Micronomics Company, Columbus, OH   6/97-9/99
Part-time Programmer's Assistant. Designed, documented, coded, and tested COBOL program subroutines for order-entry system on Novell PC network. Achieved a 95 percent average program-accuracy rate on test runs. Also cataloged and filed new programs and program patches for the company's software library.

Clermont State University, Columbus, OH   9/95-6/97
Part-time Computer Operator Aide. Using MVS system, copied files for backup. Verified accuracy of reports and scheduled print sequences. Recommended schedule changes that improved efficiency of backup procedures by 28.5 percent.

ASSOCIATIONS
Information Technology Management Association, 1995 to present
Columbus Computer Club, 1994 to present

FIGURE 14-3 Resume in reverse chronological order

Adapted from *Your Career: How to Make It Happen*, 4th edition, by Julie Griffin Levitt, South-Western Educational Publishing, Copyright 2000.

KIMI R. OKASAKI
148 Barrister Avenue   •   Tucson, Arizona 85726
(520) 555-9088   •   E-mail: KOkasaki@provider.net

OBJECTIVE   Administrative Assistant for MegaMall Property Management Company

EDUCATION

Associate of Applied Science, 2000, Community College, Tucson, AZ
  Major: Administrative Office Technology   GPA 3.6

PROFESSIONAL SKILLS

Document Preparation: Expert using MS Word, WordPerfect, PowerPoint, and Presentations. Enter text at 75 wpm and transcribe dictation at 60 wpm. Integrate tabular data and graphics into documents using Access, Paradox, Excel, and Quattro Pro. Write, format, and proofread printed and electronic business correspondence, reports, and newsletters. Research topics on the Internet (Netscape, MS Explorer).
  • Published printed and electronic newsletters and maintained correspondence for Valley Elementary School Parent-Teacher Organization (VES-PTO) for two years.

Spreadsheet Management: Set up and maintain Excel and Quattro Pro spreadsheets.
  • Designed spreadsheet to track results of three fund-raising activities for VES-PTO, which reduced reporting time by 50 percent.

Database Management: Configure, maintain, and generate reports with Access and Paradox.
  • Designed and maintained an information database to enable VES-PTO to study parent participation of 500 student families.

Bookkeeping: Perform manual (ten-key by touch at 250 spm) or computerized (Peachtree) bookkeeping functions from journal entry to end-of-period reports.
  • Maintained books for VES-PTO for two years and satisfied yearly CPA audits.
  • Computed daily cash receipts and balanced two registers as part-time sales supervisor of a department store.

Human Relations: Successfully cooperate with store managers, representatives of delivery companies and community organizations, and the general public.
  • Held positions of responsibility in four community organizations over the last eight years; chosen 1999 National Diabetes Foundation Volunteer of the Year.
  • Worked in two department stores: promoted to supervisor; trained new sales clerks; coordinated weekly inventory deliveries; provided customer service in sales and returns; attained highest part-time sales volume and had fewest sales returned.

EXPERIENCE

Community Volunteer, Tucson, AZ	December 1993-Present
Katz Department Store, Tucson, AZ	March 1992-December 1993
Value Variety, Tucson, AZ	Summers 1990, 1991

FIGURE 14-4 Resume in functional order
Adapted from *Your Career: How to Make It Happen*, 4th edition, by Julie Griffin Levitt, South-Western Educational Publishing, Copyright 2000.

Organizing Your Resume

Indicate whether each statement is true or false.

1. A resume is just a summary of a student's academic qualifications for employment.
2. An attractive, well-written resume can lead to an invitation for a job interview.
3. Leave at least a one-half inch margin on all sides of a resume.
4. If much of your work experience relates to the job you want, you should organize your resume using the functional order.

Check your answers in Appendix E.

Preparing Your Resume

Software packages, such as ResumX, are available to aid you in the writing of your resume. Typically such a package would include the following sections that could appear on a resume. The sections of a resume are shown in Figure 14-2.

Heading

The heading or beginning section should include your name, address, telephone numbers where you can be reached both day and night, and e-mail address. The following example shows a heading appropriate for a general resume.

HEATHER T. BRODY

| 53 Country Way | (501) 555-0129 (Home) |
| Bytheville, AR 72315-0105 | (501) 555-0111 (Office) |

If you are applying for a specific position, your heading might look like this (followed by an address and telephone numbers):

ELAINE WILSON'S PREPARATION
for the Position of Account Executive
with Webster and Sorrell, Inc.

Job Objective

The job objective (or career goal) is a brief statement that describes the type of position for which you are applying. It is optional. The job objective lets employers know if your interests match their needs. On the other hand, employers also can use this section to screen you out if your objective does not fit their openings. When you are unsure of exactly what the employer is seeking, you probably want to omit the job objective.

> **KEY POINT**
>
> If you send out resumes while you are away at school, you may want to show both your school and home addresses (and the corresponding telephone numbers).

Make your job objective brief, as shown in the following example:

Career Goal   To secure a position as a computer analyst with opportunity for advancement into a supervisory position.

Special Qualifications

A condensed statement of your main qualifications may be placed at the beginning of your resume so that a prospective employer will notice them. This statement should cite your strengths and achievements.

Special Qualifications   Skilled at writing computer programs using object-oriented programming languages. Extensive experience developing computer programs to analyze business expenses.

Work Experience

The section on work experience should describe, in the order that makes you look best, all work experience you have had that relates to the job you are seeking. For each job, list the name of the company or organization you worked for; the city and state; dates of employment (often included but not mandatory); the job title; and a description of your responsibilities and accomplishments. Show increases in responsibilities or pay if possible. When writing this section, use action verbs such as the following:

Action Verbs

administer	design	operate	revise	advance
develop	order	set up	analyze	direct
organize	supervise	calculate	increase	produce
supply	complete	initiate	provide	train
create	key	recommend	verify	maintain

In addition to functional order, work experience may be presented by date, by company, or by job title. Figure 14-2 contains a good example that describes work experience listed by date and by skills. The example below shows how to list your work experience by employer:

Telesystems Corporation, Lake City, Utah, Technician, March 1996 to Present. Prepare repair estimates, repair cellular phones, and answer customer inquiries. Operate testing equipment, analyze repair records, schedule customer repairs, and order parts.

The following example shows how to list work experience by job title:

Cashier. Wheeler's Variety Store, Snow City, Wyoming, October 1995 to May 1999. Assisted customers in making purchases and returns; operated electronic cash register; and handled cash, checks, and credit card transactions.

KEY POINT

You can group work experiences that are unrelated to your job objective (such as part-time or summer jobs) under a heading such as "Other Experience." Place this section after the section in which you describe your work experience.

Be honest about your job titles and work experience. Because some job applicants exaggerate their qualifications or distort work experiences on their resumes, many employers check work experience and references before hiring or immediately afterward.

KEY POINT

No matter what types of jobs you may have held in the past, you have gained skills that employers value. Similarly, as you search for a summer or part-time job, look carefully at jobs that offer the opportunities to learn or to improve the skills that you will use in your career.

When listing previous work experience on your resume, don't forget to emphasize the skills learned in part-time employment. As a cashier, for example, a person can develop money management and customer service skills.

Including extensive detail about all your work experience on your resume is not necessary. However, briefly mentioning summer and part-time jobs that are unrelated to your job objective will show prospective employers that you are hard working.

Education

If you are still in school, your education may be your strongest qualification. Begin with the most recent postsecondary school you have attended. List each school, the degree or certificate earned, the major area of study, and completion dates (month and year). Include credit and noncredit workshops, seminars, and classes if they relate to the job objective.

If you have excelled academically, include any scholarships, educational awards, and academic honors. If your grade point average (GPA) is good—at least 3.0 on a 4.0 scale—include it on the resume. List GPA as an overall average, an average in your major, or an average in your last 30 hours of schooling. Include information on military service if pertinent and if space permits. If you worked while attending school, indicate the average number of hours worked a week and indicate the percentage of your schooling you paid for yourself.

Education	Associate degree in Business Administration, May 20xx, Polk Community College, Winter Haven, Florida. Additional courses in management information systems and business communication. Worked part time while attending college. (Worked 25 hours a week while attending college to pay 100 percent of school expenses.) **Overall GPA = 3.55**

As a condition of employment, applicants frequently are asked to sign a statement that the information on their resumes and application forms is complete and accurate. If an employer learns that you have lied, you may be fired.

http://education-world.com/ is a good site for those seeking employees or a job in education. More than 500 jobs and 1,200 resumes are listed.

KEY POINT

Many employers value the leadership and technical skills gained by applicants who have served in the military.

KEY POINT

Participation in volunteer work, clubs, and other activities is a way of demonstrating leadership, diligence, and other qualities that employers look for when screening job applicants.

Activities, Interests, and Achievements

Employers are searching for applicants who are willing to work hard, who have creativity and initiative, who work well with others, and who have leadership qualities. List your activities that reflect these skills and qualities—leadership, public speaking or organizational ability, and a positive attitude.

Refer to your self-analysis (see Section 14.1) for relevant information to include in this section. The following are possible headings for this section, according to the particular information you are including:

- Achievements, awards, and honors
- Interests
- Activities and achievements
- Additional interests and qualifications

Personal Information

Personal information is optional. It includes age, gender, national origin, religion, race, disability, marital status, and number of children. In general, include personal information only if it is relevant and will help you get the job. Do not include a picture of yourself unless physical appearance is a listed job qualification (for example, for a model).

References

References are optional also. However, if you want them to be part of your resume, they should be placed on a separate page. Otherwise, you can include a notation such as "References are available upon request" at the end of your resume; however, even this notation is optional.

Some employers are interested only in work-related references; others are interested in both employment and academic references; some may want a character reference. Regardless of the type used, references should contain names, titles, addresses including ZIP codes, telephone numbers with area codes, and e-mail addresses. The following example shows an acceptable format for listing references on a separate sheet of paper:

KEY POINT

Make sure you are ready with the appropriate references when an employer asks by preparing two reference sheets. Show job references on one sheet and both job and academic references on the other. You could also have another sheet of character references.

REFERENCES FOR YING NIU

Mr. Donald Rowe	Ms. Cindy Logan	Dr. Amelia Torres
Hatfield Corporation	Brady Enterprises	Chemistry Department
33 Mitchell Street	64 West Palm Boulevard	Butte College
Chico, CA 95926-6432	Willows, CA 95988-4167	Oroville, CA 95965-1815
(916) 555-5423	(916) 429-6890	(916) 212-5005
(Employer)	(Former employer)	(College Instructor)

Before you include people as references, select those who will give you a good reference. Also, ask their permission to use them as a reference. If they agree to be a reference for you, let them know what kind of job you are applying for so that they can describe their experiences with you appropriately.

Checkpoint 4

Preparing Your Resume

Fill in the blank with the appropriate word or words.
1. The _____ is a brief statement that describes the type of job in which you are interested.
2. If you are still in school, your _____ may be your strongest section of your resume.
3. Including personal information on your resume is _____.
4. Work experience can be listed by dates, company, or _____.

Check your answers in Appendix E.

Creating Electronic Resumes

The two types of electronic resumes are scannable resumes and on-line resumes.

Objective 2

Scannable Resumes

A scannable resume is a resume that is prepared so that it becomes part of a file that is created by using scanners. To economize their search for employees, companies are using technology—scanners and specialized software. Many companies scan the resumes they receive and store the information using keywords. Then when a position opens up, a computer looks up all resumes that have "hits" in the keywords. For example, if a company were looking for an accountant, the keywords used in the search might be *accounts receivable, accounts payable, payroll, journals,* etc. If looking for a human resource manager, the key words used in the search might be *salary and benefits administration, training and development,* or *affirmative action.*

TECHNOLOGY
The trend is toward companies using computer technology to scan in resumes and using the created database to help locate qualified employees.

When submitting a scannable resume, follow these guidelines:

1. Send only originals on white paper with black ink.
2. Submit as many pages as you want (the computer does not tire when scanning).
3. Limit special effects to capitalization and bold headings. Avoid using italics, underlining, boxes, columns, or shaded areas because they sometimes confuse the computer.
4. Use font sizes 10 through 14 point only.
5. Mail flat resumes. Do not fold them because creases may make the scanner misread the resume.
6. Do not staple the resume; staples have to be removed before scanning.

The resume in Figure 14-2 on page 492 is an example of a scannable resume. Note the plain appearance of the scannable resume.

On-line Resumes

An on-line resume is a resume that is written so that it can be viewed via the Internet. This type of resume generally uses links to other screens, which expand on information that might be omitted in a one-page resume. For example, as part of work experience, the prospective employee could provide detailed job descriptions, drawings of blueprints, or other items of a portfolio. Look at Figure 14-5 on the following page for an example of the first page of an on-line resume.

You can key your resume using word-processing software, and the software will convert it to html and put it on a web site. In other words, you do not have to know how to program in html or be proficient in web design to be able to put a nice looking on-line resume on the Internet.

TECHNOLOGY

Most word processing packages contain parts that enable you to put resumes on the Internet.

Technology Is Making Us Faster but. . . .

Michelle Woelfel of Hypro Corporation said, "Today's business survives on communication. Finding ways to improve that communication, both internally and externally, gives your company a competitive advantage." Thus, technology companies strive to develop better and faster software to improve that "competitive advantage" of their users. But what impact is this technology having on the writing process?

Many college students are learning word-processing packages that will help them be more productive on the job.

When using these packages to develop a document, though, we all know that we must still proof the document before we send or submit it. However, some people proof only until they find their first mistake, and then for some reason stop proofing—leaving errors in the document that will damage their reputations. Word processing has increased the impatience of receivers. Not only do we expect a response more quickly than we used to, but we also expect that response to be perfect. After all, errors are very easy to correct. Right? Have you ever overlooked an error in one of your documents? Do you have others proofread your document?

An old Chinese proverb indicates that patience is a virtue— and it is even in the days of technology. ■

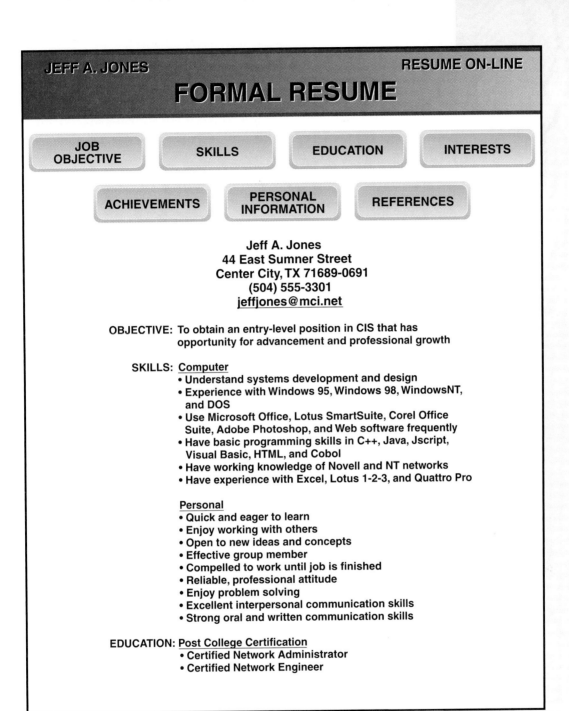

JEFF A. JONES   **RESUME ON-LINE**

FORMAL RESUME

| JOB OBJECTIVE | SKILLS | EDUCATION | INTERESTS |

| ACHIEVEMENTS | PERSONAL INFORMATION | REFERENCES |

Jeff A. Jones
44 East Sumner Street
Center City, TX 71689-0691
(504) 555-3301
jeffjones@mci.net

OBJECTIVE: To obtain an entry-level position in CIS that has opportunity for advancement and professional growth

SKILLS: <u>Computer</u>
- Understand systems development and design
- Experience with Windows 95, Windows 98, WindowsNT, and DOS
- Use Microsoft Office, Lotus SmartSuite, Corel Office Suite, Adobe Photoshop, and Web software frequently
- Have basic programming skills in C++, Java, Jscript, Visual Basic, HTML, and Cobol
- Have working knowledge of Novell and NT networks
- Have experience with Excel, Lotus 1-2-3, and Quattro Pro

<u>Personal</u>
- Quick and eager to learn
- Enjoy working with others
- Open to new ideas and concepts
- Effective group member
- Compelled to work until job is finished
- Reliable, professional attitude
- Enjoy problem solving
- Excellent interpersonal communication skills
- Strong oral and written communication skills

EDUCATION: <u>Post College Certification</u>
- Certified Network Administrator
- Certified Network Engineer

FIGURE 14-5 First page of on-line resume

CASE 14:

A n s w e r s

Responses to Questions 4 and 5 in Chapter Opener

4. **Based on his method of writing a resume, do you think Brad's resume is well written?**
    No, it is probably very poorly written. Following a resume in a book probably means that the information on the resume was not tailored for any of the jobs for which Brad applied.

5. **Why do you think Brad has not gotten any interviews?**
    Brad has probably received no invitations for interviews because he has not approached the job-getting process correctly. He did not do a self-analysis nor a market analysis. Also, he did not prepare his resume with any particular purpose in mind.

DISCUSSION QUESTIONS

1. What are the two orders for resumes? Why are there two? Should there be more?
2. What are the major advantages of an on-line resume when compared to a one-page traditional resume?

CASE 14:

S u m m a r y

Because Brad does not understand the job-getting process, he probably has severely limited his job opportunities. He does not realize that he needs to analyze himself to increase the probability of being happy in his work. He limits himself because he is restricted by not knowing where to find job openings. He does not know how to write a resume. His finding a job in which he will be satisfied is left to chance.

Chapter Summary

Section 14.1 Analyzing Yourself and the Market

1 **Analyze your personal and career goals.** By answering the questions listed on pages 480–481 about personal goals and career goals, you will have the keys to analyzing these goals. Look at your answers carefully. They provide the keys to the type of employment that will make you happy.

2 **Identify your qualifications.** Gathering your academic transcripts, letters of recommendation or commendation, previous resumes, previous job application forms, awards, test scores, and certificates will give you some ideas about your qualifications. Next, list ten skills, abilities, and accomplishments. Then look at your education, work experience, achievements and activities, special skills, and personal traits. These data should illustrate your qualifications.

3 **Analyze the job market.** To analyze the job market, find actual job openings and gather information about organizations for which you would like to work. Places to find this data are school placement offices, personal contacts, newspapers and professional publications, employment agencies, libraries, and the Internet.

4 **Research potential employers.** Before interviewing with a potential employer, research the company. If you need to, use databases, *The Wall Street Journal*, or the Internet for information. Besides gathering data about the company, make sure you want to work for that organization.

Section 14.2 Writing Your Resume

1 **Describe how to organize and prepare a resume.** Resumes can be organized in reverse chronological order or functional order. Reverse chronological order presents the most recent work experience first and then works backward toward earlier jobs. Functional order presents the most important data first and works toward the least important. The seven sections on most resumes are (1) job objective; (2) special qualifications; (3) work experience; (4) education; (5) activities, interests, and achievements; (6) personal information; and (7) references.

2 **Understand the opportunities provided by electronic resumes.** Many companies scan resumes when they receive them. Having a scannable resume that includes keywords means that you will be considered for that position. On-line resumes enable the applicant to provide a great amount of detail in a resume. This type of resume enables the reader to look at the information he or she so desires.

Critical Thinking Questions

1. Is the job-getting process difficult? Justify your answer.
2. Which is the most important—the self-analysis, the market analysis, or the resume? Justify your answer.

Applications

Part A. Write goal statements to answer the questions in the subsection titled "Personal Goals" (see page 480). List two additional questions that pertain to your personal goals. Then write goal statements that answer both of your questions. Write goal statements to answer the questions in the subsection titled "Career Goals" (see page 481). List two additional questions that pertain to your career goals. Then write goal statements that answer both of your questions.

Part B. Start your portfolio. Gather as many of the documents described in Section 14.1 as you can. Look for school transcripts, letters of recommendation and commendation, previous resumes, copies of job application forms, awards, test scores, and certificates or diplomas.

Part C. List ten skills, abilities, and accomplishments that have given you satisfaction and that make you marketable. Set up a qualifications file for this information.

Part D. (1) Select two companies or organizations you are interested in working for and list the following information: (a) name, city, and state of the home office; (b) local address and telephone number, if any; (c) classification; (d) activities; (e) size; and (f) city, state, and country location of facilities. Conduct your research using directories, annual reports, CD-ROMs, and other sources.

(2) Select one of the two organizations you studied in the first part of this exercise. Using newspapers, business magazines, the Internet, and other sources, research and list the following information: (a) current financial situation, (b) goals and philosophy, (c) company history, (d) person who owns and runs the company, and (e) recent acquisitions or expansion plans.

Part E. Select a help-wanted advertisement that interests you. Write a job objective for a resume tailored to that position.

Part F. Draft a summary of your work experience using the information in your qualifications file (see Part C). List your work experience in reverse chronological order by date.

Part G. Using the information from Part F, organize work experience in functional order according to achievements or skills.

Part H. Prepare your resume and format it according to the guidelines in Section 14.2. Tailor the contents to the job opening identified in Part E.

Editing Activities

1. Edit, paragraph, and rewrite the body of the following letter of application:

   Your company advertised for an adminstrative assistant in the December 9 issue of the Weekly Herald, which I subscribe too. I will be done with my studies in the Business Technology program at Central States Community College this month. And then I will be qualified for this position. Please consider me to be a formal applicant for this position. While attending school full time. I worked part-time as a secretary for Storrs Windows for over a year. In addition to my secretarial duties, I handled all payroll processing and petty cash. I supervised 1 clerical employee. If possible, please contact me at 555-0172 to arrange an interview at your earliest convenance. My background and education fit your requirements, and I would very much like to work for your company.

2. Proofread the following work experience section of a resume and edit it to correct any errors. Provide a revised copy.

November 99 to today	Assisstant too buyer of computers, Business Systems, Inc. in down town Atlanta, GA. Assist in in purchasing for 7 computer stores, negotiated with venders; compute price changes. Organise classes for computer trainning. Arrange for auto rentals, flite schedules, and hotel acommodations.

words@work

If you are using *words@work*, complete the activities on Finding a Job in the Workplace Success section.

Case Studies

TECHNOLOGY

1. Go to one of the Internet addresses listed on page 485 of Section 14.1 and browse through job listings until you see one that interests you and for which you might want to apply. Assume the following:

   • You are in your last term of school and will graduate in three months.
   • At the end of this term, you will have completed all courses required in your academic program.
   • Your GPA is exactly what it is now.
   • Your memberships in clubs and organizations are exactly what they are now.

   Print a copy of the advertisement you selected. Write a resume and cover letter for the position. Use the resume format that best suits your qualifications. Hand in to your instructor the advertisement, resume, and cover letter.

2. You are an assistant to a human resources director for a chain of supermarkets. Below and on the following page are parts of a resume and letter of application you received from an individual applying for the manager's position at one of your markets.

Resume Part (Reverse Chronological Order)

A. Work Experience

1999 to Present	Employed as floor sales rep for Loretta's Fashions in the Interstate Mall.
1998–99	Floor Sales Manager, Department C, SuperFoods Market, Bander, KY.
1997–98	Store Manager, SuperFoods Market, Lipson, AL.

B. Education

Graduated from Albany High School, 1992. I was in the top 5% of the class.

Graduated from Kilinger Junior College, 1994. I was in the top 10% of the class.

Graduated from Meng's Techinical College, 1997. I was the top student in the class.

Letter of Application Parts (Solicited Letter of Application)

A. Opening Sentence

> My training and qualifications make me a qualified candidate for the position you advertised recently.

B. Sentences To Sell the Applicant

1. I am very well trained as a result of my courses at Meng's Techinical College and know that I would be an asset to your company.

2. In 1997, I graduated top of the class from Meng's Techinical College. This is quiet an achievement.

3. My leadership skills were apparent while working at SuperFoods Market as store manager.

Write your boss, the human resources director, a memo in the traditional format. Make a recommendation whether or not to hire the applicant. Justify your answer by explaining what were the applicant's strengths and weaknesses. Use the correct order—direct or indirect. In a footnote to the memo, explain your choice of order.

Career Case Studies

COMMUNICATIONS FOR ENGINEERING AND INDUSTRIAL CAREERS

DIVERSITY

Jenni Zhang owns and runs a bus tour agency that caters to international clientele who want to see Disneyland, Hollywood, Beverly Hills, Las Vegas, San Francisco, and Seattle. The buses of Jenni's company are wired and equipped with earphones so that several languages are available on each tour. For example, this morning's tour of Beverly Hills was available in Thai, Japanese, Chinese, English, and French.

The visible people involved in Jenni's company are the tour bus drivers and guides, but many others also work for her. In fact, she employs about 120 people. Some are receptionists who book tours, computer technicians who keep the system up, mechanics who keep the buses in good running condition, and custodians who keep the buses and premises of the business clean.

Jenni has an opening for a receptionist whose primary responsibility will be to book tours over the phone.

1. What qualities do you think Jenni is looking for in this person?
2. What qualifications do you have for such a position?

COMMUNICATIONS FOR BUSINESS AND MARKETING CAREERS

A friend of yours, Bob Jackson, wants to apply for a position at Melvin's Department Store as the manager of the men's clothing department. He has a copy of the resume he used when he first graduated from college with a degree in geography. The work experience section of his resume is written up as follows:

> I started out at Jason's Hardware Store in September 1992 as a clerk in the electronics department. I helped customers and did a great job keeping the stock room clean and receiving freight. I got promoted to head of electronics department at the beginning of Febuary 1995. Also, someone was retiring from the electronics department, which gave me an opportunity to advance. I was head of that department for almost three years. As head, I arranged the work schedules of the department employees and was responsible for counting all inventory. I ordered merchandise from wholesalers when items need to be replinished. I sometimes had to resolve disputes with customers and employees. My current position, which I started in January 1999, is credit manager of Jason's Hardware. I evaluate the applicatons of individuals who want to buy on credit for the first time. The most credit individuals can receive at the store is $5,000. I also counsel individuals on the uses and abuses of credit.

1. Help your friend improve his resume by rewriting this section for him.
2. Describe the problems you identified with the original work experience section of his resume.

Reviewing Resumes

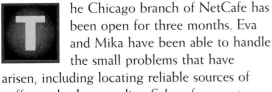

he Chicago branch of NetCafe has been open for three months. Eva and Mika have been able to handle the small problems that have arisen, including locating reliable sources of coffee and other supplies. Sales of computer services are nearly even with the income from the coffee counter, so Eva is pleased.

Mika is doing an excellent job of managing the coffee counter, but she is homesick. She wants to move back to Milwaukee. Eva hates to see Mika leave, but she understands. She misses her hometown, too, and finds excuses to go back there at least twice a month.

Now Eva must hire someone to take Mika's place. She places an ad in the *Chicago Sun-Times* and receives 48 resumes during the following two weeks. Several of the resumes contain typos, spelling mistakes, and grammar errors. It seems to Eva that applicants who are careless about their resumes would be careless managers, too.

She eliminates those resumes, along with the ones that do not describe the person's education. In her ad, Eva asked for at least two years of college. She assumes that applicants who didn't describe their education don't meet that requirement.

Eva's plan is to choose the ten best resumes and interview only those applicants.

1. Below is part of a resume from an applicant named Pat Cunningham. Analyze its strengths and weaknesses and suggest ways to improve it.

    Job Objective   To work for a company that offers opportunities for advancement.

Employment Experience

1999–present   Counter Sales, Java Hut, Naperville, IL
Serve coffee and other food products. In charge of other staff when the manager is gone.

1997–1999   5-StarTemps, Naperville, IL
Given various assignments.

Education

1992–1994   Wyoming State College
Paid own college expenses.

2. Below is part of a resume from Terry Williams. Analyze it and suggest ways to improve it.

    Job Objective   To use my skills and experience meaningfully.

Employment Experience

1998–present   Food Service Worker, City College, Chicago
Part-time position while looking for full-time work.

1997–1998   Night Crew, Burger U.S.A. Once chosen as employee of the month.

Education

1994   BS, accounting, Indiana University

3. Should Eva interview either one of these applicants? Why or why not?

chapter 15

Job Application and Interviewing Skills

15·1 Writing a Letter of Application and Completing the Application Forms

15·2 Interviewing Well and Writing the Follow-up Letter

Getting a Job and Frustration

Mercedes Suarez is discouraged and frustrated with the job-getting process. She recently graduated from a local business school and is looking for a sales position in women's fashions. She has sent out 12 resumes with letters of application that have resulted in five interviews with local employers who advertised in the paper. She believes she has done very well in the interviews, but so far there have been no offers.

As a result, Mercedes goes to her friend who works in a law firm and seeks her advice. Her friend wants to know the questions asked during Mercedes' interviews, how Mercedes responded, the questions Mercedes asked, what she wore to the interviews, and whether she wrote any follow-up letters.

Mercedes indicates that she answered all the questions honestly. For example, when the interviewers asked what she would like to be doing five years from now, Mercedes responded that she wanted to have her own dress boutique. And she brought up in all five interviews that she is engaged and that her fiancé will graduate from the local university next spring.

Mercedes goes on to say that the interviewers were very thorough, that she had been nervous, and that she did not ask any questions.

She further says that she wore the same type clothing she always wore to school—jeans, a shirt or sweater, and heels. Because she is 5'2", she wore three-inch heels to show that she was sensitive to fashion. Mercedes tells her friend that she does not know what a follow-up letter is.

Questions

1. What type of letter of application should Mercedes have written?

2. Can you tell how well Mercedes has written her resume and letter of application?

3. Did Mercedes' friend ask three good questions? Why?

4. Did Mercedes understand the interviewing process?

5. Did Mercedes dress appropriately for her interviews?

6. Would a follow-up letter have helped Mercedes get a job?

15·1 Writing a Letter of Application and Completing the Application Forms

Objectives

After completing Section 15.1, you should be able to:

1 Describe two types of application letters.

2 Describe the content of a letter of application.

3 Fill in an application form.

Objective

1

KEY POINT

An employer usually reads the letter of application before the resume. If the letter looks sloppy or disorganized, the employer may not even look at the resume.

Objective

2

Application Letter

During your job search, you will need to write letters of application, sometimes called cover letters. When you answer a help-wanted advertisement, for example, you usually should send a letter of application as well as a resume. In addition, you may send letters to prospective employers who have not advertised positions. If you are invited to an interview as a result of your letter and resume, you probably will be asked to complete an application form. Learning to write a letter of application and filling out the application form are essential to a successful job search.

Like resumes, application letters are sales tools that sell you. Application letters may be either solicited or unsolicited. A **solicited letter of application** is written to apply for a specific job opening, which has been announced or advertised. For example, you may be applying for a job advertised in the newspaper or for a job you learned about from a current employee. An **unsolicited letter of application** is written to apply for a position that has not been advertised or announced and may or may not be open.

Every letter of application has three basic parts: an opening, a body, and a closing. The opening paragraph states that you are applying for a position and captures the reader's attention, the paragraphs of the body summarize your qualifications, and the closing paragraph asks for an interview.

Opening Paragraph

The openings of a solicited and unsolicited letter of application vary a little. However, in the opening paragraphs of either type, you must capture the reader's attention so that your letter will be read. Include the following information in your opening paragraph:

1. Indicate that you are applying for a position.
2. Name the position for which you are applying.

3. Tell how you learned of the opening (solicited letter).
4. Identify your abilities (unsolicited letter).

In the opening paragraph, indicate how your background and experience can benefit the employer, as in the following example:

> Kevin Miranda, a job placement counselor at Newark College, told me about an opening for a sales associate with your company. In June, I will graduate from a certified program in marketing. My education and my three years of experience in sales qualify me for such a position. Please consider me an applicant.

Solicited Letter

If you are writing in response to an advertisement, you might open your letter as follows:

> In the July 21 issue of the *Sun-Times*, you advertised for a management trainee. My degree in management and my work experience as an assistant store manager qualify me for this position.

Often, an employee will tell you about an opening with his or her company. In such a situation, you might write an opening paragraph in the following way:

> When Terri Matsunaga, vice president of your bank, spoke to me about applying for a position as customer service representative, I became enthusiastic about the possibility of working with Second State Bank. My business administration degree and three years of customer service experience qualify me for the position.

Unsolicited Letter

An unsolicited letter of application is written to apply for a position that has not been advertised or announced and may or may not be open. Focus on your abilities in the opening paragraph of an unsolicited letter of application. You might open your letter in the following way:

> If you have an opening for an experienced truck mechanic, please consider me an applicant.

If appropriate, demonstrate your knowledge of the company's needs in an unsolicited letter:

> According to the February issue of *Changing Times*, many major companies need to fill positions for accountants. If your company has a need for accountants, I would like to be considered an applicant. I believe that my accounting degree, work experience in a CPA firm, and strong desire to succeed make me a qualified applicant.

Body Paragraphs

Your body paragraphs should convince the employer that you are right for the job. Instead of just repeating the facts presented in your

SCANS
Employability

Resources: Material and Facilities
The research into job openings and companies, discussed in Chapter 14, should help you tailor letters of application to specific positions.

KEY POINT

- When no opening has been announced or advertised, an unsolicited letter of application has to be especially persuasive and impressive.
- Like a persuasive letter, an unsolicited letter of application must have a relevant, attention-getting opening. It also must create interest and desire to persuade the reader to interview the applicant.

resume, interpret these facts for the reader. The second, and possibly third, paragraph should demonstrate that your educational preparation, work experience, and/or qualifications are relevant to the job requirements.

When you respond to a published job opening, explain how your qualifications meet those mentioned in the advertisement. For example, an advertisement may indicate that the job requires four years of experience with computerized equipment. If you worked with such equipment for three years and completed a technical course on the same subject, you would include this information in the body of your application letter.

Here's an example of an effective body paragraph that focuses on the applicant's work experience:

> As a quality control inspector, I worked closely with the plant manager to improve quality and reduce costs. During my year in this position, my department was rated Number 1 in quality while costs went down by 8 percent.

If you have not had much work experience, then concentrate on other qualifications such as your education, related activities and honors, ability to learn quickly, or enthusiasm. Note the wording of the following section:

> During my second year of college, I was awarded a Rotary scholarship. While working toward my associate degree in information systems, I was vice president of the school's Phi Beta Lambda chapter. As vice president, I organized and hosted a fund-raising event for muscular dystrophy.
>
> As a computer programmer for Datacorp, I will offer these same qualities of involvement and commitment that I demonstrated while in school.

Although the applicant in the next example has had little work experience, the applicant highlights qualities that employers value:

> While studying for my associate degree in accounting, I worked on assignments that allowed me to learn more about cost accounting. I will bring my diligence in completing my coursework to my work as an accountant with your company. Also, I have extensive experience with computer accounting programs and spreadsheets. I work well with others and enjoy being a productive team member.

You should also explain any information in your resume that may raise questions or cause a negative reaction. For example, if you took an especially long time to complete your degree, explain why in your letter. Here is an example:

> While attending college, I worked full time to support myself and pay for all school expenses. I took two courses each quarter and completed my associate degree in three years.

KEY POINT

When mentioning particular accomplishments and results, emphasize specific capabilities and achievements, but do not do it in a bragging way.

There are many companies with web sites that are eager to help you write a resume and letter of application— *some for a fee!* Using a search engine, key in "resume cover letter" and click on "search" to find such sites.

KEY POINT

When you explain any employment gaps on your resume, remember that you want to show your qualifications in the best possible light. Use the techniques you learned for conveying negative messages, and maintain a positive tone throughout your application letter.

Opening Paragraph and Body Paragraphs

Indicate whether each opening paragraph is effective or weak.

1. My considerable experience and two years of technical training make me confident that I would fit in as a medical assistant in your office.

2. I would appreciate your letting me know of any openings in your factory that I am qualified to fill.

3. Your advertisement in the February 28 *News Daily* for an office manager describes responsibilities for which I am well qualified through my college degree.

Indicate whether each body paragraph is effective or weak.

4. My 13 years of work experience at Pacific Southern have prepared me to move into a position as office manager with your company. Starting as a records clerk, I was promoted several times and now hold the position of records supervisor.

5. As my resume indicates, I will graduate from Housatonic Community Technical College in June with an associate degree in accounting. I have maintained a 3.4 grade point average while working full time as a bank teller for Midland State Bank.

6. The enclosed resume provides a complete description of my qualifications. The courses listed have given me an excellent background for the position you have available.

Check your answers in Appendix E.

Closing Paragraph

The closing paragraph should have a confident tone and ask for an interview. Make it easy for the employer to contact you for an interview by providing your telephone number again (it also should appear in the heading of your resume). Avoid the overused phrase, "May I have an interview at your convenience?" Instead, your closing paragraph should lead up to a request for an interview. Note the following closing paragraph:

> You will see from the enclosed resume that my education and experience qualify me for this position. May I have an interview with you to discuss my qualifications for the job? You may reach me at 555-0184 between 8:30 a.m. and 4:30 p.m. any weekday.

If contacting you would be difficult, consider the following closing:

> I would appreciate the opportunity to discuss my qualifications with you. Because reaching me at school is difficult, I will call you early next week to see when we can arrange an interview.

KEY POINT

The closing paragraph of a letter of application is like the action ending of a persuasive message. Use this paragraph to reinforce your main message—to ask for an interview.

If you are writing to an out-of-town company, mention if and when you will be in the area for an interview. For example:

I would appreciate the opportunity to discuss my qualifications with you while visiting Tucson next week. On Monday, I will call your office to see when we can meet.

2 Checkpoint

Closing Paragraph

Indicate whether each closing paragraph is effective or weak.

1. Because my qualifications are best described in person, I would appreciate an interview with you. Please telephone me between 2 and 5 p.m. any weekday at 555-0110 to let me know a day and time convenient for you to talk with me about this position.

2. May I come for an interview within the next two weeks? You can reach me at 555-0122 or at the above address. I look forward to discussing the possibility of joining your staff.

3. After you have reviewed my resume, I hope you will consider the possibility of putting my skills to work for your company. Please call me at (513) 555-0161, and I will try to meet with you.

4. As I complete my studies in March, I would like to know by March 10 if you have any job openings. Call me at 555-0128.

Check your answers in Appendix E.

SCANS
Employability

Resources: Materials and Facilities
Keep a copy of every letter of application you send. You can file the copies in the binder or file you set up for the company research you conducted in Chapter 14.

TECHNOLOGY
When you use a word processor or a computer to prepare an application letter, be sure to use the same letter-quality or laser printer you use for your resume. Before you print, use the spell checker to find and correct any spelling errors. Then carefully proofread your work yourself because a spell checker does not catch all errors.

General Guidelines for Application Letters

An employer will form a quick first impression of you from your letter of application. You can make your letters of application more effective by following these general guidelines:

1. Address the letter to a person. If you do not know the name of the person in charge of the department you will be joining (or in charge of employment), call the company to ask.
2. Use a simple writing style and indicate how your background and experience will benefit the employer. Make the letter brief and avoid using worn-out expressions.
3. Enclose a resume with your letter, and refer your reader to it in the body or closing paragraphs.
4. Print your letter on the same high-quality, 20-lb., white, off-white, or gray bond paper you used for your resume. Also use matching business-size envelopes.

Figure 15-1 shows a sample solicited letter of application. Figure 15-2 provides an illustration of an unsolicited letter of application.

Application Form

Most companies require prospective employees to complete an application form. An **application form** is a standardized data sheet that a company uses to compare qualifications of different job applicants. Employers invite candidates with the appropriate education and work background for an interview.

Using Sample Application Forms

If possible, fill out a sample application form for practice. If you have none, look at a copy of a form you have completed for a previous job. This sample should include information such as social security number, work experience (dates, addresses, supervisors, salaries), education (dates, schools, GPAs), and references (names, addresses, telephone numbers, and e-mail addresses—if available). If you have certifications or licenses, include the date granted and the number assigned for each.

If you obtain a copy of the company's application form in advance, copy it to practice on. Type or print neatly. Copy the completed form for your qualifications file. Figure 15-3 on page 519 shows a sample application form.

Completing the Employer's Application Form

When you visit a prospective employer, take all the information needed to complete an application form. Take with you a copy of your resume and your sample application form. Use the following suggestions when filling out an application form:

- Use a pen that writes clearly and sharply with blue or black ink.
- Skim through the application form before filling in any information to get an idea of the kinds of information you need to supply.
- Read all instructions before you start to write on the application form.
- Answer all questions on the application form. If a question or section does not apply to you, write N/A (for not applicable).
- Sign the application form to certify that all information is correct.
- Research the market so that you are aware of the salary range possible. Some application forms have questions about desired salary.
- If the application form has space for references, list the names from the reference sheet you prepared in Chapter 14.
- Take time and care in completing the application form to increase your chances of being offered the job.

Objective

TECHNOLOGY
Some employers use computers to read and store completed application forms. Applications in the computer database can be searched when the employer is seeking candidates with particular skills or qualifications.

Some application forms require prospective employees to certify that they have not omitted any significant information. Before you sign your form, check once more to make sure you have not left out anything significant.

SCANS
Employability

Resources: Materials and Facilities
Request a copy of your completed application form before leaving the employer's office. You can keep this copy for later reference.

FIGURE 15-1 (Solicited application letter)

506 Northwest Highway
Clovis, NM 88021-1304
April 30, 20—

Mrs. Sandra Markham
Director of Human Resources
Mountain Finance, Inc.
32 Commerce Way
Portales, NM 88130-5432

Dear Mrs. Markham:

My bookkeeping experience and college degree in Administrative Technologies have prepared me for the position of accounts receivable clerk that you advertised in the *Chronicle* on April 29.

In addition to more than two years of experience as a bookkeeper for a busy sales office, I recently completed an advanced workshop in collection techniques to supplement my college studies. The skills I gained from this workshop will enable me to work more effectively with Mountain Finance's customers.

As you can see from the enclosed resume, my background fits all the requirements mentioned in your advertisement. I would appreciate the opportunity to discuss my qualifications in person. After 2 p.m. on weekdays, you can reach me at (505) 555-0291.

Sincerely yours

Arnold Richter

Arnold Richter

Enclosure

FIGURE 15-1 Solicited application letter

FIGURE 15-2 (Unsolicited application letter)

175 River Road
Hartford, WI 53027-1093
November 20, 20—

Dr. Anthony Marchi
Director of Medical Services
Atlantic Manufacturing
902 Main Street
Hartford, WI 53027-2951

Dear Dr. Marchi:

The Hartford News recently reported that Atlantic Manufacturing is expanding its medical services center. With this larger facility scheduled to open next month, will you have an opening for a recent college graduate trained in physical therapy?

The skills I developed from a combination of college coursework and hands-on experience during a six-month clinical internship will enable me to assist Atlantic Manufacturing employees who require physical therapy due to work injuries. While earning my associate in science degree as a physical therapy assistant, I also completed a special research project on human motor patterns in repetitive manufacturing.

During my internship at the Hartford Clinic, I learned to use hydrotherapy, electrotherapy, massage, and chest physical therapy to treat a variety of conditions. In addition, studying under registered physical therapists who have consulted with leading Wisconsin manufacturers gave me valuable insight into the nature and treatment of assembly line injuries.

My education and internship experience, along with my desire to meet new challenges, would make me an asset to your company's medical services center. After you have reviewed the enclosed resume, could we meet to discuss my qualifications? Please call me at 555-6684.

Sincerely yours,

Anne Monaco

Anne Monaco

Enclosure

FIGURE 15-2 Unsolicited application letter

APPLICATION FOR EMPLOYMENT

Please print or type.   An Equal Opportunity Employer

Name	Address	City/State/Zip
Donna Monroe	602 Elm Street	Buffalo, NY 14240-1712

Telephone Number	Social Security Number
(716) 555-0025	123-456-7890

U.S. Citizen? Yes No	Position Applying for?	Desired Salary?
Yes	Bookkeeper	Open

WORK EXPERIENCE

Current/Most Recent Employer	Address
Corner Pharmacy	Buffalo Shopping Center, Buffalo, NY 14241-1342

Job Title	Dates of Employment from 10/96 to /Present
Cashier	

Supervisor	Salary	Reason for Leaving?
Mrs. Glenfield	$6.50/hour	Seeking full-time career position

Previous Employer	Address

Job Title	Dates of Employment from / to /

Supervisor	Salary	Reason for Leaving?

Previous Employer	Address

Job Title	Dates of Employment from / to /

Supervisor	Salary	Reason for Leaving?

EDUCATION

High School	City and State	Attended from 8/92 to 6/96
South Buffalo High School	Buffalo, NY	

GPA	Degree	Activities, Honors
B+	Diploma	Junior Achievement club member

College	City and State	Attended from 9/96 to 6/98
Lakeside Community College	Buffalo, NY	

GPA	Degree	Activities, Honors
3.5	A.S., Accounting	

SPECIAL SKILLS, LICENSES, TRAINING, OR MILITARY EXPERIENCE

Coursework in contemporary tax compliance, accounting information systems.

REFERENCES (*Do not include the names of relatives or former employers*)

Name	Address	Telephone Number
1. James Lerner (instructor)	Lakeside Community College, Buffalo, NY 14242-6415	(716)555-1100
2. Rosa Sanchez (instructor)	Lakeside Community College, Buffalo, NY 14242-6415	(716)555-1100
3. Tom Rowan (neighbor)	605 Elm Street, Buffalo, NY 14240-1714	(716)555-3854

CERTIFICATION

I certify that all information on this application is true. I understand that termination may result if any information is found to be untrue. I understand that employment is subject to passing drug tests conducted at the direction of the Company.

(sign) *Donna Monroe*   July 6, 20—

Signature   Date

Form 956 Rev. 8/98

FIGURE 15-3 Sample application form

DIVERSITY

Advertising, Business, and Language

Cultural differences include differences in language. When PepsiCo, Inc., tried to translate one of its advertisements into different languages, it ran into trouble. When translated into German, the slogan "Come alive with Pepsi" meant "Come out of the grave with Pepsi." In Asia, the translation meant "Bring your ancestors back from the dead with Pepsi."

Obviously, these translations did not work!

In France, a large American bank was trying to buy a bank from a Middle Eastern nation. The language being used for this business deal was French. In final negotiations, the American bank suggested that present loans be put in an escrow account—a common practice in such transactions.

However, the word "escrow" translates into "cheater" in some languages. The Middle Eastern businesspeople were insulted and angry—to the extent that they sold the bank to a competitor. ■

Source: O. C. Ferrell and John Fraedrich, *Business Ethics: Ethical Decision Making and Cases, 2nd edition* (Houghton Mifflin Compnay, 1994): 193.

CASE 15:
Answers

Responses to Questions 1 and 2

1. **What type of letter of application should Mercedes have written?**
   Because the position Mercedes applied for had been advertised, she should have written a solicited letter of application.

2. **Can you tell how well Mercedes has written her resume and letter of application?**
   Yes, you can tell to some extent. She must have written them well because of the number of interviews she received.

DISCUSSION QUESTIONS

1. How does a solicited letter of application differ from an unsolicited letter of application?
2. Is the format for a solicited letter of application and an unsolicited letter of application the same? If not, how do they they differ and why?
3. What is an application form and how is it used?

Interviewing Well and Writing the Follow-up Letter

Objectives

After completing Section 15.2, you should be able to:

1 Discuss the purpose of a job interview.

2 Explain how to prepare for an interview.

3 Understand the skills necessary for a successful interview.

4 Write a follow-up letter.

The Purpose of a Job Interview

Employers generally do not hire solely on the basis of a resume. They want to talk with job applicants to determine if they are qualified for the position and if they are a good fit for the company. Every applicant is competing with other applicants who want the same job. The interview process allows an employer to compare applicants and decide which person to hire.

As a job applicant, you can use the interview as an opportunity to determine if you want to work for a particular company. Use the time spent in your interview to evaluate the organization and the job through your observations and questions.

Interviews may last anywhere from 20 minutes to several hours and take place on a single day or over several days. During the interview process, you may be interviewed by one person or by several persons. How you present yourself is crucial—as with resumes, first impressions count. An interviewer often makes a decision not to hire during the first 15 seconds of an interview. That is one reason it is so important for you to be well prepared.

Objective
1

Preparing for the Job Interview

Your success in an interview depends in large part on your preparation. Preparation includes investigating the company and the position, anticipating questions that may be asked, preparing questions you want to ask, and other preliminary activities.

Objective

2

Investigate the Company and the Job

Before the interview, find out pertinent information about the company. Review the research you conducted before applying for the job and fill in any gaps about products, facilities, and other details that may be discussed during the interview.

Learn as much as you can about the job opening before you interview. Check with the person who suggested you apply at the company, ask current and former employees, or work with counselors in

TECHNOLOGY

Use your research skills to uncover additional sources of information about the job, its requirements, and general salary levels. Check to see if the company has a web site that contains job descriptions.

↓KEY POINT

- Memorizing each answer is not a good idea. Memoriza-tion prevents you from adapting answers to a particular company, job, or situation.
- Prepare questions that will reveal both positive and negative aspects of a job and a company. The answers to these questions will provide additional information to factor into your decision of whether to accept or reject the position.

↓KEY POINT

Many companies insist on seeing documentation to prove an applicant's qualifications. For example, someone who claims to be a graduate of a particular college should be prepared to bring in a final transcript or degree as proof.

your placement office to get the following information: (1) job title and responsibilities, (2) qualifications, (3) salary range and benefits, and (4) advancement opportunities.

Anticipate Questions

Before interviewing for a job, prepare yourself for probable questions from the interviewer. Nervousness during an interview is natural. However, preparing to answer typical questions will help to relieve your anxiety. Expect to be asked about your work experience, education, goals, self-concept, and relationships with others. Figure 15-4 shows a list of frequently asked questions. Write down brief but complete answers to these questions, and practice the answers, possibly taping them to hear how you sound.

Prepare Questions to Ask

During the interview, you may be asked if you have any questions. Be prepared to ask questions that demonstrate your interest and professionalism. At the same time, your questions should help you learn more about how you might fit with the position and the company. Remember, you are trying to determine if you want to accept this position if it is offered to you. Keep your questions related to the job and the company. Until you are offered a position, avoid asking questions about salary or benefits. Here are some questions you might ask:

1. What would my major responsibilities be?
2. What qualities are you seeking in the person for this job?
3. Does your company have training programs?
4. What would you like to see a person accomplish in this job?
5. What are the major tasks to be accomplished in this job?
6. What is the typical career path for someone in this job?
7. What are the company's plans for new products? new services?
8. Where are the company's major markets? Will the company be expanding to new markets?

Practice for the Interview

If possible, ask someone to videotape you in a mock interview. Viewing the interview will help you assess your interview skills, particularly your nonverbal skills (body language), and improve them. You also will be able to analyze how your answers sound to an interviewer and then make any needed changes.

Bring Appropriate Information

Take to your interview an extra copy or two of your resume and reference list, a completed sample application form (to help you fill in the employer's application form), two pens, a small notebook, a small calendar, and perhaps a portfolio containing samples of your work, transcripts, and letters of recommendation and commendation. If the interviewer asks questions related to these items, you may indicate that you have brought them with you and offer to show them.

COMMONLY ASKED INTERVIEW QUESTIONS

Educational Experiences
1. Why did you major in _____?
2. Which courses did you like best? least? Why?
3. What motivated you to seek a college education?

Work Experiences
4. Why do you want to work for our company?
5. What kind of work did you do in your last job? What were your responsibilities?
6. Describe a typical day on your last (or present) job.
7. What was the most difficult problem you encountered on your last (or present) job and how did you handle it?
8. What did you like best about your previous positions? least?
9. Why did you leave your last job (or want to leave your present job)?
10. What do you know about our company?
11. What aspects of this job appeal to you most?

Human Relations
12. What kind of people do you enjoy working with? find difficult working with?
13. How do you get along with other students? with instructors? with coworkers or supervisors?
14. In your previous jobs, how much of your work did you do on your own? How much did you do as part of a team?

Goals
15. What are your career goals?
16. Why did you choose this particular field of work?

Self-Concept
17. What are your greatest strengths? weaknesses?
18. What qualities do you need to strengthen?
19. Tell me about yourself.
20. Why do you think you are qualified for this job?
21. How do you spend your leisure time?
22. What do you consider to be your chief accomplishment in each of the jobs you have held?
23. What have your supervisors complimented you on? criticized you for?

FIGURE 15-4 Questions commonly asked in interviews

Dress for the Interview

A good appearance will show your interviewer that you are professional. Here are some pointers:

- Dress conservatively; avoid flamboyant styles or colors.
- Wear a business suit in navy, gray, or brown when interviewing for office or professional jobs. If you do not have a suit, men should wear a sport coat and tie; women should wear a dress and jacket or skirt and jacket.
- Avoid heavy fragrances and flashy jewelry. Women also should avoid bright nail polish, frilly clothes, and heavy make-up.
- Choose a conservative, attractive hair style.
- Make sure you are well groomed—good deodorant; clean clothes; polished shoes; trim, clean nails; and freshly brushed teeth.

Arrive on Time

If you are unfamiliar with the interview location, travel there before the day of the interview to learn the route. Allow plenty of time on the day of the interview. Remember, you may have to park, locate the building, and then find the right office. Allow extra time for heavy traffic or any other problems that may occur. You will not impress an interviewer if you are late; therefore, plan on arriving a few minutes early.

> **KEY POINT**
>
> If you are unsure about how to get to the interview site, ask the interviewer or the person who invited you to interview for specific directions. The interviewer (or an assistant) will gladly respond—and you can use this inquiry as another way of demonstrating your communication skills.

3 Checkpoint

Preparing for the Interview

Indicate whether each statement is true or false.
1. Before interviewing for a job, prepare yourself for probable questions from the interviewer.
2. Prepare questions to ask about the job and the company.
3. Dress casually for any interview.
4. Plan to arrive at the interview a little late.
5. All you need to take to the interview is you.

Check your answers in Appendix E.

The Interview Itself

Objective

At the interview site, you may be introduced to the interviewer by a receptionist or a secretary. As you wait in the reception area for the interview to begin, conduct yourself in a professional manner. The secretary may have an influence on whether or not you are hired. Here are some points to remember:

- Avoid smoking.
- Avoid chewing gum.
- Greet the secretary cordially.
- Avoid bringing friends or relatives to the interview.

The Introduction

Greet the interviewer with a smile and direct eye contact. Use the interviewer's name in a greeting such as "Glad to meet you, Dr. Wanamaker." A firm handshake is always appropriate and professional. Sit down only when you are asked. Then let the interviewer begin the interview and direct the discussion.

Nonverbal Skills

Your nonverbal skills are very important during the interview. From the time you meet, the interviewer will be assessing you for the job. Because the interviewer's first impression of you is crucial, you must look and act like someone the interviewer would like to hire. Focus on such nonverbal signals as posture, facial expression, gestures, and eye contact.

Posture

Carry yourself confidently. Hold your head up and keep your shoulders back and straight. Maintain good posture when you sit. To avoid slumping, make sure your back touches the back of the chair.

Facial Expression

Keep a pleasant, interested expression on your face during the interview. A warm smile sends the message that you are someone the company would like on its team.

Gestures

Keep your gestures natural. Avoid extremes such as moving stiffly, making no arm movements, or waving your hands wildly. Minimize distinctive habits such as hand twisting or leg shaking.

Eye Contact

An important nonverbal communication skill is maintaining eye contact with the interviewer. Looking at the interviewer when he or she is talking communicates that you are interested.

Listening Skills

Listen effectively so that you can answer questions and gather appropriate information. Here are some tips for effective listening during the interview:

- Concentrate on what the interviewer is saying.
- Look at the interviewer. Eye contact will let the interviewer know you are listening.

DIVERSITY

- If you are interviewing for jobs in other countries, be aware that certain hand gestures can convey different meanings in other cultures. For example, making a circle with finger and thumb usually indicates "okay" in the United States but has obscene connotations in some Hispanic cultures.
- Although direct eye contact is a sign of respect and attention in the United States, it has the opposite meaning in some other cultures. Investigate the meaning of nonverbal signals before you interview with an international company for a job in another country.

- Be observant. Notice the interviewer's body language and pick up on nonverbal cues.
- Listen eagerly. Show that you are interested by providing feedback, such as nodding or smiling, and giving verbal cues, such as saying "Yes" and "Uh-huh."
- Listen carefully for the important points so that you can respond to them later; do not interrupt the interviewer.

Interview Questions

From the time the interview begins, you will be expected to answer questions so that the interviewer can get to know you and your abilities. Speak clearly and distinctly as you answer these questions and use good grammar. The way you communicate with the interviewer indicates whether you have good communication skills—an important qualification for most jobs.

Opening Questions

Many interviewers will begin with ice-breaker questions such as, "I see that you are in the school band. What instrument do you play?" These questions are intended to put you at ease. Answer them naturally and be yourself. Well-trained interviewers want you to be comfortable and natural so they can get an accurate impression of your personality. Remember, the interviewer is as interested in finding the right person as you are in being selected for the position.

Main Questions

During the next stage, the interviewer gathers information about you by asking questions such as those in Figure 15-4. Listen to each question carefully, pause to gather your thoughts before answering, and elaborate on your answers. A simple "yes" or "no" is not enough. Use each answer as an opportunity to convince the interviewer that you are the best person for the job. Do not assume that the interviewer will learn all about you from your application form or resume. Talk about your accomplishments and abilities; employers want to hire people who are sincere, confident, and capable.

Look at the following dialogues. For the first question, the applicant can talk only about one topic (weakness). For the second question, the applicant can talk about all his or her strengths.

Interviewer:	"What is your biggest weakness?"
Applicant:	"My biggest weakness is the fear of public speaking, but to overcome this weakness, I have joined Toastmasters and am giving as many speeches as I can."
Interviewer:	"Why should we hire you?"
Applicant:	"There are several reasons you should hire me. For example, ..."

KEY POINT

- Some applicants interview with one or more managers simultaneously; therefore, you should be prepared for questions from more than one source. Some applicants meet with two, three, or more managers in rapid succession. You should be prepared to give consistent answers if asked the same question by several interviewers.
- Remember to phrase the answers you offer during an interview like a persuasive message. Reflect the interests of the receiver rather than the needs of the sender.

Illegal Questions

You may be asked personal questions that you do not want to answer. In general, you should provide only information that will be to your advantage. Federal laws such as Title VII of the Civil Rights Act of 1965 and the Americans with Disabilities Act prohibit employers from discriminating in job hiring on the basis of age, gender, national origin, religion, race, disability, marital status, number of children, or other factors unrelated to job performance. In some states, applicants may be asked about convictions but not about arrests.

The best way to handle illegal questions is to deflect them courteously, possibly providing some useful information. For example,

Interviewer: "How will your children be taken care of while you work?"

Applicant: "If you are asking if I will arrive on time and do a good job, the answer is definitely yes. I have good child care arrangements. Also, you can check my current job performance and attendance record. They are excellent."

Do not answer an inappropriate question if your response could hurt your chances of getting the job. Maintain your composure and be ready to provide information if the interviewer can show you that the question is job-related.

Interviewer: "What church do you attend?"

Applicant: "I do not understand how that question relates to my performance on the job. Can you explain?"

Figure 15-5 provides some examples of illegal interview questions. Look them over and decide how you would answer these questions if asked.

ILLEGAL INTERVIEW QUESTIONS

1. Are you married? single? divorced? widowed?
2. Do you have small children? Do you plan to have children?
3. What is your date of birth?
4. Have you ever been arrested?
5. Where were you born?
6. Where does your husband (wife, father, mother) work?
7. Are you pregnant?
8. Do you belong to a religious organization? Which one?
9. Do you rent or own your home?
10. What is your maiden name?
11. Do you have a girlfriend (boyfriend)?

FIGURE 15-5 Illegal interview questions

Salary Question

Avoid mentioning salary requirements until you receive an offer for a position. However, if the interviewer asks your requirements early in the interview, indicate that you require the standard salary for the position in question or the salary that is appropriate for your education and experience. Letting the interviewer make a salary offer rather than naming a figure yourself puts you in a better position to negotiate.

The Closing

The interviewer will provide both verbal and nonverbal signals that the interview is over. Stand up, offer a handshake, and thank the interviewer. Usually a job is not offered at this point. However, asking the interviewer when a decision will be made is appropriate.

If you are offered the job, accept it only if you are sure you want it. This decision is important, and you may need some time to consider it. If you need more time, tell the interviewer that you need to think it over because you are interviewing for other positions. Then give your answer by the agreed-upon time. Ask for the interviewer's business card before you leave; you will want to write a follow-up message.

KEY POINT

Take a moment to thank the interviewer for taking the time to explain the job in more detail or for courtesies extended.

Money Under the Table

Many businesspeople believe that a bribe is a necessary part of conducting business with international companies. A survey of American businesspeople found that 20 percent of them believe that bribes should be paid if acceptable or encouraged in the host country.

Even though a 1977 law forbids American companies from paying bribes, it does not forbid "grease" payments to foreign ministers or clerical employees of governments. Such payments are approved because of their "size" and the assumption that "they are used to persuade the recipients to perform their normal duties."

When this law was enacted, more than 400 corporations, including 117 Fortune 500 companies, reported making more than $300 million in "payments." Few companies have been prosecuted under this law since its enactment. ■

Source: O. C. Ferrell and John Fraedrich, *Business Ethics: Ethical Decision Making and Cases* (Boston: Houghton Mifflin Company, 1994), p. 200.

The Follow-up Letter

Within two days after the interview, write a brief follow-up letter thanking the interviewer. If you are sure you want the job, indicate your interest and ask for a decision. Follow-up letters are courteous and thoughtful, and they bring your name before the interviewer again.

Organize the letter as a goodwill message, as the example below illustrates:

Main Idea	Thank you for giving me the opportunity to interview yesterday for the position of legal secretary. After talking with you and seeing the office operations, I am convinced that I would like to join Powell and Martin's legal secretarial staff.
Supporting Information	During the interview, we discussed my availability for the northside office. After further consideration, I am happy to say that I would be able to work in any of the firm's locations in the city.
Helpful Closing	My education and experience make me confident that I would be able to perform the duties of the position well. If you need further information about my qualifications or have any questions, please call me at 555-7730.

Once the deadline for making a decision has passed, you may want to call the interviewer or write a second follow-up letter if you have not heard from the company. Make this second letter brief but not curt. Remind the interviewer that you still are interested in working for the company. Mention the decision date originally indicated, and politely inquire whether the interviewer needs any additional information about your qualifications to help in this decision. Close by saying that you look forward to hearing from the interviewer soon.

If you accept one job offer and within days you receive a second job offer (higher paying), the most ethical course of action is to refuse the second offer. When you keep your promises, you build a reputation as a reliable person with strong principles.

SCANS
Employability

Basic Skills: Writing
When writing follow-up letters, be sure to use the techniques for writing and formatting letters—see Chapter 6.

KEY POINT

Use the follow-up letter as a way to emphasize something positive or distinctive that will set you apart from other candidates.

Checkpoint **4**

The Interview and the Follow-up Letter

Fill in the blanks with the appropriate words.

1. Maintaining eye contact with the interviewer is an important
   _____.

2. During an interview, the best thing to do with illegal questions is to
   _____.

3. _____ ask about salary.

4. Write and mail a(an) _____ within two days of the interview.

Check your answers in Appendix E.

CASE 15:

Answers

Responses to Questions 3, 4, 5, and 6

3. Did Mercedes' friend ask three good questions?
Yes, she did. Those questions reflect an understanding of the interviewing process. They indicate that there will probably be basic questions to every interview, that she should be ready to ask questions during an interview, and that she should dress appropriately for an interview.

4. Did Mercedes understand the interviewing process?
It appears that Mercedes did not. The answers to the questions she gave hurt her chances of getting a position. For example, to say that she wants to have her own boutique in five years implies that she will one day be a competitor rather than an employee. To offer that she is getting married soon and that her husband will graduate from college next spring implies that she and her husband could be moving to where his new job will be located—again, not a good message for a prospective employer.

5. Did Mercedes dress appropriately for her interview?
No, she did not. Jeans are probably inappropriate, as are the three-inch heels. She should dress as the employer would like to see her if she were working in the store.

6. Would a follow-up letter have helped Mercedes to get a job?
Yes, if it were well done, a follow-up letter would have given her an edge on the candidates that did not send a follow-up letter.

DISCUSSION QUESTIONS

1. Which is more important—the interview or the follow-up letter?
2. Why do employers interview applicants for positions?
3. What seven steps can you take to prepare for an interview?
4. Why should you send a follow-up letter after an interview?

Summary

As illustrated by Mercedes, an effective resume and letter of application get you interviews but do not get you the job. You must understand the interviewing process, be prepared to answer basic questions, dress appropriately, and write an effective follow-up letter. To fail at any of these can result in your not getting the job.

Chapter Summary

Section 15.1 Writing Your Letter of Application and Completing the Application Form

1 **Describe the two types of application letters.** The two types of application letters are solicited and unsolicited. A solicited application letter is used when your application is sought either through a newspaper advertisement or some other means. An unsolicited application letter is used when your application has not been sought.

2 **Decribe the content of a letter of application.** The letter of application should enable the receiver to identify the position for which you are applying, why the receiver should interview you, your qualifications, and a request for an interview.

3 **Fill in an application form.** Either key or fill out an application in blue or black ink. Use a copy of your resume and your list of references as resources for responding to items on the form. Take your time when filling in the form because appearance is important.

Section 15.2 Interviewing Well and Writing the Follow-up Letter

1 **Discuss the purpose of a job interview.** From the applicant's perspective, the purpose of a job interview is to see if you want to work for the company and, if so, to get a job. From the employer's perspective, the purpose of a job interview is to see if the candidate is a good fit for the position.

2 **Explain how to prepare for a job interview.** Prepare for an interview by investigating the company and the job, anticipate questions, prepare to ask questions, practice the interview, take appropriate information with you to the interview, dress appropriately, and arrive on time.

3 **Understand the skills necessary for a successful interview.** Nonverbal and listening skills are very important during a job interview. Verbal communication skills are also critical when answering questions. Know the types of questions that may be asked and which questions are illegal.

4 **Write a follow-up letter.** The follow-up letter should be mailed within two days of the interview, and it should thank the interviewer for the interview, emphasize that you are still interested in the job, and close by saying that you look forward to hearing from the interviewer soon.

Critical Thinking Questions

1. Is the interview more important than the resume? Justify your answer.
2. Does a candidate who sends a follow-up letter have an advantage over a candidate who does not? Why or why not?

Applications

Part A. Use the company research you conducted in Chapter 14 to write an unsolicited letter of application to an employer for which you are interested in working. Address this letter to the person in charge of the department you want to join.

Part B. Use the information in your qualifications file to fill out a sample application form provided by your instructor. If you are missing any information (such as dates of employment), call your former employers to request this information.

Part C. Prepare answers to the interview questions in Figure 15-4.

Part D. Prepare your answers to the illegal interview questions in Figure 15-5. Exchange answers with a classmate and analyze the effectiveness of each answer.

TEAMWORK

Part E. Select a job that interests you and prepare five questions you would like to ask during an interview.

TEAMWORK

Part F. Team up with a classmate and stage mock interviews in which each student in turn plays the part of the interviewer and the applicant for a specific (real or imaginary) job. Videotape the interviews, if possible, and discuss each student's strengths and weaknesses after the playback.

1. Proofread and edit the following paragraph.

    In WordPerfect, your can ad a border or fill to a page or colume. To do so, select the text you want to dress up. Of your want to apply the effects to all your pages, paragraphs, or columes, don't select any text. Your formatting then affects all text from the insertion marker foreward. Border options are found, appropriately enough, on the Border tab of the Border/Fill dialoge box.

2. Proofread the following follow-up letter. Then edit and rewrite the letter.

    Thank you for taking time from your buzy schedule to interview me me for the position of assisstant head Teller. I also enjoyed the toor of your mane branch.

    As I mentioned during the interview, your computerized account system is really, really impressive. Because it is similar to the one I use in my current position at Western Bank, I am sure I could adopt to it in only a few days.

    Given my years of experience with Western Bank, I believe that I would preform well and enjoy the challenje of serveing the customers of Ansonia Savings Bank. If you need addition references or other information, please just let me know.

1. Lu Ho is almost finished with his degree program. However, he has yet to find a job in his chosen career field—nursing. While in school, Lu has worked part time as a plumber.

    Lu is questioning his career choice because he has not been able to find a full-time job in a hospital. There are plenty of private-care opportunities, but he does not want one of those.

    Because he needs an income, Lu has started interviewing for both plumber and nurse positions.
    1. How should Lu dress for the interviews for a plumber position?
    2. How should he dress for the interviews for a nurse position?
    3. Will the questions he asks of interviewers differ according to the type of position?

2. Luisa Guzman graduated from Hillside Tech two years ago with a degree in horticulture. Since graduation, she has worked for Turtle Hill Nursery and Landscape Company. Although she enjoys her job, she wants a position in which she spends more time with plant development and less time with landscaping. Presently, she is looking for such a position.

Luisa has finished her resume and is developing a letter of application. However, she knows that there are two types of these letters—solicited and unsolicited. She decides to write one of each so no matter what the situation, she will have her letter written.

1. How should the opening paragraphs of these two letters differ?
2. Write the opening paragraph for the unsolicited letter.
3. Write the opening paragraph for the solicited letter.

Career Case Studies

COMMUNICATION FOR MEDIA AND VISUAL ARTS CAREERS

Brandon Ellis has always wanted to be a television camera operator. Tomorrow, he will have an interview for just such a position. KLTY called two days ago and invited Brandon to come in for an interview.

Yesterday, he was too excited to be nervous; but when he woke up this morning, anxiety began to set in. He called you and asked if he could come over to your apartment this evening. Brandon arrives, quickly and nervously reviews his situation, and then asks, "What advice do you have for me? What do I have to say and do to get this job?"

1. What advice can you give Brandon?
2. Team up with a partner and stage a mock interview between Brandon and the interviewer.

TEAMWORK

COMMUNICATION FOR HUMAN AND SOCIAL SERVICES CAREERS

LaQuanta Jefferson had just finished a successful interview with ParData Computer Services of Dallas, Texas. She was pleased with the situation, for the job provided a good salary and full benefits. Tom Owens, the interviewer, gave LaQuanta an application form and asked her to fill it out.

As LaQuanta looked over the form, she realized that she had a pen with her but it had green ink. The form required LaQuanta to provide four references. She knew who her references were, but she did not have their addresses, telephone numbers, or e-mail addresses.

The application form also asked for her work experience and the dates of her employment. She could provide a record of her experience, but she was unsure of the dates.

1. Under the circumstances, what should LaQuanta have done? Should she have filled out the form as best she could? Should she have asked for a pen with blue or black ink? Should she have asked for permission to take the form home, fill it out, and bring it back the next day?
2. What should LaQuanta have done to be better prepared?

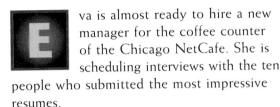
Interviewing Intelligently

Eva is almost ready to hire a new manager for the coffee counter of the Chicago NetCafe. She is scheduling interviews with the ten people who submitted the most impressive resumes.

Eva wants to be fair during the interviews, so she plans to write down the main questions she will ask each person. She will also rate each interviewee on nonverbal characteristics. In addition, Eva will evaluate the kinds of questions each person asks during the interview.

1. Below are some questions that Eva is thinking about asking. Indicate whether she should use each one. If not, explain why. Whenever possible, rewrite the question so it is more effective.
    a. What kind of experience have you had in working directly with customers?
    b. How are you going to get to work every day?
    c. What do you know about NetCafe?
    d. Why are you the best person for this job?
    e. Are you familiar with computers?
    f. How many computer classes have you taken?
    g. Do you mind working with a diverse group of people?
    h. What special skills do you bring to this job?
    i. Are you used to working on a team?

2. Put the characteristics below in order according to what you believe is their importance for the manager of the coffee counter. You can also eliminate some char-acteristics or add any missing qualities you think are important. Explain any changes you make.

    ■ friendliness
    ■ personal hygiene
    ■ timeliness
    ■ physical fitness
    ■ youthful appearance
    ■ appropriateness of clothing
    ■ stylishness of clothing
    ■ self-confidence
    ■ eye contact
    ■ lack of nervousness
    ■ ability to carry on a conversation

3. Most applicants ask questions during interviews. Evaluate each question below and explain why it should or should not be asked.
    a. What is NetCafe?
    b. What hours would I work?
    c. How much vacation would I get?
    d. Would I gain any supervisory experience?
    e. Do you plan on opening any more branches of NetCafe?
    f. How much do you pay?
    g. How much would I have to learn about computers?
    h. I don't drink coffee. Does that matter?
    i. Will I be responsible for ordering supplies?
    j. Will anyone be working at the coffee counter with me?
    k. Who would handle any problems that come up at the coffee counter?

Appendices

536

Key Terms Glossary

abbreviation a shortened form of a word or a group of words.

accessibility the ease with which customers can contact a service provider.

acknowledgment letter a letter that tells the receiver that his or her correspondence has been received.

action verb a verb that can take a direct object or an indirect object and helps to create lively, effective sentences.

active listening listening that requires understanding and remembering.

active voice verb voice and style of writing that indicates the subject of a sentence is doing the action.

adjective a word that describes a noun (person, place, or thing).

adverb a word that modifies an action verb, an adjective, or another adverb.

agenda a document that contains the order of business for a meeting.

analyses of alternatives a technical report that examines possible solutions to a problem (may contain a recommendation).

analytical report a report that analyzes a problem and may include facts, conclusions, and recommendations.

annual report a technical report required by law to be sent to internal and external stakeholders and which contains both financial and "nonfinancial" sections.

antecedent a noun to which a pronoun refers.

apostrophe a punctuation mark used to indicate the omission of a letter or number in a contraction; possession in nouns and indefinite pronouns, time, and money; and plurals of lowercase letters.

appendix a supplementary part of a formal report that contains material related to the report but is too long to be included in the body or text.

application form a standardized data sheet that a company uses to compare qualifications of different job applicants.

appositive a noun or pronoun that renames another noun or pronoun that immediately precedes it.

article the words *the, a,* or *an,* which act as adjectives.

attention line the part of a letter that directs the correspondence to a particular individual when the letter is addressed to an organization.

audience analysis the process used to analyze a receiver or receivers.

audit a formal, periodic examination of a company's accounts and financial records.

audit report a report that contains the findings when examining a company's accounts and financial records.

bar graph a graph that shows each data point as a rectangular bar; used when you want your audience to be able to compare the data represented in the graph.

bibliography a supplementary part of a formal report that provides an alphabetic list of sources used in preparing the report.

block format a letter format in which all lines start at the left margin.

body the part of a letter that contains its message.

brainstorming the act of inventing ideas without restrictions.

briefing a short informal presentation designed to keep people up to date on business activities, projects, programs, or procedures.

broken bar graph a bar graph that indicates omission of part of each bar if some quantities are so large that they would go off the chart.

business communication the communication process used in a business environment.

casual listening listening that is associated with conversation and entertainment and requires no remembering.

channel the mode a sender uses to send a message.

claim letter a special request for a refund, exchange, or discount on merchandise or services.

clause a group of words that contains a subject and a predicate.

closing paragraph a paragraph that ends a communication with a summation or reference to the main idea stated in the opening paragraph.

collection letter a letter to persuade the receiver to pay a past-due bill.

collective noun a noun that represents a group that acts as a single unit, such as *jury* or *tribe*.

colon a punctuation mark that directs the reader's attention to the material following it.

comma a punctuation mark that indicates a pause for clarity or represents an omission of words.

common noun a noun that identifies a person, place, or thing in a general way.

communication the process used to send and interpret messages.

communication barrier an obstacle to communication.

communication overload a mental condition that occurs when a person receives so many messages that he or she fails to take the time necessary to read or comprehend them.

complete predicate everything in a sentence said by, to, or about the subject, including the main verb of the sentence.

complete subject the simple subject plus all the sentence that is not part of the complete predicate.

complex sentence a sentence containing one independent clause and one or more dependent clauses.

complimentary close the formal closing or the "goodbye" of a letter.

compound adjective two or more hyphenated words that precede and modify a noun.

compound antecedent an antecedent that consists of two or more elements.

compound-complex sentence a sentence containing two or more independent clauses and one or more dependent clauses.

compound predicate two or more verbs with the same subject that are connected by conjunctions.

compound sentence a sentence containing two or more independent clauses and no dependent clauses.

compound subject two or more simple subjects joined by conjunctions.

concise brief, to the point, short.

conclusion an opinion based on the interpretation of data.

condition linking verb a verb that does not need an object or indirect object and that refers to a condition or appeals to the senses.

conjunction a word that joins two or more sentence parts.

conjunctive adverb a transitional word that joins two independent but related sentences.

consonants all letters except vowels (*a, e, i, o,* and *u*).

coordinate conjunction a word that joins words, phrases, and clauses of equal grammatical rank, such as *for, and, nor, but, or,* and *yet.*

copy notation abbreviations at the end of a letter to indicate to whom copies were sent.

copyright legal ownership of original work, whether published or unpublished.

correlative conjunction words used in pairs that connect words, phrases, and clauses of equal grammatical rank, such as *not only . . . but also, either . . . or, neither . . . nor.*

courteous request a polite way to ask for action from the receiver.

courteous words words in a business communication that are positive, considerate, and bias-free.

cross-cultural communication verbal, nonverbal, and written communication between two or more people from different cultures.

cultural diversity the differences in language, customs, values, manners, perceptions, social structures, and decision-making practices that people from different backgrounds have.

customer contact maintaining customer satisfaction by communicating in a regular and timely manner.

customer service the performance of activities to ensure customer satisfaction.

dash a punctuation mark used with nonessential elements, before a summarizing statement, with a sudden change of thought, and before a detailed listing.

data facts or findings resulting from research.

dateline line in a message that shows the date it was written.

declarative sentence a sentence that makes a statement.

demonstrative pronoun a pronoun such as *this, these, that,* and *those* that points to a specific person, place, or thing in a given sentence or answers where.

dependent clause a clause that cannot stand alone as a complete sentence.

description a verbal and visual representation.

developmental paragraph a paragraph that contains important information or explanations about the main idea of a message.

direct address a reader's name that is mentioned in the beginning, middle, or end of a sentence.

direct object a noun or pronoun directly affected by the action of a transitive verb.

direct order method of organization in which the main idea appears first, followed by supporting information; usually used for positive messages.

direct-indirect order combination method of organization when both positive and negative messages are conveyed in a business communication.

discussion outline an outline that uses information to identify topics or subtopics of the outline.

drafting the stage of the writing process during which writers use prewriting notes or organizational tools as they write their message into sentences and paragraphs.

drawing a diagram composed of lines useful for communicating a complicated idea or procedure.

edit to alter or refine a written message to improve it.

enclosure notation the word *enclosure* or its initials that indicate an item to be enclosed with the message.

enunciation the way in which a speaker sounds out each part of a word.

ethics the principles of right and wrong that guide each of us.

exclamation point a punctuation mark that follows a word, a group of words, or a sentence that shows strong emotion.

executive summary a preliminary part of a formal report that provides a brief overview of a report (sometimes called an *abstract* or *synopsis*).

extemporaneous speech sometimes called an impromptu speech, a speech given without any warning.

external barrier an obstacle to communication that lies outside the receiver or sender.

external communication communication that originates with an organization and is sent to receivers outside the organization.

external customer someone from outside the company who requests information or purchases a product or service.

external report a report written for people outside the organization.

feedback the response of a receiver to a message.

findings and analysis a part of the text or body of a report that presents the findings and supporting details and examines these results.

first-person pronouns pronouns that refer to the person who is speaking or sending the message; for example, *I, we, me, us, my, mine, our, ours, myself,* and *ourselves.*

flowchart a step-by-step diagram that shows the path of a procedure, process, or data.

follow-up letter a brief letter written to an interviewer thanking him or her for the interview.

formal communication communication that follows established lines of authority.

formal report a report that has preliminary parts and/or supplementary parts; formal reports are generally long, complex, analytical, and impersonal.

friendship letter a special type of goodwill letter that shows friendship between the sender and the receiver.

functional order a resume order that presents your accomplishments or skills in order of importance, showing the most important or impressive first.

future perfect tense verb a verb form that indicates action that will be completed at a specific point in the future.

future tense verb a verb form that expresses an action or condition yet to come.

gerund a verb form that ends in *ing* and serves as a noun.

gesture the use of the arms and hands to express an idea or feeling.

glossary a list of unfamiliar terms, abbreviations, or acronyms.

goodwill the favorable reputation an individual or business has with its customers.

goodwill letter a letter that illustrates friendship or an acknowledgement.

graph a diagram that provides a means for visually comparing data.

graphic aid a visual representation of the words in a message.

heading a word or words used in report writing that help organize and present data and help readers follow as the writer moves from point to point.

heterogeneous dissimilar; having different qualities or characteristics.

homogeneous similar; displaying the same or similar qualities or characteristics.

hyphen a punctuation mark used in dividing words, in forming compound hyphenated words, and after some prefixes.

hypothesis a possible cause or explanation of a problem.

impersonal style a writing style that allows the writer to use only third-person pronouns.

impromptu speech sometimes called an extemporaneous speech, a speech given without any warning.

indefinite pronoun a pronoun such as *one* or *each* that refers in general terms to people, places, or things.

independent clause a clause that can stand alone as a complete sentence.

indirect object a noun or pronoun that receives a transitive verb's action.

indirect order the method of organization in which the supporting information is presented before the main idea; usually used for negative and persuasive messages.

indirect question a sentence that has words in the order of a question but is actually a statement.

infinitive a verb form consisting of a present tense verb preceded by the word *to*.

informal communication communication that does not follow established lines of authority.

informal report a memo, letter, or manuscript report that has neither preliminary parts nor supplementary parts.

informational report a report that presents information (facts) and includes little or no analysis.

instructions a series of steps that tell readers how to do something.

intensive pronoun a compound pronoun form, created by joining a pronoun with *self* or *selves*, that provides emphasis in a sentence.

interjection a word or expression such as *No!* or *Help!* that has no grammatical relationship with other words in a sentence and is used to express strong emotion.

internal barrier an obstacle to communication that lies within the receiver or sender.

internal communication communication that originates and is sent to receivers within an organization.

internal customer someone who works for the same company as you do.

interrogative pronoun a pronoun such as *which* or *what*, used to begin a question that leads to a noun response.

intransitive verb a verb that does not need an object to complete the meaning of a sentence.

introduction (1) a part of the text or body of a report that contains authorization for the report, states the problem, scope of the report, limitations of the report, and/or definitions. (2) a short, informal presentation designed to introduce a speaker to his or her audience.

inverted sentence a sentence where the predicate precedes the subject.

job objective a brief statement that describes the type of work or position the writer wants.

keyword search term that relates to and helps define the research topic.

legend a key that defines the meaning for the colors or patterns used in a graphic aid.

letter a format of a message used for external documents.

letter address the part of a letter that gives the address of the receiver.

letter containing negative message a letter that contains a message that will disappoint the receiver.

letter of transmittal a preliminary part of a formal report in letter format that introduces the report to the reader.

letter report a report five pages or under and in letter format.

letterhead stationery sheets of stationery that have a company's name, address, telephone number, e-mail address, and/or logo printed on them.

line graph a graphic that displays one or more sets of data, connected by lines; useful for showing changes in a quantity or value over time.

listening the process of hearing and focusing attention to understand and remember an oral message.

main idea the central theme or most important thought in a business communication.

managerial report a report written for management.

manual a combination of instructions, explanations, descriptions, definitions, and other related information.

manuscript report an informal report in manuscript format.

map a flat representation of geographic relationships.

mechanism a synthetic object that consists of several moving parts working together to perform one or more tasks. (A dog, for example, consists of moving parts working together, but it is not a mechanism because it is not synthetic.)

memo of transmittal a preliminary part of a formal report in memo format that introduces the report to the reader.

memo report an informal, internal report five pages or under and in memo format.

memorandum a format of a message used for internal documents.

memorandums (memos) a format used for written messages sent to others in the same organization.

memorizing giving a speech entirely from memory.

message a set of symbols selected to represent a thought or an idea.

message environment the physical and/or social setting in which a message is sent.

mild command a stern request from the sender to the receiver.

minutes the official record of the proceedings of a meeting.

mixed punctuation the punctuation used in a letter that requires a colon after the salutation and a comma after the complimentary close.

modified block format a letter format in which the dateline, complimentary close, and sender's name start in the middle of the page.

multicultural having or containing people from many cultures.

multinational having to do with two or more countries.

multiple-bar graph a bar graph that compares more than one set of data at various points in time.

multiple-line graph a line graph that shows the movement of two or more quantities or values over time.

networking an informal but often effective way to locate employment opportunities by talking to personal contacts.

neutral opening an opening of a message that implies neither a positive nor a negative response to the receiver.

nominative case pronoun a pronoun, also called a *subjective case pronoun*, used as a subject or a predicate nominative.

nonessential element an interrupting expression, nonrestrictive element, or appositive that is included in a sentence.

nonrestrictive phrase or clause a phrase or clause that adds information that is not essential to the meaning of a sentence.

nonverbal communication the messages sent without or in addition to words.

nonverbal symbol a gesture, posture, facial expression, appearance, time, tone of voice, eye contact, or space used to send a message.

noun a word that names a person, place, or thing.

object something that can be seen and touched; it might be natural or synthetic.

objective what a writer wants to achieve in a business communication.

objective case pronoun a pronoun used as a direct or indirect object of a transitive verb and as an object of a preposition.

open punctuation punctuation used in a letter that has no punctuation after the salutation or the complimentary close.

opening paragraph a paragraph that identifies the subject of a business communication.

oral communication spoken communication.

order letter a letter that places an order for goods or services with the receiver.

organization chart a diagram used to illustrate the relationships and official lines of authority and communication among employees and departments of an organization.

paragraph a group of one or more sentences that expresses one idea.

paralanguage the nonverbal symbols that accompany a verbal message and reveal the difference between what is said and how it is said.

paraphrase to rephrase using different words to express the same meaning.

parenthesis a punctuation mark used in pairs to set off nonessential elements.

participle a verb form that can be used either as an adjective or as part of a verb phrase.

passive voice a verb voice and a style of writing that indicates the subject of a sentence is receiving the action.

past perfect tense verb a verb form that indicates an action that began in the past and continued to the more recent past when it was completed.

past tense verb a verb form that expresses an action that was completed.

perfect tense verb a verb form that describes the action of the main verb in relation to a specific time period, either present, past, or future.

period a punctuation mark used at the end of sentences and abbreviations and after numbers or letters in enumeration.

periodic report a managerial report that provides information at regularly scheduled intervals.

personal style a writing style that allows the writer to use all pronouns.

photograph a picture used to provide a realistic view of a specific item or place and to make the document more appealing to read.

phrase a group of words that has no subject and predicate.

pie chart a circular chart showing how the parts of a whole are distributed and how the parts relate to one another.

pitch the highness or lowness of a voice.

plagiarism presenting another person's work as your own.

plan of action a managerial report that reveals the strategies to be used when solving a problem.

portfolio a folder, computer file, notebook, or small briefcase to hold information about a person's skills, abilities, and accomplishments; information includes samples of work, transcripts, letters of recommendation, and other related items.

positive response letter a letter in which the sender responds to the receiver's request in a positive manner.

possessive case pronoun a pronoun that indicates ownership or possession.

possessive noun a noun showing possession, indicated by an apostrophe or apostrophe plus s.

postscript a sentence or paragraph added on to the bottom of a letter (after the sender's name, position, company title, enclosure notation, or copy notation) to reinforce the message in the body.

posture the way you stand or sit.

precise words exact, specific words in a business communication.

predicate everything in a sentence said by, to, or about the subject.

predicate nominative a noun or pronoun that refers to the subject and follows a form of the verb *to be*.

preliminary parts parts of a formal report that appear before its body or text.

preposition a word that usually indicates direction, position, or time and is linked to a noun or noun substitute to form a phrase.

prepositional phrase a group of words that begins with a preposition and ends with a noun or noun substitute.

present perfect tense verb a verb form that indicates continuous action from the past to the present.

present tense verb a verb form that expresses present action.

prewriting the stage of the writing process during which writers plan their message.

primary appeal the main selling point, the benefit most likely to motivate a reader to act.

primary information sources of data or information that are gathered firsthand.

primary research the gathering of fresh, new data.

process a series of events that take place over time.

process description an explanation of how something works.

pronoun a word that is a short, convenient substitute for a noun.

pronunciation the way a speaker makes a word sound.

proofreading the process of reviewing and correcting the final draft of a written message.

proper adjective a proper noun that precedes and modifies another noun.

proper noun a noun that names a specific person, place, or thing.

proposal a formal report that analyzes a problem and recommends a solution.

publish to deliver a message to the receiver, or to make a message available to the public.

qualification a skill, ability, or accomplishment that makes you fit for certain jobs.

question mark a punctuation mark used after a direct question or a series of questions.

quotation mark a punctuation mark used in pairs to set off a direct quotation, a definition, nonstandard English, a word used in an unusual way, or a title.

receiver a person or thing to whom a message is sent.

recommendation a suggestion that is based on conclusions and suggests what should be done.

redundancy needless repitition.

reference initials the initials used to identify the writer and/or the individual who keyed the message.

reflexive pronoun a compound pronoun form that ends in *self* or *selves* and refers to a noun or pronoun that appears earlier in a sentence.

reliability indicates that the information is free of error.

report a format of a message designed for a group of people.

report body a text of a report that contains its introduction, the findings and supporting details, and ending.

request denial letter a letter telling the receiver that the sender will not respond as the receiver wished.

request for proposal (RFP) a document that lists the information that must be included in a solicited proposal.

restrictive phrase or clause a phrase or clause that is essential to the meaning of a sentence.

resume a concise summary of an applicant's qualifications for employment.

reverse chronological order a resume order that presents the most recent work experience first and works backward to earlier jobs.

revise to make changes to a written message.

Robert's Rules of Order a set of rules designed to facilitate the operation of a formal meeting.

routine letter a letter in which the sender is sure the receiver will respond as the sender wants.

routine request a request for an action that will be done willingly.

sales letter a letter that tries to persuade a reader to purchase a product or service.

salutation part of a letter that acts as a greeting to the receiver.

scope the boundaries of a report (defines what will be included in a report and what will be excluded).

secondary information sources of information in published form.

secondary research the locating of data that already has been gathered.

second-person pronouns pronouns that refer to the person being spoken to or the receiver; for example, *you, your, yours,* and *yourself.*

semicolon a punctuation mark used to denote a pause that is stronger than a comma but weaker than a period.

sender a person or thing that originates a message and initiates the communication process.

sentence a group of words that contains a subject and a predicate and expresses a complete thought.

service culture a combination of customer-focused policies and attitudes that pervade a company.

signature block the part of a letter that contains the writer's signed name, keyed name, and title.

simple bar graph a bar graph that compares only one set of data.

simple horizontal bar graph a bar graph that compares only one set of data and the length of each bar indicates quantity.

simple predicate a verb that is a complete predicate.

simple sentence a sentence containing one independent clause and no dependent clauses.

simple subject the main word in the complete subject that specifically names what the sentence is about.

simple vertical bar graph a bar graph that compares only one set of data and the height of each bar indicates quantity.

simplified block format a letter format in which the salutation and complimentary close are omitted.

single-line graph a line graph that shows the movement of only one quantity or value over time.

slides visual images transferred to a 35mm film output format; slides are placed in a carousel and projected on screen using a slide projector.

solicited letter of application a type of letter of application written for a specific job opening that has been announced or advertised.

stacked bar graph a bar graph that divides each bar into the parts that contributed to each total bar.

staff report a managerial report prepared by a staff member (a subordinate to management).

standard business envelope a 9 1/2-inch by 4 1/8-inch envelope.

state-of-being linking verb a verb, frequently the verb *to be*, that does not take an object or indirect object.

status report a report used to inform management about the status of a project (sometimes called a project report).

stereotype an oversimplified belief about a group of people.

style manual a book that provides a set of guidelines for the formatting of various reports and documents.

subject a word or group of words that represents the person speaking, the person spoken to, or the person, place, or thing spoken about.

subject line an optional part of a letter or a part of a memo that declares the topic of the letter.

subordinate conjunction a word such as *when*, *unless*, and *while* that is used to join elements of unequal grammatical rank and primarily to connect dependent clauses with independent clauses.

subparts parts of parts, such as the keys on a keyboard of a computer.

summary, conclusions, and recommendations a part of the text or body of a report that summarizes the findings, draws conclusions, and makes recommendations.

supplementary parts parts of a formal report that appear after its body or text.

supporting information essential facts that explain, reinforce, or justify the main idea of a business message.

systems white paper a technical report designed to provide specific, detailed information on a technology.

table an arrangement of information into rows and columns for reference purposes.

table of contents a preliminary part of a formal report that lists the report's entire content.

technical report a written report that contains technical, detailed information.

textual presentation a speech that is read from written copy.

third-person pronouns pronouns that refer to individuals being spoken about but not personally involved in the discussion; for example, *he, she, it, they, him, her, them, his, hers, its, their, theirs, himself, herself, itself,* and *themselves.*

timeline a tool for planning and scheduling the time within which each phase of a project will be completed.

title page a preliminary part of a formal report that shows the report title; the name, title, and organization of the person for whom the report was written; the name, title, and organization of the writer; and the date the report was submitted to the receiver.

tone how a spoken message sounds.

topical outline an outline that uses headings that identify topics or subtopics of the outline in as few words as possible.

transition a word or phrase that connects sentences in paragraphs and connects paragraphs in a message.

transitive verb a verb that denotes action and requires an object.

transparencies clear acetate film on which appear visual images that are projected on screen using an overhead projector.

underscore a punctuation mark, also called an *underline,* that is sometimes used instead of italics to call attention to a word or expression.

unsolicited not asked for or requested.

unsolicited letter of application a type of letter of application written for a position that has not been advertised or announced and may or may not be open.

validity indicates that the information presented is an accurate representation of facts.

verb a word that indicates an action, condition, or state of being.

verb phrase a group of words that functions as one verb.

verb tense a form of a verb that indicates time, such as present, past, and future.

verbal symbol a word used when speaking or writing.

voice a verb form that indicates if the subject is performing the action or receiving the action of a verb.

vowels the letters *a, e, i, o,* and *u.*

webbing or clustering a creative thinking technique.

Technology Glossary

address book a feature offered with e-mail software packages that stores frequently used e-mail addresses.

analytical graphics software a set of instructions telling a computer how to convert numbers into meaningful charts and graphs.

animation movement of text or images on a slide of a computer presentation.

application software a set of instructions for a computer telling it how to perform particular functions.

audioconference a long-distance telephone conference call.

boolean operators terms such as AND, OR, and NOT that connect two or more words or phrases to either broaden or narrow the scope of a search for information.

cellular phone a portable phone that allows senders and receivers to make phone calls while away from the traditional telephone.

central processing unit the fixture that contains the computer chips that control the operating functions of a workstation.

computer a machine that performs rapid, often complex, electronic processes to facilitate or automate procedures.

computer presentation a visual aid option in which the audience sees the images from your computer that you prepared using a presentation software program.

database management software a set of instructions telling a computer how to store and retrieve information.

desktop publishing software a set of instructions telling a computer how to convert data into documents of typeset quality.

digital camera a camera that stores images digitally rather than recording them on film. Once you take your picture, you can download the photograph to your computer system, manipulate it with a graphics program, insert the photograph into a document, and print the document.

electronic mail (e-mail) a system by which written messages are sent, received, and stored by means of computers.

electronic mailbox a computer file that holds messages sent to a particular person.

electronic whiteboard using special markers to write text and draw images on an erasable whiteboard; the user can print out a hard copy of what is written on the board.

electronic workstation a computerized workstation.

emoticon an icon built by combining various letters and symbols and used to reflect emotion in personal or informal e-mail messages.

fax machine an electronic device that produces exact copies of documents sent from another fax machine.

flaming sending angry or insulting messages (usually anonymously) via e-mail.

floppy diskette a removable storage medium.

graphics software a set of instructions telling a computer how to analyze data and create visual aids to support presentations.

hard copy a communication printed on paper.

hard disk a nonremovable storage medium in a computer.

hit an item that meets a specified web search criterion.

image scanner a device that converts pictures into a digital form so they can be read by a computer.

integrated software a set of instructions telling a computer how to perform when using word processing, spreadsheets, database management, graphics, and communication packages.

Internet the name given to the current telecommunications system between networks of computers. The Internet is often called a "network of networks." The Internet will grow into the electronic superhighway of the future. The Internet is often called the Net because it is the largest computer network in the world.

landscape orientation an image positioned on a page so that the long edge of the paper is at the top of the image.

local area network a connection of computers in a building or nearby buildings.

microform a medium used to reduce the size of a document (used for storage).

mouse a hand-held device that enables the user to move quickly and efficiently on a computer screen.

multimedia presentation a computer presentation that includes text, graphics, sound, animation, and video.

office network a connection of computers within an office or between an office and employees'

homes that allow all to post items to a server; these items are available to all in the office or homes.

on-line resume a resume that is written so that it can be viewed via the Internet.

optical disk technology a technology that allows a document to be scanned into a computer, viewed on a screen, indexed for accurate retrieval, and stored on a disk.

pager an electronic device that alerts a receiver that he or she has a message.

personal computer the most common workstation (usually desktop models); also known as a microcomputer.

portrait orientation an image positioned on a page so that the short edge of the paper is at the top of the image.

presentation graphics software a set of instructions telling a computer how to create visual aids, such as transparencies and slides.

printer a machine in an electronic workstation that provides the worker with a printed copy (hardcopy) of his or her work.

real time when information is exchanged or transferred instantaneously, such as on the Internet.

scannable resume a resume that is prepared so that it becomes part of a file that is created by using scanners.

scanner a device that converts printed documents or pictures into a digital form so they can be read by a computer or word processor.

screen a monitor of an electronic workstation (allows a worker to view his or her work).

search engine a piece of software enabling you to search the Internet for information using key words; examples are Yahoo, Excite, and Lycos.

shouting using all capital letters when writing an e-mail message.

software a set of instructions to a computer on how to perform particular functions.

spamming sending mass, unsolicited e-mail messages, which are called *spam*.

spreadsheet software a set of instructions telling the computer how to set up an electronic worksheet containing rows and columns.

subject index software used to search the Web for specified information by entering one or more keywords or by browsing subject categories of selected sites.

telecommute working for a company from home using a computer, modem, telephone, fax, and the Internet.

teleconference a telephone link between two or more locations that allows for the exchange of oral messages.

truncation use of a base or root word followed by a wild card to allow software to search for more than one similar keyword.

Uniform Resource Locator (URL) an address or reference code that makes it possible for a GUI Browser like Mosaic or Netscape to locate hypertext and hypermedia documents on any WWW host server in the world.

video clip brief video feature that usually includes sound.

videoconference a conference that allows participants at different locations to see each other when exchanging messages.

virtual team a team whose members do not share a physical space and who communicate by means of telephone, videoconference, e-mail, and so on.

voice mail an oral version of e-mail or a computerized system that records a message when the receiver is not available when the call comes in.

voice recognition technology software that allows spoken words to be reproduced in printed form on a computer screen.

web ring groups of web sites linked together to form a closed ring of sites on the same topic.

wide area network a connection of computers in a nationwide or worldwide setting.

wild card a symbol, commonly an asterisk (*), that commands software to return a list of resources containing all words that begin with a root or base word.

Windows an operating system developed by Microsoft Corporation. Windows creates a graphical environment, called the desktop, on the user's computer screen. The desktop contains icons that allow the user to access software applications.

word processing software a set of instructions telling a computer how to interpret entered text, format it, revise it, and print it.

World Wide Web (WWW) a system of computers that can share information by means of hypertext links.

Appendix C

Grammar and Mechanics

Section 1: Parts of Speech

Every word in a message has a use. Understanding word usage will help you communicate more clearly and effectively. Familiarity with the parts of speech will help you choose the best word at the right time. There are eight parts of speech:

- a **noun** names a person, place, or thing
- a **pronoun** takes the place of a noun
- a **verb** is a word or phrase that describes the action, state of being, or condition of the subject
- an **adjective** modifies or describes a noun or pronoun
- an **adverb** modifies a verb, an adjective, or another adverb
- a **preposition** connects a noun or pronoun to other words in the sentence
- a **conjunction** joins words, phrases, or clauses
- an **interjection** expresses surprises or strong feeling and is not related to other words in the sentence

Nouns

A **noun** is a word used to name people, places, or things. It is helpful to sort all nouns into one of two very broad categories: *proper* and *common*.

Proper Nouns

A **proper noun** names a specific person, place, or thing. Proper nouns are always distinguished by capital letters:

Specific people:	Mary Ann	Mr. Yukimura	Ms. Mendelson
Specific places:	Seattle	Orange County	United States
Specific things:	Bic pens	Canon copiers	Ford Escort

Common Nouns

A **common noun** is a word that identifies a person, place, or thing in a general way. Here are examples of common nouns:

baseball fan	movie-goer	assets	goodwill
boy	table	joy	team

Common nouns can be *compound* (*editor in chief, vice president, son-in-law, board of directors*).

Noun Plurals

Most noun plurals may be formed by using one of three rules. The first two rules are (1) add *s* to the end of most nouns to form the plural, (2) add *es* to any singular noun that ends in *s, x, z, sh,* or *ch*.

	SINGULAR	**PLURAL**
Common Nouns	pamphlet	pamphlets
	employee	employees
Proper Nouns	Smith	the Smiths
	Corvette	Corvettes
Abbreviations	CPA	CPAs
Numbers	10	10s

SINGULAR	**PLURAL**	**SINGULAR**	**PLURAL**
lens	lenses	tax	taxes
Lopez	the Lopezes	bush	bushes
Lynch	the Lynches	wrench	wrenches

The third rule is to add an *s* to form the plural of any noun ending in *y* when the *y* follows a **vowel** (*a, e, i, o,* or *u*). Here are examples of plurals that follow this rule:

delay, delays   tray, trays
key, keys   relay, relays

With the exception of proper nouns, to form the plural of nouns that have a **consonant** (all letters except vowels) before the final *y*, change the final *y* to *i* and then add *es*.

city, cities   territory, territories

Foreign Words

Because the *s* ending is standard for English plurals, plurals that do not end in *s* may sound odd. English claims a considerable number of such words, mostly borrowed from Latin and Greek:

medium, media or mediums   alumnus, alumni
crisis, crises   matrix, matrices

Nouns Ending in *o*

Nouns that end in *o* form their plurals in one of two ways. Many simply add *s* to form their plurals. Others add *es* to form their plurals. Consider these examples:

ratio, ratios   radio, radios   piano, pianos
tomato, tomatoes   potato, potatoes   veto, vetoes

Compound Nouns

Compound nouns may be spelled as separate words; in this case, the most important word is made plural:

editor in chief, editors in chief   vice president, vice presidents

Compound nouns may be joined by hyphens; in this case, the base form is made plural:

brother-in-law, brothers-in-law

Compound nouns may be spelled as one solid word; the plural is formed by adding *s*, adding *es*, or changing the *y* to *i* and then adding *es* (depending on the word ending):

letterhead, letterheads   textbook, textbooks

Proper Names

When forming plurals, treat a proper name like any other noun with this exception: Add only *s* to all proper nouns that end in *y*; ignore the "change *y* to *i* . . ." rule with proper names.

In the following examples of proper-noun plurals, the word *the* is inserted before the plurals to simulate real-life use:

John Haggerty, the Haggertys   Rosemary Portera, the Porteras

One-Form Nouns

Some nouns have only one form. Depending on the noun, that one form may be either always plural or always singular:

Always plural: thanks, scissors, belongings
Always singular: news, mathematics, headquarters

A **collective noun**, such as *tribe* or *jury*, represents a group that usually acts as a single unit:

The *jury* eats in the cafeteria at noon.

Possessive Nouns

Possessive nouns show possession. To form the possessive, add an apostrophe plus *s* ('s) to all singular nouns, both common and proper:

man	+ 's	=	one man's opinion
Mr. Ross	+ 's	=	Mr. Ross's district
district attorney	+ 's	=	the district attorney's actions

Add only an apostrophe (') to any plural if it ends in *s*:

executives	+ '	=	three executives' goals
district attorneys	+ '	=	the district attorneys' ideas

Irregular plural nouns (such as *men, women, children,* and *alumni*) and some compound nouns are examples of plural forms that do not end in *s.* For these exceptions, add an *'s* to form their possessives; in other words, apply the rule for singular nouns:

women	+ 's	=	both women's investments
brothers-in-law	+ 's	=	my two brothers-in-law's cars

Pronouns

Pronouns are convenient substitutes for nouns, and they help to communicate the *nominative, objective,* and *possessive* forms to listeners and readers.

Personal Pronouns

A **personal pronoun** is a substitute for a noun that refers to a specific person or thing.

Nominative Case

A **nominative case pronoun** (*I, we, you, he, she, it, who, whoever*), sometimes referred to as a *subjective case pronoun,* may be used as a subject or a *predicate nominative.* A **predicate nominative** is a noun or pronoun that refers to the subject and follows a form of the verb *to be* (*am, is, are*).

Carla and *I* voted for him.

They completed the project on time.

It is *she* who received all the attention.

Kate, *who* is your boss, is generous.

Objective Case

An **objective case pronoun** (*me, us, you, him, her, it, them, whom, whomever*) may be used as a direct or indirect object of a transitive verb, which is a verb that denotes action and needs an object. A **direct object** is a noun or pronoun directly affected by the action of the verb. (They chose *me.*) An **indirect object** is a noun or pronoun that receives the verb's action. (They gave *me* a gift.) An objective case pronoun may also be used as the object of a preposition. Note these examples:

Please send *them* by express mail.

Ned bought *her* a burrito.

Give it to *whomever* you see first.

Possessive Case

A pronoun that indicates ownership or possession is a **possessive case pronoun** (*my, mine, our, ours, your, yours, his, her, hers, its, their, theirs, whose*). Unlike nouns, pronouns do not need an apostrophe to signal possession.

These are *our* folders.

The fancy clothes are *hers*.

My going to the party surprised Joe.

Intensive Pronouns

An **intensive pronoun** (*myself, yourself, herself, himself, itself, ourselves, yourselves, themselves*) is a compound pronoun form created by joining a pronoun with *self* or *selves*, such as *myself* and *yourselves*. Use intensive pronouns to provide emphasis in a sentence. For example:

I *myself* completed the project in two days.

Only you *yourselves* are responsible for this budget.

Reflexive Pronouns

A **reflexive pronoun** is also a compound pronoun form that ends in *self* or *selves*. However, a reflexive pronoun refers to a noun or pronoun that appears earlier in a sentence. For example:

We found *ourselves* reminiscing at the reunion. (The reflexive pronoun *ourselves* refers to *we*.)

Interrogative Pronouns

An **interrogative pronoun** begins a question that leads to a noun response. Interrogative pronouns are *who, whose, whom, which,* and *what.*

Who is in your office? *Whom* do you want to call you?

Whose are these? *Which* of those are important?

What are your plans?

Demonstrative Pronouns

A **demonstrative pronoun** is used to "point to" a specific person, place, or thing. The four demonstrative pronouns are *this, that, these,* and *those.*

Do you prefer *this* monitor or *that* one?

These books should be moved next to *those* shelves.

Verbs

The most important part of speech in a sentence is probably the **verb**, which expresses action, a state of being, or a condition of the subject of the sentence. No sentence is complete without a verb, and some sentences have more than one verb.

Types of Verbs

Every sentence must have a verb in order to be complete. Verbs are either *action* or *linking verbs*. Linking verbs include *state-of-being* verbs and *condition* verbs.

Action Verbs. Action verbs help to create strong, effective sentences. Action verbs may take objects and indirect objects:

> Mr. Gomez *teaches* me Finance 102.

> Juanita *purchased* a stock certificate.

> Gabrielle *wrote* legibly.

State-of-Being Linking Verbs. State-of-being linking verbs, sometimes called *to be* verbs, do not have objects or indirect objects; instead, these verbs have *predicate nominatives* and *predicate adjectives*. The verb *to be* has many different forms to denote the present, past, or future state of being. Here are some examples:

> The new president *is* Mr. Jongg. (The predicate nominative, *Mr. Jongg*, is linked to the subject by the verb *is*.)

> The old software programs *were* expensive. (The predicate adjective is *expensive*.)

Condition Verbs. A condition linking verb does not have an object or an indirect object; instead, it connects an adjective to the subject. Condition linking verbs either refer to a condition or appeal to the senses. Examples are *taste, smell, seem, appear,* and *become*.

> The assistant *appears* cooperative.

> The health food *tastes* delicious.

Verb Tenses

There are six verb tenses in English; they indicate the time an action takes place. These six tenses are categorized into two groups, simple and perfect.

Simple Tenses. The simple tenses are called *present, past,* and *future*. A **present tense verb** expresses present occurrences (what is happening now). For example:

> Computer services *sell* information.

> Georgia *is teaching* a course in merchandising.

A **past tense verb** expresses action recently completed.

> Restless, the Commander *walked* all night.

> Tammy *was visiting* her bed-ridden father.

A **future tense verb** expresses action or condition yet to come. Future tense is formed by placing the helping verb *will* before the main verb:

> I *will vote* on election day.

> The accountants *will be consulting* with their clients.

Perfect Tenses. A perfect tense verb describes the action of the main verb in relation to a specific time period that is in the past, from the past to the present, or in the future. The three perfect tenses are *present perfect*, *past perfect*, and *future perfect*. Form the perfect tense by preceding the past participle form of the main verb with either *have*, *has*, or *had*.

A **present perfect tense verb** indicates continuous action from the past to the present. *Has* or *have* precedes the past participle form of the main verb:

> George *has voted* in every election since 1986.

> They *have been jogging* every day since the beginning of the month.

A **past perfect tense verb** indicates action that began in the past and continued to the more recent past when it was completed. *Had* precedes the past participle form of the main verb:

> George *had voted* in every election until last week.

> They *had been jogging* every day until this past Monday.

A **future perfect tense verb** indicates action that will be completed at a specific point in the future. *Will have* precedes the past participle form of the main verb:

> Including next year, George *will have voted* in every election since 1986.

> By next Tuesday, they *will have been jogging* for a month.

Transitive and Intransitive Verbs

A **transitive verb** is a verb that must have an object to complete the meaning of a sentence. For example:

> Clark *suggested*. (*Suggested* what? Not complete)

> Clark *suggested a profitable method*. (Complete)

An **intransitive verb** is a verb that does not need an object to complete the meaning of a sentence. For example:

> The recruits *laughed.*

> The merchandise *is* here.

> He *will be* treasurer. (*Treasurer* is a predicate nominative.)

Active and Passive Voice

Voice indicates whether the subject is doing the action or receiving the action of a verb. **Active voice** means that the subject of a sentence is doing the action.

> John *completed* his report using his computer.

> The young sprinter *won* the race.

For the most part, use the active voice in business writing. The active voice creates a clear, sharp picture in the listener's or reader's mind.

Passive voice means that the subject of a sentence is receiving the action. The passive voice is formed with the past participle and a form of the verb *to be.*

> The report *was completed* by John.

> The race *was won* by the young sprinter.

Verbals

A **verbal** is a verb form used as a noun, adjective, or adverb. The three verbals are *infinitives, gerunds,* and *participles.*

Infinitive. An **infinitive** is a verb form that functions as a noun, an adjective, or an adverb, but not as a verb: An infinitive is formed by placing the word *to* in front of a present tense verb.

> *To run* like the wind is Jaime's dream. (noun—subject)

> Evan wants *to graduate* from West Point with honors. (noun—direct object)

> Drew's job is *to feed* his aunt's nine cats. (noun—predicate nominative)

> Her desire *to become* principal is noble. (adjective—"*what kind* of desire?")

> Racine International was founded *to promote* world peace. (adverb—"was founded *why?*")

Gerund. A **gerund** is an *-ing* verb form that functions as a noun. *Sleeping, renting,* and *building* are examples of gerunds. Gerunds may be used in a phrase that contains the gerund, an object, and its modifiers.

> *Avoiding* the awful truth was her tendency. (subject)

> Su Yung's career is *refurbishing* boats. (predicate nominative)

Every Friday, they love *swimming* at the YMCA. (direct object)

Telly's habit, *falling* off to sleep, gets him into trouble in class. (appositive)

His talent for *guessing* someone's age is uncanny. (object of preposition)

Participle. A participle is a verb form that can be used either as an adjective or as part of a verb phrase. The *present participle* is always formed by adding *ing*. The *past participle* is usually formed by adding *d* or *ed* to the present tense of a regular verb; or it may have an irregular form. The *perfect participle* always functions as an adjective and always is formed by combining *having* with the past participle of the verb.

Casey has a *snoring* dog on her front porch. (present participle as adjective)

Tanya and Sam are *thinking* about moving. (present participle in verb phrase)

There were six *launched* satellites that summer. (past participle as adjective)

This is a *broken* arrow. (irregular past participle as adjective)

Having noticed the change in Gina, he married her. (perfect participle as subject)

Clara, *having studied* highland dancing, entered the contest. (appositive)

Adjectives

An **adjective** is a word that describes or limits nouns or noun substitutes (pronouns, gerund phrases, and infinitive phrases). Adjectives answer the following questions about nouns:

1. Which one? *this* proposal, *those* appointments
2. How many? *six* calls, *few* tourists
3. What kind? *ambitious* student, *creative* teacher

She is reading a *well-written, suspenseful* book. (The adjectives *well-written* and *suspenseful* describe *book*.)

Casey's stylish suit was perfect for *Dot's* wedding. (The adjectives *Casey's stylish* describe *suit*; *Dot's* modifies *wedding*.)

Articles

Although classified as adjectives, the words *the, a,* and *an* are also called **articles.** *The* denotes a specific noun or pronoun. *A* or *an* denote a nonspecific noun or pronoun.

Place the article *the* before *a* noun to designate that the noun is specific, not general:

The man (a specific man)   *The* toy (a specific toy)

Place the article *a* before *a* noun that begins with a consonant sound to designate that the noun is general, not specific:

A man (a nonspecific man)   *A* toy (a nonspecific toy)

Place the article *an* before a noun that begins with the sound of a vowel:

an honorable leader   *an* attractive child

Nouns and Pronouns Used as Adjectives

Nouns or pronouns that precede and modify other nouns and answer questions such as *which one* or *what kind* are used as adjectives:

Luis had four *theater* tickets. (Usually a noun, *theater* serves as an adjective describing the "kind" of tickets.)

Did you see *my mathematics* assignment? (The pronoun *my* and the noun *mathematics* are used as adjectives to identify which assignment.)

Proper Adjectives

Proper nouns that precede and modify other nouns serve as **proper adjectives**. Begin proper adjectives with capitals.

Burton is proud of his *New York* accent.

Our family thoroughly enjoys *Thanksgiving* dinner.

Compound Adjectives

A **compound adjective** is two or more hyphenated words that precede and modify nouns:

The *well-known* mystery writer is signing copies of his book.

Vivian is selling *long-term* health care insurance policies.

Comparison of Regular Adjectives

Adjectives have three *degrees* for comparison: the *positive* degree, the *comparative* degree, and the *superlative* degree.

To create the comparative degree of regular adjectives, either add *er* or *more* or add *er* or *less* to the positive degree form. To create the superlative degree of regular adjectives, either add *est* or *most* or add *est* or *least* to the positive degree form.

Use the positive degree to describe one item:

> The box is a **big** carton.
>
> Ryan is an **efficient** worker.

Also use the positive degree to express equality:

> He is as **big** as you.

Use the comparative degree to describe two items:

> The box is a **bigger** carton than the first one.
>
> Ryan is **less efficient** than Charles.

Use the superlative degree to describe three or more items:

> The box is the **biggest** carton of the three.
>
> Ryan is the **least efficient** of the new employees.

Comparison of Irregular Adjectives

A few frequently used adjectives do not form their comparisons in the usual manner (adding *er* or *more, est* or *most*). Examples are *good, bad, little, many,* and *much.* Note this breakdown:

POSITIVE DEGREE	COMPARATIVE DEGREE	SUPERLATIVE DEGREE
good book	better book	best book
bad result	worse result	worst result
little amount	less amount	least amount
many reports	more reports	most reports
much laughter	more laughter	most laughter

Absolute Adjectives

Some adjectives cannot be compared because they do not have degrees; they are already at the maximum level of their potential. These adjectives are referred to as **absolute adjectives**. Some examples are *immaculate, perfect, square, round, complete, excellent,* and *unique.* When you use these words in your sentences, use them alone or precede them with the terms "more nearly" or "most nearly." For example:

> Your yard is *more nearly square* than your neighbor's.
>
> The food at Tim's restaurant is *excellent.*

Adverbs

An **adverb** is a word that modifies an action verb, an adjective, or another adverb. Most adverbs end in *ly*. An adverb answers the questions *how, when, where, how often,* or *to what extent*:

How? He wrote the paper *correctly.*

When? He wrote the report *yesterday.*

Where? He wrote the report *here.*

How often? He wrote the report *twice.*

To what extent? How? He wrote the report *very quickly.*

Modifying Action Verbs

Adverbs modify action verbs but not linking verbs. Linking verbs are modified by adjectives, as in "She *appears* **happy**" or "George *is* **intelligent**." Action verbs require adverbs:

She gave it to me *gladly.*

The dog sat up and begged *just once.*

Modifying Adjectives

An adverb usually answers the question *to what extent* about an adjective that it modifies:

The cookies Granny bakes are *very* good. (The adverb *very* describes the adjective *good*.)

That new project is *tremendously* complex. (The adverb *tremendously* describes the adjective *complex*.)

Modifying Other Adverbs

An adverb also can answer the question *to what extent* about another adverb in a sentence:

The grammar school pupil did her work *too quickly.* (The adverb *too* modifies the adverb *quickly*.)

We purchased the new printer *very recently.* (The adverb *very* modifies the adverb *recently*.)

Accompanying Verb Phrases

Because adverbs modify action verbs and verb phrases that include action verbs, adverbs such as *never* or *always* frequently appear in the middle of verb phrases.

Ned is *always* writing e-mail messages.

That has *already* been ordered.

Conjunctive Adverbs

A special group of adverbs called *conjunctive adverbs* includes words such as *therefore, moreover, however, nevertheless,* and *furthermore.* A **conjunctive**

adverb is a transitional word that joins two independent but related sentences.

> They remained at work late; *therefore*, they were able to complete the project.

> The student works after school as a messenger; *moreover*, she waits on tables in the evening.

Comparison of Adverbs

Like adjectives, adverbs have three degrees of comparison: *positive, comparative*, and *superlative*. Adverbs usually show their comparative form by adding *er* or *more* or *less* to the simple form (positive degree). Adverbs show their superlative form by adding *est* or *most* or *least* to the simple form. Here are examples:

POSITIVE DEGREE	COMPARATIVE DEGREE	SUPERLATIVE DEGREE
arrived *late*	arrived *later* than she	arrived *latest* of all
clearly written	*more clearly* written	*most clearly* written
acted *greedily*	acted *less greedily*	acted *least greedily*
keyed *fast*	keyed *faster* than he	keyed *fastest* of all

Prepositions

A **preposition** is a word that usually indicates direction, position, or time. A preposition is linked to a noun or noun substitute to form a phrase.

Direction: She walked *into* the classroom.

Position: She stood *behind* the open gate.

Time: She left work *before* lunch.

The following list contains some of the most commonly used prepositions:

about	behind	for	through
above	below	from	to
across	beneath	in	toward
after	beside	into	under
against	between	like	until
along	beyond	of	up
among	by	off	upon
around	concerning	on	with
at	during	out	within
before	except	over	without

The Role of the Preposition

Prepositions introduce phrases called **prepositional phrases**. A prepositional phrase begins with a preposition and ends with a noun or noun substitute that functions as the *object* of the preposition. In addition, one or more adjectives that modify the object may appear in a prepositional phrase. Here are examples:

> Place the carton *behind* the tall cabinet. (The preposition is *behind*; the object is the noun *cabinet*; *the tall* are modifiers; the prepositional phrase is *behind the tall cabinet.*)

> Gary believes that learning a spreadsheet software program is *beyond* him. (The preposition is *beyond*; the object is the pronoun *him*; the prepositional phrase is *beyond him.*)

Prepositional Phrases Used as Adjectives

Prepositional phrases may be used to modify nouns and noun substitutes in sentences. Prepositional phrases can have the same function as adjectives and answer questions such as *what kind* or *which one* about the words they modify. Here are examples:

> Robert is *among those* here. (The prepositional phrase *among those* modifies the noun *Robert.*)

> They, *without a doubt*, are the most considerate people I have ever met. (The prepositional phrase *without a doubt* modifies the pronoun *they.*)

Prepositional Phrases Used as Adverbs

Prepositional phrases may be used to modify action verbs, adjectives, or adverbs. Prepositional phrases can have the same function as adverbs and answer questions such as *when, where, why, how,* or *to what extent* about the words they modify.

> *After lunch*, Marla filed the papers. (The prepositional phrase *after lunch* answers the question *when* about the verb *filed.*)

> Ms. Torres is very knowledgeable *about the subject*. (The prepositional phrase *about the subject* modifies the adjective *knowledgeable.*)

Special Considerations When Using Prepositions

This section discusses guidelines for using *over* and *opposite* and omitting *of* after *off*, *at* or *to* after *where*, *for* after *like*, and prepositions at the end of sentences.

Use of *Over*

Omit *with* after *over*:

INCORRECT	**CORRECT**
We want this project *over with*.	We want this project *over*.

Omitting *Of* after *Off*

Eliminate the word *of* after the word *off* in sentences.

INCORRECT
Flo took the book *off of* the shelf.

CORRECT
Flo took the book *off* the shelf.

Omitting *At* or *To* after *Where*

Eliminate the words *at* and *to* after the word *where*.

INCORRECT
Where should I deliver the bag *at*?

Where did the children go *to*?

CORRECT
Where should I deliver the bag?

Where did the children go?

Use of *Opposite*

Do not add the word *to* after the preposition *opposite*.

INCORRECT
The school is opposite *to*
the township building.

CORRECT
The school is opposite
the township building.

Conjunctions

A **conjunction** is a word that joins two or more words, phrases, or clauses.

> Clara *and* Jose worked overtime.
>
> Not only Clara *but also* Jose worked overtime.
>
> *When* Clara worked overtime, Jose joined her.

Each of the previous sentences illustrates a different kind of conjunction. The first sentence uses a *coordinate conjunction;* the second sentence, a *correlative conjunction;* the third sentence, a *subordinate conjunction.*

Coordinate Conjunctions

A **coordinate conjunction** joins words, phrases, and clauses of equal grammatical rank. *Equal grammatical rank* means that the connected elements are the same part of speech. For example, the connected elements may be nouns, verbs, prepositional phrases, or independent clauses. The coordinate conjunctions are *for, and, nor, but, so, or,* and *yet.* The following list presents guidelines for using coordinate conjunctions and includes examples of their use.

> Leo is studying computer science, *for* he plans to be a systems analyst. (The conjunction *for* joins two independent clauses.)
>
> The teacher *and* the principal spoke outside the room. (The conjunction *and* joins two nouns.)
>
> Max did *not* agree with Craig, *nor* did he agree to take part in the arrangements. (The conjunction *nor* joins two clauses.)

Tien wanted to attend the workshop, *but* she couldn't spare the time. (The conjunction *but* joins two clauses.)

Janice loves him, *so* she said she would marry him. (The conjunction *so* joins two clauses.)

They plan to swim *or* to hike this weekend. (The conjunction *or* joins two verbs.)

Philippa says she loves to travel, *yet* she has never been on an airplane. (The conjunction *yet* joins two clauses.)

Correlative Conjunctions

A **correlative conjunction**, like a coordinate conjunction, is a word that connects words, phrases, and clauses of equal grammatical rank. Correlative conjunctions differ from coordinate conjunctions because they are always used in pairs for emphasis. The following pairs are the most commonly used correlative conjunctions:

both . . . and   neither . . . nor   either . . . or   not only . . . but also

These sentences illustrate the use of correlative conjunctions:

Both Greg *and* Barbara applied for the teaching position.

Either Greg *or* Barbara applied for the teaching position.

Neither Greg *nor* Barbara applied for the teaching position.

Not only Greg *but also* Barbara applied for the teaching position.

Subordinate Conjunctions

A **subordinate conjunction** joins elements of unequal grammatical rank. It is used primarily to connect dependent clauses with independent clauses. Here's a list that shows common subordinate conjunctions:

after	as though	provided	though	whenever
although	because	since	unless	where
as	before	so that	until	while
as if	if	that	when	

Here are some sentences that use subordinate conjunctions:

Although we couldn't attend, we sent a donation.

They saw her *as* they were leaving the factory.

As if we could solve the problems, the men asked us for help.

Jules and Beth will visit *provided* they are allowed.

Interjections

An **interjection** is a word or expression that has no grammatical relationship with other words in a sentence. An interjection is used primarily to express strong emotion; therefore, it is often followed by an exclamation point.

Hey, get your coffee cup off my monitor!

Help! Do you hear that daily from your customers?

Don't pass this by. *No*, the opportunity is too good.

Your idea is sure to work. *Super*!

In specific situations such as sales promotions, interjections add color and vitality. However, interjections should not be used routinely in business writing.

Applications

Part A. Write ten sentences using each of the following proper, common, and possessive nouns.

1. bank	6. Mr. Smith
2. Bank	7. Mr. Smith's
3. college	8. memo's
4. College	9. telephones'
5. children	10. editor in chief's

Part B. Correct any errors in nominative, objective, and possessive case personal pronouns.

1. Gloria's outdated typewriter was her to keep.
2. Did May ask for the operator whom assisted her?
3. We voted for they for treasurer and parliamentarian.
4. It's Appendix F is incomplete.
5. Him working on the budget keeps him busy.

Part C. Select the correct word(s) in each sentence.

1. The spreadsheet software is the (easier, easiest) of the two.
2. As a team, Keely and Rex are (more smarter, smarter, smartest) than Lyle and Nita.
3. That is a (well-known, well known) film.
4. Her color monitor is (incredibly, incredible) expensive.
5. Do you feel (bad, badly) about Karl's promotion?
6. Of all the students, Tina worked (more intelligently, most intelligently).
7. The toddlers are (real, really, realy) happy to swim.
8. He saw in the memo (that, where) the topic was already covered.

Part D. Correct any errors in preposition or conjunction usage.

1. The report was divided between Karen, Lee, and Gia.
2. Who has been elected beside Ms. Gianetti?
3. Su-Yung climbed in the car to find a flashlight.
4. Where are the folding chairs at?
5. Neither the head of the department or the editor found the spelling error.
6. Being that Tom is broke, he can't go to the play.
7. The child listened attentively and with enthusiasm.
8. Drew didn't bring the sheet music for he knew the words.
9. Because we hear the go-ahead, we will not start to work.
10. Evan needed either a scholarship and a grant.

Editing and Proofreading Applications

I. Correct all errors in adverbs, adjectives, and spelling in the contents of this memo sent to all sales agents.

In the last few months' we have been great effected by the suddenly decline of the stock and bond markets. Our sales adgents are complaining most bitterly then ever about they're decreasing commission's. We want you to know that we full understand your discontent and your surprise about the unexpectedly downturn in the economy.

Be assure that we are watching the situation careful and will due everything we can to see that your income is not affected to severe in the coming months.

Mean while, encourage you're clients to sell their holdings cautious and assure them that you will monitor their accounts dayly and keep them apprised frequent. We all look foreword to a rapidly recovery in the markets and in the economy.

II. Correct all errors in preposition usage, spelling, and word usage in the following message.

As you know, our company will be relocating on the very near future. We has sold the building, the buisiness, and the inventory as of March 1. All employees will start this week to prepare for our move to Lafayette Creek, which is between 15 miles from here, opposite to the Methodist church. The store to the new location is newest and more modern then this one, and you will enjoy the cleaner and best surroundings. We plan to occupy the new premises during June 1.

Because the new store is only 15 miles a way, commuting should continue to be easy for everyone. You will also be happy to hear that starting June 1, the day of the grand openning, all employees will receive a 1 percent pay raise.

You will be sent additional details in regards to the move within the next two weeks. Our relocation should be benificial for everyone, and we are certain that all employees will be very pleased when the move is over with.

III. Write a one-paragraph description of a person sitting near you in class or of an interesting relative you have. Use adjectives and adverbs to enliven your description of how that person looks or what that person does. Then underline the adjectives and circle the adverbs that you have used. Upon rereading and reflection, could you edit your writing to be more precise or more colorful?

Section 2: Sentence Parts and Sentence Structure

A **sentence** is a group of related words that contains a *subject* and a *predicate* and expresses a complete thought. The sentence is the core of all communication. When forming sentences, the parts of speech are arranged into subjects and predicates.

The Subject in a Sentence

A **subject** is either the person who is speaking, the person who is spoken to, or the person, place, or thing spoken about.

Simple Subject

The **simple subject** is the main word in the *complete subject* that specifically names what the sentence is about. The simple subject of a sentence is never in a prepositional phrase. Here are examples with the simple subject in italics:

> *John*, the young journalist, writes articles.

> The *chair* behind the girl is vacant.

Complete Subject

The **complete subject** includes the simple subject plus all the sentence that is not part of the *complete predicate*. The complete subjects are in italics in these sentences:

> *John* writes articles.

> *John, the young journalist,* has written articles.

Compound Subject

A **compound subject** is two or more simple subjects joined by conjunctions such as *and, or, nor, not only/but also,* and *both/and.*

> *John* and *Sally* work for our company.

> His *brother* or my *sister* will accompany us.

When two nouns in a subject refer to one person, the article *the* (or *a*) is omitted before the second noun:

> The *teacher* and *counselor* is my friend.

When two nouns in a subject refer to two people, the article *the* (or *a*) is placed before both nouns:

> The *teacher* and the *counselor* are my friends.

The Predicate in a Sentence

The discussion of a predicate is divided into three brief parts: the simple predicate, the complete predicate, and a compound predicate.

Simple Predicate

The **simple predicate** is the verb in the *complete predicate*.

John *writes* articles.

John, the young journalist, *has written* articles.

Complete Predicate

The **complete predicate** is everything in the sentence said by, to, or about the subject; it always includes the main verb of the sentence. Whatever is not included in the *complete subject* of a sentence belongs in the *complete predicate*.

John *writes articles*.

John, the young journalist, *has written articles*.

Compound Predicate

A **compound predicate** consists of two or more verbs with the same subject. The verbs are connected by conjunctions such as *and, or, nor, not only/but also*, and *both/and*.

John and Sally *discussed* the matter and *concluded* that we are handling this situation incorrectly.

The engineer not only *complained* but also *refused* to finish the project.

Objects and Subject Complements

Objects and **subject complements** help to complete the thought expressed by a subject and simple predicate.

Objects

An **object** is a noun, pronoun, a clause or phrase that functions as a noun. It may be direct or indirect.

A **direct object** helps complete the meaning of a sentence by receiving the action of the verb. In fact, only action verbs can take direct objects. Direct objects answer the questions *what?* or *whom?* raised by the subject and its predicate:

Louis closed the *door*. (Louis closed *what?*)

The boy lost his *mother*. (The boy lost *whom?*)

An **indirect object** receives the action that the verb makes on the direct object; you cannot have an indirect object without a direct object. Neither the direct object nor the indirect object can be part of a prepositional phrase.

The indirect object usually answers the question *to whom is this action being directed?* You can locate the indirect object by inverting the sentence and adding *to*. Here, the direct object is in *italics* and the indirect object is in **bold**.

Michiko gave **Thomas** the *candy bar*. (The candy bar was given by Michiko *to* Thomas.)

Nancy brought the **twins** their *broccoli*. (The broccoli was brought *to* the twins by Nancy.)

Subject Complements

A **subject complement** is either a noun or pronoun that renames the subject or an adjective that describes the subject. In either case, it always follows a state-of-being or linking verb (such as *am, is, are, was, were, has been, seems, appears, feels, smells, sounds, looks,* and *tastes*). In these examples, the subject and subject complement are in *italics* and the linking verb is in **bold**.

Petersmeyer **is** an honest *banker.* (The noun *banker* renames *Petersmeyer.*)

We **have been** *sleepy* before. (The adjective *sleepy* describes *we.*)

Her *writing* **appears** *magical.* (The adjective *magical* describes *writing.*)

Clauses, Phrases, and Fragments

A **clause** is a group of words with a subject and a predicate; a **phrase** is a group of words with no subject or predicate.

Clauses

A clause is labeled **independent** if it can stand alone as a complete sentence:

One of our sales managers has developed an excellent training manual. [This is an independent clause with a complete subject (*One of our sales managers*) and a complete predicate (the rest of the sentence).]

A clause is labeled **dependent** if it cannot stand alone as a complete sentence. For example:

which we plan to use in all future training sessions

This dependent clause must be attached to an independent clause to make any sense:

One of our sales managers has developed an excellent training manual, *which we plan to use in all future training sessions.*

Phrases

A **phrase** is a group of related words that does not contain both a subject and a predicate.

A **verb phrase** is a group of words that functions as one verb. For example:

Frederico *will be finished* when we call him.

The IBC Corporation *has been supplying* us with these products.

A **prepositional phrase** is a group of words that begins with a preposition and ends with a noun or a noun substitute.

Place both cartons *on the desk.*

The boxes *in the office* belong *to him.*

Phrases add detail, interest, variety, and power to your writing. Compare:

> Horace writes.

> An avid storyteller, Horace writes shocking, turn-of-the-century ghost tales for impressionable teenagers.

Here are some other kinds of phrases:

> **Noun phrases:** her yellowed teeth/John's funny sweater

> **Adjective phrases:** smooth and juicy/below average/self-styled

> **Participial phrases:** moving quickly/having been elected

> **Infinitive phrases:** to wonder/to purchase/to be detained

Verb Phrases

Frequently, sentences have a main verb and helping verbs. The combination of a main verb, either action or linking, preceded by a helping verb or verbs forms a verb phrase. The most common helping verbs are forms of the verb *to be* and forms of the verb *to have*. Examples are *is, are, was, were, has, have,* and *had*. For example:

> Sally *spoke* to her peers. (The verb is *spoke*.)

> Sally *has spoken* to her peers. (The main verb is *spoken*; the helping verb is *has*; thus the verb phrase is *has spoken*.)

Additional helping verbs include *can, could, may, might, must, ought, should, will,* and *would*. For example:

> Sally *could have spoken* to her peers. (The main verb is *spoken*; the helping verbs are *could have*; the verb phrase is *could have spoken*.)

For a verb to be classified as a helping verb, it must have a main verb to help. Compare these sentences:

> Jim *has assisted* Ms. Quinn. (The helping verb *has* precedes the main verb *assisted*.)

> Jim *has* a new computer. (The verb is *has*.)

> Jane *will be looking* for it. (The helping verb *will be* precedes the main verb *looking*.)

> Jane *will be* here. (The linking verb is *will be*.)

Fragments

A **fragment** is an incomplete sentence that may or may not have meaning. Fragments that have meaning in context (*Good luck on your trip!*) can be used in business messages. However, do not use fragments that have no meaning:

Fragment: Sam, the vice president's brother.

Sentence: Sam, the vice president's brother, got a hefty raise.

Fragment: Because the beds were uncomfortable.

Sentence: Because the beds were uncomfortable, Goldilocks slept on the floor.

Sentence Structures

Your communications will be more stimulating if you vary the types of sentences you write. There are four basic **sentence structures**, which are classified on the basis of the number and type of clauses they have.

Recall that the two types of clauses are independent (main) and dependent (subordinate). As an effective business communicator, you can put emphasis on an idea by placing it in an independent clause, or you can de-emphasize it by placing it in a dependent clause.

The Simple Sentence

A **simple sentence** contains one independent clause and no dependent clauses. There may be any number of phrases in a simple sentence. Especially in business writing, a simple sentence can be a clear, direct way to present an idea because there are no distracting dependent clauses. However, if overused, too many simple sentences in one paragraph can sound monotone or abrupt. Here are some examples of simple sentences:

Pavarotti sings. (simple sentence)

Pavarotti and Domingo sing. (simple sentence with compound subject)

Pavarotti sings and acts. (simple sentence with compound predicate)

Luciano Pavarotti, the exquisite Italian tenor, sings like an angel. (simple sentence with various phrases)

The Compound Sentence

A **compound sentence** contains two or more independent clauses and no dependent clauses. In other words, two main ideas share equal importance. Note in these examples that the two independent clauses are joined by a coordinating conjunction, a conjunctive adverb, or a semicolon:

Mr. Feinstein is the founder, and he was the first president of FSI.

Are you going to the farmer's market, or are you going to the grocery store?

It's getting late; however, I am glad to stay here and finish this project.

Erin loves to ride horses; Connor loves to draw horses.

The Complex Sentence

A **complex sentence** contains one independent clause and one or more dependent clauses. In this structure, one or more ideas are dependent upon the main idea. The less important or negative ideas can be de-emphasized by using the complex sentence structure. Or the dependent clauses can give detail and support to the main clause. In these examples, the dependent clauses are in *italics*.

> *Although it is important to proofread a written message*, many people feel they do not have the time.

> Dan, *who cannot swim*, hates wading in Lake Waldo *because he thinks it is polluted.*

> You should understand *that Karen and Tim are happily married.*

The Compound-Complex Sentence

A **compound-complex sentence** contains two or more independent clauses and one or more dependent clauses. This structure offers the business writer a variety of ways to present ideas and emphasize or de-emphasize details. Because this structure can become long and complicated, be careful how you use it in business communications. In these examples, the independent clauses are in **bold** and the dependent clauses are in *italics*:

> *Since Noni left the folders on the desk*, **her assistant decided to finish up**, and **he did a good job**, *even though he was dead tired.*

> **Sierra and Casey**, *who are cousins*, **play together often**; however, **their fathers**, *who are brothers*, **don't see enough of each other** *because they both travel so much.*

Subject-Verb Agreement

Good communicators make sure that their subjects and verbs always agree (*he walks, they walk*). Grammatical errors in subject-verb agreement offend the receiver and label the person who erred as a careless writer or speaker.

Agreement in Number

Third-person singular pronouns and singular nouns require a singular verb that ends in *s* when the present tense is used.

> Joy *telephones* her parents daily.

> Ari *drives* to his client's warehouse every Monday.

Third-person plural pronouns and plural nouns require a plural verb that does not end in *s* when the present tense is used. For example:

> Joy's parents *telephone* her daily.

> The musicians *record* their music when they have a chance.

Agreement in an Inverted Sentence

If a sentence is **inverted** (predicate precedes subject), putting the sentence in normal order will help you check subject-verb agreement:

INVERTED ORDER	**NORMAL ORDER**
In the recruit's many strengths *lies* her *admiration*.	Her *admiration lies* in the recruit's many strengths.
In the box *are* two *bags* of apples.	Two *bags* of apples *are* in the box.

Intervening Phrases

Intervening words do not affect subject-verb agreement and should be ignored. Note these examples with the intervening words in **bold** and the subjects and verbs in *italics*:

> The *manager* **of the sports teams** *is traveling* to New Orleans.

> The *members* **of the audience** *have* different reactions.

In the first example, the singular subject *manager* requires the singular verb *is traveling*. In the second example, the plural subject *members* requires the plural verb *have*. Here are two additional examples:

> A *professor*, **rather than the college administrators**, *represents* the institution at the convention.

> My *assistants*, **along with the company comptroller**, *work* overtime on this project.

A Number, The Number

When used as a subject, the expression *a number* is considered to be plural and needs a plural verb:

> *A number* of inquiries **come** to our office each day.

> There **are** *a number* of tourists at our concert.

When used as a subject, the expression *the number* is considered to be singular and needs a singular verb:

> *The number* of inquiries **has decreased** since last month.

> *The number* of attorneys in Philadelphia **is** on the rise.

Names of Companies

Names of companies are usually considered singular. Although a firm's name may end in *s* or include more than one individual's name, it is still one business.

> *Gordon, Rodriguez, and Ramirez* **is representing** the plaintiff.

> *Silkowski and Daughters* **manufactures** computer chips.

Amounts

An amount that is plural in form takes a singular verb if the amount is considered to be one item:

One hundred dollars **is** a generous wedding gift.

Two dollars **is** given to the six-year-old child for every baby tooth.

An amount that is plural in form takes a plural verb if the amount is considered to be more than one item:

Fifty-one dollar bills **are** in my wallet.

Compound Subjects Joined by *And*

Because errors in subject-verb agreement commonly occur with compound subjects, take a careful look at some special guidelines.

1. Usually a compound subject joined by *and* is plural and requires a plural verb.

   Mei-ling and Yuan **are visiting** their parents in Wuxi.

2. Sometimes compound subjects are treated as one item and require a singular verb.

   Peanut butter and jelly **is** popular in the grammar school.

3. If *each, every, many a,* or *many an* precedes a compound noun, always use a singular verb. For example:

   Many an investor and homeowner **has supported** this tax increase.

Compound Subjects Joined by *Or/Nor*

When a compound subject is joined by *or, nor, either/or,* or *neither/nor,* the verb agrees with the subject that is closest to the verb:

Tracey or *Hal* **seems** to be well qualified for the position.

Either George or *his sisters* **are** catering the buffet.

Neither the supervisors nor *the security guard* **has seen** the criminal.

Pronoun-Antecedent Agreement

The noun or noun phrase that is replaced by the pronoun is called the **antecedent** of the pronoun. The pronoun must agree with its antecedent in person, number, and gender.

Person: Use a first-person pronoun to represent the persons speaking (*I, we*). Use a second-person pronoun to represent the persons spoken to (*you*). Use a third-person pronoun to represent the persons spoken about (*he, she, it, they*).

Number: Use a singular pronoun (*he, she*) to refer to an antecedent that is a singular noun. Use a plural pronoun (*they*) to refer to an antecedent that is a plural noun.

Gender: Use a masculine pronoun (*his*) to refer to an antecedent that is a masculine noun. Use a feminine pronoun (*her*) to refer to an antecedent that is a feminine noun. Use a gender-neutral pronoun (such as *it*) to refer to an antecedent that is a gender-neutral noun (such as *table*).

In the following examples, the antecedents are in *italics* and the pronouns are in **bold**:

John encouraged **his** staff.

Anyone can state **his** or **her** opinion on the matter.

The British *man* **who** completed the two projects received a promotion.

Third-Person Pronoun Agreement

Writers do not have many problems matching first- and second-person pronouns with their antecedents. On occasion communicators find that third-person pronouns present problems in gender and number.

The gender of the antecedent in a sentence is not always obvious. For example, nouns such as *manager, nurse, astronaut, president, systems analyst,* or *worker* could apply to either gender. Here are two alternative solutions:

1. Use both masculine and feminine pronouns to agree with an antecedent if its gender is unknown:

    A good *manager* consults with **his** or **her** staff.

    A *doctor* tends to **his** or **her** patients without favoritism.

2. Change the antecedent to a plural form and use the gender-neutral plural pronoun *their*:

    The *students* completed **their** software installation on time.

    The *astronauts* cooperate 100 percent with **their** peers at NASA.

A problem may arise when applying the number-agreement principle to a collective noun (*jury, panel, committee*). You must first determine whether the group is acting as a unit or individually. Note these examples:

The *committee* submitted **its** report. (acting as a single unit)

The *police* were given **their** assignments. (acting as individuals)

The *members* of the Board of Directors volunteered **their** opinions.

Remember, nouns such as *school, company,* or *corporation* are always singular even though they employ many people.

Compound Antecedents

A **compound antecedent** is an antecedent that consists of two or more elements. "Agreement in number" may present a problem if an antecedent is compound. To eliminate errors when this occurs, follow these three principles.

1. When two or more elements are connected by *and*, use a plural pronoun to refer to the antecedent:

    After *David and I* drafted the proposal, **we** sent it to Ms. Jones.

    The manager and the word processor planned **their** itinerary.

2. If two or more elements of a compound antecedent are joined by *or/nor, either/or,* and *neither/nor,* (a) use a singular pronoun if all elements are singular; and (b) use a plural pronoun if all elements are plural. Here are some examples:

    Singular: *Faye or Tom* can work on **her or his** papers now.

    Neither Lars nor Hal has completed **his** book report.

    Plural: *The trainees or their supervisors* will finish **their** statistical computations.

    Neither the men nor the women plan to share **their** profits on the sale.

3. If elements are connected by *or/nor, either/or,* or *neither/nor* and one part of the antecedent is singular and the other is plural, the pronoun must agree with the part that is closest to the verb:

    Singular: *Neither the boxers nor the manager* expressed **his** (or **her**) opinion.

    Either the engineers or the architect will give **her** (or **him**) suggestions for renovation.

    If applicable, place the plural item last and use a plural verb and pronoun:

    Plural: *Neither the manager nor the boxers* expressed **their** opinions.

    Either the architect or the engineers will give **their** suggestions for renovation.

Indefinite Pronoun Agreement

An **indefinite pronoun** refers in *general* terms to people, places, and things. Some pronouns in this category are always *singular*, such as *one, each, every, anybody,* and *anything*:

Every auditor had an opportunity to ask **his** or **her** questions.

Each of the data operators is concerned about **his** or **her** job.

Other indefinite pronouns are always plural, such as *many, few, both,* and *several*:

> *Many* will hand in **their** questionnaires.

> *Few* accountants receive **their** CPAs.

Some indefinite pronouns, such as *all, any, some, more,* and *most,* can be either singular or plural depending on the noun or object of the preposition that follows them:

> **Singular:** *Most of the report* had **its** spelling checked.

> **Plural:** *Most of the reports* have **their** spelling checked.

Parallel Construction

Another kind of agreement is parallel construction. A construction that is not parallel will have a conjunction that joins unmatched elements. An adverb may be joined to a prepositional phrase, or a verb phrase may be joined to a noun. Constructions that are not parallel are ungrammatical. Note these examples:

> **Incorrect:** Customers want *not only* good service *but also* to be treated with courtesy. (A correlative conjunction joins a noun with an infinitive verb phrase, which is an unparallel construction.)

> **Correct:** Customers want *not only* good service *but also* courtesy. Or Customers want *not only* to receive good service *but also* to be treated with courtesy.

> **Incorrect:** The expert works cleverly *and* with speed. (A coordinate conjunction joins an adverb with a prepositional phrase, which is not a parallel construction.)

> **Correct:** The expert works cleverly *and* speedily. Or The expert works speedily *when* a deadline is approaching.

> **Incorrect:** Jack is responsible for washing, ironing, and to fold the clothes. (an unparallel series)

> **Correct:** Jack is responsible for washing, ironing, and folding the clothes.

> **Incorrect:** His territory is larger than the Brainerd Realty Company. (confusing comparison)

> **Correct:** His territory is larger than the Brainerd Realty Company's territory.

Applications

Part A. Identify the simple or compound subject in each sentence.

1. The two actors with several years of training are more professional.
2. Neither the tellers nor the loan officers understand the directive.
3. Every one of the secretaries worked overtime on Monday.
4. Both of the team members that were benched were also fined.
5. Stan and Chloe's sister won a merit scholarship.

Part B. Identify the simple or compound predicate in each sentence.

1. Each of us has her suit pressed and ready to wear.
2. The employees have listened carefully and have heeded our advice.
3. Some of the report is intelligible and appropriate.
4. The residents will scrape the walls and woodwork before painting them.
5. Careful reading, enjoying both the plot and its development, enhances the reader's enjoyment.

Part C. Correct any errors in verb form.

1. All executives has been offered early retirement incentives.
2. Where is the speaker and the introducer sitting on the stage?
3. The committee were unified in the decision.
4. Neither of her remarks were meaningful.
5. While keying in the data, Hal and Julia was distracted by the noise.
6. The seashore house, together with the furnishings, are a very tempting purchase.
7. Priscilla, while looking for the missing proposals, have found the documents prepared by Tilden.
8. Neither Ms. Huang nor her former students plans to attend the reunion.

Part D. Correct the errors in pronoun-antecedent agreement. Write your answers on a sheet of paper.

1. Every student took their seat in the auditorium.
2. After one works so diligently to finish the project on time, we expect it to be accepted by the administration.
3. Each of the retailers changed their mind about the display.
4. Either Ms. Morganti or Mr. Gold is going to state their side of the story.
5. The leaders of the federation offered its opinions on the matter.
6. Tonick Bros., Inc., submitted their bid for repaving the road.
7. Maya and I, which suggested the renovation, have been assigned to draw up the plans.

Editing and Proofreading Applications

I. Correct all errors in pronoun agreement, word usage, and spelling in the following excerpt of a report. Write a corrected copy.

In order to collect data and the opinions of the township residents, a house-to-house survey was completed the weeks of July 10 and July 17. Here are some of the findings: (1) most household have two or more dependants which are still in school; (2) some of the residence either disapproved off or were not willing to give his or her opinions about the township recretional areas; (3) a few people surveyed had all ready recieved questions such as this in the mail and had all ready returned the three-page questionairre to the township building; (4) most township familys whom have lived here 15 or more year's support the ideas of the township directors; (5) all those surveyed congratulated themselves for putting up with the recent construcsion in there neighborhood; and (6) adherence to the scooper-dooper policy, who had been put in force in March, is not a problem for him or her.

Overall, those people in this township are extremely cooperative and indicate that they will continue they're support of are leaders.

II. Correct all errors in subject-verb agreement and spelling in the contents of the following message.

To provide you with an additional opportunity to enhance you're financial security and over come any retirement fund deficeincy, the Board of Directors have unanimously voted to institute a new stock purchase plan effective Febuary 1. This plan are voluntary and provide you with a chance to acquire company stock. Heres important information about the offer:

1. You can elects to make contributions through payroll deduction's.

2. The dollar amount you contributes are applied toward the purchase price of the stock. You will receives a 5 percent discount on the market price; the company pay all brokerage fees.

3. As soon as you receives a stock certificate, you begin to earn dividend's and may vote as a stockholder.

All staff members, including recent hires, is eligable. If you is interested in this investment opportunity, just fill in the attached questionnairre and return it to Room 264 within 20 days. If their is any questions you want answered, call me at Ext. 1234.

Section 3: Punctuation

For readers to interpret your ideas and inquiries precisely as you intend, you need to use correct punctuation in every message you write. Punctuation tells your readers where one thought ends and the next begins; punctuation clarifies and adds emphasis.

Punctuation includes external marks such as periods, question marks, and exclamation points. Punctuation also includes internal marks such as commas, semicolons, colons, quotation marks, parentheses, dashes, apostrophes, and hyphens.

The Period

A **period** can be used to indicate the end of a sentence, to indicate the end of an abbreviation, and to accompany an enumeration.

Periods at the End of Sentences

A period is used at the end of a declarative sentence, a mild command, an indirect question, and a courteous request.

A **declarative sentence** makes a statement:

Gloria and Ralph are upgrading their software programs.

The choir members will sing in Italy during the holiday season.

A **mild command** is a stern request from the writer to the reader:

You should watch your step or you will fall.

Return the defective hard disk to the plant today.

An **indirect question** is a statement that contains a reference to a question:

They inquired how your parents are feeling since their accident.

The judge asked if the prosecutor had any more questions for the witness.

A **courteous request** is a polite way to ask for action on the part of the reader; it does not ask for a *yes* or *no* answer:

May I have an interview when convenient.

Would you be kind enough to revise the proposal and return the corrected copy to me as soon as possible.

Periods with Abbreviations

Periods are placed after many commonly used abbreviations to indicate that the words are shortened forms of longer words:

Mr. (Mister)	Jr. (Junior)	Dr. (Doctor)
Ltd. (Limited)	Inc. (Incorporated)	Sr. (Senior)

Periods in Enumerations

When numbers or letters are used in a vertical list, periods are placed after each number or letter:

Your child will need the following items for the outing:

1. one change of clothing
2. bathing suit, swim cap, sandals, towel, and sunscreen lotion
3. snack money

The Question Mark

A **question mark** is used after a direct question and after each part in a series of questions. The response may be a single word, or it may be one or more sentences.

Question Marks after Direct Questions

Use a question mark after a complete or incomplete sentence that asks a direct question. For example:

Do you agree that summer seems to pass more quickly than winter?

Have you considered relocating to find suitable employment?

Question Marks in a Series

Occasionally a series of questions may be useful in your writing. For emphasis, follow each segment in the series with a question mark:

Were all the votes counted? all the winners notified? all the losers contacted?

Did she apply to Temple University? to Boston College? to Florida International University? to Miami Dade Community College?

The Exclamation Point

An **exclamation point** is a mark of punctuation that follows a word, a group of words, or a sentence that shows strong emotion. When an expression shows excitement, urgency, or anger, the exclamation point, together with the words, conveys the strong emotion intended by the writer:

Quick! Here's an opportunity to make money!

I'll never do that again!

Use exclamations and exclamation points sparingly in all writing, but especially in business communications. Because exclamations signify strong emotion, they lose their impact if overused.

The Comma

External punctuation marks tell the reader whether a sentence is a statement, question, or exclamation. Internal punctuation marks clarify the message intended by the writer. Of all the internal punctuation marks discussed here, the comma is without a doubt the most frequently used and misused.

Commas are used with introductory elements, independent clauses, nonessential elements, direct addresses, numbers, abbreviations, and repeated words. Commas also are inserted in a series and between adjectives. In addition, commas are used to indicate the omission of words and to promote clarity in sentences.

With Introductory Elements in Sentences

Insert a comma after an introductory word, phrase, or clause:

> *Meanwhile,* I will begin the next phase of the project. *Nevertheless,* I think we can attend the meeting. (Introductory word)

> *Before running,* the teenager warms up the leg muscles. (Introductory phrase)

> *In the long run,* the cutback will be beneficial. (Introductory phrase)

> *Because we have no record of the sale,* we cannot help you. (Introductory clause)

> *Although he was not present,* his influence was evident. (Introductory clause)

With Independent Clauses in Compound Sentences

When independent clauses in a compound sentence are joined by a coordinate conjunction such as *for, and, nor, but, or,* or *yet,* precede the conjunction with a comma:

> I will go to the hockey game on Friday, *or* I will babysit for my niece.

> The new order forms are on legal-size paper, *and* the quantity we bought should last us a while.

> We thought he was guilty at first, *but* now we have changed our minds.

When each independent clause in a compound sentence has fewer than four words, no comma is needed:

> Yoshi spoke and they responded.

> I rode but he walked.

With Nonessential Elements

Nonessential elements are set off from the rest of a sentence with commas. Examples of **nonessential elements** are interrupting expressions, nonrestrictive elements, and appositives. Nonessential elements include information that may be interesting but is not necessary to the meaning or the structure of a sentence.

To determine if the information is essential, temporarily omit it. If the meaning of the sentence stays the same, set off the nonessential word, phrase, or clause with commas.

Interrupting Expression. Any expression that is nonessential and interrupts the flow of a sentence is set off with commas:

> The most interesting part of the movie, I believe, is the entrance of the ex-wife. (The expression *I believe* is not needed.)

> He should, on the other hand, separate the items in the box. (The expression *on the other hand* is not needed.)

Nonrestrictive Element. A nonrestrictive **phrase or clause** adds information that is not essential to the meaning of the sentence:

> Jeffrey Chang, who graduated from Loyola, is my neighbor. (The clause that begins with *who* is not needed.)

> We plan to order Part 643, which Steve recommended. (The clause that begins with *which* is not needed.)

A phrase or clause that is essential to the meaning of a sentence is called a **restrictive phrase** or a **restrictive clause** and is not set off with commas:

> Ask the nurse who was on duty that night.

> The man who was just hired is part of my team.

Appositive. An **appositive** is a noun or noun substitute that renames and refers to a preceding noun. Appositives provide additional information that is not necessary to the meaning of a sentence. They are set off from the rest of the sentence with commas:

> The paper contained the forecasts for the next quarter, July through September. (*July through September* tells which quarter.)

> Ruby Muñoz, the councilwoman, is soliciting suggestions to bring up in council. (The phrase *the councilwoman* refers to and renames *Ruby Muñoz*.)

An appositive that is only one word is not set off with commas:

> My brother Mario is touring the factory.

With Direct Address

To personalize a message, a writer may use **direct address** by mentioning the reader's first or last name in the beginning, middle, or end of a sentence. Because the name is not needed to convey the meaning of the sentence, it is set off with commas:

> *Dr. Oakes*, you have been exceedingly helpful to my family.

> Have I told you, *Gwen*, that we appreciate your purchase?

In a Series

Use a comma to separate three or more items in a series of words, phrases, or clauses. Although some experts omit the comma before a conjunction in a series, we recommend that you include the comma to avoid confusion:

> Evan's college essay was thoughtful, humorous, and brief.

I will be going to the movies, to the mall, or to my grandparents' home Saturday evening.

Wake up early, prepare and serve breakfast, and take the children to the school bus.

Note: Use semicolons to separate items within a list that already contain commas:

Those in attendance were Lan Choy, President; Larry Tripp, Vice President; Rob Healy, Secretary; and Juanita Hall, Treasurer.

Between Adjectives

Use a comma between two adjectives that modify the same noun when the coordinate conjunction *and* is omitted. If the word *and* wouldn't make sense between the adjectives, do not insert a comma:

The short, thin teenager envied the tall, husky football players. (*Short and thin* and *tall and husky* make sense; insert a comma between each set of adjectives to show that *and* is omitted.)

Janet's royal blue suit is inappropriate attire for a job interview. (*Royal and blue* does not make sense; do not insert a comma.)

With Omission of Words

Occasionally, a writer may omit words that are understood by the reader. Inserting a comma at the point of omission provides clarity:

The treasurer is Johnetta; the secretary, Garth; and the vice president, Warren. (The word *is* is omitted twice in the sentence; commas are inserted at the points of omission.)

In Numbers

Use commas to indicate a whole number in units of three whether in money or items:

$2,468   34,235 hot dogs   526,230 pins   278,249

For Clarity

Occasionally, a sentence requires a comma for no reason other than to ensure clarity.

Not Clear   Shortly after the teacher left the classroom.
Clear   Shortly after, the teacher left the classroom.

With Abbreviations

Writers who use abbreviations such as *etc.*, *Jr.*, *Sr.*, and *Inc.* should be familiar with the following comma rules concerning these abbreviations:

Rule 1:   In a series, insert a comma before *etc.* when it appears at the end of a sentence, and use commas before and after *etc.* when it appears in the middle of a sentence. For example:

We will be taking camping clothes: shorts, boots, swimwear, etc.

Rule 2: Generally, place a comma before *Jr.*, *Sr.*, and *Inc.* when the abbreviations appear in a name. Also insert commas after the abbreviations in the middle of a sentence. For example:

Harry Larkin, *Jr.*, was elected to the presidency.

Able, *Inc.*, is owned by a conglomerate in New York.

The Semicolon

A **semicolon** is a form of punctuation used to denote a pause. Semicolons are stronger than commas but weaker than periods.

Between Independent Clauses

Use a semicolon between two related independent clauses instead of using a comma and a coordinate conjunction:

George is studying economics; his brother Dave is majoring in accounting.

Elaine will attend the July convention; she then will vacation in Lofton.

Before Conjunctive Adverbs

Use a semicolon before a conjunctive adverb (*moreover, nevertheless, however, consequently*) that joins two independent clauses. Conjunctive adverbs, which function as transitional expressions, introduce the second clause. Note these examples:

His report is too long; therefore, he cannot submit it until he revises it.

Getting information from Amtrak can be easy; however, the voice-mail system tends to confuse some callers.

In a Series

Use a semicolon before expressions such as *for example* (e.g.), *that is* (i.e.), and *for instance* when they introduce a list of examples:

You can attend some interesting functions; for example, an art show, a dance performance, or a special film screening.

They must follow smart money management principles; that is, save part of their income, make purchases they can afford, and avoid buying inferior goods.

In Compound Sentences

Use a semicolon before a coordinate conjunction in a compound sentence when either or both of the clauses have internal commas and the sentence might be misread if a comma is inserted before the conjunction.

I requested a return call, information about a particular check, and the teller's extension number; instead, I received a past-due notice, a reference to the wrong check, and an incorrect telephone number.

On Wednesday, March 12, 2000, the group will meet; but Florio will not officiate.

In a Series Containing Commas

Use semicolons to separate items in a series when an item or items contain commas:

> The mortgage company has branches in Newport, Rhode Island; Atlanta, Georgia; and Chicago, Illinois.

> In attendance were Acklin, the chairman; Ikuko, the treasurer; Maria, the corresponding secretary; and Sean, the parliamentarian.

The Colon

A **colon** is a form of punctuation that directs the reader's attention to the material that follows it. The material that follows the colon completes or explains the information that precedes the colon.

Before a Series

Use a colon when the words *the following, as follows,* and *are these* are near the end or at the end of a sentence that introduces a series of items:

> Each person will need the following at the meeting: a computer, a printer, a set of instructions, and a writing tablet.

> The new automobile's special features are as follows: antilock brakes, a built-in CD player, and leather upholstery.

Before a List

Use a colon before a vertical, itemized list. As with a series, the words *the following, as follows,* or *are these* may precede the colon:

> Your instructions for Sunday are these:
>
> 1. Open the office at 9 a.m.
>
> 2. Check Saturday's mail, and call me if Pinder's check arrived.
>
> 3. Answer the telephone until noon.

Before a Long Quotation

Use a colon to introduce a long quotation of more than two lines.

> Chien remarked: "When I think of my home in Beijing, I can just picture the hundreds of people riding their bicycles to work early in the morning and returning from work late in the evening."

Between Special Independent Clauses

Use a colon to separate two independent clauses when the second clause explains the first. In the following situations, a colon replaces a semicolon:

> Lucia is a skilled artist: She won an award for sketching animals.

> Here is one way to improve your sense of humor: Recall experiences that seemed serious at the time, and realize how funny they actually were.

After a Salutation

When using mixed punctuation in a letter, use a colon after a salutation. For example:

Dear Sir: Dear Dr. Santiago: Dear Ms. Linden:

In Time Designations

Use a colon between the hour and the minutes when the time is expressed in numerals:

Let's meet at 11:30 a.m. in the lobby of the office building.

The Dash

A **dash**, formed by keying two unspaced hyphens, is an informal punctuation mark. A dash is used with appositives or other nonessential elements that contain commas, before a summarizing statement, with a sudden change of thought, or before a detailed listing.

With Nonessential Elements

For emphasis, use a dash to set off appositives and other nonessential elements from the rest of the sentence. Some of the nonessential elements may have internal commas:

The stockbroker's office—newly equipped, nicely decorated, and spacious—is perfect for the hospitality reception.

Before a Summarizing Statement

Use a dash after a listing at the beginning of a sentence that is followed by a summarizing statement. Summarizing statements usually begin with the words *all* or *these*:

A nurturing manner, a love of people, and an unselfish attitude—these are three traits school counselors need.

Precision in mechanics, vocabulary, and facts—all are necessary for effective communications.

With a Sudden Change of Thought

Use a dash to indicate a sudden change of thought or a sudden break in a sentence:

Here is the perfect suit for work—and it's on sale, too!

"Then we both agree that—oh no, now what's wrong?" asked Amy.

Before a Detailed Listing

Use a dash to set off a listing or an explanation that provides details or examples:

The restaurant features exotic desserts—Polynesian pudding, Hawaiian coconut sherbet, and Samoan almond supreme cake.

Do your graduates have employable skills—excellent oral communications, keyboarding at least 70 wpm, and desktop publishing experience?

The Hyphen

A **hyphen** is a punctuation mark used after some prefixes and in forming some compound words.

After Prefixes

Use a hyphen after prefixes in some words. If you are unsure whether a word needs a hyphen, consult a dictionary. Note these examples:

ex-president	pro-American	semi-invalid
de-emphasize	co-coordinator	

In Compound Words

Use a hyphen in some compound words. In the English language some compound words are written as one word, others are written as two words, and others are hyphenated. Here are some examples of hyphenated compound words:

up-to-date reports	self-confident speaker
well-informed reporter	two-year-old child
Abe's mother-in-law	one-half the members

Some compound adjectives, such as *up to date*, *well informed*, and *two year old*, are hyphenated if they precede the noun they modify, but they are not hyphenated if they follow the noun:

The report is up to date.

Our up-to-date equipment improves productivity.

Quotation Marks

Quotation marks indicate a direct quotation, a definition, nonstandard English, a word or phrase used in an unusual way, or a title.

With Direct Quotations

When stating someone's exact words, enclose the words within opening and closing quotation marks. For example:

Betty exclaimed, "It's getting late; let's go!"

"We'll leave now," answered Jeff. "We don't want to miss the train."

Within Quotations

Use single quotation marks to enclose a quotation within a quotation:

Amanda stated, "They listened carefully to the president when he said, 'Our competition is getting ahead of us.' "

With Other Punctuation Marks

When placing ending quotation marks, follow these guidelines.

Rule 1: Place periods and commas within ending quotation marks:

"I concur," said the investor, "with your suggestion."

Rule 2: Place semicolons and colons outside ending quotation marks:

> His best lecture is called "Psychoanalysis in the 1990s"; have you had an opportunity to hear it?

> This is the "beauty of San Diego": ideal temperatures and clear skies.

Rule 3: Place question marks and exclamation points inside the ending quotation marks when the quoted material is a question or an exclamation:

> She shouted, "Watch out!"

> He replied, "What's happening?"

Rule 4: Place question marks and exclamation points outside the ending quotation marks when the sentence, but not the quoted material, is a question or an exclamation:

> Did Lydia actually say, "I will attend the seminar"?

> What a deplorable situation; he's just "goofing off"!

With Definitions and Nonstandard English

Use quotation marks to designate a term that is defined in the same sentence in which the term appears:

> A "couch potato" is someone who watches television all day and all evening.

Use quotation marks to enclose slang words or expressions:

> He referred to his car as a "dumb bunny."

With Titles

Use quotation marks to enclose the titles of parts of whole works such as magazine articles and chapters. Quotation marks also are used to enclose titles of lectures, songs, sermons, and short poems. Here are examples:

> I read the article "The New Subcompact Cars" in *Consumer's Digest*.

> Gregory's lecture "E-Mail Versus Voice-Mail" created a stir in the audience.

Parentheses

A **parenthesis** is used in pairs to set off nonessential words, phrases, or clauses. The pair is called *parentheses*. Parentheses also are used with monetary designations, abbreviations that follow names, references and directions, and numerals and letters accompanying a list.

With Nonessential Elements

De-emphasize nonessential elements by placing them in parentheses. When the items in parentheses appear at the end of a sentence, place the external punctuation mark after the ending parenthesis:

A high percentage of the alumni (73 percent of those surveyed) opposed changing the name of the college.

We received a visit from our ex-president (1997–1998).

When an item in parentheses is *intentionally* a complete sentence, capitalize the first word and end the item with an internal punctuation mark:

Luis and Ramona relocated to Brooklyn. (Didn't you meet them in San Juan?)

When a dependent clause is followed by an item or items within parentheses, place the comma after the ending parenthesis:

When they arrive at the airport (around 6 p.m.), George will meet them.

With Monetary Designations and Abbreviations

Primarily in legal documents, parentheses are used to enclose a numerical designation ($500) following a verbal designation of money. For example:

Mr. Chin has deposited the sum of five hundred dollars ($500) in your escrow account.

In addition, parentheses are used with abbreviations that follow names:

The Association for Business Communication (ABC) had selected Clifford Chung as its Interim Executive Director.

With References and Directions

Use parentheses to set off both references and directions to minimize their importance in a sentence:

You may consult the appendix (page 345) for the correct format.

This trip (see the enclosed brochure) is a once-in-a-lifetime opportunity.

With Numerals and Letters Accompanying a List

When numerals or letters are used to list items in a sentence, parentheses may be used to enclose the numerals or letters:

Please include (a) your date of birth, (b) your social security number, and (c) your mother's maiden name.

The Underscore

The **underscore**, also known as the *underline*, calls attention to a word or expression. The underscore is used with titles of complete works or with foreign expressions. In word processing software, italics is used instead of the underscore. For those cases when a document is handwritten or typewritten, this section provides guidelines for using underscores.

With Titles

If you cannot utilize italics, use an underscore with titles of complete works that are published as individual items. Examples of complete works include books, magazines, newspapers, and plays. In addition, use an underscore with the name of a film, television program, aircraft, cruise ship, sculpture, or painting:

> Will television programs such as <u>All in the Family</u> and <u>Cheers</u> ever be forgotten?

> The stockbroker reads <u>The Wall Street Journal</u> every morning before the market opens.

With Foreign Expressions

Use an underscore or italics to distinguish foreign expressions from standard English vocabulary:

> Her baked goods are <u>par excellence</u>; no better pastries exist.

The Apostrophe

The **apostrophe** is used primarily to indicate the omission of one or more letters or numbers in a contraction, to indicate possession in nouns and indefinite pronouns, or to denote time and money.

In Contractions

Although sometimes considered overly informal, contractions are accepted in today's business world by many communicators. We recommend, however, using contractions sparingly. To indicate a contraction, insert an apostrophe in the space where the missing letter or letters belong. For example:

> don't (do not)   didn't (did not)   we'll (we will)

To indicate an omission in a number, insert an apostrophe in the space where the missing number or numbers belong:

> Martin graduated in '99. (1999)

> The reunion was planned for this year but rescheduled for '02. (2002)

In Possession

Apostrophes are used in the possessive case in nouns to indicate possession:

> The *boy's* suit needs pressing. (singular possessive)

> The *boys'* suits need pressing. (plural possessive)

Add an 's to an indefinite pronoun such as *someone* or *everyone* to show possession. In compound words, add the apostrophe to the last word to indicate possession. For example:

> *Someone's* monitor has been left on.

> My *brother-in-law's* education prepared him for his career.

In Time and Money

Add an ' or 's to *dollar, day, week, month,* and *year* to indicate each word's relationship with the noun that follows it. For example:

A *week's* salary is needed to pay the rent.

Buy ten *dollars'* worth of produce at the farmer's market.

In Plurals

Add an 's to lowercase letters and to some abbreviations to form the plural. For example:

We sometimes find it difficult to distinguish her *a's* from her *o's.*

Do not include so many *etc.'s* in your listings.

Applications

Part A. Select the correct external punctuation for each sentence.

1. Why continue with this line of discussion at this time (!/?/.)
2. The teacher asked the class what year the Concorde had its first flight (!/?/.)
3. May I hear from you without delay (!/?/.)
4. The systems analyst praised the new software (!/?/.)
5. Yea! We won the World Series (!/?/.)

Part B. Insert commas in the following sentences.

1. Therefore we will not meet until the end of the year.
2. I think however that she will accept the hardware equipment proposal.
3. He wanted to be a doctor but his grades were not high enough.
4. Clara who is a computer whiz is upgrading her equipment.
5. After we left work we went directly to the restaurant.

Part C. Delete unnecessary commas in the following sentences.

1. George, the teller, closed his window, and counted his money.
2. If I were going on vacation, I could get ready to leave, now.
3. She bakes, and cooks, and sews during her spare time.
4. For the spring, I plan to buy a new, navy, blue suit.
5. Speaking out of turn, is a rude way to participate.

Part D. Insert all missing internal and external punctuation.

1. The trip starts in Osaka said the travel agent You are then taken to the cruise ship in Kobe

2. They have an impossible commute every day 80 miles
3. The mens suits womens dresses and childrens snowsuits are ready to be inventoried
4. A weeks wages are needed to pay for the Encyclopedia Atlas and Illustrations
5. Before you traveled to Korea did you read her most recent article What Present Day South Koreans Think About America

Editing and Proofreading Applications

I. Insert commas and periods where needed, delete unnecessary commas and periods, and correct errors in word usage and spelling.

Now, that I have calm down I am writing to tell you that I believe I was justify in the matter we discussed Friday, being penalized for not working overtime last weekend, does not seem like a fare penalty.

I do understand, that I had agreed to put in over time hours, when they were needed but last weekend my twin son's where three years old and they expected me to attend they're birthday party, if I had known several weeks' ago that I had to work on June 7 I would have arrange for a substitute, or changed the party date. With such little notice I were unable to make any last minute arrangements

I know I was wrong when I went over your head to talk with Howard your supervisor and apologize for doing so. Can we discuss this farther?

II. Revise the following message by adding semicolons, colons, dashes, hyphens, and external punctuation. Also correct misspelled words.

Charlotte, this note is to apolagize for not forewarding your tax bill in fact, I sincerly want to make it up to you Could you meet me in my office at 1015 on Tuesday I will have it ready for you then

I think that I must be getting forgetful or is it that I'm just over worked I promise that next year I will send your bill on time furthermore, I will send you two copies for your personal record's

When I spoke with my assistant about the error, she implied that she had double checked to see that all bills had been mailed I guess that she only spot checked her records. Please let me know if Tuesday, August 10, is conveneint for you my assistant, Gladys Small my secretary, Gerard Alvarez and I will give you the tax bill and go over all your records for the last twelve month's.

III. Revise the following message by adding quotation marks, parentheses, underscores, apostrophes, and external punctuation where needed. In addition, correct all misspelled words and incorrect word usage.

Because my husband and me both have IRA accounts in your fund, I thought you would be interest to know that we are becoming increasing displeased with one fase of your operation. When I had spoke with one of your representatives, she said, All you half to do to have your funds transfer to your bank is to have the bank send an IRA Transfer Form to us. The directions are clearly outlined in our booklet How to Transfer Funds.

I read the booklet and had the bank Fidelity Fiduciary Bank mailed the correctly filled-in form to your company The fund's still have'nt been transferred. Another one of your representatives told me on the telephone, Because a bank administrater did'nt sign the form, we have to return it to your bank for a signature. This stipulation did not appear in the book let I was told to read.

Aparent, your company makes it easy to deposit money in your IRA funds, but makes it difficult for customers when they want to transfer money out of one of the funds When my friends ask me if I would reccommend your company, I would have to tell them, Not at the present time

Section 4: Style

The basic rules for abbreviation, capitalization, and number usage may be called elements of writing style. Writers who are concerned about these three aspects of their business and personal writing will minimize the number of distractions in a message and bring consistency to their writing.

Abbreviations

An **abbreviation** is a shortened form of a word or a group of words. Shortened forms are used sparingly in business letters because they sometimes obscure the writer's meaning and also present an informality that may offend the reader.

Shortened forms that apply to business writing include courtesy titles, *Jr.* and *Sr.* designations, and initials; professional titles and academic degrees; addresses and states; and names of companies, organizations, and government departments. In addition, abbreviations such as *a.m.*, *p.m.*, *Co.*, *Inc.*, *Corp.*, and *Ltd.* appear in business communications. Notice that although many abbreviations are followed by periods, some abbreviations are not.

Courtesy Titles and Family Designations

Abbreviate a personal title that precedes a person's name. For example:

> *Messrs.* White and Rome represent our firm at the negotiations. (The title *Messrs.* is the plural of the title *Mr.*)

> We will interview *Ms.* Violeta Ruiz. (*Ms.* is a title for a woman that omits reference to marital status; it does not have a full-length form. *Ms.* is not an abbreviation for *Miss* or *Mrs.*)

Abbreviate family designations such as *junior* and *senior* that appear after a person's name. Commas usually set off the family designations:

> Carl Brockman, *Jr.*, is the first speaker on the program.

Sometimes people use an **initial** to indicate the first letter of their first name or middle name:

> *I. H.* Roth uses his first and middle initials, not his first name.

> Gladys *S.* Blackwood insists that her middle initial appear on all correspondence.

Professional Titles

Some professional titles are abbreviated in business writing. Note these examples:

> *Dr.* Sergio Silva is an internist in private practice.

> The company lawyer, Sonia Ramos, *Esq.*, has an office on the eleventh floor. (The title *Esq.* is set off with commas.)

Academic and Professional Degrees

Abbreviate academic and professional degrees that follow a person's name:

Luisa Barnes, *Ed.D.*   Letitia Anderson, *M.D.*

Steven Joffe, *Ph.D.*   Edwin Jeffreys, *D.D.S.*

Addresses

In business correspondence, do not abbreviate words such as *street, avenue, boulevard, road, north, south, east,* and *west*. However, do abbreviate compass designations after street names:

Our new address is 123 *South* Main *Street*.

The meeting will take place at 4 Spring *Boulevard*.

Our president lives at 1605 Bird Lane *NW*.

States

Two-letter postal abbreviations appear in all capital letters without punctuation. Use these abbreviations with the appropriate nine-digit ZIP codes in your correspondence.

Two-letter postal abbreviations are used in full addresses within the text of a letter but are not used when a state name appears in a sentence by itself:

Please send to Ms. Lucy Sands, 1004 Clemens Avenue, Roslyn, *PA* 19001-4356.

The cellular phone will have to be shipped directly to *Pennsylvania*.

Companies, Organizations, and Government Departments

You may abbreviate the names of some well-known companies and organizations if the institutions themselves use the abbreviations. This policy also applies to U.S. government departments:

ABC	American Broadcasting Company
AMA	American Medical Association (or American Management Association)
FBI	Federal Bureau of Investigation
IBM	International Business Machines
IRS	Internal Revenue Service
YWCA	Young Women's Christian Association

Company, Incorporated, Corporation, Limited

The abbreviations *Co., Inc., Corp.,* or *Ltd.* may be used in a company name if the company uses it as part of its official name:

Our accountant previously worked for Mobil Oil *Corp.*

The British firm Lourdes, *Ltd.*, distributes this product.

Do not abbreviate *company, incorporated, corporation,* or *limited* when it appears in lowercase letters in a sentence:

> One firm has *incorporated* into the other.

> She now owns her own software development *company*.

Expressions of Time

The abbreviations *a.m.* and *p.m.* may be used to designate time when they accompany numerals:

> The next meeting is called for 8 *a.m.* on Tuesday.

Familiar Business Abbreviations

Here are more examples of abbreviations, some of which tend to be used in informal business communications such as memos:

A.I.A.	Associate of the Institute of Actuaries
ASAP	as soon as possible
CEO	chief executive officer
C.O.D.	cash on delivery (c.o.d. and COD also are used)
EST	Eastern Standard Time
FYI	for your information
GNP	Gross National Product
P/E	price-to-earnings ratio
P.O. Box	Post Office Box
vs.	versus

Miscellaneous Abbreviations

Some abbreviations used in statistical documents should not be used in business letters. They include the following:

mfg.	manufacturing	reg.	registered
bal.	balance	mdse.	merchandise
pd.	paid	whlse.	wholesale

Other abbreviations such as *No.* (Number) and *Acct.* (Account) may be used in technical documents and also in business correspondence when they are followed by numerals:

> Please refer to our check *No.* 654.

> This information pertains to *Acct.* 6J843.

Units of Measure

The following abbreviations, though not acceptable in standard business correspondence, are widely used in technical documents:

mph	miles per hour	in.	inches
oz.	ounce	ft.	feet
lb.	pound	kg.	kilogram
cm.	centimeter	yd.	yard

Days and Months

In lists and business forms, the abbreviations for days and for months are acceptable. These abbreviations are not acceptable in general business correspondence. Here are the abbreviated forms:

Monday	Mon.	Tuesday	Tues.	Wednesday	Wed.
Thursday	Thurs.	Friday	Fri.	Saturday	Sat.
Sunday	Sun.				

January	Jan.	February	Feb.	March	Mar.
April	Apr.	August	Aug.	September	Sept.
October	Oct.	November	Nov.	December	Dec.

The months of May, June, and July do not have abbreviated forms.

Capitalization

A **capital letter** is used in the first word of a sentence, quotation, salutation, complimentary close, and outline. Further, capitalize titles of persons, written works, and proper nouns.

To Begin a Sentence and to Begin a Quotation

To indicate the beginning of a sentence, capitalize the first letter of the first word. For example:

> *The* tax collector is at the door.

> *When* did this problem begin?

When a complete sentence that states a rule or emphasizes a statement is preceded by a colon, capitalize the first letter of the first word:

> It is a perfect beach day: *The* sun is out, the breeze is warm, and the temperature is balmy.

Capitalize the first word of a direct quotation. For example:

> He said, "*Let* me help you perform the end-of-month audit."

Do not capitalize the second part of an interrupted direct quotation:

> "We should congratulate Gail," James stated, "*on* her recent promotion."

In a Salutation and Complimentary Close

In a business letter, capitalize the first letter of the first word, the person's title, and the proper name in a salutation. Also capitalize the first word in a complimentary close. Here are some examples:

Dear Sir	Ladies and Gentlemen	Dear Ms. Morales
Yours very truly	Very truly yours	Sincerely

Titles of Persons

Capitalize professional titles that precede proper names. For example:

> *Dr.* Nancy Musi   *Governor* Louis Ramos

Capitalize professional titles that do not precede proper names but that refer to specific, well-known individuals:

> The *President* is concerned with the uprising in Europe. (refers to the President of the United States)

Generally, do not capitalize a job title that follows a name. For example:

> Tanya Blank is the *marketing manager* for our company.

Titles of Written Works

Capitalize all words in report headings and the titles of books, magazines, newspapers, articles, movies, television programs, songs, poems, reports, and chapters except for the following: 1. the articles *the*, *a*, or *an*; 2. short conjunctions—three or fewer letters; 3. short prepositions (even the word *to* in an infinitive)—three or fewer letters.

Here are some examples:

> *U.S. News and World Report* (magazine)

> *How to Succeed in Business Without Really Trying* (movie)

Capitalize an article, a short conjunction, or a short preposition when it is the first or last word in a heading or title:

> *The Far Pavilions*

> *As You Like It*

Proper Nouns and *I*

Capitalize the names of specific people, places, and things in written communications. Also, always capitalize the pronoun *I*, wherever it appears in a sentence:

> Gia and *I* are always together.

Names of People. Capitalize all proper names and nicknames. For example:

> *Yoko Tanaka* is a professor at the university.

> The baseball player is called *Crime Dog*.

Capitalize all titles of family members when the titles are used as proper nouns and are not preceded by a possessive noun or pronoun. Do not capitalize titles for family members, however, if they are preceded by a possessive noun or pronoun:

> Let's visit *Grandmother* this morning.

> Are you accompanying *Mother* and *Father* on the trip?

> Bertha's *sister* is about to be hired.

> My *grandfather* started this business.

Names of Places. Capitalize the names of streets, parks, buildings, bodies of water, cities, states, and countries:

He lives at 106 *Green Street*. (street)

The *Ledger Building* was destroyed in the fire. (building)

Have you crossed the *Atlantic Ocean* on the cruise ship? (body of water)

I have not visited *Jackson, Mississippi*. (city and state)

Names of Things. Capitalize the proper names of historical events, companies, documents, organizations, institutions, government departments, periods in history, course titles, and automobiles:

She is a veteran of *World War II*. (historical event)

Walt is a systems analyst for the *General Electric Company*. (company)

Have you studied the *Constitution* of the United States? (document)

I graduated from *Furness Junior High School* in 1995. (institution)

Glenda enrolled in *Physics 103*. (course title)

Suzanne's new car is a *Ford Taurus*. (automobile)

Capitalize some adjectives that are derived from proper nouns. Refer to your dictionary:

Several excellent *Spanish* students are enrolled in my class.

Do I detect a *Bostonian* accent?

Capitalize most nouns that precede numbers or letters. For example:

Flight 643	Chapter VI	Vitamin C
Chart 6J	Invoice 1675	Check 563

Exceptions to this guideline include *line, paragraph, verse, size, page,* and *note* when they precede numbers or letters. For example:

line 4	paragraph 2	verse 16-5
size 10	page 24	note 14

Commercial Products

Do not capitalize common nouns that refer to, but are not part of, a proper noun. For example:

Bic pen	Maytag dishwasher	Breyers ice cream

Points of the Compass

Capitalize compass points (*north, south, east,* and *west*) when they refer to a geographical area or a definite region. Do not capitalize compass points, however, when they indicate a direction or a nonspecific location. For example:

The corporate office is in the *South*.

Travel *east* to the river and then drive *south* to the farm.

Months, Days, and Holidays

Capitalize the months of the year, the days of the week, and the names of holidays. Note the examples on the following page.

In *December*, we are having a company party on a *Monday* or *Tuesday*.

Where are you having your *Fourth of July* picnic?

Seasons of the Year

Do not capitalize summer, fall (autumn), winter, or spring unless a specific designation accompanies the season. For example:

Our *Spring Blockbuster Sale* begins March 21.

Old Man Winter is just around the corner.

After this icy *winter*, we are looking forward to *spring*.

The leaves turn beautiful colors in the *fall*.

Nationalities, Races, Religions, and Languages

Capitalize the names of nationalities (American), races (Caucasian), religions (Catholicism), and languages (Latin). Note these sentences:

Many *Mexican* tourists visit San Diego.

Black History Month attracts noted *African-American* speakers.

Students learned about *Judaism*, *Christianity*, and *Buddhism* in Comparative Religion 101.

Her job at the World Bank requires her to learn both *French* and *Russian*.

Deities

Capitalize nouns that refer to a deity. For example:

God   the Almighty   Lord   Allah   Buddha

Academic Degrees

Because academic degrees such as Doctor of Philosophy and Doctor of Education are capitalized, also capitalize the abbreviated degrees:

Leonard, a consultant, has *Ed.D.* printed on his business stationery.

Hyphenated Names and Words

Apply the guidelines for capitalizing single names and words to hyphenated names and words. Capitalize elements of hyphenated words if they are proper nouns (Leonard Cross-Townsend) or proper adjectives (Atlanta-Chicago train). Do not capitalize prefixes or suffixes added to proper words (mid-Atlantic flight).

Number Expression

Because numbers are used in most business communications, writers must present them accurately and clearly to the reader. In correspondence, writers commonly refer to quantities, dollar amounts, percentages, dates, addresses, time, invoice numbers, and similar items. In reports and proposals, tables, charts, and graphs frequently accompany statistics. Numbers generally are written in *word style* in more formal and literary communications. *Numeral style* generally is used for routine business and personal writing.

Ten-and-Under/Eleven-and-Over Rule

Write quantities of ten and under in words. For example:

Mail *three* copies of the proposal to us.

We rented a *four*-bedroom house in the mountains.

Write quantities of eleven and over in numerals. For example:

Would you buy *25* yellow-lined writing tablets for them?

Charles received *16* inquiries the first day of the session.

One exception to the ten-and-under/eleven-and-over rule involves indefinite or approximate numbers. Use words to express these numbers in a sentence. For example:

Several *thousand* people attended the concert.

Around *thirty-five* students complained to the department head.

Use words for numbers in a sentence that includes two or more related numbers all ten and under. If the numbers are all eleven and over, use numerals:

Daniel has written *five* articles, *one* anthology, and *three* textbook chapters since 1998.

Please bring to the meeting *15* copies of the report, *20* copies of the names and addresses, and *25* copies of the newsletter.

When two or more related numbers are included in a sentence—some of which are ten and under and some of which are eleven and over—use numerals for all numbers. For example:

Our inventory list of paint shows *18* cans of white, *24* cans of eggshell, and *9* cans of light blue.

Consecutive Numbers

When two related numbers appear next to each other in a sentence, write the shorter number in words and the other in numerals:

Ms. Chan received *160 two*-inch samples.

Oscar brought *twelve 36*-inch pieces to the classroom.

Consecutive Unrelated Numbers

If two unrelated numbers appear next to each other in a sentence, separate them with a comma to avoid confusion. For example:

In *1997, 18* of the girls made the All-State Team.

Numbers to Begin Sentences

Use words to express a number at the beginning of a sentence. If a number is very long, rewrite the sentence:

Eighty-one questionnaires were returned.

A total of *5,243* employees applied for the new health-care benefit. (Rewrite the sentence to avoid spelling out *5,243* at the beginning of a sentence.)

Numbers in Dates

When the day follows the month, express the day in numerals. For example:

Kim's presentation is *March 26.*

Use ordinals (*d* or *th*) with the day when the day precedes the month and when the month and the year are omitted. Write out ordinal (*first*) or use numerals (*1st*) if the month is omitted. Use numerals if the month is not omitted. Note these sentences:

The *26th of March* is her graduation date.

Your letter of the *26th* arrived today.

Numbers in Addresses

In ordinary text, use numerals to express house and building numbers except for the number *one*. For example:

One East Grayson Place   6743 North Market Road

Use words for streets numbered first through tenth and numerals with ordinals for streets numbered 11th and over.:

210 West *Fifth* Avenue   634 South *21st* Street

Numbers with Money

Write sums of $1 or more in numerals preceded by a dollar sign ($):

The baseball game program costs $5.

Our total expenses are *$5.00* for the program and *$3.50* for a soda and a snack. (Insert a decimal and zeros after *$5* for consistency within the sentence.)

For sums less than one dollar, use numerals followed by the word *cents*. For example:

The small tablet costs *75 cents.*

In a series of amounts in the same sentence, use a consistent format:

Be sure to budget *$57.00* for the textbook, *$3.50* for the pens and marker, and *$0.99* for the paper clips. (All amounts must use the same format.)

Write approximate amounts in words. For example:

A few *hundred dollars* should cover the cost of the trip.

Use a combination of words and numerals to express very large amounts of money:

> They won a *$20 million* state lottery last Tuesday.

Numbers with Percentages, Decimals, and Fractions

Use numerals followed by the word *percent* (not %) to express percentages.

> The department store is offering a 40 percent discount.

Always express decimals in numerals. A zero placed at the left of a decimal point prevents the reader from overlooking the decimal point:

> 0.364   0.457   .064

Express simple fractions in words. For example:

> A *one-half*-inch length is more than adequate.

> We will need *three-quarters* of an hour to travel.

Express mixed numbers in either a fraction or a decimal unless they appear first in a sentence. Note these examples:

> The job will take *2.5* hours to complete.

> *Two and one-half* pounds of coffee are enough for the group.

Numbers with Time

Use numerals before *a.m.* and *p.m.*, but use words before *o'clock*. To express the time on the hour, omit the colon and two zeros before *a.m.* or *p.m.*:

> One session begins at *9 a.m.*; the other begins at *1 p.m.*

> A *ten o'clock* meeting could extend past noon.

Applications

Part A. Correct any misuse of abbreviations in these sentences.

1. My sister who lives in SC and my brother who lives in NC try to visit each other once a yr.
2. The Y.M.C.A. is sponsoring a trip to NY for local orgns.
3. The U.S. government office is closed Sat. afternoon and all day Sun.
4. We will check your Jan. acct. bal. for you as you requested.
5. Doctor Lloyd Servino and Mister Ian Johnson are the first two people on the waiting list.

Part B. Correct errors in capitalization and insert external punctuation in the following sentences.

1. do you know that the Second annual office equipment association conference will meet in Oakland, california, the third week of April
2. The spiegel Catalog is worth every penny it costs
3. When you go to Washington, dc, visit the air and space museum and the national gallery of art
4. The national spelling bee champion was told, "you are a true scholar"
5. Some native floridians prefer Skiing in colorado to Surfing in miami

Part C. Identify errors in number expression and word usage in the following sentences, and write the corrected sentences on a sheet of paper.

1. Yesterday, they order four alternators and 8 snow tires.
2. Approximately 200 people responded at the help-wanted advertisement.
3. 11 of the athletes will sit on the bench or return to the minor leagues.
4. The Cromwell Company shipped 8 two-hundred-volt batteries tomorrow.
5. We still has 13 reams of letterhead paper, six large boxes of printed envelopes, and 15 reams of copy paper.

Part D. Identify errors in number expression, capitalization, and word usage in the following sentences. Write the corrected sentences on a sheet of paper.

1. In 2002 100 of are middle managers will work out of our indianapolis office.
2. Responds to this inquiry by september 12th to earn the 1% discount.
3. The new office at 1 East munroe street will accommodates our present staff.
4. The united states Navy have a budget of well over 7,000,000 dollars.
5. He said, "representative Baldwin of the Twenty 2nd Congressional district support this bill."

Editing and Proofreading Applications

I. Proofread the following message. Eliminate errors in abbreviations and spelling, and insert external punctuation. Prepare a corrected copy.

On Mon., Aug. 1, I sent you a letter asking for the procedures' to follow to pay off my mtge. loan You sent me a reply on Fri. of the same week, telling me that the bal. due on the loan was $2,003.94 minus $694 left in my escrow acct.

I dont want to be a nusance, but I still have these few unanswered questions,

1. Should I deduct the escrow acct. bal. from the mtge. loan bal. and send you a chk. for the diference

2. Should I mail my pymt. to this address or to the NJ address were I usually send my mtge. pymt.

II. Proofread and correct all errors in number expression, word usage, and spelling in the following message. Prepare a revised copy.

On Saturday the 10 of August, I visit your fashion consultant and ordered 2 pairs of jeans, three blouse's, 1 fall dress, and two professional outfits for work. She promised me that I would recieve the clothes from the distributor at September eighth. This is the 2nd time that a order have gone to a wrong address.

I live at 1 Oak Drive in Tarrytown. When the cloths finally arrive on the 18, I noticed that they had been sent to Ten Ox Drive in Tarrytown and then forwarded to me. In nineteen ninety-nine, 11 items was ordered from the same consultant, and a mixup in my address occurred at that time. 2 errors in shipments is too many for me.

If you do not apologize by 10/1/99, you may have to cross my name of you're list of customers. Because it appears that my purchase of five hundred and thirty-five dollars is not important enough for you to get my address strait, I am thinking of going elsewhere to get the same two percent discount and recieve my clothes in 1/2 the number of days. Please consider my position in this matter and also help yourselve by eliminating this one weakness in you operation.

Section 5: Words Frequently Misused

Below is an alphabetized list of words that are misused frequently in business communication. To help you understand how to use these words, the list provides a definition of each word and an example of its usage.

a lot *n.* many (Note that *a lot* consists of two words.)
  Ex. She owns a lot of books.

accept *v.* to agree to; to receive
  Ex. He will accept your recommendation.

addition *n.* increase; enlargement; part or thing added
  Ex. With the addition of the family room, the house is more comfortable.
  Ex. The new addition to the hospital provides more office space for the medical staff.

advice *n.* counsel
  Ex. The college counselor's advice helped the student.

advise *v.* to give advice; to inform
  Ex. The attorney will advise you to write a will.

affect *v.* to influence
  Ex. His new contract will affect his annual income.

all ready *adj.* completely prepared
  Ex. The auditors are all ready to discuss their findings.

all together *adj.* in a group; in unison
  Ex. Let us sing all together so that our voices ring out.

allot *v.* to give or share in arbitrary amounts; to apportion
  Ex. They will allot each speaker only five minutes.

allude *v.* to refer to something not specifically mentioned
  Ex. Did the article allude to her disinterest in the new product without actually stating it?

already *adv.* by or before a specified or implied time
  Ex. He already called the bank officer.

altogether *adv.* completely or thoroughly
  Ex. Raising the budget is altogether unwise in today's economy.

ascent *n.* the act of climbing or rising
  Ex. The ascent to the top of the mountain was difficult.

assent *v.* to agree or to accept a proposal or an opinion
  Ex. We assent to your idea.

assure *v.* to make sure
  Ex. We assure you that you can count on our support.

capital *n.* money invested
    Ex. How much capital was invested in the business?

capitol *n.* a government building
    Ex. She took her class to the capitol in Harrisburg.

choose *v.* to select based on judgment
    Ex. They will choose Ted because of his skill and knowledge.

chose *v.* past tense of choose
    Ex. Art chose Gloria to be on his team.

cite *v.* to acknowledge; to quote as a reference
    Ex. You were asked to cite directly from your resource book.

complement *n.* anything that completes a whole; *v.* to complete or make perfect
    Ex. *(n.)* A complement of certified public accountants would enhance your staff.
    Ex. *(v.)* Her new hat will complement the outfit.

compliment *n.* recognition; praise; flattery; *v.* to praise
    Ex. *(n.)* The supervisor's compliment pleased the clerks.
    Ex. *(v.)* He will compliment his employees when they work overtime.

consul *n.* an official appointed by the government to live in a foreign city to attend to the interests of the official's country
    Ex. The consul from France helped the French tourists who had lost their passports.

continual *adj.* taking place in close succession; frequently repeated
    Ex. The continual interruptions annoyed the music listeners.

continuous *adj.* without break or let up
    Ex. The waterfall's continuous flow of water captivated the onlookers.

cooperation *n.* assistance; help
    Ex. The cooperation of the parties is necessary in this situation.

corporation *n.* type of business organization
    Ex. The four doctors formed a corporation to practice medicine.

council *n.* group of people called together to provide counsel
    Ex. The vote of the council was divided.

counsel *n.* advice; *v.* to provide advice
    Ex. *(n.)* We must obtain legal counsel before we make a decision.
    Ex. *(v.)* Who is going to counsel them on the matter?

decent *adj.* correct; proper
    Ex. We will accept any decent offer for the property.

descent *n.* going from a high level to a lower level
    Ex. The descent of the asset's value is quite remarkable.

desert *v.* to abandon; *n.* a barren geographical area
  Ex. *(v.)* Don't desert a family that needs your support.
  Ex. *(n.)* He drove through the desert in the early morning hours.

dessert *n.* a course at the end of a meal
  Ex. Chocolate ice cream is her favorite dessert.

disburse *v.* to make payments; to allot
  Ex. We will disburse the money after the project is completed.

disperse *v.* to distribute
  Ex. Did they disperse the pamphlets at the conference?

dissent *n.* disagreement
  Ex. The situation caused dissent between the parent and the teenager.

edition *n.* an issue of a book or newspaper
  Ex. The author is working on the second edition of his book.

effect *n.* the result or outcome; *v.* to bring about
  Ex. *(n.)* All the employees felt the effect of the redistribution.
  Ex. *(v.)* The new leadership will effect massive changes.

elude *v.* to escape notice or detection
  Ex. By changing the subject, he was able to elude criticism.

ensure *v.* to make sure; to guarantee
  Ex. Bail is set to ensure the appearance of defendants in court.

envelop *v.* to surround; to cover completely
  Ex. The fog will envelop the area at daybreak.

envelope *n.* containers for letters, reports, and so forth
  Ex. Send the memorandum in an interoffice envelope.

except *prep.* with the exclusion of; other than
  Ex. All staff members attended except Timothy.

farther *adj.* more distant
  Ex. Her home is farther from the school than Art's home.

forth *adv.* forward; onward
  Ex. From that day forth, he arrived at the airport one hour before depar-
  ture time.

fourth *adj.* any one of four equal parts; the item following the first
three in a series
  Ex. Randi is the fourth person to ask the same question.

further *adv.* to a greater degree or extent
  Ex. No further suggestions will be accepted.

hear *v.* perceive by the ear
  Ex. Speak loudly so that everyone can hear you.

here *adv.* in or at this place
  Ex. Are all the speakers here?

hoard *v.* to collect and keep
>Ex. Aunt Rose does hoard all scarce items.

horde *n.* a huge crowd
>Ex. A horde of people blocked the street to prevent entrance.

insure *v.* to secure from harm; to guarantee life or property
>Ex. The company will not insure people who are poor risks.

its *pron.* possessive pronoun form of *it*
>Ex. When did you see its paw prints?

it's contraction for *it is*
>Ex. It's supposed to rain the day of our annual picnic.

lay *v.* to place; to put (transitive verb—requires an object)
>Ex. Lay the dictionary on my desk.

lie *v.* to recline; to remain (intransitive verb—no object required)
>Ex. Glenn will lie down on the sofa.

loose *adj.* not restrained; not fastened
>Ex. The dogs are loose again despite all our efforts.

lose *v.* to fail to win; to be deprived of
>Ex. I play the lottery but always lose.

medal *n.* a badge of honor
>Ex. Faye deserves a medal for her kindness to others.

meddle *v.* to interfere
>Ex. Do not meddle with your children's business.

metal *n.* a mineral substance
>Ex. That item is made from metal not wood.

passed *v.* past tense of pass
>Ex. Sashi passed the final examination with a high grade.

past *adj.* finished; gone by
>Ex. The past season was good for the local retailers.

personal *adj.* private; not public or general
>Ex. Are you interested in my personal opinion on this subject?

personnel *n.* the staff of an organization
>Ex. A change in personnel is due the first of next month.

principal *n.* the amount of the money borrowed in a loan; the head official in a court proceeding or school; *adj.* most important or influential
>Ex. *(n.)* The principal of the mortgage is about to be paid off. Ms. Landis is the new principal at the high school.
>Ex. *(adj.)* What is the principal textbook used in biology?

principle *n.* a basic belief or truth
>Ex. Follow this principle to solve your first problem.

quiet *adj.* still; calm
  Ex. A librarian prefers quiet rooms to accommodate the readers.

quit *v.* to stop; to discontinue
  Ex. John will quit his job when he returns to college.

quite *adv.* very or fairly; positively
  Ex. Miranda is quite ill and will not be able to attend.

sight *n.* the ability to see; vision
  Ex. Joe's sight has improved with the treatment.

site *n.* a place; a plot of land
  Ex. On what site are you planning to build?

stationary *adj.* fixed; unmovable
  Ex. That huge piece of equipment is stationary.

stationery *n.* paper for letters and envelopes
  Ex. The company is having new stationery printed.

taught *v.* past tense of teach
  Ex. Len's father taught in the public schools in her city.

taut *adj.* tight
  Ex. Make sure that the ropes are taut in order to hold the items.

than *conj.* in comparison with; *prep.* except; besides
  Ex. *(conj.)* Sean is older than Maria.
  Ex. *(prep.)* It was none other than Gayle who wallpapered the house.

their *pron.* plural possessive form of they
  Ex. Their reports are on the receptionist's desk.

then *adv.* at that time
  Ex. We will be ready then to discuss another investment.

there *adv.* in or at that place
  Ex. Bob hesitates to go there to have his car repaired.

they're contraction for *they are*
  Ex. They're interested in traveling to Spain this summer.

to *prep.* in the direction of
  Ex. Go to the corner of South and Prescott Avenues.

too *adv.* also; excessively
  Ex. Too many opinions are being offered.

two *adj.* the number 2
  Ex. Two girls are being added to the team.

weather *n.* atmospheric condition at a certain time and place
  Ex. Presently, the weather is very nice; however, tomorrow it is suppose
  to rain.

whether *conj.* if it be the case; in either case
  Ex. Whether Toni comes by air or car, she will arrive on time.

your *pron.* possessive form of you (may be singular or plural)
  Ex. (singular) Your report card arrived in the mail.
  Ex. (plural) Let me help you with your roles before the auditions begin.

you're contraction for *you are*
  Ex. You're very well qualified for the job.

Applications

Part A. Choose the appropriate word to fit the meaning of each sentence.

1. After his long day, Peter only wanted to (lay, lie) down.
2. (Whether, Weather) or not Tom runs for office is undecided.
3. Despite her many years playing hide-and-seek, Pilar could not (elude, allude) her children.
4. Can you please direct me to the (personal, personnel) department?
5. This time Catherine wanted to buy a (medal, metal, meddle) golf club.
6. Jonathan was afraid his belt was (to, two, too) (loose, lose).
7. Heinrich was the first to (cite, sight, site) his favorite author.
8. Tan, will (you're, your) family be coming to the formal dinner?

Part B. In each sentence, correct the words, if any, that are misused.

1. Roy put the capitol fund papers altogether in one pile.
2. After the tornado had past, Lorna was relieved that she had assured her principle belongings.
3. Bobby thinks they're is already to much noise.
4. What affect does the company's forth rule have on it's staff?
5. Does Dr. Racine council anyone of the executives at the McDougal Cooperation?
6. Jane complemented Marc on his sand-colored dessert attire.
7. Did you here that the envelops don't quit match the stationary?
8. James insured Betty Sue that he could swim further then she.
9. Did he advise you on whether that score was your personal best?
10. For his birthday, he choose to invite a hoard of people to the party.

Editing and Proofreading Applications

What is wrong with the following phrases or clauses? Decide and then rewrite them correctly.

1. on 45 minutes notice
2. a three year old horse
3. Hear comes Mister Jon Woolner!
4. an S.B.A. disaster loan
5. a first addition Jane Austen novel
6. a jewish holiday
7. the 24 of Aug.
8. On page 329 25 references apply.
9. Please except they're apology.
10. how to affect a change

Appendix D

Documenting Other Sources: Citation Styles

Whenever you use someone else's material you must document your sources. Sources should be documented in a manner that makes it easy for readers to locate additional information about the material and in an acceptable citation style.

Types of Citations

Most source documentation falls within two categories: that which appears within the text and that which appears at the end of a document. The **in-text reference** provides immediate identification of the source of the material and makes it easy for the reader to locate more detailed information at the end of the report.

Reference lists, **works cited lists**, and **bibliographies** appear at the end of a document. All three lists contain the information necessary for the reader to locate the original source material. Reference lists include only information used to support the material discussed in the document. A works cited list must include all the works cited within the report. Work cited lists are sometimes labeled as Literature Cited, Works Consulted, or Bibliography. A bibliography is not as limited as a reference list. A bibliography may include related material, background information, and additional readings. It is also acceptable to annotate a bibliography.

Citation Styles

Three of the most widely used documentation styles are from the American Psychological Association (APA), the Modern Language Association of America (MLA), and the University of Chicago Press' *The Chicago Manual of Style*. Following is a brief description of each group's citation guidelines.

APA

The APA style is the style most often used in reports produced by individuals in the social and physical sciences. For in-text citations, the APA style calls for a simple author-date format (Henson & Means, 2000). An APA-style bibliography or reference list is alphabetized by the author's last name. Figure D-1 shows the correct presentation of references using the APA style.

MLA

The MLA style is the standard for many writers in business, industry, government, and the media. In the MLA style, in-text citations refer the reader to a comprehensive Works Cited List at the end of the document. The format of the in-text citation is author-page (Henson 365). Figure D-2 shows acceptable reference format using the MLA style.

Reference Type	Reference Format
Annual Report	Willamette Company, Incorporated. (2000). *2000 Annual Report*. Seattle, WA: The Willamette Company, Incorporated.
Book, one author	Logan, P. (1998). *Small Winners*. New York: Stallings Publishing Co.
Book, two authors	Parker, Erica M., and T. M. Gauge (1998). *Winning Is Not the Only Thing*, Phoenix, AZ: McDougle Press.
Book, edited	David, Gill A. (Ed.) (1999). *The Horse that Won the World*. Kansas City, MO: Lopes and Kinner Publishing.
Brochure	Collision Center. (2000). *Accidents Do Happen*. [Brochure]. Ruston, LA: Louisiana's Collision Center.
CD-ROM encyclopedia article, one author	Lee, Tyler (1996). Filing Systems. *FileProof '99* [CD-ROM]. Silcon Valley, CA: FoolProof Systems, Inc.
Encyclopedia article, one author	Callens, Elizabeth (1999). Database systems. *The Computer's Users Encyclopedia*, Dallas, TX: Automated Press.
Film, videotape, or audiotape	*Successful Computer System Projects*. (1999). [Film]. Atlanta, GA: Systems Development Resource Center.
Government publication	U.S. Department of Defense. (2000). *The Cost of the B-1 Bomber*. Washington, DC: National Press, Inc.
Internet, Web	Combining ethics and your travel. (1999). *Ethnic-o-Travel*. [On-line]. Available: **http://www.travelsites.com/dogood.htm**. Cited 1999 May 13.
Interview	Susanboy, Martha, professor, Clever City State (1996, January 12). Interview by author. Clever City, UT.
Journal article	Jiang, J. J. (1998). Systems success and communication. *The Journal of Computer Intelligence 9*, 112–117.
Magazine article	Johnson, K. (1998, April 10). Losing and the loser psychology. *Successful Challenging 45*, 43–45.
Newspaper article, no author	"Is the weather really cyclical?" (1998, December 28). *Ruston Daily Journal*, p. B–7.
Newspaper article, one author	Marks, Amy. (1998, December 21). "Successful weddings in Modesto." *Modesto Daily Times*, C–12.
On-line newspaper	Adams, B. M. (1999, February 10). "The exciting international lawyer." [On-line]. *Lawyers Journal 34*, 23–26. Available: **http://www.alajournal.com/realworld.htm**.

FIGURE D-1 References using the APA Style

Reference Type	Reference Format
Annual Report	Willamette Company, Incorporated. *2000 Annual Report*. Seattle, WA: The Willamette Company, Incorporated.
Book, one author	Logan, P. *Small Winners*. New York: Stallings Publishing Co., 1998.
Book, two authors	Parker, Erica M., and T. M. Gauge. *Winning Is Not the Only Thing*. Phoenix, AZ: McDougle Press, 1998.
Book, edited	David, Gill A. (Ed.). *The Horse that Won the World*. Kansas City, MO: Lopes and Kinner Publishing.
Brochure	Collision Center. (2000). *Accidents Do Happen*. [Brochure]. Ruston, LA: Louisiana's Collision Center.
Encyclopedia article, one author	Callens, Elizabeth. "Database Systems." *The Computer's Users Encyclopedia*. 1999 ed.
Film, videotape, or audiotape	*Successful Computer System Projects*. Film. Atlanta, GA: Systems Development Resource Center, 1999.
Government publication	U.S. Department of Defense. *The Cost of the B-1 Bomber*. Washington, DC: National Press, Inc., 2000.
Internet, Web	"Combining Ethics and Your Travel." *Ethnic-o-Travel* (1999). On-line. Internet. Available: **http://www.travelsites.com/dogood.htm**. 4 Mar. 1999.
Interview	Susanboy, Martha. Personal Interview. 12 January 1999. Jiang, J. J.
Journal article	"Systems Success and Communication." *The Journal of Computer Intelligence 9* (1998): 112–117.
Magazine article	Johnson, K. "Losing and the loser psychology." *Successful Challenging* 15 Aug. 1999: 43–45.
Newspaper article, no author	"Is the Weather Really Cyclical?" *Ruston Daily Journal* 28 December 1998: B–7.
Newspaper article, one author	Marks, Amy. "Successful weddings in Modesto." *Modesto Daily Times* 21 December 1998: C-12.

FIGURE D-2 References using MLA style

The Chicago Manual of Style

The Chicago Manual Style is the reference guide for most publishers and editors. *The Chicago Manual of Style* supports both a documentary-note style and an author-date style. Figure D-3 shows examples of both styles. In the documentary-note system (see the Newspaper reference in Figure D-3), the writer provides notes and retrieval information about the source information in a parenthetical note. This style can eliminate the need for a comprehensive bibliography. Similar to the in-text reference style of the APA, the author-date in-text style of *The Chicago Manual of Style* provides a relatively unobtrusive pointer to a more detailed reference list at the end of the document.

For More Information

Style guidelines for the three sources referenced in this appendix cover almost every aspect of writing and editing. To learn more about each, you may want to check your local bookstore or the World Wide Web. How do you choose which style to use? As the notes on these styles indicate, different subject areas may have different conventions for crediting source material. For example, the American Mathematical Style has its own set of conventions for presenting citations and other information. You should use the style most acceptable to your subject area or organization.

Book, one author
Logan, P. 1998. *Small winners*. New York: Stallings Publishing Co.

Book, two authors
Parker, Erica M. and T. M. Guage. 1998. *Winning Is Not the Only Thing*. Pheonix, AZ: McDougle Press.

Journal article
Jiang, J. J. 1998. Systems success and communication. *The Journal of Computer Intelligence 9*: 112–117.

Magazine article
Johnson, K. 1998. Losing and the loser psychology. Successful Challenging, 10 April, 43–45.

Newspaper
This type of citation is commonly incorporated into the text of the report; for example,

An article in the *Modesto Daily Times* of December 21, 1998 describes recent weddings in the Modesto area. Common elements in these weddings included . . . .

Unpublished interview
Susanboy, Martha. 1996. Interviewed by author. Clever City, UT, 12 January 1996.

FIGURE D-3 References using *The Chicago Manual of Style*

Appendix E

Answers to Checkpoints

CHAPTER 1

Checkpoint 1 The Purposes and Process of Communication

1. Verbal and nonverbal.
2. Channel is very important. Channel selection can determine the success or failure of a message.
3. a. To establish or build goodwill
   b. To establish or build goodwill, to share information, and to build self-esteem
   c. To establish or build goodwill, to persuade, and to share information

Checkpoint 2 Usage of Communication Media

1. Speaking—this mode enhances your chances of getting the response you want.
2. Writing and Speaking—writing because you want a written record and speaking because you want to build your interpersonal relationship with your supervisor.
3. Speaking—this mode enables you to build your interpersonal relationship with your subordinate.
4. Speaking and Writing—speaking because you want to make sure that Anna understands the severity of her mistake and writing so that you have written record for her personnel file.

Checkpoint 3 Responsibilities of Participants

1. Receiver
2. Sender
3. Sender
4. Receiver
5. Sender

Checkpoint 4 Forms of Communication

1. Lateral, internal, oral
2. N/A, external, written
3. Upward, internal, written
4. Upward, internal, written
5. Upward, internal, written

Checkpoint 5 Barriers to Communication

1. Internal
2. External
3. External
4. Internal
5. Internal

Checkpoint 6 Production of Documents

1. c
2. e
3. d
4. a
5. b
6. f

Checkpoint 7 Sending and Storing Electronic Messages

1. e
2. a
3. f
4. c
5. b
6. d
7. g

CHAPTER 2

Checkpoint 1 The World as a Global Workplace

1. a
2. b

Checkpoint 2 Cultural Differences

1. False; 2. False; 3. False; 4. True; 5. False; 6. True; 7. True

Checkpoint 3 Cross-Cultural Communication

1. helps (but may not be feasible)
2. hinders
3. may hinder
4. hinders
5. helps
6. helps

Checkpoint 4 Strategies for Global Communication

1. False; 2. True; 3. False; 4. True

Checkpoint 5 Other Diversities in the Workplace

1. elderly
2. female
3. Jewish

Checkpoint 6 Working Effectively in Teams

1. effective; 2. ineffective; 3. effective; 4. ineffective; 5. effective

CHAPTER 3

Checkpoint 1 The Roles of Nonverbal Communication

1. True
2. True
3. False
4. True
5. True

Checkpoint 2 Nonverbal Symbols

1. True
2. True
3. True
4. False
5. True

Checkpoint 3 Your Image and Nonverbal Symbols

1. True
2. True
3. False
4. True
5. True

Checkpoint 4 The Importance and Nature of Listening

1. True
2. False
3. True
4. False
5. True

Checkpoint 5 Effective Listening

1. False
2. False
3. True
4. True
5. False

CHAPTER 4

Checkpoint 1 The Writing Process

1. prewriting, drafting, revising, editing and proofreading, publishing or presenting
2. The writer conducts research, gathers data, or collects information; and considers purpose, audience, length, and medium.
3. purpose, audience, length, medium

Checkpoint 2 Identify the Objective of a Message

1. inform
2. persuade
3. record/inform
4. request
5. inform

Checkpoint 3 Plan the Message for the Receiver

Answers may vary.

1. Have your ID card ready to show the guard so that he will quickly admit you.
2. Your new, custom-printed business cards are ready.
3. Your stay at Dalton's B&B should be a pleasant one. If you are unsatisfied, you will receive a coupon for a free dinner.

Checkpoint 4 Organizing Messages

1. direct
2. direct
3. indirect
4. indirect

Checkpoint 5 Drafting

1. Shannon should circle the word and check it later.
2. Austin should jot a note to himself and get the figures after he finishes drafting.
3. Stephanie should go back to the prewriting stage and brainstorm further ideas.

Checkpoint 6 Courteous Words
Answers may vary.

1. Please bring me the report.
2. Reverend Chang will conduct the session.
3. The attorney was an expert trial lawyer.
4. The professor has Lyme disease.
5. Employees requesting family leave must file the required paperwork at least one month prior to their requested leave.

Checkpoint 7 Appropriate Words
Answers will vary.

1. Topek motor scooters get 30 miles to the gallon.
2. Please ask Bill to reserve the hotel for our conference.
3. I do not know if I will apply for that job.
4. Customers who place their orders by November 30 receive a gift.

Checkpoint 8 Unnecessary Elements
1. Overall, in my opinion, by far, qualified, that is open
2. many helpful new, for work
3. that was

Checkpoint 9 Complete and Clear Paragraphs
1. 2, 1, 3
2. *This, Since*

Checkpoint 10 Editing
Memo should tell where the forms are available. Second sentence should be split into two. Second and third sentences should be more formal.

Checkpoint 11 Proofreading
1. it's
2. dr.; the the
3. salary; be will announced.
4. breaks. brakes
5. busniess

Checkpoint 12 Publishing
1. It should be error-free, and its message should be suited to its audience.
2. The paper should be good quality and neat, the ink should be dark, and the margins should be even.
3. Using a sans serif font, perhaps in boldface, makes a heading stand out.

Checkpoint 13 Enhancing Your Message
1. In addition to adding visual appeal, graphics can add information, make a concept easier to grasp, or summarize complex information.
2. Each graphic should have a number and a title or caption. Number all graphics consecutively. Captions and titles should be parallel—that is, always use a sentence fragment or a complete sentence to identify or label graphics. In the text of the report, refer to the graphic by number just before the graphic appears. Place the graphic as close to the reference as possible.
3. If you borrow ideas or data from another source, you must give credit to that source.
4. Before you add graphics to your written message, you should think about who makes up your audience and tailor your message and graphics to that group. Make sure the graphics are helpful, not just decorative, and that they enhance your message rather than detract from it.

CHAPTER 5

Checkpoint 1 Uses of Memos
1. to state policy and to inform
2. to inform
3. to promote goodwill
4. to provide a record

Checkpoint 2 Traditional and Simplified Memo Formats
1. False
2. True
3. False
4. True
5. True

Checkpoint 3 E-Mail Abuses

1. shouting
2. subjects
3. spam
4. paragraph

Checkpoint 4 Agendas

1. True
2. False
3. False
4. True

CHAPTER 6

Checkpoint 1 Letter Parts

1. subject line
2. enclosure notation
3. salutation
4. copy notation
5. complimentary close

Checkpoint 2 Letter Formats and Business Envelopes

1. True
2. False
3. False
4. True
5. False

Checkpoint 3 The Main Idea

1. Poor—does not introduce or reveal the main idea and is not receiver-oriented
2. Poor—does not introduce or reveal the main idea
3. Good
4. Poor—does not introduce or reveal the main idea
5. Good

Checkpoint 4 Goodwill Closings

1. Poor—is not receiver-oriented
2. Good
3. Good
4. Poor—is not receiver-oriented and does not help the receiver
5. Poor—is not receiver-oriented and repeats already-given information

Checkpoint 5 Letters with Neutral or Positive Messages

1. False
2. True
3. False
4. True
5. False

Checkpoint 6 Neutral Openings

1. Poor—does not identify the topic of the letter
2. Good—introduces the topic of the letter and does not infer a positive or negative response
3. Poor—implies the answer will give the receiver what he or she wants
4. Good—introduces the topic of the letter and does not infer a positive or negative response
5. Poor—implies that the answer is *no*

Checkpoint 7 Reasons for the Negative Message

1. Good—provides a logical reason for the negative response
2. Good—provides a logical, receiver-oriented reason for the negative response
3. Poor—provides a reason that is sender-oriented, not receiver-oriented
4. Poor—provides a reason that is too short and company-oriented rather than receiver-oriented
5. Good—provides a customer-oriented, logical reason for the negative response

Checkpoint 8 The Negative Message

1. Your order will be sent September 5.
2. Hand in your assignment when it is finished.
3. If he had been more qualified, he would have been hired.
4. When the new shipment comes in, your paper will be sent to you immediately.
5. If the lead singer were well, the concert would go on as planned.

Checkpoint 9 The Closing

1. Poor—uses the word *hope* and does not contain a soft sale
2. Good—contains a soft sale, provides motivation for the receiver to say *yes*, and makes his or her response easy
3. Good—tries to help even while providing a negative response
4. Poor—contains an apology and does not contain a soft sale
5. Good—offers another option

CHAPTER 7

Checkpoint 1 Steps in a Search for Information
1. False
2. False
3. False
4. True
5. True

Checkpoint 2 Planning the Search
1. timeline
2. webbing or clustering
3. Keywords
4. backward
5. broaden; narrow

Checkpoint 3 Sources of Information
1. True
2. False
3. False
4. True
5. True

Checkpoint 4 Finding It on the Web
1. Web address
2. *
3. AND, OR, NOT
4. Alta Vista
5. base or root word

Checkpoint 5 Using Information
1. False
2. True
3. False
4. True
5. True

CHAPTER 8

Checkpoint 1 Purposes and Placement of Graphic Aids
1. d
2. False. The main factor to consider when placing a graphic aid is where the reader would prefer and most benefit from its placement.
3. (b) title, (d) source

Checkpoint 2 Developing Graphic Aids
1. flowchart
2. table
3. map
4. drawing
5. photograph
6. organization chart
7. pie chart
8. line graph
9. bar graph

Checkpoint 3 Using Visual Aids for Oral Presentations
1. c
2. True
3. (b) points, (c) practice, (d) face

CHAPTER 9

Checkpoint 1 Planning Reports
1. True
2. False
3. False
4. True
5. False

Checkpoint 2 Collecting and Analyzing Data
1. True
2. True
3. True
4. True
5. False

Checkpoint 3 Organizing and Writing Informal Reports
1. True
2. False
3. True
4. True
5. False

Checkpoint 4 Formatting Informal Reports
1. True
2. True
3. False
4. True
5. True
6. False

CHAPTER 10

Checkpoint 1 Planning, Organizing, and Writing Formal Reports
1. False
2. True
3. False
4. False
5. True

Checkpoint 2 Formatting Formal Reports
1. style manual
2. one inch
3. fourth level
4. noun
5. indented

Checkpoint 3 Managerial Reports
1. e
2. a
3. b
4. d
5. c

Checkpoint 4 Technical Reports
1. True
2. False
3. False
4. True
5. False

CHAPTER 11

Checkpoint 1 Writing Effective Steps
1. a. Check to make sure that the warehouse has enough stock to fill the order.
   b. Send the pink copy of the invoice to the shipping department.
2. Reorder Part 103A when only five boxes remain in stock.
3. Enter the customer's name.
   The screen will display that customer's purchase history.

Checkpoint 2 Making Information Accessible in Manuals
1. False
2. True
3. False

Checkpoint 3 Writing an Object or Mechanism Description
1. pebbly
2. to the left of
3. loose

Checkpoint 4 Writing a Process Description
1. False
2. True
3. False
4. False

Checkpoint 5 Beginning a Persuasive Message
1. Poor
2. Poor
3. Poor
4. Good

Checkpoint 6 Describing Benefits
1. Poor
2. Poor
3. Good
4. Poor

Checkpoint 7 Writing Collection Letters
1. Urgency stage
2. Reminder stage
3. Strong reminder stage
4. Discussion stage

Checkpoint 8 Writing Persuasively
1. False
2. False
3. True
4. True

CHAPTER 12

Checkpoint 1 Short and Formal Oral Presentations
1. short, uniform
2. report/written report
3. attention-getter
4. sentence
5. summary

Checkpoint 2 Delivery of Oral Presentations
1. delivery
2. Visual aids
3. Nonverbal symbols
4. Good posture
5. small group

Checkpoint 3 Effective Participation and Organization
1. False
2. False
3. False
4. True
5. True

Checkpoint 4 Lead Meetings Effectively
1. purpose/objective
2. handling difficult people
3. participate/contribute
4. postpone
5. Summaries

CHAPTER 13

Checkpoint 1 Customer Service and Contact
1. Response A
2. Response B
3. Response A

Checkpoint 2 Customer Interaction
1. poor
2. quality
3. quality
4. poor

Checkpoint 3 Customer Service and Ethics
1. True
2. False
3. False
4. False
5. True

Checkpoint 4 Technology and Effective Communication with Customers
1. cellular telephone
2. e-mail
3. fax

Checkpoint 5 One-on-One Communication
1. enunciation
2. pitch
3. pronunciation
4. tone

Checkpoint 6 Telephone Communication
1. poor
2. poor
3. good

CHAPTER 14

Checkpoint 1 Analyzing Your Goals and Qualifications
1. False
2. True
3. True
4. False

Checkpoint 2 Analyzing the Job Market
1. interviewing with that company
2. file
3. networking
4. Internet

Checkpoint 3 Organizing Your Resume
1. False
2. True
3. False
4. False

Checkpoint 4 Preparing Your Resume
1. job objective
2. education
3. optional
4. job title

CHAPTER 15

Checkpoint 1 Opening Paragraph and Body Paragraphs
1. Effective
2. Weak—doesn't name the position applying for
3. Effective
4. Effective
5. Effective
6. Weak—too general, doesn't explain specific qualifications

Checkpoint 2 Closing Paragraph
1. Effective
2. Weak—does not lead up to question
3. Weak—unsure tone (hope, try)
4. Weak—does not ask for an interview, just asks if there are openings

Checkpoint 3 Preparing for the Interview
1. True
2. True
3. False
4. False

Checkpoint 4 The Interview and the Follow-up Letter
1. nonverbal symbol/cue
2. deflect them courteously
3. Do not
4. follow-up letter

Index

Note: The letter *f* following a page number indicates that the term appears in a figure.